THE OCCULT IN RUSSIAN AND SOVIET CULTURE

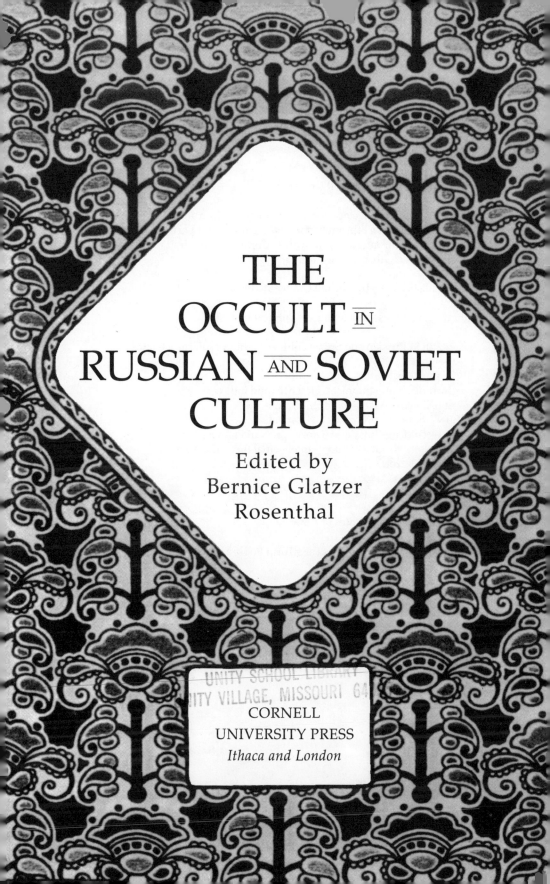

THE
OCCULT IN
RUSSIAN AND SOVIET
CULTURE

Edited by
Bernice Glatzer
Rosenthal

CORNELL
UNIVERSITY PRESS
Ithaca and London

First published 1997 by Cornell University Press.

Library of Congress Cataloging-in-Publication Data

The occult in Russian and Soviet culture / edited by Bernice Glatzer
  Rosenthal.
  468 p.   cm. : ; ill, ¹⁄₀₂
    Includes bibliographical references and index.
    ISBN 0-8014-3258-8 (cloth : alk. paper). —
  ISBN 0-8014-8331-X (pbk. : alk. paper)
    1. Occultism—Russia—History.   2. National socialism and
  occultism.   3. Soviet Union—Intellectual life.   I. Rosenthal,
  Bernice Glatzer.
  BF1434.R8023   1997
  133'.0947—dc20   96-27566

CONTENTS

Contents

ACKNOWLEDGMENTS

This book grows out of the research conference "The Occult and Modern Russian and Soviet Culture," held at Fordham University in June 1991. Grateful acknowledgment is made to the National Endowment for the Humanities (an independent federal agency), Fordham University, the National Council for Soviet and East European Research, IREX, the Soros Foundation, and the Institute for Modern Russia Culture. These agencies are not responsible for the findings of this conference or for any of the interpretations herein.

Grateful acknowledgment is also made to Henryk Baran, Kenneth Brostrom, Irena Belobravtseva, Pamela Davidson, Charlotte Douglas, Daniel Entin, William Fletcher, Viacheslav Vsevolodovich Ivanov, Valentin Kuklev, Irina Kulyus, Lauren Leighton, Arkady Rovner, Svetlana Semenova, and Wojtiech Zalewski for their presentations; to John Ackerman, Nina Melechen, Susan Ray, and the anonymous referees of Cornell University Press for their suggestions; to the staff of the Slavic and Baltic Division of the New York Public Library; and to the reference and interlibrary loan librarians of Fordham University. The editor also expresses appreciation to the University Seminars at Columbia University for assistance in the preparation of this manuscript for publication. Material drawn from this work was presented to the Columbia University Seminars on the History of Legal and Political Thought and on Slavic Culture and History.

Transliteration follows the Library of Congress system with the exceptions of names ending in -ii, which are transliterated as ending in -y, and the familiar English spellings of such well-known names as Maxim Gorky, Mayakovsky, Meyerhold, and Sinyavsky.

B. G. R.

THE OCCULT IN RUSSIAN AND SOVIET CULTURE

INTRODUCTION

Bernice Glatzer Rosenthal

T he occult was a remarkably integral part of prerevolutionary Russian and Soviet culture. Occult doctrines appealed to artists, writers, and political activists.[1] Symbolism, the dominant aesthetic of the Silver Age, was grounded in the occult. Avant-garde poets and painters were intrigued by the idea of a fourth dimension. Philosophers and lay theologians explored the occult in their quest for new religious truths. The occult concept of the androgyne helped inspire revaluations of traditional gender roles and of sexuality per se. Early Russian psychologists studied hypnotic suggestion and thought transfer, subjects then associated with the occult. Occult ideas underlay the political ideology of the extreme right and informed the left doctrines of Mystical Anarchism and God-building.

After the Bolshevik Revolution, many people who once had vested their hopes in religion and magic turned to science and technology instead. The Bolsheviks adapted occult ideas, symbols, and techniques to political propaganda. Occult and quasi-occult ideas nourished early Soviet utopianism, per-

---

1. The literature on the occult in Russian painting and literature is already substantial. See the following articles in *The Spiritual in Modern art*, ed. Maurice Tuchman and Stephanie Barron (Los Angeles and New York, 1986): John Bowlt, "Esoteric Culture and Russian Society"; Charlotte Douglas, "Beyond Reason: Malevich, Matuishin, and Their Circles"; Linda Dalrymple Henderson, "Mysticism, Romanticism, and the Fourth Dimension"; and Edward Kasinec and Boris Kerdimum, "Occult Literature in Russia." See also Sexton Ringbohm, *The Sounding Cosmos* (Abo, Finland, 1970); Thomas Berry, *Spiritualism in Tsarist Society and Literature* (Baltimore, 1985); Amy Mandelker and Roberta Reeder, eds., *The Supernatural in Russian and Baltic Literature* (Columbus, 1988); Maria Carlson, *"No Religion Higher than Truth": The Theosophic Movement in Russia* (Princeton, 1992); and Ingrid Ehrhardt, ed., *Okkultismus und Avant-garde: Von Munch bis Mondrian, 1900–1915* (Frankfurt, 1995), which contains several articles on Russia.

vaded literature and the arts, and contributed to the Lenin cult. In Stalin's time, subliminal communication techniques pioneered by the Symbolists and others were systematized and incorporated into the official aesthetic of Socialist Realism. Stalinist political culture treated Stalin as a master magician and recycled the occult conspiracy theories of the prerevolutionary right. The occult revival so obvious in present-day Russia is in many respects a replay of the one that occurred a century ago; the same doctrines are being recirculated.

This book describes the occult revival of the late nineteenth and early twentieth centuries, identifies occult ideas and symbols in the art, thought, and culture of late imperial Russia, and delineates their transformations and applications in the Soviet period. In doing so, it brings to light hitherto unrecognized elements in Russian and Soviet culture, raises new issues for research and discussion, and contributes to the ongoing re-visioning of twentieth-century Russian history.

What exactly is the occult? Etymologically the word means that which is covered or hidden. "Occult" is often used interchangeably with "esoteric"—that which is meant for a select few or for the initiated. But many occultists make no attempt to hide their views (some actively proselytize them), and many religions have an initiation rite of some sort. There are areas of contiguity between the occult and religion and between both of them and mysticism. To give but one example, occult doctrines and practices often depend on religious dogmas, rituals, and symbols, but employ them differently. We can, however, identify four basic elements that together, as Antoine Faivre notes, form a "particular constellation" that is "endowed with relative autonomy and is detached from theology proper," and also from mysticism: correspondences, living nature, imagination and mediation, and transmutation. These interrelated elements indicate how occultists perceive the world. In other words, the occult is a cosmology.[2]

In this volume, the occult (or esoteric) encompasses (1) alchemy, astrology, and magic, which were actually called the "occult sciences" in the Renaissance (medicine was too, but we do not treat it as such in this book); (2) Jewish and Christian Kabbala; and (3) the post-Renaissance doctrines of Rosicrucianism, Spiritualism, Theosophy, and Anthroposophy.[3] The Rosicrucians, an esoteric order allegedly founded in the fifteenth century by one Christian Rosenkreuz, laid claim to various forms of occult knowledge and power, including alchemy

---

2. Antoine Faivre, "Introduction I," in *Modern Esoteric Spirituality*, ed. Antoine Faivre and Jacob Needleman (New York, 1992), pp. xiii, xv–xx.

3. These doctrines in turn incorporate elements of rival religions of the ancient Mediterranean world in the second to fourth centuries: Hermeticism, Gnosticism, Neoplatonism, and Christianity, which had much in common. See Antoine Faivre, "Ancient and Medieval Sources of Modern Esoteric Movements," in Faivre and Needleman, *Modern Esoteric Spirituality*, p. 3.

and the mysteries of "the East"; they paid particular attention to teachings attributed to the Egyptian god Thoth, whom the Greeks called Hermes Trismegistus (Thrice-Great Hermes) and whose writings they preserved in Greek. Although these writings treated astrology and magic, they were believed to anticipate Christian revelation. According to the doctrine of *prisca theologica* (primitive theology), the first glimmerings of Christian truth were planted in Egypt, and these truths are as important as those written in the Old Testament. From this doctrine stems the mystique of Egypt found in Freemasonry, Theosophy, and Anthroposophy, the pyramid as a symbol of rebirth, the cult of the Great Pyramid, and the idea of a sacred geometry. Freemasonry is not an occult doctrine, though it does contain occult elements, partly by way of Rosicrucianism; but its sacred geometry is based on the Temple of Solomon, which allegedly the first Freemasons built. Spiritualism was promoted as a science, but its central features—communication with other worlds and reliance on mediums—are among the elements of the occult.

The idea of *correspondences* stems from the ancient idea of macrocosm, the great world, and microcosm, the world in miniature or the human being viewed as an epitome of the universe. The idea of correspondences implies a rejection of ontological dualisms, binary oppositions, and linear causality in favor of resolution, an included middle (or higher harmony), and synchronicity. Symbolic and real correspondences are said to connect all parts of the visible and invisible world: "That which is above is like that which is below, to perpetuate the mystery of the one thing"—often shortened to "As above, so below"—according to the Emerald Table of Hermes Trismegistus. These correspondences are more or less veiled at first glance; they have to be decoded. Everything in the universe is a symbol or a sign. Everything harbors and manifests mystery. Astrology and other forms of divination, such as palm reading, numerology, and tarot cards, are based on correspondences. So are witchcraft and sorcery, gematria (a prekabbalistic method of biblical exegesis and prophesy based on the numerical value of each letter), sacred numbers, and the magical power of the Word. The capital letter signifies the Word's divine origin. Manipulation of one part of a correspondence affects the other part.

Nature is said to be essentially alive in all its aspects and to occupy the central position in a complex, plural, multilayered, and hierarchical cosmos, which can be decoded. The idea of a *living nature* underlies the Renaissance concept of magic, according to which the magician or magus has theoretical knowledge of the network of sympathies or antipathies that bind the things of nature, and also knows how to apply this knowledge in a concrete, practical way. He can reestablish physical or psychological harmony, for example, by using talismans, stones, metals, or plants. The basic principle here is analogy rather than direct cause and effect or logic, but it is manipulation all the same. The idea of a living nature has multiple ramifications, including animal magnetism, cosmic "sympathies," "antipathies," and "vibrations"; a universe of musical or numerical harmonies; homeopathy and other forms of "natural medicine"; forms of *magia naturalis,* a complex notion at the intersection of magic and science; and a primal substance or energy of some sort (e.g., an *anima mundi*) that underlies all being. Also related to a living nature is esoteric *Naturphilosophie,* which holds that nature is subject to exile and will participate in salvation. The cosmic pantheism of Friedrich von Schelling (1775–1854) contains such esoteric elements. Some occult doctrines associate living nature with the biblical Sophia, Divine Wisdom; others, with the fallen Sophia of the Gnostics.

Imagination and *mediation* are complementary. Imagination enables the seer to penetrate the surface of appearances in order to make the connections (perceive the correspondences) between the visible and invisible worlds. Human "transmitters" of sacred mysteries—magi, high priests, gurus—use a special kind of imagination or intuition to reveal and to employ mediation of all kinds—rituals, symbolic images, and intermediary spirits, such as angels and demons. Transmitters of secret knowledge can also be "initiators"—that is, originators of new knowledge. Mediation is one of the features that distinguishes esotericism from mysticism. Not always, but in general esotericists prefer to stay on Jacob's ladder, along with angels and other beings, rather than proceed above to direct union with God—the goal of mystics who follow a Judeo-Christian model.[4] The exaltation of the imagination as an "organ of the soul," a tool for the knowledge of the self, of the world, and of myth, made occult doctrines particularly appealing to artists.

As alchemists used the term, *transmutation* meant the passage of a thing from one level to another or the metamorphosis of its elements into other elements. According to the alchemists, transmutation of lead into gold or silver requires that active knowledge (gnosis) work together with inner experience (or active imagination). Such illuminated knowledge promotes a "second birth" and elevates the secular element to the religious level of God, who created all higher things out of lower ones (as he formed Adam from the dust of the earth).

Two other elements are often juxtaposed with the basic four. The practice of concordance, a feature of modern esotericism, involves not only eliminating differences or discovering harmonies between different religious traditions but acquiring an all-encompassing higher knowledge. *Transmission* is the passing on of secret knowledge from a master or a recognized authority to a disciple or novice by an established tradition and its confirmation by an initiation ritual. One reason that medicine was considered an occult science is that it had a body of "hidden" lore that had to be learned. Occultism is often called "occult science" or "secret science" because it has rules, principles, opera-

4. Faivre, "Introduction I," p. xvii.

tions—all of which must be mastered. These rules are not arbitrary. The visions and direct revelations of the mystic, by contrast, are uniquely personal. Transmission is especially important to secret esoteric groups.

Despite their ancient lineage, occult beliefs are neither monolithic nor unchanging. They are recycled, overlayered with new ideas, and brought to bear on the issues that concern people at the moment, whenever that moment may be. The Renaissance occultist and physician Paracelsus (Theophrastus of Hohenheim, 1493–1541) introduced the idea of secular progress. In the seventeenth and eighteenth centuries, occultists wished to counter "soulless" or "mechanical" rationalism. Emanuel Swedenborg (1688–1772) preached the primacy of extrasensory perception and emphasized correspondences in *The Secret of the Universe* and *The Apocalypse Revealed.* Nineteenth-century occultists objected to materialism and tried to personalize an increasingly impersonal world. Some of them hoped to reconcile science and religion, even using the language of science to "prove" their doctrines. The psychological orientation of modern occultism is another feature that distinguishes it from mysticism; mystics seek union with God, not knowledge of the self.[5]

In all ages, occultists have concerned themselves with phenomena that seem to transcend rational explanation, whether scientific or otherwise, but the explanations they offer are distinct from the beliefs commonly designated as religious and from the efforts of philosophers to explain psychic or emotional phenomena that cannot be empirically verified. Viewed in philosophical terms, occult doctrines are ways of ordering the world, postulates of unifying principles that underlie apparently disparate phenomena. They reflect a desire to go beneath or rise above material reality and to deal with such intangible essences as mind, soul, and spirit. The occult also has a practical side, which is revealed when individuals attempt to enlist invisible or supernatural forces, divine or diabolic, to attain health, wealth, love, and other personal goals.

Political and cultural considerations determine what is considered occult at a particular time and place. Occultists were often persecuted by the official churches, as much for political as for religious reasons: the churches wanted to be the sole interpreters of dogma. Once Gnosticism was declared a heresy, for example, it had to be hidden, though most Gnostics considered themselves to be Christians. Gnostic teachings and symbols became part of occult lore. Among them were the androgyne, symbolizing the unity of male and female, and Uroboros, a serpent biting its tail. The circle thus formed symbolizes the unity of good and evil and their continuous transmutation, good coming out of evil and vice versa, as distinct from and opposed to an absolute moral code. Occult doctrines vary in their conceptions of good and evil. Modern occultism has a countercultural aura, in part because it exalts the "spiritual wisdom" of

5. Jacob Needleman, Introduction II, in Faivre and Needleman, *Modern Esoteric Spirituality,* pp. xxiii–xiv.

Egypt, Persia, India, China, and Tibet. This exoticism is attractive to persons who find the established wisdom of their own society inadequate. Prerevolutionary Russian artists were fascinated by Siberian shamanism and by the beliefs and rituals of the pagan Slavs. The shamanism of Native Americans (Amerindians) is part of the cluster of ideas favored by the contemporary New Age movement. Occult doctrines can be a conduit for practices that are not at all occult in the culture of their origin. Relaxation techniques drawn from yoga, for example, and such forms of alternative medicine as acupuncture were introduced to the West as part of esoteric lore.

Some people in every age are drawn to the occult, but occultism as a popular phenomenon is correlated with periods of political and social upheaval, cultural confusion, and spiritual quest. At such times, old values and beliefs lose their credibility. New questions arise which the dominant belief does not answer or spiritual yearnings develop which the institutionalized church does not satisfy. Until a new belief is established, the occult, with its vision of an immutable world, deepens or supplements the verities of established religion and seems to offer stability and salvation. Renaissance Italy was torn between medieval Catholicism and revived paganism; political, social, and religious conflicts in seventeenth-century England were exacerbated by the apocalyptic expectations evoked by the date 1666 (666 is the number of the Beast); and in the late nineteenth and early twentieth centuries all Europe was bedeviled by a host of new problems for which neither Christianity nor Enlightenment ideals seemed to offer solutions.

The occultism that flourishes in such periods can be seen as a response to the spiritual disorientation and cultural confusion that accompanies the death of the myth (the dominant belief). In the process of establishing a new myth, its devotees suppress and marginalize the occult. Thomas Kuhn's explication of the structure of scientific revolutions describes a very similar process.[6] Eventually anomalies arise that the accepted scientific paradigm cannot explain. As anomalies accumulate, the credibility of the dominant paradigm is undermined. New paradigms are posited. Ultimately one of them prevails, displacing its rivals or selectively appropriating some of their features. The scientific revolution that Kuhn describes began in the Renaissance and culminated in the seventeenth century with the triumph of the Newtonian system, the epistemological foundation of the Enlightenment. Among these rival paradigms were scientific theories that were subsequently associated with the occult. In Kuhn's model, they were rejected alternate paradigms. James Webb even defines occultism as *"rejected knowledge."*[7] The revolution in physics in the late nineteenth and early twentieth centuries challenged the Newtonian paradigm,

6. Thomas Kuhn, *The Structure of Scientific Revolutions* (Chicago, 1970).
7. James Webb, *The Occult Underground* (La Salle, Ill., 1974), p. 191.

but did not displace it. The occult revival discussed in this volume occurred during those same years.

The vogue of the occult that arose in late nineteenth-century Russia was a response to such Europe-wide trends as the fading appeal of institutionalized Christianity, but the vogue was also a response to a series of shocks peculiar to Russia or most intensely felt there. First there was Russia's diplomatic isolation and subsequent defeat in the Crimean War (1854–55). Then the abolition of serfdom in 1861 contributed greatly to the decline of the gentry while at the same time it left the peasants disappointed. The perceived inadequacy of the emancipation settlement was a major factor in the development of the revolutionary intelligentsia, men and women committed to abolishing the autocracy and instituting a just society, although they disagreed on exactly what a just society entailed and how to achieve it. Some resorted to terror, killing off scores of government officials in an attempt to make the system unworkable and to inspire revolution. Instead, their assassination of Tsar Alexander II in March 1881 horrified educated society and ushered in two decades of reaction.

But other revolutionary forces were at work. The government-sponsored industrialization drive of the 1890s transformed the economy at a pace unprecedented in Europe, creating numerous dislocations and undermining long-established social and political structures and the beliefs that sanctioned them. Not only Orthodoxy, the state religion, but Populism, the agrarian socialism based on the peasant commune—the "ruling idea" of the intelligentsia—was called into question. For some people, Marxism filled the ideological vacuum. Others sought answers in occult doctrines and, around the turn of the century, in Christian eschatology, frequently combining the two. Russia's unexpected defeat in the Russo-Japanese War (1904–5) and the Revolution of 1905 confirmed and exacerbated the sense of an all-pervasive crisis and the imminent end of the old world. The tsar's promise of a duma (a parliament with limited powers) in October 1905 satisfied some revolutionaries, but others continued the struggle by various means. The homemade bombs revolutionaries used to kill government officials also killed innocent bystanders, creating a climate of fear. The government responded to terrorism with reprisals and martial law. Even so, violence continued. The prime minister, Petr Stolypin, was assassinated in 1911. World War I brought terrible suffering and humiliating defeats to Russia. The revolution of February 1917 and the Bolshevik Revolution in October destroyed the social order along with the autocracy.

Among the carriers of occultism in prerevolutionary Russia were artists and writers who rejected the official ideology of church and state, and found the positivism and materialism of the intelligentsia inadequate as well. These people drew on the French occult revival and the new occult doctrines of Spiritualism, Theosophy, and Anthroposophy, combining them with occult beliefs and

Bernice Glatzer Rosenthal

practices indigenous to Russia and with popular culture generally. Let us briefly survey these Western imports.

The French occult revival involved a rediscovery and popularization of alchemy, magic, and Kabbala. Its progenitor was Eliphas Lévi (pseudonym of Alphonse Louis Constant, 1804–75), a defrocked priest but a lifelong Catholic. Lévi and his followers wrote books on magic, astrology, palmistry, and tarot cards, and translated into French the classics of late medieval and early modern European occultism and mysticism. He found an enthusiastic public for Agrippa von Nettesheim (1486–1535), Paracelsus, Swedenborg, and Jakob Boehme (1575–1624). By the 1890s French occultists had fragmented into rival schools, some Catholic, others vehemently anti-Catholic. Paris was the cultural capital of the Western world and educated Europeans could read French. The most popular occult writers, such as Papus (Gérard Encausse, 1865–1916), were translated into many languages, including Russian, and attracted a mass audience.

Spiritualism affirms the continued existence of "the dead" and the ability of the living to communicate with them through specially gifted mediums. Spiritualism with a capital *S* refers to a doctrine and a movement, as distinct from "spiritualism" as a search for the spiritual, or as an antonym of "materialism." The doctrine achieved tremendous popularity among people of all classes, including the highest circles of the royal courts of England, Germany, and Russia, because it responded to people's unmet spiritual needs.[8] Born in 1848 near Rochester, New York, the center of the "Burned-Over District," Spiritualism achieved its greatest impact in England, home of the Industrial Revolution and of Charles Darwin.[9] Darwin's theory of evolution evoked tremendous religious anxiety because it seemed to contradict the biblical account of creation, deny personal immortality, and reduce humankind to a species in the animal kingdom, condemned to an endless struggle for survival. Spiritualism comforted people. It did not require them to renounce Christianity; it used scientific language and methodology to "prove" its claims; and it accommodated a wide range of views—political radicalism, political conservatism, vegetarianism, homeopathic medicine. It fostered interest in parapsychology. The utopian socialist Robert Owen (1771–1858) was a Spiritualist in later life. Spiritualism also lent itself to parlor games: people sat in a darkened room, held hands, and listened for mysterious raps and knocks. The Frenchman

8. Tolstoy alluded to spiritualist séances in his novels and ridiculed them in his play *Plody prosveshchenia* (The fruits of enlightenment). Dostoevsky alluded to Spiritualism in his novels.

9. Spiritualism was the creation of the Fox sisters, who later admitted it was a hoax. The Burned-Over District, a poor farming region, got its name because it was seared so many times by the fires of religious enthusiasm. Social unrest and economic instability created a state of mind susceptible to intense religious emotion. Enthusiastic sects flourished in this area, which was also the birthplace of Mormonism.

Allan Kardec (1803–69) combined Spiritualism with reincarnation. In Germany, Spiritualism was proselytized by Baron Karl Du Prel (1839–99), editor and publisher of *Psychische Studien* in Leipzig. Du Prel collaborated with Russian Spiritualists who published the journal *Rebus*. The philosopher Vladimir Soloviev (1853–1900), his brother Vsevolod Soloviev (1849–1903), and the Symbolist poet Valery Briusov (1873–1924) were interested in Spiritualism. Vsevolod Soloviev wrote a novel called *Velikii Rozenkreitser* (The great Rosicrucian, 1892) and corresponded with Elena Blavatsky. Many occultists were similarly eclectic. Spiritualism had the most adherents, but Theosophy and Anthroposophy had greater influence on art and thought.

Theosophy was founded by Elena Blavatsky (1831–91), who began her occult career as a Spiritualist, and Colonel Henry Olcott in New York in 1875. They soon relocated to India, and their home in Adyar (near Madras) became the headquarters of a worldwide movement. "Theosophy" with a capital *T* refers to her doctrine, as distinct from "theosophy," divine wisdom, which is often used as a synonym for speculative mysticism. Blavatsky taught that one eternal truth, "the Secret Doctrine," which she claimed to have learned from "mahatmas" in the Himalayas, was given to humankind at the creation but had fragmented into different religions and become adulterated by materialism. Purportedly a world religion, Theosophy incorporated elements of Christianity, medieval and Renaissance occultism, the mystery religions of ancient Greece, Hinduism, and Buddhism, but was closest to Buddhism. When Blavatsky's successor, Annie Besant (1847–1933), proclaimed a young Hindu boy, Krishnamurti, as an avatar of the coming Christ in 1908, Rudolf Steiner (1861–1925), then a prominent German Theosophist, and his followers left the society. A few years later, Steiner founded a new movement, which he called Anthroposophy. Actually a Christianized form of Theosophy, Anthroposophy taught that the birth of Jesus was the central event in the evolution of the cosmos, which Steiner saw in both physical and spiritual terms. He called Anthroposophy "spiritual science" and claimed that it reconciled religion, philosophy, and science.

As these doctrines spread throughout Europe, devotees adapted them to their own personal situation and cultural heritage. French occultism featured alchemy and magic and depended on Catholic rituals and symbols. The Satanist black mass, for example, was an inversion of the Catholic mass. German occultists rediscovered their own mystical and occult tradition—Meister Eckhardt (c. 1260–1327), Boehme, Franz von Baader, Pietism, Goethe's interest in alchemy and magic. German Romanticism is replete with occult elements. Irish Theosophists emphasized Celtic folklore and myth to counteract the dominant English culture. In both Ireland and England, early Theosophical propaganda was aggressively anti-Christian.

Russians combined Western doctrines with their own religious and cultural heritage, and with apocalypticism and messianism. The Orthodox Church did not discourage personal religious experience or speculative mysticism. Gnostic elements, laundered by the Greek fathers, became embedded in Orthodoxy in the sixth century and were reinforced in the late sixteenth and early seventeenth centuries by Boehme's thought, which was popular in the Orthodox seminaries. Boehme's thought, very likely in combination with mystical Freemasonry, which Russians learned about in the eighteenth century, influenced the reformer Count Mikhail Speransky (1772–1839) and the Slavophile Ivan Kireevsky (1806–56), whose father was a Mason.[10] Boehme also influenced Russia's greatest philosopher, Vladimir Soloviev, and through him the art and thought of the early twentieth century. Boehme and Schelling had exalted Sophia, but the mystical eroticism of Vladimir Soloviev's poems to her was unique.

Orthodox theologians had long disparaged rationalism as a thing of the "Latin West." In the 1840s this theme was taken up by the Slavophiles, a group of intellectuals who maintained that Western ideas and institutions were not suited to Russia (despite their own indebtedness to German Romanticism). By the end of the nineteenth century, some Russians were associating rationalism with the "bourgeois West." Attempts to define a distinct Russian identity led to a new appreciation of native folktales, myths, and legends, many of which featured supernatural beings and forces that derived from the peasant *dvoeverie* (dual faith). *Dvoeverie* combined the pantheism of the pagan Slavs with Christianity; its basic distinction was not between good and evil but between clean and unclean. The peasant's universe was populated by all sorts of nature spirits—*rusalki* (mermaids), wood sprites (*leshie*), creatures who inhabited house and barn—and all had to be propitiated.[11] Such beings accorded well with the occultists' living nature, and so were easily assimilated into an occult paradigm. Witches and sorcerers prevented "spoiling," warded off the evil eye, and cast spells on love objects, enemies, and rivals. The craft of these mediators relied on correspondences.

Persons interested in the occult were receptive to all sorts of extrarational beliefs and practices. The Symbolists regarded the orgiastic rituals of certain mystical sectarian groups as survivals of the Dionysian cults and, paradoxically, as expressing authentic Christianity.[12] Some Symbolists made pilgrimages to Lake Svetloiar, the site of the legendary city of Kitezh, which sank to the

10. Zdenek V. David, "The Influence of Jacob Boehme on Russian Religious Thought," *Slavic Review,* March 1962, pp. 43–64. On Freemasonry, see Stephen Baehr, *The Paradise Myth* (Stanford, 1991), esp. pp. 90–111.

11. Linda Ivanits, *Russian Folk Belief* (Armonk, N.Y., 1989). For the *rusalka* in Russian legend and literature, see Maria Deppermann, "Rusalka—Nixe der Slawen," in *Sehnsucht und Sirene,* ed. Irmgard Roebling (Pfaffenweiler, 1992), esp. pp. 285–88, on the Symbolists.

12. Details are found in William John Comer, "The Russian Religious Dissenters and the Literary Culture of the Symbolist Generation," Ph.D. diss., University of California, Berkeley, 1992.

bottom of the lake at the time of the Mongol invasion and was to remain invisible until the second coming of Christ. Some revolutionaries viewed the sectarians as potential political allies because they, too, hated the establishment. Artists and writers of various schools were fascinated by shamanism. By coincidence, studies of shamanism written by revolutionaries exiled to Siberia appeared in the early 1900s. The shaman has supernatural powers; he leaves his body and in a trance (sometimes induced by drugs) proceeds to other worlds in order to learn how to heal this one. In other words, he is a transmitter. The great Soviet film director Sergei Eisenstein (1898–1948) was interested in the altered consciousness induced by shamanistic practices, including the use of hallucinatory drugs, and shamanistic symbols can be seen in his films. Eisenstein was initiated into a Rosicrucian order in 1918, and read widely in alchemy.

Many Russians in the late nineteenth and early twentieth centuries were also attracted to the philosophy of Nikolai Fedorov (1828–1903), who maintained that the "common task" of humanity was to resurrect, by means of science, its dead fathers from particles scattered in the cosmic dust. Fedor Dostoevsky, Lev Tolstoy, and Vladimir Soloviev were among his admirers, as were the Nietzschean Marxists Maxim Gorky (1868–1936), Anatoly Lunacharsky (1875–1933), Aleksandr Bogdanov (1873–1928), and the Futurist poet Vladimir Mayakovsky (1893–1930). Despite Fedorov's invocation of science and technology and his emphasis on abolishing the distinction between the learned and the unlearned, his was a special science of the Gnostic type and there are definite parallels between his thought and the occult. Fedorov's "common task" was like an alchemical Great Work in which transmutation is achieved by science rather than the philosopher's stone. He advocated colonizing space to accommodate the increase in population when the dead were resurrected, harnessing solar energy, controlling the climate, and transforming nature by such means as irrigating Arabia with icebergs hauled from the Arctic. He predicted cloning and prosthetic organs (not organ transplants—the resurrected would need their organs). Fedorov's vision of the regulation of nature appealed to worshipers of technology. According to V. V. Ivanov, Fedorov set the agenda for Soviet science.[13]

Fedorov turned his back on the female principle that most Russians found so appealing. Not for him the Great Mother; he yearned for no Sophia. He never married and, so far as is known, never had a sexual relationship of any kind. Throughout his work he treats the sex drive as a negative natural force that man must regulate. As George M. Young Jr. notes in Chapter 7 of this book, Fedorov is the most patriarchal of Russian thinkers. He is also an authoritarian thinker. Men and women perform their tasks in labor armies, and

13. V. V. Ivanov, remarks at the conference "The Occult in Modern Russian and Soviet Culture," Fordham University, June 1991.

Fedorov's entire project is supervised by a tsar-autocrat. No one can refuse to join in. Reproduction ceases so that people may devote all their energies to resurrection. Women sew together the particles and clean or purify the bodies—important roles, but traditional "woman's work." Fedorov's utopia is asexual but not androgynous.

In Russia and Western Europe alike, occult doctrines appealed first of all to people unsatisfied by institutional religion but uncomfortable with rationalism and materialism. They also appealed to people who were marginalized or disempowered by existing social or political structures. Among them were artists, women, and political radicals of the left and the right. There were devotees of the occult at all levels of society. It was not unusual for Spiritualists to attend Theosophist meetings and vice versa, and for occultists of different persuasions to be friends. Some occultists saw themselves as part of a universal movement that dissolved denominational and national boundaries in a higher harmony. Others fused occultism with racism. Occultism, it bears repeating, accommodated a wide range of political and social views. The occult tenet that the individual is a microcosm of the macrocosm, for example, supported cults of the self at one extreme and mandated self-renunciation at the other. In between were various schemes that tried to balance individual freedom and social harmony.

The Symbolists and the Decadents (interrelated movements that began in France in the 1880s) rejected realism, naturalism, and positivism to withdraw from society and cultivated their feelings. Fascinated by the ineffable, they explored the world inside the human heart, finding evil and perversity there (hence "decadent"), and experimented with the subliminal effect of sensations on the psyche, paying particular attention to sound. Mysterious occult forces, sinister but suggestive of a higher realm, haunt their works. Symbolist poetry works by subtle suggestions and subliminal associations. So do Symbolist paintings and plays.

Symbolism is based on the occult idea of correspondences. Assuming that the phenomenal world is but a reflection of a deeper or higher reality, the Symbolists frequently quoted Charles Baudelaire's poem "Correspondences," which contains the line "Man passes through forests of symbols," and Johann Wolfgang von Goethe's statement "Everything that exists is just a symbol." Incidentally, Goethe and Baudelaire were both readers of Swedenborg. Also basic to Symbolism is belief in the magic power of the word, a tenet that can be traced back to ancient Egypt and is perpetuated in the Kabbala. The Decadent poet Arthur Rimbaud wrote about "the alchemy of the word," to which he attributed transmutative powers, and preached derangement of the senses as a means to new insights. In the twentieth century, the Surrealist poet André Breton consecrated the unconscious and bestowed upon language the powers and rewards usually associated with magic. Baudelaire and the Symbolists were devotees of Richard Wagner's operas, which they understood in terms of alchemical transmutation, and also, because of their complexity, in terms of the alchemists' "Great Work," complete with an act of sacrificial purification at the end.

Persons interested in the occult found philosophical support in the irrational epistemologies of Arthur Schopenhauer (1788–1860), Richard Wagner (1813–83), Friedrich Nietzsche (1844–1900), and Henri Bergson (1859–1941). Schopenhauer believed in the existence of the supernatural. Particularly striking is the correlation between the occult and Nietzsche; almost invariably persons interested in one were interested in the other. Occultists' rejection of rationalism, their emphasis on training the will and on expanding human powers, and their belief (in some cases) that humankind is evolving toward a new kind of being, a god-man, attracted them to Nietzsche, and Nietzscheans were attracted to the occult for the same reasons. Annie Besant proclaimed, "Nietzsche belongs distinctly to us!" even though she objected to his emphasis on "brute energy."[14] She was also (at different times) a Fabian socialist, a leader of the Malthusian League, and an advocate of women's rights—all causes that transgressed conventional norms in one way or another. Nietzsche himself stated: "Do you really believe that the sciences would have originated and grown if the way had not been prepared by magicians, alchemists, astrologers and witches whose promises and pretensions first had to create a thirst, a hunger, a taste for *hidden* and *forbidden* powers?"[15] Bergson was personally interested in psychic phenomena and was president of the French Society for Psychic Research. His sister was married to a member of the Hermetic Society of the Golden Dawn, the group to which the Irish poet William Butler Yeats belonged. Occultists appreciated Bergson's concept of an "élan vital" and his intuitive philosophy.

Occultists maintained that the revolution in physics which seemed to dematerialize matter confirmed their tenet of a primal substance or energy that infuses all being. The French scientist F. Jollivet-Castelot interpreted the unity of matter in explicitly alchemical terms. "At the dawn of the nineteenth century, triumphant materialism, led astray by immoderate love of excessive Analysis, denied Alchemy, the same Alchemy to which this dying century returns, eager in its decline for mysticism and for synthesis." His scientific program was "to militate for the Unity of Matter and therefore the possibility of transmutation."[16] Other innovations and discoveries—radio waves, X-rays, and new theories of the atom—were taken by occultists as empirical proof that

14. Quoted in Webb, *Occult Underground*, p. 108n. For Russia, see Maria Carlson, "Armchair Anarchists and Salon Supermen: Russian Occultists Read Nietzsche," in *Nietzsche and Soviet Culture*, ed. Bernice Glatzer Rosenthal (Cambridge, 1994), pp. 107–24.

15. Friedrich Nietzsche, *The Gay Science* (New York, 1974), p. 240.

16. Quoted in François Bonardel, "Alchemical Esotericism," in Faivre and Needleman, *Modern Esoteric Spirituality*, p. 88.

normal optical experiences were illusory; authentic reality lay beyond or beneath matter. Claude Bragdon, an American architect and Theosophist, and Charles Hinton, an untenured mathematics instructor at Princeton, regarded the fourth dimension, a mathematical concept represented by the cube, as our higher and immortal self. The Russian Theosophist Petr Uspensky (1878–1947) translated Hinton's *Fourth Dimension* into Russian in 1915 and summarized Hinton's ideas in his own books *Chetvertoe izmerenie* (The fourth dimension, 1910) and *Tertium organum* (1911). For Uspensky, the fourth dimension was the way to escape from death into the real world of the spirit. He also wrote about yoga, the symbols of the tarot cards, and conversations with the devil.[17]

That astronomy grew out of astrology and chemistry out of alchemy is well known, but the links between the occult and modern psychology are yet to be generally recognized.[18] Occult doctrines appealed to people who were interested in what was then called the "inner man," the soul or the psyche, which rationalists and empiricists neglected or even disdained. The Spiritualists conducted psychic research. The research agenda of the new discipline of psychology included investigation of subjects still associated with the occult, such as the nature of psychic phenomena, mental telepathy, parapsychology, hypnosis, the transcendence of the mind-body dichotomy, and the interpretation of dreams. Sigmund Freud referred approvingly to Du Prel in his first major work, *The Interpretation of Dreams* (1900), and stated that the "contributions of amateur psychologists" to the subject of psychical activities "are not to be despised." In the 1914 edition, Freud added a reference to the "brilliant mystic Du Prel."[19] Some psychologists posited the existence of N-rays, a mental counterpart to X-rays, as the mode of thought transfer.

Occultists had a great deal to say about sexuality, but they did not speak with one voice. Some occultists interpreted the Gnostic ideal of the androgyne to support rejection of the family, rigid gender roles, and sexual repression, and to sanction bisexuality, homosexuality, and lesbianism. Blavatsky, for her part, maintained that modern society overemphasized the sex drive to the detriment of spirituality. She advocated sexual restraint in marriage and opposed birth control because it interfered with reincarnation. Besant deferred to Blavatsky's views after she became a Theosophist and resigned from the

17. Petr Uspenskie, *Iskanie novoi zhizni: Chto takoe ioga* (St. Petersburg, 1913); *Razgovory s diavolom: Okkul'tnye rasskazy* (Petrograd, 1916); *Simvoly Taro* (St. Petersburg, 1912).

18. Henri F. Ellenberger, *The Discovery of the Unconscious* (New York, 1970); David Bakan, *Sigmund Freud and the Jewish Mystical Tradition* (Princeton, 1958); Karl Jung, *Psychology and Alchemy* (1944), trans. R. F. C. Hall (Princeton, 1968). Also Edward Edinger, *Anatomy of the Psyche: Alchemical Symbolism in Psychotherapy* (La Salle, Ill., 1985); James Webb, "The Hermetic Academy," in *The Occult Establishment* (La Salle, Ill., 1976), pp. 345–416; George Devereux, *Psychoanalysis and the Occult* (New York, 1953); Alan Gauld, *The Foundations of Psychical Research* (London, 1968).

19. Sigmund Freud, *The Interpretation of Dreams* (New York, 1965), p. 96.

Malthusian League. The downgrading of sexuality appealed to women who sought to make feminism respectable by dissociating it from free love, or who wished to create a sexually uncharged public sphere, or who equated sex with original sin, or who regarded sex as a chore in an era when good women were presumed not to enjoy it. Some male occultists were unabashed misogynists who promoted fasting and sexual abstinence to strengthen the will and concentrate the powers of the male, which they believed were dispersed by ejaculation.

Occult doctrines had a special attraction to women because they foregrounded such stereotypically "female" qualities as intuition. Women were thought to have a special gift for mediumship. Spiritualist séances enabled women to voice their inner experiences and to be heard in a male-dominated world.[20] Women constituted a large proportion of the members and leaders of the various Theosophical and Anthroposophical societies, especially the former. Many of these women were also active in philanthropic and humanitarian causes and in the women's movement. Many female Russian Theosophists had their own businesses or careers, especially in the arts. Occultists often claimed that woman had special healing powers, implicitly challenging the male medical establishment.

Most occultists were apolitical, but people who felt alienated from the existing order for any reason tended to cluster together in what James Webb calls a "progressive underground," united principally by opposition to the powers that were. Constantly, Webb writes, "we find socialists and occultists running in harness."[21] There are clear occult elements in the fantastic cosmology of Charles Fourier (1772–1837) and in the Saint-Simonians' mystique of Egypt. Fourier's system is based on his Law of Passional Attraction, a series of correspondences in nature which hold the universe in harmony and which can be applied to human society. His obsession with calculation and enumeration suggests an interest in numerology (he may have had a private system), for he never rounded off his figures. Fourier's desire to control the climate anticipates Fedorov's, which it may have influenced, for Fourier's thought was well known in Russia. Flora Tristan (1803–44), the celebrated proponent of woman's liberation as a part of worker liberation, knew Fourier in his last years and offered him her services; she also studied the works of the Saint-Simonians. Eliphas Lévi was briefly associated with the Saint-Simonians and was romantically involved with Flora Tristan. In 1848 the *Revue du magnétisme*

---

20. Alex Owen, *The Darkened Room* (Philadelphia, 1990); Janet Oppenheim, *The Other World* (Cambridge, 1985).

21. Webb, *Occult Underground*, pp. 192, 344–45, 353–57. Philippe Muray, in *Le Dix-neuvième Siècle à travers les âges* (Paris, 1984), refers to the confluence of occultism and socialism as "OCSOC" and emphasizes its repressive aspects—a universally regimented human order based on the principle of harmony, imposed by an elite that possesses true knowledge (gnosis) and would impose it on others.

declared its support for the revolution. In the 1870s the London-based Spiritualist club Isis became a rallying point for émigré socialists, and its journal, *Lucifer,* edited by Blavatsky, regularly recommended the *Revue socialiste* to its readers.

Particularly noteworthy is the association of feminism, socialism, and the occult. Fourier preached sexual freedom and the abolition of marriage and the family. The Saint-Simonians preached the "liberation of the flesh" and called for both a male and a female pope, the male representing reason and the female emotion, which the Saint-Simonians deemed higher than intellect. One of their leaders, Barthélemy Prosper Enfantin (1796–1864), predicted a female messiah, and in 1833 led his followers to Egypt, where he expected her to appear. Such beliefs are not necessarily feminism, but they do indicate a desire to go beyond God the Father. Victoria Woodhull, Lilly Braun (the German Marxist feminist), and Margaret Sanger (the American birth control advocate) were all interested in the occult. Sanger used astrology to guide her life. Woodhull was president of the American Association of Spiritualists in the 1870s and a committed socialist. In 1872 she published the first English translation of the *Communist Manifesto* and tried to persuade Karl Marx that the goals of Spiritualism were the same as those of the International Workingman's Association.

By the end of the nineteenth century, the links between occultism and socialism had all but vanished in Western Europe. Marxist socialists were committed to reason and to a materialistic interpretation of history. Many were de facto revisionists, working for reform rather than revolution. The Fabian socialists were allied to the British labor movement, which stressed bread-and-butter issues. Some Spiritualists and Theosophists joined movements for political or social reform or to prevent cruelty to animals, or to encourage nonviolence, but they couched their arguments in humane rather than occult terms.

In the nineteenth century, occultism as such smacked too much of heresy and satanism for the traditional Christian right. Viewing occultism in solely negative terms, these Christians blamed the French Revolution and subsequent upheavals on a Masonic conspiracy. In the 1880s, however, occultism was taken up by a new force, the radical right, and became intertwined with anti-Semitism. The word "anti-Semitism" was coined in 1879 to justify hatred of Jews on "scientific" rather than religious grounds. Edouard Drumont, author of *La France juive* (1886) and one of the major instigators of the charges against Alfred Dreyfus, was a key figure in this transition. Deeply involved in the occult, he carried around a mandrake root and read the palms of the workers employed by his newspaper, *La Libre parole,* which propagated the notion that Jews were a hostile, alien element conspiring to destroy France and rule the world. The "Masonic conspiracy" became the "Judeo-Masonic conspiracy." It was during the furor over the Dreyfus case that the materials that served as the basis for the infamous forgery *The Protocols of the Elders of Zion* were fabricated. Juliana Glinka, the person who apparently carried the forgery to Russia, was a member of the French Theosophical Society and a secret agent of the Russian government. Presumably she accepted Blavatsky's racial theories of history, which included the tenet that Jews and gypsies were relics of obsolete root races.

The Monist religion of Ernst Haeckel (1834–1919) fused nature worship (sun worship in particular) with Darwinism, anti-Semitism, anti-Christianity, eugenics, euthanasia, and *volkisch* thought. By the beginning of the twentieth century, Haeckel had admirers all over Europe. In January 1906 he founded the Monist League. This was not a fringe group; its members included a winner of the Nobel Prize in physical chemistry, Friedrich Wilhelm Ostwald (1853–1932); the physicist and philosopher Ernst Mach (1838–1916); the sociologist Ferdinand Tönnies, author of *Gemeinschaft und Gesellschaft* 1887), published in English as *Community and Society;* Rudolf Steiner (briefly); and the dancer Isadora Duncan.[22] Not necessarily in agreement with Haeckel in every respect, these people were seeking some sort of natural religion as an alternative to Christianity. Ostwald became president of the Monist League in 1911, two years after he won the Nobel Prize.

All of these occult doctrines pervaded the art and thought of late imperial Russia. Particularly important in their dissemination were the Symbolists and their associates, the post-Symbolist avant-garde, and the Nietzschean Marxists Gorky and Lunacharsky.

For the Symbolists, occult symbols had intrinsic meaning and religious, philosophical, and sociopolitical ramifications. Occult doctrines reinforced the Symbolists' rejection of rationalism and positivism, inspired mythopoesis, and sustained their exaltation of imagination over reason, of art over science, of the subjective over the objective, and of the "inner man" over material well-being and legal rights. They regarded art as a theurgy, a concept that stems from the Latin *theurgia* and Greek *theourgia* (sorcery), originally a system of magic practiced by Egyptian Platonists to communicate with beneficent spirits and produce miraculous effects with their aid. In the Christian era "theurgy" came to stand for white magic, the practice of calling on God and his angels to bring about the ends one desired, as opposed to black magic, whose practitioners appealed to Satan and his minions.

The writer Dmitry Merezhkovsky (1865–1941) had learned about Symbolism and Nietzsche in Paris in the early 1890s and popularized them in Russia. Interpreting Symbolism as a "new idealism," he expected it to lead to higher spiritual truths, to revitalize Russian culture, and to reunite the artist and the

---

22. Daniel Gassman, *The Scientific Origins of National Socialism: Social Darwinism, Ernst Haeckel and the German Monist League* (London, 1971); Richard Noll, *The Jung Cult: Origins of a Charismatic Movement* (Princeton, 1994), pp. 48–50.

people. The most prominent Symbolist poets were Konstantin Bal'mont (1867–1942), Valery Briusov (1873–1924), Andrei Bely (1880–1934), Aleksandr Blok (1880–1921), Viacheslav Ivanov (1866–1949), Maksimilian Voloshin (1877–1932), and Zinaida Gippius (Merezhkovsky's wife, 1869–1945). Associated with them were the writers Aleksei Remizov (1877–1957), Fedor Sologub (1863–1927), and Vasily Rozanov (1856–1919); the painter Mikhail Vrubel' (1856–1910); the composer Alexander Scriabin (1872–1915); and the future Soviet director Vsevolod Meyerhold (1874–1940). All of them were indebted to Nietzsche.[23]

Symbolist poets used words incantationally to create a mood and to transport the listener to "other worlds than ours." Unlike their French counterparts, the Russians regarded the Word as a palpable entity, a concept found in Russian Orthodoxy. Except for Briusov, they believed that the Symbolists had a mission—to pronounce the New Word and thereby create a new world. The belief that the world was created from sound, from the spoken word, appears in many occult doctrines and is echoed in French poststructuralism.

Astrological, Masonic, and Theosophical symbols decorate the journals in which the Symbolists published: *Mir iskusstva* (The World of Art, 1899–1904), founded by Sergei Diaghilev, future impresario of the Ballets Russes; Briusov's journal, *Vesy* (The scales or The balance, 1904–9)—the title refers to the astrological sign Libra; and *Zolotoe runo* (The golden fleece, 1906–9). Bely read widely in occult literature, cast his own horoscope, and took his chart very seriously. Briusov and Aleksandr Dobroliubov (1874–1944?) reputedly experimented with black magic and drugs. Dobroliubov returned to Orthodoxy in 1905 and became a monk. The path he chose was similar to that followed by the French occultist J. K. Huysmans, author of the Decadent novel *A rebours* (1884), published in English as *Against the Grain*.

Merezhkovsky and Gippius returned to religion around 1900—not to what Merezhkovsky disdained as "historical Christianity" but to a new apocalyptic interpretation based on the assumption that the second coming of Christ was imminent and that Christ himself would grant humankind a third testament, a new revelation. Still interested in the occult, Merezhkovsky found it a reservoir of wisdom suppressed by the established churches, an indicator of signs and portents of the approaching end, and a guide to eternal symbols and to the hidden meaning of the Bible and the Apocrypha.

To spread their views, in 1901 Merezhkovsky, Gippius, and their associate Dmitry Filosofov (1872–1940) founded the Religious-Philosophical Society of St. Petersburg, which became a gathering place for intellectuals interested in religion, the so-called God-seekers (*Bogoiskateli*). Most Symbolists became God-seekers, but the movement encompassed diverse trends. The philoso-

---

23. See Bernice Glatzer Rosenthal, ed. *Nietzsche in Russia* (Princeton, 1986).

phers Nikolai Berdiaev (1874–1948) and Sergei Bulgakov (1871–1944), both former Marxists turned neo-Kantians, and the future priest-theologian Pavel Florensky (1882–1937) appreciated Symbolism but were not Symbolists.

Almost all of these people were interested in Theosophy at one time or another, as a way to reconcile religion, art, and philosophy. Theosophy provided a structured worldview that could accommodate other forms of mysticism, and Theosophy's claim to a world religion freed its followers of the need to renounce Christianity. Blavatsky's statement "As God creates, so can man create" appealed to artists who hoped to design a new reality in their own image. That Blavatsky was born in the Russian Empire (in Ukraine) probably enhanced the appeal of her ideas. *Rebus* serialized her works in the 1890s. The Religious-Philosophical Society devoted its entire session on November 24, 1909, to Theosophy. The Theosophists, for their part, were interested in God-seeking and quoted its leaders. Merezhkovsky objected to Theosophy because it lacked a personal God, but he appreciated mystical Freemasonry, and he was fascinated by the mystical sectarians. He and Gippius made a pilgrimage to Lake Svetloiar in 1902. There they discussed religious matters with sectarian leaders, and later they corresponded with them. The influence of Anthroposophy is clear in Merezhkovsky's books *Taina trekh* (The secret of the three), about ancient Egypt and Babylon, and *Taina zapada* (The secret of the West), about Atlantis, both written in emigration. Anna Mintslova, who claimed to be Steiner's emissary to Russia, was a major influence on Andrei Bely and briefly on Viacheslav Ivanov.[24] Bely was even baptized by Steiner.

Berdiaev's book *Smysl' tvorchestva* (1916), translated as *The Meaning of the Creative Act*, includes among its chapters "Creativity and Mysticism: Occultism and Magic" and "Man, Microcosm and Macrocosm." In *Tipy religioznoi mysli v Rossii* (Types of religious thought in Russia), a collection of articles written before the Bolshevik Revolution, Berdiaev treated Theosophy, Anthroposophy, Fedorov, and occult themes in Bely's novels. Berdiaev considered Christian mysticism superior to magic and occultism because it sought to create a higher world, as distinct from merely harnessing the forces of nature. But he was sympathetic to magic and occultism nevertheless, because they departed from the "mechanical worldview" of the Enlightenment. He opposed the institution of the family as yoking men and women to "necessity" and the endless chain of birth and death. *Smysl' tvorchestva* and *Filosofiia svobody* (The philosophy of freedom, 1909) exude an almost Gnostic rejection of matter and of the flesh. Sergei Bulgakov referred positively to magic in

---

24. Maria Carlson, "Ivanov-Belyj-Mintslova: The Mystic Triangle," in *Cultura e memoria: Atti del Terzo Simposio Internazionale dediccato a Vjacheslav Ivanov*, ed. Fausto Malcovati (Florence, 1988), 1:63–79. For Bely's interest in astrology, see Carlson, *"The Silver Dove,"* in *Andrey Bely: Spirit of Symbolism*, ed. John E. Malmstad (Ithaca, 1987), pp. 62–69.

general and to the Kabbalistic concept of Adam Kadmon (primordial man) in particular. Florensky came to consider occultism demonic, and he denigrated Theosophy as positivism, but the footnotes to his magnum opus, *Stolp i utver-zhdenie istiny* (The pillar and affirmation of truth, 1914), indicate that he read everything he could find on the subject. Occult elements, including a mystique of blood, permeate the theological essays he wrote between 1917 and 1923. Florensky and Bulgakov based their cosmologies on Sophia, Divine Wisdom or the Eternal Feminine; the Symbolists exalted her in their poems.

An unsystematized mix of occult ideas informed the new artistic and literary movements that developed after 1909.[25] Futurism was arguably the most important of the new movements, for it achieved quasi-official status in the early Soviet period. The Futurists sought direct contact with reality (unmediated by symbols), but they shared the Symbolists' belief that the Word was a palpable entity with theurgical properties. Fascinated by the nomadic peoples of Asian Russia and by primitive cultures in general, they saw themselves as shamans rather than as high priests. Paradoxically, they were enthralled equally by technology and by the fourth dimension.[26] *Zaum*—literally "beyond the mind"—the transrational language that some of them tried to create, was inspired in part by the incantational language of the shaman and by the glossolalia (speaking in tongues) of the mystic sectarians.

The Futurist poet Velimir Khlebnikov (1885–1922) was also interested in occult botany (the magical power of certain herbs), in ancient Egypt, and in divination. The Egyptian concept of the *ka* (a mysterious life force that lives on in the grave) appears in his writings. His belief that changing the letters of a word (e.g., "exploiter" to "explorer") actually creates a new entity recalls the Kabbalistic practice of *temurah* (which can be traced back to ancient Egypt)—substitution, transposition, or altering of letters of words to create a new reality or to predict the future. For the latter purpose, Khlebnikov propounded laws of history based on elaborate numerical calculations, which he revised when they proved inaccurate.

Avant-garde painters such as Kazimir Malevich (1878–1935), founder of Suprematism, believed that geometric forms, especially the cube, represented the structure that underlies the visible world. Imbued with the mystique of the fourth dimension and seeking to achieve transparency, they tried to develop pictorial means of transcending material reality. They also tried to depict sounds, colors, and smells, and to capture the vibrations and atmospheric dynamism that they believed made up the world. Vasily Kandinsky (1866–

25. The debt of Acmeist poets to the occult requires research. Nikolai Gumilev (1866–1921), for one, was interested in it as part of a more general interest in exoticism.

26. See the articles by Henderson and Douglas cited in n. 1. For the primitivist painter Mikhail Larionov (1881–1964) see Anthony Parton, *Mikhail Larionov and the Russian Avant-Garde* (Princeton, 1993), p. 137.

1944) tried to paint invisible essences, to go beneath and beyond material phenomena to reach a greater spiritual reality. A trained ethnographer, he viewed the artist as a kind of shaman, a healer.[27] Themes and images drawn from shamanism, Theosophy, the *dvoeverie,* apocalyptic Christianity, Russian icons, and German Expressionism permeate his work. The pictorial kaleidoscope of Marc Chagall (1887–1985) included themes and images drawn from the Kabbala, Hasidic mysticism, and Jewish folklore.

Futurist and other avant-garde architecture was informed by the occult idea of a sacred geometry and by the Freemasons' concept of God as the Grand Architect (for which some visionaries substituted themselves). The use of glass as an artistic and architectural medium was an application of the ideal of transparency.

A prominent feature of the post-1909 cultural scene was heightened interest in China, India, and Tibet (partly because of the Russo-Japanese war) and in exoticism generally. Two new occult systems foregrounded Oriental religions and yogic practices. George Gurdjieff (1886–1949) developed a unique system that included Islamic mysticism (Sufism), yoga, his own form of numerology, and a vision of the world and the body as machines. Uspensky began to work with Gurdjieff around 1915. They emigrated (separately) after the Bolshevik Revolution and continued to work together until the mid-1920s, when Uspensky began to develop his own system of a Fourth Way. The painter and poet Nikolai Rerikh (Roerich; 1874–1947) synthesized European and Asian esoteric and spiritual thought in an illustrated book of poems, *Tsvety morii* (The flowers of Moria, 1921), and in *Agni-yoga* (there is no such system in India), both written in emigration. *Agni-yoga* includes discussions of health, education, daily life, and human relationships. There is tremendous interest in his thought, and in Gurdjieff's and Uspensky's as well, in present-day Russia.

Artists and writers of peasant origin such as the sculptor Sergei Konenkov (1874–1971), future winner of the Lenin Prize, and the poets Sergei Esenin (1895–1925) and Nikolai Kluiev (1877–1937), both of Old Believer families, featured occult images and themes in their work, thereby replicating and aestheticizing the folk idea of a living nature. Urban intellectuals such as Bely hailed the work of the "peasant poets" as authentic expressions of the folk spirit. The shamanistic image of the world tree was the subject of Konenkov's last work.

Interest in the occult cut across ideological lines. The Nietzschean Marxists Gorky and Lunacharsky were interested in Theosophy, partly because of their own spiritual quest, partly because aspects of Theosophy were compatible

---

27. Peg Weiss, "Kandinsky and Old Russia: An Ethnographic Exploration," in *The Documented Image,* ed. Gabriele Weisberg, Lavrinda Dixon, and Antje B. Lemke (Syracuse, 1987); idem, *Kandinsky and Old Russia* (New Haven, 1995).

with socialism. Theosophy did not posit a personal God; it condemned egoism and the accumulation of material goods, and it preached commitment to labor. Lev Tolstoy was interested in Theosophy for the same reasons and the Theosophists in turn were attracted to his ethic of nonviolence. Maria Carlson maintains that Gorky's "vision of a New Nature and a New World, subsequently assimilated to its socialist expression as the Radiant Future, is fundamentally theosophic."[28] Irene Masing-Delic and Michael Hagemeister emphasize the Fedorovian aspects of Gorky's vision of abolishing death.[29] There are clear occult elements in the poetry and plays of the young Lunacharsky, including references to the "astral spirit."[30] He had a detailed knowledge of demonology, even wrote about white magic. As late as 1919, when he was commissar of enlightenment, Lunacharsky wrote an occult play called *Vassilisa the Wise,* the beginning of a projected trilogy. Anna Larina recalls that Lunacharsky "took an interest in palmistry." In 1932, he asked to see her palm, scrutinized it, and predicted a "terrible fate." Six years later she was arrested after her husband, Nikolai Bukharin (1888–1938), co-ruler with Stalin in the 1920s, was executed. She spent decades in a forced labor camp.[31]

During the Revolution of 1905, Gorky and Lunacharsky developed a Marxist surrogate religion (to which Lenin strenuously objected) called God-building (*Bogostroitel'stvo*). The term challenged God-seeking and advanced the Feuerbachian idea that God is a purely human construct. God-building has been described as a "movement of secular rejuvenation with mystery cult aspects."[32] Gorky and Lunacharsky based their surrogate religion (their myth, in Nietzschean terms) on empiriocriticism, a positivist phenomenology that Ernst Mach and Richard Avenarius (1843–96) created independently of each other which sought to transcend the spirit-matter dichotomy—that is, to overcome ontological dualism. A component of God-building was Wilhelm Ostwald's theory of Energetism, which reduced the world to energy in various states of transformation; for Ostwald energy was the primal substance in a Monist universe, and it was eternal and immortal, since it can be neither created nor destroyed. Empiriomonism and Energetism were not occult doctrines, but aspects of them could be assimilated into a quasi-occult paradigm. Mach was a socialist, an atheist, and an opponent of individualism; his theory that thoughts

28. Carlson, *"No Religion Higher than Truth,"* p. 160.

29. Irene Masing-Delic, *Abolishing Death* (Stanford, 1991), pp. 123–54; Michael Hagemeister, *Nikolaj Fedorov* (Munich, 1989), passim.

30. A. L. Tait, *Lunacharsky: Poet of the Revolution (1875–1907)* (Birmingham, 1984), pp. 31, 35, 62, 64, 101. Kaluga, where Lunacharsky was in exile, was a center of occultism.

31. Anna Larina, *This I Cannot Forget: The Memoirs of Nikolai Bukharin's Widow,* trans. Gary Kern (New York, 1993), p. 143. Larina goes on: "Although I may not have fully believed in his fortune-telling, I was upset for a while. . . . I told my mother about it the same day and she never forgot. Many years later, after my release from the camp, she recalled it over and over."

32. Noll, *Jung Cult,* p. 54.

and deeds live on in a kind of social immortality after the individual dies was perceived, rightly or wrongly, as a version of the occult tenet that the individual is but a microcosm of the macrocosm. Ostwald believed that individual atoms die but the collective in all its generations lives on through "self-sacrifice for the sake of humanity."[33] The God-builders promised collective immortality as a way of overcoming people's fear of death. Impressed by Nietzsche's vision of self-forgetting in the cultic ecstasy of the Dionysian rites, they wanted to induce people to abandon their private interests and fight and die for socialism.

On the popular level, interest in the occult surged. The Revolution of 1905 brought some civil liberties to Russia; the censorship laws were relaxed, and such groups as the Theosophists were permitted to organize. Private quests became public. Until 1905, *Rebus* was the only legally published journal that dealt exclusively with the occult, though *Voprosy filosofii i psikhologii* (Problems of philosophy and psychology) and Briusov's journal *Vesy* carried articles and book reviews on the occult and related subjects, and listed meetings and lectures in their chronicles of current events. After 1905, scores of new journals were founded, among them *Vestnik teosofii* (Herald of Theosophy), *Izida* (Isis), and *Sfinks* (Sphinx). Around 1910, new "Eastern" occult themes began to appear in popular literature. Dr. Badmaev's restorative "Tibetan powders" were in great demand. Popular occultism was partly a fad and partly entertainment (mediums and fortune-tellers held forth at social gatherings), but it was also a response to spiritual and cultural confusion and to the traumas of war and revolution.

In 1905 and again in 1917, occultism was part of a cluster of ideas that inspired a mystical revolutionism based on the belief that great earthly events such as revolution reflect a realignment of cosmic forces. Revolution, then, had eschatological significance. Its result would be a "new heaven and a new earth" peopled by a new kind of human being and characterized by a new kind of society cemented by love, common ideals, and sacrifice.

The Bolshevik Revolution did not quash interest in the occult. Some prerevolutionary occult ideas and symbols were transformed along more "scientific" lines. Mingled with compatible concepts, they permeated early Soviet art, literature, thought, and science. Soviet political activists who did not believe in the occult used symbols, themes, and techniques drawn from it for agitation and propaganda. Further transformed, some of them were incorporated in the official culture of Stalin's time.

One of the appeals of the occult has always been the power it claims to place in human hands. The Bolsheviks' daring seizure of power in October and their victory against what seemed to be overwhelming odds in the Civil War (1918–20) led some Bolsheviks to think of themselves as wonder-workers, people

33. Robert Williams, *The Other Bolsheviks* (Bloomington, 1986), p. 43.

who could do anything—a propensity that Lenin decried as "Communist arrogance" (*Komchvanstvo*). The first five-year plan (1928–33) stimulated expectations of manmade miracles. On another level, one upheaval after another made people receptive to occult explanations. The brutal and bloody civil war ruined the economy and resulted in millions of deaths from starvation and epidemics. Then in March 1921 Lenin instituted his New Economic Policy (NEP). This partial restoration of capitalism confused and dismayed many people, among them many Bolsheviks. That summer Lenin's health began to fail. The following May he suffered the first of a series of debilitating strokes. The struggle to succeed him was already under way when he died on January 21, 1924. After defeating the "Left Opposition," Stalin radicalized their program and turned on the Party's "right." In 1929, proclaiming "a great break" (*velikii perelom*), he reformulated the first five-year plan to feature all-out industrialization, war on the kulaks (the so-called rich peasants), and the forced collectivization of agriculture. Cultural revolution, an intrinsic part of the plan from its inception, was intensified. As chaos ensued, mishaps and shortages were blamed on "wreckers" and "saboteurs." Millions of peasants were starved to death in the "terror-famine" (Robert Conquest's term) of 1932–33. And these upheavals were followed by the great purge and terror, which "revealed" that trusted Old Bolsheviks were traitors, wiped out the leadership strata, and condemned millions of people to slave labor and premature death.

In the years immediately after the Bolshevik Revolution, the Free Philosophical Academy (Vol'fila) in Petrograd and the Moscow Spiritual Academy provided forums for the discussion of Theosophy, Anthroposophy, and other occult doctrines. Theosophists and Anthroposophists found employment in Soviet cultural institutions, including TEO, the theatrical division of the Commissariat of Enlightenment; IZO, the fine arts division; and Proletkult (Proletarian culture), an organization founded outside the Party by Bogdanov, Lunacharsky, and others just before the October Revolution. Its purpose was to liberate the proletariat spiritually and culturally from the bourgeois past. Many occultists accepted the Bolshevik Revolution as a "leap" event into another world. Bely believed, on the basis of his understanding of Anthroposophy, that the Bolshevik Revolution was part of a negative apocalypse, and that a positive apocalypse would follow.

The partial return of capitalism led Bolsheviks to fear a revival of bourgeois thought. All ideas that conflicted with materialism had to go. Theosophy and Anthroposophy joined religion as targets of ridicule and vilification. Berdiaev, Bulgakov, and other religious philosophers were exiled. Occult circles went underground. Yet we find clear suggestions of Anthroposophy and also of Fedorov's and Florensky's thought in the theories of the Soviet psychologist Aaron Zalkind, who believed that a "new man" with new organs and new sensibilities was being formed.

Lev Trotsky's attempts to debunk the occult demonstrates his familiarity with it and his concern about its popularity. In *Literatura i revoliutsiia* (*Literature and Revolution*) he attacked Anthroposophy. In *Voprosy byta* (*Problems of Everyday Life*) he provided (presumably with tongue in check) an elliptical astrological analysis of the birth of Marxism and the revolutions of 1848, linking both to the discovery of the planet Neptune in the orbit of Uranus; Uranus is the planet of revolution and Neptune is associated with ideals or inspirations that stem from the unconscious. In the same essay Trotsky praised Mendeleev's periodic table (as compared to the "mumbo-jumbo of the alchemists") and claimed that because chemistry is the science of the transmutation of elements, it is the science of revolution, "hostile to every kind of absolute or conservative thinking cast in immobile categories."[34] Incidentally, Mendeleev did not confine his interests to chemistry; in 1875–76 he headed a commission to study mediumistic phenomena, which debunked Spiritualism—a fact that was known to many occultists.

Occult themes and symbols permeated early Soviet literature. Aleksei Tolstoy's novel *Aelita* (1922–23) is about a Soviet citizen who arrives on Mars in the midst of a revolution and falls in love with a Martian. The novel combines science fiction, a genre with its own assumptions and cosmology, with ideas derived from Theosophy, Anthroposophy, Fedorov, and Cosmism. The novels of Vera Kryzhanovskaia, a socially prominent Spiritualist and writer before the Revolution, similarly mix science fiction and the occult; *Smert' planety* (The death of the planet, 1925) enjoyed a wide audience. Gothic horror films were popular before the Revolution and remained so in the 1920s, when private filming was again legalized, even though the Party denounced them as catering to the superstitions of the masses. Numerological codes and gematria appear in Boris Pilniak's *Golyi god* (*The Naked Year*, 1919), in Evgeny Zamiatin's *My* (*We*, 1919), and in the works of Mikhail Bulgakov. The genre of Zamiatin's *My*, the utopian or dystopian novel, is different from science fiction and from fictional treatments of occult themes, but it can overlap both, as it does in this case. Bulgakov's "Rokovye iaitsa" ("The Fatal Eggs") and *Sobach'e serdtse* (*Heart of a Dog*) describe misguided attempts at transmutation without using that term. Bulgakov was satirizing the pretensions of "scientists" who were experimenting on Russia. His masterpiece, *The Master and Margarita* (written in the 1930s), is laden with occult ideas and symbols drawn from magic, alchemy, and Freemasonry. All sides in the literary wars of the 1920s acknowledged the incantational and theurgical properties of the Word; at issue was whose word would prevail.

The actor and theatrical director Mikhail Chekhov staged Bely's *Petersburg*

---

34. Leon Trotsky, "Dialectical Materialism and Science" (1925), in *Problems of Everyday Life* (New York, 1973), pp. 210–11, 217, and 219, where he quotes Mendeleev: "There is no way of seeing how there can be a limit to man's knowledge and mastery of matter."

(which abounds in Anthroposophic and other occult symbolism) and two other Anthroposophist plays at the second Moscow Art Theater in 1925, and he incorporated Steiner's idea of a higher self in his acting and Anthroposophical motifs in his stage designs. Also important in early Soviet theater was the Anthroposophical concept of eurythmy (not to be confused with Jacques Dalcroze's eurythmics). Both systems stress rhythmic bodily movements, but eurythmics was a system of musical education, whereas eurythmy was said to express cosmic verities. Gurdjieff developed his own variant of rhythmic exercises based on assumptions similar to those of eurythmy. Margarita Sabashnikova, wife of the Symbolist writer Maksimilian Voloshin, taught eurythmy at Steiner's Anthroposophical colony at Dornach. After the Bolshevik Revolution, she returned to Russia and gave demonstrations that attracted many theatrical people. It is possible that Meyerhold attended, for in the biomechanics he directed his actors to perform, the discerning theatergoer could recognize the influence of eurythmy as well as of eurythmics, and the time-motion studies of Frederick Taylor, then enjoying a vogue in the USSR.

In the utopian atmosphere of the 1920s, the boundary between magic and science faded. Consonant with the slogan "Science is the religion of the Soviet Union," technology became the force that would rescue Russians from poverty and backwardness, build socialism, and create a beautiful, happy, and prosperous new world. Magic and fantasy are prominent in the writings of Iury Olesha, Vsevolod Ivanov, Marietta Shaginian, Olga Forsh, Andrei Platonov, and Ilia Ehrenburg, as well as of Aleksei Tolstoy. In Shaginian's novel *Mess-Mend* (1924; the title is the same in English), for example, the evil occult forces of capitalism are defeated by the benevolent occult forces of Soviet technology. Platonov, the son of a railroad worker who was also an inventor, simply loved machines. His favorite was "the machine of light—an invisible machine of the invisible ether," which is invented by several of his characters.[35] Ether, according to Blavatsky, pervades the universe; it is the source from which all things come and to which they will return. In Platonov's use of a term that has occult as well as scientific significance we see the confluence of the two realms. We know that Platonov was interested in Gurdjieff's *Naturphilosophie* and in Fedorov's thought. In his *Chevengur* and *Kotlovan* (*The Foundation Pit*) there is also a "'death machine,' a specially designed place on the earth's surface where everything is defined by signs of death, by overexertion and exhaustion. . . . One machine constantly produces the living out of the dead, while the other produces the dead out of the living."[36] In *Iuvenil'noe more* (The juve-

35. Valery Podoroga, "The Eunuch of the Soul," in *Late Soviet Culture*, ed. Thomas Lahusen with Gene Kuperman (Durham, 1993), p. 222.

36. Ibid. See also Elena Tolstaia-Segal, "Naturfilosofskie temy v tvorchestve Platonova," *Slavica Hierosolymita* 4 (1979): 223–54, and "Ideologicheskie konteksty Platonova," *Russian Literature* 9 (1981): 231–80.

nile sea, 1934), corpses are put to use: human remains are recycled, so that nothing is lost. Life ends in death and is sustained by death, in a kind of alchemical Uroboros. Thomas Seifrid refers to Platonov's sense of the "alienness of the body," constituted of "dead matter," which the soul finds itself condemned to inhabit.[37] Note the similarity to the Gnostic idea of the soul ensnared in matter.

Fedorov's thought appealed to worshipers of technology inside and outside the Communist Party. Trotsky envisioned "building people's palaces on the peaks of Mont Blanc and at the bottom of the Atlantic," and redesigning the human body to prevent the "wearing out of organs and tissues."[38] Bogdanov's ultimately fatal experiments in blood transfusion were inspired in part by Fedorov's ideas. Occult ideas can also be seen in the writings of Olga Forsh (a former Theosophist) and of Mikhail Prishvin (whose writings on nature suggest esoteric *Naturphilosophie*).

Related to Fedorov's ideas, directly and indirectly, was a new doctrine, Cosmism, roughly a cosmic philosophy based on the occult idea of microcosm and macrocosm. The Cosmists embraced and hoped to transform the world. They shared the Gnostics' view of the earth as a prison, but believed they could harness cosmic forces and energies to end the earthly captivity and overcome death. In the 1920s the Cosmists founded a research academy. Among its members were K. E. Tsiolkovsky, the "father of Soviet space travel" (1857–1935); V. I. Vernadsky, the founder of biogeochemistry; A. L. Chizhevsky, a historian of philosophy; V. N. Chekrygin, a painter; and A. K. Gorsky, a philosopher.[39] Connected to the Petrograd group of Cosmists, which declared immortality to be a "human right," was Leonid Vasiliev (1891–1966), later the most prominent Soviet parapsychologist. The last line of a manifesto circulated in 1920, "Dead of all countries, unite!" intrigued the Soviet historian Mikhail Pokrovsky (1868–1932). Christianity, said Pokrovsky, preached a spiritual victory over death; the Communist state should use science to achieve a physical victory.[40]

In Stalin's time, occult themes and techniques detached from their doctrinal base became part of the official culture. The prominence given to the "conquest of nature" in the first and second five-year plans and the attempts to transform the climate of Asia after World War II smack of Fedorov, even though his

---

37. Thomas Seifrid, *Andrei Platonov: Uncertainties of Spirit* (Cambridge, 1992), p. 108.

38. Leon Trotsky, *Literature and Revolution* (New York, 1971), pp. 251, 254–55.

39. Excerpts from their writings are included in the anthology *Russkii kozmizm*, ed. S. G. Semenova and A. G. Gacheva (Moscow, 1993). Also included are excerpts from Fedorov, Vladimir Soloviev, Berdiaev, Bulgakov, and Florensky. Semenova is a leading Russian exponent of Fedorov's thought. Kendell Bailes, *Science and Russian Culture in an Age of Revolution: V. I. Vernadsky and His School* (Bloomington, 1990), ignores Vernadsky's religious-philosophical views.

40. S. Frederick Starr, *Melnikov: Solo Architect in a Mass Society* (Princeton, 1978), p. 248.

writings were relegated to the closed shelves of libraries.[41] Fedorov was definitely an influence on the poet Nikolai Zabolotsky (1903–58), who hailed collectivization as a giant step toward a technological utopia and triumph over death. He was a firm believer in astrology, and was convinced that the Age of Aquarius was at hand.[42] The occult themes of Soviet literature of the 1920s were transformed into the magical or fantastic elements that observers have noted in Socialist Realism. Stalin himself was invested with occult powers.

After Stalin's death, occult and related themes were used counterculturally, to criticize Soviet reality.[43] In *On Socialist Realism (Chto takoe sotsialisticheskii realizm,* c. 1956) Andrei Sinyavsky (Abram Tertz) wrote that realism of any kind was inadequate to describe the Soviet present; for that some sort of phantasmagoric art would be necessary, a type of art "that will teach us to be truthful with the aid of the absurd and the fantastic."[44] As models, Sinyavsky offered E. T. A. Hoffmann, Fedor Dostoevsky, Francisco Goya, Chagall, and Mayakovsky. In Sinyavsky's novel *Liubimov* (1962–63), published in English as *The Make-Peace Experiment,* time and space cease to be stable categories; a small Russian provincial town suddenly steps into a different dimension and becomes an arena for all sorts of occult happenings. In *Spokoinoi nochi (Good-night,* 1983), the ghost of Stalin appears in a labor camp.[45] In Iury Trifonov's novel *Drugaia zhizn'* (Another life, 1975) the hero, desperate to find the "threads" of history (in other words, to know the truth), turns to parapsychology; at a séance the medium calls up the spirit of Herzen, who misspells three words! In Tengis Abuladze's film *Repentance (Pokaianie,* 1984) the villain, a composite Stalin-Hitler-Mussolini, will not stay buried. The Village Prose movement, a group of writers that draw on "luminous" memories of their childhood to evoke a thousand-year-old pattern of life that is disappearing as they write, have resurrected the forest and house spirits of the folkloric occult as a kind of counterweight to contemporary culture, Soviet and Western. The works of Vladimir Lichutin, author of "Poslednii koldun" (The last wizard), include long digres-

41. There is a parallel here to Nietzsche, whose works were banned but whose ideas were quietly appropriated. See Rosenthal, *Nietzsche and Soviet Culture.*

42. Zabolotsky's works did not become part of official culture for reasons that cannot be gone into here. For occult themes in his work, see Darra Goldstein, *Nikolai Zabolotsky* (Cambridge, 1993), pp. 277–78; see also p. 281 for Zabolotsky's idea of a living rock.

43. Latin American magical realist writers such as Gabriel García Marquez use the occult in a similar way. Their works were translated into Russian in the Brezhnev era and became very popular.

44. Abram Tertz [Andrei Sinyavsky], *On Socialist Realism,* trans. George Dennis (1959; New York, 1960), pp. 94–95.

45. For details on Sinyavsky, see Catherine Nepomyashchy, *The Poetics of Crime: An Approach to the Writings of Abram Tertz* (New Haven, 1995); and Edith Clowes, *Russian Experimental Fiction: Resisting Ideology after Utopia* (Princeton, 1993), passim.

sions on pagan gods.[46] Of course, the use of occult themes is not always politically or ideologically motivated; sometimes it is simply entertainment. Writers and editors realize that the occult sells and give the public what it wants.

Destalinization and the collapse of communism created favorable conditions for the occult revival that is so apparent in Russia today. Open interest in the occult surged in the Gorbachev years (1985–91). *Moskovskaia pravda* went so far as to publish Gorbachev's horoscope (he was born under the sign of Pisces).[47] On September 10, 1989, the *New York Times* introduced its readers to Dzhuna Davitashvili, the faith healer who attended Leonid Brezhnev, and Anatoly Kashpirovsky, whose prime-time TV program (now off the air) featured faith healing at a distance.[48] One Soviet scholar told me that Brezhnev's enemies managed to have Davitashvili's Moscow residence permit revoked, and that soon thereafter, bereft of her ministrations, Brezhnev died. Kashpirovsky claimed that all people have a "biocomputer" inside their body which can be programmed from afar. His healing séances attracted television audiences of 300 million in the Soviet Union and Eastern Europe, and filled huge concert halls and football stadiums. Some of his admirers believed that he could heal the nation as well. There are indications that the Communist Party officials who ran state television hoped that Kashpirovsky's teleséances would serve as a "grand diversion," to distract people's attention from the plummeting economy and end the talk of an imminent apocalypse or a new Time of Troubles.[49] Gorbachev himself publicly endorsed the "Rerikh idea" (a kind of spiritual communism) in 1987 and helped establish a center for Rerikh studies, conferences, and exhibitions in Moscow. There are at least five hundred Rerikh societies in Russia today.

Contemporary Russian occultism is a highly variegated and diffuse phenomenon. "White Christian magic" is popular; at a time when medicine is scarce and the quality of medical care available to ordinary people is poor, the psychic healing it offers appears as a practical benefit. Old occult doctrines have been rediscovered and new doctrines are proliferating. Theosophists, Anthroposophists, and followers of Gurdjieff and Uspensky have emerged from the underground. The Symbolists and the God-seekers are in vogue, so the occult ideas embedded in their writings are finding a new audience. Fedorov readings are regularly scheduled in the Russian State Library. Fedorov's statement that nature is a temporary enemy but an eternal friend has won him

---

46. For a full discussion of the Village Prose movement, see Kathleen Parthe, *Russian Village Prose* (Princeton, 1992).

47. Reported in *New York Times*, January 11, 1989.

48. The article was headed "Around Gorbachev, Centrifugal Forces." On October 12, 1989, the *Washington Post* did the same in an article headed "Soviets Under a Spell."

49. David Remnick, *Lenin's Tomb* (New York, 1994), pp. 256–58.

high regard as an ecologist. Cosmism is prominent on the contemporary occult scene, replete with UFOs and other novel elements. The new occult system expounded by Daniil Andreev in *Roza mira* (The rose of the world) arouses widespread interest; conceived while he was in the Gulag, it circulated in samizdat in the 1980s and was published in 1991. Incidentally, the Rose of the World is a female entity; much like Sophia, she will unite humankind. Also published in 1991 was an expanded edition of Eremei Parnov's *Tron Liutsifera: Kriticheskie ocherki magii i okkul'tizma* (The throne of Lucifer: Critical sketches of magic and occultism, 1985). Books and pamphlets on astrology, yoga, UFOs, tarot, palmistry, numerology, and the interpretation of dreams are prominently displayed on bookstands in the metro stations and on the streets along with Russian translations of Western books, such as Carlos Castaneda's descriptions of Native American shamanism, which were popular among student rebels in the United States in the 1960s. One also finds Shirley MacLaine's books and other New Age works by Western writers. Numerology is much more popular in Russia than it ever was in the United States; perhaps this vogue is a legacy of prerevolutionary and Soviet scientism and the esteem for "objective" numbers.

Occultism in late imperial Russia was not simply a passing fad; it had a profound and enduring impact on Russian and Soviet thought and culture. In a transition period when people were open to new ideas, occultism helped inspire new literary and artistic schools, and provided a language and symbols in which people could articulate their feelings and expectations. Occultism did not cause, but it surely contributed to, the repudiation of values associated with the status quo, by stimulating the quest for a new cosmology, a new vision of the human being and of the individual's place in the world. Occult doctrines motivated scholarly studies of Asian religions and cultures. The space travel and climate control that Fedorov advocated topped the Soviet scientific research agenda. The Soviets pioneered in research on extrasensory perception and other forms of parapsychology, and not only for political purposes. Kirlian photography (photographs of auras) was used for medical diagnosis and in the training of Soviet athletes for the Olympic Games.

Sociopolitically, however, the effects of occultism were uniformly negative. The occult idea of the individual as a microcosm of the macrocosm undercut the idea of the rights of the individual. The occult tenet that earthly events are but reflections of cosmic processes (substitute historical processes to incorporate Marxism in an occult paradigm) induced passivity and fatalism in some people, but in others it inspired utopian visions, eschatological expectations, and attempts to rid the world of evil. Rightists demonized the Jews; in Stalin's time, the occult conspirators were "wreckers," "kulaks," and "traitors."

What of the contemporary occult revival? If history is any guide, occultism will fade as stability is restored. Some ideas will lie dormant until the next general crisis and others will find a place as the established wisdom of a new era.

The subject of the occult in modern Russian and Soviet culture is so vast and requires so much specialized expertise that a single scholar could not hope to do it justice. The chapters in this volume are pieces of a mosaic, and though some pieces are still missing (research is needed on music and architecture), the contours and major features of the picture are now clear.[50] Some chapters are informational; others are interpretive and even speculative, as is appropriate for a book intended to raise new issues for research and discussion.

Part I, "Ancient Beliefs in Modern Times," focuses on three strands of the variegated weave that makes up the Russian occult legacy. In Chapter 1 W. F. Ryan surveys the old Russian sources of magic and divination. Linda J. Ivanits discusses Turgenev's, Bely's, and Solzhenitsyn's use of the occult in Chapter 2, "Three Instances of the Peasant Occult in Russian Literature: Intelligentsia Encounters *Narod*." Judith Deutsch Kornblatt explains Vladimir Soloviev's attraction to and interpretation of the Kabbala and its misrepresentation by some of his successors in Chapter 3, "Russian Religious Thought and the Jewish Kabbala."

Part II explores the varieties of early twentieth-century occultism. Kristi Groberg focuses on Satanism as a literary and artistic theme in Chapter 4, "'The Shade of Lucifer's Dark Wing': Satanism in Silver Age Russia." In Chapter 5, "Fashionable Occultism: Spiritualism, Theosophy, Freemasonry, and Hermeticism in Fin-de-Siècle Russia," Maria Carlson describes the occult beliefs that were most in vogue at the turn of the twentieth century. In Chapter 6, "Anthroposophy in Russia," Renata von Maydell explains the appeal of Anthroposophy to Russians and examines the Anthroposophists' extensive cultural and social activism during and after the revolutions of 1917.

Part III, "From Magic to 'Science,'" treats a hitherto unexplored aspect of early Soviet utopianism, the transfer to science and technology of hopes formerly invested in magic. In Chapter 7, "Fedorov's Transformations of the Occult," George M. Young Jr. shows that although Fedorov publicly disparaged the entire esoteric tradition, he shared a good many of its assumptions and goals. In Chapter 8, "Russian Cosmism in the 1920s and Today," Michael Hagemeister explains the nature of Cosmism, an eclectic and utopian doctrine at the margins of science which featured a "right to immortality." In Chapter 9, "Technology as Esoteric Cosmology in Early Soviet Literature," Anthony J. Vanchu discusses the works of Andrei Platonov and Marietta Shaginian.

Part IV, "Transformations of the Occult in Stalin's Time," reveals hitherto unexpected sources of Soviet culture in the 1930s and 1940s. In Chapter 10,

---

50. Numerology and the idea of a living nature may have helped shape N. D. Kondratiev's (1892–1938) theory of economic cycles (the Kondratiev wave) in agroeconomics.

Irina Gutkin traces the transformation and politicization of the magic of words from Symbolism to Futurism to Socialist Realism. In Chapter 11, "An Occult Source of Socialist Realism: Gorky and Theories of Thought Transference," Mikhail Agursky argues that Maxim Gorky seized on the idea of mental telepathy because of its potential to inspire the masses. In Chapter 12, "Sergei Eisenstein's Gnostic Circle," Håkan Lövgren documents and explains the famed director's interest in alchemy and Rosicrucianism, and their effect on his art. In Chapter 13, "The Occult in the Prose of Vsevolod Ivanov," Valentina Brougher shows that Ivanov, best known for a novella about Red partisans in the Civil War, also wrote about the occult and related phenomena, and not simply as literary tropes; he was deeply interested in philosophy and religion.

Part V, "The Occult since Stalin," demonstrates the remarkable vitality of ideas long banished. In Chapter 14, "Daniil Andreev and the Russian Mysticism of Femininity," Mikhail Epstein introduces Western readers to Daniil Andreev's occult doctrine and discusses Andreev's revival of Sophia, the Eternal Feminine. In Chapter 15, "The Occult in Russia Today," Holly DeNio Stephens surveys the most prominent occult trends and the rise of new prophets, movements, and healers.

"Instead of a Conclusion" consists of just one chapter. "Political Implications of the Early Twentieth-Century Occult Revival," Chapter 16, brings together aspects of the earlier chapters and of my own research to argue that before the Bolshevik Revolution, occult ideas pervaded both the utopianism and political maximalism of the left and the racism and obscurantism of the right, and that after the Revolution occult-derived ideas and symbols pervaded early Soviet utopianism and were instrumentalized by a political elite.

The Appendix directs scholars to source materials. Here Edward Kasinec, Robert H. Davis Jr., and Maria Carlson provide a guide to the rich corpus of literature produced by Russian occultists at home and abroad.

PART ONE

ANCIENT BELIEFS
IN MODERN TIMES

CHAPTER ONE

MAGIC AND DIVINATION
Old Russian Sources

W. F. Ryan

For the purposes of this chapter I intend "Russia" to include Kievan, Muscovite, and imperial Russia, and occasionally Belorussia and Ukraine also—in fact, the East Slavic part of "Slavia Orthodoxa." I shall refrain from attempting a definition of "magic": the difficulty of finding definitions and constructing historical models that satisfactorily distinguish between magic, religion, and science has given rise to a great deal of literature and I do not propose here to add to this debate. I will only say that no general modern study has so far been attempted for Russia, although a good deal has been written on various aspects of it.[1]

1. To avoid excessive annotation I list here the scholars and works most consulted, without comment on their comparative worth. At the level of oral literature, folk belief, and custom, especially in the modern period, the literature is extensive. Most works will be found listed in the appropriate sections of the various volumes of *Russkii fol'klor: Bibliograficheskii ukazatel'*. Since this chapter deals only marginally with this aspect of folk belief, I refer the reader only to the most recent book-length study: Linda J. Ivanits, *Russian Folk Belief* (New York and London, 1989). On witchcraft and the law see N. N. Novombergskii, *Koldovstvo v Moskovskoi Rusi XVII veka* (St. Petersburg, 1906); Ardalion Popov, *Sud i nakazaniia za prestupleniia protiv very i nravstvennosti po russkomu pravu* (Kazan, 1904); Russell Zguta, "Witchcraft Trials in Seventeenth-Century Russia," *American Historical Review* 82, no. 2 (1977): 1187–1207. On magic and medicine: V. M. Florinskii, *Russkie prostonarodnye travniki i lechebniki* (Kazan, 1879); L. F. Zmeev, *Russkie vrachebniki*, Pamiatniki drevnei pis'mennosti i iskusstva, no. 112 (St. Petersburg, 1895); G. Popov, *Russkaia narodno-bytovaia meditsina* (St. Petersburg, 1903). On texts and the text-historical aspects of the subject see principally A. N. Pypin, *Lozhnye i otrechennye knigi russkoi stariny*, pt. 3 of *Pamiatniki starinnoi russkoi literatury, izdannye G. Kushelev-Bezborodko* (St. Petersburg, 1862); N. Tikhonravov, *Pamiatniki otrechennoi russkoi literatury* (Moscow, 1863; London, 1973); M. N. Speranskii, *Iz istorii otrechennykh*, 4 vols., Pamiatniki drevnei pis'mennosti i iskusstva, nos. 129, 131, 137, 171 (St. Petersburg, 1899–1908); A. I. Sobolevskii, *Perevodnaia literatura Moskovskoi Rusi XVI–XVII vv.* (St. Petersburg, 1903). After

With divination the problem is not so much one of concept as of classification, although even here difficulties arise. Although it is fairly easy to see that most divination is an attempt to predict something or to reach a correct decision about it rather than to cause it, the means of achieving a prediction may differ little from the magic employed to obtain a result or prevent a prediction from being realized. At another level, it is frequently difficult to distinguish between divination and games or popular pastimes, and to decide to what extent weather or agricultural predictions are divination and to what extent they are prognosis based on past observation, and whether physiognomy is divination or a protoscience. Normally I have inclined to inclusiveness, although most recent classifications of divination have been conceptual;[2] though I do not dissent from this approach, I have, as with magic, allowed the availability of evidence to guide my presentation of the material. As the title of this chapter indicates, the emphasis is on textual evidence, and therefore inevitably on intercultural transmission.

The historiography of magic and divination in Russia has passed through many stages, from the antiquarian and folkloric in the eighteenth and early nineteenth centuries, through the comparative mythological, medical historical, and various ethnographic and anthropological approaches, to the semiotic approach of the school of Lotman and Uspensky. In general the treatment of the subject in both imperial Russia and the Soviet Union has usually been colored by intellectual or ecclesiastical disapproval and a didactic eagerness to bring enlightenment to the masses. Some Soviet scholars adoped a kind of jovial Slavophile neopaganism, a *fol'kloristika* designed to appease the authorities by being scornful of organized religion in the approved manner but to defend the intrinsic interest of the subject by emphasizing the robust poetry of indigenous pagan mythology and the earthy wisdom and patriotism of the Russian peasant. Because of the self-congratulating nationalism of this approach, together with the enforced cultural isolation of Soviet scholarship in the Stalin period and its aftermath, few scholars knew much of what was

---

this chapter was written there appeared an excellent survey of magic in "Slavia Orthodoxa": Robert Mathiesen, "Magic in Slavia Orthodoxa: The Written Tradition," in *Byzantine Magic*, ed. Henry Maguire, pp. 155–77 (Dumbarton Oaks, 1955). Mathiesen's discussion is more theoretical and comparative than mine and not restricted to the Russian evidence. On more recent textual and history of science aspects of the subject: Ihor Ševčenko, "Remarks on the Diffusion of Byzantine Scientific and Pseudo-Scientific Literature among the Orthodox Slavs," *Slavonic and East European Review* 59, no. 3 (1981): 321–45; M. D. Grmek, *Les Sciences dans les manuscrits slaves orientaux du moyen âge*, Conférences du Palais de la Découverte, ser. D, no. 66 (Paris, 1959); T. Rainov, *Nauka v Rossii XI–XVII vekov* (Moscow and Leningrad, 1940).

2. I have in mind in particular the article on divination by Evan Zuesse in the *Encyclopedia of Religion*, ed. Mircea Eliade (New York and London, 1987), and Åke Hullkrantz, "Divinationsformer: En klassifikation," in *Nordisk folktro Studiertillägnade Carl-Herman Tillhagen 17 Dec. 1976* (= Nordisk museet, 1976), pp. 49–70.

happening outside the Soviet Union, and even fewer ventured to refer to foreign research except to condemn it. Most of the more valuable Soviet writing on the subject of magic was in fact produced under the headings of archaeology, literature, semiotics, folk medicine, and folklore. How post-Soviet Russian scholarship will treat the subject is not yet clear.

ASTROLOGICAL AND RELATED TEXTS

The various lists of books banned by the Russian Orthodox Church invariably carry a prohibition of astrology.[3] This position, however, must be regarded as a topos carried over from the Greek source texts. A fairly early example is the Novgorod *Kormchaia* (canon law code) of 1280, which condemns "astrological nativities." In fact the lack of geometry and the absence of even the concept of angular measurement made the understanding and development of mathematical astrology an impossibility, and there is no evidence that anyone in Russia ever constructed a horoscope before the seventeenth century. Nevertheless, the concept of astrology was certainly known, and not necessarily disapproved. The Bible, Bible commentaries, and a variety of apocryphal and historical texts contain references to astrology. In particular we may note the legends in the chronographs and in a work such as the *Palaia* or the *Tale of Afroditian*, which tells of Seth or Enoch being given the secrets of the heavens, and the conversion of the wizard Balaam into a Persian magus who bequeathed his books of astrology to the Three Kings, thus enabling them to identify the star of Bethlehem.

The Alexander legend, perhaps the most popular nonreligious text of medieval Russia and one that was still extant in the nineteenth century, contains a fairly extensive passage about the practice of magic and astrology by Nectanebus, the magician king of Egypt who was, according to the story, the true father of Alexander the Great, to whom he bequeathed his arcane knowledge. And Alexander, one may recall, became, in the official ideology of the sixteenth century, part of the pedigree of Rurik, the first prince of Kiev. Likewise, the Russian version of the pseudo-Aristotelian *Secretum secretorum*, a late fifteenth- or early sixteenth-century "mirror of princes" translated from Hebrew and found in the libraries of princes and patriarchs, contains an explicit claim about

3. For a basic bibliography of Russian literature on astrology see O. P. Khromov, "Astronomiia i astrologiia v Drevnei Rossii: Materialy k bibliografii," in *Estestvennonauchnye predstavleniia Drevnei Rusi* (Moscow, 1988), pp. 290–310. The subject of the lists of banned books was analyzed most completely by A. I. Iatsimirskii, *Bibliograficheskii obzor apokrifov v iuzhnoslavianskoi i russkoi pis'mennosti*, vol. 1, *Apokrify vetkhozavetnye* (Petrograd, 1921). For corrections to Iatsimirskii and more recent material see N. A. Kobiak, "Indeksy otrechennykh i zapreshchennykh knig v russkoi pis'mennosti," in *Drevnerusskaia literatura: Istochnikovedeniia* (Leningrad, 1984), pp. 45–54, and "Indeks lozhnykh knig i drevnerusskii chitatel'," in *Khristianstvo i tserkov' v Rossii feodal'nogo perioda* (Novosibirsk, 1989), pp. 352–63.

astrology and the inevitable influence of the stars on character, and states that familiarity with astrology is essential for a ruler. This compendium of political, medical, and magical advice, ostensibly written by Aristotle for Alexander the Great, contained the most extensive collection of magical and divinatory information to be found in any Old Russian text. It will be mentioned again in connection with other topics.[4]

But whatever the literary references to astrology, the nearest we get to its actual practice in medieval Russia is a belief in celestial portents and a few fairly basic calendrical and meteorological divination texts.

CELESTIAL PORTENTS

The notion of celestial phenomena as portents was familiar to the Russians not only from the Bible but also from the *De bello contra Judaeos* of Flavius Josephus and from the chronicle of George Hamartolos, which copies from Josephus the episode in which the fall of Jerusalem is heralded by the appearance of a comet. The Slavonic version, which dates from the eleventh century (manuscripts are extant in Russia from the fifteenth), describes the portent as "a star above the city, like a spear, which remained all summer, and its name was Komitis, which means all hairy." Thereafter comets are regularly noted in the Russian chronicles, usually as portents of disaster, and are usually described as being "like a spear," "bearded," or "hairy," although these terms are probably often conventions rather than descriptions of their actual appearance.

Although literary evidence for belief in that other universal celestial portent of disaster, the eclipse, occurs quite early in Russian literature, in the *Tale of the Campaign of Prince Igor* (possibly late twelfth century, if indeed it is genuine), I know of no divinatory text in Russian relating to eclipses.

METEOROLOGICAL AND CALENDRICAL DIVINATION

For the magical and divinatory aspects of the subject we have to turn to a different category of text, small works of prognostication involving a degree of astronomical, meteorological, and calendrical information. These are the *Brontologion,* or *Gromnik (Gromovnik)* in Slavonic; the *Seismologion,* which in Slavonic texts is integral with the *Gromnik* and has no separate title; the *Selenodromion (Lunnik* in Slavonic); the *Kalandologion (Koliadnik* in Slavonic); and a variety of smaller texts. These works all originated in the ancient world with the astrologers and magicians of Mesopotamia, and very similar texts can be

4. See W. F. Ryan, "The Old Russian Version of the Pseudo-Aristotelian *Secretum secretorum,*" *Slavonic and East European Review* 56, no. 2 (1978): 242–60.

found in the *Liber de ostentis*, the Byzantine anthology of such material which was compiled by Johannes Lydus in the sixth century.

Some of these works are known in South Slavonic manuscripts from at least the thirteenth century. In Russia they appear to have gained currency from the later fifteenth century onward, together with other nonastrological divinatory texts of Byzantine or presumed Byzantine origin, such as the *Trepetnik* (divination from involuntary movements), *Lopatochnik* (scapulimancy), the Divinatory Psalter, the geomancy ascribed to Samuel, and the dice divination ascribed to King David, which are discussed elsewhere. L. Delatte mentions the prevalence of texts of this kind in the monastic libraries of Mount Athos,[5] and it seems fairly clear that literature of this nature was the province of the lesser clergy in later Byzantium and among the Orthodox of the Balkans and Mediterranean area, and began to spread in Russia after the fall of Constantinople. It is obvious from the catalogues of manuscripts in Russian, Bulgarian, Serbian, and Romanian collections that the Byzantine influence in this field continued into the post-Byzantine and modern periods.

Texts of this kind, though quite clearly primitive by comparison with elaborate Byzantine horoscopes, are nevertheless not easy to place in binary cultural models of "high" and "low" culture. An emperor as sophisticated as Constantine Porphyrogenitus in the tenth century recommends in his *De ceremoniis aulae Byzantinae* that emperors should always take with them on their campaigns a *Biblion sunantimatikon* (possibly this is the *Putnik* of the Russian indexes of banned books), a dream book (*Oneirocriticon*), a thunder book (*Brontologion*), and an earthquake book (*Seismologion*). This can hardly be considered a "low" cultural context.

The simple astrological and divinatory texts such as the *Brontologion* have a continuous existence from late antiquity to the present day. They do not in themselves have a "cultural level"; they simply circulate in different kinds of society at different times. In Russia they flourish mainly in monastic manuscript miscellanies, and begin to be restricted to the level of popular culture only in the seventeenth century, when a distinct "educated" culture begins to emerge.

THUNDER DIVINATION: THE *GROMNIK*

The Slavonic text of the *Gromnik* (or *Gromovnik*) is derived from a Byzantine source, as apparently are the Georgian and Hebrew versions.[6] The Slavonic

---

5. L. Delatte, "Note sur les manuscrits astrologiques du Mont Athos," in *Annuaire d l'Institut de philologie et d'histoire orientales et slaves*, vol. 11 (1951), p. 110.

6. The main study is still V. N. Peretts, "Materialy k istorii apokrifa i legend. 1. Istoriia Gromnika. Vvedenie, slavianskie i evreiskie teksty," *Zapiski Istoriko-filologicheskogo fakul'teta Imp. Sanktpeterburgskogo universiteta* 65, no. 1 (1899).

versions, first recorded from the thirteenth century in Bulgaria but probably not before the fifteenth century in Russia, are usually ascribed to the seventh-century Byzantine emperor Heraclius, as are many of the Greek versions found in the *Corpus codicum astrologorum graecorum*, although one manuscript ascribes it to "Moses the Thunder Witness." In the *Gromnik* predictions are made from the sign of the zodiac or from the day of the lunar month on which thunder occurs. As with the other small "astrological" pieces, there is little uniformity of text, details being altered to suit localities, but all are clearly in the Byzantine tradition until the eighteenth century, when texts are often markedly different from the earlier versions and may be newer importations from the West. The last appearance of the *Gromnik* appears to have been on toffee papers of the Zhurkin factory at the end of the nineteenth century. Books of thunder divination are regularly condemned in the Russian indexes of banned books from the fourteenth to the eighteenth century.

MOON DIVINATION: THE *LUNNIK*

The word *lunnik* (moon book) is used as the title of quite disparate texts, both in the original manuscripts and by later scholars.[7] It may even be applied to the innocuous lunar tables used in the calculation of the church calendar.

A number of manuscript miscellanies, especially the medical compendia derived from the Western *Hortus sanitatis* tradition and circulating in Russia from the sixteenth century onward, contain *lunaria*, a set of predictions for days of the lunar month, with an Old Testament event attached to each. These Russian texts, though varying in detail, all belong to group 2 of Christoph Weisser's classification of German and Latin texts.[8] This tradition of Old Testament *lunaria* is now accepted as an adaptation, probably by a Jew, of a more ancient system of divination originally involving classical mythology.

CALENDAR PREDICTIONS: THE *KOLIADNIK*

The *koliadnik* takes a variety of forms but essentially is a set of predictions arranged for the days of the week in which Christmas, the New Year, or some other feast occurs. Its earliest occurrence is in a Greek manuscript of the apocryphal 4 Esdras, and there are many subsequent Latin and vernacular versions. In the South and East Slavonic versions (usually in fact Church Slavonic), usually known as *koliadniki* (*koliada*, from Latin *kalendae*, with cognates

7. For a general but not always reliable study see V. N. Peretts, "Materialy k istorii apokrifa i legendy: K istorii Lunnika," *Izvestiia Otdeleniia russkogo iazyka i slovesnosti* (1901), pp. 1–126.

8. Christoph Weisser, *Studien zum mittelalterlichen Krankheitslunar: Ein Beitrag zu Geschichte laienastrologischer Fachprosa* (= Würzburger medizinhistorische Forschungen, vol. 21) (Pattensen, 1982), pp. 18, 67–68.

in other Slavonic languages, means the Christmas period and festivities), this text is ascribed to the prophet Esdras, as it is in many of the Greek *kalandologia*, Western European, and Hebrew versions. Copies are known from the thirteenth century in Bulgaria, including one made for Tsar Aleksander Asen, and later in Serbian versions. They are found from the fifteenth century onward in Russia. Like most texts of this type, *koliadniki* vary considerably in content and wording, but their similarities are sufficient to suggest that all the East and South Slavonic versions are in the same tradition and derive from Byzantine Greek models.

LUCKY AND UNLUCKY DAYS

The classical world and Byzantium had several traditions of calendrical superstition, the simplest of which is the ascription of good and bad luck to odd and even dates, a process that may be elaborated by a variety of types of number and letter magic. "Egyptian days," the unlucky *dies aegyptici*, originally two in each month, go back to before the third century A.D. and were well known throughout Europe in the Middle Ages, although belief in them was regularly condemned by the Church.

Among the Slavs this belief found literary expression from the very beginning of their Christian history. The earliest calendrical advice given in an East Slav manuscript is in the *Izbornik Sviatoslava* of 1073, which gives a list of prohibitions of food, drink, and ablutions at certain times in each month in the article on the Roman months. The more specific "good and bad days" texts take a variety of forms, almost always short articles in miscellanies or at the end of psalters. They cannot easily be dated, but many examples are probably derived from one of the encyclopedic miscellanies of Kiril Belozersky, founder of the monastery at Belozero at the end of the fourteenth century. These works contain calendrical and eschatological information about the end of the millennium and the coming of the Antichrist; medical and dietary advice for the four seasons; a lunar almanac giving the times of the moon's waxing and waning and of eclipses; a list of the hours in each day on which planting and sowing, pruning, tree-felling, slaughtering of cattle, bloodletting, haircutting, and so on may be done with advantage, and the days on which they should not be attempted.

The Byzantine tradition is reinforced in Russia from the sixteenth century onward by Western influences such as the *Hortus sanitatis* literature, almanacs (which normally listed good and bad days), and calendars designating days that were favorable for bloodletting. It is perhaps worth noting that Western almanacs of the fifteenth, sixteenth, and seventeenth centuries (and to a lesser degree ever since) included precisely the same kinds of divination as the Russian manuscripts: "Erra Pater" almanacs, for example, contain lucky and unlucky days, thunder divination, lunar divination, and calendrical divination.

ALMANACS

In the sixteenth century the *Almanac nova* of Johannes Stöffler was translated, probably by Nicolaus Bülow, Tsar Ivan III's physician. Its introduction acquainted the Russians with the astrology of Alchabitius, an Arab astrologer widely known in the West. This almanac occasioned the first reasoned attack on astrology in Russia, by Maksim the Greek, on the familiar ground that it derogated from God's omniscience, and for another reason quite novel in Russia, that it had been condemned by Aristotle. Maksim's work was influential and was copied for centuries after his death; it found an echo in the seventeenth century in Avvakum's scathing remarks about *almanashniki* (almanac-mongers), although in this case the target was more probably the almanacs that were translated for Tsar Aleksei Mikhailovich.

Calendars and almanacs with some astronomical and astrological content (the signs of the zodiac, the dates of eclipses, propitious times for bloodletting, and so on) were published in the Grand Duchy of Lithuania. The *Malaia podorozhnaia knizhitsa*, for example, published in Vilna by the Italian-educated Belorussian scholar Francis Skarina, included the zodiac and dates of eclipses, taken from Johannes Stöffler's calculations, which probably prompted the remark in the 1598 Ostrog Psalter that calendars were not to be used for "astrological magic." Calendars of saints' days (*sviattsy*), also carrying such information, were printed in Vilna in 1601 and in Kiev in 1628.

In Muscovy, however, no further almanacs seem to have appeared until the reign of Aleksei Mikhailovich, in the second half of the seventeenth century. This tsar was fascinated by astrology and astronomy and had translations made of a variety of foreign almanacs, presumably for use by himself and his advisers. Most of these works were not known to the populace in general, to judge from the small number of copies known. Among the translated almanacs (often titled *Kalendar'* or *Mesiatseslov*) of the seventeenth and early eighteenth centuries were translations from Polish and a series of late seventeenth-century translations of Swedish almanacs by the Swedish royal mathematician Johann Heinrich Focht. The Russian court at this time must have been sufficiently familiar with astrology for the court poet, the cleric Simeon Polotsky (d. 1680), to risk elaborate baroque poetry on the Western model, complete with classical allusions and astrological symbolism. His *Orel rossiiskii* (The Russian eagle), a glorification of the Russian ruler, uses extended astrological imagery and cannot be understood without some knowledge of astrology and classical mythology. Polotsky was for a long time considered to be the author of a not entirely positive horoscope of the future Peter the Great, but doubt has now been cast on this attribution.[9]

The first native Russian almanac was that of General James Bruce, Peter the

9. See V. P. Pluzhnikov and R. A. Simonov, "Goroskop Petra I," *Trudy Otdela drevnerusskoi literatury* 43 (1990): 82–100.

Great's scientific adviser. Bruce (Iakov Villimovich Brius), Russia's first astronomer and constructor of its first observatory, was popularly regarded as a wizard who possessed the "water of life" and a "black book" that would cause demons to appear and offer their services to anyone who chanced to open and read it. He also published Russia's first printed almanac, which, together with astronomical information, contained astrological predictions of the kind commonly found in Western European almanacs. Indeed, Bruce has the dubious distinction of joining Aristotle and Albertus Magnus as the eponym for a whole subgenre of popular pseudoscientific literature. As far as I can discover, the last almanac to carry his name, *Briusov kalendar' na 200 let*, was published in St. Petersburg in 1912.[10]

LATER ORIENTAL TEXTS

The seventeenth century in Russia also sees the appearance of several strange little texts of Oriental and Jewish origin. One is a set of zodiac predictions based on the Oriental animal zodiac, not otherwise found in European astrology, which is stated to be of "Polovtsian" or "Uighur" origin. It is usually diagrammed as either a circle or a hand.[11] Another is a curious divinatory text, extant in seventeenth- and eighteenth-century manuscript miscellanies, about a star called Aravan (a corruption of Aravoth, the empty heaven in the Slavonic Enoch), sometimes replaced by other apocryphal stars called Chigir and Kolo, which are otherwise found in a peculiar "Solomonic" text with evident Jewish elements. A closely analogous Byzantine text is known but appears not to be the source.[12]

GEOMANCY: THE *RAFLI* AND OTHER TEXTS

"Geomancy" has several meanings. Two of them apply to divinatory systems known in Russia: earthquake divination, known from the fourteenth century onward in a Balkan Slav translation of the Greek *Seismologion*, which is found as part of the thunder divination text, the *Gromnik*; and the more widely known divinatory system, which will be discussed here, based on the interpretation of arbitrarily drawn series of dots, originally in sand but later on other media.

The word *Rafli* is not found in the earliest lists of banned books but appears

10. For a full account of Bruce in English see V. Boss, *Newton and Russia* (Cambridge, Mass., 1972).

11. W. F. Ryan, "The Oriental Duodenary Animal Cycle in Old Russian Manuscripts," *Oxford Slavonic Papers*, n.s. 4 (1971): 12–20.

12. For details see W. F. Ryan, "Solomon, SATOR, Acrostics and Leo the Wise in Russia," *Oxford Slavonic Papers*, n.s. 19 (1986): 46–61, esp. 56–57.

first in lists of forbidden books and practices in two sixteenth-century texts: the *Domostroi* (a manual of domestic behavior), which condemns "spell-casting and wizardry and amulets, stargazing, Rafli, almanacs, black-bookery, crow-cawing, Six Wings, thunder arrows, lightning stones, magic bones," and more, and the *Stoglav* or record of the Council of One Hundred Chapters convened by Ivan IV in Moscow in 1551, which condemns the following "evil heresies" (as in most lists of this kind, it is not always clear whether books or practices are being referred to): "rafli, Six Wings, crow-cawing, astronomy, zodiac, almanac, stargazing, Aristotle, the Gates of Aristotle."

Only recently has it become possible to say definitely what the Old Russian *Rafli* was. Indeed, the first Russian text to be published which purported to be the *Rafli* (despite the absence of the word from the text)[13] was in fact not a geomancy but a quite different form of divination involving three dice.

THE GEOMANCY ASCRIBED TO THE PROPHET SAMUEL OR KHAIL

This semigeomantic text, usually ascribed to the prophet Samuel, is first known in Slavonic in Serbian versions of the fifteenth century. It presents essentially the sixteen figures and predictions of geomancy, shorn of all further derived figures and associations, with no astrological element, and with a selection procedure drawn from bibliomancy, as in some Western lot books. A fifteenth-century Byzantine text is almost identical, even to the prophet Khail and the unusual names for some of the houses. This type of divination, whether or not it derives ultimately from an Arabic source, seems to have been common, at least in late Byzantium, and its transmission to the Orthodox Slavs is unproblematic. Similar semigeomantic texts exist in the West.

THE *RAFLI* OF IVAN RYKOV

Recently a text was published which not only calls itself *Rafli* but is in fact an elaborate geomancy.[14] It is unusual in many respects: it is long, it has a named Russian author, it is of apparently Oriental origin but obviously was rewritten extensively for a Russian Christian readership, and it forms part of a compendium of divinatory texts. Its author was one Ivan Rykov, probably a cleric in the entourage of Ivan IV.

This manuscript, which is quite remarkable in a Russian context, is known

---

13. See A. N. Pypin, *Lozhnye i otrechennye knigi russkoi stariny*, pt. 3 of *Pamiatniki starinnoi russkoi literatury, izdannye G. Kushelev-Bezborodko* (St. Petersburg, 1862), pp. 161–66.

14. A. A. Turilov and A. V. Chernetsov, "Otrechennaia kniga Rafli," *Trudy Otdela drevnerusskoi literatury* 50 (1985): 260–344. This discussion is expanded in R. A. Simonov, A. A. Turilov, and A. V. Chernetsov, *Drevnerusskaia knizhnost': Estestvennonauchnye i sokrovennye znaniia v Rossii XVI v., sviazannye s Ivanom Rykovym* (Moscow, 1994).

only in one copy and calls for considerable revision of the received view of the extent of Russian esoteric knowledge in the sixteenth century. Clearly it is a conflation of several texts: a major manual of geomancy, possibly with some Jewish influence ("Shmoil" for "Samuel" and "gates" for "chapters," as in several other Russian texts translated from Hebrew), considerably reworked for a Russian milieu, and with many protestations of its religious orthodoxy; a minor arithmomancy of Byzantine origin; and a collection of basic astrological texts of late Byzantine provenance.

OTHER TEXTS

Evidence of a geomantic consultation in Russia is to be seen in an illustration in the late fifteenth-century illuminated chronicle known as the Radziwill or Königsberg Chronicle. Here, below a battle scene, is an almost complete geomantic consultation in its characteristic triangular shape. The compiler of this prediction, which appears to be of the same date as the main text of the manuscript, must have been familiar with a full geomantic text, such as Rykov's *Rafli* (or possibly a Western European manual, in view of other Western influences in the manuscript), and not simply a basic text of the prophet Samuel / Khail type.[15]

This is the sum of the evidence for the existence of geomancy in Russia, and one might therefore conclude that geomancy was not widespread. It is possible, however, that the practice was more popular than the extant written evidence indicates—in the eighteenth century Tatischev talks of the charlatans who practice casting dice or beans, drawing dots on paper, and pouring wax or tin, and during the reign of the enlightened Catherine the Great "drawing on the ground" (presumably geomancy) was included in a list of magical practices that were made criminal offenses.

ALCHEMY AND THE VIRTUES OF STONES

The Orthodox Slavs had access to at least part of the same ancient lapidary lore as had medieval Western Europe.[16] The stones listed in the Bible (the twelve stones in the breastplate of the high priest in Exodus 28:17–20, the covering of the king of Tyre in Ezekiel 28:13, and the stones in the foundations of the Heavenly City in Revelations 21:19–20) naturally gave rise to exegetical speculation and symbolic or magical interpretation. The discussion by the

15. See A. V. Chernetsov, "Ob odnom risunke Radzivillovskoi letopisi," *Sovetskaia arkheologiia*, 1977, no. 4, pp. 301–6.

16. Much of the material presented in this section has appeared in a more detailed study: W. F. Ryan, "Alchemy and the Virtues of Stones in Muscovy," in *Alchemy and Chemistry in the 16th and 17th Centuries*, ed. P. Rattansi and A. Clericuzio (Dordrecht, 1994), pp. 149–59.

fourth-century bishop Epiphanius of Salamis, in his *De duodecim gemmis quae erant in veste aaronis liber*, of the origin and virtues of the stones in the breast-plate of the high priest, together with the reference to them in the *De bello contra Judaeos* of Josephus and the *Physiologus*, appear to be the source for their further appearance in the twelfth- or thirteenth-century Slavonic version of the *Christian Topography* of Cosmas Indicopleustes (a work that had almost canonical status in Muscovy), the chronicle of George Hamartolos, the *Hexaemeron* of John the exarch of Bulgaria in the tenth century, the florilegium called the *Izbornik Sviatoslava* of 1073, and the *Aleksandriia*, as well as the later *Tale of the Indian Kingdom* and the *Life of Stefan of Perm* by Epifanii Premudryi.

Alchemy, however, in any of its manifestations—whether concerned with mystical and kabbalistic notions, with the philosopher's stone and transmutation, or with universal solvents and panacaeas—seems not to have been available to the Russians, if the surviving literature is a fair guide, before the translation from Hebrew of the pseudo-Aristotelian *Secretum secretorum*. This work praises alchemy as a great art, describes the medical and magical properties of several precious stones, and gives instructions for making gold and silver and for the making of planetary talismans.[17] The concept of such talismans was not entirely new to the East Slavs: a description, taken from the Byzantine chronicle of George Hamartolos, of the methods used by Apollonius of Tyana to protect cities from scorpions and earthquakes appears in the twelfth-century *Russian Primary Chronicle* under the year 912.

The various magico-medical properties of stones given in many of the *lechebniki* or medical manuals of the sixteenth and seventeenth centuries are derived either from the *Secretum* or from the *Hortus sanitatis* tradition.

In the sixteenth century the subject of alchemy and the magical properties of stones acquired great interest. Ivan the Terrible, who, like his grandfather Vasily III, consulted Finnish magicians, had a knowledge of the virtues of the precious stones set in his staff, as is recorded by Sir Jerome Horsey, the English merchant and diplomat. Not long afterward, in 1586, Tsar Boris Godunov offered the fabulous salary of £2,000 a year, with a house and all provisions free, to John Dee, the English magus and mathematical adviser to the Muscovy Company, to enter his service. Dee's son Arthur, who was also an alchemist, did in fact go to Moscow and had a successful career there as a court physician.[18] He actually wrote his major alchemical work, the *Arcana arcanorum*, in Moscow.

Interest in alchemy was common throughout Europe in the sixteenth and seventeenth centuries, and after Paracelsus the growth of iatrochemistry

17. See W. F. Ryan, "Alchemy, Magic, Poisons and the Virtues of Stones in the Old Russian *Secretum Secretorum*," *Ambix* 37, no. 1 (1990): 46–54.

18. See N. A. Figurovskii, "The Alchemist and Physician Arthur Dee," *Ambix* 1 (1965): 33–51.

would have made it inevitable that a good proportion of the physicians who sought their fortunes in Muscovy (and many were little more than adventurers) could have pretended to at least some alchemical doctrine, not to mention astrology and other arcane skills—indeed, it seems to have been a required part of their qualifications.

The existence of official *alkimisty* (most, apparently, foreign) in the Tsar's Apothecary Department (*Aptekarskii prikaz*) in the seventeenth century, perhaps dating back to the time of Ivan the Terrible in the sixteenth century, suggests at first sight official promotion of alchemy, but in fact the duties of these "alchemists" seem to have extended no further than the preparation of medicines and the enormous quantities of distilled cordials consumed by the tsar's household.

Other aspects of Western European Hermeticism were not entirely unknown in seventeenth-century Muscovy—the Western-educated court poet and cleric Simeon Polotsky owned John Dee's *Monas hieroglyphica* and Caussin's *Symbolica aegiptiana sapientia,* and the Greek clerical adventurer in Russian service Paisis Ligarides refers in a letter to "the prophetic sphinx" and "Trismegistus Mercurius." Tsar Aleksei himself had a picture of an obelisk with hieroglyphs.

James Bruce's considerable scientific library certainly included several alchemical works, but no further Russian alchemical manuscripts were produced, as far as I can tell, until the appearance of Freemasons and Rosicrucians in the eighteenth century. Some of these men made translations of Basil Valentine, Roger Bacon, John Fludd, Paracelsus, and others, and they must have been the main consumers of the extraordinary stock of Western European alchemical and occult literature that was kept by the Rosicrucian Nikolai Novikov, the publisher, printer, bookseller, and leading figure of the Enlightenment in Catherine the Great's reign; this collection was confiscated by order of the Moscow censor. Only a handful of alchemical works was published in Russian in the eighteenth century, three of them by the Moscow Rosicrucian I. V. Lopukhin.

NUMBER AND LETTER MAGIC

Russians engaged in a variety of practices that involved numbers, letters, calculations, tables, wheels of fortune, dice, cards, and various other systematic fortune-telling devices. Few of these practices made their way into texts. Playing cards were a relatively late introduction from the West—their divinatory use is not mentioned before the eighteenth century. The tarot seems not to have been known before the late nineteenth century; a wide variety is now available in Russian bookshops. Wheels of fortune, such as the popular print called *Krug Solomona,* were probably also an eighteenth-century Western innovation.

DICE DIVINATION

Varieties of dice are found quite early in Russia, but only rarely are they described as being used for divinatory purposes. Ecclesiastical denunciations of them, which begin as early as the second century, in the Russian church were usually made in the context of gambling. One dice divination text, however, is usually acribed to King David. Most writers who commented on the *Rafli* had assumed that it was a book of dice divination, but in fact it is now established that the *Rafli* was a geomancy and the term should not be applied to the *Gadaniia Tsaria Davida* (Oracle of King David). A very similar seventeenth-century Belorussian version of the King David text was also published. For those unable or too lazy to interpret the dice, the text itself could be used as a *zagovor* or spell, and possession of amulets and divinatory texts, including the King David text, was part of the incriminating evidence against a priest at a Synodal court in 1770.

The text could well be of Western origin. All attested copies of it are late, as are references in the literature, and the only Byzantine dice text of which I am aware is an astrological work with no similarity to the Russian text. Texts of this kind are common in Western Europe, many of them stemming from Lorenzo Spirito's *Libro della ventura ouer libro della sorte* (1483).

The predictions in the *Gadaniia Tsaria Davida* are arranged in descending numerical order: 666, 665, 664 . . . 111. Individual predictions are about fifty words long; typically they consist of a quotation from a psalm or description of an incident in the Bible or religious, sometimes apocryphal, literature or folktales, then an interpretation, sometimes with a proverb, and sometimes with a final statement as to whether the cast indicated good fortune or not. The predictions offer advice on a limited number of subjects: almost all advise on the outcome of an illness, most also advise on journeys, and may also have a prediction for domestic life, a move to a new home, loss, enemies, or general well-being.

NUMBER MAGIC

It might be expected that the system of alphabetical numerals used by the South and East Slavs, which was a variant of the Greek system, would lend itself very easily to number magic. In fact, apart from some examples of onomancy, number symbolism and number magic were not much developed in Russian texts, partly perhaps because knowledge of mathematics itself was rather limited. A recent study has shown that the names of various Russian systems of cryptography could well be derived from the Jewish Kabbala, but for any Russian interest in kabbalistic gematria we must wait until the Rosicrucians of the eighteenth and nineteenth centuries. This is not to say, of course, that numbers played no part in popular beliefs: as in other culture areas, Russian belief attributes significance to odds and evens, days of the week and of the month, threefold repetition, and so on.

ONOMANCY

The "number of the beast," 666, from the Apocalypse, was well known in Russia and much employed in Old Believer circles in eighteenth- and nineteenth-century Russia,[19] but the earliest example of a systematic onomantic text in Old Russian literature is to be found in the pseudo-Aristotelian *Secretum secretorum.* In this system of divination one adds up the numerical values of the letters in the names of two antagonists, divides the totals by nine, and compares the results in a table that will predict the winner. According to the *Secretum,* Aristotle used the table when he gave advice to Alexander, but despite Alexander's pleas, the secret was not revealed to him until Aristotle decided to write down all his secret wisdom for his illustrious pupil's benefit. Some copies of the Russian text include two pairs of names, Alexander and Porus, and Nestor and Lyaeus, as examples of the efficacy of the system.[20]

MAGIC WORDS

Russian spells and texts in general contain fewer specifically magic words or names than their equivalents in other languages. Where *voces magicae* do occur, they are as often as not transliterated and garbled Greek, as in Anglo-Saxon texts. The SATOR square and ABRACADABRA, almost certainly imports from Western Europe, are found from the sixteenth century onward. Native Slavonic magic words are comparatively few; the commonest in Russian is *chur,* originally a line or boundary but used in a variety of games and magical rituals to mean "Keep away!" Another rare example is the word *chernobyl* (Artemisia vulgaris, a variety of the herb wormwood), which is recorded in several nineteenth-century accounts of popular magic and has acquired a terrible modern significance from the catastrophe at the nuclear power station in the town of that name. The word was on no account to be used when one was conjuring with the aid of the Queen of Serpents or else the spell would be broken!

19. For a survey see W. F. Ryan, "The Great Beast in Russia: Aleister Crowley's Theatrical Tour in 1913 and His Beastly Writings on Russia," in *Symbolism and After: Essays on Russian Poetry in Honour of Georgette Donchin,* ed. Arnold McMillin (Bristol, 1992), pp. 137–61.

20. See W. F. Ryan, "The Onomantic Table in the Old Russian *Secreta secretorum,*" *Slavonic and East European Review* 49 (1971): 603–6, and "The Passion of St. Demetrius and the Secret of Secrets: An Onomantic Interpolation," *Cyrillomethodianum* 8–9 (1984–85): 59–65.

BIBLIOMANCY

In Russia the commonest form of divination involving words is bibliomancy. The practice of using randomly selected passages in books to predict the future was well known in antiquity, in Byzantium, in the Muslim world, and in medieval and even modern Europe. In the Western world the commonest works to be used for this purpose were the works of Vergil (the famous *sortes Virgilianae*), the Psalter, and the Bible. In Russia, where the Bible in a single volume was less common than in the West, the Psalter was the scriptural work most likely to be found in a Russian home (it was the book from which many people learned to read; it is often found with a calendar at the end), and was the book usually used for bibliomancy, although the Gospels are known to have been used also. The practice came to Russia from Byzantium by way of the South Slavs and was almost certainly already in use in Kievan Russia.

In some cases the selection process could be quite complicated and compounded with other magical or divinatory procedures; in others the use of the book was itself a selection device in some other kind of divination—for selecting an answer from an "oracle" or preexisting list of predictions, for example.

The practice of psalmomancy was condemned by the church: Russian manuals for confessors list it among the evil practices about which penitents should be questioned.

A Psalter can be used for divination in several ways. It may be simply part of a hallowing process otherwise incidental to the divination. In the geomantic text of Ivan Rykov, for example, the diviner or appellant is advised before proceeding to the geomancy to "fast, bathe, then with a pure and humble heart take the Gospels or Psalter, sing the trisagion three times, pray to God, and cross yourself with the Gospels or Psalter."

The Psalter may be used as a divinatory device but without reference to its text (onomancy presupposes literacy). One such practice involves saying a prayer, taking a key and tying the ring end to the Psalter, then asking a passerby to suspend the Psalter by lifting it with the index finger under the ward of the key. If the Psalter turns, this is a good omen; if not, a bad one.

The Psalter may be opened at random either by the diviner or by a random passerby. The text may then be read from the top, or a passage or line or letter chosen by a previous random selection, either by a passerby or by some other method, may be read and interpreted as desired. A variant of this method, in which a "wise woman" opens the Psalter with a knife, is also used to discover thieves. Often the procedure involves rotating the book three times above the head before commencing the divination, a practice also known in Western Europe and in Islam.

Extracts (first lines) of the Psalms could be copied into *tetradki* (divinatory booklets) and used for fortune-telling; in 1647 a cathedral clerk admitted in court having such a booklet and telling fortunes from it by throwing a piece of wax.

The Psalter may be used in conjunction with a set of oracular statements. This is the *Gadatel'nyi psaltyr'* or Divinatory Psalter proper.

Texts as Amulets

The use of texts as amulets should perhaps be seen as an extension of word magic. The use of the King David dice oracle has already been mentioned in this respect, but more common are religious, usually apocryphal texts. The number of apocryphal texts used as amulets is considerable: *The Tale of Adam and Eve, About the Tree of the Cross, About Heaven, The Lament of Adam, Adam's Letter, About the Head of Adam, The Dream of the Virgin, The Jerusalem Scroll (Sunday Letter), The Journey of the Virgin through Hell, The Twelve Fridays.*[21] In fact, it is clear from catalogues of Russian manuscript collections that the very many copies of the *Dream of the Virgin* from the eighteenth century to the present day more often than not also contain the *Jerusalem Scroll* and the *Twelve Fridays.* I have not found actual cases of the use of all these texts as amulets.

THE DREAM OF THE VIRGIN

The commonest epistolary amulet in Russia, *The Dream of the Virgin*, is perhaps one of the most recent. It is probably of medieval Latin origin; it is known in several languages and may well have come to Russia from Poland, perhaps via Belorussia, where it was known from the sixteenth century. It was very popular in the Balkans, where it is still current, and in Romania.

Not surprisingly, there are very many recorded examples; the latest I have found is dated 1940.

The *Dream* was found in most Russian peasant homes: it was carried everywhere as an amulet, on appearances at court, on visits to comfort the dying; it was placed under the pillow of sick persons, and it would bring a blessing to anyone who copied it nine times and gave it to nine people (in other words, an early version of the chain letter). In the home it was normally kept behind the icon case.

Despite its innocuous nature, possession of the text was punishable, and it often figured in cases that came before both ecclesiastical and civil courts, and in repressive measures taken against schismatics.

21. This list is given in A. N. Minkh, "Narodnye obychai, obriady, sueveriia, predrassudki krest'ian Saratovskoi gubernii," *Zapiski Imperatorskogo Russkogo Geograficheskogo obschestva po otdeleniiu etnografii* 9, no. 2 (1890): 51.

MAGIC SQUARES

Another kind of textual amulet is the ubiquitous and ancient SATOR AREPO magic square, which began in classical antiquity, arrived in Russia at the end of the fifteenth century, and was variously used there as a calendrical mnemonic, a key to a set of Bible aphorisms, and a magic spell.[22]

SPELLS AND MAGIC PRAYERS

The subject of spells and magic prayers is too big for a general chapter, and I mention them here only insofar as they can be found as written texts. There are many kinds of Russian spell in the form of Christian prayers but with magical, folkloric, or at least distinctly uncanonical elements in them. As in Western Europe, such prayers may often differ little from ecclesiastically acceptable prayers, and may be found interspersed with them. For example, the *Bol'shoi trebnik* of the seventeenth-century metropolitan of Kiev Peter Mogila, published in 1641, contains many prayers that are in fact *zagovory;* and in this practice the author was only following a long-established manuscript tradition in Greek and Slavonic euchologia. These prayers are usually classified in Russian as *lozhnye molitvy* (false prayers) or *zagovory* (usually translated as "spell," sometimes as "incantation," because, with the exception of the special category of whispered spells, they were often intoned like an ecclesiastical chant), although *zagovory* also encompasses spells that have no Christian content and indeed that are known in some cases to come from pagan areas in contact with Russia, or from the Latin West.

Zagovory are essentially magic formulas intended to fulfill the wishes of the persons employing them, to protect them, or to exorcize evil spirits (which may be identified as illness). The church condemned the use of *zagovory* very early. Grand Prince Vladimir's *ustav* (church statute) in the late eleventh century listed it with witchcraft as one of the crimes an ecclesiastical court could try, and Moisei, archbishop of Novgorod in the middle of the fourteenth century, listed among reprehensible practices "the writing of Greek words on apples and placing them on the altar during mass" and various magical practices employed by people about to go fishing or hunting, or seeking audience with the prince. The placing of items on the altar so that they might acquire magical power was evidently a widespread practice and was still incurring episcopal condemnation in the sixteenth century at the Stoglav council.

The fact that the church condemned *zagovory* does not mean that the clergy did not resort to them. Indeed, as priests were more likely than their parishioners to be literate and to be called to the bedside of the sick, they were often specified as being necessary for the reading of a *zagovor,* and, as we have seen,

22. For details see Ryan, "Solomon, SATOR" (n. 12 above).

were occasionally taken to court for possession of written copies. Like many other aspects of magic and witchcraft, *zagovory* appear to be at their most popular in Russia in the seventeenth century at all levels of society, although it is quite possible that heightened political and religious sensitivity, higher levels of literacy, and the better documentation of the period make this only appear to be the case. They were still widely used thereafter, and at one time books of *zagovory* were kept in most Russian homes, rather as were recipe books or books of domestic medicine (from which they often differed only in detail). These books of *zagovory* are not so common in the manuscript collections of Russia as might be expected, partly perhaps because as domestic items of everyday use they were kept until they fell apart, partly because, as I mentioned earlier, from the time of Peter the Great onward possession of such books was technically illegal, and any that were found were supposed to be burned.

Dream Books

A distinct category of divinatory book is the dream book, or *sonnik*. Although these works are mentioned in both Byzantine and Russian indexes of banned books, and the notion of prophetic dreams was certainly known from the earliest times in Russia (the *Tale of Prince Igor* is a famous example), no such text in Old Russian is known, and we have no hard evidence that there ever was one. The earliest extant East Slavonic dream books are seventeenth-century Belorussian translations from Polish; they seem not to have had currency in Muscovy. The dream books or fortune-telling compendia with dream elements which were published in dozens of editions in Russia in the eighteenth and nineteenth centuries were part of the general influx in that period of popular fortune-telling books from Western Europe, or were local derivatives of them.[23] Under Catherine the Great dream interpretation (often a function of the local wizard [*koldun*] or village "wise woman") was made a criminal offense, together with various other kinds of divination and witchcraft.

The predictions of these dream books become inextricably entwined with popular dream beliefs and the various induced dream predictions of Russian popular divination (usually divination of marital prospects) which were originally part of a different tradition.

Physiognomy and Palmomancy

A variety of methods of prognostication involved the human body.

23. For more detailed discussion see W. F. Ryan and Faith Wigzell, "Gullible Girls and Dreadful Dreams: Zhukovskii, Pushkin and Popular Divination," *Slavonic and East European Review* 70, no. 4 (1992): 647–69.

PHYSIOGNOMY

The literature of Kievan Rus' is ignorant of physiognomy, apart from some elements in the florilegia of Ioann the exarch of Bulgaria.

Full treatises on the subject arrived in the fifteenth or sixteenth century with the translation of the Hebrew version of the pseudo-Aristotelian *Secretum secretorum* in the Grand Duchy of Lithuania and its subsequent dissemination in Muscovy. The Hebrew version used by the translator was special in that it had interpolated within it most of the medical works of Maimonides and the physiognomy of Rhazes, of which a Hebrew version had been made by Shem Tov ben Yitzhak. The Rhazes text immediately follows the physiognomical text of the *Secretum* proper, so that readers had before them almost the whole of Arabic teaching on the subject.

In fact, these two physiognomical texts are not magical or divinatory in a direct sense, apart perhaps from warnings to avoid dwarfs and men with blue eyes, which smack rather of popular superstition. They are rather medical treatises designed to enable the ostensible recipients of the texts, Alexander and Mansur respectively, to make intelligent judgments in their choice of the men who served them and in diplomacy. Nevertheless, at the level of learned magic they were an important innovation in Russia: they are placed immediately after the onomantic section of the *Secretum,* and together with the astrological and alchemical sections they represent a deterministic view of life quite at odds with the church's teaching on divine omnipotence and individual free will. They are, moreover, part of a notion, new to Russia, of esoteric wisdom recorded in secret books for the eyes of the elect only.

The physiognomic sections of the *Secretum* took on an independent existence and can be found separated from their parent text in a number of florilegia. They were supplemented in the seventeenth century by a translation of Michael Scot's *Liber physionomiae.*

PALMOMANCY

A more specifically divinatory approach to the human body is palmomancy, or divination from twitches and itches in various parts of the body, an ancient and apparently universal method of divination. At the level of Russian popular sayings and beliefs a large number of examples of this lore can be found, some of which are familiar in other languages, including English. The manuscript tradition is still unclear and palmomancy in Russia must be considered more as a corpus of popular beliefs than as a literary tradition.[24]

24. For texts see M. N. Speranskii, *Iz istorii otrechennoi literatury. II. Trepetnik,* Pamiatniki drevnei pis'mennosti i iskusstva, no. 131 (St. Petersburg, 1899). Speransky's research was placed in a wider context by Hermann Diels, who also provided German translations of

THE *VOLKHOVNIK*

The *Volkhovnik*, or "Book of the Wizard," is listed in Russian indexes of banned books from the fifteenth century onward, together with a whole series of natural omens ("if a door creaks," "if a mouse gnaws your clothes," etc.) which can be found across European literature and popular belief from Pliny to modern America. In fact, it seems that the compilers of the indexes included the omens that appear in the *Volkhovnik* as the titles of separate works, thus greatly confusing the issue.[25]

No copy of a work with this title survives, but Latin astrological manuscripts from the eleventh and thirteenth centuries titled "Tabula prenostica Salomonis" give precisely the same list of omens as appear in the Russian indexes. It appears, then, that there is a manuscript tradition of such a text, but where it originated and whether it actually existed in Russian translation cannot be established. One can only say that most of the omens are well known in Russian folk belief.

SCAPULIMANCY: THE *LOPATOCHNIK*

The practice of scapulimancy, or divination from markings on a sheep's shoulderblade, is known in many cultures: among the various indigenous peoples of Central Asia, North Africa, China, Japan, North America, and several parts of Europe, including the Slavonic area. Although it is a relatively primitive form of divination, manuscript manuals for its practice exist in Latin and Arabic, and it is described in Greek. All Arabic and Latin texts prescribe boiling the bone (the "noncalcinating" method). Mongol, Chinese, Japanese, and Native American methods all involve baking, as does the Russian and the presumably Byzantine method described in a text attributed to Psellus. There is only one Slavonic text and it exists in only one copy,[26] in the early sixteenth-century Belorussian manuscript miscellany that includes the earliest known copy of the Old Russian *Secretum secretorum*. It is ascribed to one Peter the Egyptian and is closest in content to the Byzantine description of Psellus. Its origin is still mysterious and it appears to have had no literary influence, although it is listed along with the *Volkhovnik* and *Trepetnik* in seventeenth-century indexes of banned books.

European (including Slavonic) and Oriental *Zuckungsbücher*; see Hermann Diels, "Beiträge zur Zuckungsliteratur des Okzidents und Orients," *Abhandlungen der Königlichen Preussischen Akademie der Wissenschaften* (1907 and 1908).

25. See W. F. Ryan, "What Was the *Volkhovnik*? New Light on a Banned Book," *Slavonic and East European Review* 68, no. 4 (1991): 718–23.

26. Published in M. N. Speranskii, *Iz istorii otrechennykh knig. III. Lopatochnik*, Pamiatniki drevnei pis'mennosti i iskusstva, no. 136 (St. Petersburg, 1900).

The Survival of Magical Texts and Practices

I have been concerned here primarily with the *textual* tradition of magic and divination in premodern Russia; it follows that the male clergy were the principal producers and perhaps consumers of these materials. But textual magic and popular magic are often intertwined, and there is plenty of evidence from Kievan Rus' onward that women were frequently to be found as professional magicians and fortune-tellers, a role that was often combined with that of midwife. Since the eighteenth century the urban professional fortune-teller seems to have been most commonly a woman, and nonprofessional ritualized popular divination, in particular at the Christmas period and largely concerned with marital prospects, was also more commonly, but not exclusively, a matter for women. The more serious matter of demonic and malefic magic, or protection from it, was more often the province of the male witch or *koldun*, who played a specific role in village life. This complicated subject, however, is outside the scope of this chapter.

The magic of the *volkhvy* (evidently all male) of ancient Russia, as described in the generally hostile chronicles and ecclesiastical literature, may or may not be closely identified with the religion or religions of the ancient Slavs—the evidence is tenuous and its interpretation varies greatly. Certainly many of the modern folk beliefs and magical practices can be shown to have considerable antiquity and may indeed go back to pre-Christian times. The historical origins of the practitioners of popular magic, the *kolduny* in their various forms, both male and female, who certainly still exist in considerable numbers, may also be ancient, but it is impossible to be sure. Indeed, it is very improbable that the many terms for magician in Russian denote the same thing at different times and places. On the other hand, we have to take note of the close analogies with beliefs and practices from classical antiquity, Byzantium, and the medieval West, not to mention the clearly demonstrable imports and adaptations of imports. By adaptations I have in mind both artefacts such as *zmeevik* amulets, which develop Slavonic forms, and texts such as the *Volkhovnik*, which supply popular omens. Folk magic is eclectic and syncretistic.

If the oldest strand of magical belief and practice is or may be pre-Christian and devoid of written texts, the next, the Byzantine, is largely textual and ostensibly Christian in that many divination texts are ascribed to biblical figures. Christian texts such as Gospel books and Psalters were, and still are, used for divination; and, of course, through the Bible and other translated literature, both Christian and non-Christian, Russians became aware of the prevalence in biblical times of various kinds of magic and divination, and even of their apparent efficacy. As we have seen, local adaptation may take place: Russian icons may be used as palladia and vexilla, like their Byzantine precursors; calendrical weather and crop predictions may be adapted to make a pun on or a rhyme for a Greek saint's name in its Russian form.

The Byzantine divinatory texts that came to Russia are of a very basic kind and may well not have been known in Russia before the late fifteenth century. There is no evidence of the existence in Russia of Byzantine black magic, alchemy, or mathematical astrology. The "Christian" strand in popular magic and divination continues to the present day, sometimes even in textual form in magical prayer spells, thunder divination texts, and lists of good and bad days, which can be found in fairly modern Old Believer manuscript miscellanies.

The late fifteenth and early sixteenth centuries see the first Jewish influence via Poland and the Grand Duchy of Lithania, and the beginnings of Western influence. The Jewish influence appears to be entirely textual and restricted to intellectual circles: the main texts are the *Secretum secretorum* and, possibly, the *Rafli*. The first offers a defense of astrology and alchemy, a system of onomancy, instruction in the making of talismans and the magical properties of precious stones, and two systems of physiognomy. The latest copy of which I am aware was written in the eighteenth century. Parts of it had a continuing existence in popular medical compendia certainly into the nineteenth century, but as far as I know it has left no other mark in popular belief. The second is a major geomantic text, as yet incompletely researched but with strong evidence of a Jewish origin, found in a compendium of divinatory practices. It appears not to have been copied further, but geomancy as a practice evidently continued, for it was banned in the eighteenth century under a law of Catherine the Great. I have no evidence that it is still practiced, but bean divination, which is similar, was in use until recent times and is probably still practiced.

Western textual influence also begins at the end of the fifteenth century with the translation of almanacs, which have a strong astrological component, and of manuals of popular medicine, many of which contain magical recipes, or at least refer to magical properties of plants and stones. These works are still occasionally being discovered in provincial households. Neither the Western nor the Jewish *grimoires* or manuals of black magic seem to have been known.

Western influence grows markedly in the seventeenth century, still for the most part in the area of almanacs and popular medicine. This period also sees the introduction of the first dream books from Poland, and an increase in the number of texts used as amulets, notably the *Dream of the Virgin*. Dream books and religious texts are still in use as amulets today. The seventeenth century was also the time of increase in prosecution for witchcraft (involving men rather more often than women), which was often associated with treason, and of the adoption of capital punishment for practicing magic.

Legal sanctions, including the death penalty for demonic magic, continue in the eighteenth century with Peter the Great's military code. Catherine's enactments later in the eighteenth century are more in line with Enlightenment thought and ban various magical practices as fraudulent. This remained the attitude of Russian law up to the Revolution. The eighteenth century also brings secular publishing and a great increase in the number of almanacs, notably the famous Bruce calendar, books of divination and fortune-telling, and dream books, many of them printed on the presses of the Academy, Moscow University, and the Cadet Corps. These books, as their titles often indicate, were usually only semiserious and were intended as much to serve as pastimes as to cater to popular superstition. Nevertheless, they were undoubtedly a part of popular belief in many sections of the population, including the gentry, into the next century, as witness Vasily Zhukovsky's *Svetlana* and Chapter 5 of Pushkin's *Evgeny Onegin*. Indeed, Tatiana's dream and catalogue of beliefs and methods of divination is a fine example of the coexistence of beliefs and practices from many sources, popular and literary, native and foreign. And it serves as a reminder that many of the popular magical and divinatory practices (and to a lesser extent texts) are associated either with particularly magic times of the year (the midwinter *sviatki* or Christmas and New Year period and the midsummer St. John's Day) or with marriage, and often with both.

The eighteenth century also sees the beginning of interest in Western occult, spiritualistic, and esoteric literature. These works were still flourishing at the time of the 1917 Revolution, together with more popular eighteenth-century texts such as *The Circle of Solomon* and the Bruce calendar, and all these genres are even now having a revival as one of the less enlightened by-products of the end of the Soviet system and current Western influence.

It is probably fair to say that by the nineteenth and early twentieth centuries, the nature and role of magic and divination in Russia were much the same as they were in other parts of Europe, although, of course, patterns of social acceptance varied widely across the continent. In the Russian countryside many of the ancient popular beliefs and practices were identical with those to be found among the rural populations of other European countries. Some popular literature of the fortune-telling kind survived from the period of Byzantine influence, but mostly it was derived from the fortune-telling and almanac literature of Western Europe and was to be found in rural and urban populations alike.

At the level of the intelligentsia, not only were foreign and classical languages fairly well known, but extensive translation from Western European languages, which had begun in the eighteenth century, made much of the occult literature of the West available to educated Russians. These people probably differed from their Western counterparts only in that their experience of popular magic and divination was likely to have been more extensive than that of the average urban educated person in England or France.

CHAPTER TWO
THREE INSTANCES OF THE PEASANT OCCULT IN RUSSIAN LITERATURE

Intelligentsia Encounters *Narod*

Linda J. Ivanits

The ancient folk apprehension of the universe as alive and seething with a multitude of harmful powers has provided Russian literature with a seemingly inexhaustible source of occult lore. Coming from the Westernized upper classes and intelligentsia, most nineteenth-century writers lived in a cultural atmosphere light-years away from that of the peasants, whose worldview retained a strong pagan stamp. Yet the peasants' age-old storehouse of beliefs about harmful spirits, corpses, and sorcerers—in the folk idiom "the unclean force" (*nechistaia sila*)—percolated upward and entered the fictions of writers of the most diverse literary and political tendencies. Nor does the use of the folk occult seem to require a particular religious stamp: it occurs in writers known to be agnostic or indifferent to religion (Pushkin, Turgenev) as well as in those considered apologists for Christianity (Gogol, Dostoevsky).

Clearly the folk occult serves multiple functions in literature. Here I shall discuss its artistic use as a vehicle for exploring relations between the educated elite and the masses. I shall examine three works that are built on the pattern of an encounter between the intelligentsia and the peasantry: Ivan Turgenev's sketch "Bezhin lug" (Bezhin meadow, 1851), Andrei Bely's novel *Serebrianyi golub'* (*The Silver Dove*, 1909), and Aleksandr Solzhenitsyn's story "Matrenin dvor" (Matrena's home, 1963). These works fall into three distinct eras in Russian cultural history: the pre-emancipation period, when the burning issue among the intelligentsia was serfdom; the years of upheaval and apocalyptic expectations at the turn of the century; and the immediate post-Stalin period. In each of these works so widely separated in time, notions about the unclean force function to obscure, at least temporarily, the educated narrator's or hero's understanding of the folk. My primary concern is to explore the way each writer incorporates the peasant occult into his overall artistic vision in treating the problem of the intelligentsia and the people.

"Bezhin lug" appeared initially as a separate sketch in *Sovremennik* (The contemporary) for February 1851 and then entered the first book edition of *Zapiski okhotnika* (published in English as *Memoirs of a Sportsman*) in 1852. Upon the appearance in 1847 of the earliest of Turgenev's sketches, "Khor i Kalinych," Vissarion Belinsky encouraged him to continue with this genre. In the course of the next four years, Turgenev furnished *Sovremennik* twenty additional sketches, most of which he wrote abroad.[1] As a series of portraits of the Russian peasantry, the sketches belonged to the growing literature of the "Natural School," which called for the treatment of lower-class life. It was not the novelty of Turgenev's theme that brought his work such a favorable response. Indeed, the reading public of the late 1840s was already familiar with Vladimir Dal''s peasant stories, with their strong ethnographic bent, and Dmitry Grigorovich's works, with their depictions of the hardships of village life. Turgenev's strength lay in his superior craftsmanship and his penchant for drawing peasants not as popular types but as distinct individuals. Iury Lebedev terms this Turgenev's "Copernican revolution," for though his peasants are serfs, "slavery has not turned them into slaves."[2]

Though *Zapiski okhotnika* is by no means an open call to rebellion, from its first appearance it was perceived as a blow to serfdom. It employs what Frank Seeley terms the "most subtle" mode of indictment by holding up a mirror and letting the reflection speak for itself.[3] Several nonliterary factors also contributed to the political reading of the work, not the least being Turgenev's position as a liberal Westernizer and his association with Belinsky. The cumulative effect of the sketches published together was sufficient to cause the Moscow censor, Prince V. V. Lvov, to be dismissed from his post.[4] No second edition of *Zapiski okhotnika* could appear during the reign of Nicholas I; but Alexander II was supposedly favorably inclined toward the work, which may have exerted some influence on the Great Emancipation.[5] Later in his life Turgenev himself fueled a tradition that the sketches were his fulfillment of a "Hannibalic oath" sworn in his youth against the oppression of serfdom.[6] Perhaps the most vigorous opponent of the view that the sketches represent a civic response to the social evils of the 1840s is Leonid Grossman; in his opinion, the work is Turge-

1. For the publication history of *Zapiski okhotnika* see Frank F. Seeley, *Turgenev: A Reading of His Fiction* (Cambridge, 1991), pp. 101–2.

2. Iurii Lebedev, "Kniga veka: O khudozhestvennom mire 'Zapisok okhotnika' I. S. Turgeneva," in his *V seredine veka* (Moscow, 1988), p. 54.

3. Seeley, *Turgenev*, p. 102.

4. Ibid.; Lebedev, "Kniga veka," p. 56.

5. Leonard Shapiro, *Turgenev: His Life and Times* (Cambridge, Mass., 1982), p. 66.

6. Seeley, *Turgenev*, p. 102.

nev's aesthetic solution to the need for a new theme and style in view of the weakness of his previous lyrics and narrative poems.[7] The truth, no doubt, lies between these extremes, for *Zapiski okhotnika* represents both a new aesthetic direction for Turgenev and a form of political commentary.[8]

In "Bezhin lug" it is the sensitive and deeply humane depiction of five peasant boys that has been considered implicitly critical of serfdom. From our point of view, it is significant that the folk occult is integral to the boys' portraits; they take shape as they tell a series of miniature horror stories about spirits, harmful corpses, and the Antichrist.[9] The hunter-narrator, who is lost in Tula province in July and by chance spends the night with the boys on Bezhin meadow, overhears these stories and forms his judgments about the boys in relation to them. Turgenev has chosen to maintain the ethnographic authenticity of this material, which takes the form of thirteen *bylichki*, or brief accounts of meetings between villagers and various spirits or ghosts.[10] The narratives as a whole provide a sort of compendium of folk belief about the unclean force; they include encounters with the *domovoi* (house spirit), *leshii* (forest spirit), *rusalka* (female spirit of the water, forest and fields), *vodianoi* (a malicious water spirit), and dead people.[11] A particularly poignant note is struck by the account of how a former playmate, Vasia, drowned in the river next to Bezhin meadow; and a jocular touch is added when twelve-year-old Pavlushka relates how a villager returning home with a tub on his head was mistaken for the Antichrist (here called Trishka, p. 106).

As they tell their stories the boys acquire their individual traits.[12] Fedia's reluctance to participate fully in the storytelling reflects his status as the oldest (about fourteen) and the wealthiest (his shirt is new and unpatched, his boots are his own). Iliusha is the chattiest and the most versed in village traditions; most of the stories come from him. Vania, about seven, is the youngest and, it

7. Leonid Grossman, "Turgenev's Early Genre," in *Critical Essays on Ivan Turgenev,* ed. David A. Lowe (Boston, 1988), pp. 63–73.

8. See, e.g., Dale E. Peterson, "The Origin and End of Turgenev's *Sportsman's Notebook:* The Poetics and Politics of a Precarious Balance," in *Russian Literature,* vol. 16 (Amsterdam, 1984), pp. 347–58.

9. I. S. Turgenev, "Bezhin lug," in *Polnoe sobranie sochinenii i pisem v dvadtsati vos'mi tomakh* (Moscow and Leningrad, 1963), 4:92–113. All further references to "Bezhin lug" are to this edition and are indicated by page number in the text.

10. On the stories as *bylichki* see N. A. Nikolina, "Kompozitsionno-stilisticheskoe svoeobrazie rasskaza I. S. Turgeneva 'Bezhin lug,'" *Russkii iazyk v shkole,* 1983, no. 4 (July–August), p. 55. On specifications for the genre see E. V. Pomerantseva, *Mifologicheskie personazhi v russkom fol'klore* (Moscow, 1975), pp. 5–6. For an interesting discussion of various other stories in *Zapiski okhotnika* that would seem to envision the village boys of "Bezhin lug" as "mythmakers" see Irene Masing-Delic, "Philosophy, Myth, and Art in Turgenev's *Notes of a Hunter,*" *Russian Review* 50 (October 1991): 437–50.

11. For more complete discussions of these spirits see Linda J. Ivanits, *Russian Folk Belief* (Armonk, N.Y., 1989).

12. See esp. S. E. Shatalov, *"Zapiski okhotnika" I. S. Turgeneva* (Stalinabad, 1960), pp. 68–75.

appears, the most horrified, for his usual reaction is to curl up under his matting. Pavlushka, though physically unattractive and poor, has caught the eye of the narrator by his natural intelligence and bravery. It is he who recognizes the sound of the pike jumping in the river and the cry of the heron, and it is he who gallops off alone after what he thinks may be a wolf and goes by himself to the river in which Vasia drowned. There he believes he hears the voice of the drowned child summoning him, and on returning he expresses the peasant conviction that one cannot escape fate (p. 111).

Pavlushka's casually uttered aphorism foreshadows the story's end: a brief mention that within the year he fell from a horse and died. Patricia Carden argues persuasively that the hunter's experience on the meadow must be interpreted from the point of view of this tailpiece, and from this vantage "Bezhin lug" is more than a story about the charm of Russian peasant boys; it becomes a meditation on life's deepest mysteries—fate and death.[13] As we shall see, material connected to the folk occult enters into this meditation.

Within the spacial imagery of the sketch, the storytelling is located at the center of the human and safe: in the area immediately around the fire.[14] The edge of the area lit by the fire seems to be marked off by a "black veil." Beyond lies darkness, its silence broken from time to time by eerie sounds that interrupt the stories. The narrator has stumbled through the unfamiliar landscape before he espies the light. His emergence onto the familiar meadow signifies that he is no longer lost, but has reasserted control "over whatever dark forces had been implied in his earlier failures of recognition."[15] No wonder, then, that when he contemplates the relation of the area illumined by the fire to what lies beyond, the narrator concludes that "darkness [*mrak*] was struggling with light" (p. 96).

However "safe" the locus of the storytelling, the contents of the boys' tales relate to the area of darkness. They represent the actual beliefs of peasants about frightening and inexplicable events. The hunter-narrator, listening in silence while pretending to sleep, views these stories from a distance that is both intellectual and aesthetic; they offer a quaint, archaic vision of the universe that he cannot share. Turgenev's technique, then, is to segregate the narrator from the boys on the basis not only of class but also of their respective

---

13. Patricia Carden, "Finding the Way to Bezhin Meadow: Turgenev's Imitations of Mortality," *Slavic Review* 36 (September 1977): 455–58.

14. Commentators tend to stress the importance of spacial imagery in "Bezhin lug." See ibid., pp. 459–60, and Victor Ripp, *Turgenev's Russia from "Notes of a Hunter" to "Fathers and Sons"* (Ithaca, 1980), pp. 72–73. Rimvydas Silbajoris, "Images and Structures in Turgenev's *Sportsman's Notebook,*" *Slavic and East European Journal* 28 (Summer 1984): 182, notes: "We see the hunter entering a kind of bewitched inner space, an enchanted place, bordered by a river and a ravine, circumscribed by the limits of light from the boys' campfire and ruled by sorrow and death enveloped in a veil of poetry and myth."

15. Carden, "Finding the Way," p. 457.

"codes" for coming to terms with the unknown. N. A. Nikolina implies this dichotomy when she asserts that "Bezhin lug" develops through the juxtaposition of two sets of images: on the one hand the miraculously fantastic (connected with the boys' stories) and on the other the narrator's perceptions of nature.[16] Though sympathetic, the narrator knows better than to believe these village tales, and his estimations of the boys reflect the strictness of their adherence to the belief system sketched out in their stories. Hence his dislike for Iliusha and his fondness for the brave and quasi-skeptical Pavlushka, who is the most prone to seek a natural explanation for the nocturnal sounds and to give a humorous twist to a belief story. In general, the reader shares the narrator's stance, with the result that the horror a believing peasant audience would feel disappears.

What the hunter-narrator fails to understand at a conscious level is that the boys' stories are related thematically to the terrifying ordeal he has just experienced. Nikolina thinks that all their stories are linked by the concepts of "destruction" (*gibel'*) and "fear" (*strakh*).[17] But surely these concepts apply equally to the hunter's nocturnal journey, which found him on the edge of an abyss just before he emerged onto the meadow (p. 95). From a peasant's perspective, the narrator strayed into the realm of the unclean force, most likely that of the *leshii*, who supposedly led people astray, sometimes depositing them in a swampy pit or on the edge of a ravine.[18] The bats and birds the lost narrator encounters are no doubt to be associated with harmful powers, and the pile of white stones at the bottom of a pot-shaped ravine that he stumbles upon is the sort of unusual landmark regarded as fraught with the supernatural, a theme caught up in the boys' stories about clean and unclean places.[19]

Pavlushka emerges as a traveler between two worlds. He mediates between the "safe" world of the campfire (of which he is the keeper)[20] and the frightening world beyond the "black veil" (into which he ventures), between the narrator's unbelieving stance (his story of Trishka, his penchant for identifying sounds) and the peasant worldview (his belief that Vasia has summoned him from the river). His death, too, in a sense, cuts through both the narrator's and the boys' modes of coming to terms with the unknown, for, on the one hand, it fulfills the prediction implicit in his hearing of Vasia's voice, and on the other, it defies the portent of death by drowning. Carden suggests another important meaning of this brief ending: it shatters the sense of confidence and mastery of environment that the narrator experiences in the first closure—a morning full of the promise of another perfect summer day rounded out by the pastoral

16. Nikolina, "Svoeobrazie rasskaza 'Bezhin lug,' " p. 54.

17. Ibid., p. 56.

18. Pomerantseva, *Mifologicheskie personazhi*, pp. 35–36.

19. Silbajoris, "Images and Structures," p. 185.

20. Nikolina, "Svoeobrazie rasskaza 'Bezhin lug,' " p. 58.

scene of the boys driving the horses back to the village. The irony is that these horses serve as the means of Pavlushka's death.[21]

"Bezhin lug" ends on the same note of uncertainty that the narrator experienced when he was lost. The reader by now suspects that behind the boys' narratives and the hunter's nocturnal gropings lies the great mystery of their common impotence in the face of destiny and death. While he was on the meadow, the stories connected with folk occult allowed the narrator, listening with the critical stance of an unbeliever, to maintain a false sense of security; they thus served to mask his deep human bond with the children. Only Pavlushka breaks through this mask, though on an emotional rather than cognitive level. It is his death, both fulfilling and nullifying predictions based on folk superstition, that forces a reevaluation of the stories told on Bezhin meadow and makes it impossible to regard them as pure village superstitions totally disconnected from the deeper questions of human existence.

Andrei Bely's novel *Serebrianyi golub'* (*The Silver Dove*) first appeared in *Vesy* (The scales) in 1909 and then was published as a book 1910. The initial volume of a projected trilogy under the general title *Vostok ili zapad* (East or west), it concerns the destructive "Mongol" Russia of the East as perceived in the *narod*. The second volume, *Peterburg*, stresses the suprarational, Western aspect of the intelligentsia, and the third, intended as a synthesis of the first two under the title *Nevidimyi grad* (The invisible city), was never written.[22] *The Silver Dove* has sometimes been termed Bely's "most conventional" prose fiction, probably because it contains a story line that is easy to follow, irrespective of the distortion and deformation that govern language use and the depiction of characters.[23] Its setting is provincial Russia in the summer of 1905, though it more truly reflects the despondent mood of the intelligentsia several years later, as they struggled to come to grips with the failure of the Revolution of 1905.[24] Interposed within the text are bits and fragments of political and social realia of the time (references to strikers, to student radicals [*skubenty*], 2:190]), and hanging over the entire cosmos is an atmosphere of impending cataclysm, reflecting the apocalyptic mood among the Symbolists of this era.[25] Yet one can take the atmosphere of doom in *The Silver Dove* too seriously. James Rice

21. Carden, "Finding the Way," p. 461.

22. See Maria Carlson, "*The Silver Dove*," in *Andrey Bely: Spirit of Symbolism*, ed. John E. Malmstad (Ithaca, 1987), pp. 60–61.

23. See, e.g., Vladimir E. Alexandrov, *Andrei Bely: The Major Symbolist Fiction* (Cambridge, Mass., 1985), p. 68.

24. Carlson, "*Silver Dove*," p. 66.

25. Andrei Belyi [Boris Bugaev], *Serebrianyi golub'* (Munich, 1967), 1:282, 2:146, 156, and elsewhere. All further references to *The Silver Dove* are to this edition and are indicated by page number in the text. On apocalyptic mood see Carlson, "*Silver Dove*," p. 66, and Bernice Glatzer Rosenthal, "Eschatology and the Appeal of Revolution: Merezhkovsky, Bely, Blok," *California Slavic Studies* 11 (1980): 105–40.

rightly points out the strong elements of self-parody and humor in the work.[26] *The Silver Dove* may be read as something of a spoof on the question of European versus native (folk) Russia with a good measure of irony directed at those who recast history exclusively in terms of West versus East, whose anticipations of a new age were dashed by the failure of the Revolution of 1905 (Bely's own included), and who sought salvation through blind, mystical faith in "the people." The narrative concerns the involvement of Petr Darialsky, a somewhat muddleheaded and oversexed member of the intelligentsia, with a religious sect known as the Doves. His search for Russia leads him to abandon his aristocratic fiancée, Katia, for a pockmarked peasant woman named Matrena, who lives with the old carpenter Kudeiarov. Kudeiarov heads the Doves and has plotted to bring Darialsky and Matrena together so that they may engender a "Dove child," or world redeemer. The novel ends with Darialsky's ritual murder.

In the battle between West and East occurring within the hero, two occults offset each other. Darialsky's friend Shmidt, a Theosophist, explains that according to his horoscope, Saturn threatens him with destruction, but it is still not too late to turn from his dangerous path (2:12). Darialsky, shaken and mindful of an earlier time when Shmidt's "blinding path of secret knowledge" had greater attraction for him, looks out the window and sees Russia: "white, gray, red huts, shirts etched out against the meadow and a song; and in a red shirt winding his way across the meadow to the priest the carpenter; and the tender, caressing sky" (2:14–15).[27] It is this second, "Eastern" occult, residing in the depths of the Russian folk, that proves more potent and ultimately brings entrapment and destruction.

The folk occult permeates the novel's highly theatrical topography, which has its westernmost limit in Gugolevo, where Katia lives, and extends eastward through Tselebeevo, the center of the action, to Likhov by way of a road that is controlled by some sort of "mysterious power" (*nevedomaia sila*). After Likhov comes the end of the earth, the abyss. This abyss, inasmuch as it seems to merge with the waters of the village pond, may have something to do with the condition of the universe prior to creation (normally imagined as a watery expanse) in Russian folk legends, though it may relate as well to the Tatarus of Greek myth (thus catching up Darialsky's training in the classics and constituting one of the multiple strains of imagery that run through the text); its blueness seems to be Bely's own idiosyncratic addition based on a personal experience, and this blueness is reflected in the bottomless depths of Matrena's eyes.[28] Like the cosmos of folk superstition, which is buzzing with an endless

26. James Rice, "Andrej Belyj's *Silver Dove:* The Black Depths of Blue Space, or Who Stole the Baroness's Diamonds?" in *Mnemozina: Studia literaria russica in honorem Vsevolod Setchkarev,* ed. Joachim Baer and Norman Ingham (Munich, 1974), pp. 301–16.

27. E.g., Carlson, "*Silver Dove,*" pp. 69–73 and elsewhere.

28. Alexandrov, *Andrei Bely,* p. 72.

number of hostile spirits, the world of the novel is saturated with demons awaiting their chance to destroy the hero.

The critical consensus is that Likhov, the name of the central locus of the Doves, comes from *likhoi*, "evil" or "devil."[29] The choice of a bathhouse as the place of worship is an additional signal of the Doves' tie to the demonic, for in folk belief the bathhouse was a gathering place for evil spirits.[30] Matrena's name links her with Mother Earth (*mat'*) and Mary.[31] Her innately lascivious nature plus the mandate that she spend her summer making love to Darialsky catch up the orgiastic quality often attributed to the worship ("Christly love") of sectarians.[32] That this "heretical" Madonna is really in league with the powers of evil, as is made clear by the many references to her as a witch (*ved'ma*), suggests that Bely was familiar with the popular tendency to regard sectarians as witches, sorcerers, and werewolves.[33] Kudeiarov is an obvious sorcerer, and commentators have noted that his name is suggestive of *kudel'* (tow), thereby pointing to the mysterious web he casts over all with whom he is in contact, and with *kudesnik*, a term used for "sorcerer" in medieval times.[34] It is highly probable that Kudeiarov also relates to Kudeiar, a legendary brigand known in the central Black Earth provinces (especially Orel), where his name came to designate the demonic guardian spirit of buried treasure.[35] Kudeiarov's brigandry involves his scheme to gain for the Doves the wealth of the merchant Eropegin, whom he is slowly poisoning, and he dreams as well of gaining Katia's money once Darialsky has fulfilled his purpose with Matrena.

In *The Silver Dove* demonic powers infect vegetation and objects as well as people. Bushes in particular acquire a sinister quality.[36] Those lining the road between Tselebeevo and Likhov seem to come alive as they "wail" and "dance" ("kustiki vskhlipyvali, pliasali," 1:74); and when Eropegin's wife, Fekla Matveena, drives along this road, bushes and stumps acquire the likeness of the devil while the wind whistles, driving dry dust against her (2:55). As Darialsky gropes his way to Gugolevo through the deep forest (termed *dremuchii*, as in the fairy tale), bushes seem to surround him, whisper at him;

29. E.g., Carlson, *"Silver Dove,"* p. 76.

30. Ivanits, *Russian Folk Belief,* p. 59.

31. Carlson, *"Silver Dove,"* pp. 72, 74.

32. Paul Miliukov, *Religion and the Church,* vol. 1 of *Outlines of Russian Culture,* trans. V. Ughet and E. Davis (New York, 1942), pp. 90, 92.

33. P. I. Mel'nikov-Pecherskii, "Tainye sekty," in *Polnoe sobranie sochinenii* (St. Petersburg, 1909), 6:255.

34. Carlson, *"Silver Dove,"* pp. 73–74.

35. S. V. Maksimov, *Nechistaia sila: Nevedomaia sila,* vol. 18 of *Sobranie sochinenii* (St. Petersburg, 1908–13), pp. 175–76.

36. Aleksandrov, *Andrei Bely,* p. 71; J. D. Elsworth, *Andrey Bely: A Critical Study of the Novels* (Cambridge, Mass., 1983), p. 67.

and as he stands over an accursed place (*nad prokliatym mestom*), the pock-marked face of Matrena, whom he has encountered for the first time this day, seems to rise up from behind a bush and merge with the falling moon, which looks at him between the bushes (1:127–30). Toward the end of the novel Darialsky fully comprehends that he is doomed when he sees Kudeiarov and the evil coppersmith-Dove Sukhorukov emerging from a bush (2:167–68). Folk traditions envisioned devils as appearing and disappearing "through the earth" (*skvoz' zemliu*) by means of holes running down to hell and sometimes located under bushes or stumps.[37] In a tale about an evil wife, for example, we learn that a peasant stumbled on such a "bottomless pit" under a currant bush.[38] It seems likely that the connection of bushes and stumps with the demonic builds on this superstition.

After leaving Gugolevo, Darialsky lives in the forest, using a hollow oak as the locus for his trysts with Matrena. Having symbolically placed himself under the dominion of the hostile powers against which he had recently uttered a halfhearted charm ("God will arise. . . . You, Katia, chase away the devil, get rid of the devil" ["Da, voskresnet Bog. . . . Katia . . . ty progoni besa: ty otzheni besa . . . "], 1:127), he acquires a new identity within this realm. This transformation is indicated by his unshaven, unkempt appearance, by Katia's vision of him as a werewolf (*oboroten'*, 1:214–15), and by references to him as a "wolf" (*volk*, 2:185). As a forest resident, he is the one who now emerges from the bushes to meet the witch Matrena (1:271). No wonder the village shopkeeper Ivan Stepanov claims that a spell has been cast on the "gentleman" from Gugolevo (*okoldovali*, 2:10), for in folk belief, the transformation of a person into a beast (*oborotnichestvo*) was a result of sorcery.[39] We can speculate about a bond between Darialsky and the *leshii* during his forest sojourn, for in popular tradition this spirit entered into sexual liaisons with village women and was the master of wolves, but the strange headgear of fir branches he adopts suggests an even closer association with a Greek satyr, or even Pan himself, with whose stories he has recently bored Katia.[40] Such a comparison highlights the instinctive, Dionysian nature of Darialsky's forest existence.

Connections among "bush," "shaggy," and "dust" intensify the sense that the natural world of the novel is malevolent. This linkage is established early in the novel, before Darialsky appears: "then the bush along the side of the road would sob, and shaggy dust would jump forth" ("togda vskhlipnet pridorozhnyi kustik, da kosmatyi vskochet prakh," 1:11). Here the word used for dust—*prakh* instead of the more usual *pyl'*—is doubly threatening because

37. Maksimov, *Nechistaia sila*, p. 260.

38. A. N. Afanas'ev, *Narodnye skazki*, vol. 2 of *Narodnye russkie skazki i legendy* (Berlin, 1922), p. 367.

39. Maksimov, *Nechistaia sila*, p. 122.

40. See Rice, "Belyj's *Silver Dove*," pp. 308–9, 312–13.

of its association with "dust to dust." In folk superstition dust (especially in columns) indicates the presence of the unclean force, and the term *kosmatyi* (shaggy) often modifies the devil.[41] Dust driven by the wind into Fekla Matveevna's eyes (2:55), the dusty hoarfrost that "breathes" on Kudeiarov as he makes his way to Likhov (1:73), the dust the resident of Tselebeevo wipes from his face with a sweaty sleeve (1:9), the cloud of dust that accompanies the "red devil"–automobile into Tselebeevo (2:18), and all other mentions of dust acquire menacing overtones and suggest the impending doom hanging over the world of the novel. The concept of shagginess is realized most specifically in the "shaggy one" (*kosmach*), a Dove who serves as Kudeiarov's worker and is an obvious demonic power. On the early pages of the novel, shagginess is integrated into the scene that best foreshadows Darialsky's destruction. He senses in the mirrorlike surface of the village pond a merger of blue sky and water; a birch by the pond seems to stretch out its shaggy (*lokhmatye*) arms, and he longs to throw himself down and look into the depths, through the branches, through the shining spider web (*kudel' pauka*). In folklore *lokhmatyi*, a synonym of *kosmatyi*, is also used of the devil; in one tale a rich man recognizes his nocturnal visitor as the devil himself on seeing his shaggy hand (*lokhmataia ruka*).[42] Here the implication is that the shaggy hands of the devil and Kudeiarov's web have already trapped Darialsky. When immediately afterward Darialsky muses, "Devil take me, what else do I need?" ("Chego mne, chort menia poberi, nado," 1:18), he is, in a sense, acquiescing to these powers.

The early action of *The Silver Dove* occurs around Trinity. The apparent significance of this holiday is that the Pentecost / Trinity season is sacred to the Doves. But it is also significant in folk belief. In the peasant calendar, this was the great spring celebration of new vegetation; it involved rites connected with birch trees, the dead, and the ceremonial banishment of the *rusalka*, and an entire series of prohibitions intended to protect villagers from the unclean force.[43] Of course, the imagery indicating that vegetation has fallen prey to the unclean force subverts the very sense of this holiday. The woman (Matrena?) doing her laundry as Darialsky passes the village pond is violating a prohibition on doing women's work on Trinity Day, and Darialsky will break a ban on entering the forest on his return to Gugolevo. Nor can the Trinity Day church service protect him from the dark powers of Matrena, who, just as he steps forth to kiss the cross, enters his soul "as a cloud, a storm, a tigress, a werewolf [*oboroten'*]" (1:21).[44] After the service, as he drowsily makes his way to the

41. Pomerantseva, *Mifologicheskie personazhi*, p. 118.

42. N. Onchukov, *Severnie skazki* (St. Petersburg, 1909), p. 498.

43. D. K. Zelenin, *Ocherki russkoi mifologii: Umershie neestestvennoiu smert'iu i rusalki* (Petrograd, 1916), 1:217–82.

44. For more on *oboroten'* see S. A. Torakev, *Religioznye verovaniia vostochnoslavianskikh narodov XIX–nachala XX v.* (Moscow and Leningrad, 1957), pp. 44–45, and Maksimov, *Nechistaia sila*, pp. 121–24.

priest's house, he passes the cemetery and overhears the churchwarden (who has just appeared from behind a bush) abusing a village spinster by insulting her father's memory: "We should dig up his bones and empty out the place. . . . Did you come to visit your daddy? Is there anything to visit—bet his remains have all rotted" (1:23). From the perspective of Trinity Week rituals, this is another desecration of the holiday. Darialsky, though somewhat befuddled, seems to recognize deviltry here (*d'iavol'shchina*), and he utters a quick prayer: "Save us from the midday demon" (1:23). The reference may be to the midday spirit of popular lore, who is connected to noon heat and sunstroke, and also to sixteenth-century apocryphal prayers of Old Believers.[45] If so, its inclusion here, joining folkloric and sectarian imagery, is yet another foreshadowing of Darialsky's entrapment.

This list of allusions to the folk occult is by no means exhaustive, for the networks of associations in the novel make it possible to find such imagery on virtually every page.[46] Thus, for example, a casual, seemingly irrelevant tavern conversation about a dying witch who passes her powers on to a reed because she cannot find a suitable person echoes the theme of infected vegetation (1:66). Significant, too, is the use of the term "one-eyed" (*odnoglaznyi*) to animate and describe a house: "a one-eyed house would squint with a clear pupil by day, with an evil pupil would squint from behind the thick bushes" (1:10). Since in the folk tradition *odnoglaznyi* is sometimes combined with *likho*, the use of this word both prepares for the mention of the town Likhov and creates the expectation that it will be an evil place.[47] When, during a riot, a peasant complains that the overseer has "spoiled" several of the village girls, he uses the highly charged term for casting a spell (*portit'*, 1:183). Of course, here its primary meaning is that the overseer has seduced the girls; the irony is that Darialsky's sexual escapades with Matrena, whom he acknowledges to be a witch, are precisely the means of his "spoiling," and they are being carried out under the auspices of the sorcerer Kudeiarov. Finally, we should note that Darialsky is not only the victim of his own casually uttered curse ("Devil take me . . . ," 1:18); he is the victim of a sort of "parental" curse as well. Here the perpetrator is not the uncanny Kudeiarov but the narrator himself, who, trying

45. Felix J. Oinas, "Russian *Poludnica* 'Midday Spirit,'" in *Essays on Russian Folklore and Mythology* (Columbus, Ohio, 1985), pp. 103–10, esp. 109n. In addition, one cannot rule out the possible influence of the "noonday scourge" of Psalm 91:6 (in the Russian translation Psalm 90:6, "zarazy, opustoshaiuschei v polden'").

46. On various other networks of imagery, especially those involving sound and color, see Andrew Barratt, "Mystification and Initiation in *Serebriannyj golub'*: Belyi, the Reader, and the Symbolist Novel," in *Andrey Bely Centenary Papers*, ed. Boris Christa (Amsterdam, 1980), pp. 135–45; Thomas Beyer Jr., "Andrej Belyj's 'The Magic of Words' and *The Silver Dove*," *Slavic and East European Journal* 22, no. 4 (1978): 464–72; Carlson, "*Silver Dove*"; and Rice, "Belyj's *Silver Dove*."

47. See "Likho odnoglaznoe" in Afanas'ev, *Narodnye skazki*, pp. 155–56.

to explain his character, concludes simply, "But the devil take him. . . . Let him disappear without a trace" ("No, chert s nim. . . . Da, propadi propadom on" (1:178). This curse has the dual function of handing the hero over to the darker powers of the Russian folk and at the same time reminding the reader that his existence is in any case spectral, emanating as it does from the creating and controlling consciousness of the artist.

Published in the January 1963 issue of *Novyi mir* (New world), Aleksandr Solzhenitsyn's "Matrenin dvor" is one of a handful of his works that actually appeared in the Soviet Union. The setting here is the period after Stalin's death, when the largely autobiographical narrator, who has spent time in the Gulag and then in exile in Kazakhstan, has been allowed to return to rural central Russia. Though it would be difficult to imagine two works more different in style and temperament, "Matrenin dvor," like *The Silver Dove*, takes a member of the intelligentsia to the folk on an intentional search for Russia. Here the question implicit in the narrator's search for the real, primordial (*nutrianaia, kondovaia*) Russia is whether anything of value remains after forty years of Soviet rule. But in spite of the havoc communism has wreaked on the Russian land, the quest in Solzhenitsyn's story is ultimately successful. The narrator comes to understand that he has found the object of his search not in what he had thought constituted the real Russia—the central Russian landscape, the quiet rustle of the forest, the quaint sounds of the regional dialect— but in the person of an old woman named Matrena. Having witnessed her harsh life and cruel death in a train accident, the narrator proclaims her "that proverbial righteous person [*pravednik*] without whom a village cannot stand."[48] On the whole, critics have viewed this summary statement as the key to the story and considered Matrena a Christian saint, an Old Russian "icon" that survived miraculously into the Soviet era.[49] This emphasis, however correct, has tended to downplay the significance of the peasant occult in her presentation, for the narrator's earlier attempt to come to grips with her spirituality led him to conclude that she was basically a "pagan" (*iazychnitsa*) in whom "superstitions held sway" (p. 210).

An entire series of folk superstitions attends her depiction, firmly anchoring her in the spirit world of the nineteenth-century peasant. Her beliefs that a snowstorm signals that someone has committed suicide by hanging and that if

48. Aleksandr Solzhenitsyn, "Matrenin dvor," in *Sobranie sochinenii v shesti tomakh* (Frankfurt am Main, 1970), 1:231. The proverb, as given in Vladimir Dal', *Tolkovyi slovar' zhivogo velikorusskogo iazyka*, 4 vols. (St. Petersburg and Moscow, 1881), 3:380, equates *pravednik* with *sviatoi* (saint): "Ne stoit gorod bez sviatogo, selenie bez pravednika."

49. Irina Corten, "Solzhenitsyn's Matrena and Rasputin's Dar'ja: Two Studies in Russian Peasant Spirituality," *Russian Language Journal* 33 (Winter 1979): 85–98; Robert Louis Jackson, " 'Matryona's Home': The Making of a Russian Icon," in *Solzhenitsyn: A Collection of Critical Essays*, ed. Kathryn B. Feuer (Englewood Cliffs, N.J., 1976) pp. 60–70.

someone steps into the garden on the feast of the Beheading of John the Baptist there will be no harvest are among the thousands of omens that actually pervaded every aspect of village life.[50] Her fear of lightning accords with peasant notions about the angry prophet Elijah, whose bolts, supposedly aimed at devils, often caused crop damage and fire.[51] Her fear of the herder and the tailor is probably connected to folk notions that attributed occult powers to fellow villagers with special or unusual skills. The shepherd in particular was regarded as a sorcerer because he supposedly concluded a pact with the *leshii* for help with the herd.[52] Sheryl Spitz intimates that Matrena's superstitious fear of trains may reflect the peasant tendency to demonize them by viewing them as fire-breathing dragons.[53]

No occasion in village life elicited greater fear of harmful magic than a wedding, and multiple precautions were taken to protect the bride from sorcery.[54] From this perspective, the details surrounding Matrena's marriage are ominous. She marries the wrong man; the ceremony takes place at the wrong time; and immediately afterward she violates a prohibition connected to women's work. When her fiancé, Faddei, fails to return from World War I, Matrena accepts the proposal of his younger brother, Efim. The wedding takes place at an inauspicious time, during the peak season for fieldwork (after St. Peter's Day, June 29), and not at the more traditional time, at the end of the harvest (after the feast of the Intercession, October 1). After her wedding, Matrena goes "straight to the stove," though custom forbids a bride to attend the hearth during the first year in her husband's home.[55] When all six of her children die, the village concludes that she is the victim of "spoiling" (*porcha; portsiia* in Matrena's peculiar idiom, p. 216). The attempted cure accords with the cure called for when the "spoiling" was thought to be caused by an unclean animal sucking the victim's vital forces: Matrena is taken to a holy woman, who tries to make her cough up a frog.[56]

Folk imagery suggests the overwhelming presence in Matrena's life of some evil power. That power seems to be connected to Faddei, whose violence and possessiveness contrast sharply with her mildness and lack of acquisitiveness. Robert Jackson asserts that "this strange figure carries out the motif of demonism in the story" and that he emerges out of the "core of Russia" as an embodi-

---

50. Maksimov, *Krestnaia sila*, vol. 17 of *Sobranie sochinenii*, pp. 201–5.

51. Ivanits, *Russian Folk Belief*, pp. 29–30.

52. Tokarev, *Religioznye verovaniia*, pp. 31–34.

53. Sheryl A. Spitz, "The Impact of Structure in Solzhenitsyn's 'Matryona's Home,'" *Russian Review* 36 (April 1977): 171.

54. Maksimov, *Nechistaia sila*, pp. 132–33.

55. P. I. Kushner, *The Village of Viriatino*, trans. and ed. Sula Benet (Garden City, N.Y., 1970), p. 96.

56. N. A. Nikitina, "K voprosu o russkikh koldunakh," *Sbornik Muzeia antropologii i etnografii*, vol. 7 (Leningrad, 1928), p. 316.

ment of the dark forces in Russian life.[57] On the plane of everyday reality Matrena's "spoiling" finds its implementation in her unfortunate family life, the series of injustices she suffers at the hands of officials and relatives, and finally in her brutal death and dismemberment. The moment that best captures the meaning of her "spoiling" occurs when Faddei returns from captivity and finds her married to his brother. In a scene whose memory still terrifies Matrena forty years later, he threatens, "If it weren't my own brother, I'd chop you both to pieces," and then he declares he will marry only a woman who has the same name as Matrena (p. 215). Critics have suggested that the substitute Matrena functions much like the classic doppelgänger in draining the life force from the original; she bears six children, and all survive.[58] The uncanniness of the interaction between these two women is also indicated by the second Matrena's lament over the dead body of the first: "And forgive me, wretched woman that I am. Oh-oh! You've gone to your mother, and, no doubt, you'll come for me! Oh-oh!" (p. 226).

The folk occult in "Matrenin dvor" deepens the spiritual struggle, for it suggests that what is at issue is a conflict not merely between the Soviet era, which has failed to improve the peasant's lot, and a somewhat idealized pre-revolutionary Russia, but between the universal forces of good and evil. The story's references to peasant superstition and the implicit assumption that the unclean force is a powerful factor in human life imply that the acquisitiveness and materialism of the villagers are linked to the demonic. That this force is pervasive enough to be the norm in the village is clear from the narrator's remark that many were like Faddei. Matrena's life has passed in this environment, and she has lacked defenses against it. The narrator's curious statement that she does not make the sign of the cross may be meaningful here, for in folk superstition, the sign of the cross was the weapon most frequently used against the unclean force. Its absence is a sign of her vulnerability. So is the unexplained disappearance of her pot during the blessing of water on the feast of the Baptism of Christ. We are told "it was as if an unclean spirit carried it off" (p. 210). Peasants relied on holy water for various healing and protective purposes, so if one interprets this loss according to folk notions, it signifies that Matrena has been left unprotected against the powers of evil for the coming year.[59]

The ubiquitous presence of evil coupled with Matrena's defenselessness hints at the essence of her spirituality and contains the clue to the shift in the narrator's understanding of her: he sees her no longer as pagan but as righteous. Between his two assessments, he has discovered Faddei, who provides a necessary contrast. Artistically, the contrast is suggested by the use of darkness

---

57. Jackson, " 'Matryona's Home,' " pp. 67, 62.
58. Spitz, "Impact of Structure," p. 178, and Jackson, " 'Matryona's Home,' " p. 62.
59. Ivanits, *Russian Folk Belief,* p. 42.

and light.[60] Faddei's black hair, beard, and mustache, signs of his connection with the "powers of darkness," run counter to Matrena's "radiant smile" and to the white scarf surrounding her peaceful face as she lies in her coffin (p. 225). Solzhenitsyn tends to present Matrena framed in a darkness from which she sometimes steps forth, as when she emerges from the half-darkness into a rosy light on telling the narrator the story of her past (p. 214). Nor is it accidental that the narrator's final pronouncement is presented in terms of light imagery: Matrena's sister-in-law, who remembers only bad things about her, "lit up" (*osvetila*, p. 230) her image from a new angle and made it possible for the narrator to understand her as a righteous one. The darkness surrounding Matrena, related symbolically to the peasant occult and, on a more realistic level, to Faddei and the values he represents, provides the background against which her image comes into proper focus. It also suggests an understanding of her within the Russian Orthodox tradition. Threatened by Faddei, unable to bear children of her own, despised and marginalized by her neighbors and family, whose relationship with her turned on getting her to work for nothing, and finally asked by Faddei to break the walls of the house in which she has lived for forty years, Matrena retains her cheerful temperament and her kindliness, and yields to the desires of others. Her passivity in the face of greed and possessiveness suggests that she is, as Irina Corten has argued, an embodiment of Russian kenoticism, saintliness through nonresistance to evil.[61]

The folk occult provides a vast, homegrown system of imagery that authors can incorporate according to their individual visions and the needs of particular works. While all the works we have examined use the peasant occult in exploring the problem of intelligentsia versus folk, each reacts to a distinct cultural-historical situation and integrates the occult according to its specific tasks. The actual content of this occult, we might note, changed minimally in the better than a hundred years between "Bezhin lug" and "Matrenin dvor."[62] In the three works examined, the most evident common function of the folk occult is characterization: peasant superstitions occupy an important place in the portrayals of Turgenev's boys, Bely's Kudeiarov and Matrena, and Sol-

60. Jackson, " 'Matryona's Home,' " and Spitz, "Impact of Structure," underscore the visual quality of Matrena's depiction. Jackson suggests that the entire story is structured around the polarities of image or "icon" (*obraz*) and disfiguration, deformity (*bezobrazie*). Spitz points out the importance of the theme of photography, connected with the narrator's attempts to capture Matrena's radiance on film, in accentuating the darkness-light contrast that eventually brings Matrena into true focus (pp. 173–74, 179–81).

61. Corten, "Matrena and Dar'ja," p. 91; see George P. Fedotov, *The Russian Religious Mind: Kievan Christianity* (New York, 1960), pp. 94–113.

62. Much of the ancient heritage survives to the present day in part of Russia. See R. P. Matveeva, ed., *Mifologicheskie rasskazy russkogo naseleniia vostochnoi Sibiri*, comp. V. P. Zinov'ev (Novosibirsk, 1987).

zhenitsyn's Matrena. These works share as well the sense that the narrator or hero, who is not a believer in popular superstition, has strayed into an alien world in his encounter with the peasantry. And this world is, in fact, Russia.

The differences in the uses of the folk occult in these works are especially significant, for they indicate the flexibility that this system of imagery offers. Only in *The Silver Dove* does it function to create a sense of the presence of a malevolent supernatural force that will destroy the hero, a presence that is counteracted, if weakly, by references to Theosophy. The folk occult in this work enters into the creation and parody of an atmosphere of eschatological expectation and despondency that characterized Symbolist brooding after the Revolution of 1905.

In "Bezhin lug" the implied worldview is that of the educated, not particularly religious European narrator, and not of the boys, for whom the universe is saturated with the unclean force. Here the folk occult enters into the meditative dimension of the work, for it first masks and then, on reprospection, reveals the common vulnerability in the face of death and the viscissitudes of fate that the narrator shares with these peasant children. It is precisely in this discovery of their shared humanity that the work becomes implicitly critical of serfdom.

Solzhenitsyn's work, to a far greater degree than the other two, has an intentional moral dimension; the artist takes pains to transmit a correct understanding of the nature of good and evil. In "Matrenin dvor" the folk occult deepens the spiritual dimension of Matrena's life by suggesting that she, though engulfed by dark forces, has somehow managed to retain her humanity and goodness. The educated narrator, who does not share her belief in "spoiling" and various omens, guides the reader in perceiving this great evil not as a literal intrusion of the unclean force into daily life but as the greed and violence of ordinary people.

CHAPTER THREE
RUSSIAN RELIGIOUS THOUGHT AND THE JEWISH KABBALA

Judith Deutsch Kornblatt

Amid the post-Soviet chaos, it has become clear that Russian libraries house a variety of lost and as yet uncatalogued manuscripts on
Jewish mysticism. The authors of those texts, as well as the Jewish
scholars who are rediscovering them, would be surprised to learn
that for a brief historical moment an effort was made to reconcile Jewish Kabbala with the apparently quite different and sometimes hostile theology of
Russian Orthodoxy. The prophet of reconciliation, Vladimir Soloviev, was the
most influential thinker in the religious renaissance at the end of the nineteenth and beginning of the twentieth centuries. He was drawn to both the
speculative mysticism and the traditional practice of Judaism as a cornerstone
of his ideal Universal Church, the church that he believed was destined to
reconcile all opposites—East and West, male and female, heaven and earth.

Curiously, Soloviev's interest in Kabbala coincided with a time when the
"Jewish question" grew ever more pressing within the Russian empire, and his
work on Jewish mysticism therefore takes on political as well as theological
significance. Ultimately, Soloviev's writings on the Kabbala and his repeated
use of kabbalistic terminology point to the philosopher's effort to legitimate
Jewish mysticism as a system that, though outside of the church and largely
unknown to Russian society, could nonetheless inform and possibly reform
Russia and the Orthodox Church through its ancient message of the relationship between God and humanity. For us, an understanding of the unrecognized place of Kabbala in modern Russian religious thought may help explain
some of modern Orthodoxy's mystical message. A revelation of the reasons

I thank the National Endowment for the Humanities and the Hewlett Foundation at the
University of Wisconsin for generous grants to pursue research for this chapter.

Judith Deutsch Kornblatt

why the relationship between Kabbala and Orthodoxy remained unrecognized after Soloviev may also explain why the return to the occult in Russia today often has a decidedly un-Solovievan and anti-Jewish cast.

The second half of the nineteenth century witnessed a crisis in the Russian Orthodox Church. As one historian comments: "Diocesan administration suffered from venality, malfeasance, and arbitrariness; the seminaries were a shambles, afflicted with poverty and pedagogical disarray; the parish clergy had become a virtual caste, impoverished, isolated, and disparaged."[1] It is no wonder that educated Russians searched for authority outside the official church, turning in some cases to Western positivism or revolutionary ideology and in others to occult explanations for the meaning of an increasingly chaotic universe.

Soloviev was no exception. While investigating and ultimately rejecting European philosophy for his master's thesis, aptly titled "Krizis zapadnoi filosofii (Protiv pozitivistov)" (The crisis of Western philosophy [against the positivists], 1874), he became curious about the occult sciences, Eastern thought, and ancient religion. In 1875 Soloviev requested leave from his duties as docent at Moscow University to travel to London and study "Indian, gnostic, and medieval philosophy," and, as his correspondence reveals, to participate in the English occult scene.[2] He was disappointed in what he found there, it turns out, for he wrote to his friend Dmitry Tsertelev: "Local spiritualism (and thus spiritualism in general, since London is its center) is in an absolutely pitiful state. I have seen famous mediums as well as famous spiritists, and don't know which of them are worse."[3]

Nonetheless, Soloviev continued his private investigation of esoteric beliefs. Examples of automatic writing, references to alchemical symbols, and occult diagrams fill the notebook that he compiled during his trip abroad. With a believer's zeal he penned: "Kabbala and Neoplatonism. Boehme and Swedenborg. Schelling and I."[4] At this point, Soloviev clearly understood Kabbala as a hidden, occult phenomenon, and he sought the key to initiation. As he discovered more convergences with his own intuition of God through study, however, he came to accept Kabbala as a mystical doctrine, legitimately correlative to Orthodoxy, with its truth available to all.

1. Gregory L. Freeze, "Revolt from Below: A Priest's Manifesto on the Crisis in Russian Orthodoxy (1858–59)," in *Russian Orthodoxy under the Old Regime*, ed. Robert L. Nichols and Theofanis George Stavrou (Minneapolis, 1978), p. 90.
2. Quoted in S. M. Luk'ianov, *O Vladimire Solov'eve v ego molodye gody: Materialy k biografii* (Petrograd, 1921), 3:64.
3. Vladimir Solov'ev, *Pis'ma,* ed. E. L. Radlov (Petrograd, 1923), 2:229; reprinted in *Sobranie sochinenii V. S. Solov'eva: Pis'ma i prilozhenie* (Brussels, 1970). All other references to Soloviev are from *Sobranie sochinenii Vladimira Sergeevicha Solov'eva,* ed. S. M. Solov'ev and E. L. Radlov (St. Petersburg, 1911; rpt. Brussels, 1969), hereafter cited parenthetically in the text as *SS.*
4. For a discussion of the notebooks, see S. M. Solov'ev, *Zhizn' i tvorcheskaia evoliutsiia Vladimira Solov'eva* (Brussels, 1977), pp. 118–21.

By way of context, we must remember that Soloviev shocked his liberal friends by studying at the orthodox Moscow Spiritual Academy after his graduation from university. The voracious scholar believed until his death that *all* the research and writing he undertook, including his much-criticized rapprochement with Catholicism, only supported the true and eternal Orthodox Church. His flirtation with non-Orthodox doctrines was fully consistent with his belief in the holistic nature of Russian Orthodoxy, of the "wholeness" (*tsel'nost'* or *sobornost'*) of its worldview. Thus Soloviev's encounter with the occult, as well as with the aspects of mystical Judaism that he came to dissociate from occult doctrines, may have had more "orthodox" roots than that of less scholarly as well as less pious intellectuals of his time. What may have been rebellion against stultified ecclesiastic dogma for some people was for Soloviev confirmation of the intimate relationship between God, humanity, and the Russian Church.

Soloviev cultivated his interest in Kabbala in particular on his trip to London, and he continued to nurture it throughout the next twenty-five years of his life. Before Soloviev's publications on it, most Russians had, at best, vague notions about the Jewish Kabbala. Kabbalistic ideas had entered Russian intellectual circles in the nineteenth century indirectly through German Romanticism and Schelling, and many mystical aspects of Russian as well as European Romanticism found confirmation in the popular quasi-kabbalistic writings of the Protestant mystic Jacob Boehme.[5] Somewhat more directly, kabbalistic texts written or edited by Christian cabalists (who typically adopted the French spelling) had been collected in the eighteenth century by the Freemason N. I. Novikov. Throughout the nineteenth century, the Masons propagated kabbalistic terminology and symbolism without necessarily distinguishing Kabbala from other esoteric systems. Consequently, late nineteenth-century occultists and esoteric faddists tended to meld all mystical schools into a large and bizarre puzzle. The founder of Theosophy, Elena Blavatsky, would not have been alone in believing that "Swayambhuva, the unknown essence of the Brahmans, is identical with En-Soph, the unknown essence of the kabalists [sic]," and that "strictly speaking, it is difficult to view the Jewish *Book of Genesis* otherwise than as a chip from the trunk of the mundane tree of universal Cosmogony, rendered in Oriental allegories."[6]

5. For a brief comparison of Boehme and Kabbala, see Gershom G. Scholem, *Major Trends in Jewish Mysticism* (New York, 1961), pp. 237–38. For a thorough study of Boehme in Russia, see Zdenek V. David, "The Influence of Jacob Boehme on Russian Religious Thought," *Slavic Review* 21, no. 1 (1962): 43–64. See also Nikolai Berdiaev, "Iz etiudov o Iakove Beme," *Put'*, no. 20 (February 1930), pp. 47–79, and no. 21 (April 1930), pp. 34–62.

6. H. P. Blavatsky, *Isis Unveiled: A Master-Key to the Mysteries of Ancient and Modern Science and Theology*, vol. 2, *Theology* (Pasedena, 1960), pp. 214, 216. Soloviev severely criticized *Isis Unveiled:* "In my whole life I have never read a more obscure and disjointed book" (*Pis'ma*, 4:290–91, and *SS*, 6:394–98). See also "Retsenziia na knigu E. P. Blavatskoi: *The Key to Theosophy*," in *SS*, 6:291.

Blavatsky aside, most modern scholars agree that Kabbala is a historical phenomenon. Although symbols from different mystical or occult schools may interact—and in the present case the figure of Wisdom is a good example—they are best understood in the context in which they developed and in relation to the belief systems and ritual practices that give them expression. Jewish mysticism is inseparable from Jewish tradition, and is impossible to study adequately without at least the degree of knowledge of Judaism that Soloviev, for one, acquired. Its writings refer back to biblical, Talmudic, and midrashic texts, and by the nineteenth century some of its theology and liturgy had made their way into normative Jewish practice. We should also recognize a distinction between certain techniques of "practical kabbala"—breathing, counting, manipulation of the names of God, repetitive prayer—which have much in common with other occult practices, and the theology of "speculative Kabbala," which more interested the mature Soloviev.[7]

In 1896, Soloviev wrote the preface to an article by a Hebraist, Baron David Günzburg, titled "Kabbala: The Mystical Philosophy of the Jews," and arranged for its publication in the prestigious journal *Voprosy filosofii i psikhologii* (Problems in philosophy and psychology).[8] Günzburg's article, its preface, and Soloviev's entry on Kabbala in the Brokgauz-Efron encyclopedia (Soloviev had originally solicited Günzburg to write this more popular entry) all attempt to establish the theological integrity of Kabbala, thus disentangling it from Masonry and Theosophy, from heretical Christian Gnosticism and the various hidden teachings that so fascinated Soloviev's contemporaries. Discussing a subject that his fellow Russians considered occult, Soloviev hinted at the similarities between Kabbala and Orthodoxy, and noted the legitimate claims of Jewish tradition to the God-man relationship that Soloviev himself proclaimed as essential for the future ideal theocracy in Russia.

A short introduction to kabbalistic theology is necessary in order to analyze Soloviev's interest in Jewish mysticism and his belief in the affinity between Kabbala and Russian Orthodoxy. That analysis, in turn, leads to speculation about the failure of Soloviev's heirs in Russian thought to continue their mentor's study of Kabbala, and about the changing cultural atmosphere in which the term "Jewish cabal" took on increasingly sinister and specifically unchristian and anti-Russian connotations.

THE JEWISH KABBALA: HISTORY AND THEOLOGY

The Russian term *kabala*, as Günzburg's article tells us, was familiar to nineteenth-century Russian readers in the meaning of indentured servitude or

---

7. See Gershom G. Scholem, *Kabbalah* (New York, 1974), pp. 182–89.

8. David Gintsburg, "Kabbala, misticheskaia filosofiia evreev," *Voprosy filosofii i psikhologii* 33 (1896): 277–300. The preface alone is reprinted in *SS*, 12:332–34.

bail, and probably came into the Russian language through Muslim sources. Although Günzburg is incorrect in connecting this *kabala* to the Hebrew term meaning "tradition" or "that which is received," his etymology serves his and Soloviev's larger purpose: to demonstrate the antiquity of Kabbala to an audience for whom the foreign-sounding *kabalistka* had come to mean little more than "magic."[9] Pushkin was the most famous propagator of this latter meaning in his story of the occult, "The Queen of Spades," where Kabbala is mentioned in the same mysterious tone as Mephistopheles, hypnotism, and "demonic powers."[10]

Kabbala actually refers to a mystical practice that involves contemplation of the names of God found in Hebrew Scripture, often through numerical manipulation of the letters of the Hebrew alphabet. Kabbala is based on a theology that attempts to speak of God positively, rather than in the apophatic or negative terms of most postbiblical theology (i.e., "God is *not* limited," "God is *not* mortal"), and that aims at an explanation of God's intimate relationship with creation. Its most intense development came in thirteenth-century Spain, with the dissemination of the *Zohar* or *Book of Splendor*, and in sixteenth-century Safed, in Palestine, within the school of Isaac Luria.[11]

The *Zohar*, which Soloviev probably read in Latin translation on his London trip, was written or perhaps partially compiled by Moses ben Shemtov de León, but it was attributed to a great sage of the Talmudic period, Shimon bar Yohai. Its theology contrasts both to the theism of rabbinic Judaism and even more to the medieval Jewish philosophers' insistence on God's radical transcendence.[12] God does have a transcendent aspect in Kabbala: Ein-Sof or "That Which Has No End," sometimes called the Root of Roots, the Cause of Causes, and the Concealed One. Ein-Sof, however, "gives birth" to an elaborate system of *sefirot*, something similar but not identical to hypostases or members of the divine pleroma that are no longer concealed, but disclosed. *Sefirot* are "outer layers of the hidden dimension of God to which they are intimately bound"; they are referred to as the garments, colors, faces, limbs, crowns, or names of God, and are associated with various biblical personalities.[13] The *sefirot* interact in a way reminiscent of a human family, so that Hokhmah (Wisdom), the

9. For etymology, see Maks Fasmer, *Etimologicheskii slovar' russkogo iazyka*, trans. O. N. Trubachev (Moscow, 1967), 2:148–49.

10. For Pushkin's use of *kabal'nyi* and *kabalistika*, see *Slovar' iazyka Pushkina*, ed. V. N. Sidorov (Moscow, 1957), 2:266.

11. For background on Kabbala, see the works of Gershom G. Scholem: *Major Trends* and *Kabbalah*, cited above; *Jewish Gnosticism, Merkabah Mysticism, and Talmudic Tradition* (New York, 1960); and *On Kabbalah and Its Symbolism* (New York, 1965). See also the work of Moshe Idel, esp. *Kabbalah: New Perspectives* (New Haven, 1988).

12. Lawrence Fine makes this point in "Kabbalistic Texts," in *Back to the Sources: Reading the Classic Jewish Texts*, ed. Barry Holtz (New York, 1984), p. 316. This essay is a concise but scholarly introduction to Kabbala for the laity.

13. Ibid., p. 319.

second *sefirah*, impregnates the third, Binah (Knowledge), who, as Upper Mother, gives birth to the lower seven *sefirot*. The lower *sefirot* are often distinguished by gender, and two of them, the male Tiferet (Beauty) and the female Shekhinah (Divine Presence, sometimes called Malkhut, or Kingship), duplicate the sexual activity of the upper *sefirot* and unite in sexual intercourse through the vehicle of Yesod (Foundation), the phallus.[14] Thus divine energy flows downward undiminished, as creation and procreation. Shekhinah, although still fully a part of the Godhead and in fact the culmination of the internal divine unfolding, becomes the hinge between us and God. (See Figure 3.1.)

The exalted status of Shekhinah together with her intimate connection to humanity clearly differentiate Kabbala from both Neoplatonism and Gnosticism, which also elaborate schemes of emanations from an unknowable divine source. In Neoplatonism, the emanations diminish in energy and importance as they descend toward humanity. In Gnosticism, the lower members of the pleroma break away from the supreme deity in a cosmic fall, utterly alienating the transcendent spirit from the created world, dominion of the Demiurge. Neoplatonism thus emphasizes the unity of the divine, Gnosticism the dualism of the cosmos, while Kabbala insists on a dynamic and organic interrelationship of the one and the many.

Aside from the ascription of femaleness to divinity and the corresponding assertion that sex is a divine activity, perhaps the most radical element of Kabbala is its insistence on the correspondence between our world and that of God, for we are not outside the theogonic chain, but rather a vital link in it. In fact, our actions on earth intimately affect the makeup and relationships of the divine *sefirot*. As the *Zohar* states: "Any activity below stimulates a corresponding activity above."[15]

According to Kabbala, the *sefirot* interacted in harmony before Adam's fall. Unlike traditional readings of Genesis 3, the Fall took place within the divine realm itself, causing an imbalance between the *sefirot* of Hesed (Mercy) and Din (Judgment), so that the light of the former no longer mediated the harshness of the latter. As a result, the lovers Tiferet and Shekhinah were separated, and with their separation Shekhinah was exiled. Humanity's task is to reunite the two through righteous and merciful fulfillment of the commandments, through charity, and through prayer. Our deeds stimulate the *sefirot* and can

14. For an important essay on Shekhinah's female role, see Gershom G. Scholem, *"Schechina: Das passiv-weibliche Moment in der Gottheit,"* in *Von der Mystischen Gestalt der Gottheit: Studien zu Grundbegriffen der Kabbala* (Frankfurt am Main, 1977), pp. 135–92.

15. *Zohar* 3:31b, translated in the extensive but still incomplete set: *The Zohar*, trans. Harry Sperling and Maurice Simon, 5 vols. (London, 1984), 4:385. For a more poetic translation with invaluable notes, see the selections in *Zohar: The Book of Enlightenment*, trans. Daniel Chanan Matt (New York, 1983). Gershom G. Scholem translated a handful of entries, but without sufficient notes, in *Zohar: The Book of Splendor* (New York, 1949).

THE TEN SEFIROT

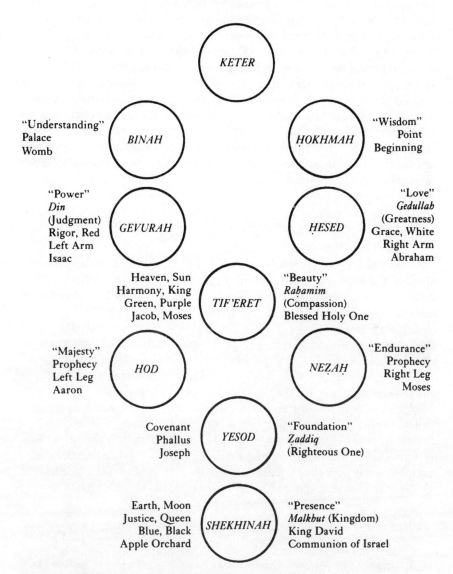

Figure 3.1. The ten *sefirot*. From *Zohar: The Book of Enlightenment,* trans. Daniel Chanan Matt (New York: Paulist Press, 1983). Copyright © 1983 by Daniel Chanan Matt. Reprinted by permission of Paulist Press.

reverse Adam's sin, reuniting God to Itself. Thus the ethical and the mystical are inseparable in Kabbala. To follow the daily laws, many of which are ethically oriented ("Love your neighbor as yourself," "Allow widows and orphans to glean from your fields"), is to unite with God.

Despite its reputation in Christian circles as an occult teaching, and without regard to certain antinomian offshoots, Kabbala was not really "hidden," but integrated into Jewish life and laws. Traditionally only male Jews over forty were considered learned enough in Torah and Talmud to undertake study of the mystical and therefore potentially dangerous texts. But kabbalistic mystics were not aged hermits. They were family men and activists within their communities who believed that the "healing of the universe," or *tikkun olam*, depended on them and their actions. It was this mystical rather than occult aspect of Kabbala that attracted Soloviev.

SOLOVIEV'S ATTRACTION TO KABBALA: GODMANHOOD AND ADAM KADMON

For anyone familiar with both the ethical and the metaphysical teachings of Vladimir Soloviev, the points of contact between Kabbala and Soloviev's doctrine of *bogochelovechestvo* (Godmanhood) should be clear. Soloviev was by no means a kabbalist, just as he was not a Gnostic, a papist, or a Theosophist, as some have claimed, but he did research Kabbala rather extensively, and he learned Hebrew to read Scripture in the original and to study Talmud with his tutor and friend Faivel' Gets.[16] Observed in the British Museum poring over illustrations in a text on Kabbala, Soloviev was heard to say: "In every line of this book there is more life than in all of European scholarship."[17]

Soloviev himself recognized that the Greek name Sophia, which he adopted for his mystical vision of communion between the Trinity and the self, is a direct translation of the Hebrew term *Hokhmah*, Wisdom. It is also, as we saw, the name of the second *sefirah* of Kabbala. Is it a coincidence that Soloviev's central vision of Sophia appeared to him in the British Museum, while he read the *Zohar* or another text of Kabbala?[18] Although Soloviev's Sophia ultimately

---

16. See Faivel' Bentsilovich Gets, "Ob otnoshenii Vl. S. Solov'eva k evreiskomu voprosu," *Voprosy filosofii i psikhologii* 56 (1901): 159–98. The correspondence between Gets and Soloviev can be found in *Pis'ma*, 2:134–91.

17. I. I. Ianzhul, "Vospominaniia I. I. Ianzhula o perezhitom i vidennom," *Russkaia starina* 141 (1910): 481–82. The British Museum houses a large number of kabbalistic manuscripts (see Gerhard Scholem, *Einige kabbalistische Handschriften im Britischen Museum* [Jerusalem, 1932]), but Soloviev did not know Hebrew or Aramaic at the time and probably made use of the Latin translation of Christian Freiherr Knorr von Rosenroth, *Kabbala denudata*, vol. 1 (Sulzbach, 1677); vol. 2 (Frankfurt, 1684). The two volumes were reprinted in *Kabbala denudata* (New York, 1974).

18. Soloviev describes his visions in the long poem "Tri svidaniia" (*SS*, 12:80–86). See also

is not identical to the Hokhmah of Kabbala, the resemblance of many basic kabbalistic premises to Soloviev's statements on the structure of reality, the cosmogonic process, and human institutions all point to Kabbala as a source for his vocabulary and as confirmation of his mystical intuitions about the relationship of God and man.[19] All the more reason, then, that Soloviev should seek to legitimate the doctrine of Kabbala within the history of religion, and to distance kabbalistic practice from occult charlatanism and heretical mysticism.

The introduction to Günzburg's article demonstrates the affinity between Kabbala and Soloviev's teaching. In it Soloviev praises Kabbala as a "whole and unique worldview" ("tseloe svoeobraznoe mirosozertsanie," *SS*, 12:332). The "wholeness" of Orthodoxy was one of the cornerstones of late nineteenth-century Russian religious philosophy, and to call Kabbala *tseloe* was significant praise indeed. The syncretism of Kabbala no doubt appealed to Soloviev's own highly synthetic mind, especially in view of the Neoplatonic and Gnostic influence on both systems. Yet Soloviev warns against overemphasizing the influence of Neoplatonism, since Kabbala ultimately goes deeper than its "superficial branches," and is grounded through its roots in ancient and biblical thought (*SS*, 12:332).

Soloviev further emphasizes the "special and essential realism" and the "integrated monism" of Kabbala (*SS*, 12:332). The central paradox that both Kabbala and Soloviev must confront is the justification of essentially dualistic and triadic concepts within a system dedicated to monotheism. Soloviev's frequent references to the Trinitarian and Christological heresies of the early church raise the specter of polytheism, especially in his main works on Sophia: *Rossiia i vselenskaia tserkov'* (Russia and the universal church; French version 1889, Russian translation 1911) and *Chteniia o bogochelovechestve* (Lectures on Godmanhood, 1877–81). He reconciles the paradox not by blind assertion of the oneness of God but by the development of a doctrine of wholeness that takes as its ideal the Russian Orthodox concept of *sobornost'*, or "multiplicity in unity."[20] The church on earth and in heaven, Sophia, and the Godhead Itself are all fully integrated and organic wholes with a nonetheless multipartite (usually triadic) structure. "All that is," claims Soloviev, "is by necessity both one and many" (*SS*, 3:61).

Like Soloviev, Kabbala integrates a universal mystical tradition that views the world in threes, and does so by the development of its system of *sefirot* emerging from Ein-Sof, often organized into three triads, with the tenth *sefirah*,

---

the poems "Vsia v lazuri segodnia iavilas'" and "U tsaritsy moei est' vysokii dvorets" (*SS*, 12:12).

19. For more on Soloviev's interest in Kabbala, see my article "Solov'ev's Androgynous Sophia and the Jewish Kabbalah," *Slavic Review* 50 (Fall 1991): 487–96.

20. See A. S. Khomiakov, "Tserkov' odna," in *Polnoe sobranie sochinenii*, 8 vols. (Moscow, 1900–1904), 2:1–26.

Shekhinah, including the other nine. The following description appears early in the *Zohar:*

> Three emerge from one; one stands in three;
> enters between two; two suckle one;
> one suckles many sides.
> Thus all is one.[21]

Neither system accepts the static Godhead of Eastern mysticism or the unmoving Prime Mover of Greek philosophy. For both Kabbala and Soloviev, God can indeed seem to be many, for the divine world is in perpetual movement, constantly relating to and interrelating with aspects of itself. A modern scholar of Jewish mysticism writes of the *Zohar:* "Portrayed through a myriad of symbols and described in countless patterns of pairing and unification, the *sefirot* have the effect of transforming the God of static oneness, as portrayed in most of Western theology, into a deity of vibrant and dynamic unity, manifest in ever-changing patterns."[22]

Dualism is a more pressing problem; Soloviev would not need to criticize it so often were it not uncomfortably close to the traditions on which he draws. If God is transcendent, how is it possible to avoid a picture of the universe in which earth is opposed to heaven, evil to good, ugliness to beauty? If God is immanent, how do you distinguish your theology from a pantheism that too easily turns into either the polytheism avoided by a doctrine of *sobornost'* or the atheistic humanism of the nineteenth century against which Soloviev also rails? Both Soloviev and Kabbala approach the problem of dualism with the assertion that God and creation are essentially united. Humanity is integrally connected to the cosmogonic and theogonic worlds; we are its last extension and a vital step in the redemption, or in fact deification, of nature and the reunion of all: *tikkun olam*. In Soloviev's words: "In the thought of the God of heaven and earth, the higher world and the lower world were created together and have a single base, which is essential Wisdom—the unconditional unity of all. The unity of heaven and earth, posited on the base (*reshit* [a kabbalistic name for Hokhmah]), in the beginning of the creative act, must be realized factually by means of the cosmogonic and historical process, leading to the perfect manifestation of that unity in the Kingdom of God (*malkhut* [Shekhinah])" (*SS*, 11:302).

From this intimate connection between humanity and God emerges the next point of contact between Soloviev and Kabbala: the anthropomorphism of the Kabbala, which Soloviev called its crowning height, or *zavershenie* (*SS*, 12:333). Kabbalistic texts sometimes depict the *sefirot* as an androgynous hu-

---

21. *Zohar* 1:32b, in Matt, *Zohar*, p. 21.

22. Arthur Green, Introduction to Menahem Nahum, *Upright Practices, The Light of the Eyes* (New York, 1982), p. 10.

man body, with the first *sefirah*, Keter (Crown), as the head, and the lower *sefirot* representing the shoulders, breast, arms, genitals, and legs. Together they describe Adam Kadmon, or Primordial Man, and God is therefore depicted in the image and likeness of collective humanity. As Gershom Scholem writes: "The Biblical word that man was created in the image of God means two things to the Kabbalist: first, that the power of the Sefiroth, the paradigm of divine life, exists and is active also in man. Secondly, that the world of the Sefiroth, that is to say the world of God the Creator, is capable of being visualized under the image of man the created."[23]

For Soloviev, who here follows Orthodox doctrine, to be born in the image and likeness of God is to retain Godlike unity. The Orthodox Church might distinguish between the divine and the human realms, but not between spirit and flesh, as Western theology does, following Augustine. Physical matter is not inherently sinful for Soloviev, and Kabbala's virtual deification of the flesh (within the bounds of Torah law) must have been particularly appealing to him. Traditional Judaism stresses the importance of sexual relations between married couples, including a commandment for a husband to attend to the pleasure of his wife. For the kabbalist, sexual relations on Friday night are one way for the male mystic to unite with Shekhinah. As one scholar remarks: "Kabbalists considered the sexual act as an act that gives life," and "Marriage and sexual union have an enormous impact on the upper world"; "perfect sexual union truly influences the divine presence."[24]

Soloviev directly links erotic love with the transfiguration of the flesh into a divine-human being, claiming that Eros can lead us along five possible paths, the highest of which is the path toward the image and likeness of God, the union of male and female principles in androgyny, and the establishment of a whole human being (*tselyi chelovek*) based on a *spiritual-bodily* principle (*nachalo dukhovno-telesnoe*) (*SS*, 9:234). Soloviev asserts not only that Christ "became man" (*vochelovechilsia*), suggesting that he manifested human reason, but that he "became flesh" (*voplotilsia*), reaffirming the sanctity of matter (*SS*, 3:170). The incarnation of Christ demonstrates the natural movement toward the sanctification of the flesh; his transfiguration into spiritual light then further proves the potential deification of that flesh: God became man so that man might become God.[25]

A natural outgrowth of Soloviev's belief in deification through transfiguration is his interest in human institutions, or those means by which humanity

23. Scholem, *Major Trends*, p. 215.

24. Moshe Idel, "Métaphores et pratiques sexuelles dans la Cabale," in *Lettre sur la sainteté: Le Secret de la relation entre l'homme et la femme dans la Cabale*, trans. Charles Mopsik (Paris, 1986), pp. 344, 347, 336.

25. For more on this doctrine, see Vladimir Lossky, *In the Image and Likeness of God* (Crestwood, N.Y., 1974), p. 97; and Timothy Ware, *The Orthodox Church* (New York, 1963, 1978), pp. 236–42.

can influence the created world in which we will be united with God. We see this optimistic belief in social action perhaps most clearly in Soloviev's critique of Plato, whom otherwise he considers a mentor (see especially his lengthy essay "Zhiznennaia drama Platona" (The life drama of Plato, 1898). Plato falls short of greatness for Soloviev, for, "although anticipating social *truth*, Plato's idealism did not possess the *means* to its accomplishment and he could not give *life* to his idea" (*SS*, 9:318). All Russian religious philosophy insists on the role of action, a task or *zadacha* whose accomplishment will mean the reunion of God and creation. As in Kabbala, we must participate in the cosmogonic as well as the historical process in order to achieve Soloviev's ideal of Godmanhood.

Perhaps the most important reason for Soloviev's attraction to Kabbala cannot be found in similarities in mystical convictions, or in the emphasis on sexuality, or even in the ultimate reliance on human institutions in the process of the deification of creation, although this was one of Soloviev's strongest convictions. Elements of all these ideas can be found in Soloviev's affinity with esoteric and mystical systems other than Kabbala. Rather, the attraction lies in the very people who historically carried the tradition of Kabbala: the Jews. The Jewish people and their institutions held a special place in all aspects of Soloviev's philosophy, and it is not surprising that their mystical practices should seem so appealing to this prophet of the Universal Church. *Christian* cabala is rarely mentioned by Soloviev, although its development in Europe had a significant influence on Renaissance and modern Western philosophy, and its teachings found their way into Russian thought through Freemasonry, as mentioned above. Apparently only "authentic" Jewish Kabbala carried the authority of Soloviev's beloved Hebrew prophets and could help structure his ideal theocracy.

Soloviev idealized the Solomonic period of Jewish history, when, according to the Russian philosopher, priest, prophet, and king exerted equal control over the people of Israel and elicited equal love from them. "Within the Jewish theocracy," Soloviev writes in *Rossiia i vselenskaia tserkov'*, "all three social powers revealed themselves in the proper harmonic relationship, and thus prefigured and prepared for the kingdom of the true Messiah" (*SS*, 9:326). Although the Solomonic kingdom lasted no more than a few decades, it proved to Soloviev the potential for a theocratic social structure that could welcome the Godman and bring about Godmanhood.

According to Soloviev, Christ was born to Jewish parents precisely because of the contradictory combination of the Jews' "deep religiousness" (their total devotion to God) and their strong "sense of self" (their exclusive egoism) united with an "extreme materialism" (*SS*, 4:142). The first characteristic suggests the sacred, the latter two, presumably, the profane. The combination of the three, however, demonstrates that the Jewish people embodied the principle of Godmanhood even before the advent of the Godman; they properly demonstrated the true connection between the material and divine realms, entering into a covenant with God as with an equal partner: "as two beings, although not of equal strength, nonetheless morally akin" (*SS*, 4:144). Furthermore:

> Firmly believing in the Essence of God, Israel attracted to itself the divine man-ifestation and His revelation. Believing also in themselves, Israel could enter into a *personal* relationship with Yehova. It [Israel] could stand before Him face to face, confirm a covenant with Him, and serve Him as an active partner instead of a passive instrument. Finally, by the strength of that active faith striving toward the final realization of its spiritual principle through the purification of material nature, Israel prepared in its midst a pure and holy abode for the incar-nation of God the Word. (*SS*, 4:150)

The Jews' mistake, according to Soloviev, rests simply on the fact that their sense of self came to outbalance their religiousness, so that they failed to recognize Christ as the physical embodiment of their own inner principles. Despite their failure to accept Jesus, however, they remain the Chosen People, chosen by God not arbitrarily but reciprocally, because *they* first chose God (*SS*, 4:144). God, asserts Soloviev, wants a partner, not a slave, in the development of Godmanhood and the deification of nature.

In short, Jewish Kabbala may have been particularly appealing to Soloviev precisely because it is *Jewish*, and then, in confirmation of Soloviev's own reading of Jewish institutions, because it stresses the *active* role of humanity in the establishment of Godmanhood. The theology of Kabbala and its cos-mogonic system, with the coincidence of the terms Hokhmah/Sophia, no doubt compelled Soloviev to seek in its vocabulary an expression of his own mystical intuitions regarding divine-human interaction.

SOLOVIEV'S LEGACY: SAMPLES AND TRENDS

Soloviev's followers, among both the Symbolist poets and those theologians called Sophiologists, reclaimed Soloviev's early interest in the occult, and their esoteric seekings responded to an acute sense of imminent disaster and the loss of Orthodox religious values that Soloviev had rightly identified. Despite frequent reference to Kabbala, however, Soloviev's heirs for the most part did not have enough knowledge of kabbalistic teachings to separate Kabbala from the dualism of Gnosticism or to save it from disappearing into other esoteric systems. Furthermore, the poets and theologians of the twentieth century rarely began with the Judeophilia of Soloviev, even though interest in the Jews was high in the period before and during World War I.[26] The significance of their statements on Judaism and Jewish mysticism, therefore, is more historical

26. See, e.g., L. Andreev, M. Gor'kii, and F. Sologub, eds., *Shchit: Literaturnyi sbornik*, 3d ed. (Moscow, 1916).

Judith Deutsch Kornblatt

than theological, since they speak to the rapidly changing political climate in prewar and revolutionary Russia.

"The historian," wrote Nikolai Berdiaev in 1919, "must discover within himself the deep layers of the ancient Jewish world in order to grasp its history."[27] Berdiaev stressed, however, that those layers are no more important, in fact even less so, than an awareness of the influence of the Hellenic world and of Greek history. Therefore, the Jew to this student of Soloviev is not the model for ideal communication between humanity and God, but only one element in the development of modern historical consciousness. In Berdiaev's view, furthermore, Christ's incarnation brought on a radically transformed period in history, so that contemporary Jews not only are mistaken in their refusal to see Godmanhood incarnate in the Godman, as Soloviev explains Judaism's error, but are cut off entirely from the spirituality of their biblical forefather Abraham.

Sergei Soloviev, the philosopher's nephew and perhaps most devoted, if eccentric, follower, argued against Berdiaev's and others' tendency to denigrate the influence of Judaism on Christianity. Yet he also distinguished sharply between the "true" Judaism of Abraham and Moses and that of those "followers of the Talmud and Kabbala" who had perverted the meaning of the Bible. For Sergei Soloviev, "the consequent mortification of the law of Moses, its perversion in the Talmud, clearly demonstrates that the Jews had lost their God. With the appearance of the Kabbala, Judaism assumes elements of the Babylonian magic that Israel fought against, and in the fighting strengthened its own religious consciousness."[28]

Pavel Florensky and Sergei Bulgakov, theologians who expanded on Soloviev's Sophiology, both refer to Kabbala when they seek the origins of Sophia/Hokhmah. Like Soloviev, Florensky points to Jewish philosophy and theology as confirmation of the sanctity of nature. Nonetheless, "only Christianity gave birth to a hitherto unseen love of creation and inflicted on the heart a wound of loving compassion for all of existence. A 'feeling for nature' . . . is a feeling entirely Christian, and decidedly unthinkable outside of Christianity."[29]

The "holy body" of which Florensky speaks elsewhere is therefore not Adam Kadmon, and did not, as Soloviev claimed, exist historically before the coming of Christ within the Jewish social organization, expressed in the Jews' activist mysticism. Florensky includes Ein-Sof in that "boundless and great Nothingness of mystics outside of Christianity," but in so doing does not

27. Nikolai Berdiaev, *Smysl istorii: Opyt filosofii chelovecheskoi sud'by*, 2d ed. (Paris, 1969), p. 31.

28. Sergei Solov'ev, "Religioznoe znachenie evreistva," in *Bogoslovskie i kriticheskie ocherki: Sobranie statei i publichnykh lektsii* (Moscow, 1916), pp. 49, 53.

29. Pavel Florenskii, *Stolp i utverzhdenie istiny: Opyt pravoslavnoi feoditsei v dvenadtsati pis'makh* (Paris, 1989), pp. 279–82, 288. He also points to Kabbala as expressing the triadic nature of the human spirit (p. 731).

distinguish the kabbalistic notion from the Buddhist or Neoplatonic, as Soloviev did.[30]

In *The Wisdom of God*, an authorized English collection of Sergei Bulgakov's main teachings on Sophia, Bulgakov defines Sophia's aspect of the "Wisdom of God" as the Hebrew Hokhmah, and the "Glory of God" as Shekhinah. His designation suggests an acquaintance with Soloviev's work on Kabbala, especially in *Rossiia i vselenskaia tserkov'*, but does not demonstrate any real understanding of the theology of classical Kabbala, for Bulgakov essentially conflates Wisdom and Glory, ignoring their specific roles vis-à-vis the other *sefirot*. Even more telling, Bulgakov mentions only the biblical sources for the Hebrew terms and not the kabbalistic ones, although Shekhinah is not a "person" or even a divine principle in the Bible, but simply the term for the presence or "indwelling" of God.[31]

It is possible that Florensky and Bulgakov, especially after he was accused of unorthodox Sophiology, were forced to defend the Christian aspects of their Sophia.[32] When they asserted the ancient source of Sophia, biblical passages were therefore more acceptable than kabbalistic ones, and more easily reconciled with Orthodox doctrine. Even Gnostic sources were more legitimate, not to mention better known to Florensky and Bulgakov, for some of the Church Fathers had flirted with Gnosticism. And when Florensky and Bulgakov turned to patristic sources to confirm the presence of Sophia in the piety of the early church, they filtered biblical readings through Christian interpretations. In general, they did not investigate Jewish mysticism to any significant extent, and, unlike Soloviev, the later Sophiologists viewed neither the Jews' mysticism nor their social structure as a model for the true, ecumenical Russian Church.[33]

In view of the mystical aspects of Sophia worship by Aleksandr Blok and Andrei Bely, it would seem natural for Soloviev's heirs among the Symbolists to look to Kabbala. But without a concurrent search within Orthodoxy for the basis of Godmanhood—a search that culminated in Soloviev's validation of *Jewish* history and mysticism—the Symbolists' understanding of Kabbala ironically sank back into what Soloviev had labeled charlatanism, and the teachings on Sophia/Hokhmah approached the dualism of Gnosticism from

30. Ibid., p. 312.

31. Sergius Bulgakov, *The Wisdom of God: A Brief Summary of Sophiology* (New York and London, 1937), pp. 47, 50, 53–54. For an explanation of the changing meaning of Shekhinah in Jewish theology, see Kornblatt, "Solov'ev's Androgynous Sophia," p. 495, n. 31.

32. For a discussion of the controversy surrounding Bulgakov's Sophiology, see Samuel D. Cioran, *Vladimir Solov'ev and the Knighthood of the Divine Sophia* (Waterloo, Ont., 1977), pp. 247–72.

33. This is not intended to be a complete survey of writings on the Jews by Berdiaev, Bulgakov, and Florensky. The first two turned again to the "Jewish question" in the late 1930s. A thorough study of Judaism, Jewry, and modern Russian religious thought is currently under way.

which Soloviev had tried to distinguish it. According to Berdiaev, who here substitutes "Christ" for Soloviev's "Godman": "The Russian poet/Sophia-worshipers for the most part believed in Sophia without believing in Christ. This Sophia is not at all wise and is alien to Christ. Blok's 'Beautiful Lady' is this unrecognizable Sophia, who eternally seduces and eternally deceives; her image splits in two."[34]

Berdiaev is here oversimplifying, and his statement about Christ may be more applicable to Blok than to Bely,[35] but the fact remains that the poets of the early twentieth century demonstrate gnostic/dualistic rather than kabbalistic tendencies, and their knowledge of Kabbala itself was limited to textbooks that equated Kabbala with all other occult systems, of the sort disseminated by Madame Blavatsky and the Theosophical movement.[36]

From this brief survey we can conclude that among Soloviev's followers neither the Symbolists nor the philosophers in the Russian religious renaissance had as profound a knowledge of Kabbala or of Judaism as their mentor did. The Sophia of the Symbolists lost her organic multiplicity, and with it her ability to form the hinge between heaven and humanity. She could no longer help define God as well as flesh in positive terms. The Sophia of the later Sophiologists, especially Florensky and Bulgakov, retained her multiplicity but found her authentication in patristics and Russian piety, and only incidentally in Jewish traditional or mystical texts.

It is possible that Vasily Rozanov most closely follows Soloviev's interest in the Jews, and thus in Jewish mysticism, although he more often repudiated Soloviev than praised him.[37] Nowhere is Soloviev's legacy more obvious than in Rozanov's association of Judaism with positive sexuality (however abstract the concept of sexuality may have been for Soloviev), and sexuality, in turn, with divine interaction.

Nonetheless, Rozanov's approach to Jewish mysticism differed radically from his predecessor's. In a brilliant if perverse anti-Semitic work that might be translated as "The Olfactory and Tactile Attitude of the Jews toward Blood," Rozanov includes a lengthy essay by a scholar he identifies only as S. D-sky, apparently "one of two individuals, totally unrelated and hitherto unknown to me," who helped Rozanov "prove" that the Jews killed the Christian youth

---

34. Berdiaev here compares the Sophia of the poets to that of Boehme. "Iz etiudov o Iakove Beme: Etiud II," *Put'*, no. 21 (April 1930), p. 55.

35. See David M. Bethea, "Aspects of the Biblical Plot in the Age of Symbolism: Blok, Bely, and the Poetics of Revelation," in *Christianity and Its Role in the Culture of the Eastern Slavs in Modern Times: Ideologies, Institutions, Cultural Life*, ed. Robert Hughes, Boris Gasparov, and Irina Paperno (Berkeley, 1995). I thank Professor Bethea for allowing me to see this article in manuscript.

36. Cioran argues for Gnostic influences on Soloviev in *Solov'ev and the Knighthood*, but exaggerates them by reading the philosopher back through the eyes of Blok and Bely.

37. See Emanuel Glouberman, "Vasilii Rozanov: The Antisemitism of a Russian Judeophile," *Jewish Social Studies* 38, no. 2 (1976): 123.

Andrusha Iushchinsky in a ritual human sacrifice. "The purpose of this essay," writes D-sky, "is to determine the connection between the 13 wounds [on Iushchinsky's head] and the text of the *Zohar*." He claims to identify Hebrew letters when lines are drawn from one stab wound to the next, and develops an elaborate discussion of the occult meaning of those letters—that is, of "Judaic cryptography," as Rozanov himself refers to the Hebrew alphabet in the essay that opens the book.[38]

D-sky's sources, however, are less than reliable. He includes a diagram of the *sefirot* taken, uncredited, from the medieval occultist Agrippa, whose "creative" interpretation of Kabbala influenced many Christian cabalists.[39] (See Figure 3.2.) He draws on various occult tracts,[40] a pamphlet by one Mr. Uranus titled *Ubiistvo Iushchinskago i kabbala* (Iushchinsky's murder and the Kabbala, 1913), and supposed translations of the *Zohar* by a Hebraist, Isaak Markon, and a Catholic priest, Justin Bonaventura Pranaitis. This is the same Pranaitis who testified for the prosecution in the Beilis case. D-sky then demonstrates with parallel passages from Markon and Pranaitis how the Jewish translator "censored" passages that "prove" the existence of ancient Hebrew (and thus modern Eastern European Jewish!) human sacrifice.[41]

Rozanov's reliance on D-sky's treatise, with its spurious scholarship and, at best, support from unnamed occultists and Christian cabalists, suggests how far Rozanov had traveled from Soloviev's effort to legitimate the Jewish Kabbala and to show its organic relation to Orthodoxy. In fact, Rozanov returns to the more popular "Masonic" or "Theosophical" understanding of the Kabbala as only one of many occult systems that could be used either for white or, in the case Rozanov cites, decidedly black magic.

Whether or not Rozanov's anti-Semitic tracts represented the author's personal belief at the time (Rozanov asked forgiveness of the Jews on his deathbed), they clearly fed a growing belief among some Russians that the Jews of the world were assembled in a secret "cabal" that was profoundly anti-Christian and anti-Russian. The numerous publications in Russia of *The Protocols of the Elders of Zion*, the work of the Black Hundreds, and the increasing number of accusations against the Jews as revolutionaries (from the right) and

38. Vasilii Rozanov, *Oboniatel'noe i osiazatel'noe otnoshenie evreev k krovi* (St. Petersburg, 1914), pp. viii, 217. Rozanov also thanks "one scholarly friend," who in all likelihood was Pavel Florensky. For information on the murder in question, see Maurice Samuel, *Blood Accusation: The Strange History of the Beiliss Case* (New York, 1966).

39. Rozanov, *Oboniatel'noe i osiazatel'noe otnoshenie*, p. 222a.

40. He cites in part "E. Lévi, L. Lucas, Papus, d'Alveïdre, Christian and others" (ibid., p. 247). Pseudo-scholarly footnotes include such noninformation as "See various treatises on Kabbala" and "See various treatises on astrology" (pp. 231, 232).

41. No reference can be found to the Markon translation, and, as far as I can determine, Pranaitis never translated the *Zohar*, but he did publish an attack on the Talmud in St. Petersburg; it has been translated into English as *The Talmud Unmasked: The Secret Rabbinical Teachings Concerning Christians* (New York, 1939).

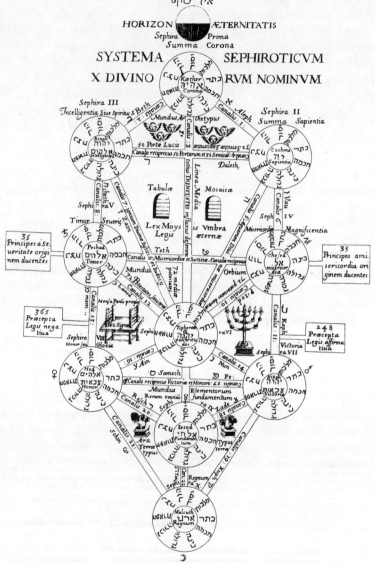

Figure 3.2. A sixteenth-century diagram of the *sefirot*. From Henricus Cornelius Agrippa ab Nettesheym, *De occulta philosophia.*

as blood-sucking capitalists (from the left) all rely on a belief in the conspiratorial and satanic cult of the Jews, to which the term "Kabbala" became firmly attached in the years after Soloviev's death.[42]

In a great historical irony, just at the time when Soloviev and Russian religious thought were experiencing a revival, Rozanov's words found a forum in glasnost Russia, exemplified by the statement of a leader of the anti-Semitic organization Pamiat'. All of Russia's disorder, he explains, can be traced to the fact that

> we live under what is in essence a kabbalistic, foreign heraldry. As long as the walls of the Kremlin are marked with the sign of the Antichrist, there will be no order in our state. Why? Take any textbook on Kabbala, or on astrology, and you will see that the astronomical sign of the five-pointed star has ancient significance. It was then stolen through India and became a purely magical, astrological, kabbalistic sign. Furthermore, the five-pointed star burns in Masonic lodges.[43]

It would be wrong, however, to end on the occult ravings of a madman who represents, one hopes, only a small percentage of the Russian public. To find one more explanation for Soloviev's ultimate failure to distinguish Kabbala from other mystical teachings and to incorporate it into Russian thought, we must look again to the Günzburg article that Soloviev introduced. Here we find the influence of Jewish as well as Russian cultural changes.

In the century and a half before Soloviev, kabbalistic teachings experienced a third age of flowering, similar to the periods of the *Zohar* and the Lurianic school in Safed. Eastern European Hasidism of the eighteenth century was an outgrowth of earlier Kabbala, and developed especially a cult of Shekhinah, the *sefirah* that, together with Hokhmah, Soloviev equated with Sophia. Hasidism's mystical aspects and its insistence on the divinization of humanity indeed have much in common with traditional (as well as sectarian) Russian Orthodoxy, and especially with the Orthodoxy expressed by late nineteenth- and early twentieth-century Russian religious philosophers.

As Soloviev points out in *Evreistvo i khristianskii vopros* (Jewry and the Christian Question), the Russian Empire in the modern period was home to the largest population of Jews in the world, and the phenomenon of Hasidism seems likely to have had some influence on the Russian Orthodox popula-

---

42. For a classic study of the *Protocols of the Elders of Zion*, see Norman Cohn, *Warrant for Genocide: The Myth of the Jewish World-Conspiracy and the Protocols of the Elders of Zion* (London, 1967). For a discussion of modern anti-Semitism and its ambiguously reactionary *and* radical base, see Paul Lawrence Rose, *Revolutionary Antisemitism in Germany from Kant to Wagner* (Princeton, 1990).

43. Aleksandr Terekhov, "Portret na Pamiat'" (interview with D. D. Vasiliev), *Ogonek* 20 (May 1990): 12.

tion.[44] Yet Günzburg's article carefully differentiates "pure" Kabbala from "evil" Hasidism, thus rejecting the Hasids as carriers of the authentic teaching that Soloviev wanted to propagate. The Hasidim are hypocrites, claims Günzburg, and Kabbala ultimately "caused the greatest of evils through the appearance of the miracle worker BeSHT (Ba'al-Shem-Tov, the Master of the Good Name), who invented Hasidism . . . , developed sanctimoniousness to the detriment of science, gave free rein to superstition, and created a whole throng of sincere and insincere *tsaddikim* [spiritual leaders]."[45]

Günzburg's rejection of later Jewish mysticism stems from an aspect of Jewish history in the nineteenth century: the spread into Russia of "Enlightenment Judaism," or the Haskalah. The so-called enlightened Jews distanced themselves from the rural, uneducated population in which Hasidism flourished, as well as from the old-fashioned Talmudic scholars who refused any suggestion of assimilation (and also criticized Hasidism). But it was these secular Jews of the city, bitter enemies of anything reeking of Jewish backwardness, who forged ties with the liberal Russian intelligentsia, and who entered into the artistic and political circles of early twentieth-century Russia.

Instead of following Soloviev and seeking the similarities between Orthodoxy and Judaism, especially in their mystical incarnations, most liberal Russian and Jewish intellectuals of the time sought a common language in socialism and revolution. Many actors in the Russian religious renaissance in fact recognized the relationship between the Marxism of their youth and the religion into which they had been reborn. As Bulgakov wrote, "My present idealistic world outlook . . . strives to deepen and to substantiate precisely that social ideal which is inscribed on the banner of Marxism and which constitutes its very soul."[46] "However strange it may seem at first glance," wrote Berdiaev, "the ideological and, later, the religious current among us . . . came in fact from the bowels of Marxism."[47] Yet it was "precisely the messianic, religious, myth-creating aspect of Marxism" that took hold in Russia.[48] Those messianic aspects, as Soloviev had shown, united Russian Orthodoxy and Kabbala rather than separated them.

Had the early Soviet leaders who rejected religion of any kind been able to see that the roots of socialism coincide with the Solovievan *and* kabbalistic

44. See Raphael Patai, *The Jewish Mind* (New York, 1977), pp. 182–91.

45. Gintsburg, "Kabbala," p. 299. For another negative assessment of Hasidism, see M. M. Filipov, "Maimonid i kabbala," *Vek* 10 (1882): 156–58, where the author speaks of the "infection of Hasidism."

46. Sergei Bulgakov, *Ot marksizma k idealizmu* (St. Petersburg, 1903), p. vi, quoted in E. A. Stepanova, "Exhausted Marxism: An Examination of Marxist Doctrine in the Traditions of Russian Religious Philosophy," *Soviet Studies in Philosophy* 29, no. 4 (1991): 9.

47. Nikolai Berdiaev, *Istoki i smysl russkogo kommunizma* (Paris, 1955), p. 90, quoted in K. M. Kantor, "Two Designs of Universal History," *Soviet Studies in Philosophy* 29, no. 4 (1991): 37 (Russian text: "Dva proekta vsemirnoi istorii," *Voprosy filosofii* 2 [1990]: 76–86).

48. Stepanova, "Exhausted Marxism," p. 18.

principles of the deification of humanity, the glorification of matter, belief in communal responsibility for "healing" the universe, and the essentially divine nature of social activism, they might have recognized the truly mystical nature of their practical program. Instead, the suppressed mystical aspects of the Russian worldview, whether expressed in Orthodox, Marxist, or kabbalistic terms, went underground, and emerged only in their occult manifestations. Kabbala never regained its legitimate meaning in the Soviet Union. Now, after the discrediting of Soviet ideology and the revival of research on the "idealist" thinkers of the Russian religious revival, Jewish mysticism still has little attraction for Russian scholars. The term *kabala* remains connected to black magic and to unchristian, anti-Russian activities. *The Protocols of the Elders of Zion* has a new audience that fears the "Jewish cabal," and piles of authentic kabbalistic texts remain uncatalogued in damp, unventilated libraries.

PART TWO
VARIETIES OF EARLY TWENTIETH-CENTURY OCCULTISM

CHAPTER FOUR
"THE SHADE OF LUCIFER'S DARK WING"

Satanism in Silver Age Russia

Kristi A. Groberg

atanism was one facet of the occult movement in Silver Age Russia (c. 1890–1914). There is a dearth of concrete evidence on the actual practice of Satan worship, black magic, and the black mass; what does exist is secondhand: rumor, gossip, epithet, or literary artefact. Yet fascination with the satanic and with what it suggested left visible traces. This interest was first aroused by the general revival of the occult in Europe, the fin-de-siècle rediscovery of Lucifer and Mephistopheles as Romantic heroic figures, and the rise of French Symbolist and Decadent satanism in the last half of the nineteenth century.[1] In Russia, these strains met with the resurgent popularity

1. Volumes have been written on the integration of the Symbolist and Decadent schools; here I use the terms almost interchangeably to account for the intense cross-fertilization, but with a slight bow to the negative, nihilistic connotations of Decadence. David R. Schaffer, "The Religious Component of Russian Symbolism," in *Studies in Honor of Xenia Gasiorowska,* ed. L. G. Leighton (Columbus, 1982), p. 89, claims Christian philosophy is the basis of Russian Symbolism, whereas satanism, demonism, and anti-Christian views form the basis of Russian Decadence. More realistic is Renato Poggioli, *The Poets of Russia, 1890–1930* (Cambridge, Mass., 1960), p. 148, who notes "the tendency on the part of the genuine Symbolists to yield no less supinely than their Decadent brethren to the temptations of the demonic and the seductions of Satanism, to the superstitious worship of the blind and dark forces of the underworld." On satanism in the European experience, see John Senior, *The Way Down and Out: The Occult in Symbolist Literature* (Ithaca, 1959); Christopher McIntosh, *Eliphas Lévi and the French Occult Revival* (London, 1975), pp. 177–218; Gerhard Zacharias, *Satanskult und schwarze Messe: Ein Beitrag zur Phänomenologie der Religion* (Wiesbaden, 1964). Among the Russian favorites were Victor Hugo's *Fin de Satan* (begun 1854, published 1886), Charles Baudelaire's *Fleurs du mal* (1857, 1886, 1890), Lautréamont's *Maldoror* (1868), Gustave Flaubert's *Tentation de saint Antoine* (1878, 1900), Jules Barbey d'Aurevilly's *Diaboliques* (1874, 1882), Joséphin Péladin's *Vice suprême* (1884), Arthur Rimbaud's *Saison en enfer* (1886), and *Les Sataniques* of their favorite illustrator, Félicien Rops (1883), as well as "serious studies" such

of the Gothic novel, Goethe, and Edgar Allan Poe, the theme of Satan as the projection of intellectual pride in the works of prominent Russian novelists, and the discovery of Nietzsche. The result was a convergence of the occult with religious and philosophical questions about the nature of evil, as well as a preoccupation with evil for its own sake.

In the manner of the French occultist Symbolists who tried to prove the existence of Satan worship and the black mass in 1890s Paris, I came across only the spoor of what might have been Satan worship in Silver Age Russia. If it did indeed exist, we probably will never learn very much about it, because it is a noteworthy paradox that the incidence of references to Satan and explicit images of him seem to be in inverse proportion to the seriousness of the belief in him. To profess certain ideas or practices (or to be rumored to have professed them) is not necessarily to hold or manifest them. Serious occultists may not have expressed their spiritual investigations through the arts, possibly to avoid notice (in imperial Russia the threat of arrest loomed) or the trivialization of their ideas. Nonetheless, we need to take account of the fact that perceptions about the existence of satanism, whether or not they reflected actuality, are still valid as perceptions.

Receptivity to the satanic found its expression primarily through multivalent symbolic imagery in literature, art, and music, and secondarily through behavior. Often inextricably intertwined, these expressions reflect disaffection from and rebellion against established norms: sociocultural mores, religion, politics, and artistic forms. In short, the same things that drove people to the occult in general drew them to the satanic: they may have said they were seeking answers their culture could not provide, but more often than not they used the satanic as an expression of protest. The symbol was—of course— Satan, the Devil, or any one of an assortment of demons from the biblical to the folkloric; more sophisticated were images (directly related to the popularity of Goethe and Nietzsche) of Mephistopheles, the figure of embodied evil, and of Lucifer, the Romantically tragic fallen angel.[2] The behavioral posture, a reaction against norms considered outmoded or obsolete, was at its simplest nothing more than youth-culture rebellion: a sensationalist response by a youthful group who saw satanism, in Georgette Donchin's words, as "a daring innovation, a reflection of *their* times, the last word in modernism, [and] a

---

as J.-K. Huysmans's *Là-bas* (1891), Stanislas de Guaita's *Serpent de la Genèse* (*Le Temple de Satan* and *La Clef de la magie noire*, 1891), Bois's *Petites Religions de Paris* and *Satanisme et la magie* (both 1894), and *Le Diable et l'occultisme* (1896) of Papus (Gérard Encausse).

2. On demons and devils in Russian folklore, see Erna V. Pomerantsova, *Mifologicheskie personazhi v russkom fol'klore* (Moscow, 1975), pp. 118–49. An encyclopedic work on the Symbolist image, which does not deal with prose, is now available: Aage A. Hansen-Löve, *Der russische Symbolismus: System und Entfaltung der poetischen Motive: Diabolischer Symbolismus* (Vienna, 1990).

necessary component of their intensity of feeling."[3] The rebellious nature of satanism was often expressed through outré behavior—costumes, drugs, talk of suicide—through which the young (and later not so young) could practice escapism and remove themselves from the world they abhorred, yet at the same time mock that world to which they ultimately belonged. Artists sought to upset predominant sensibilities and express unconscious desires, but they also wanted to sell their work, and, then as now, nothing sold better than sensationalism, particularly if it was coupled with satanism. It was, as the critic Georgy Chulkov realized, a point of departure (*iskhod*).[4]

Others (often the same individuals at a different point in time) turned to satanism as one aspect of a spiritual *renovatio*.[5] The historian of religions Mircea Eliade asserts that the rejection of sociopolitical structures and moral values is common to all youth cultures and always has religious meaning.[6] A shift to the occult as subject matter for literature and art is symptomatic of disaffection from orthodox belief (in this case Christianity) and is often accompanied by a sense of remorse, as if the intellectual had dispensed with a God in whom it was impossible to believe, but whose absence was also disconcerting. The turn to Satan as a cultural hero can then justify the existence of evil in the world and explain why human beings and the societies they create are imperfect and limited.[7] The Faust motif, for example, recurs explicitly and implicitly in fantasy and fiction because it reflects the yearning for an absolute.[8] In Russia as elsewhere, the fascination with personifications of evil went far beyond the teachings of the Russian Orthodox Church and in some cases produced active sympathy with the satanic figure. As the poet Ellis queried, "Is not Satan better than a large part of the human race we try to save from him?"[9] Did intellectuals, as Dmitry Merezhkovsky (1865–1941) suggested, feel compelled to choose between God and the Devil?[10]

The occult was extremely important to the Symbolists (the main carriers of the idea of satanism) and to the circles that gathered around them. From the 1890s through at least 1910, and perhaps as late as 1915, they stood apart as the

3. Georgette Donchin, *The Influence of French Symbolism on Russian Poetry* (The Hague, 1958), pp. 144–45.

4. Georgii Chulkov, "Iskhod," *Zolotoe runo*, 1908, pp. 99–104.

5. See Jean Pierrot, "Religious Unease—Satanism," in *The Decadent Imagination, 1880–1900*, trans. Derek Coltman (Chicago, 1981), pp. 89–92.

6. Mircea Eliade, "Some Observations on European Witchcraft," *History of Religions* 14 (1975): 172.

7. Mircea Eliade, "The Occult and the Modern World," in his *Occultism, Witchcraft, and Cultural Fashions* (Chicago, 1976), p. 56.

8. See Rosemary Jackson, *Fantasy: The Literature of Subversion* (London, 1981), p. 62.

9. Ellis [Lev Kobylinskii], "O sovremennom simvolizme, o 'deistve' i o 'cherte,' " *Vesy*, 1909, no. 1, p. 82.

10. D. S. Merezhkovskii, "Bes ili Bog?" *Obrazovanie*, 1908, no. 8, pp. 91–96.

literary, artistic, and musical avant-garde. After the 1890s, this segment of educated society reacted to literary stagnation, the bureaucratization of the Russian Orthodox Church, and political repression in the wake of Alexander II's assassination (1881) by turning away from unpleasant realities. Their form of political protest against the institutionalization of the rationalist-industrial-bourgeois social order was in many ways a nihilistic program of rejection. They thus responded in an irrational way to their rationalist society, in which the establishment used Christianity as a convenient means to manage the social order. As Aleksandr Blok (1880–1921) claimed, all that artists could do in response was accept the Devil's truth, the essential minus, and the theme of mysticism (not a religious theme, he insisted).[11] Eager to remove literary taboos and broaden their personal experiences, the Symbolists began to explore the dark recesses of human nature and of the world around them. In the process, once fearful and threatening cultural elements were to some degree demystified. Early Symbolists, who took a mystical or sociocultural interest in evil, and the Decadents, who cultivated the demonic and encouraged others to believe that they practiced black magic, became for literary conservatives and the religious right the very symbols of society's decay. But the reverse was also true: Symbolists and Decadents believed that church and state and the bureaucrats who operated them were truly evil as well. This attitude intensified in the politicized years after the abortive revolution of 1905. Satan as the embodiment of evil and Satan as the consummate rebel against authority became complementary strains that bridged the gap between the spiritual occult and the demonic occult. To some extent, the Symbolists' fascination with Satan can be interpreted as an attempt to legitimize much of what was illegitimate about satanic mythology. Disillusioned with Christianity, in search of evidence of the Unknown and a direct relationship with the Creator, the Symbolists and Decadents were drawn to the "devilish beauty that attracts from below"; even the "most vacuous demonism," claimed the critic Akim Volynsky (1863–1926), was distinguished by a thirst for religious truth.[12]

The fascination with Satan was often colored by apocalyptic ideas engendered by the Russian sociopolitical crisis and by visions of the Nietzschean *Übermensch* (Superman), or of the Antichrist, who reversed "good" and "evil." The religious philosopher Vladimir Soloviev (1853–1900) was in many ways the spiritual father of this zeitgeist because Christian theology, spiritualism, occultism, and demonism were realities in his metaphysical worldview. Between 1898 and his death in 1900, he became increasingly disillusioned with Christianity as a unifying force for the modern world; at this time, he began to

11. See Avril Pyman, "Aleksandr Blok: The Tragedy of Two Truths," in *Aleksandr Blok Centennial Conference,* ed. W. N. Vickery (Columbus, Ohio, 1984), p. 10.

12. Akim Volynskii [A. L. Flekser], "Dekadenstvo i simvolizm," in *Borba za idealizm* (St. Petersburg, 1900), p. 384.

experience visions of demons and devils, and believed that he had actually confronted Satan in the flesh. His final work is the eschatological *Kratkaia povest' ob Antikhriste* (A short tale of the Antichrist, 1899). Merezhkovsky, author of the trilogy *Khrist i Antikhrist* (Christ and Antichrist, 1895–1905), which reveals his knowledge of occult systems, including black magic, progressed from Decadence to a mystical religious quest in the years before 1900. In the early poetic corpus of his wife, Zinaida Gippius (1869–1945), who sympathized with the rebellious Satan, the Devil as tempter and evil incarnate is often victorious; yet her attraction to Satan was balanced by her profound belief in God.[13] Vasily Rozanov (1856–1919) argued for the importance of the juxtaposition of gods and demons.[14] Their compatriot Viacheslav Ivanov (1866–1949) wrote that "without opposition to the Deity" there could be no mystical life.[15] Together they and a group of like-minded intellectuals with mystical leanings sought a new religious consciousness and a new church in the years after 1900.

Among a broad cross section of artists, fascination with the satanic became an almost cultic response to the chaos that followed the failed revolution of 1905. Their responses were highly individual and varied over time. Many of these artists were the educated children of the newly wealthy merchant class or of upper-middle-class intellectuals; some were aristocrats; and with few exceptions they were male.[16] To a man they were allied with or sympathetic to the political left. The poet Konstantin Bal'mont (1867–1942)—a devotee of the French Symbolists, Poe, and Nietzsche—was exiled to France from 1905 to 1913 for his antitsarist poetry. His dissolute lifestyle and contempt for the good fostered rumors about the Decadents; yet his *Zlye chary: Kniga zakliaty* (Evil spells: A book of exorcisms, 1906) was an attempt to connect his metaphorical vision of "the darkness of 1905" to the occult.[17] Although the poems are based

13. Gippius believed that she encountered the Devil throughout her life; in a letter to Dmitry Filosofov she wrote, "You know that I struggle against the devil, but he is close to me, he speaks to me, I can hear his voice": quoted in Temira Pachmuss, *Zinaida Hippius: An Intellectual Profile* (Carbondale, Ill., 1971), p. 145. Her first poem on the Devil is "Grizelda" (1895); on her sympathy with the Devil, see esp. her poems "Bozhiia tvar" (God's creature, 1902) and "V chertu" (Into a line, 1905); on Gippius's Devil poems as spiritual in content, see Olga Matich, "The Religious Poetry of Zinaida Gippius" (Ph.D. diss., UCLA, 1969), p. 184; Pachmuss, *Zinaida Hippius*, pp. 27, 144–45, and her Introduction to *Selected Works of Zinaida Gippius*, trans. and ed. Temira Pachmuss (Urbana, 1972), p. 19.

14. Vasili Rozanov, "Kontsy i nachala 'bozhestvennoe' i 'demonicheskoe' bogii i demony," *Mir iskusstva*, 1902, no. 8, pp. 122–37.

15. Viacheslav Ivanov, *Po zvezdam* (St. Petersburg, 1903), p. 103.

16. Eugen Weber, "Decadence on a Private Income," *Journal of Contemporary History* 17, no. 1 (1982): 1, writes that because many such European youths did not have to work, they were bored enough to explore the outer fringes of culture.

17. See Evgenii Anichkov, "Konstantin Bal'mont," in *Russkaia literatura XX veka, 1890–1910*, ed. S. A. Vengerov (Moscow, 1914), 1:82. On Bal'mont's contempt for the good, see his earlier poem "Golos d'iavola" (Voice of the Devil, 1903).

on curses and incantations from Slavic mythology and folklore, the book was confiscated by the censors on the basis of its political tone. Blok, like Dostoevsky, identified the Devil with the bourgeois: "Go away from me, Satan. Go away from me, bourgeois."[18] In 1906 he warned that a fat female spider (a common symbol of Satan) had encased everything in a web of gray boredom; only the Decadents noticed the destruction, but their cries fell on deaf ears, and even they were poisoned by the spider venom: they lost first God, then their world, and finally themselves.[19]

The political nature of the satanist theme, as well as the desire to shock through artistic expression, was affirmed in the proliferation of satanic themes after the dismissal of Konstantin Pobedonostsev (the powerful procurator general of the Holy Synod of the Russian Orthodox Church) and the relaxation of government censorship allowed for a more public presentation of sexual imagery. The correspondence between satanism and sexual imagery or pornography was noted at the time: Rozanov wrote in 1904 that Symbolists were drawn to the erotic in a "disfigured, strange, and shamelessly naked form."[20] Gippius claimed that social circumstances, including the stifling of expressions of individuality by censorship, were the cause of Symbolist erotomania.[21] According to the writer Andrei Bely (1880–1934), the "myth" of Decadent debauchery grew out of a calculated effort to shock the bourgeoisie with satanism and pornography; the reading public and its nonsymbolist critics recognized this fact as well.[22] An expressionistic psychological urge—a concern with satanic prurience for its own sake—was commonly expressed in trivialized images, such as Konstantin Somov's vignette (Figure 4.1) in which a sleeping woman in a seductive pose awaits the incubus (a male demon who takes sexual liberties with a woman while she sleeps) with obvious pleasure. In satirical journals published in the aftermath of Bloody Sunday (January 1905), frightening or unpalatable social realities were often represented as devilish, vampiric creatures, sometimes ravishing a woman—usually Mother Russia. In Figure 4.2, published in the immediate aftermath of Bloody Sunday, a toad sucks the life force from a woman's breast as she lies helpless on her back. The choice of a toad as Satan reflects the conclusion of Milton's *Paradise Lost* (popular in Russia at that time),[23] in which Satan is transformed into a grotesque toad and a serpent. If this image represents the impotence of good and the power of evil

18. Quoted in Valentin Boss, *Milton and the Rise of Russian Satanism* (Toronto, 1991), p. 106.

19. Aleksandr Blok, "Bezvremenie," *Zolotoe runo*, 1906, nos. 11–12, pp. 107–14.

20. Vasilii Rozanov, *Dekadenty* (St. Petersburg, 1904), p. 5.

21. Z. N. Gippius, "Notes sur la littérature russe de notre temps," *Mercure de France* 1, no. 1 (1908): 73–79.

22. Andrei Belyi [Boris Bugaev], *Nachalo veka* (Moscow and Leningrad, 1933; Chicago, 1966), p. 280. Scathing criticism came from Georgii S. Novopolin, *Pornograficheskii element v russkoi literature, 1907–1909* (St. Petersburg, 1909).

23. Boss, *Milton and Russian Satanism*, p. 137.

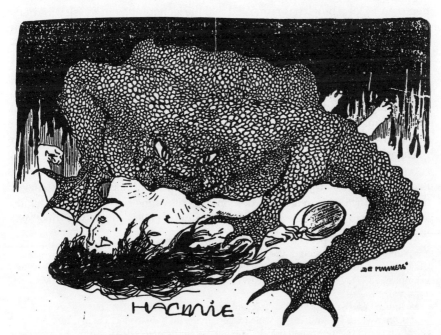

Figure 4.1. (above) Konstantin Somov, *Incubus.* Pen-and-ink endpiece in *Zolotoe runo* (Moscow), 1906, no. 2. Courtesy Slavic and East European Library, University of Illinois, Urbana-Champaign.

Figure 4.2. Nasil'no (Force). Illustration in *Voshebnyi fonar'* (St. Petersburg), 1905, no. 3 (January 25), p. 2. Courtesy Slavic and East European Library, University of Illinois, Urbana-Champaign.

on Bloody Sunday, why is the violated female eroticized? Figures 4.3, 4.4, and 4.5 are from satirical journals printed in 1906, after censorship was relaxed. In Figure 4.3 a woman is about to be martyred on a cross by a demonic reptilian beast; she looks seductive rather than fearful, and one breast is exposed. The artist was probably influenced by Félicien Rops's engravings in *Les Sataniques* (1883), of which "Le Calvaire" (Calvary) (Figure 4.6) is one. In Figure 4.4 the female victim, obviously Mother Russia, has her breast mutilated by a monstrous winged being who "pacifies" her by killing her; the corpse is peaceful—she even smiles. In Figure 4.5 we see yet another eroticized female victim; she too appears peaceful (or dead) as serpent-like creatures bite at her breasts. Granted that these demonic creatures represent political fears and perhaps actual government officials, we still must ask why the victim is an eroticized woman. Has she "asked for it"? Such questions need to be addressed. According to one literary historian, the fears that surface in such responses to crisis reflect "the shadow on the edges of bourgeois culture" and are variously identified, as we have seen, as "black, mad, primitive, criminal, socially deprived, deviant, crippled, or (when sexually assertive) female"; through this primal approach, very real social fears can be dealt with "in the name of exorcising the demonic."[24] John Bowlt has remarked that the iconography in Russian journals of the period indicates less the artists' social consciences than their psychological fascination with Decadent motifs; images of sex and violence are "symptoms or gestures of a deeper, more essential impulse" and constitute "a protest against the taboos of a given society."[25] Satan's sexual attraction—and the disturbing consequences of physical intimacy with Satan—is one such taboo, and infringements on it prompted strong reactions by political authorities and the Russian public alike.

As in the fin-de-siècle France described by Eugen Weber, the general climate of chaos and transition, sin and vice, "at least in some circles," were the measures of "a civilization whose refinement was mirrored in its corruption."[26] In Leonid Andreev's (1871–1919) drama *Chernye maski* (The black masks, 1907), the title characters represent the demonic agents of the collective unconscious and the human subconscious.[27] To Fedor Sologub (1863–1927)—who, like An-

24. Jackson, *Fantasy*, pp. 121–22.

25. John E. Bowlt, "Through the Glass Darkly: Images of Decadence in Early Twentieth-Century Russian Art," *Journal of Contemporary History* 17, no. 1 (1982): 103, 95, 98; for other examples see V. Shleev, *Revoliutsiia 1905–07 godov i izobrazitel'noe iskusstvo*, 2 vols. (Moscow, 1977–78).

26. Eugen Weber, *France fin de siècle* (Cambridge, Mass., 1986), pp. 39–40.

27. Other works by Andreev in which Satan toys with humans include his story "Pokoi" (Rest, 1911) and the unfinished novel "Dnevnik Satany" (Satan's diary, 1919), in which people ultimately prove to be more evil than Satan. Demons, devils, fallen angels, and grotesque monsters form the subject matter of Andreev's paintings; see Richard Davies, ed., *Photographs of a Russsian Writer* (London, 1989). On Andreev as a follower of French Decadence, a suicidal alcoholic (from his teens), and a nonbeliever, see H. H. King, *Dostoevsky and Andreyev: Gazers upon the Abyss* (New York, 1936).

Figure 4.3. N. Kriuev, back cover of *Pchela* (St. Petersburg), 1906, no. 1. Courtesy Slavic and East European Library, University of Illinois, Urbana-Champaign.

dreev, was deeply influenced by Victor Hugo, Charles Baudelaire, Joris-Karl Huysmans, and other French satanists (as well as by Goethe and Nietzsche)— the world was more evil than good and the underworld was controlled by Satan, whom Sologub called "Father." He expressed his disillusionment with Russian society and the perversity of political and behavioral shortcomings in the satirical novel *Melkii bes* (The petty demon, 1905), which shocked and excited his audiences, and in the trilogy *Tvorimaia legenda* (The created legend,

Figure 4.4. "He seems to have pacified her . . . " Front cover of *Vampir* (St. Petersburg), 1906, no. 1. Courtesy Slavic and East European Library, University of Illinois, Urbana-Champaign.

Figure 4.5. Levap, front cover of *Satiricheskoe obozrenie* (St. Petersburg), 1906, no. 1. Courtesy Slavic and East European Library, University of Illinois, Urbana-Champaign.

Figure 4.6. Félicien Rops, *Le Calvaire* (1882). Engraving for the series *Les Sataniques* (1883).

1907–13), which a modern Russian critic says colored the "bloody nightmare of a recent time with shades of mysticism."[28] Sologub's poetry is more to the point. In "Kogda ia v burnom more plaval" (When I was sailing on a stormy sea, 1902), a man in crisis calls on the Devil to be his savior, and in exchange dedicates his life to him. His 1907 poem "Chertovy kacheli" (The Devil's swing, 1907) describes life as a swing propelled by the Devil; the rider is Everyman, his fate decided by the Devil's whims. In these and other poems, the poet is a sorcerer who casts spells to attain self-divination in a world populated by witches, demons, and monsters.[29] Gippius's short story "Ivan Ivanovich i chert" (Ivan Ivanovich and the Devil, 1906) portrays the Devil as the great Mephistophelian tempter of human weakness. Her novel *Chertova kukla* (The Devil's doll, 1908), patterned on Dostoevsky's *Besy* (The devils, 1867), portrays human beings as Satan's puppets who are unable to respond to societal problems in any way. Highly political (although she considered it social and ethical), it is her response to post-1905 reactionary trends and addresses the fatal failure of political and spiritual leaders of the Russian left to build a new society and a new church out of the ashes of 1905.[30]

During 1906–8, the years Bely described as "inhumanly vile,"[31] even Symbolists who claimed to have an apolitical program turned to the satanic. In May and June 1906, Nikolai Riabushinsky ran an advertisement in his journal *Zolotoe runo* (Golden fleece) soliciting poetry, prose, art, and criticism for a special edition dedicated to the Devil. He received ninety-two entries—a telling indication of the timeliness of the theme. All sixty-one written entries were part of a contest judged by—among others—Blok, Ivanov, and Valery Briusov.[32] The two first prizes went to Aleksei Remizov, author of the satanic mystery play *Besovskoe deistvo* (A devilish act, 1907), for his short story "Chertik" (Little devil) and to Mikhail Kuzmin for the story "Iz pisem devitsy Klary Val'mon k

28. Sologub's *Melkii bes* was serialized in *Voprosy zhizni*, 1905, nos. 6–11, and published in its entirety in 1907. On the novel as "mimetic of his society" and as a response "to the sociopolitical and ideological conditions peculiar to Russia at the time," see Judith M. Mills, "Expanding Critical Contexts: Sologub's *Petty Demon*," *Slavic and East European Journal* 28, no. 1 (1984): 21. *Tvorimaia legenda* was serialized 1907–13, published in its entirety in 1914. The quote is from A. A. Izmailov, *Literaturnyi Olimp* (Moscow, 1991), pp. 309–10; cf. Donchin, *Influence of French Symbolism*, pp. 136–40.

29. See Fedor Sologub, "Demony poetov," *Pereval*, 1907, no. 5, pp. 48–51, and no. 12, pp. 46–50.

30. Poggioli, *Poets of Russia*, p. 112; cf. Vladimir Zlobin, "Gippius i chert," *Novyi zhurnal*, 1967, no. 86, pp. 63–75. Simon Karlinsky, "Introduction: Who Was Zinaida Gippius?" in Vladimir Zlobin, *A Difficult Soul: Zinaida Gippius*, ed. Simon Karlinsky (Berkeley, 1980), p. 19, describes her oeuvre as "religiously heretical, politically radical, and sexually unconventional."

31. Bely to Blok, in *Aleksandr Blok i Andrei Belyi: Perepiska*, ed. V. N. Orlov (Moscow, 1940; Munich, 1969), p. 261.

32. See "Otchet zhivri po konkursu 'Zolotogo runa' na temu 'D'iavol,'" *Zolotoe runo*, 1907, no. 1, p. 74. *Zolotoe runo* did claim to be apolitical, but its artists and writers also contributed to satirical political journals in the post-1905 period, often under assumed names.

Rozaly Tiutel'maier" (From the letters of Claire Valmont to Rosalie Toutelle-Meyer), in which Claire falls in love with and is impregnated by Satan.[33] The second prize went to A. E. Kondratiev, known for his demonic prose in the literary journals of his day. The art jurists judged thirty-one entries, including works by such well-known artists as Ivan Bilibin, Mstislav Dobuzhinsky, Sergei Sudeikin, Vasily Miliutin, and Pavel Kuznetsov; yet Riabushinsky, who hosted a suicide club in the Moscow mansion he called the Black Swan, felt that none of them captured the essence of the Devil well enough to merit the first prize.[34]

The January 1907 issue of *Zolotoe runo* opens with artworks submitted for the competition, including the feminine imagery of Kuznetsov's *Rozhdenie—sliianie s misticheskoi siloi atmosfery: Probuzhdenie D'iavola* (Birth—fusion with the mystical force in the atmosphere: The rousing of the Devil), which the critic Sergei Makovsky claimed "haunts one by its morbid move toward a mysticism of sin."[35] Dobuzhinsky's *D'iavol* (The Devil, Figure 4.7) is also included. John Bowlt has suggested that when this work—he calls it "the most striking description of the Symbolists' *taedium vitae*"—is viewed upside down, the demonic spider can be read as a predatory female.[36] Dobuzhinsky may have been responding to Blok's comments of 1906 with regard to a satanic female spider devouring Russia.[37] The theme of the Devil continues through a series of twenty-six reproductions of ancient Russian apocalyptical paintings, miniatures, and icon fragments that illustrate Aleksandr Uspensky's article "Bes" (The Devil). There follow Nikolai Feofilaktov's erotic painting *D'iavol* and Léon (Lev) Bakst's *Portret Andreia Belago* (Portrait of Andrei Bely).[38] Among the poems, belletristic contributions, and articles are Anatoly Dobrokhotov's poem "D'iavol," S. Golovachevsky's "Otkrovenie D'iavol" (*sic*, Revelation of the Devil), P. Potemkin's "D'iavol," Erazm Shtein's poem "Zmii" (The serpent), Sologub's "Chelovek cheloveku—D'iavol" (Man to man—the Devil),

---

33. Aleksei Remizov's *Besovskoe deistvo nad nekym muzhem, a takzhe prenie zhivota so smertiiu* was produced in 1907 by Vsevolod Meyerhold and Kommissarzhevsky in St. Petersburg, with stage sets by Mstislav Dobuzhinsky. See also Remizov's "Pozhar," *Zolotoe runo*, 1906, pp. 54–60, and "Moskva: Demony," *Novosele*, 1949, nos. 39–41, pp. 1–15; the latter discusses Andreev and Briusov as demonic figures. Kuzmin wrote in his sensational novel *Kryla* (Moscow, 1907), pp. 261–62, that "one can steal and fornicate in any faith, but to understand *Faust* and use a rosary in prayer with conviction, that's inconceivable—or else, God knows, it teases the Devil."

34. See John E. Bowlt, "Nikolai Riabushinsky: Playboy of the Eastern World," *Apollo* 98, no. 142 (1973): 486–93.

35. *Zolotoe runo*, 1907, no. 5, pp. 25–26.

36. John E. Bowlt, *The Silver Age* (Newtonville, Mass., 1982), p. 265.

37. A. A. Blok, "Bezvremenie," *Zolotoe runo*, 1906, nos. 11–12, pp. 107–14.

38. This is not the more famous head-and-shoulders portrait of Bely, executed in black and red chalk by Léon Bakst, in which Irina Gutkina tells me the satanic was read in Bely's eyes; cf. N. N. Valentinov, *Dva goda s simvolistami* (Stanford, 1969), p. 11. The *Zolotoe runo* portrait is of a standing Bely who looks quite grim.

Figure 4.7. Mstislav Dobuzhinsky, *D'iavol* (The devil). Pen-and-ink drawing in *Zolotoe runo* (Moscow), 1907, no. 1. Courtesy Slavic and East European Library, University of Illinois, Urbana-Champaign.

and three brief articles on music, one of which comments on the theme of Satan in contemporary opera and other musical genres.[39]

Mephistopheles and Lucifer were often used to give a face to the Symbolist idea of the artist as magus or theurgist. Both personae, rife with correspondences, were beloved by the Symbolists. Prominent writers and artists identified with them, at times affected the pose, and so were perceived by their peers and their public as embodiments of Mephistopheles and Lucifer. In the fin-de-siècle literary and artistic world, appearance and behavior as well as cultural product dictated what was satanic. Among the most vivid of such figures are the writer Valery Briusov (1873–1924) and the artist Mikhail Vrubel' (1856–1910). Although separated by a generation, each came into his own in the years after 1900: Briusov rejected religion outright and acted as the master of his own universe, but Vrubel' rejected Christianity after personal reflection; Briusov pretended to be political when it suited his ends to do so, whereas Vrubel' was politically uncommitted but expressed his vision of the end of the old order in the will to destroy; each was influenced by the work of Goethe and Nietzsche; each knew Milton's Satan and Lermontov's Demon well. Despite the fact that they were almost polar opposites—Briusov's life imitated art in a calculated manner, whereas Vrubel''s art so faithfully imitated his psychic inner life that it escaped his control—each recognized in the other an intense attraction to the demonic.

Mephistopheles, the consummate black magician of Goethe's *Faust*, personifies satanic evil, destructiveness, and nihilism. His power, rooted in the darkest levels of the mind, focuses on the exaltation of the human being to godly stature. Goethe may have been popular with the Symbolists because he identified imagination with the demonic, portrayed the artist as magus, and repeatedly spoke of demonic assaults on gifted men.[40] The Mephistophelian image, with its Nietzschean overtones, had broad appeal in Russia. Nowhere was this fascination with the demonic more evident than in Fedor Chaliapin's three-decade campaign (1893–1928) to put a truly evil Mephistopheles on the stage. Promotional photographs and widely circulated playbills (Figure 4.8) show the gradual progression of Chaliapin's Mephistopheles from a facile dandy to a powerful personification of evil.[41] He first performed Mephistopheles, the pivotal role of his career, in Gounod's 1859 opera *Faust* in 1894. Within a few years, Chaliapin began to sing the lead role in Boito's 1868 opera *Mefistofele*. He

39. I. A. S., "Satana v muzyke," *Zolotoe runo*, 1907, no. 1, pp. 65–67, focuses on the popularity of Charles Gounod's *Faust*, Anton Rubinstein's *Demon*, and Arrigo Boito's *Mefistofele* as performed by Fedor Chaliapin.

40. Camille Paglia, *Sexual Personae* (New York, 1991), p. 255, claims that "all of *Faust* is a Walpurgisnacht, a return to the occult" (p. 255), and that Goethe expanded the sexual commentary of the historical Faust story (p. 253).

41. See the photographs reproduced in Victor Borovsky, *Chaliapin* (New York, 1986), pp. 163, 165, 167, 277, 279, 287, 290, 291, 293, 296, 299, 301, 303.

Figure 4.8. Chaliapin as Mephistopheles in Gounod's *Faust*, 1895 (*left*) and 1915 (*right*).

gravitated to Boito's music because he felt that it was more demonic than Gounod's and thus allowed him to develop a characterization based on the darkest instincts of the human spirit. Boito's music eventually inspired Chaliapin to seek to play Mephistopheles dressed in nothing but bronze body paint, but the censors disapproved. The pose that Chaliapin struck onstage in 1901 found its way in 1906 onto the cover of the post-1905 satirical journal *Mefistofel'* (Figure 4.9)—an image much more sinister than Ivan Bilibin's logo (a laughing folkloric devil) for the short-lived satirical journal *Adskaia pochta* (Hellish post, 1906). After seeing Chaliapin perform the satanic role of Bertram in Giacomo Meyerbeer's opera *Robert le diable* in 1894, Vrubel' executed a bronze sculpture consisting of four life-sized figures for the Gothic entrance hall of the Morozov mansion in Moscow, depicting a scene from the third act of the opera, in which the spirits of evil nuns are transformed into beautiful women, who then dance in a graveyard at night. For the same mansion Vrubel'

Figure 4.9. Chaliapin as Mephistopheles in Gounod's *Faust,* 1901 (*left*), and Mstislav Dobuzhinsky's front cover for the journal *Mefistofel'* (St. Petersburg), 1906, no. 1 (*right*). Courtesy Slavic and East European Library, University of Illinois, Urbana-Champaign.

prepared a series of decorative panels on the theme of Mephistopheles; one is his *Polet Fausta i Mefistofelia* (Flight of Faust and Mephistopheles, 1896).

The first writer to act out satanic decadence appeared on the St. Petersburg literary scene in 1891 in the salons of Liubov' Gurevich, Gippius, and Sologub. Aleksandr Dobroliubov, an aesthete influenced by Poe and Baudelaire, was a fifteen-year-old gymnasium student at the time he adopted a Mephistophelian persona. He became an opium addict, wore only black, and lived in a small windowless room replete with black walls and symbolic objects that he claimed to use in the worship of Satan. Rumor had it that he was expelled from the university for successfully imposing his fixation with suicide on several female students. Then, around 1895, he experienced a spiritual revelation, forswore the Devil, and became a Christian sectarian.[42] The subject of his *Sobranie stikhov* (Collected verse, 1900) is a spiritual inertia that was the direct result of his drug and alcohol abuse and his self-imposed isolation. Dobroliubov is an interesting case: his satanism was clearly in imitation of the French Decadents—he idolized Huysmans's antihero Des Esseintes—and he got into it very young and at the beginning of the vogue for it. Outré behavior among intellectually precocious youths was nothing new, but in Dobroliubov's case the three short years (1895–98) it took him to immerse himself deeply in sectarian Christianity make his satanism appear to be a phase in a spiritual quest—"a sin flowing from faith," as his fellow traveler Vladimir Gippius so aptly put it.[43]

Dobroliubov's most lasting legacy to Russian satanism was his influence on Briusov, another young aspiring aesthete, whom he met in 1894 (the same year he became close to Bal'mont). Briusov began in his teens to mold himself into the image of the Decadent magus; the texts of his movement were the French Decadents, his appearance, the behavior he affected to draw others into his circle, and his own writings. He went on to create a powerful physical image, his personal aura of mystery enhanced by the Baudelairean statement that God and the Devil were the same to him, the frequent séances of his spiritualist circle, and his contributions to the spiritualist journal *Rebus*.[44] Dressed severely in black, his black beard trimmed to a point, Briusov reminded contemporaries of his favorite Decadent literary themes: Bely, whose poem "Mag" (The magus, 1903) portrays Briusov as a seer, believed that he practiced demonology and black magic and referred to him as the "Fiend" (*Vraga*); Bal'mont dedicated a cycle of fifteen poems titled "Khudozhnik-D'iavol" (The artist-devil, 1903) to him; Ivanov believed that he was inescapably trapped in a state of evil; Gippius wrote that no one expressed devilish eroticism better than he did.[45] Blok thought Briusov looked like a painting by Félicien Rops, as S. A. Vinogradov's

42. On drug use (opium, ether, hashish) among the Russian literary crowd, see Sergei Makovskii, *Stranitsy khudozhestvennoi kritiki* (St. Petersburg, 1909), 3:6. On Dobroliubov's behavior, cf. Z. N. Gippius, "Filosofiia liubvi," *Mir iskusstva*, May 1901, pp. 28–33; L. Ia. Gurevich, "Istoriia 'Severnogo Vestnika,'" in Vengerov, *Russkaia literatura*, 1:254–55; and Joan D. Grossman, "Aleksandr Dobroliubov: The Making of a Decadent," Introduction to Dobroliubov's *Sochinenie* (Berkeley, 1981), pp. 7–18.

43. V. V. Gippius, "Aleksandr Dobroliubov," in Vengerov, *Russkaia literatura*, 1:284.

44. On the séances of Briusov and others, see V. S. Akatov, *O positivnykh osnovakh noveishego spiritualizma* (Moscow, 1909); Sergei R. Mintslov, *Debri zhizni* (Berlin, 1929) and *Peterburg v 1903–1910 godakh* (Riga, 1931). Mintslov, a civil servant and historical novelist, was the brother of Anna R. Mintslova; see Maria Carlson, "Ivanov-Belyj-Minclova: The Mystical Triangle," in *Cultura e memoria*, ed. Fausto Malcovati (Florence, 1988), pp. 63–79.

45. Andrei Belyi, "Vospominaniia ob A. A. Bloke," *Zapiski mechtatelei*, 1922, no. 6, pp. 105–6, 152–53, and *Nachalo veka*, pp. 276–87. On Ivanov, see Pamela Davidson, *The Poetic Imagination of Vyacheslav Ivanov* (Cambridge, 1989), pp. 174–82; Gippius, "Notes sur la littérature russe," pp. 76–77, and "Oderzhimyi (o Briusove)," in *Zhivye litsa*, ed. L. A. Liatsky (Prague, 1925; Munich, 1971), 1:73–117, esp. 92.

portrait (Figure 4.10) corroborates.[46] Briusov did nothing to dispel these impressions, and his public image and demonic behavior led others to perceive of him as a black magician (*chernomag*). He has been assessed as a "power and success worshipper"[47]—a view that complements Richard Cavendish's theory that the driving force behind black magic or perceived black magic is the magus's "hunger for power" and his willingness to resort to anything—"gestures, drink, drugs, sex"—to achieve it.[48] Clearly Briusov set out to acquire the behavior, and found that it fitted his personality.[49]

The most arresting aspect of Briusov's satanism was a cultivated amoralism in which life imitated art.[50] It was most obvious in his relationship with Nina Petrovskaia (1884–1928), a young belletrist and poet. The wife of the publicist Sergei Sokolov, she came to Briusov (himself a married man) as a nineteen-year-old Symbolist groupie—that is, by way of earlier affairs with Bal'mont

46. Briusov was repeatedly portrayed as demonic in photographs, drawings, paintings, and sculptures until his death; Fig. 4.10 is reproduced in *Literaturnoe nasledstvo*, 1976, no. 85, p. 157. Rops's popularity in Russia can be traced from the reproduction of two engravings, *L'Incantation* (1878) and *Pornokratès* (the ruler of Pierre Joseph Proudhon's "Pornocracy" led by a pig, the bestial representative of all sexual evil, 1896), in *Mir iskusstva*, 1989, no. 1. His influence can be seen in the engraver Vasily Miliutin's album *Grekh* (St. Petersburg, 1909) and the art of Konstantin Somov and Nikolai Feofilaktov. He was the subject of a study by the Decadent playwright Nikolai Evreinov (*Rops* [St. Petersburg, 1910]), and his works were used to illustrate the literary collection *Satanizm* (Moscow, 1913). Blok was acquainted with Rops's work, so one must wonder: Did his poem "Nochnaia fialka" (The night violet, 1907) relate to Rops's etching *Femme à la violette noire* (1880)? Both connect the colors black and violet to the image of the seductively fatal prostitute. The Futurist poet Velimir Khlebnikov also was influenced by Rops; with Aleksei Kruchenykh he composed *Igra v Adu* (A game in Hell, 1912), which describes a card game between sinners and devils—a theme from Russia's *lubok* heritage—illustrated by Natalia Goncharova's Devil prints.

47. Victor Erlich, "The Maker and the Seer: Two Russian Symbolists," in *The Double Image* (Baltimore, 1964), p. 92.

48. Richard Cavendish, *The Black Arts* (New York, 1967), p. 7. For elaborations, see Benjamin Walker, *Sex and the Supernatural* (London, 1970); Francis King, *Sexuality, Magic, and Perversion* (London, 1971); and Gordon Wellesley, *Sex and the Occult* (London, 1973).

49. Henry A. Murray, "The Personality and Career of Satan," *Journal of Social Issues* 18, no. 4 (1962): 50–51, suggests that the term "Satan Complex" be used to describe personalities marked by a compulsion to acquire personal power and to debase the self and the opposite sex through theme, image, and behavior. Phillips Stevens, "New Legends: Some Perspectives from Anthropology," *Western Folklore* 49 (1990): 128, writes that some deviant individuals are attracted to satanism as a source of power and enhanced identity and then attempt to act it out.

50. See Danylo Struck, "The Great Escape: Principal Themes in Valerii Briusov's Poetry," *Slavic and East European Journal* 12 (1968): 409, 414. Donchin, *Influence of French Symbolism*, p. 141, connects Briusov's amoralism directly to Baudelaire. Imagery related to Briusov, who decorated his apartment with Nikolai Feofilaktov's pornographic drawings, is often prurient. See Sergei Gorodetsky's watercolor *The Round Table*, reproduced in Vera Stravinsky and Robert Craft, *Stravinsky in Pictures and Documents* (New York, 1978), pl. 10; it shows Briusov with a naked dead woman draped over his wineglass.

Figure 4.10. S. A. Vinogradov's pencil portrait of Valery Briusov (1906).

and Bely. In the late phase of a failed infatuation with Bely in the autumn of 1904, she turned for revenge to Briusov, who, she metaphorically wrote, offered "a chalice of dark, astringent wine . . . and said, 'Drink!' "[51] Rumors flew that together they conducted black magic rituals and concocted spells to revive Bely's interest in her, but fell in love with each other instead. Thus began "a protracted seven-year affair that led each of them into the morass of mental illness, morphine addiction, and suicide pacts."[52]

In Petrovskaia's memoirs, she writes that her own literary work—most of which deals with the demonic—was influenced by French occultism and Symbolism, the "demonism" of Sologub, the "maniacal religiosity" of Bely, the "mysticism" of Blok, and the "eroticism" of Bal'mont. The memoirs treat Briusov as a competent practitioner of the "dark sciences" and Petrovskaia's relationship with him as a pact with the Devil. She believed that together they were "children of evil" who drowned the crisis of 1905 in wine and exotic music.[53] Her life ended in suicide—like those of the poets Viktor Gofman, who at age twenty-one (1911) followed Briusov's advice in the matter, and Nadezhda L'vova, who shot herself in 1913 over a failed affair with Briusov. All three, in the eyes of their mutual friend V. F. Khodasevich, were bewitched by Briusov's invitation to a "solipsistic Walpurgisnacht."[54]

Out of the Bely-Petrovskaia-Briusov ménage à trois evolved Briusov's historical novel *Ognennyi angel* (The fiery angel, 1907–8). Briusov set his novel in sixteenth-century Germany and illustrated it with selections from *La Grande Danse macabre des hommes et des femmes* (1486). Originally titled *Ved'ma* (The witch), it is the story of a woman's surrender to a demonic possession brought on by the angelic persona of a fiery angel (a disguised demon modeled on Bely). The woman, Renata—whose insanity ends in religious madness, and who is imprisoned, tried, and condemned as a witch—is based on Petrovskaia.[55] Briusov describes Renata's psychoerotic episodes of demonic posses-

51. Petrovskaia papers, RGALI (Moscow), f. 376, op. 1, ed. khr. 3, as quoted in Joan D. Grossman, "Russian Symbolism and the Year 1905: The Case of Valery Bryusov," *Slavonic and East European Review* 61, no. 3 (1983): 350. Grossman concludes that Briusov's pessimism after 1905 had less to do with the failed revolution than with the series of crises between him and Petrovskaia.

52. Kristi Groberg, "Nina Ivanovna Petrovskaia," in *Dictionary of Russian Women Writers*, ed. M. Ledkovsky et al. (Westport, Conn., 1994), p. 500. Both Briusov and Petrovskaia were hospitalized on numerous occasions.

53. See the selections published by Iu. A. Krasovsky: Nina I. Petrovskaia, "Iz 'Vospominanii,' " *Literaturnoe nasledstvo*, 1976, no. 85, pp. 775, 781–82.

54. V. F. Khodasevich, "Briusov: Otryvki iz vospominanii," *Sovremennye zapiski*, 1924, no. 23, p. 221, and "Konets Renaty" and "Briusov," in *Nekropol'* (Brussels, 1939; Paris, 1976), pp. 7–25, 26–60; see also Konstantin V. Mochul'skii, *Valerii Briusov* (Paris, 1962), pp. 102–3, 155–56.

55. See S. S. Grechishkin and A. V. Lavrov, "Biograficheskie istochniki romana Briusova *Ognennyi angel*," *Wiener slawistische Almanach*, 1978, nos. 1, pp. 79–107, and 2, pp. 73–96. *Ognennyi angel*, first serialized in *Vesy* (1907–8), was printed as a complete novel by Briusov's

sion in exactly the same terms that the sensational French fin-de-siècle psychiatrist Jean-Martin Charcot (1825–93) used to describe his patients. Charcot's medical interests lay in the realm of hysterical mental illness (by the 1880s thought to be a "woman's disease"); his subjects were the female inmates of a Parisian hospital-asylum, most of them homeless prostitutes or destitute women who suffered from mental illness, tuberculosis, or syphilis. Charcot, whose private passion was demonic imagery in art, and who enhanced his artistic speculations with his own concoction of morphine and codeine, had his patients sketched and photographed during what he termed "abnormal states": in satanic possession and religious ecstasy, during exorcism and seizure, and under hypnosis.[56] These exploitive and widely published images were sources of artistic inspiration for Félicien Rops.[57] Doubtless they influenced Briusov as well, as his contemporary Liubov' Gurevich noted in her 1910 critique of *Ognennyi angel*.[58] Charcot's work was of great interest in Russia, where the relationship between genius and madness was explored by Nikolai Bazhenov, a psychiatrist and a friendly rival of Briusov's and, like Briusov, a self-proclaimed expert on the female sex.[59] Such correspondences suggest that there was a deeper psychological reason for what Pierre Hart calls the "ahistorical themes of sexual obsession and mental instability" presented in *Ognennyi angel*.[60] Perverse eroticism, realized in the femme fatale

---

own publishing concern (Skorpio) in 1908, when Petrovskaia left Briusov (but not for good), went to Paris, and converted to Roman Catholicism, taking the name Renata. Of interest here is Ellis's poem to *Ognennyi angel* in his *Stigmata* (Moscow, 1911), p. 113.

56. See Jean-Martin Charcot and Paul Richer, *Les Démoniaques dans l'art* (Paris, 1887; Amsterdam, 1972); this work contains drawings of "supernatural possession" and "satanic convulsions" (Charcot's terms); photographs are in Désirée Bourneville and Paul Regnard, *L'Iconographie photographique de la Salpêtrière*, 3 vols. (Paris, 1877–80); similar images reached the public on a yearly basis through Charcot's serialized *Nouvelle Iconographie de la Salpêtrière* (Paris, 1888–93).

57. See Georges Didi-Huberman, *Invention de l'hystérie* (Paris, 1982), pp. 114–15, 120–21, 159–60. On Rops as a pornographic satanist, see the remarks of his contemporaries: Joséphin Péladin, *L'Art ochlocratique* (Paris, 1888), p. 50, and J.-K. Huysmans, *Certains* (Paris, 1889), pp. 100–108. For iconographic readings of Rops's satanic feminine imagery, see "Little Dictionary round about Félicien Rops," in *L'Exposition Félicien Rops* (London, 1971), pp. 244–52.

58. Liubov' Gurevich, "Dalnozorkie," *Russkaia mysl'*, 1910, no. 3, pp. 143–55.

59. See N. N. Bazhenov, *Psykhiatricheskie besedy na literaturnye i obshchestvennye temy* (Moscow, 1903), which includes an essay on Baudelaire. These concerns are reflected also in the French psychologist/psychic Charles F. Richet's *Somnambulizm, demonizm i iady intellekta* (Moscow, 1885). Cf. Joan D. Grossman, "Genius and Madness: The Return of the Romantic Concept of the Poet in Russia at the End of the Nineteenth Century," in *American Contributions to the Seventh International Congress of Slavists*, ed. Victor Terras (The Hague, 1973), 2:247–60.

60. Pierre Hart, "Time Transmuted: Merezhkovskij and Brjusov's Historical Novels," *Slavic and East European Journal* 31, no. 2 (1987): 196. For more on *Ognennyi angel*, see Brigitte Flickinger, *Valerij Brjusov: Dichtung als Magie, Kritische Analyse des "Feurigen Engels"* (Munich, 1976); Joachim T. Baer, "Symbolism and Stylized Prose in Russia and Poland: Brjusov's

Figure 4.11. (*left*) Mikhail Vrubel', *Liubov' i golod* (Love and hunger, 1883–84). Watercolor. Russian State Museum, St. Petersburg. (*right*) Félicien Rops, *Mors syphilitica* (1892). Etching.

or the demonic feminine, went hand in hand with the fashionable view of modern woman as "poisonous," but it was also a cultural response to the fear of women (possibly a reaction to feminism) and of syphilis, for which there

Ognennyi angel and W. Berents' *Zywe Ramienie*," in *American Contributions to the Ninth International Congress of Slavists*, ed. M. S. Flier (Columbus, Ohio, 1983), pp. 19–38; Joan D. Grossman, *Valery Bryusov and the Riddle of Russian Decadence* (Berkeley, 1985); Julian W. Connolly, "Briusov's *The Fiery Angel:* By Love Possessed," *Selecta* 8 (1987): 102–8.

was no cure at the time.[61] (See Figure 4.11.) Rops, whose influence on the Russian Symbolists cannot be ignored, was blatant in his misogyny: "Man is possessed by woman, and woman is possessed by the Devil."[62]

In *Ognennyi angel*, the narrator, Ruprecht (read Briusov), agrees to risk eternal damnation and participate in a black mass to reach the source of Renata's demonic possession. He annoints himself with magical oils and flies to the black mass on a broomstick, with plans to question the Devil during his initiation rite. When his questions go unanswered, Ruprecht—who encounters Dr. Faustus and Mephistopheles on his travels—turns to the study of occult science under the direction of the historical figure Agrippa von Nettesheim (1486–1535). Briusov may have borrowed the trappings of the black mass from Goethe's *Faust*, Barbey d'Aurevilly's *Diaboliques* (1874, 1882), Huysmans's *Là-bas* (1891), Guaita's *Temple de Satan* (1891), or the Walpurgisnacht scenes in Modest Musorgsky's tone poem *Night on Bald Mountain* (*Noch' na lysoi gore*, 1867); or he may have learned about them during the course of his own intensive study of postmedieval magic.[63] Literary descriptions of the black mass include Roman Catholic religious imagery and usually present Satan as a counterculture hero. Such a vocabulary, often extracted from a female source under torture, is provided by the inquisitor; the "witch" has only to affirm it. Woman, always the instrument of Satan and a pivotal figure in the black mass, is portrayed as a sexually perverse creature who responds to sadistic aggres-

61. On the recognition of the demonic femme fatale as a perverse manifestation of the cultural climate by an art critic of the time, see Baron N. N. Vrangel'," "Liubov'naia mechta sovremennykh russkikh khudozhnikov," *Apollon*, 1909, no. 2, pp. 30–45. Cf. Samuel D. Cioran, "The Triumph of the Demonic Feminine," in *Vladimir Solov'ev and the Knighthood of the Divine Sophia* (Waterloo, Ont., 1977), pp. 238–42. T. A. Riazanovskii, *Demonologiia v drevnerusskoi literature* (Moscow, 1915), pp. 61–62, remarks that women are most susceptible to satanic forces. On the importance of syphilis to literary themes in the fin de siècle, see Patrick Lasowski, *Syphilis* (Paris, 1982), which notes the alarming tendency of the Symbolists to link pleasure and death, sex and self-destruction; cf. Bram Dijkstra, *Idols of Perversity: Fantasies of Feminine Evil in Fin de Siècle Culture* (New York, 1986).

62. As quoted in Gilbert Lascault, "Contradictions de Félicien Rops," in *Félicien Rops*, ed. R. L. Delevoy et al. (Brussels, 1985), p. 22.

63. Musorgsky borrowed his black mass from Georgii Mengden's *Ved'ma* (a libretto now lost) and from his own reading of Matvei Khotinsky's popular exposés of sorcery, witchcraft, and magic in Russia: *Rasskazy o temnykh premetakh o volshebstve natural'noi magii, obmanakh, chuvstv, sueveriiakh fokusnichestve, koldunakh, ved'makh, i t.p.* (St. Petersburg, 1861) and *Charodeistvo i tainstvennaia v noveishee vremia* (St. Petersburg, 1866). The subtitles of *Night on Bald Mountain* are *Assembly of the Witches; Cortège of Satan; Black Mass;* and *Sabbat*. See Edward R. Reilly, "The First Extant Version of *Night on Bare Mountain*," in *Musorgsky: In Memoriam, 1881–1981*, ed. M. H. Brown (Ann Arbor, 1982), pp. 135–62. Briusov's study of black magic focused on Agrippa; see his "Oklevetannyi uchenyi" 1908), in Zhosef Ors, *Agrippa Nettesgeimsky*, trans. B. Runt, ed. V. Ia. Briusov (Moscow, 1913), pp. 7–16; and "Agrippa Nettesgeimsky," *Russkaia mysl'*, 1911, no. 2, pp. 234–37.

sion.[64] This scenario appears in the work of the poet Mirra Lokhvitskaia (1869–1905), who was Bal'mont's lover and a friend to Briusov. In the play *In nomine Domini* (1904, based on a witchcraft trial of 1610–11) Lokhvitskaia describes a woman's conversion to Christianity under torture and her coerced confession of seduction by the forces of black magic.[65] Briusov and Lokhvitskaia were not the first among their contemporaries to describe the black mass. The main character of Gippius's story "Ved'ma" (1898) is a woman who yearns to participate in a witch's sabbath. And Merezhkovsky included a black mass in his historical novel *Voskresshie bogi: Leonardo da-Vinchi* (Rebirth of the gods: Leonardo da Vinci, 1896); his character Monna Cassandra, drugged into hallucinating flight, attends a black mass to become the bride of Satan.

Sergei Prokofiev resurrected *Ognennyi angel'* as the subject and title of his third opera. As a teenager, Prokofiev (1891–1953), already the idol-smashing *enfant terrible* of a new musical generation, gravitated to the Poe-like qualities of Bal'mont's poetry (some of which he set to music in 1910–11) and to Briusov's writings. When his composition *Navazhdeniia* (*Suggestion diabolique*, 1908) was first performed in public (he was sixteen), a critic suggested that its title be changed to "Wild Pandemonium of Dirty Devils in Hell."[66] Prokofiev did not begin to compose *Ognennyi angel* until 1919, when he read Briusov's novel. To one critic, who recognized it as "sadomasochistic," Prokofiev's operatic interpretation did not concentrate enough on the "more important psychological sexual motivations" provided in Briusov's novel.[67]

Derived from the same *ménage à trois* as *Ognennyi angel* but more concerned

---

64. Robert W. Anderson, "The History of Witchcraft: A Review with Some Psychiatric Comments," *American Journal of Psychiatry* 126, no. 12 (1970): 1727, 1733; George Rosen, "Psychopathology in the Social Process," pt. 2, "Dance Frenzies, Demonic Possession, Revival Movements and Similar So-Called Psychic Epidemics: An Interpretation," *Bulletin of the History of Medicine* 36 (1962): 13–44.

65. As a poet, Lokhvitskaia did not hesitate to equate Satan with God; she peopled her poems and dramas in verse with witches and evil spirits, and drew heavily on the symbolism of the color black. See Kristi Groberg, "Mirra Aleksandrovna Lokhvitskaia," in Ledkovsky et al., *Dictionary of Russian Women Writers*, pp. 381–84.

66. *Novyi den'*, January 2, 1909, as quoted in Nicolas Slonimsky, *Music in 1900* (New York, 1968), p. 135.

67. Harlow Robinson, *Sergei Prokofiev* (New York, 1987), pp. 154–55. The music was reworked as his Third Symphony, a "demonological orgy" through which it eventually became well known, although the opera was not staged until 1955. See "Venice: Angel and Cockfight," *Opera News*, October 31, 1955, pp. 18–19; Hans Swarenski, "Sergei Prokofieff's *The Flaming Angel*," *Tempo* 39 (1956): 16–27; Alan Jefferson, "The Angel of Fire," *Music & Musicians* 13, no. 12 (1965): 32–35; Anthony Payne, "Prokofiev's *The Fiery Angel*," *Tempo* 74 (1965): 21–23; Rita McAllister, "Natural and Supernatural in *The Fiery Angel*," *Musical Times* 111, no. 1530 (1970): 785–89; and Harlow Robinson, "The Operas of Sergei Prokofiev and Their Literary Sources" (Ph.D. diss., University of California, Berkeley, 1980). In the second section of Prokofiev's *Scythian Suite* (1914–15), titled "Chuzhbog and the Dance of the Evil Spirits," we again hear the demonic in his music.

with the Russian experience was Bely's occult novel *Serebrianyi golub'* (1909), which has been translated as *The Silver Dove*. Under the influence of the demonic female Matrena (inspired by Petrovskaia), the protagonist, Darialsky (perhaps modeled on Aleksandr Dobroliubov), succumbs to the dark force (*temnaia sila*). Its evil—manifest in a heretical Christian cult—draws him to his death in the town of Likhov (*likhoi* = evil), a site overrun with pigs (manifestations of the Devil in both Western Christian symbolism and Russian folklore). In the Symbolist spirit that recognized the "magic of words" (*magiia slov*), Bely carefully chose his vocabulary to connect symbol to sound and create an incantation: acoustic complexes invert the spiritual *d-u-kh* to produce the arcane *k/q-u-d* (Demon est Deus inversus) for a vocabulary that emphasizes, through meaning and sound, the pervasiveness of the demonic.[68]

Like Briusov and Maksimilian Voloshin,[69] Bely was well read in Western occultism and had a collection of books on the subject; yet he also imagined evil sorcery to be a pagan urge deep within the Russian psyche. His English translator sees in the character Darialsky the struggle for a "spiritual and intellectual solution for Russian backwardness, Russian darkness, Russian evil" as he succumbs to the "dark elemental earth forces which lie at the base of the Russian ethos."[70] Blok, who said that he himself simultaneously was the Devil and was attracted to the Devil both as a real force and as a concept,[71] believed that a dark, diabolical force—born of folk magic, spells, and incantations—was afoot in Russia. Sorcerers, witches, wizards, and magicians, he said, expose the dark light of demonism within the "pure poetry" of folk spells and incantations[72]—themes that surface in his poems about Russia. Briusov claimed that the demonic came into Blok's poems in 1907 with creatures "personifying the pagan principles."[73] Merezhkovsky too interpreted black magic as one manifestation of highly illusory pagan forces. This so-called dark force was of considerable concern to intellectuals and occultists at the turn of the century, and may be seen as a shift in interest from the Satan of the West to the Satan of the East. The many efforts of intellectuals to reach out to and learn from the peasantry were colored by a deep fear that a powerful primeval force might be tapped into and released. Sergei Maksimov was interested in the

68. See Maria Carlson, *"The Silver Dove,"* in *Andrey Bely: Spirit of Symbolism*, ed. John E. Malmstad (Ithaca, 1987), pp. 71–74.

69. See Maksimilian Voloshin, "Demony razrusheniia i zla," *Zolotoe runo*, 1908, no. 6, pp. 59–68.

70. See George Reavey's preface to his translation of Andrei Bely, *The Silver Dove* (New York, 1974), p. viii.

71. See Franklin D. Reeve, *Aleksandr Blok: Between Image and Idea* (New York and London, 1962), pp. 129–30.

72. Andrei Belyi, "Poeziia zagovorov i zaklinanii" (1906), in his *Sobranie sochinenii*, ed. Victor N. Orlov et al. (Moscow and Leningrad, 1960), 5:36–65.

73. Valerii Briusov, "Alexander Blok," in *Blok: An Anthology of Essays and Memoirs*, ed. Lucy Vogel (Ann Arbor, 1982), p. 108.

remnants of ancient fertility cults (projected as evil) in Russian Orthodoxy, as well as in the continued presence of evil beliefs and their relation to modernity—all found in *The Silver Dove*.[74] The theme continued as late as 1914, when Mikhail Lodyzhensky's *Temnaia sila* expanded on the psychological implications of demonic mysticism and the dark side of man's nature.[75] Some of this fascination came out of the teachings of Elena Blavatsky's Theosophy and Rudolf Steiner's Anthroposophy. The latter names Ahriman and Lucifer as personifications of the spirits of materialism and pride. Of these "dark forces," Lucifer more subtly seduces humanity to overestimate its spiritual powers, and it is he that dominates modern philosophy, literature, and art.

Thus, at the same time that Mephistophelian imagery appears prominently in the arts, the figure of Lucifer was equally well received. Lucifer's image was generally presented as a spiritualistic occult icon: as the archrebel against God, Lucifer was symbolic of humanity's fall from grace. He was considered the Prometheus of Christian mythology and hailed as the vindicator of freedom of thought and as a defiant yet sympathetic symbol of protest. Alexander Scriabin (1871–1915)—whose biographer says unequivocally that "Black Masses were seriously practised and believed in" in Silver Age Russia— was drawn to the Promethean qualities of the figure of Satan, and in fact referred to Prometheus as both a satanic Mephistopheles and Lucifer, the archrebel.[76] In the spirit of Nietzsche, Scriabin envisioned all three figures as archrebels whose defiance of God inspires humanity to become its own Almighty. The titanic evil coloration in his music began with *Poème satanique* 1903), continued through many pieces including his Ninth Sonata (subtitled "Black Mass"), and culminated in *Prométhée: Poème de feu* (c. 1909). He was an adherent of Blavatsky's Theosophy, which accepts Satan as God's adversary, a symbol of occult wisdom on earth. Scriabin's erotic megalomania, "his diabolism, and his quest for the *mysterium* were part and parcel of his response to the political realities and cultural climate of his time.[77] Like Chaliapin, he brought

74. Sergei Maksimov, *Nechistaia, nevedomaia i krestnaia sila* (St. Petersburg, 1903), pp. 3–29 on the Devil.

75. Mikhail Lodyzhenskii, *Temnaia sila* (St. Petersburg, 1914), vol. 3 of *Misticheskaia trilogiia*. Lodyzhensky, a friend of Volynsky and the occultist P. D. Uspensky (seeker of the fourth dimension and author of *Razgovory s diavolom: Okkultnye rasskazy* [Conversations with the Devil: Occult stories, 1916]), considered himself a religious mystic.

76. Faubion Bowers, *The New Scriabin* (New York, 1973), p. 121. Bowers describes the "devilish experiments" of others in Scriabin's circle (Bal'mont, Briusov, et al.), especially the painter Nikolai Shperling, who, as part of a "spiritual exercise" to study the effects of degradation on his soul, drank the blood and ate the flesh of wounded and dead soldiers during World War I.

77. Leonid Sabaneef, "A. N. Scriabin—A Memoir," *Russian Review* 25, no. 3 (1966): 260. See also Leonid Sabaneev, " 'Prometheus' von Skriabin," *Die blaue Reiter*, 1914, no. 2, pp. 57–68; Boris Shloezer, *Skriabin* (Berlin, 1923); Malcolm Brown, "Scriabin and Russian 'Mystic' Symbolism," *19th Century Music* 3 (1979): 42–51; Ralph E. Matlaw, "Scriabin and Russian Symbol-

symbolic images of Satan before the public through his extremely popular performance art.

The theme of the Demon—a rebellious Luciferian fallen angel with Mephistophelian overtones, but also representative of the Greek *daemon*—was a prominent part of satanism in fin-de-siècle Russian culture, albeit one that demonstrates more clearly the spiritual aspects of the fascination with Satan. The Demon had earlier entered Russian Romantic literature in the "Demon" poems of Aleksandr Pushkin (1799–1837), who under the influence of Goethe sought artistic expression for a profound personal experience of "life-killing skepticism," which was to him "the evil demon of our age."[78] The Demon as a figure of rebellion was further explored by Mikhail Lermontov (1814–41), whose epic poem *Demon* (1841) drew on Goethe's Mephistopheles, Milton's Lucifer, and Byron's Fatal Man.[79] In Lermontov's poem, the Demon (a fallen angel), doomed to fly endlessly through the universe, chances to see the Georgian princess Tamara, who kindles his interest in terrestrial beauty. The Demon's evil wishes kill Tamara's fiancé, and she takes refuge in a convent. Yet even here she is not safe, for the Demon pursues her into her convent cell, persuades her to surrender to his love, and kills her with his kiss ("Alas, the evil spirit triumphed! The deadly venom of his kiss instantly penetrated her breast").[80] According to Merezhkovsky, Lermontov was the first to raise "the religious question of evil," and all Russian literature after him that revolves around the concept of demonic temptation tries "to lay bare Lermontov's Demon."[81]

The theme of the Demon became popular in the closing decades of the nineteenth century and through the early years of the twentieth. It was the subject of Anton Rubinstein's opera *Demon* (1871–72), which portrays the Demon as a creature of darkness who, propelled by lust, seeks redemption in the love of a mortal woman.[82] In addition, there was a series of tableaux vivants by

ism," *Comparative Literature* 31, no. 1 (1979): 1–23; Ann M. Lane, "Bal'mont and Skriabin: The Artist as Superman," in *Nietzsche in Russia*, ed. Bernice Glatzer Rosenthal (Princeton, 1986), pp. 195–218.

78. P. V. Annenkov, *A. S. Pushkin v Aleksandrovskoi epokhe* (Moscow, 1874), p. 153, as quoted in André von Gronicka, *The Russian Image of Goethe* (Philadelphia, 1968), p. 86.

79. N. L. Brodski, *M. Lermontov* (Moscow, 1945), p. 297, writes that Goethe's Mephisto is the role model for Lermontov's Demon; Gronicka, *Russian Image of Goethe*, pp. 86–87, says that Byron's Fatal Man is the dominant influence, but that Goethe's Mephisto marks Lermontov's Demon with the traits of nihilistic doubt, cynicism, and hatred; Aline Isdebsky-Pritchard, *The Art of Mikhail Vrubel', 1856–1910* (Ann Arbor, 1982), p. 120, writes that Lermontov's Demon is Milton's Satan, as does Boss, *Milton and Russian Satanism*, p. 133.

80. Mikhail Lermontov, *Demon, vostochnaia povest'* (Moscow, 1964), p. 61.

81. Dmitrii Merezhkovskii, *Izbrannye stati: Simvolizm, Gogol', Lermontov* (Munich, 1972), pp. 312, 315. For another example, see idem, *Gogol' i chert* (St. Petersburg, 1906), serialized earlier as "Sud'by Gogolia," *Novyi put'*, 1903, nos. 1–3.

82. Rubinstein, who decorated his apartment with (nothing but) a large bust of Mephistopheles, was fascinated by the figures of Lucifer and the Demon; he composed a symphonic

the Mamontov theatrical circle (1878), a satanic painting by the illustrator and eroticist Mihály Zichi, another by the realist Konstantin Makovsky (1889), and Alfred Eberling's haunting illustrations to a deluxe edition of Lermontov's poem (1910).[83] But by far the Demon's most culturally attuned publicist was the innovative painter Mikhail Vrubel'. After seeing Rubinstein's opera, Vrubel' reread Lermontov's poem; by 1885 he had fixed on the Demon as the central figure of his oeuvre. Because he reinforced the psychological element in his paintings and sculpture and depicted the Demon as the human soul in eternal struggle with its own mutinous spirit, Vrubel''s biographer concludes that he was attracted to the dynamic, very modern juxtaposition of psychological vignettes in Lermontov's poem.[84]

Vrubel' first painted the Demon in 1885. His illustrations for Lermontov's *Demon* were commissioned for a special jubilee edition of the poem published in 1890.[85] The years 1899–1902 were a period of intense activity during which he worked exclusively on interpretations of the Demon. His infamous *Demon poverzhennyi* (The Demon cast down, 1902; Figure 4.12) may have been the prototype for the cover illustration for a 1906 issue of *Satiricheskoe obozrenie* (Satirical review; Figure 4.13), a political cartoon by "Levap" that depicts an eroticized woman attacked by a devilish figure. The victim, her face expressing anguish and her body and peacock-feather wings clearly broken, is remarkably like Vrubel''s fallen Demon (who, although androgynous, shares characteristics with the fin-de-siècle femme fatale).[86] Vrubel' was at this time overtaken by mental illness brought on by tertiary syphilis (and probably abuse of narcotics and alcohol as well), and the Symbolists sympathetically considered

quartet titled *Faust,* and an oratorio, *Paradise Lost;* see Catherine D. Bowen, *"Free Artist"* (Boston, 1961), pp. 116, 256–57, 280, 370.

83. For these and other examples see Nikolai P. Pakhomov, *Lermontov v izobrazitel'nom iskusstve* (Moscow and Leningrad, 1940), pp. 108–28, 240–47.

84. Isdebsky-Pritchard, *Art of Mikhail Vrubel',* p. 95, and idem, "Art for Philosophy's Sake: Vrubel' against 'the Herd,'" in Rosenthal, *Nietzsche in Russia,* pp. 219–48. Cf. Sergei Durylin, "Vrubel'; Lermontov," *Literaturnoe nasledstvo,* 1948, nos. 45–46, pp. 541–62; and Patricia P. Brodsky, "The Demons of Lermontov and Vrubel'," *Slavic and East European Arts* 6, no. 2 (1990): 16–31. Fluent in several languages and well versed in Western art, Vrubel' attended art exhibits in Europe and was in all likelihood familiar with the work of the French Symbolist painter Odilon Redon, whose oeuvre is so like his own. Redon's illustrations for the 1890 edition of Baudelaire's *Fleurs du mal* depict Satan as a fallen angel; his haunting *Gloire et louange à Satan* (Glory and praise to Satan) is reproduced as *Satana* (Prince of Hell) in the Russian Symbolist periodical *Vesy,* 1904, no. 12, p. 52.

85. On Vrubel''s illustrations see D. E. Maksimov, *Poeziia Lermontova* (Moscow and Leningrad, 1964), pp. 247–65; Petr Suzdalev, "Demon Vrubelia," *Panorama iskusstv,* 1979, no. 78, pp. 101–38, and idem, *Vrubel' i Lermontov* (Moscow, 1980), pp. 168–88.

86. Isdebsky-Pritchard, *Art of Mikhail Vrubel',* p. 106, writes that Vrubel''s Demon is related to the femme fatale image as it was emerging in other European paintings of the period, particularly the paintings of Dante Gabriel Rossetti: "Vrubel''s transformation of the Demon into a malevolent womanly type may, on one level, be explained by his ambivalence toward women." See also pp. 118, 121.

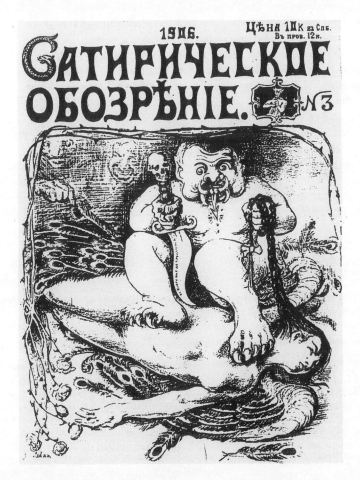

Figure 4.12. (above) Mikhail Vrubel', *Demon poverzhennyi* (The demon cast down, 1902). Oil on canvas. Tretiakov Gallery, Moscow.

Figure 4.13. Levap, front cover of *Satiricheskoe obozrenie*, 1906, no. 3.

him a mad genius. At the Usoltsev clinic in Moscow's exclusive Petrovsky Park from 1904 to 1906 he continued to explore the Demon under the watchful eye of his psychiatrist, Dr. Pavel Karpov, who later featured Vrubel' and his Demon in a book on the creativity of mentally unstable patients.[87] A contemporary, the writer and critic Georgy Chulkov, expressed the theory that primordial chaos, the affirmation of individuality, and humanity's satanic fall were Vrubel''s primary themes and that the Demon personified them.[88] It is true that Vrubel' was attracted by hedonism, "but in him," writes Valentin Boss, "the urge was in continuous tension with his spiritual quest, of which the Demon became the visible expression."[89] His last commissioned work, to be owned by Nikolai Riabushinsky, was an unfinished portrait (1906) of Briusov.[90]

Chaliapin, who first saw Vrubel''s *Demon poverzhennyi* on exhibit in 1902, popularized the figure of the Demon when he sang the role in Rubinstein's opera between 1904 and 1906. "My Demon," he wrote, "is taken from Vrubel''s," and indeed, in his interpretation the Demon was a mighty, primeval Promethean being rejected by God and humanity.[91] Chaliapin was only one among many Russian bassos who sang the role; enormous numbers of Russians attended the various productions of the opera, and its merits were publicly debated in the periodical press.

The Symbolists considered Vrubel' one of them by virtue of his willingness to make the dangerous descent into the unconscious, and his Demon was therefore attractive both as an antihero and as a spiritual model. And, like the Symbolists, Vrubel' was preoccupied by the moral fragmentation of his society.[92] Briusov, not surprisingly, was drawn to the Demons of both Lermontov and Vrubel'. As early as the 1890s, he immersed himself in Lermontov's poetry, knew and could recite *Demon*, and began an essay on types of the Demon in literature.[93] At age twenty-two, already a hardened opportunist, he turned to Lermontov's demon as the type of sated experience. His own poem "M. A.

87. Pavel I. Karpov, *Tvorchestvo dushevnobolnykh i ego vliianie na razvitie nauki, iskusstva i tekhniki* (Moscow and Leningrad, 1926), pp. 119–20 (pl. 7).

88. Georgii Chulkov, "Moskva i Demon," *Zolotoe runo*, 1909, no. 6, pp. 71–74. Chulkov later continued the theme in *Satana i Roman* (Moscow, 1915).

89. Boss, *Milton and Russian Satanism*, pp. 130–31.

90. For Briusov's take on the portrait, which he hated, see his "Posledniaia rabota Vrubelia," *Iskusstvo*, 1912, nos. 11–12, pp. 369–78; cf. Petrovskaia, "Iz 'Vospominanii,'" p. 784.

91. Fedor I. Shaliapin, *Maska i dusha* (Paris, 1932), pp. 328–29. Chaliapin claimed that the Demon caused his severe insomnia and haunted his dreams; see A. Serebrov, "Demon," in *Fedor Ivanovich Shaliapin*, ed. E. A. Groseva (Moscow, 1960), p. 254. Konstantin Korovin's stage settings for Chaliapin's interpretation of Rubinstein's *Demon* were derived from Vrubel''s concept; see also Aleksandr Golovin's Vrubel'ian portrait of Chaliapin in the role of Rubinstein's Demon (1904), reproduced in Borovsky, *Chaliapin*, p. 367.

92. See John E. Bowlt, "Russian Symbolism and the 'Blue Rose' Movement," *Slavic and East European Review* 51, no. 123 (1973): 163.

93. See Valerii Briusov, "Moia iunost'," *Iz moei zhizni* (Moscow, 1927), p. 74.

Vrubel'ia" (1906) dwells on Vrubel''s vision.[94] Blok, who physically resembled Vrubel''s Demon and who pursued the Demon in his own poetry, was profoundly moved by Lermontov's Demon and Vrubel''s interpretive image. He believed that he understood the link between the two demons and the root of the demonic idea in the individual experiences of both Lermontov and Vrubel', and he interpreted their Demons as "symbols of our times"—representatives of the spirit of revolt against society, intermediaries between this and other worlds, and sympathetic projections of the artist. He saw Vrubel' as a fallen angel whose beautiful Demon is a prophet who has betrayed his religious calling.[95] For Blok, the fact that *Demon poverzhennyi* was never given final form was an admirable rejection of absolutes.[96] He wrote two poems titled "Demon"—one after Vrubel''s funeral (1910) and the second in 1916. In the first, the Demon is human and world-weary; here we can note that Blok envisioned his own "Neznakomka" (The stranger, 1906), a spectral femme fatale, as a counterpart to Vrubel''s fallen angel, and that he related them to the 1905 Revolution.[97] In Blok's second poem, the Demon is a Mephistophelian figure empowered by an evil creative will.[98] The Demon held grave importance for Gippius as well, and was prototypical of her concept of evil and of the place of the Devil in this world.[99] In her short story "On—belyi" (He—white, 1912) the Devil is an angel who grieves over human spiritual torment in the manner of the Demon. In our time, James Billington has remarked that "Vrubel was trying to have the devil make his appearance," and that in him "the sensualists of late imperial Russia found their patron saint."[100]

94. Valerii Briusov, "M. A. Vrubel'ia," *Zolotoe runo*, 1906, no. 1, p. 7.

95. See Aleksandr Blok, "O sovremennom sostoianii russkogo simvolizma," *Apollon*, 1910, no. 8, p. 22. On Blok's Demon poems, see I. T. Kruk, "Obraz Demona v poezy Bloka," in *Russkaia literatura XX veka* (Kaluga, 1968), pp. 212–26. One wonders if Blok, who, like Vrubel', suffered from alcoholism and venereal disease, related to Vrubel' in terms of these diseases (with reference to societal ills and the demonic double as individual experience).

96. See his eulogy at Vrubel''s funeral, "Pamiati Vrubelia," *Iskusstvo i pechatnoe delo*, 1910, nos. 8–9, pp. 307–9.

97. D. E. Maksimov, "Aleksandr Blok i revoliutsiia 1905 goda," in *Revoliutsiia 1905 goda i russkaia literatura*, ed. V. A. Desnitsov and K. D. Muratova (Moscow and Leningrad, 1956), pp. 246–79. Baudelaire brought the subject of syphilis into his poetry; Blok did so only symbolically. Rops (who did not have the disease) first expressed the fin-de-siècle fear of syphilis in his graphic images of women. I am thinking of Rops's *Mors syphilitica*, so like Vrubel''s earlier *Liubov' i golod* (Fig. 4.11). See François Beamish-Thiriet, "The Myth of Woman in Baudelaire and Blok" (Ph.D. diss., University of Washington, 1973), for a revealing interpretation.

98. Such an approach to human failure in relation to the Demon was central to the creative work of both Vrubel' and Blok; see Richard H. Byrns, "The Artistic Worlds of Vrubel and Blok," *Slavic and East European Journal* 23, no. 1 (1979): 47–48. For more on the Demon in Blok's dreams and in his vision of the dangers of mysticism, see Avril Pyman, *The Life of Aleksandr Blok* (Oxford, 1980), 2:142–47.

99. See Vladimir Zlobin, "Gippius and the Problem of Evil," in his *Difficult Soul*, pp. 66–68.

100. James Billington, *The Icon and the Axe* (New York, 1970), p. 504. I prefer to agree with

A project that marked the final phase of Symbolist satanism was the literary collection *Satanizm* (1913), illustrated with engravings by Félicien Rops. Among the translations of satanic theme pieces by Baudelaire, Barbey d'Aurevilly, and Anatole France and such works as Stanislaw Przybyszewski's "Sinagoga Satana" (Synagogue of Satan, a European name for a witches' sabbath) are scattered poems, stories, and articles by Russian writers. We find Mikhail Artsybashev's article "Ideia D'iavola" (The idea of the Devil), Briusov's poems "Zhenshchine" (To a woman) and "Lamia" (The witch), Sergei Makovsky's "Iz pesen Astarte" (From the song of Astarte), the critic Nikolai Abramovich's article "Khudozhniki satanizma" (Artists of satanism), and short stories by Sologub and others. *Satanizm* brought together a cross section of prose, poetry, and imagery by the European satanists popular at the end of the nineteenth century, as well as a core group of Russians under their influence, and so provides a microcosm of the movement from that perspective.[101]

It would be comforting to accept satanism as a component of the general Russian fin-de-siècle spiritual *renovatio* and the search for truth. But, however well this approach may define the Symbolist-Decadent sense of ennui (the feeling Sâr Péladin addressed when he noted that "at these moments in history when a civilization is coming to an end, the central fact is spiritual nausea"),[102] it does not address the perversity so common to the "satanists" I have discussed. Constantine Ponomareff has said that "the intrinsic nihilism of the symbolist sensibility cannot be glossed over by dwelling on its liberating impulses for renewal."[103] He raises an important point, because the rationale for satanism (rebellion against the social structure, a search for religion, ennui) does not necessarily touch on the deeper reasons for the fascination with Satan and the behavior that sometimes accompanies it, which are rooted in the practitioner's subconscious. Artists, musicians, and the literati expressed a hysterical interest in cultural problems; yet this interest was, in effect, almost all theory and little or no practice. Symbolists responded artistically to the burning social questions of the time, but they were an extremely small fraction of the Russian populace and they did little to make a difference. Interested in ideas and subject matter, they were critics who addressed the suffering of the masses while safely ensconced in their own aristocratic or bourgeois worlds (the very ones they rebelled against): many lived comfortably on family al-

---

most Vrubel' scholars, who interpret his Demon as a *daemon* (Vrubel''s own, in fact) and not the Devil per se, but nonetheless in Vrubel''s time his Demon was perceived as a satanic figure.

101. One wonders if its publication prompted Anatoly B., in "Peterburgskie satanisty," *Golos Moskvy,* 1913, no. 34 (reprinted in *Rebus,* 1913, no. 8), to comment that Petersburg was rife with satanists, Luciferians, and black magicians.

102. Sâr Péladin, *Le Vice suprême* (Paris, 1884), p. 58.

103. Constantine Ponomareff, *On the Dark Side of Russian Literature, 1709–1910* (New York and Bern, 1987), p. 219.

lowances or were in government service. They engaged in their rebellious "underground" satanism as a way to reject the society's values, but it was also an excuse for exciting and unusual forms of self-indulgence. Jean Pierrot has described this phenomenon in Europe as "spiritual anxiety"—a mode of guilt exacerbated by the consciousness of evil and sin that Satan embodies.[104] In Russia this "moral guilt" may have been no more than the Symbolists' affirmation that they did not "go to the people" for anything other than source material. As Ivanov wrote, such extreme self-affirmation was, plain and simple, the demonic "wish to be as gods."[105]

104. Pierrot, *Decadent Imagination*, pp. 90–97.
105. Ivanov, *Po zvezdam*, pp. 307, 325.

CHAPTER FIVE
FASHIONABLE OCCULTISM

Spiritualism, Theosophy, Freemasonry, and
Hermeticism in Fin-de-Siècle Russia

Maria Carlson

For many years critics have relegated to footnotes or simply ignored Spiritualism, Theosophy, Hermeticism, and other forms of popular occultism as they relate to the fin de siècle in general and to Russian culture in particular.[1] Yet an investigation of turn-of-the-century cultural documents (literary works, paintings, philosophical essays, memoirs, newspaper articles) reveals that the occult excited an extraordinary amount of interest among educated Russians of the emerging middle class. For many of these people, fashionable occultism was a form of entertainment—they loved the frisson of fear at confronting the unknown, for example, or the excitement of holding hands without censure in a darkened room during a séance. Others seriously accepted it as representing the cutting edge of contemporary natural science or the revelation of a profound religious philosophy. Some found its otherworldliness consoling in a world where God had been pronounced dead. Others made satisfying journalistic careers by ridiculing the popular rage for the occult. Passionately defended or violently defamed, occultism permeated the atmosphere of upper- and middle-class Russian society and was one more manifestation of the general spiritual hunger that generated the phenomenon we call the Russian religious renaissance.[2]

1. The one exception is Freemasonry, which attracted a great deal of attention because of the visibility of several Masons in the Russian Provisional Government and the implicit political connotations of membership in their organization (as a "mysterious and secret society," Freemasonry was not unique in being viewed as a politically subversive force).

2. While the occult movements discussed in this chapter appealed primarily to the gentry and the professional middle classes, "boulevard mysticism" exercised its power over the imagination of the lower classes, who shared a passion for fortune-telling, some forms of astrology, palmistry, dream interpretation, exhibitions of public hypnosis, and various supernatural phenomena.

Spiritualism

Of the three most popular occult movements, Spiritualism had the largest number of adherents, both serious and dilettante. Today we tend to forget that in 1900 the number of avowed Spiritualists throughout the world actually soared into the millions. Briefly, Spiritualism is a belief in the continued existence of the personality after death in a higher, spiritual body, and the ability of the living to communicate with the spirits of the departed through a human channel, or medium. The medium assists the spirits to make their presence known through a variety of physical and mental phenomena—rapping, table-turning, automatic writing, spirit voices, luminous phenomena, apports, levitation, clairvoyance, divination, telepathy, and even ectoplasmic materialization.

The idea of spiritualism is ancient, but the modern Spiritualist movement can be quite precisely dated to March 31, 1848, when two young sisters, Kate and Margaret Fox, spoke with the spirit of a murdered peddler in a farmhouse in Hydesville, New York. Within a very few years Spiritualism had swept the United States and become the rage in Europe, attracting the attention of the educated public and making such diverse converts as the art nouveau artist Alphonse Mucha, the actress Sarah Bernhardt, the writers Victor Hugo, Arthur Conan Doyle, and Elizabeth Barrett Browning, Queen Victoria, and members of the Russian, German, and French courts, not to mention an army of ordinary people.

Modern Spiritualism took two forms. Scientific Spiritualism (also called Anglo-American Spiritualism), regardless of its occult trappings, was essentially positivistic in its insistence that Spiritualist phenomena could be scientifically investigated and would eventually be explained by modern science; nevertheless, the moral and ethical dimension inherent in its assumptions should not be overlooked. Mystical Spiritualism, or *Spiritisme,* originated in France by Allan Kardec (Hippolyte Léon Denizard Rivail, 1804–69), more closely resembled an alternative religion, lacking the scientific dimension but espousing a doctrine of compulsory reincarnation not present in Anglo-American Spiritualism. Thus the late nineteenth-century spiritualist phenomenon appealed both to the "scientific" mind and to the religious-philosophical mind.

By the late 1850s both Spiritualism and Spiritism had reached Russia. Initially this phenomenon was concentrated in a small group of adherents centered on the salon of Count Grigory Kushelev-Bezborodko. The count was a friend of Daniel Dunglas Home (1833–86), Spiritualism's most famous physical medium and the only one never to have been exposed as a fraud. Home visited Kushelev-Bezborodko in Russia several times, married the count's sister-in-law (in St. Petersburg, with the popular French author Alexandre Dumas as best man), and gave séances for the enthusiastic court of Alexander

II; many members of the royal family and retinue were devoted adherents of Spiritualism.

On his frequent visits to Russia, Home often stayed at the home of the writer A. K. Tolstoy (1817–75; not to be confused with the Soviet writer A. N. Tolstoy), who was deeply immersed in occult studies. Other members of Tolstoy's circle who shared his interests were the philosopher Vladimir Soloviev (1853–1900), the writer and dictionary compiler Vladimir Dal' (1801–72), and Pamfil Iurkevich (1826–74), professor of philosophy at Moscow University. D. D. Home and Spiritualism even entered Russian literature, courtesy of Lev Tolstoy, who had met Home in Paris in 1857 and used him as a model for the medium Landau in his novel *Anna Karenina* (1877). Tolstoy also parodied the popular passion for spiritualism in his ironically titled comedy *Plody prosveshcheniia* (The fruits of enlightenment, 1891).

After 1875, Russian Spiritualism was dominated by Aleksandr Nikolaevich Aksakov (1823–1903), the nephew of the writer Sergei Timofeevich Aksakov and a younger cousin of the Slavophiles Ivan and Konstantin Aksakov. Highly esteemed in both European and Russian Spiritualist and aristocratic circles, Aleksandr Aksakov was an exclusively scientific Spiritualist. Encountering difficulties in publishing materials on spiritualism and animal magnetism in Russia, he founded the respected journal *Psychische Studien* in Leipzig in 1874; the Leipzig press published both original and translated materials on spiritualism and animal magnetism.

During the nineteenth century, selected European books on spiritualist and occult topics could be imported into Russia from abroad, but they could not be published in Russia without approval by the strict church censorship (*dukhovnaia tsenzura*), into whose purview all "spiritual" materials came. Not surprisingly, the Orthodox Church viewed the occult revival in all its aspects as pernicious and inimical to Christianity. Original works and translations dealing with the "scientific" and "medical" aspects of animal magnetism and hypnotism, however, were published in Russia, including Aksakov's own *Animizm i spiritizm;* originally published in Leipzig); books dealing with more heretical pseudo-religious and occult topics were less likely to receive permission for publication in Russia until after the censorship reforms of 1905.

Aksakov bent his considerable intellectual and financial efforts toward popularizing Spiritualism in Russia. Together with Mikhail Butlerov (1828–86) and Nikolai Vagner (1829–1907), two science professors at the Imperial University in St. Petersburg, Aksakov moved Spiritualism out of private parlors and into the press. In the winter of 1875–76 the Imperial University in St. Petersburg formed a Scientific Commission for the Study of Mediumistic Phenomena. It was headed by the famous chemist Dmitry Mendeleev (1834–1907; father of the periodic table; later the symbolist poet Aleksandr Blok's father-in-law) and included Aleksandr Aksakov as well as Professors Butlerov and Vagner. Forty séances were planned, but only eight had taken place before the commission was torn apart by scandal. Mendeleev, who had a very low opinion of Spiritualism, had decided to sabotage the séances and publish his conclusions before the experiment had barely started.[3] Letters of protest against such unscientific behavior, written by both pro- and anti-Spiritualists, flooded the press. Spiritualism seemed to take on a new scientific legitimacy. The Spiritualists even managed to change some minds: some twenty years later, Professor Mendeleev would publish a "there are more things in heaven and earth" recantation and even become the Russian representative to the Institut Psychique Internationale in Paris in 1900.[4]

By 1881, in spite of the church's strict "spiritual censorship," Viktor Pribytkov, a leading St. Petersburg Spiritualist, founded the first Russian Spiritualist journal, *Rebus,* which appeared weekly from October 1881 through 1917. Disguised as a games magazine to circumvent the censorship, *Rebus* eventually garnered thousands of subscribers. After the censorship reforms that followed the Revolution of 1905, the Russian Spiritualists were able to register officially as a society. *Rebus,* their primary organ, was soon joined by other Spiritualist journals: *Golos vseobshchei liubvi* (The voice of universal love), *Ottuda* (From beyond), *Spiritualist, Vestnik okkul'tizma i spiritizma* (Herald of occultism and spiritualism), *Voprosy psikhizma i spiritualisticheskoi filosofii* (Problems of psychism and spiritualist philosophy), and *Zhizn' dukha* (Life of the spirit). None were as long-lived or as important as *Rebus,* but their mere number is suggestive. These journals were quite cosmopolitan and informed interested Russian readers on everything from animal magnetism, telepathy, and somnambulism to automatic writing and *Naturphilosophie.* They printed the reports of the London Society for Psychical Research, articles by leading European scholars and occultists, and occult belles-lettres by European and Russian authors.

The Russian Spiritualist movement grew apace. Sponsored by *Rebus,* the Society of Russian Spiritualists held its own congress in Moscow, October 20–27, 1906. More than 400 Russian Spiritualists attended; 300 more were turned away for lack of space. Vladimir Bykov, editor of *Spiritualist* and several other Spiritualist journals and president of the Moscow Circle of Dogmatic Spiritualists, estimated that there were more than 1,600 individual "spirit circles" in Moscow and St. Petersburg alone at the turn of the century.[5]

Spiritualism exerted a considerable influence on Russian middle- and upper-class society, culling its adherents primarily from the civil service and the military (the largest single category), the professions (including academe), and the independently wealthy; it appealed equally to men and women. The cre-

3. Dmitrii Mendeleev, *Materialy dlia suzhdeniia o spiritizme* (St. Petersburg, 1876).

4. Viktor Pribytkov, "Professor Mendeleev priznaet mediumicheskie iavleniia (iz moei besedy s nim o spiritizme)," *Rebus,* 1894, no. 1, p. 4.

5. Vladimir Bykov, *Spiritizm pod sudom nauki* (Moscow, 1914), p. 77.

ative intelligentsia also found it compelling. Among those who found Spiritualism of some interest were the Symbolist writer Valery Briusov (who occasionally contributed to *Rebus*); the Argonauts (a group of young Moscow Symbolists), Nina Petrovskaia, Nikolai Kiselev, and Mikhail Sizov (both Kiselev and Sizov were officers of the Society of Russian Spiritualists). Highly visible members of the Russian spiritualist movement were the popular novelists Vsevolod Soloviev, Andrei Zarin, Ivan Karyshev (the "Russian Kardec"), and Vera Kryzhanovskaia; their popular novels and stories, based on spiritualist and occult themes, are quite interesting and have yet to be investigated by scholars.[6]

THEOSOPHY

Although not so widespread or so numerically strong as the Spiritualist movement, Theosophy was the most intellectually important of the fashionable occult trends of the late nineteenth century.[7] Spiritists in particular were attracted to Theosophy (and to the Hermetic arts as well); for that matter, membership among the occult groups was generally fluid.

"Theosophy" (from the Greek for divine wisdom) in the wider sense refers to various systems of mystic gnosis reflected in Buddhism, Neoplatonism, mystery religions, and the speculative mysticism of such philosophers as Jacob Boehme, Emanuel Swedenborg, and Vladimir Soloviev. In the narrower sense, Theosophy is a pseudoreligious movement founded on November 17, 1875, in New York City by an eccentric Russian expatriate named Elena Blavatsky (1831–91). Assisted by her Spiritualist friend Colonel Henry Olcott (1832–1907), this woman of genius (or notorious charlatan, depending on one's point of view) created the Theosophical Society, an organization that within twenty-five years could boast of tens of thousands of members worldwide. Theosophy

---

6. See, for example, Andrei Zarin's *Spirit* (1902) and *Dar Satany* (1906); A. A. fon Nol'de's *Okkul'tnye rasskazy* (1913; the Nol'de family was well known in Moscow for their Spiritualist interests); and Vsevolod Soloviev's *Velikii Rozenkreitser, Volkhvy* (both 1896), and other novels with occult themes. The most famous spiritualist author, however, was Vera Kryzhanovskaia, who wrote dozens of popular occult novels with spiritualist themes; even her pseudonym, Rochester, was derived from her spirit guide. See especially her *Magi* (1902), *Gnev Bozhii* (1909), *Adskie chary* (1910), *V inom mire* (1910), and *Smert' planety* (1911). Her books invariably went through numerous editions. Various spiritualist phenomena play a role in Valerii Briusov's novel *Ognennyi angel* (1908); Briusov also planned but never completed a novel to be called *Medium*. Some negative aspects of Spiritualism are also closely associated with the character of Kudeiarov in Andrei Belyi's *Serebrianyi golub'* (1909); spiritualist references are sprinkled throughout the poetry and prose of the Russian Silver Age.

7. The various aspects of Theosophy (historical, cultural, and doctrinal) are discussed at greater length in Maria Carlson, *"No Religion Higher than Truth": A History of the Theosophical Movement in Russia, 1875–1922* (Princeton, 1993).

soon spread to Russia, and attracted numerous adherents there from the middle and gentry classes.

The primary aim of the Theosophical Society, as its charter stated, was to form the nucleus of a Universal Brotherhood of Humanity, without distinction by race, color, creed, or caste. Its subsidiary goals were to sponsor the study of comparative religion, philosophy, and science; to demonstrate the importance of such study; and to investigate the unexplained laws of nature and the psychic powers latent in humanity.

Theosophists define their doctrine as a syncretic, mystical religious-philosophical system, a "synthesis of Science, Religion, and Philosophy," supposedly based on an ancient esoteric tradition that Mme Blavatsky called the "Secret Doctrine" or the "Wisdom Religion." Through "comparative esotericism" (the study of all the religious and occult doctrines of the past), Blavatsky's Theosophy claimed to distill out the universal mother doctrine that ageless adepts had been jealously guarding from the uninitiated for thousands of years. Mme Blavatsky called these adepts "mahatmas," or "masters." These ancient sages, she claimed, lived in a special lodge somewhere in the Himalayas and in the natural way had little truck with the rest of the world. In the last quarter of the nineteenth century, however, this "Brotherhood of the White Lodge, the Hierarchy of Adepts who watch over and guide the evolution of humanity, and who have preserved these truths unimpaired," decided that the time had come for some of these truths to be gradually revealed through certain chosen vessels.[8] The first chosen vessel turned out to be Mme Blavatsky herself. She explicated her wisdom religion in her two major Theosophical texts, *Isis Unveiled* (1877) and *The Secret Doctrine* (1888), claiming that these epics of Theosophical thought were "dictated" to her by the mahatmas, with whom she was in direct psychic communication.

Mme Blavatsky's new Theosophy seemed to offer an alternative to the dominant materialism, rationalism, and positivism of the nineteenth century. Sometimes called Neo-Buddhism, Theosophy strikes the modern student as an eclectic, syncretic, dogmatic doctrine, strongly pantheistic and heavily laced with exotic Buddhist thought and vocabulary. Combining bits and pieces of Neoplatonism, Brahminism, Buddhism, Kabbalism, Rosicrucianism, Hermeticism, and other occult doctrines, past and present, in a frequently undiscriminating philosophical mélange, Theosophy attempted to create a "scientific" religion, a modern gnosis, based on absolute *knowledge* of things spiritual rather than on *faith*. Under its Neo-Buddhism lies an essentially Judeo-Christian moral ethic tempered by spiritual Darwinism (survival of those with the "fittest" spirit, or most advanced spiritual development). One might describe Theosophy as an attempt to disguise positivism as religion, an attempt that was seductive indeed in its own time, in view of the psychic

8. Annie Besant, *Ancient Wisdom* (1897; Adyar, Madras, 1977), p. 41.

tension produced at the fin de siècle by the seemingly unresolvable dichotomy between science and religion.

Although the Theosophical Society was founded in New York in 1875 and spread quickly throughout the world (in spite of the numerous scandals and exposés that followed in its formidable founder's wake), the Russian Theosophical Society was not officially registered and chartered in St. Petersburg until September 30 (O.S.), 1908. Nevertheless, Theosophy existed in Russia before the official registration of the society, for Russians who traveled abroad became members of the national sections of the society in England, Belgium, Germany, and France. News of the movement and articles about Theosophy, mostly critical, appeared in Russian journals as early as the 1880s. Documented private Theosophical circles existed in major Russian cities from the 1890s, but, again, they were either independents or unofficial affiliates of European branches of the society. The Russian church censorship saw Theosophy's Oriental passivity and its Buddhistic pantheism as highly inimical to Christianity, so not until after the censorship reforms of 1905 was it possible for the Russian Theosophists to publish their own journal, *Vestnik teosofii* (Herald of Theosophy), and register the Theosophical Society with the government.

The organizational meeting of the Russian Theosophical Society was held on November 17, 1908. Anna Kamenskaia (1867–1952), a leading Russian Theosophist with close ties to the English section, was elected president. She was ably assisted by her friends and colleagues Elena Pisareva and Anna Filosofova (1837–1912), a prominent name in the Russian women's movement. Filosofova was a pioneer of both Russian feminism and the Russian Theosophical Movement, as well as one of Russia's leading philanthropists.[9] The Russian Theosophists were enthusiastically involved in a variety of humanitarian projects: women's rights, progressive education, housing for the proletariat, charity work, vegetarian cafeterias and dormitories for the unemployed and the poor, and hospital work. This connection of Theosophy and feminism was not at all unusual; such movements were attractive to an emerging class of professional and financially independent women. The convergence of Theosophy, feminism, and social gospel could also be found in England and the United States.

More than one hundred members attended the first organizational meeting of the Russian Theosophical Society in St. Petersburg. Within a year, subchapters were opened in Kaluga, Moscow, and Kiev. An active Theosophical community in Smolensk, unaffiliated with St. Petersburg, published its own journal, *Teosofskaia zhizn'* (Theosophical life). By 1910 there were probably several

9. With Dr. A. N. Shabanova, Filosofova helped to organize the first All-Russian Women's Congress in 1908. She also maintained a high profile among the artistic elite: she was acquainted with the Symbolists Dmitry Merezhkovsky and Zinaida Gippius; she was the mother of the critic and minor philosopher Dmitry Filosofov; and she was an aunt of the impresario Sergei Diaghilev.

thousand Russian Theosophists, the majority of them women.[10] Many people who were interested in Theosophy were hesitant to register, since membership in what was officially perceived as an anti-Christian organization could still affect one's professional and social life in Russia. The registered Theosophists, however, were an active lot, and eventually covered the Russian cities of Moscow, St. Petersburg, Kaluga, Kiev, Rostov-on-the-Don, Yalta, Kharkov, and Poltava with Theosophical pamphlets; their lectures (the Theosophists were indefatigable lecturers) were remarkably well attended.

Although Theosophy has a strong element of Buddhism in it, the Russian explication of Theosophy owed as much to Vladimir Soloviev, Fedor Dostoevsky, and Lev Tolstoy (himself no stranger to Buddhist thought) as it did to the Bhagavad Gita or the Hindu mystics. Russian Theosophy shared the strong messianic streak that characterized other Russian "God-seeking" movements of the early twentieth century and embraced the social utopianism of the God-builders as well, although these movements did not share Theosophy's Buddhist assumptions. Theosophy, too, sought the synthesis of *narod* and intelligentsia in a form of mystical populism and admired such young intellectuals as Viktor Danilov and Aleksandr Dobroliubov, both Decadent poets who left the intellectual life of the capital to found religious sects in the Russian countryside. It also looked for answers to questions of faith and knowledge beyond the confines of official church dogma. Though part of a larger international movement, Russian Theosophy preserved a fundamentally nationalistic and messianic coloring, which no doubt accounts for a great deal of its appeal to certain elements within the God-seeking intelligentsia, who saw in Theosophy confirmation of their own eclectic and syncretic patterns of religious and creative thought.

Not all Russian intellectuals came under Theosophy's spell. In November 1909, when the Russian Theosophical Society's president, Anna Kamenskaia, was the invited speaker at a meeting of the St. Petersburg Religious-Philosophical Society, she was condescendingly baited by Dmitry Merezhkovsky, the novelist and philosopher who advocated his own nontraditional religious philosophy of the Third Revelation. Nevertheless, several leading members of the Russian creative intelligentsia were involved in Theosophy, using its imagery in their work, using its worldview to inform their own, and finding in its cosmogony the roots of their own creative process. They included (at various times) Andrei Bely, who later came under the spell of Rudolf Steiner and embraced his Christianized, Western form of Theosophy, Anthroposophy; the writer and translator Ellis (Bely's friend Lev Kobylinsky), the

---

10. The impetus for Spiritualism, by contrast, came from women (the Fox sisters) but the movement was dominated by men, and its Russian (and Western) adherents seem to have been evenly divided between the sexes. Theosophy was founded by a woman and its strongest leaders were women; its membership was dominated by women.

quintessential unsettled seeker, who sampled everything from Marxism to Catholic mysticism, and tasted of Theosophy as well; Aleksei Petrovsky, Mikhail Sizov, Nikolai Kiselev, and especially Pavel Batiushkov, all members of the Argonaut or Musaget circle; Anna Mintslova, a Blavatsky look-alike who Theosophized the mystically inclined Viacheslav Ivanov; the writers and philosophers P. D. Uspensky and Nikolai Berdiaev, who subsequently went on to other things: Uspensky became a modern guru, attempting to reconcile Occidental rationalism and Oriental mysticism, while Berdiaev was still refuting Theosophical doctrine as late as 1935; the novelist Olga Forsh in her impetuous youth; the poet Maks Voloshin and his wife, the painter Margarita Sabashnikova, who later turned to Anthroposophy; the composer Alexander Scriabin and the poet Konstantin Bal'mont, who remained Theosophists until their deaths; and the painter Vasily Kandinsky, whose modern art incorporated elements as diverse as Theosophical color theory and Siberian shamanism.

The Theosophists, like the Spiritualists and other occultists, did not fare well after the Bolshevik coup. The occult societies were persecuted from 1918 and all were closed by official decree in 1922; in the 1930s those members who had not emigrated were arrested. At the urging of Annie Besant, then president of the International Theosophical Society, Anna Kamenskaia decided to flee, and in the summer of 1921 she and a colleague made their way illegally to Finland, then to Belgium, and finally were sent by Mrs. Besant to Geneva. From there Anna Kamenskaia managed to reorganize the Russian Theosophical Society (Outside Russia) by 1924; it was rechartered by the Adyar Headquarters of the Theosophical Society on January 1, 1926. Kamenskaia ran the worldwide Russian branch from Geneva until her death in 1952, publishing the Geneva *Vestnik teosofii*, which united Russian Theosophists in China, Yugoslavia, North and South America, Europe, and even the East Indies. This tireless woman also acquired a doctorate and taught Buddhist philosophy at the University of Geneva. She and the Geneva Theosophists continued to work with various humanitarian organizations, including the League of Nations, as well as with various other peace, relief, and vegetarian organizations.

FREEMASONRY

Some reliable information is available about Russian Theosophy and Spiritualism, but the same cannot be said of Freemasonry. Writing about Freemasonry in Russia (or anywhere else) is a difficult task; there is both a wealth and a dearth of information, and little of it is reliable. Much of what we "know" is based on hearsay and anecdotal evidence provided by individuals and units who have only one small piece of a much larger mosaic and extrapolate freely and not always informedly about the contours and content of the larger picture. It is best to approach any text purporting to deal with Russian Masonry skeptically, as many such texts are contradictory and of uncertain accuracy.

A. V. Semeka has written that "in all the history of Russian culture it seems that there is no more tangled and complicated question than the one of the origin and subsequent development of Freemasonry in Russia."[11] Here, as in the case of most information about occult movements, caveat lector.

Even the definition of Freemasonry poses difficulties. A rite or an individual lodge of the brotherhood may be concerned with religious philosophy, occultism, ethics, morality, or philanthropy. The Masonic rituals and their symbolism derive from a broad range of mystic and occult systems, including Kabbala, Hermeticism, Alchemy, the ancient mystery religions, Gnosticism, Christianity, and Swedenborgianism. Like Theosophy, Masonry is eclectic and syncretic; "the Masonic idea is that religion is absolute, everlasting and unchanging; that it is not a dogma, or a collection of dogmas, but rather reverence and humility before the awful Ideas of Infinity and Eternity; a sense of subjection to the great law of Justice which stretches through the universe, and of obligation to love and serve man on earth, and God in heaven."[12] To this end Masonry, like Theosophy, freely adopts elements from a variety of religious systems and creates a diverse system of rituals. It emphasizes the concept of mystic "Quest" and uses the terminology of knighthood as a central metaphor for its strong initiatory features, which are constellated in a central pageant of figurative Death, Resurrection, and Rebirth and expressed through a complex system of arcane symbols.[13]

The actual origin of Freemasonry in Russia remains unclear, although most sources credit Captain John Philips and the Grand Lodge of England with introducing the order into Russia in 1731.[14] Although Philips was named provincial grand master for all Russia, his authority was limited to British and other European Masons living abroad. Not until 1740, when General James Keith replaced Philips as provincial grand master, were Russian members probably admitted to the "Craft," and then only in small numbers.

The first evidence of serious Russian involvement in Freemasonry appears

11. A. V. Semeka, "Russkoe masonstvo v XVIII veke," in *Masonstvo v ego proshlom i nastoiashchem*, ed. S. P. Mel'gunov and N. P. Sidorov, 2 vols. (1914; Moscow, 1991), 1:124.

12. Robert Macoy, *General History, Cyclopedia and Dictionary of Freemasonry* (New York, 1870), p. 324.

13. The images of knighthood, quest, beautiful lady, etc., so prevalent in Russian Symbolism, derive from many sources: revived literary and artistic interest in the medieval period, interest in Arthurian legend, renewed interest in courtoisie, the mystic operas of Richard Wagner. But another, completely overlooked source of such imagery was speculative Freemasonry, which claims a chivalric origin; perhaps even more relevant is the symbolism of its Rosicrucian variant, or emblematic Freemasonry.

14. See Macoy, *General History*, and A. E. Waite, *A New Encyclopedia of Freemasonry (Ars Magna Latomorum)*, 2 vols. in 1 (1937; New York, 1970). Needless to say, numerous apocryphal tales circulated about the early Russian Masons, including a popular story that Peter the Great had been initiated in England during his Grand Embassy; Semeka, "Russkoe masonstvo," suggests that the rumor started because the Masons held Peter in high regard as embodying the Enlightenment ideal of "transfiguring action" (p. 126).

only after 1750, with the founding of the Russian lodge Zur Verschwiegenheit; a second Russian lodge, Parfaite Union, appeared in 1771, followed by more than a dozen others during the 1770s. Between 1731 and 1771 Russians were not intensely drawn to Freemasonry, and it was considered an essentially "European amusement," associated initially with the British and subsequently with the ethnic and Russified Germans who filled the court of the empress Elizabeth (1741–61). Apathy was replaced by great enthusiasm during the early years of Catherine's reign (1762–96), as the more sophisticated, better-educated, and well-traveled cream of Petersburg male society, including the leading princely families (the Golitsyns, Trubetskoys, Vorontsovs, Gagarins, and Shcherbatovs), were attracted to Masonry.

The subsequent popularity of the Russian Masonic movement in the late eighteenth and early nineteenth centuries cannot be denied. Distinguished political and literary figures, including Count Ivan Perfil'evich Elagin (1725–94), a social lion and friend of Catherine the Great; the judge and social thinker Ivan Vladimirovich Lopukhin (1756–1816); the influential courtier and diplomat Count Nikita Ivanovich Panin (1718–83); Tsar Peter III; Catherine's generals Aleksandr Suvorov (1730–1800) and Prince Mikhail Kutuzov (1745–1813); her favorite, Grigory Orlov (1734–1783); the writer and publisher Nikolai Novikov (1744–1818); the popular dramatists Vladimir Lukin (1737–94), Denis Fonvizin (1744–92), and Aleksandr Griboedov (1795–1829); the poet Vasily Maikov (1728–78); the writers Aleksandr Sumarokov (1717–77) and Mikhail Kheraskov (1733–1807); the social thinkers Aleksandr Radishchev (1749–1802) and Petr Chaadaev (1794–1856); the belletrist and historian Nikolai Karamzin (1766–1826); and the Russian national poet, Aleksandr Pushkin (1799–1837), as well as his father and grandfather, were all active Masons. Many of the Decembrists belonged to Masonic lodges, as did Konstantin Pavlovich, the older brother of Nicholas I. These Russian Masons, whether of the politicized or mystical stamp, were the spiritual godfathers of both the Westernizer and Slavophile intelligentsia.

Russian Freemasonry flourished during the 1770s and 1780s. There were two fundamental systems, the Prussian Zinnendorf system (Berlin) and the English system, with a few independents, constituting some 100 named lodges.[15] Both eventually came under the authority of Count Ivan Elagin, Russia's most famous Mason; on February 26, 1772, the English Grand Lodge named him provincial grand master. Shortly afterward (in 1776) the Prussian lodges were subsumed under his English aegis as English-Prussian Masonic relations readjusted themselves. The merger was not successful. In 1784 the Elagin lodges closed without explanation and with the members' agreement. Certainly one

---

15. The English Masons had a three-degree system, essentially humanitarian, philanthropic, and rational; the German Zinnendorf system consisted of initially seven degrees, later nine, and was based on mystical Pietism.

determinant here was the fact that Russian Freemasonry was limited in the number of degrees it could award, and preference eventually went to the Prussian-Swedish system.

Russian Freemasonry was essentially divided into rational St. Petersburg Masonry and mystical Moscow Masonry. An important role in its subsequent development was played by Johann Georg Schwarz (1751–84), a German Freemason who in 1779 was named a professor at Moscow University. An occultist, alchemist, and disciple of the German mystic Jacob Boehme, Schwarz introduced the Western mystical tradition into Russia through his translations; after 1781 he established a Russian branch of the Order of Rosicrucians (authorized by Prussian Masonic circles). A close colleague of Nikolai Novikov's, Schwarz through his work and influence paved the way for the Russian Schellingians of the early nineteenth century and moved the Masonic center of weight from St. Petersburg to Moscow. The eighteenth-century Russian culture, having borrowed Enlightenment rationalism and Voltairean skepticism from the West (thus shutting the door on traditional religion), also borrowed Freemasonry, the West's mystical-religious response to excessive rationalism. The Masonic influence, in its more antirational, individualistic, mystical, and symbolic branches, would lead naturally into Sentimentalism and Romanticism; its more rational, politicized branches would lead into the liberalism of the Decembrist movement.

The relationship between the Masonic lodges and the Russian court in the eighteenth century was relatively neutral at the beginning. Elizabeth looked benignly on the Craft, and Tsar Peter III was himself a Freemason and conducted his own lodge. During the early years of Catherine II's reign, Russian Masons succeeded in organizing into a national grand lodge. But concerned by the possible political ramifications of secret societies in the aftermath of the American and French revolutions, Catherine II, who initially had been sympathetic to Freemasonry, banned all Masonic activity by the end of her reign. Her interdiction was supported by her son Paul, but Masonic activities continued, albeit quietly. Whether or not Catherine's grandson, Alexander I, was an initiate remains unknown, but Masonic lodges flourished during his reign after 1808. The lodges united again under the authority of the Prussian-Swedish grand lodge Vladimir zur Ordnung until 1815, when the preference again went to the three-degree Astrea of the English system. The two parallel systems existed until 1822, representing an estimated 3,300 influential members.[16] In 1822 Alexander I unexpectedly issued a decree prohibiting all secret societies in general and closing Masonic lodges in particular.

16. James Clark, *Modern Encyclopedia of Russian and Soviet History,* ed. Joseph L. Wieczynski, vol. 12 (Gulf Breeze, 1981), p. 16. Although almost half of the members were foreigners, this number is nevertheless impressive, given the small number of educated Russian elite. An additional 5,000 Masons were in Poland and the Baltic.

From 1822 until the end of the nineteenth century, the Russian Masonic lodges remained more or less dutifully dormant. Some of them continued their philanthropic activities without attracting official scrutiny; others met at great risk and in secret. Officially forbidden, the movement also survived by taking an active part in European lodge life. Many Russians became members of lodges in France, England, and particularly Germany. By the turn of the century, with the renewal of interest in things occult and mystical, Russian Freemasonry emerged again to become popular in all its manifestations (political, social, esoteric, etc.).

Russian Masonry came into its own again after the October Manifesto of 1905 eased many restrictions, and Russian Masonry experienced a revival between 1905 and 1908, aided particularly by the French Freemasons. Between 1906 and 1908 a Russian scholar living in France, Maksim Kovalevsky, established two major Russian lodges (Vozrozhdenie in Moscow and Poliarnaia Zvezda in St. Petersburg) under the aegis of Le Grand Orient of France. Their members included Nikolai Bazhenov, Vasily Nemirovich-Danchenko, Evgeny Anichkov, Ivan Loris-Mel'nikov, Prince Sergei Urusov, and others (lawyers, university professors, doctors, writers, other professionals, and civic leaders). These lodges were soon overshadowed by others with more politicized agendas, and there seems to be little question but that Masonic lodges played a role in the events of 1916–17.

After 1911 national Russian Masonic lodges proliferated in every area of the Russian empire, in parallel with the Spiritualist societies, Theosophical branches, and other occult movements. The exoteric Masons even assayed their own journal, the short-lived *Russkii Frank-Mason: Svobodnyi kamenshchik* (Russian Freemason), in 1908. Unlike the earlier lodges, which were exclusively male, many post-1911 lodges accepted women as members. They tended to be highly politicized, leaning toward the liberal or moderate left.

By February 1917 there were twenty-eight known major (and many more minor) Masonic lodges in Russia, together boasting some 2,500 members. The movement had permeated every level of Russian professional and intellectual life. Nina Berberova points out that "at this time—from the start of the First World War and right up to February 1917—there was no profession, institution, civic or private society, organization, or group in Russia without Masons."[17]

The Masonic phenomenon in Russia was not monolithic. The lodges varied not only in their rites and the degrees they recognized but in their purposes and doctrines. Untangling them is frankly impossible, at least for the uninitiated. The whole is complicated by the fact that Russian Freemasonry, like European Freemasonry, had always been closely associated with Rosicrucianism, Martinism, Theosophy, and other occult movements.

17. Nina Berberova, *Liudi i lozhi: Russkie masony XX stoletiia* (New York, 1986), p. 20.

Although the Masons claim to trace their ritualistic roots back to the master craftsmen who built the Temple of Solomon ("operative Masonry"), some Masonic orders have claimed that the origin of "speculative Masonry" (emblematic, symbolic, or "Free" Masonry) actually lay in medieval Rosicrucianism.[18] "Rosicrucianism" is one of those indeterminate concepts capable of multiple definitions. The term may be used as a synonym for Hermeticism, or mystical alchemy, or it may refer to a probably mythical fifteenth-century esoteric order founded by one Christian Rosenkreutz, who traveled to the Orient to learn its mysteries. Rudolf Steiner's Anthroposophy identified the concept with a Western-style occult initiation heavily characterized by esoteric Christian features. Meanwhile, eclectic Freemasonry incorporated some aspects of Rosicrucianism as well. Since several of the earliest English Freemasons (Robert Fludd, Elias Ashmole, and other seventeenth-century initiates) were alchemists, we should not be surprised. Like Freemasonry and Theosophy, Rosicrucianism claimed to have preserved and transmitted ancient truths unimpaired from the distant Gnostic past to modern initiates. Various Masonic rites have orders or degrees of the Rosy Cross (or Rose Croix).

A new complication was added with Martinism, which is, very generally speaking, a merging of Freemasonry and Rosicrucianism. The Martinists saw themselves as direct heirs of the medieval Rosicrucians. Martinism embraced all forms of occultism, although in its more exoteric form it focused almost exclusively on ethics. Members were called knights (*rytsari*), even "knights of Christ." "The contemporary Martinists represent a secular Christian order of knights," wrote an anonymous occultist in a 1910 Russian study of Martinism.[19] Martinism does contain strong elements of esoteric Christianity, but was always strongly anticlerical and anti-Catholic.

The Martinist order was organized by Louis Claude de Saint-Martin (1743–1803), a French Rosicrucian who saw himself as "Guardian of the Secret Legends of Antiquity" transmitted by the Brotherhood of the Rosicrucians and other secret societies. His Martinism included materials from Jacob Boehme, Martínez Pasquales, the tarot, Hermeticism, alchemy, and Christian mystical theology, to mention only a few of its sources. It struck a cord with many Russian Masons; Lopukhin first published Saint-Martin's *Des erreurs et de la vérité* (1775) in Russian translation in 1785, and this small volume by *le philosophe inconnu* soon became an influential text in late eighteenth-century Russian Masonic circles.

---

18. Speculative or "Free" Masonry has been defined as "the scientific application and the religious consecration of the rules and principles, the technical language and the implements and materials, of operative Masonry to the worship of God as the Grand Architect of the universe, and the purification of the heart and the inculcation of the dogmas of a religious philosophy": Macoy, *General History,* p. 277, 1st pagination.

19. "Orden Martinistov: Istoricheskii ocherk," *Izida,* 1910, no. 1, p. 14.

Late nineteenth-century Martinism was closely allied with the Ordre Kabbalistique de la Rose-Croix, founded by the marquis Stanislas de Guaita (1860–97), a French Decadent occultist, in the 1880s. In 1910 the head of both the Martinists and the Ordre de la Rose-Croix was Gérard Encausse (1865–1916), better known by his "occult" name, Papus. Papus was the author of dozens of the best-known occult texts of the late nineteenth and early twentieth centuries, an expert on everything from alchemy to Kabbala to the tarot. He also held high-ranking Masonic and Rosicrucian posts, was the head of the Faculté des Sciences Hermétiques of the Université Libre des Hautes Etudes in Paris, and briefly served as a member of the General Council of the Theosophical Society. That all these streams converged in a single individual gives some indication of their doctrinal similarities.

Papus reestablished and updated the Martinist order, which soon achieved great popularity in Russia and Italy. Between 1900 and 1905, on one of several visits to Russia, Papus reputedly established a Martinist lodge at the court in St. Petersburg, together with another occultist, Dr. Philippe (Philippe Nizier-Anthèlme Vachod, also Maître Philippe de Lyon, 1849–1905), the monk Grigory Rasputin's predecessor as "friend" to the court of Nicholas II. Rumors persist that Tsar Nicholas II belonged to the Lodge of the Cross and Star; his uncles Nikolai Nikolaevich and Petr Nikolaevich, as well as the grand duke Georgy Mikhailovich, were members. It is true that Martinism had become very popular in Russia by 1905; it waned after 1916.

Close ties also existed between the Russian Masonic lodges (especially those of the more mystical Rosicrucian bent) at the turn of the century and certain of the more esoteric Theosophical circles. Mme Blavatsky herself claimed to belong to an obscure Masonic order called the Royal Oriental Order of Sat B'hai, and Dr. Rudolf Steiner, Annie Besant, the Reverend C. W. Leadbeater, and other prominent Theosophists were associated with various Masonic orders. Many Russian Theosophists belonged to various lodges, both at home and abroad. Nina Berberova even claims that "the Lucifer Lodge, founded about 1910 and very short lived, was close to the Martinists. According to certain documents, not entirely reliable, several Symbolist poets belonged to it, including Viacheslav Ivanov, [Valery] Briusov, [Andrei] Bely, and Bely's friend A[leksei] Petrovsky."[20] Her claim has some foundation.[21]

The Soviets first politicized and then attempted to destroy all trace of the Russian Masonic movement. We may never know the entire extent of this fascinating movement in Russia. Like other popular occult movements, however, it left its mark on the Russian national psyche.

20. Berberova, *Liudi i lozhi*, p. 228.

21. Viacheslav Ivanov and Andrei Bely were certainly involved by Anna Mintslova in a Rosicrucian venture in 1909–10; for more information, see Maria Carlson, "Ivanov-Belyj-Minclova: The Mystical Triangle," in *Cultura e Memoria*, ed. Fausto Malcovati (Florence, 1988), pp. 63–79.

HERMETICISM

The least known and least documented of the four fashionable occult movements in Russia was Hermeticism. "Hermeticism" can be broadly or narrowly defined. In its broadest sense, the term may refer to any occult (in this case "sealed" or "cloistered" [hermetic]) teachings; in its most specific sense, "Hermeticism" refers to a specific body of mystery wisdom, gnostic in spirit, purportedly written by Hermes Trismegistus (Thrice-Great Hermes) sometime between the third century B.C. and the first century A.D. Like many occult systems, Hermeticism provides its more sophisticated and knowledgeable practitioners with an esoteric religious-philosophical system and satisfies less sophisticated tastes with an exoteric system of astrological, magical, and alchemical arts more suited to popular consumption.

Russian Hermeticism was the heir of the French occult revival of the second half of the nineteenth century; it signaled a reaction against the prevailing scientific positivism and gained particular popularity among the French Decadents and Symbolists.[22] Its recognized leader was Eliphas Lévi (Alphonse-Louis Constant, 1810–75), a defrocked French priest who had a long-standing interest in occult and mystical philosophy. Starting almost alone, he gathered around him a group of devout if eccentric disciples, and soon made France the vanguard of the occult renascence. His studies, although vague, Romantic, and often contradictory, became increasingly popular and are considered occult classics even today.

Not only was Eliphas Lévi himself an important figure of the French occult revival, but his occult works, especially his *Histoire de la magie* (1860), influenced the work of many others. Lévi and the French occultists had an important influence on the Symbolist writers (Baudelaire, Rimbaud, Verlaine, Villiers de L'Isle-Adam, and Huysmans), the painters of the Salon de la Rose-Croix, the Nabis (especially Paul Serusier and Paul Ranson), Odilon Redon, Puvis de Chavannes, Gustave Moreau, and Jean Delville, as well as on the Dutch artist Jan Toorop, the English Pre-Raphaelites, the scandalous poets Algernon Charles Swinburne and Oscar Wilde, and, both directly and indirectly, the Russian Decadents. The British writer Edward Bulwer-Lytton, a Rosicrucian, put Lévi and his philosophy into his popular novels. The Hermetic Order of the Golden Dawn, whose members included the Theosophically inclined Irish poet William Butler Yeats and the scholar A. E. Waite, attempted to synthesize the vast and bewildering body of occult material into a system, using Eliphas Lévi's works as its foundation. Many other occultists based their studies on Lévi's; even the wonderfully eccentric Mme Blavatsky leaned heavily on

22. For literary-intellectual connections, see Philippe Jullian, *Dreamers of Decadence*, trans. Robert Baldick (London, 1971), and Jean Pierrot, *The Decadent Imagination, 1880–1900*, trans. Derek Coltman (Chicago, 1981).

Lévi's work for her own Theosophical classics, injecting Hermetic materials into her highly syncretic Theosophical doctrine.

The French occult revival, once started, generated interest in many mystical systems. Gnosticism, ancient Hermeticism, medieval philosophical alchemy, astrology (traditional and Oriental), Kabbala, Eastern mysticism, black and white magic, Rosicrucianism, the tarot, and some forms of mystical Freemasonry were rediscovered and popularized under the rubric of "Hermetic arts." As the French occult revival configured French Decadence and Symbolism in the arts in France, so it acted on the arts of Russia.

These interests, intersecting with the rage for Spiritualism, in turn generated additional curiosity about chiromancy, hypnotism, somnambulism, geomancy, phrenology, and fortune-telling. These more sensational forms of popular occultism entertained the middle and lower classes, whether predigested for them by Sofia Tukholka, whose popular handbook *Okkul'tizm i magiia* (Occultism and magic) went through numerous editions, or retold for them by Vladimir Zapriagaev, who made a small fortune by paraphrasing European and American occult texts in Russian and issuing ephemerides for Russian astrologers.[23] As in our own fin de siècle, books on dream interpretation, fortune-telling, horoscopes, magic, chiromancy, witchcraft, and hypnotism sold steadily and well.

An important figure in the history of Russian hermetic interests was the ubiquitous Papus (Gérard Encausse), the leading French occult scholar of the fin de siècle. Eleven of his many works on Kabbala, alchemy, spiritualism, Rosicrucianism, Freemasonry, and the tarot were translated into Russian. His Faculté des Sciences Hermétiques attracted Russian students to its occult curriculum, which became the basis of numerous private courses of occult study in Russia. Papus, with his influential Masonic and Rosicrucian connections, served as an important link between Russian occultists and the French occult revival.

Though the Hermetic arts in their elite manifestation were popular with a certain refined audience in Russia, this audience was small and its influence was minimal. The Russian Hermeticists, headed by Ivan Antoshevsky and Aleksandr Troianovsky, published their own journal, *Izida: Ezhemesiachnyi zhurnal okkul'tnykh nauk* (Isis: Monthly journal of occult sciences, 1909–16) and subsidized the translation and publication of occult classics, but they maintained a very low profile in Russian public life. They distinguished themselves and their "serious occult labors" from the more "fashionable" Hermeticists who made the front pages, such as Czeslaw von Czinski (who published under

---

23. Among Zapriagaev's occult best-sellers were *Svet Egipta* (Viaz'ma, 1906) and *Astrologiia v nashi dni* (Viaz'ma, 1908), a paraphrase of Thomas Burgoyne's *Light of Egypt; or The Science of the Soul and the Stars,* 2 vols. (1889–1900). The works were very popular in Russia.

the pseudonym Punar Bhava). Czinski, calling himself a professor of occult sciences and a disciple of Papus, made outrageous claims about his esoteric abilities and offered to initiate St. Petersburg occultists into the most elite occult and Masonic organizations for only 500 rubles. Although he had patrons in high places, Czinski was eventually forced by the authorities to leave St. Petersburg and Russia.

Unlike the clannish Spiritualists, Theosophists, and Masons, the Hermeticists, who viewed themselves as truly serious occultists, tended to study independently, to avoid organizations and societies, and to work in secret. As the "scholarly" occultists, they contributed to the culture of the period by providing primary materials, translating European occult classics into Russian, doing bibliographic work, and rescuing ancient texts from oblivion. The materials they compiled were frequently used by the Theosophists and others.

CONCLUSION

The impact of the various popular occult movements on Russian fin-de-siècle society and culture was more significant than is generally realized today. Occultism offered everything from popular entertainment and literary inspiration to scientific adventurousness and philosophical stimulation; in some cases it even served as a substitute for religion. The popularity of the occult in Russia is attested to by the publication of more than thirty Russian journals and well over 800 discrete book titles (exclusive of belles-lettres) dealing with such subjects between 1881 and 1918.

As in Europe, the widespread Russian interest in the fashionable forms of occultism was a middle- and upper-class response to the larger crisis of culture and consciousness broadly experienced by a European society tired of scientific empiricism and positivism. Séances, mediums, mahatmas, and magic were more fun than Marx and Mendeleev and soon became part of the language of daily communication. Modern scholars who become more aware of the esoteric and occult interests of European and Russian fin-de-siècle society (a subject most twentieth-century historians have chosen to ignore) will be able to decipher more easily the elusive and frequently puzzling images and references in the art and literature of the period, and to entertain new perspectives and interpretive possibilities that will allow them to approach fin-de-siècle culture and society with increased understanding and insight.

CHAPTER SIX
ANTHROPOSOPHY IN RUSSIA
Renata von Maydell

In December 1990 the Anthroposophical Society in Russia—successor to the Russian Anthroposophical Society, which functioned from 1913 to 1923—held its first meeting. In the early decades of this century, Anthroposophy was part of a philosophical and literary discussion shaped by Symbolism; today its followers focus on applying its precepts as guides to action in a country where all paths to a fulfilling social life seem to have come to a dead end. Once again interest in Anthroposophy is growing in the midst of radical social changes and revolutionary events; now again Anthroposophy stands not only for a weltanschauung but for close contact with Western Europe.

When Rudolf Steiner (1861–1925) reflected on the history of civilization, he envisioned a special role for Russia, because he considered Russia the country that could best embody the spirit of a new cultural epoch. In Russia Anthroposophy developed beyond the mere study of an esoteric doctrine and its theory of knowledge. Anthroposophy sought to evaluate Russian and Soviet reality concretely, to interpret Russia's historical development in the context of world history, and to become the basis of action for Russian cultural activities. Russian Anthroposophy is more than a variant of the Anthroposophical movement. Russia occupies a prominent place in the Anthroposophical conception of culture.

In 1902 Steiner became general secretary of the newly founded German section of the Theosophical Society. Regarding Christianity as superior to other religions, he argued against the Theosophists' practice of assigning equal importance to Hinduism and Buddhism. When the Theosophists proclaimed the Hindu boy Krishnamurti a reincarnation of Christ in 1912, the German section of the Theosophical Society withdrew from the organization and most of its members followed Steiner into the Anthroposophical Society.

According to the Anthroposophical doctrine established by Steiner, the development of the human capacity for cognition leads to a progressive revelation of the spiritual being in the world and in man (Steiner, a man of his time, used "man" in the generic sense). This was the basis of the Anthroposophical striving for holistic completeness in the development of personality, on the one hand, and in the social context of the community, on the other. Steiner described the ideal of a threefold human being, developed in every respect, who realized his or her inner capacities of thinking, feeling, and acting in the material, spiritual, and metaphysical worlds.[1]

According to Steiner, only a community of harmoniously developed personalities who had undergone this training could succeed in the tasks that would face humanity in the future. A relationship would have to be established between spirit and matter, science and mysticism, religion and civilization, philosophy and concrete action. Anthroposophy offered the possibility of applying a holistic, idealistic doctrine practically, concretely, in education, agriculture, medicine, religion, art, and politics. Steiner divided the "social organism" into three realms, which he linked to the slogan of the French Revolution: culture was related to liberty, politics and law to equality, and economy to fraternity. Each of these fields was to develop independently within the framework of a triadic society.[2]

Steiner structured the history of civilization in seven (post-Atlantean) periods: Indian, ancient Persian, Egyptian-Chaldean, Greek-Roman, Central European, Slavic, and American. According to his scheme, humanity stood at the end of the fifth, the Central European period—that is, at the threshold of the sixth, Slavic period. The fifth post-Atlantean epoch began in the first half of the fifteenth century among the Germanic peoples. It manifested itself through an increase in individualism and through a growing interest in the sciences and technology. Around the year 3500, this era of perception was to be succeeded by the sixth epoch, the epoch of the "Spirit Self," in which the charac-

1. Rudolf Steiner refers here to the anthropological understanding of ancient Greece. The trinity of body, soul, and spirit constitutes the basis of his philosophy of cognition. In his *Wie erlangt man Erkenntnisse der höheren Welten* (Dornach, 1982; published in English as *Knowledge of the Higher Worlds—How Is It Achieved* [London, 1985]) he describes a way of grasping areas of metaphysics by exact thinking and self-training.

2. See Rudolf Steiner, *Die Kernpunkte der sozialen Frage in den Lebensnotwendigkeiten der Gegenwart und Zukunft* (Dornach, 1919); published in English as *Towards Social Renewal: Back Issues of the Social Question* (London, 1977). A Russian translation of his earlier essay "Geisteswissenschaft und soziale Frage" (1905–6) was published in *Vestnik teosofii* as early as 1912; in 1917 the publisher Dukhovnoe Znanie issued it in book form. Here Steiner combined Theosophical and social questions and formulated his "fundamental social law," aimed at the separation of labor and income: everyone is to work for the community and to be supported by the community without respect to his or her labor.

teristics of the Slavic people were to prevail: a sense of community, selflessness, patience, and the ability to accept higher truth.[3]

These qualities constitute the basis and the "seed" of the world spirit's incarnation in the Russian people; according to Steiner, the broad Russian masses already carried in them the seed of the coming civilization. Steiner used the image of "seed" repeatedly to describe the state of Russia's development; that is, the "embryonic, nuclear state of the East" as opposed to the "hypertrophy" of the West.[4] The spirit of the Russian people was "young and fresh in its hopes" and "yet to confront its task."[5] This task, to suffuse all aspects of life with a new meaning, would be realized only in the course of history. Steiner called the Russian a child, in whose very soul one could find the questions that must be answered if humanity was to master its future. From these Russian character traits Steiner derived the capability of holistic thinking. In the Russian way of thinking, as he saw it, two opposing concepts can hold sway simultaneously, so that rationality was mysticism and mysticism was rationality. "The Russian does not have the slightest understanding of what Westerners call 'reasonableness.' He is accessible to what could be termed 'revelation.' Basically, he will accept and integrate into the contents of his soul anything he owes to a kind of revelation."[6]

Another characteristic of the Russian people manifested itself in its understanding of Christ, Steiner claimed. The Russians had kept their souls open to the "continuous influx of the Christ-impulse."[7] That is how they became Christ's own people; Christ was present in them as an aura, determining their thoughts and feelings (for the soul has no physical appearance, and can be discerned only by the spiritual eye). The evidence of this impulse can be seen in Vladimir Soloviev's understanding of Christ, which was like "the dawn announcing the rise of a new civilization."[8] In Soloviev's philosophy Steiner

3. Rudolf Steiner, *Menschenschicksale und Völkerschicksale*, vol. 157 of *Rudolf Steiner Gesamtausgabe* (hereafter *RSGA*) (Dornach, 1981), lecture of January 17, 1915, p. 89; published in English as *Destinies of Individuals and Nations* (London, 1987). See also Sergej O. Prokofieff, *Die geistigen Quellen Osteuropas und die künftigen Mysterien des Heiligen Gral* (Dornach, 1989).

4. See Rudolf Steiner, *Menschliche und menschheitliche Entwicklungswahrheiten*, vol. 176 of *RSGA* (Dornach, 1982), July 24 1917, p. 189; published in English as *Aspects of Human Evolution* (New York, 1987). See also *Menschenschicksale und Völkerschicksale*, June 22, 1915, p. 279; *Geschichtliche Symptomatologie*, vol. 185 of *RSGA* (Dornach, 1987), October 20, 1918, p. 72; published in English as *From Symptom to Reality in Modern History* (London, 1976).

5. Rudolf Steiner, *Die okkulten Grundlagen der Bhagavad Gita*, vol. 146 of *RSGA* (Dornach, 1962), June 5, 1913, p. 87; published in English as *Occult Significance of the Bhagavad Gita* (New York, 1985).

6. Rudolf Steiner, *Die neue Geistigkeit und das Christus-Erlebnis des zwanzigsten Jahrhunderts*, vol. 200 of *RSGA* (Dornach, 1970), October 23, 1920, p. 60; published in English as *New Spirituality and the Christ Experience of the Twentieth Century* (London, 1988).

7. Steiner, *Geschichtliche Symptomatologie*, November 2, 1918, p. 184.

8. Rudolf Steiner, *Die Mission einzelner Volksseelen*, vol. 121 of *RSGA* (Dornach, 1962), June 16, 1910, p. 178; published in English as *The Mission of Folk-souls* (London, 1970).

saw the seed of the philosophy of the "Spirit Self" of the sixth epoch, for here the religious and philosophical worldviews merged; Soloviev's philosophy spoke the language of religion, while his religion strove to be a philosophical worldview.[9] And, according to Steiner, this was where the superiority of the Russian philosophy over the aging Western philosophy lay: it transcended Hegel's and Kant's views, the fruit of the fifth epoch, because it transcended the limits of reason and it built a basis for a new holistic understanding.

In order to develop its capacities and to fulfill its mission, Steiner said, the Russian people needed contact with the West; the "female East" should be impregnated by the "male West." Intellectuality and technology, the achievement and problem of the fifth epoch of civilization, had led the life force to stagnate in Europe. Meanwhile this life force was at work in Russia, but was so lacking in form that it could fall into chaos. That was why Steiner felt that Russia depended on a Western awareness of form and consciousness. "To imagine that the East, at its present state, would develop on its own would be comparable to the foolish hope of a woman who wanted to have a child without a man."[10] In the past, Eastern Europe had proved its receptiveness to the West; Steiner pointed to the reception of the Byzantine religion in Russia.[11] Thus the Slavic peoples showed that they were also capable of absorbing higher truths—that is, the spirit of the sixth epoch.

Steiner thus gave Russia a perspective on its future that included a reconsideration of its roots. His conception of the world harmonized with the tension built up by the Russian dualism of renovation and conservation, East and West. For the Russian Anthroposophists, Steiner embodied Western ideas, the "foreign," as well as Slavic thought, their own, since he linked the Eastern mysticism of Theosophy with Christian doctrine and a rationalistic Western approach. Moreover, certain elements of the Anthroposophical worldview corresponded with trends within the Russian intelligentsia: the striving for an all-comprising synthesis and a holistic worldview reflected Russian efforts to create an action-oriented philosophy—a philosophy that would enable an idealistic conception of the world to be applied to concrete actions. Steiner was an ardent student of Russian literature and philosophy, including the literature that influenced the Russian intelligentsia at the beginning of the century.[12] This

9. Rudolf Steiner, *Der Goetheanumgedanke inmitten der Kulturkrisis der Gegenwart: Ausgewählte Aufsätze, 1921–1925*, vol. 36 of *RSGA* (Dornach, 1961), p. 64.

10. Steiner, *Menschenschicksale und Völkerschicksale*, January 17, 1915, p. 88.

11. Rudolf Steiner, *Die geistigen Hintergründe des ersten Weltkrieges*, vol. 174b of *RSGA* (Dornach, 1973), March 12, 1916, p. 140.

12. Steiner was extremely well read. His studies of Goethe are central to his work. He sees what he calls "Goetheanism"—Goethe's method of cognition and his manner of artistic productivity—as a counterpart to a rational, merely analytical philosophy, such as Kant's. He was introduced to Russian literature mainly by his wife, Marie von Sivers (1867–1948), whose German family had settled in Russia. Von Sivers played a major role in the development of eurythmy and in the Anthroposophical movement. She read to Steiner the Russian

study led to a certain spiritual closeness between Steiner and Andrei Bely, even before the two had met.

Interest in Anthroposophy was not limited to any particular social stratum in Russia. The majority of followers, however, came from a secure background, from circles that offered an opportunity to concentrate on spiritual questions and the financial resources for travel to the West. Most Anthroposophists were poets, artists, scientists, teachers, and doctors. About half of the active members were women. In Anthroposophy the intelligentsia continued their attempt to achieve a convergence of secular and spiritual culture. Many Russian Anthroposophists saw themselves as part of the tradition of the Symbolists, who had helped create religious-philosophical meetings and societies at the beginning of the century. Theosophy is rarely compatible with the Russian Orthodox faith, but Anthroposophy is strongly oriented toward Christianity, embodies a way that leads to a new Christianity, and thus is easier to reconcile with Christian traditions.

Steiner saw a symbolic significance in the fact that Anthroposophy in Russia evolved out of contacts that members of the intelligentsia maintained with the West: in 1912 he said that Anthroposophy, whose roots are to be found in Russia (he was referring to the Ukrainian Elena Blavatsky), should return to Russia by way of India, the Americas, and Europe, thereby coming full circle.[13]

As early as 1913, interest in Steiner led to the founding of the Vladimir Soloviev Russian Anthroposophical Society in Moscow. Even before Steiner broke from the Theosophical Society, a division had opened up between Russian Theosophical groups that were oriented toward England and those that were allied with the Russian Symbolists. The latter groups had met mainly through the Symbolist publishing house Musaget, headed by Emily Karlovich Medtner, and were already oriented toward Germany. These meetings provided the framework for courses and workshops on the philosophy and literature of Symbolism as well as on the Theosophical worldview (based on Steiner's work). Bely and his friend Lev Kobylinsky-Ellis influenced these activities significantly.[14]

---

classics as well as contemporary literature. He reflected a lot on Soloviev, Dostoevsky, Tolstoy, and the Slavophile writers, especially Aleksei Khomiakov. Bely remembered that von Sivers read Steiner the works of Aleksandr Pushkin, Aleksei Koltsov, and Vladimir Soloviev, and that Steiner recited, inter alia, Dmitry Merezhkovsky and Akim Flekser-Volynsky. According to Bely, Steiner was also familiar with the works of such contemporary philosophers as Sergei Bulgakov, Nikolai Berdiaev, and Dmitry Filosofov, and he thought highly of Russian folk art. See Andrei Belyi, *Vospominaniia o Shteinere* (Paris, 1982), pp. 31, 71, 72, 292.

13. Rudolf Steiner, *Die geistigen Wesenheiten in den Himmelskörpern und Naturreichen*, vol. 136, of *RSGA* (Dornach, 1960), April 11, 1912, p. 202; published in English as *The Spiritual Beings in the Heavenly Bodies* (Hastings, E. Sussex, 1989). He depicts Blavatsky as a woman with Russian characteristics who went to extremes, did not think logically, and remained childlike, but precisely for that reason was receptive to higher powers.

14. See Victor B. Fedjuschin, *Russlands Sehnsucht nach Spiritualität: Theosophie, Anthro-*

Many members of the Musaget staff attended the Theosophical discussions and workshops, which were held in the apartment of the economist Boris Pavlovich Grigorov (1883–1945) and his wife, Nadezhda Afanasieva Grigorova, née Baryshkina (1885–1964). They got to know Steiner in Bern in 1910 and from then on stayed in close contact with the Theosophical / Anthroposophical movement in Germany. Many members of their circle traveled to Helsinki, Germany, and Switzerland to hear Steiner speak. From 1913 to 1917 people and information flowed constantly between the Swiss town of Dornach, the center of Anthroposophy, and Russia. Many Russians went to Dornach to help in the construction of the first "Goetheanum," Steiner's headquarters.[15] During that time the Anthroposophical Society in Moscow organized a large variety of meetings and lectures presided over by Grigorov, Bely, Klavdiia Nikolaevna Vasileva (1886–1970, Bely's future wife),[16] and the literary critic Mikhail Pavlovich Stoliarov (1888–1937). In addition, the Anthroposophists founded a publishing house, Dukhovnoe Znanie (Spiritual knowledge), which from 1912 to 1920 published translations of Steiner's work and other Anthroposophical literature.

The February Revolution was generally well received by the Russian Anthroposophists, who hoped it would enable them to spread Anthroposophical ideas further and even to implement them in some areas of social life, especially in the arts and in educational theory. The artist Margarita Vasilevna Sabashnikova-Voloshina (1882–1973) remembered those days as a period of particular freedom, for one could spread Anthroposophy in public lectures,

posophie, Rudolf Steiner und die Russen (Schaffhausen, 1988), pp. 98–102. Medtner, although critical of Anthroposophy, thought highly of Bely's work and opened the publishing house as a platform for discussions, which in turn led to the publication of Ellis [Lev Kobylinskii], *Vigilemus!* (Moscow, 1914) and of Volfing [Emilii Medtner], *Razmyshlenii o Gete. Kniga pervaia. Razbor vzgliadov R. Shteinera v sviazi s voprosami krititsizma, simvolizma i okkul'tizma* (Moscow, 1914). Belyi replied to Medtner in *Rudolf Shteiner i Gete v mirovozzrenii sovremennosti: Otvet Emiliiu Metneru na ego pervyi tom "Razmyshlenii o Gete"* (Moscow, 1917). The controversy led eventually to the schism between Medtner and the Anthroposophists. Medtner's papers (RO, RGB, f. 167) contain extensive correspondence on this topic. The polemics about those two works were kindled by Evgeny Trubetskoi, Ivan Il'in, and Sergei Bulgakov. This affair demonstrates Steiner's role in shaping the discussion on Goethe among the Russian intelligentsia.

15. The foundation stone of the first Goetheanum was laid in the fall of 1913 in Dornach, south of Basel. The building, featuring twin wooden cupolas, was erected according to Steiner's plans and under his supervision. Anthroposophists of many nationalities participated in the building, among them a large Russian group. In 1920 the first events took place in this "Free Academy of Spiritual Sciences." The building was destroyed by fire on New Year's Eve, 1922. In 1928 the second Goetheanum was inaugurated. A concrete building, it was based on plans made by Steiner shortly before his death. The Goetheanum is still the center of the Anthroposophical movement.

16. On her relation to Steiner, see Klawdija Bugaeva, *Wie eine russische Seele Rudolf Steiner erlebte*, trans. Elisabeth Ohlmann–v. Pusirewsky (Basel, 1987).

whereas before it had been restricted by the tsar's censorship.[17] Some Anthroposophists related Steiner's statements about Russia to the revolution, and they began to see the "worldwide significance of the Russian social revolution, this lightning flash, this eruption of the Russian people's soul and the anticipation of its spiritual-historical mission."[18] Some Russian Anthroposophists returned home from Dornach in 1917 to participate in campaigns for enlightenment and civilization (Steiner himself had engaged in the same kind of activity between 1899 and 1905, when he was teaching at the Berlin Workers' School, founded by Karl Liebknecht). Bely described his attitude toward his own cultural work this way: "In the changes I saw possibilities for the true Anthroposophist to implement cultural work according to the new principles in Russia. It is his task to take an active part in his country."[19] Bely saw Anthroposophy as "the predestination of the new civilization in Russia . . . the way is now free for Anthroposophy in Russia."[20]

Even though cultural work and campaigns for enlightenment were often their only sources of income and the living and working conditions were extremely hard, the Anthroposophists went about their work with passion and enthusiasm, which waned only under growing pressure from the state after the October Revolution.[21] When Sabashnikova was offered a job with Proletkult, she felt it was "the fulfillment of my soul's most profound desire to open art up to our people. I came from Dornach, from the source of the new artistic impulses, and I was allowed to work at a place that could set the standards for the proletariat all over Russia." Sabashnikova had returned to Russia in 1917 and worked in the painting department at Proletkult and in the drama department of Narkompros; she also gave lectures at the Anthropo-

---

17. Margarita Woloschin, *Die grüne Schlange: Lebenserinnerungen einer Malerin* (Frankfurt, 1987), p. 309. See also Ruth Moering, Dorothea Rapp, and Rosemarie Wermbter, *Margarita Woloschins Leben und Werk* (Stuttgart, 1982). Sabashnikova met Steiner in 1905 and became one of his followers. Both she and her husband, Maksimilian Voloshin, helped to build the first Goetheanum. She spent the years 1917 to 1922 in revolutionary Russia, then went to live in Germany.

18. Mariia Zhemchuzhnikova, "Vospominaniia o Moskovskom Antroposofskom Obshchestve (1917–23 gg.)," *Minuvshee*, vol. 6 (Paris, 1988), p. 106.

19. Andrei Belyi, *Pochemu ia stal simvolistom i pochemu ia ne perestal im byt' vo vsech fazakh moego ideinogo i khudozhestvennogo razvitiia* (1928; Ann Arbor, 1982), p. 108.

20. Andrej Bjely, "Die Anthroposophie und Rußland," *Die Drei* (Stuttgart), 1922, no. 5, p. 384.

21. In the following years a discussion emerged among the emigrants about Steiner's possible influence on the decision of Russian Anthroposophists to return to their revolutionary homeland. Valentin Zubov maintained that Trifon Trapeznikov had gone to Moscow because Steiner had welcomed the Revolution ("Institut istorii iskusstv: Stranitsy vospominanii," *Mosty*, 1963, no. 10, p. 374). Asia Turgeneva argued that Steiner had welcomed the Revolution as liberation from the autocracy, but that he had seen trouble ahead for Russia ("Po povodu 'Instituta istorii iskusstv,'" *Mosty*, 1968, no. 12, p. 360). Like Bely, Trapeznikov returned to Moscow in response to the military draft.

sophical Society in Moscow and taught eurythmy.[22] The Steiners had launched this motion art, "visible speech or visible music," in 1912, on the basis of Goethe's theory of metamorphosis—the idea that the whole of an organism is included in each of its parts. Thus the cosmic laws are included in every human organ, and through eurythmy one came into contact with the cosmos. Eurythmy was said to make spiritual laws and the qualities of language or music visible by gesture and movement, and to raise them to an artistic experience that exerted its influence on the entire human being. Sabashnikova was instructed by the first eurythmist, Lory Smits. From 1914 on, eurythmy instruction was offered at the Goetheanum by the Russian Anthroposophist Tatiana Kiseleva (1881–1970), who herself made significant contributions to its development.[23]

Like Sabashnikova, the art historian Trifon Georgievich Trapeznikov (1882–1926) returned to Moscow from Dornach in 1917; he was one of the leading organizers of the movement for the preservation of monuments between 1918 and 1924. This department of Narkompros was engaged in preserving Russia's cultural heritage, protecting it from pillage and registering the artworks held by the clergy and by private persons. The iconoclasm inherent in the Revolution had hardly been launched before it was countered by a movement to preserve the Russian artistic heritage.[24] For an Anthroposophist, to preserve works of art was to preserve the basis of Russian culture for the future tasks of the Russian people. After 1917 Stoliarov was busy lecturing at the Institute of the Word, the Palace of the Arts, and the State Academy of the Arts; in addition, he directed a literary studio in Proletkult.[25] The poet Nikolai Nikolaevich Belotsvetov (1892–1950), who stayed in Moscow until 1920, engaged in similar activities, lecturing on the metaphysical significance of the Revolution. In his lecture "Anthroposophy and Russian Reality" he called for the Revolution to be transformed into "Russian reality" with the help of Steiner's book *Wie erlangt man Erkenntnisse der höheren Welten* (How to attain knowledge of the higher world).[26]

Bely, who left Dornach in 1916 to return to Russia, was outstanding in his

22. Woloschin, *Die grüne Schlange*, p. 314. Through her official activities she established contact with Anatoly Lunacharsky, who, she reports, had been an enthusiastic reader of Steiner but was now detaching himself from him (p. 320).

23. From 1927 to 1939 Kiseleva taught eurythmy in Paris. See Tatiana Kisseleff, *Eurythmie-Arbeit mit Rudolf Steiner* (Basel, 1982). Bely wrote to Asia Turgeneva about his participation in Sabashnikova's eurythmy class; see George Nivat, "Lettres d'Andrej Belyj à la famille d' 'Asja,'" *Cahiers du monde russe et soviétique*) 18, nos. 1–2 (1977): 139.

24. See Richard Stites, *Revolutionary Dreams: Utopian Vision and Experimental Life in the Russian Revolution* (Oxford, 1989), pp. 76–78.

25. GAKhN, in RGALI, f. 941, op. 10, d. 597.

26. RO, RGB, f. 24. Belotsvetov's lectures for the society were published in his *Religiia tvorcheskoi voli: Chetyre lektsii o kulture budushchego, chitannye v Russkom Antroposofskom Obshchestve v 1915 g.* (Petrograd, 1915).

zeal to combine cultural and Anthroposophical activities. He participated in a great variety of projects, appeared at literary conferences and discussions, worked in the drama department of Narkompros and in Proletkult, and was active in the Anthroposophical Society.[27]

Before the Revolution Steiner had often expressed disapproval of the Russian monarchy, which he considered alien to the character of the Russian people; from 1918 on he criticized Bolshevism as an unhealthy combination of Western abstract thinking and Eastern mysticism.[28] At this time, however, only a few of his statements reached Russia from Dornach, because of the complicated postal and travel situation that prevailed from 1917 to 1920. Factions emerged in the Anthroposophical Society in Moscow when the group tried to decide how to deal with the political changes. Grigorov wanted to go on as before, discussing Steiner's lectures in small groups dedicated to the perfection of the self, out of the public eye. Many Anthroposophists feared that if they took that course, Russian Anthroposophy would become a sect rather than an important part of cultural life.[29] Bely, Trapeznikov, Stoliarov, Sabashnikova, and Klavdiia Vasilieva all took this stance. They decided to establish a new group, which they named for Mikhail Lomonosov, because they considered him to be representative of the Russian Enlightenment, and because his literary and scientific activities linked him with both East and West.[30] The members of the Lomonosov group maintained contacts with representatives of other movements, such as Lev Tolstoy's disciples, whom they joined as habitués of the Moscow vegetarian café.

The discussion of how an Anthroposophist should deal with the public after the Revolution also determined the course of the Anthroposophical group in Petrograd. Like the Russian Anthroposophical Society in Moscow, the Petrograd group had been established in 1913. One of its leading organizers was

27. On his activity in the Anthroposophical Society see John E. Malmstad, "Andrei Belyi i antroposofiia," *Minuvshee*, vol. 9 (Paris, 1990), pp. 473–81. Bely's relation to Anthroposophy has been the subject of numerous studies.

28. Steiner explained autocracy in Russia as a consequence of Mongol rule. See Steiner, *Entwicklungsgeschichtliche Unterlagen zur Bildung eines sozialen Urteils*, vol. 185a of *RSGA* (Dornach, 1963), November 23, 1910, p. 193. He rejected the alliance between tsarism and the Russian Orthodox Church (*Geschichtliche Symptomatologie*, November 3, 1918, p. 220). On Bolshevism see Steiner, *Drei Perspektiven der Anthroposophie: Kulturphänomene*, vol. 225 of *RSGA* (Dornach, 1990), July 15, 1923, pp. 124–32. According to Steiner, Russia now fervently welcomed this combination: *Geisteswissenschaft als Erkenntnis der Grundimpulse sozialer Gestaltung*, vol. 199 of *RSGA* (Dornach, 1985), August 21, 1920, pp. 112–13; published in English as *Spiritual Science as a Foundation for Social Forms* (London, 1986).

29. From 1917 to 1923 the Anthroposophists in Western Europe concentrated on applying Anthroposophical ideas to education, medicine, and social life. Attempts to initiate a parallel development in Russia were unsuccessful in the aftermath of the Bolshevik Revolution.

30. See Steiner, *Zeitgeschichtliche Betrachtungen*, vol. 174 of *RSGA* (Dornach, 1966), January 28, 1917, 2:168; published in English as *The Karma of Untruthfulness* (London, 1992).

Boris Alekseevich Leman (1880–1945), who was associated with Symbolist circles and published under the pseudonym Boris Diks.[31] Another leading figure was the poet Elizaveta Ivanovna Vasilieva (1887–1928), who published under the pseudonym Cherubina de Gabriak.[32] They both maintained a correspondence with Dornach and forwarded Anthroposophical news, books, and lecture cycles to Koktebel and other places.[33] From 1914 on the group met in Elizaveta Vasilieva's home, studied Steiner's writings, and supported a small bookshop that specialized in the Anthroposophical works published by Dukhovnoe Znanie. In the discussion that led to the split with the Lomonosov group, Leman agreed with Grigorov that intensive study in small groups was more important than public relations.[34]

Rather than secede, members of the Petrograd group took part in founding a new forum, Vol'fila (Vol'naia filosofskaia assotsiatsiia, or Free philosophical association), where they opened discussions of Anthroposophical ideas to the public. Vol'fila tried to combine socialist cultural work and idealistic philosophy; it was designed as a research and teaching facility, a place for the intelligentsia to meet and the public to be informed. It was founded in 1919 in Petrograd by Ivanov-Razumnik, Bely, and Blok—the writers who called themselves the Scythians, who hoped for a spiritual revolution to follow the political one.[35] From 1920 on, Vol'fila had its own rooms and accommodated a large number of working groups.[36] Audiences numbering as many as a thousand are said to have attended its lectures on Sundays, when poets, artists, musicians, and scientists spoke on a wide range of subjects related to cultural

31. Leman, who took an interest in Theosophy before joining the Anthroposophists in St. Petersburg, published poetry in Symbolist journals. During the 1920s he lived for awhile in Krasnodar, where he lectured at the university. Back in Leningrad he continued with Anthroposophical work. In the 1930s he was exiled to Tashkent. He died in 1945, probably in Alma-Ata.

32. In 1921 Vasilieva spent a year in Krasnodar, where she worked with Samuil Marshak in a theater for children. Their plays were published in *Teatr dlia detei: Sbornik p'es* (Krasnodar, 1922). Leman wrote the Foreword. Until her arrest in 1927 she was a central figure in Anthroposophical work (illegal from 1923) in Leningrad. In 1928 she died in Tashkent. Zakhar Davydov and Vladimir Kupchenko, "Maksimilian Voloshin: Rasskaz o Cherubine de Gabriak," in *Pamiatniki Kultury: Novye otkrytiia* (Moscow, 1989), pp. 41–61; Vladimir Glotser and Elizaveta Vasileva, "Dve veshchi v mire dlia menia vsegda byli samimi sviatymi: Stikhi i liubov'," *Novyi mir*, 1988, no. 12, pp. 132–70.

33. Their letters to Maksimilian Voloshin are in IRLI, f. 562.

34. See Leman's letters to the Grigorovs in RO RGB, f. 636.

35. The Scythians were a loosely organized group of writers who produced no defined philosophical system but were concerned about the integration of East and West, revolution and world destruction, and the role of the arts in changing society. Scythianism united the concepts of Russian Symbolism with the ideas of the Socialist Revolutionaries. The group published two volumes: *Skify* (Scythians), 1917 and 1918. See Stefani Hope Hoffman, "Scythianism: A Cultural Vision in Revolutionary Russia" (Ph.D. diss., Columbia University, 1975).

36. See Nina Gagen-Torn, "Vol'fila: Volno-Filosofskaia Assotsiatsiia v Leningrade v 1920–1922 gg.," *Voprosy filosofii*, 1990, no. 4, p. 90.

philosophy. On Mondays lectures were given for a smaller public composed largely of Vol'fila members. The remaining days of the week were reserved for courses and workshops on Symbolism, mathematics, the philosophy of Marxism, anarchism, and various other belief systems.[37]

Vol'fila was the main public forum for the discussion of Anthroposophical themes.[38] Sabashnikova, who spent 1921 in Petrograd, organized a Vol'fila workshop on Anthroposophy.[39] Bely was ambivalent about Leman's Anthroposophical group, so Vol'fila became his forum for Anthroposophical activities when he visited Petrograd. He spread Anthroposophical ideas in his Sunday lectures and led workshops dealing with Anthroposophical subjects, such as his "Course on Spiritual Culture" and "Anthroposophy as a Means of Perception."

Among those who attended these circles were Sabashnikova, Olga Dmitrievna Forsh (1873–1963), the art historian Elena Iulievna Fekhner (1900–1985), the sculptor Sofia Gitmanovna Kaplun (1901–1962), and her future husband, the author and translator Sergei Dmitrievich Spassky (1889–1956). In a letter to Bely, Kaplun called these circles the "core" of Anthroposophical work in Petrograd.[40] Vol'fila was not, however, an exclusively Anthroposophical forum; one Sunday in 1921, for example, the philologist Lev Vasilievich Pumpiansky (1891–1940) critically analyzed Steiner's ideas on the "social question."

After Bely and Sabashnikova left Petrograd—he in 1921, she in 1922—some Anthroposophists remained in Vol'fila, which continued to function up to 1924.[41] Others joined the Leman group and assembled at Elizaveta Vasilieva's.[42] Among them was the sinologist Iulian Konstantinovich Shutsky.[43]

---

37. See "Vol'naia filosofskaia assotsiatsiia," *Kniga i revoliutsiia*, 1920, no. 2, p. 92. On the popularity of Vol'fila's meetings see also Aaron Shteinberg, *Druz'ia moikh rannikh let (1911–1928)* (Paris, 1991), pp. 46–47.

38. In questionnaires filled out by Vol'fila members in 1919–20 (when Vol'fila is said to have had about 350 members), Anthroposophy placed fourth in members' interest, after philosophy, religion, and literature. These questionnaires are preserved among the Ivanov-Razumnik papers in IRLI.

39. The opening of the workshop was announced in February 1921 (IRLI, f. 79, op. 1, d. 5, l. 23).

40. Spasskii to Belyi, October 20, 1928, RO, RGB, f. 25, p. 23, d. 4, l. 5.

41. The Ivanov-Razumnik papers include the last statutes of Vol'fila (1924); officially the organization no longer existed: IRLI, f. 79, op. 2, d. 12, ll. 1–8ob. For its last activities and attempts to resurrect it in the 1920s, see Ivanov-Razumnik's letters to Bely in RO RGB, f. 25, op. 16, d. 6b, ll. 28–31, 53ob.

42. In the summer of 1922 Leman wrote to Sergei Grigorov (Boris's brother) that he was working with the former Sabashnikova group: RO, RGB, f. 636, op. 1, d. 19, l. 8.

43. Shutsky, a disciple of the Sinologist Vasily Alekseev, was a specialist in classical and medieval Chinese philosophy. He worked in various research institutes and lectured at Leningrad University. See Artem Kobzev, "Pobeda sinikh chertei (o Iu. K. Shutskom)," *Problemy dal'nego vostoka*, 1989, no. 4, pp. 142–56; Natalia Griakalova, "Strikhotvoreniia E. I. Vasilevoi, posviaschennye Iu. K. Shutskomu," *Russkaia literatura*, 1988, no. 4, pp. 200–205.

In October 1921, Bely founded a Moscow branch of Vol'fila, which was largely influenced by members of the Lomonosov group. Shortly thereafter he left for Berlin (where he established yet another branch of Vol'fila), and Stoliarov became chairman of the Moscow Vol'fila. Its activities were extremely limited and it disbanded the next year.

In 1923 the study of Anthroposophy became illegal, but Steiner's ideas continued to be influential. The actor Mikhail Aleksandrovich Chekhov (1891–1955), for instance, was an ardent student of Steiner's work and sought to combine his ideas with Stanislavsky's method of acting (he had worked under Stanislavsky at the Moscow Art Theater since 1913) in a new concept of the theater.[44] Following Steiner's views on the art of language and motion, Chekhov considered language to be not only a means of communication but a manifestation of various spheres. The laws of the extrasensory world were reflected in language. According to Steiner, the historical shift in linguistic sounds depended on the development of the extrasensory world. The extrasensory world therefore had an impact on the development of language and even on the development of the organs of speech. At the same time, language expressed the speaker's relationship with the world, both as an individual and as part of the collectivity of the nation. On this basis Chekhov believed that the designation "I" expressed the relationship between the nation and the individual. The Russian *ia* expressed openness and perceptiveness, whereas the English "I" was directed toward the earth. In place of perceptiveness one found resoluteness. These ideas were connected with the belief that every individual sound had a life of its own, its own gestures, which existed independently of human beings, but could be embodied by them. Vowels corresponded to emotions, desires, and passions, whereas consonants imitated the outer world.[45]

Artistic movement was meant to give expression to the nature of language, and the artist should approach the higher nature of language. Chekhov regarded eurythmy, which he himself practiced and to which he ascribed importance in his theoretical discourse, as a model of such an awakening of the higher nature of language. In contrast to Stanislavsky, who believed that actors must experience their roles personally and subjectively in order to identify with the characters they were portraying, Chekhov held that actors should get rid of their personal experiences, so that their roles would appear before their

44. Chekhov describes his experience with Anthroposophy in his memoirs and letters. See Mikhail Chekhov, "Zhizn' i vstrechi," *Novyi zhurnal*, nos. 7–9 (1944) and 10 (1945). The Soviet edition lacks some paragraphs dealing with Anthroposophy; see Chekhov, *Literaturnoe nasledie*, 2 vols. (Moscow, 1986), 1:150–267. See also "Pis'ma M. A. Chekhova," *Novyi zhurnal*, no. 132 (1978), pp. 146–60. The most extensive publication of his memoirs is Michail A. Cechov, *Leben und Begegnungen: Autobiographische Schriften* (Stuttgart, 1992). Chekhov audited Steiner's lectures in Berlin in 1922 and in Arnhem in 1924.

45. See Chekhov, "Zhizn' i vstrechi," *Novyi zhurnal*, no. 9 (1944), pp. 34–37.

inner eyes as independent beings. Every role had its own existence. The actor should not create the role but allow it to shape him. In general the actor should concentrate not on outward action but on spiritual-psychical processes and how they were manifested in life on earth. The aim of acting was to penetrate the role with the knowledge of spiritual science. The activity of the actor, who captured the laws of the earth and the cosmos through his gestures, who brought the extrasensory world to the stage, came close to that of a priest.[46] Chekhov invested his artistic activity with a high degree of spiritual and moral value. Thus he understood Shakespeare's *Hamlet* as a symbolic drama with characters that had already died, so that the action took place beyond this world.[47]

The non-Anthroposophical audience appreciated the imaginativeness of Chekhov's role interpretation.[48] In his book *To the Actor* Chekhov gave practical instructions on training an actor, based on Steiner's cognitive approach.[49] When Bely's dramatization of his novel *Peterburg* premiered at the Moscow Art Theater's Second Studio in November 1925, Chekhov played the role of Ableukhov.[50] He and Bely conducted a workshop on rhythm, motion, and language, where students practiced eurythmy and studied the formation of language and its role in art on the basis of Steiner's ideas.

In lectures delivered in factories and other public places during the early years of the Revolution, Chekhov discussed the spiritual background to his ideas on the art of acting. In 1925 he was accused of mysticism and occultism, and Narkompros ordered him to stop spreading Steiner's ideas.[51] Discouraged, Chekhov took the occasion of a trip to Germany in July 1928 to leave the Soviet Union for good.[52] In the following years the repressions of Anthroposo-

46. At times Chekhov himself considered becoming a priest; see Fedjuschin, *Russlands Sehnsucht nach Spiritualität*, pp. 269–70; Margarita Woloschin, "Michael Tschechow zum Gedenken," *Das Goetheanum*, 1956, no. 6, p. 45.

47. Solomon Volkov, ed., *Testimony: The Memoirs of Dmitri Shostakovich* (New York, 1979), p. 88.

48. See Pavel Markov, *O teatre* (Moscow, 1974), 2:298–307.

49. The first version of the book, which exists only in typescript, was written in 1942 in English. An amended version appeared in 1953: *To the Actor: On the Technique of Acting* (New York, 1953). The Russian version, *O technike aktera*, was published in Chekhov's *Literaturnoe nasledie*, vol. 2.

50. See John E. Malmstad, "Posleslovie," in Andrei Belyi, *Gibel' senatora (Peterburg): Istoricheskaia drama* (Berkeley, 1986), pp. 203–37. On Bely's relationship with Chekhov (they met in 1921), see Leonid Dolgopolov, "A. Belyi o postanovke 'istoricheskoi dramy' 'Peterburg' na stsene MKhAT-2," *Russkaia literatura*, 1977, no. 2, pp. 173–76; Mariia Kozlova, " 'Menia udivliaet etot chelovek . . . ' (Pis'ma Andreia Belogo k Mikhailu Chekhovu)," in *Vstrechi s proshlym* (Moscow, 1982), pp. 224–43.

51. See Chekhov, "Zhizn' i vstrechi," *Vozdushnye puti*, 1963, no. 3, pp. 173–90.

52. Chekhov worked with Max Reinhardt in Berlin and later in Vienna. Eventually he settled in the United States, where he founded a drama center, appeared in films, and gave acting lessons. He never abandoned Anthroposophy. See, e.g., "Pis'ma M. A. Chekhova,"

phists intensified and many Russian Anthroposophists ended their lives in Soviet labor camps.[53]

For decades Anthroposophy could be discussed only in small conspirational groups.[54] It was not until the summer of 1969 that a larger meeting of Anthroposophists was held. Out of that meeting emerged the nucleus of the Anthroposophical movement in Moscow: they studied Steiner's works, and later on, during the 1980s, supported various Anthroposophical initiatives in Russia. Since 1988 the number of such initiatives has risen steadily. A eurythmy studio was opened in Moscow and numerous public eurythmy performances were given;[55] in the spring of 1989 the Aristotle Club organized seminars on Steiner's Waldorf pedagogy, public lectures, and children's groups;[56] seminars are now held on homeopathic medicine, biodynamic farming, and Anthroposophical architecture, music, and art.[57] New editions of Steiner's works are being sold in the streets of Moscow. The law on associations that went into effect on January 1, 1991, permitted the Anthroposophical Society in Russia to open its doors in Moscow, and branches were established in St. Petersburg and Odessa.[58] The society is part of the International Anthropo-

---

Novyi zhurnal, no. 132 (1978), pp. 146–60. In August 1992 actors, stage managers, playwrights, and drama coaches from Germany, the United States, Ireland, Poland, and Russia gathered in Berlin for the first international Chekhov conference.

53. Chekhov suspected a connection between his departure and the repressions; see Chekhov, "Zhizn' i vstrechi," *Novyi zhurnal,* no. 10 (1945), pp. 49–50. On repressions against the Anthroposophists around Bely see Gleb Struve, "K biografii Andreia Belogo: Tri dokumenty," *Novyi zhurnal,* no. 124 (1976), pp. 152–62.

54. Material that has recently become available indicates that such circles were surprisingly numerous. Reports in the papers of Marie von Sivers Steiner at Dornach indicate that the Anthroposophy group in Leningrad had about seventy members in the late 1920s.

55. See Tille Barkhoff, "Eurythmie-Studio Moskau," *Was in der Anthroposophischen Gesellschaft vorgeht,* 1991, no. 27, pp. 161–62; Wolfgang Veit, "Eurythmie im Lande der Revolution und des klassischen Balletts: Eindrücke von dem Rußland-Gastspiel der Goetheanum-Bühne und des Eurythmeum Stuttgart," *Das Goetheanum,* 1990, no. 49, pp. 439–42.

56. Waldorf schools, based on Steiner's ideas about the reformation of the social order, are found throughout Europe, the United States, Canada, some South American countries, South Africa, Australia, and New Zealand. The first Waldorf school in Moscow was opened in 1992. See Felix Stöcklin, "Waldorfskij Utschitjelskij Seminar: Von der Eröffnung eines Waldorflehrerseminars in Moskau," *Das Goetheanum,* 1990, no. 47, pp. 417–19.

57. Study of all these subjects is based on Steiner's holistic weltanschauung. Homeopathic medicine assumes a variety of entities within the human being. Noncooperation of these entities leads to diseases. The aim of biodynamic farming is the recovery of the soil, plants, animals, and human beings through obediences to cosmic and earthly laws; such harmful influences as chemical fertilizers are to be avoided. The aim of Steiner's architectural method is to create a suitable and healing environment for human beings on the basis of spiritual science.

58. Anthroposophy also gained followers in Siberia, Ukraine, Armenia, and Latvia, and especially in Estonia and in Georgia, when the former president Sviad Gamsakhurdia was an Anthroposophist; see Ramon Brüll, " 'Erst müssen wir unabhängig sein, danach können wir neue Ideen realisieren': Interview mit dem georgischen Präsidenten Swiad Gamsachurdia,"

sophical Society (with headquarters in Dornach) but also regards itself as the successor of the Russian Anthroposophical Society of 1913–23. So far the first of those links seems to be dominant: the various initiatives are strongly supported by the Western Anthroposophical movement, whereas analysis of Russian history has only just begun. Yet the prominent role of Russia in Anthroposophy is once again clear.[59]

Info3, 1991, nos. 7–8, pp. 23–25. Georgia became less hospitable to Anthroposophy after Gamsakhurdia was overthrown.

59. " . . . without Russia, Anthroposophy cannot develop its full importance in the world . . . and we will be greeted as long-expected guests in the West": Genady Bondarev, "Konets veka: Krizis tsivilizatsii i zadachi antroposofov," in *Antroposofiia*, vol. 2 (Moscow, 1991), p. 4. Bondarev was one of the organizers of Anthroposophical work in the Soviet Union during the 1970s; see also his *Stimme aus dem Osten* (Basel, 1992).

PART THREE

FROM MAGIC TO "SCIENCE"

CHAPTER SEVEN
FEDOROV'S TRANSFORMATIONS OF THE OCCULT

George M. Young Jr.

Nikolai Fedorovich Fedorov (1828/29–1903) was, in Sergei Bulgakov's phrase, "an enigmatic thinker."[1] One of several illegitimate children of a Gagarin prince and an unknown neighbor woman, Fedorov grew up on both sides of the great social divide in nineteenth-century Russia. His first years were spent as partly an outsider and partly an insider on an eminent family's country estate. He attended the prestigious Richelieu Lyceum, but owing, as he later put it, to an "act of insubordination," he did not receive his diploma. Instead of following a diplomatic or high government administrative career, as might be expected of a "complete" Gagarin, he spent the next several years teaching elementary history and geography in village schools in central Russia. By the mid-1860s, when he was in his late thirties, Fedorov had arrived at the basic original ideas that he would spend the rest of his life developing and elaborating. In 1868 he went to Moscow to work in the library of the Rumiantsev Museum, where his erudition, eccentricity, and diligence became legendary. He lived in a closet-sized room as an ascetic bachelor, wore the same clothes winter and summer, slept on a humpback trunk, ate very little, refused all promotion, and gave away most of his meager salary to "the poor." Called "the Moscow Socrates," Fedorov published almost nothing during his lifetime but expounded his ideas orally to a small group of devoted friends and followers. Through these disciples his ideas became known to Dostoevsky, who endorsed them "as if they were my own," and Soloviev, who considered Fedorov's resurrection

---

1. For a general introduction to Fedorov's life and writings, see my *Nikolai F. Fedorov: An Introduction* (Belmont, Mass., 1979). Two outstanding works are Michael Hagemeister, *Nikolaj Fedorov: Studien zu Leben, Werk und Wirkung* (Munich, 1989); and Svetlana Semenova, *Nikolai Fedorov: Tvorchestvo zhizni* (Moscow, 1990).

project "the first forward movement of the human spirit along the path of Christ."[2] Lev Tolstoy, the future rocket pioneer Konstantin Tsiolkovsky, and many other eminent library patrons became acquainted with and fascinated by Fedorov and his ideas.

After his death, two of his disciples, N. P. Peterson and V. A. Kozhevnikov, published a two-volume edition of his dictated writings under the title *Filosofiia obshchago dela* (Philosophy of the common task). Only 480 copies of the works were printed, stamped "Not for sale," and distributed without charge to libraries and individuals who requested them. Despite this paucity of written texts, and despite their incompatibility with emerging Soviet doctrine, Fedorov's ideas became surprisingly well known among small but important circles of Russian intellectuals.[3] His great theme was immanent universal resurrection, the full and literal restoration of the dead to life, a task or "project" to be accomplished by human ingenuity and effort. According to Fedorov, resurrection of the dead is not only a scientific possibility but a moral duty. We must, in his view, bend all effort toward this end, and only by engaging all humankind in this single task of resurrection can we hope to solve such apparently unrelated problems as war, poverty, and the destruction of the environment. Parts of Fedorov's project that were most ridiculed during his own day include his calls for space travel, genetic engineering, and gradual prolongation of human life and health until eventually universal immortality is achieved—a most literal version of the age-old dream of restoring paradise on earth.

But while his "project" has been viewed as a grand synthesis, a culmination of Russian, Christian, and socialist ideas, individual parts of that project have inevitably raised the Russian, Christian, and socialist eyebrow—his ideas work and yet do not work as philosophy, theology, sociology, or history. The combinations of religion and technology, social radicalism and patriarchal rigidity, nationalism and cosmism, fantasy and literalism have as often given an impression of intellectual misalliance as of felicitous conjunction. But if Fedorov was a controversial eccentric, was he also an occultist?

V. V. Zenkovsky has suggested that in Fedorov's ideas we can find traces of an occultism prevalent among Russian Freemasons of the eighteenth century.[4] Georges Florovsky and others have found in some of Fedorov's ideas hints of magic and sorcery.[5] Although consideration of Fedorov's thought in relation to the occult has never amounted to more than a brief passing comment, his work

2. Young, *Nikolai F. Fedorov*, p. 8.

3. Irene Masing-Delic, *Abolishing Death: A Salvation Myth of Russian Twentieth-Century Literature* (Stanford, 1992), discusses the impact of Fedorov's idea on major Russian writers of the twentieth century.

4. V. V. Zenkovskii, *Istoriia russkoi filosofii* (Paris, 1950), 2:131–47; English ed.: *A History of Russian Philosophy* (New York, 1953), 2:588–604.

5. Georgii Florovskii, "Proekt mnimogo dela," *Sovremennye zapiski* (Paris), 1935, no. 59, pp. 399–414 (reprinted in slightly condensed form in *Puti russkogo bogosloviia* [Paris, 1937], pp. 322–30).

does share several points with occult writings. A difficulty is that while Fedo-rov's work addresses many topics traditionally associated with the occult, he does not cite occult sources, or even mention esoteric literature except to dis-parage it. Although as an illegitimate grandson he was brought up in the home of Ivan Alekseevich Gagarin, one of the leading Freemasons of Catherine's time, and though the universal invisible "brotherhood of man" is one of his fundamental themes, Fedorov almost nowhere mentions the Masonic idea.[6] Rereading Fedorov in search of traces of esotericism in his writings, one con-stantly finds everywhere hints and circumstantial evidence, but no direct con-nections. Fedorov's ties to the invisible world remain themselves invisible.

But not only his relation to the occult is obscure. Believing that ideas did not really belong to individuals but should be the common property of all, he seldom cited any sources at all in his writings and generally mentioned the names of authors or schools of thought only when he wished to challenge them. Among patrons of the Rumiantsev Museum Fedorov's erudition was legendary; he was reputed to be familiar with the contents of every book and pamphlet in the collection. So it would be no surprise to find that he knew a great deal about the occult, and it would be characteristic of him to omit references to sources of ideas that he wished to incorporate in his own. My purpose, then, is not to try to prove influences and borrowings, but rather to speak of confluences, shared concerns, overlaps; not to try to demonstrate that Fedorov was or was not a high-level secret mahatma, but rather to consider how Fedorov transformed or "Fedorovized" occult themes. These points of contact include the notion of a hidden reality, a fascination with the Orient, the transformation of matter and the elimination of temporality, the achievement of total enlightenment, the recovery of lost knowledge, and the restoration of ancient geographic power centers.

One feature of most occult speculation is the belief that within or behind our mundane, everyday reality lies another reality that is more interesting, more important, and ultimately "more real" than the everyday. As P. D. Uspensky explained:

All views on life are divided into two categories on this point. There are concep-tions of the world which are entirely based on the idea that we live in a house in which there is some secret, some buried treasure, some hidden store of precious things, which somebody at some time may find and which occasionally has in fact been found. And then from this point of view, the whole aim and the whole meaning of life consist in the search for this treasure, because without it all the

6. An exception: Freemasonry is an "artificial, extremely antipopulist society, constructed on the principles of the eighteenth century": *Filosofiia obshchago dela: Stat'i, mysli, i pis'ma Nikolaia Fedorovicha Fedorova,* ed. V. A. Kozhevnikov and N. P. Peterson, 2 vols. (1906, 1913; Farnborough, Hants., 1970), 1:529. Hereafter this edition is referred to parenthetically in the text by volume and page number.

rest has no value. And there are other theories and systems in which there is no idea of 'treasure trove', for which all alike is visible and clear, or all alike invisible and obscure.[7]

Further developing the same idea, he writes:

> According to this idea, humanity is regarded as two concentric circles. All humanity which we know and to which we belong forms the outer circle. All the history of humanity that we know is the history of the outer circle. But within this circle there is another, of which men of the outer circle know nothing, and the existence of which they only sometimes dimly suspect, although the life of the outer circle in its most important manifestations, and particularly in its *evolution*, is actually guided by the inner circle. The inner or the esoteric circle forms, as it were, a life within life, a mystery, a secret in the life of humanity.
>
> The outer or exoteric humanity, to which we belong, is like the leaves on a tree that change every year. In spite of this they consider themselves the centre of life, not understanding that the tree has a trunk and roots, and that besides leaves it bears flowers and fruit.
>
> The esoteric circle is, as it were, humanity, within humanity, and is the brain, or rather the immortal soul, of humanity, where all the attainments, all the results, all the achievements, of all cultures and all civilisations are preserved.[8]

Uspensky's remarks, published in 1931, could not have been a direct source for Fedorov, but the idea is so fundamental and common to the occult tradition that Fedorov, who died in 1903, did not need special uncanny powers to be familiar with the basic concept. Fedorov's version of the circle within the circle offers, within ordinary reality, a projected ideal reality that it is our human task to realize. Instead of the occultist's secret treasure known only to its initiated guardians, Fedorov would have a treasure now ignored by all but potentially accessible to all. For Fedorov, the path from ordinary to ideal reality consists not in secret rites or blind forces of evolution but in shared, conscious, open labor, a universal assignment to use all means known and knowable to accomplish the single goal of resurrecting the dead. For Fedorov, the guiding consciousness is not that of illuminati in an esoteric school but the most common painful awareness of mortality that anyone can feel, as Fedorov himself must have felt early in life, on losing a member of one's family. For Fedorov, the treasure is hidden only because we ignore it; we look everywhere but in the right direction. The people most aware of the ideal reality are not the educated,

---

7. P. D. Ouspensky, *A New Model of the Universe* (New York, 1931), p. 14. I cite Uspensky at length not because he was a source for Fedorov but because he is an articulate and convenient spokesman for an occult tradition that originated long before Fedorov and extended long after him.

8. Ibid., p. 19.

initiated elite but the simplest and least learned peasants, those who have lost and are still losing the most in the human struggle with nature.

In Fedorov's world "as it is," we are all subject to nature and death, but we all bear within us not only a longing for but an ability to project and realize the world "as it ought to be," that is, a world without suffering and death, a world in which we are not nature's victims but its regulator and partner. In traditional occult thought, the hidden reality becomes visible only to certain "seers" or mediums under special circumstances, such as trances. But for Fedorov, human effort, properly directed, will actually replace the currently visible reality with the one currently hidden. And everyone will participate in the replacement. Those who are now utterly unaware of even the possibility of a higher reality will become aware not by intellectual persuasion but by actual hands-on experience in resurrecting their ancestors. Lost secrets of the past will no longer be either lost or secret when, for example, the very builders of Stonehenge can actually be brought back to life to tell us how and why they did it.

Another fundamental element in much nineteenth- and twentieth-century occult literature is its Orientalist bias, the notion that a higher wisdom exists east or south of the Mediterranean: in Egypt, India, Tibet, Ceylon, Central Asia, Persia, wherever nonwestern traditions of wisdom could best be rediscovered.

Fedorov found little to admire in the mysterious Orient of his occultist contemporaries. For him, Buddhism was too much a turning away from the world "as it is" and Hinduism too much an embracing of it. The Islam of the dervishes was a whirlwind of destruction. Jewish Kabbalists were exclusivist to an unhealthy extreme. The one Oriental doctrine worth borrowing from was the religion of the ancient Iranians as outlined in the Zend-Avesta. Here he found an active struggle of good against evil, forces of light against dark; here he found genuine paradigms for the attainment of immortality and the resurrection of the dead. The *frasho kerete* (1:346–48) or "end of the present state of the world, the Last Day," served Fedorov as a model for his project of restoring paradise.[9] And, as a scholar of the Avesta has pointed out, "The gap separating 'this earth' from 'yon heaven' as the text expresses it, is not unbridgeable. In addition to the intermediary of Fire, there also exists the cosmic mountain arising from earth and heaven, the Meru of the Indians, called the Alburz by the Iranians."[10] The Indo-Iranian ideas of the cosmic mountain and the bridgeable gap are central to Fedorov's spiritual geography. In his system, the mythical Meru-Alburz is actually the Pamirs, where, according to local legend, the Garden of Eden once flourished, and where Adam was originally buried.

9. Mary Boyce, *Zoroastrians: Their Religious Beliefs and Practices* (London, 1979), p. xvi.
10. William W. Malandra, ed., *An Introduction to Ancient Iranian Religion: Readings from the Avesta and Achaemenid Inscriptions* (Minneapolis, 1983), p. 11.

Another point that links Fedorov to the ancient Iranians is the idea of truth as a connectedness.

> In addition to this word for 'truth' [*sat*], there existed another, partly synony-mous word, *rta. . . .* The etymology of this word has been the subject of much dispute, but it probably derives from a verb *ar*—'to join.' *Rta-* is a neuter noun basically meaning 'connection.' Like *Satya*, *rta-* implies a 'connection' with the real, with the proper or characteristic order of things. As such it has two basic meanings in Indo-Iranian: (1) 'truth'; (2) 'cosmic order.' *Rta-* is perhaps the most important concept in Aryan religion, since it embodies the basic principle by which the entire cosmos, physical as well as ethical, behaves.[11]

To Fedorov, truth is certainly a connectedness. The current state of the world is false precisely because everything is disconnected, disintegrated, unre-lated—the world is wrong because *rodstvo*, kinship, does not obtain. To set the world straight again, *rodstvo* must be restored—again, literally, by resurrection of all the dead back to and including our common ancestor.

Fedorov presents his project as a Christian task, but the aspects of Christian thought dearest to Fedorov are those that overlap most with ancient Iranian religious thought. As Georges Dumezil has shown, the Iranians may have been the first to emphasize the idea of immortality and resurrection.

> Yim and Kau Us . . . were created immortal and became mortal through their own fault; it was for having tried to conquer heaven that Kay Us lost this pre-cious gift. . . . These texts render it likely that the Indo-Iranian prototype already contained, besides the power to save us from imminent or effective death, this mastery of the aging process, which the Indic and Iranian derivates present in two different forms.[12]

Fedorov viewed the ancient Iranians as the forebears of the Slavs: conti-nental, as opposed to insular or peninsular; agricultural, as opposed to no-madic; overcoming enemies by absorbing them rather than by driving them out (1:366–68).

Zoroastrianism is the only predecessor of Christianity that Fedorov cites with much approval. He quotes the Zend-Avesta, uses Avestan terminology, and incorporates fundamental Indo-Iranian concepts into his project. Par-ticularly important here are the ideas of regulating the aging process and our role as partners of the gods in maintaining cosmic order. In ancient Iranian religious texts, the story of an old man who enters a gate, drinks from a foun-tain, climbs a peak (usually Alburz, which in Fedorov becomes Pamir), or drinks an herbal preparation and turns back into a youth of fifteen recurs

---

11. Ibid., p. 13.

12. Georges Dumezil, *The Plight of a Sorcerer*, ed. Jaan Puhvel and David Weeks (Berkeley, 1986), p. 69.

frequently. Fedorov often put more stock in folktales than in academic treatises, arguing that folktales at least give voice to common human longings and mythic truths. The means of rejuvenation described in the ancient Indo-Iranian tales, the ingesting of haoma or of soma, magic words or potions, are dismissed outright as inadequate for Fedorov's task. But the goals of life posited in the Indo-Iranian texts are the goals that Fedorov would have us turn our energies and technological advances toward in our day and in the days to come.

The literature of alchemy can be considered another ingredient in Fedorov's project. Though he does not directly discuss the "cloudy clauses" of Paracelsus, Hermes Trismegistus, or any of the other classics of alchemical literature,[13] Fedorov shares with the alchemists a faith in our ability to transform matter and correct the processes of nature, a desire to redesign the human being according to a higher model, a belief that the search for immortal life must begin in the laboratory, and an inclination toward a hermaphroditic ideal. The first principle in Hermes Trismegistus' Emerald Table is: "It is true without lie, certain and most veritable, that what is below is like what is above and that what is above is like what is below."[14] In Fedorov's thought, what is above is always like what is below, the projected task is the same everywhere and on every scale, the dust of ancestors inheres in both the smallest and largest particles in the universe. One belief of alchemists both in Europe and in Asia was that ores, and indeed all natural things, tended toward an ideal (gold) that would be achieved over a long time by natural "maturation," but that could be accelerated by human art.[15] The alchemist attempted to help nature achieve its true purposes sooner than it could achieve them on its own. Fedorov would go further to state that we should not merely accelerate natural processes but redirect natural force to realize divine intent. Without humankind, nature is blind and destructive. Humankind, for Fedorov, is not only nature's assistant but nature's regulator and guide. For Fedorov, lead will not eventually turn to gold on its own, but needs us to project the idea of the transformation to gold, and to see that the project of transformation is realized. In an oft-repeated phrase, Fedorov states: "Nature is for us a temporary enemy, but an eternal friend" (2:247).

As Mircea Eliade, among others, has noted, by seeking to transform base metal into pure, the alchemist also seeks to refashion himself from base elements into pure.

> For his part, the alchemist pursues the transmutation of the body and dreams of indefinitely prolonging its youth, strength and suppleness. In both cases—tantra

13. "The Ordinall of Alchimy. Written by Thomas Norton of Bristoll," in Elias Ashmole, *Theatrum Chemicum Britannicum* (1652; London, 1967), p. 8.

14. Cited in Stanislas Klossowski de Rola, *Alchemy: The Secret Art* (London, 1973), p. 15.

15. Mircea Eliade, *The Forge and the Crucible* (New York, 1971), p. 47.

yoga and alchemy—the process of the transmutation of the body comprises an experience of initiatory death and resurrection. . . . In addition, both Tantrist and alchemist strive to dominate "matter." They do not withdraw from the world as do the ascetic and metaphysician, but dream of conquering it and changing its ontological regime. In short, there is good ground for seeing in the tantric *sadhana,* and in the work of the alchemist, parallel efforts to free themselves from the laws of Time, to "decondition" their existence and gain absolute freedom.[16]

Fedorov's task of resurrection would also free us from the laws of time, and the task of resurrecting, like the alchemist's labor to obtain the philosopher's stone, would be a purifying endeavor: as one resurrects one's ancestors, one resurrects oneself, finding immortality as one gives it. Fedorov does not speak of calcination, solution, separation, conjunction, putrefaction, congelation, cibation, sublimation, fermentation, exaltation, multiplication, and projection of mercury and sulphur, sun and moon, moist and dry, warm and cold, male and female, as the alchemists do, but in a section called "The Sanitary Question" (1:276–84, 2:316–18) he does address some of the same processes and finds a place for them in his task. Generally, where the alchemist attempts to work with and through the natural processes of decay and regeneration, Fedorov projects a future without decomposition and death, an eternity in which the risen world will never need to fall again, in which everything lost will be returned, and replacement, the messy business of conception and childbirth, will no longer be necessary. The alchemist and Fedorov both emphasize the need to contain and control the war of natural opposites, whether within the glass beaker or throughout the universe. For the alchemist this war leads to an exalted conjunction and its issue, the sublime hermaphrodite. For Fedorov the ideal union is an asexual one of a brother who is not a father with a daughter who is not a mother, both sexes united in the task not of reproducing offspring but of resurrecting the dead parents. In some alchemical illustrations, the two halves of the royal hermaphrodite embrace face to face. If Fedorov were illustrated, the two halves would be back to back, leaving all digits free for the serious task of gathering ancestral particles.

The great difference between Fedorov and most other Christian thinkers is similar to that between the Western alchemist and the Indian yogi. The goal is much the same for all, but for Fedorov and the alchemist the way leads through the laboratory. One does not withdraw from nature or tolerate or transcend it, one tinkers with it in the hope of mastering and improving it. For the most part, Fedorov sets goals for humankind and indicates the technological means without going into too much detail. But when he does elaborate on the technological details, his ideas do resemble some of the alchemical recipes published in Elias Ashmole's *Theatrum Chemicum Britannicum* (1652). Here is a fifteenth-century description of the uses of liquor:

16. Ibid., pp. 11–13, 129.

> Liquor is the Comfort of this Werke;
> Liquor giveth evidence to a Clerke
> Thereby to fasten his Elements,
> And Also to loose them for some intents;
> Liquor conjoyneth Male with Female Wife,
> And causeth dead things to resort to Life,
> Liquors clenseth with their ablution,
> Liquors to our *Stone* be Cheefe nutrition;
> Without Liquor no Meate is good;
> Liquors conveieth all Aliment and Food
> To every part of Mans Body,
> And so thei doe with us in Alkimy.[17]

For liquor substitute electromagnetic current, and Fedorov's speculations on the possible effects of a series of transcontinental rings of telegraph wires do not sound that different from the speculations of the fifteenth-century alchemist: "In this regard, perhaps, the possibility opens for action upon the earth in its entirety: a transcontinental highway brings up the necessity of a transcontinental telegraph across the great ocean, and then it can link up with the existing transcontinental telegraph and with it can form the first electrical ring around the earth. Wouldn't this ring electrify the globe by the action of magnetism?" (1:54).

Further, Fedorov speculates that a series of such rings arranged in a spiral could turn the earth, a natural magnet, into an electromagnet, which could be used to control storm belts, indeed to create a new "meteorological equator," and when used in conjunction with "a globe-encircling wire supported by balloons with lightning rods," could create a controlled weather environment for the entire earth. This, really, is alchemy in a global laboratory with lightning bolts instead of little clouds and sparks popping in a double pelican retort. Fedorov too writes of the need to regulate the dry and the humid, the hot and the cold, the up and the down—all in the quest for eternal life. The difference is that alchemy is a secret that a master may in his entire life pass on to a single worthy aspirant, whereas Fedorov viewed his task as an open teaching, a basic science, which could be and should be studied and adopted by all.

For Fedorov, as for the occult tradition, total enlightenment is a major objective. But Fedorov's idea of total enlightenment is knowledge "by all, of all" (1:7), "through all" (1:320), and "for the sake of all" (1:36, 118). Total enlightenment is not an individual grail quest, as it is in most esoteric systems, but a long mass project leading to a kind of universal omniscience. For Fedorov, "cosmic

---

17. Ashmole, *Theatrum Chemicum Britannicum*, p. 76. I cite this work not to suggest that Fedorov knew it and was influenced by it but merely as an example of alchemical writing for those not familiar with the genre.

consciousness" is not the result of secret initiation followed by individual spiritual development along a guarded path, but is instead, essentially, family knowledge—what everyone knows about and through everyone else who ever lived in the universe. Fedorov's quarrel with Spiritualism and occultism is not with the awakening sought, and not with the desire to go beyond natural earthly limits. Rather, the problem with any esoteric system is that super-natural knowledge is limited to a select few. Only those chosen or deemed worthy are allowed to pursue the knowledge that everyone would like to have. Or, as the alchemist says:

> The first Paine is to remember in minde
> How many seeken, and how few doe finde,
> And yet noe man may this Science wynn,
> But it be tought him before that he beginn. . . .
> Yet teaching maie not surely availe,
> But that sometime shall happ a man to faile;
> As all that be now dead and gone
> Failed before theie found our *Stone*.[18]

For Fedorov, all must join the task of knowledge and labor, or the task will fail. Only if all join in will all be resurrected, and only if all are resurrected will all be known to all. Fedorov acknowledges that the desire for occult knowledge is a legitimate desire, and the task for those interested in the occult is to accomplish in reality with science and to pass on to all feats that have here-tofore been claimed by pseudoscience and cloaked in mystery that prevented examination, confirmation, and replication by legitimate investigators (1:285). Even such phenomena as hauntings and the materialization of spirits repre-sent, to Fedorov, manifestations of genuine human concerns. To the modern person, as to the savage, the dead return, sometimes as ghosts, sometimes, if unburied or unburned, as microbes bearing disease and infection, to remind us that life is not for the present generation only, to make us feel again that we were created not for the simple enjoyment of the present moment but for a higher purpose. Whether as painful memories of loved ones no longer with us or as terrifying faces flickering in the forest beyond a campfire, the dead reap-pear to tell us what is missing in our lives, and what we must now do to restore ourselves to wholeness. That we are more successful in ignoring these appari-tions does not make us superior to the savage. In our own way we also say: "Stay asleep, don't come back, don't trouble our enjoyment of life." But the dead will not leave us alone, "they must constantly remind us of our solidarity with them" (1:286).

The focus for all ancient lost power and knowledge for Fedorov is not At-lantis but the Pamir mountain range. Now as all we metaphysicians know,

18. Ibid., p. 76.

there are mountains and there are magic mountains. The difference is that the magic ones occupy what Mircea Eliade has called "Sacred Space." As he has written: "For religious man, space is not homogeneous; he experiences interruptions, breaks in it; some parts of space are qualitatively different from others."[19] Or, as P. D. Uspensky has suggested:

> There are differences in stone, in wood, in iron, in paper, which no chemistry will ever detect: but these differences exist, and there are men who feel and understand them. . . . The mast of a ship, a gallows, a crucifix at a crossroads on the steppes—they may be made of the same kind of wood, but in reality they are different objects made of different material. That which we see, touch, investigate, is nothing more than "the circles on the plane," made by the coin and the candle. They are only the shadows of real things, the substance of which is contained in their function. The shadow of a sailor, of a hangman, and of an ascetic may be quite similar—it is impossible to distinguish them by their shadows, just as it is impossible to find any difference between the wood of a mast, of a gallows, and of a cross by chemical analysis. But they are different men and different objects—their shadows only are equal and similar.[20]

So mountains may appear the same, but behind their shadows they are fundamentally different. When a prophet says that he has been to the Mountain we know he means something other than the bumper sticker that proclaims: "This Car Climbed Mt. Washington."

Fedorov's magic mountain was not Olympos or Ararat or Mount Horeb, but, as I mentioned earlier, the unlikely Pamirs in what is now Kirgizstan and Tadzhikistan, the high border country where the former USSR meets Afghanistan and China. This is one of the most desolate spots on earth, a range of icy, windswept 24,000-foot summits loved only by mountain climbers, goats, and Fedorov. But even before Fedorov, this region was a center of mysteries, wonders, and legends. Marco Polo, for instance, wrote that the pasturage in the Pamir foothills was the richest in the world, that only a few days' grazing hereabout could turn even the scrawniest bags of bones into sleek steeds and fat beeves. The Pamiri natives of the valleys belong to an early branch of Indo-European-speaking people whose dialect of Iranian has been described by specialists as a particularly pure and ancient variety. Since Alexander the Great's time, European, Middle Eastern, and Asian travelers have brought back from the Pamirs tales of finding in hidden valleys people who live well past a hundred years, one-eyed cyclopean people, blue-eyed, yellow-haired people, beasts long extinct elsewhere. Early Islamic literature names this as one of the seven gates of Paradise. In the deserts that stretch north of the Pamir range, along the silk trails of the caravans, the nineteenth-century traveler

19. Mircea Eliade, *The Sacred and the Profane* (New York, 1957), p. 20.
20. P. D. Ouspensky, *Tertium Organum* (New York, 1970), p. 141.

Arminus Vambery and thirty years later Sven Hedin passed beside the minarets of ancient cities buried in the shifting sands, and long after Fedorov, George Gurdjieff (who probably did not know Fedorov's work) set much of his *Meetings with Remarkable Men* in this very region.

Fedorov probably learned about the Pamirs near the end of the nineteenth century on visits to his friend N. P. Peterson, who was a judge in the Russian Central Asian provinces. In his published writings and in letters to his friends and disciples Peterson and Kozhevnikov, Fedorov defines the Pamir range as the focal point for all human mourning. Here, according to local legend, was the original site of Eden, and the visible desolation in contrast to biblical and other lush images of the garden emphasizes what we have lost and how great a task of restoration remains. Present Pamir is Golgotha, a mountain of skulls. The Pamir range is to the world what the Alps have been to Europe, a spine dividing people from people, language from language, a symbol of all that must be surmounted in the task to make humankind one (1:161–68).

A treaty that Russia had signed with England concerning the Pamirs and the Hindu Kush demonstrated to Fedorov that perhaps the world was at last waking up to the international significance of the region. Fedorov proposed a joint Anglo-Russian archaeological expedition to the Pamirs in search of common ancestral remains as a first step toward restoring the wasteland to a garden, and he projected as a task for international linguistics the rediscovery of the original language of the first Pamiri, which, he believed, would also turn out to be the original language of all Indo-Europeans, and indeed the language of Adam and Eve. When reacquired, Ur-Pamiri would be the natural language of all, uniting peoples and races better than any artificial language such as Esperanto possibly could. Ignored by the world today, Pamir would be the focus of universal attention on the last day of the resurrection project, when Adam and Eve would once again find themselves alive in Eden. Atlantis, Fedorov believed, writing about both Plato and the Theosophists' revival of interest in lost continents, was a lost power center for philosophers only. Pamir was the lost power center for all people, and if the energies that were going into attempts to rediscover Atlantis were turned toward Pamir, we would be closer to the beginning of the common task:

> The history of Pamir is the history of the patriarchal, familial way of life, for the sake of which kinship represents the highest ideal projective form; the history of Pamir, for which there are as yet no sources, is not political history, not civil history, not the history of civilization, rather it is a history of decline, of unbrotherhood, to be studied in fundamentals, but precisely such a study of unbrotherhood can lead the way to the means of the restoration of kinship. (1:348)

Fedorov's writings, then, share many points of interest with traditional literature of the occult. In one notable way, however, Fedorov differs from other major Russian thinkers interested in the occult: he does not worship at the shrine of the Great Mother. In some respects, he is indeed, the most patriarchal of all Russian thinkers: unity, order, control, regulation, restoration, autocracy, strict devotion to a narrow task, return of the past—these are Fedorov's passwords. His "supramoralism" is the opposite of any kind of sophiology. If anything, he calls for the reimposition of the great masculine over any great feminine principle. But having said that, we must also note that in his idea of daughterhood, Fedorov gives women as important a role as men in the project of resurrection. Models for women include Mary Magdalene, the female equivalent of the Prodigal Son, and Ruth and all other women who have married outside their tribe or race or clan, helping to restore unity to fragmented humankind. Fedorov does not ignore the role of women either in today's world or in tomorrow's project of resurrection. In general, he is not a woman-hater, he does not despise the female sex, but rather wishes to control the sex drive and all natural forces that turn people of both sexes into greedy, lustful, parent-forgetting, infantile individuals. He believed that humankind was already well on the way to creating a worldwide debauched playground that he called "pornocracy." Men and women suffer from the same natural condition, and the remedy for sexism (in which sex becomes everything) is a brotherhood and sisterhood, a sonship and daughterhood in which one's sex eventually becomes irrelevant. Fedorov's ideal is not so much misogynist as asexual. He stands for restoration, against reproduction.[21]

In discussing Gnosticism, mysticism, Theosophy, or any branch or twig of the long and broad esoteric tradition, Fedorov always finds fault with the exclusivity and obscurity of the writing rather than with the goals or underlying motives. The failure of esoteric teaching is that, by definition, it is directed only toward a few selected adepts rather than toward humankind at large. The paradox is that while supposedly directed toward an elite few, occult literature in general usually manages to reach a mass audience; while Fedorov's works, expounding the "common" task and directed in theory toward all people, were written in such a cryptic and enigmatic fashion, published in such small editions, and distributed to so few selected institutions and individuals that, at least until the last few years, they have existed as *de facto* classic examples of a truly esoteric tradition of knowledge. If Fedorov's intention was to open discussion on matters previously closed, the results have only recently begun to match the intent. For most of the world beyond our small circle of listeners and readers, Fedorov's treasure remains buried, and Fedorov occupies the unsought position of occultist in spite of himself.

21. See my *Nikolai F. Fedorov*, pp. 117–18. And for an interesting if one-sided and contrarian argument that Fedorov's entire project is a fantastic homosexual paradise, see Boris Paramonov, "Nechistii dukh," *Novoe russkoe slovo*, July 2, 1989, p. 6.

CHAPTER EIGHT
RUSSIAN COSMISM
IN THE 1920s AND TODAY

Michael Hagemeister

"Russian cosmism" and "Russian cosmic thinking" are terms indicative of a broad intellectual movement in contemporary Russia which has scarcely been noticed in the West. The movement was heralded by a wave of publications on anthropocosmism, sociocosmism, biocosmism, astrocosmism, sophiocosmism, colorcosmism, cosmic aesthetics, cosmic ecology, and other related topics. Beginning in 1988, a series of conferences on Russian cosmism generated enough material to fill several volumes.[1] Indeed, there is hardly an area of interest that has not been related to cosmism, whether it be icon painting, yoga, Kant's philosophy, the ethnic question, or the ozone layer.

What lies at the heart of this flourishing interest in cosmism? Stated briefly, Russian cosmism is based on a holistic and anthropocentric view of the universe which presupposes a teleologically determined—and thus meaningful—evolution; its adherents strive to redefine the role of humankind in a universe

I am indebted to Brian Poole for help in translating this article.

1. *Russkii kosmizm i noosfera: Tezisy dokladov Vsesoiuznoi konferentsii, Moskva, 1989,* 2 vols. (Moscow, 1989); *Obshchee delo: Sbornik dokladov, predstavlennykh na I Vsesoiuznye Fedorovskie chteniia, 1988 g.* (Moscow, 1990); *Russkii kosmizm: Po materialam II i III Vsesoiuznykh Fedorovskikh chtenii, 1989–1990 gg.,* 2 vols. (Moscow, 1990); L. B. Fesenkova, ed., *Russkii kosmizm i sovremennost': Sbornik statei* (Moscow, 1990). See also the *Trudy* of the annual *Tsiolkovskie chteniia* (Tsiolkovsky lectures) in Kaluga. The term "Russian cosmism" as a characterization of a national tradition of thought appeared in the early 1970s, whereas the expressions "cosmic thinking," "cosmic consciousness," "cosmic history," and "cosmic philosophy" (*philosophie cosmique*) go back to nineteenth-century mysticism and occultism (Carl Du Prel, Max Théon [Louis M. Bimstein], Elena Blavatsky, Annie Besant, Petr Uspensky) as well as to evolutionary philosophy. See, e.g., John Fiske's *Outlines of Cosmic Philosophy* (1874) and Richard M. Bucke's *Cosmic Consciousness: A Study in the Evolution of the Human Mind* (1901).

that lacks a divine plan for salvation, thus acknowledging the threat of self-destruction. As rational beings who are evolving out of the living matter (*zhivoe veshchestvo*) of the earth, human beings appear destined to become a decisive factor in cosmic evolution—a collective cosmic self-consciousness, active agent, and potential perfector. Cosmic evolution is thus dependent on human action to reach its goal, which is perfection, or wholeness. By failing to act, or failing to act correctly, humankind dooms the world to catastrophe. According to cosmism, the world is in a phase of transition from the "biosphere" (the sphere of living matter) to the "noosphere" (the sphere of reason). During this phase the active unification and organization of the whole of humankind (the *razumnoe zhivoe veshchestvo* or "living matter endowed with reason") into a single organism is said to result in a higher "planetarian consciousness" capable of guiding further development reasonably and ethically (in line with "cosmic ethics"), changing and perfecting the universe, overcoming disease and death, and finally bringing forth an immortal human race.

Cosmism is thus a highly speculative concept couched in vague terminology, a belief in progress whose popularity today reflects the increasing awareness of crisis and the need for a theory that assumes the world to be a rational entity with humankind at its center. Adherents define it as an original product of the Russian mind, an essential element of the "Russian idea" now so often invoked. The specifically national character of this worldview is said to be rooted in the uniquely Russian archetype of "all-unity" (*vseedinstvo*). Cosmists maintain that Konstantin Tsiolkovsky (1857–1935), Vladimir Vernadsky (1863–1945), and Aleksandr Chizhevsky (1897–1964) are the major representatives of their national tradition of "cosmic thinking" in this century.[2] Related thoughts are found in the philosophical conceptions of Vladimir Soloviev (1853–1900) and Pavel Florensky (1882–1937). Nikolai Fedorov (1828/29–1903), author of *Filosofiia obshchego dela* (Philosophy of the common task, 1906/1913), is considered to be the founder of this tradition.[3]

2. See, e.g., F. I. Girenok, *Russkie kosmisty* (Moscow, 1990); V. N. Dudenkov, *Russkii kosmizm: Filosofiia nadezhdy i spaseniia* (St. Petersburg, 1992); O. D. Kurakina, *Russkii kosmizm: K probleme sinteza nauki, filosofii i religii* (Moscow, 1992) and *Russkii kosmizm kak sotsiokul'turnyi fenomen* (Moscow, 1993); S. G. Semenova, "Russkii kosmizm," *Svobodnaia mysl'*, 1992, no. 17, pp. 81–97; S. G. Semenova and A. G. Gacheva, ed., *Russkii kosmizm: Antologiia filosofskoi mysli* (Moscow, 1993); A. I. Aleshin, "Kosmizm russkii," in *Russkaia filosofiia: Malyi entsiklopedicheskii slovar'* (Moscow, 1995), pp. 274–82. There is a vast literature on Tsiolkovsky and his scientific work, but a comprehensive and reliable biography remains to be written. On Vernadsky's life and work, see I. I. Mochalov, *Vladimir Ivanovich Vernadskii, 1863–1945* (Moscow, 1982); and Kendall E. Bailes, *Science and Russian Culture in an Age of Revolutions: V. I. Vernadsky and His Scientific School, 1863–1945* (Bloomington, 1990). On A. L. Chizhevsky, see his memoirs, *Vsia zhizn'* (Moscow, 1974); and V. N. Iagodinskii, *Aleksandr Leonidovich Chizhevskii, 1897–1964* (Moscow, 1987).

3. On Fedorov's life, philosophy, and its influence, see George M. Young Jr., *Nikolai F. Fedorov: An Introduction* (Belmont, Mass., 1979); Michael Hagemeister, *Nikolaj Fedorov: Studien*

Russian cosmism is, to be sure, an unconventional way of interpreting our world (perhaps justly described by the Soviet philosopher Vladimir Filatov as an example of an "alternative science").[4] To call it occult would seem an exaggeration. Yet the cosmists have always shared points of contact with occult and esoteric thought and tendencies.

On the theoretical level it is possible to isolate a large degree of contact between cosmism and the occult, even of agreement. Thus cosmism's underlying belief in the omnipotence of science and technology is rooted in the idea of the magic power of (occult) knowledge. The idea of self-perfection and self-deification, including the realization of immortality and the revival of the dead, has a long occult and Gnostic tradition. The belief in and the practice of science as a means to uncover hitherto concealed, all-powerful psychic, nervous, or cosmic energies appears to be especially characteristic. As we shall see, the conceptions of the cosmists contain, beyond the pseudoscientific elements, theosophic and pan-psychic influences.

Occasionally it is possible to isolate personal contacts, as in the case of Fedorov's follower Aleksandr Gorsky (who, while evincing his own occult leanings, maintained contact with Theosophists and Anthroposophists) and Leonid Vasiliev (a prominent psychic researcher who during the 1920s was connected with a group of so-called Biocosmists and was also a friend of the cosmist Chizhevsky, himself among the closest colleagues of Tsiolkovsky).

Finally, it is possible to localize the contacts between Russian cosmism and occult and esoteric tendencies: the city of Kaluga was a center of both cosmic thought and the Russian Theosophical movement.

Research in this field has scarcely begun. During the Soviet period of Russian history, many documents, especially in the area of pseudoscientific, occult, and esoteric thought, were repressed, falsified, or destroyed. Whatever survived or was handed down through the underground has only recently been rediscovered, largely in the interest of quenching the metaphysical thirst for meaning and for orientation. By comparison, the tendencies that may be called Promethean or God-building colluded very early with the ruling ideology, and they are now being defended loudly by adherents in an attempt to stave off its demise. Russian cosmism partakes of all these currents—the pseudoscientific, occult, and esoteric, as well as the Promethean or God-building—and this connection explains its recent rediscovery and propagation.

The link connecting cosmism with the occult and esoteric was particularly strong in the 1920s. Today, under the influence of the centrifugal forces of

---

zu Leben, Werk und Wirkung (Munich, 1989); Svetlana Semenova, *Nikolai Fedorov: Tvorchestvo zhizni* (Moscow, 1990).

4. V. P. Filatov, "Ob idee al'ternativnoi nauki," in *Zabluzhdaiushchiisia razum? Mnogoobrazie vnenauchnogo znaniia,* ed. I. T. Kasavin (Moscow, 1990), pp. 152–74.

chaos and disintegration, Russian cosmists have focused their thoughts on harmony and order. The 1920s was, by contrast, a decade saturated with utopian projects in which the Promethean bent toward world transformation and world domination prevailed.[5] There was a widespread expectation that science, art, and technology, freed from the ties of conflicting particular interests and for the first time functioning for the benefit of all humanity, would take an unprecedented upswing, pave the way for a "bright future," and transcend the final barrier blocking the gate to the realm of freedom—human limitations in space and time. Related to this idea were plans for expansion into outer space and for the regulation of geological, meteorological, and cosmic processes, all leading to the bold vision of a complete restructuring and domination of the universe, the creation of an all-powerful "new man," the abolition of death, and the resurrection of the dead.

The revolutionary belief in the omnipotence of the liberated human being erased all the lines that traditionally separated science and magic. What used to be the business of magicians, sorcerers, and alchemists now became the task of scientists and engineers: the conquest of natural laws, the absolute domination over space and time, the advance into new dimensions, and, above all, the fight against death—the last relic of unconquered nature that prevented mortals from becoming godlike. According to the writer and engineer Andrei Platonov (1899–1951), "thought" would "easily and quickly destroy death by its systematic work, science."[6]

This optimism was particularly strong among the former adherents of God-building (*bogostroitel'stvo*). Gorky was convinced that humankind would sooner or later achieve immortality. Another God-builder, the historian Nikolai Rozhkov (1868–1927), not only believed in the immortality of future generations but also preached the resurrection of the dead with the aid of science and technology.[7] Although, when put into practice, resurrection never went beyond the resuscitation of infusoria or frozen fish and amphibia (if one can give credence to the corresponding reports), optimism was strong enough to motivate preparations to preserve Lenin's corpse for future resurrection. That, at least, is the way many people interpreted the measures taken after Lenin's

5. See Richard Stites, *Revolutionary Dreams: Utopian Vision and Experimental Life in the Russian Revolution* (New York, 1989); and, more specifically, V. Baidin, " 'Kosmicheskii bunt' russkogo avangarda," in *Rossiiskii ezhegodnik '90*, vol. 2 (Moscow, 1990), pp. 181–207.

6. A. P. Platonov, "Kul'tura proletariata" (1920), quoted in Sh. Liubushkina, "Ideia bessmertiia u rannego Platonova," *Russian Literature* 23 (1988): 412. On the (black) magic origin and character of modern science and technology, see, e.g., N. A. Berdiaev, *Smysl tvorchestva* (Moscow, 1916), esp. chap. 13. Regarding the themes of fighting death and achieving physical immortality, see Irene Masing-Delic, *Abolishing Death: A Salvation Myth of Russian Twentieth-Century Literature* (Stanford, 1992).

7. N. A. Rozhkov, *Osnovy nauchnoi filosofii* (St. Petersburg, 1911), pp. 130–32, and *Smysl i krasota zhizni: Etiud iz prakticheskoi filosofii* (Petrograd and Moscow, 1923), p. 19.

death. Witness the testimony of Zhachev, the protagonist in Platonov's novel *Kotlovan* (The foundation pit, 1929/30):

> "Prushevsky! Will the successes of higher science be capable of resurrecting the rotting corpses of men?"
> "No," Prushevsky said.
> "You're lying," Zhachev objected. . . . "Marxism can do anything. Why do you think Lenin lies in Moscow perfectly intact? He is waiting for science, he wants to rise from the dead."[8]

Nowhere is the goal of overcoming death and resurrecting the dead given more detailed treatment than in Fedorov's description of the "common task," and nowhere is this goal based on a firmer moral conviction. As a rational being, man is able, indeed obliged, to work to transform everything natural (and therefore transitory) including himself into an intransitory synthetic creation of reason. By bringing himself and his external environment into his control and turning it into a work of art, man rids himself of all divisiveness, destruction, and mortality. Upon humans' actions depends not only their own deliverance but also the salvation and perfection of the entire universe.

The realization of Fedorov's project does not, however, presume to restrict itself to "superhuman" individuals or to a select group of chosen ("the righteous"). On the contrary: the combined efforts of all humankind, living and dead, are required in order to vanquish death and perfect the universe, since perfection and immortality are morally justified only if all without exception are comprehended in the action intended to nullify historically accumulated injustice and suffering. Thus all "brothers" are called upon to unite fraternally and combine all their scientific and technical skills in the project of physically resurrecting their deceased forefathers. Fedorov's innerworldly paradise attains perfection through the unification of all humankind—a paradise created by all and for all, in which there are no damned, no victims of history.

The means of attaining "all-unity" lies in the resurrection that mankind consciously effects with the help of science and technology and that is progressively directed toward the conscious re-creation (*soznatel'noe vossozdanie*) of all our ancestors. Fedorov regards this as an exclusively physical process—tracking down, collecting, and synthesizing the smallest of particles. The product is a consummate work of art that, as the creation of a rational being, is immortal and perfect.

In the search for the dispersed particles of their ancestors, humans will, according to Fedorov, expand out into space—and here, too, the resurrected

8. A. P. Platonov, *Kotlovan. Iuvenil'noe more* (Moscow, 1987), p. 97. One is reminded of Lenin's famous dictum "The doctrine of Marx is omnipotent because it is true": V. I. Lenin, *Polnoe sobranie sochinenii*, 5th ed. (Moscow, 1961), 23:43.

will take up residence, inhabiting the universe with reason and transforming it into a work of art. Resurrection and the conquest of the universe are dependent on each other, "since without the control of the heavens, the simultaneous existence of generations is not possible, although, on the other hand, without resurrection it is not possible to achieve complete control of the heavens."[9] By uniting all generations and settling throughout the universe, Fedorov maintains, men will overcome all borders of space and time, becoming not just omniscient and omnipotent, but also omnipresent and immortal:

> The resurrection of all mankind will result in a complete victory over space and time. The transition "from earth to the heavens" is a victory, a triumph over space (or successive omnipresence). The transition from death to life, or the simultaneous coexistence *of all ages of time* (generations), the coexistence of their succession, is a triumph over time.[10]

With this goal in mind, Fedorov developed a multitude of bold technical projects, beginning with the control and regulation of atmospheric processes and the use of new energy sources, and continuing right through to the transformation of the earth into a gigantic spaceship with which humans could then cruise through the universe and populate other planets. Precisely such utopian projects—especially in the early postrevolutionary years—found an eager following, although almost without exception the moral foundation of these projects—which was actually Fedorov's main interest—dropped out of the picture as their popularity grew.

The followers and disciples of Nikolai Fedorov, the so-called *fedorovtsy*, who assembled in Moscow at the beginning of the 1920s[11] were mainly fascinated by the technical aspects of Fedorov's ideas on the resurrection of the dead and on the transformation and colonization of the universe, and tried to combine them with the latest scientific and technological achievements, paying special attention to the resurrection of the dead. An impressive graphic illustration of the first stage of this process—the search for the particles and traces of the dead ancestors on earth and in the universe—is given in the charcoal drawing *Nachalo vnekhramovogo deistviia* (The beginning of extra-ecclesiastical activity, 1921/22; see Figure 8.1) by the artist and Fedorov follower Vasily Chekrygin (1897–1922).[12] *Deistvie* is also used to mean liturgy.

In expectation of the future resurrection of the dead, the Fedorov adherent Nikolai Setnitsky (1888–1937), an economist, philosopher, and writer, demanded the abolition of the modern practice of disposing of corpses by cremation or burial outside the towns, and a return to more traditional forms of

9. N. F. Fedorov, *Filosofiia obshchego dela,* 2 vols. (1906–13; Farnborough, Hants., 1970), 1:283.
10. Ibid., 2:351.
11. For details, see Hagemeister, *Nikolaj Fedorov,* pp. 343–62.
12. For more on Chekrygin, see ibid., pp. 286–99.

Figure 8.1. V. N. Chekrygin's *Nachalo vnekhramovogo deistviia* (1921 / 22) depicts "the beginning of extra-ecclesiastical activity"—the search for traces of dead ancestors on earth and in the universe, so that they may be resurrected.

funerals based on the belief in resurrection and so requiring the preservation of the dead body. As a model worthy of imitation he cited the embalming of Lenin's corpse and its preservation in the center of Moscow. According to Setnitsky, less prominent contemporaries could look forward to their eventual resurrection in a "world cemetery" (*mirovoi nekropol'*), which was to be located in the permafrost regions of the North.[13]

Setnitsky's lively and largely unpublished correspondence in the 1920s and '30s demonstrates that he attempted to engage Gorky as a propagandist for Fedorov's ideas. Gorky, who hated death and called for its abolition, showed some interest, but could never accept the thought of a material and individual resuscitation of the dead. Fedorov's doctrine, however, was not always interpreted in a materialistic and scientific way. Among those who were interested in Fedorov during the 1920s were the World War I general Aleksei Brusilov (1853–1926), who had a strong penchant for occultism and Theosophy, and was married to one of Elena Blavatsky's nieces; the writer Olga Forsh (1873–1961), who had worked on Buddhism, Theosophy, Gnosticism, and occultism; and the historian and theologian Iuliia Danzas (1879–1942), a noted specialist in Gnosis and occultism who had been for some time a Theosophist and a member of a St. Petersburg Martinist order.[14]

The central figure of the Moscow *fedorovtsy* was the rather obscure philosopher and poet Aleksandr Gorsky (who wrote variously as Gornostaev and Ostromirov; 1886–1943), whose work shows distinct references to occult and esoteric thought.[15] As a youth, Gorsky became acquainted with Karl von Reichenbach's (1788–1869) pseudoscientific doctrine of "odic force" and soon came under the powerful influence of the American journalist and popular philosopher Prentice Mulford (1834–91), who maintained that the individual, by controlling and applying the creative power of thought, could achieve health, longevity, and even physical immortality. Later, at the Moscow Theological Academy, Gorsky became a disciple of Pavel Florensky, who was a specialist in occult traditions and whose own worldview contained a large measure of magical and Gnostic features (one need only consider his studies on the magic of words and the occult energies of names). In the 1920s Gorsky maintained contact with Nikolai Rerikh (1874–1947) and with a group of cosmist painters called Amaravella. During the late '30s and early '40s Gorsky

---

13. N. A. S[etnits]kii, "O smerti i pogrebenii," *Vselenskoe delo*, sb. 2 (Riga, 1934), pp. 141–46. On Setnitsky, see Hagemeister, *Nikolaj Fedorov*.

14. See Hagemeister, *Nikolaj Fedorov*, esp. pp. 366, 371–79, 389–93, 396–403. For A. A. Brusilov's interest in the occult and Theosophy, and for his marriage to Nadezhda Zhelikhovskaia, Mme Blavatsky's niece, see his memoirs, *Moi vospominaniia* (Moscow and Leningrad, 1929), pp. 31, 33–35, and Iurii Sokolov, *Krasnaia zvezda ili krest'?: Zhizn' i sud'ba generala Brusilova* (Moscow, 1994), pp. 27–29, 114–15; on Forsh see A. V. Tamarchenko, *Ol'ga Forsh* (Moscow and Leningrad, 1966), pp. 31–42, 47–49; on Danzas see Mikhail Agurskii, "M. Gor'kii i Iu. N. Danzas," *Minuvshee* (Paris), 1988, no. 5, pp. 360–61.

15. For details on Gorsky's life and work, see Hagemeister, *Nikolaj Fedorov*.

lived in Kaluga, a center for Russian cosmism and esoteric thought. In 1943 he was accused of having led a secret Anthroposophy group there.[16]

The Leningrad historian Nikolai Antsiferov, who met Gorsky in a labor camp on the White Sea Canal in the early 1930s, noted in his memoirs that Gorsky

> was an assiduous follower of the teachings of Fedorov and his theory of the "common task." Death is not a law of life; it must be overcome. One must be chaste. Chastity is a precondition for the immortality of the flesh. But the goal is not only personal immortality. Death must be overcome once and for all, and it is the obligation of all the living to resurrect the dead. That is the "common task." And Gorsky maintained his chastity, and what's more, he remained . . . chaste in his marriage. . . . Whenever someone died, in Gorsky's eyes, he committed an unworthy deed. Gorsky himself firmly believed that he would not die. He believed it beyond the shadow of a doubt.[17]

In the 1920s Gorsky wrote a book he called "Ogromnyi ocherk" (An enormous sketch), which has not yet been published and which is said to be his magnum opus. In a peculiar continuation of Fedorov's idea of "positive chastity" (the redirection of sexual energy toward the restoration of life to the dead), Gorsky speculated about the transformation and sublimation of sexual energy into a powerful creative potential for the perfection of humanity, the abolition of death, and the conquering and restructuring of the universe. In these speculations he alluded to the ideas of Reichenbach and especially Mulford as well as to contemporary theories: Freud's doctrine of instinctual drives is obviously present, and the assumption of "sexual energy" that can be accumulated and transformed reminds one of Wilhelm Reich's theory of (cosmic) orgone energy and its applications.[18] It is clear that Gorsky was familiar with the research and theories on the "psycho-physical radiation of the brain" and the transformation of human nervous energy. And he knew the book by the German analytic chemist Ludwig Staudenmaier (1865–1933) *Die Magie als experimentelle Naturwissenschaft* (Magic as experimental natural science), in which magic phenomena are related back to the transformation of nervous energy.

16. A. V. Belov and D. A. Karpov, *Mistika na sluzhbe antikommunizma* (Moscow, 1978), pp. 19–20.

17. N. P. Antsiferov, *Iz dum o bylom: Vospominaniia* (Moscow, 1992), p. 378. On the connection between physical immortality and asexuality (ranging from chastity to castration) in Russian folk and sectarian belief as well as in utopian thought, see Aleksandr Etkind, "Russkie skoptsy: Opyt istorii," *Zvezda*, 1995, no. 4, esp. pp. 150–53; and Eric Naiman, "Historectomies: On the Metaphysics of Reproduction in a Utopian Age," in *Sexuality and the Body in Russian Culture*, ed. Jane T. Costlow et al. (Stanford, 1993), pp. 255–76.

18. See W. Edward Mann, *Orgone, Reich and Eros: Wilhelm Reich's Theory of Life Energy* (New York, 1973), who also gives a good overview of energy theories. Reich's influence in the Soviet Union is yet to be investigated.

The search for occult forces and energies springing from the human organism played a major role in a wide range of plans to expand human power, and led to a myriad of experiments and bold speculation in the margins of regular science. At the institute of the biophysicist Petr Lazarev (1878–1942), attempts were made not only to transform "nervous energy"—which was thought to be emitted by the human organism in the form of electromagnetic waves—into light and heat but also to use it in the form of mental suggestion and telepathy as a means of direct communication and to employ it for moving and transforming objects (telekinesis). The physiologist Sergei Beknev wrote in 1923 that in the future, simply by controlling the transformation of nervous energy into other forms of energy, people not only would become sources of light and heat whenever they wished but would also directly affect matter and change its structure.[19]

The conception of an effective "psycho-physical" or "nervous" energy had become popular in Russia around the turn of the century primarily through the philosophical writings of the German chemist Wilhelm Ostwald (1853–1932), who claimed that energy, and not matter, was the basic principle of all natural phenomena. In 1904 the neurologist Naum Kotik began his research on "psycho-physical energy" in Odessa. He claimed that this energy was generated in the brain and redirected into the extremities. One of the astounding attributes of this energy was supposed to be its ability to pass into objects (paper, for example), where it could be stored and transported. With the help of this energy, thoughts and feelings could be conveyed (telepathy); in higher concentration it could be a carrier for mass suggestion.[20] In connection with Kotik's research, Maxim Gorky wrote in 1912: "Every year more and more thought-energy accumulates in the world, and I am convinced that this energy—which, while possibly related to light or electricity, has its own unique inherent qualities—will one day be able to effect things we cannot even imagine today."[21]

19. S. A. Beknev, *Gipoteza o nervnoi energii i ee znachenie v dele obrazovaniia rabochikh kollektivov maksimal'noi proizvoditel'nosti truda* (Moscow, 1923).

20. Naum Genrikhovich Kotik, born October 26, 1876, in Odessa, graduated in 1901 from Berlin University (his doctoral thesis contains a short curriculum vitae); he settled in Odessa, where he practiced as an internist and pediatrician. But he was more preoccupied with experimental research in telepathy and brain radiation. His major works are *Emanatsiia psikhofizicheskoi energii: Eksperimental'noe issledovanie iavlenii mediumizma, iasnovideniia i myslennogo vnusheniia v sviazi s voprosom o radioaktivnosti mozga* (Moscow, 1907); *Neposredstvennaia peredacha myslei: Eksperimental'noe issledovanie* (Moscow, 1908; 2d ed., 1912). Kotik was mentioned in *Rossiiskii meditsinskii spisok* (Petrograd, 1916); no references to Kotik can be found after this date. (For the last piece of information I am indebted to the L. L. Vasiliev Fund of Parapsychology, Moscow.)

21. M. Gor'kii, "Izdaleka" (V), in *Nesobrannye literaturno-kriticheskie stat'i* (Moscow, 1941), p. 434. See also Heinz Setzer, "Die Bedeutung der Energielehre für die Literaturkonzeption Maksim Gor'kijs nach der ersten russischen Revolution," *Welt der Slaven* 25 (1980): 394–427;

Again borrowing from Kotik, Gorky formulated in 1919 an idea that seems to anticipate the concept of the "noosphere": "Besides the atmosphere and the photosphere, our entire planet is enveloped in a sphere of spiritual creation, a manifold, iridescent emanation of our energy. . . ."[22]

Fedorov had already presumed that "nervous energy" was comparable to or even identical with electricity and that physical expressions of psychological processes could be transmitted by means of electric current.[23] In the 1920s and '30s the assumption of physically measurable brain radiation (the "brain radio") formed the basis for the pioneering studies of the Leningrad physiologist Leonid Vasiliev (1891–1966) in long-distance telepathy. In 1921 Vasiliev joined the Petrograd Institute for Brain Research, founded and directed by the noted physiological psychologist Vladimir Bekhterev (1857–1927). Bekhterev had a keen interest in hypnosis and mental suggestion, and was currently attempting, with the help of the animal trainer Vladimir Durov, to convey movement commands to trained dogs by mental suggestion. On Bekhterev's initiative a special commission was founded in 1922 to study the problem of mental suggestion. After Bekhterev's death, Vasiliev continued their research and later became one of the leading Soviet psychical researchers.[24]

In November 1922 we find Vasiliev's name among the contributors to a magazine called *Bessmertie* (Immortality). It was the organ of the Petrograd Biocosmists-Immortalists, who, under the motto "Immortalism and Interplanetarianism," proclaimed two basic human rights: the right to exist (*pravo na bytie*) and the right of unimpended movement (*pravo na peredvizhenie*). In effect they postulated the immediate abolition of bondage to time and space: now that the social revolution had been accomplished, it was time to put the abolition of death, the colonization of the universe, and the resurrection of the dead on the agenda.[25] This demand appeared at the time of Lenin's death to be an immediate necessity: "The consciousness of the workers and the oppressed all

Mikhail Agurskii, "Velikii eretik: Gor'kii kak religioznyj myslitel'," *Voprosy filosofii*, 1991, no. 8, pp. 54–74, on Kotik esp. 63–64.

22. M. Gor'kii, "Vsemirnaia literatura," in *Nesobrannye stat'i*, p. 276.

23. Fedorov, *Filosofiia obshchego dela*, 1:328, 331.

24. An extensive report on the research program on mental suggestion in the 1920s and '30s can be found in L. L. Vasil'ev, *Eksperimental'nye issledovaniia myslennogo vnusheniia* (Leningrad, 1962); see also his *Tainstvennye iavleniia chelovecheskoi psikhiki* (Moscow, 1959; 2d ed., 1963; 3d ed., 1964) and *Vnushenie na rasstoianii: Zametki fiziologa* (Moscow, 1962). All these books have been translated into English and several other languages.

25. A. Iaroslavskii, "Kosmicheskii Maksimalizm," *Bessmertie* (Petrograd), November 25, 1922, p. 2; cf. "Deklarativnaia rezoliutsiia," *Izvestiia VTsIK*, January 4, 1922, p. 3. For more on the Biocosmists, see Michael Hagemeister, "Die 'Biokosmisten'—Anarchismus und Maximalismus in der frühen Sowjetzeit," in *Studia slavica in honorem viri doctissimi Olexa Horbatsch*, ed. G. Freidhof et al., vol. 1, pt. 1 (Munich, 1983), pp. 61–76; idem, *Nikolaj Fedorov*, pp. 300–317.

over the world," went the argument of the Biocosmists, "could never reconcile itself with the fact of Lenin's death."[26]

The Biocosmists, a rather small group of anarchists and poets, had first become prominent in Moscow around 1920 under the leadership of Aleksandr Sviatogor (pseudonym of A. F. Agienko, whose dates are unknown); in 1922 a Petrograd group seceded under the leadership of Aleksandr Iaroslavsky (1897–ca. 1930). In their struggle against death and for the conquest of space the Biocosmists tried to recruit such prominent scientists as the Viennese physiologist Eugen Steinach (1861–1944), who concentrated on experiments on the revitalization and rejuvenation of organisms; Albert Einstein, whose theory of relativity promised "the domination and reversion of time" and whose famous equation, $E = mc^2$, became a sort of universal formula of almost magical power; and finally the cosmist thinker and pioneer of space rocketry Konstantin Tsiolkovsky, who lived in Kaluga.

When he joined the Petrograd Biocosmists at the beginning of the 1920s, the telepathy researcher Leonid Vasiliev was a close friend of the biophysicist, historian, and cosmist painter and poet Aleksandr Chizhevsky, who further developed the theory of the influence of cosmic factors (cosmic radiation and periodic sunspot activity) on the behavior of organized human masses as well as on the universal historical process—a theory that was widely discussed at the time. Chizhevsky's assertion of a causal relationship between the eleven-year cycle in the appearance of sunspots and the intensity of social unrest, wars, revolutions, and even epidemics shows obvious connections with astrology and the occult fascination with prophecy.[27] No wonder Marxist critics condemned his search for what they called a "transcendent factor of the historical process" as leading to "cosmic fatalism." In the 1920s Chizhevsky was a collaborator and close confidant of Konstantin Tsiolkovsky; he edited and published some of Tsiolkovsky's works and tried to generate a forum for his astronautical projects. It may have been Chizhevsky who inspired Vasiliev's interest in Biocosmism at that time.[28]

The obscure provincial town of Kaluga was not only one of the centers of the Russian Theosophical movement and (since 1908) the residence of its Lotos publishing house, but also home base for the famous cosmist thinker and "grandfather of Russian space travel" Konstantin Tsiolkovsky, who spent most of his life there and died there in 1935.[29] Tsiolkovsky, the "eccentric from Ka-

26. A. Sviatogor et al., "Golos anarkhistov," *Izvestiia TsIK SSSR*, January 27, 1924, p. 5.

27. A. L. Chizhevskii, *Fizicheskie faktory istoricheskogo protsessa* (1924; Kaluga, 1992); idem, *Zemnoe ekho solnechnykh bur'*, 2d ed. (Moscow, 1976); idem, *Kosmicheskii pul's zhizni: Zemlia v ob"iatiiakh solntsa. Geliotaraksiia* (Moscow, 1995). For connections with astrology, see Michel Gauquelin, *The Cosmic Clocks: From Astrology to a Modern Science* (Chicago, 1967; London and New York, 1969) and *The Scientific Basis of Astrology* (New York, 1969).

28. Chizhevskii, *Vsia zhizn'*, pp. 181–82.

29. Aleksandr Chizhevsky and the Fedorovite Aleksandr Gorsky also lived in Kaluga for some time. Kaluga's attraction for cosmists and occultists has been explained by the impact

luga" (*kaluzhskii chudak*), has often been called a disciple of Fedorov. This allegation, however, raises serious questions. Tsiolkovsky did indeed meet Fedorov at the age of sixteen when he was studying in the Chertkov library in Moscow, but we do not know whether Fedorov discussed his ideas with him. Tsiolkovsky himself says that he learned about Fedorov's ideas only ten years after Fedorov had died.[30] It is well known that Tsiolkovsky cultivated his image as an original thinker and thus almost always left his sources unacknowledged. In any case, his space projects were more likely inspired by Jules Verne and Camille Flammarion, and do not reveal any direct influence of Fedorov. Indeed, Tsiolkovsky's solution to the problem of death is, as we shall see, directly opposed to Fedorov's claim for the *material* permanence of the *individual*. Tsiolkovsky's uneven and, on the whole, rather primitive philosophical views obviously have very little in common with Fedorov's.

Tsiolkovsky called himself a Biocosmist and a "panpsychist," and claimed to "acknowledge the sensitivity of the whole universe." He referred to the cosmos as an "animal being" (*zhivotnoe*); the world and the solar systems were for him enormous, soul-endowed organisms. He also believed in the existence of conscious, intelligent beings more perfect than humans but nearly incorporeal, ethereal, and therefore incomprehensible to us. He even believed that these beings, obviously closely related to the angels, send messages to humans using atmospheric or heavenly symbols, and averred that he himself was twice a witness to such events.[31] Tsiolkovsky expounded upon his "cosmic philosophy" (*kosmicheskaia filosofiia*) in a naive didactic tone in numerous brochures with such titles as *Nirvana* (1914), *Prichina kosmosa* (The cause of the cosmos, 1925), *Monizm vselennoi* (The Monism of the universe, 1925), *Volia vselennoi: Neizvestnye razumnye sily* (The will of the universe: Unknown rational powers, 1928), and *Nauchnaia etika* (Scientific ethics, 1930), which he published himself in Kaluga.[32]

A detailed study of these works (not to mention the unpublished manuscripts buried in the archives of the Russian Academy of Sciences, among them a positivistic exegesis of the four Gospels) gives credence to what has so far only occasionally been mentioned—that the philosophy of this Russian astro-

---

of a meteor on the outskirts of the city: Vladimir Lytkin, vice-director of the K. Tsiolkovsky State Museum for the History of Cosmonautics in Kaluga, personal communication, Kaluga, May 18, 1992.

30. See K. N. Altaiskii [K. N. Korolev], "Moskovskaia iunost' Tsiolkovskogo," *Moskva*, 1966, no. 9, pp. 181–82.

31. See K. E. Tsiolkovskii, *Volia vselennoi: Neizvestnye razumnye sily* (Kaluga, 1928), pp. 9, 22–23.

32. These thin brochures had only a small circulation and have thus become bibliographic rarities. An edition of Tsiolkovsky's works in 10 volumes is now in preparation under the direction of the Russian Academy of Sciences. Three volumes of cosmic-philosophical, religious, and socio-utopian works, edited by N. K. Gavriushin, are planned. Vladimir Kaziutinsky, personal communication, Moscow, May 15, 1992.

nautical pioneer and hero of Soviet propaganda is rife with ideas of eternally "lively and happy atoms," of the sensitivity of matter, of the conscious energy inherent in all matter striving for further development, perfection, and happiness; ideas that constitute a peculiar synthesis of vitalism and monadology with Theosophical, Buddhist, and pan-psychic thought.[33] This is especially apparent in Tsiolkovsky's solution to the problem of death: a human being is nothing more than a temporary "realm of immortal atoms" (*gosudarstvo bessmertnych atomov*), which are scattered at death only to be reconfigured, according to the cosmic law of evolution and the quest for happiness, into more perfect, blissful "realms":

> Death therefore is simply one of the illusions of the weak human mind. Death does not exist. . . . The universe is constructed in such a way that not only is it itself immortal, but also all its parts, in the form of living, blessed beings. There is no beginning and no end to the universe, and thus no beginning and no end to life and to bliss.[34]

A study of Tsiolkovsky's philosophy would shed new light on the Soviet space program—a program that was supposed to open the cosmic way to the transfiguration and perfection of humanity, and finally to eternal salvation. The advancement into space was intended not merely to expand human powers and capabilities but also to rebuild the human body in order to accommodate it to the conditions of life in the cosmos. This development, in turn, was supposed to bring forth a generation of superhumans who would be to us what we are to a unicellular organism. Ultimately, the human race would lose its corporeality and individuality and turn into a kind of radiation, "immortal in time and infinite in space."[35]

33. See N. K. Gavriushin, "Kosmicheskii put' k 'vechnomu blazhenstvu' (K. E. Tsiolkovskii i mifologiia tekhnokratii)," *Voprosy filosofii*, 1992, no. 6, pp. 125–31. In this respect it is remarkable that the German rocket pioneers and engineers Hermann Ganswindt (1856–1934), Hermann Oberth (1894–1989), and Max Valier (1895–1930) were also engaged in extensive metaphysical and occult speculation, and were fascinated by paranormal phenomena. Valier not only developed powerful rocket engines but also followed the pseudoscientific cosmic ice theory and published an extensive *Okkulte Weltallslehre* [Occult doctrine of the universe] (Munich, 1922), in which he described the universe as a "living and besouled organism," in accordance with the Hermetic doctrine of the microcosm and macrocosm.

34. Tsiolkovskii, *Volia vselennoi*, p. 7; see also his *Nauchnaia etika*, pp. 24–32. Tsiolkovsky's conception comes close to the idea—developed by some of the Theosophists—of the "permanent atom," which passes from one incarnation to another.

35. A. L. Chizhevskii, "Stranitsy vospominanii o K. E. Tsiolkovskom," *Khimiia i zhizn'*, 1977, no. 1, pp. 23–32. According to the Moscow scientist V. N. Kozitsky, Tsiolkovsky's "radiant humanity" (*luchistoe chelovechestvo*) already exists in the form of the earth's magnetic field, which he supposes to be a sort of collective supermemory in which all information (along with thoughts, feelings, and efforts) are recorded and kept alive. See V. N. Kozitskii, "Gipoteza o sushchnosti noosfery," in *Russkii kosmizm: Po materialam II i III Fedorovskikh chtenii*, 2:96–

In 1990 the Institute for Philosophy of the Academy of Sciences published a collection of essays titled *Russkii kosmizm i sovremennost'* (Russian cosmism and the contemporary world), which begins with the words "Currently Russian cosmism has gained enormous popularity." This is certainly no exaggeration. Russian cosmism has found its way into every branch of the media, and is being avidly researched at institutes and discussed at scientific conferences.

Still, the popularity has an unmistakably strong nonprofessional coloration. Most of the people who have organized themselves into circles and societies (often bearing sectarian traits) to meet and devote themselves to the study and dissemination of the ideas of Fedorov, Tsiolkovsky, Vernadsky, and Chizhevsky are not scientists.

The artworks of the Russian cosmists—especially of the 1920s—have also been rediscovered and praised. Iury Linnik (b. 1944), a self-proclaimed "cosmist poet and philosopher," has founded a Museum of Cosmic Art in Karelia where he is collecting the paintings of the cosmist group Amaravella (1923–30); he is also attempting to supplement Russian cosmism with the ideas of Elena Blavatsky and the occult doctrine of Agni-yoga recorded by Elena and Nikolai Rerikh.[36] In Kaluga the annual Tsiolkovsky lectures have for years provided a forum for the discussion of pseudoscientific and even occult theories. More recently, the Theosophists have reappeared; despite the fact that they are dependent on the reprints produced in Riga—their own libraries and archives were dispersed or destroyed long ago—they are contributing to the revival of Kaluga's long-standing esoteric and cosmic traditions.

There are manifold connections between the contemporary cosmists and other groups and movements within the flourishing religious, philosophical, and occult subculture in Russia—the followers of George Gurdjieff (c. 1877–1949) and Petr Uspensky (1878–1947), the adherents of Lev Gumilev's (1912–92) highly speculative biocosmic theory of ethnogenesis, and the devotees of Daniil Andreev's (1906–59) even more speculative historiosophy, to name just a few. Russian cosmism seems to be just as intriguing to the so-called *ivanovtsy*, the followers of the prominent health freak Porfiry Ivanov (1898–1983)—the "messenger of the Cosmos" (*poslannik Kosmosa*)—as it is to environmentalists and lifestyle reformers, pacifists and vegetarians.[37]

The ideas of the cosmists have become especially significant in the wake of the lively discussions over the existence of extraterrestrials and unidentified flying objects (in Russian *nepoznannye letaiushchie ob''ekty*, or NLOs). While

---

98. Kozitsky's hypothesis reminds one of Rupert Sheldrake's highly controversial theory of "morphogenetic fields."

36. See Iu. V. Linnik, "Amaravella," *Sever*, 1981, no. 11, pp. 108–14; idem, *Amaravella: Katalog vystavki* (Petrozavodsk, 1989); idem, *V poiskakh Shambaly* (Petrozavodsk, 1992).

37. Examples can be found in the often eccentric contributions to the Fedorov Lectures (*Fedorovskie Chteniia*) that have been held annually since 1988.

Orthodox theologians dutifully interpret such phenomena as the contemporary apparitions of evil spirits, the UFOlogists and parapsychologists, researching on the borderlines of traditional science, refer increasingly to the theories of Vernadsky, Tsiolkovsky, Chizhevsky, and even Fedorov.[38]

Much of the syncretic ideology currently propagated under the label of "cosmism" appears to be a Russian variant of Western New Age thinking, since both are rooted in the same traditions of pseudoscientific utopian and occult and esoteric thought. Take the holistic-organic conceptions of James Lovelock or Gregory Bateson; their works are proof that concepts such as "planetarian consciousness," "noosphere," "ecology of the mind," and the so-called Gaia theory, which supposes the earth to be a self-regulating organism, have become standard terminology for both Western New Age ideologists and the modern Russian cosmists Nikita Moiseev, Fedor Girenok, and Vlail Kaznacheev, to name only the most prominent exponents.[39]

In connection with these movements, the concept of the "noosphere" has become something of a fad. The term "noosphere" was coined in the 1920s by the French mathematician and Bergsonian Edouard Le Roy (1870–1954) and popularized by Pierre Teilhard de Chardin (1881–1955). With their work in mind, Vernadsky developed his own conception of the noosphere, defining it as a new phase of evolution brought about by conscious human activity—a conception that Vernadsky sketched shortly before his death in 1945.[40] Esoteric publishing houses, informal groups, and pseudoscientific organizations are among those who call themselves *noosfera*. For a few years now the N. D. Zelinsky Center for the Protection of the Noosphere has been at work in

38. See, e.g., Ieromonach Serafim [Rouz (Rose)], *NLO: Nepoznannye letaiushchie ob"ekty v svete pravoslavnoi very* (Moscow, 1991); *Neperiodicheskie bystroprotekaiushchie iavleniia v okruzhaiushchei srede* (Tomsk, 1990).

39. See, e.g., James Lovelock, *The Ages of Gaia: A Biography of Our Living Earth* (New York and London, 1988); Lawrence E. Joseph, *Gaia: The Growth of an Idea* (New York, 1990); N. N. Moiseev, "U rokovoi cherty," *Oktiabr'*, 1988, no. 3, pp. 163–78; idem, "Ekologiia, nravstvennost' i politika," *Voprosy filosofii*, 1989, no. 5, pp. 3–25; idem, *Chelovek i noosfera* (Moscow, 1990; an English translation called *The Sphere of Reason: Vernadsky and the Gaia System* has been announced); V. P. Kaznacheev, *Uchenie V. I. Vernadskogo o biosfere i noosfere* (Novosibirsk, 1989); Moiseev and E. A. Spirin, *Kosmoplanetarnyi fenomen cheloveka: Problemy kompleksnogo izucheniia* (Novosibirsk, 1991). Vlail Petrovich Kaznacheev, who is a member of the Russian Academy of Medical Sciences and director of the Institute of Clinical and Experimental Medicine in Novosibirsk, conducts parapsychological experiments on "bioinformation"; see his "Opinion on Principles of PSI," in *Study Guide to UFOs, Psychic and Paranormal Phenomena in the USSR*, ed. Antonio Huneeus (New York, 1990), pp. 75–79.

40. See V. I. Vernadskii, *Biosfera i noosfera* (Moscow, 1989) and *Nauchnaia mysl' kak planetnoe iavlenie* (Moscow, 1991). Although the publications of Vernadsky's late works on natural philosophy were generally mutilated by censorship, it has nevertheless been apparent that these works cannot be subsumed by vulgar materialist interpretation. Regrettably, Kendall Bailes, in *Science and Russian Culture*—the first biography of Vernadsky to be published in any Western country—hardly ever deals with Vernadsky's philosophy and his theories of the noosphere, and he fails to mention the cosmism for which Vernadsky is so revered in Russia.

the heart of Moscow; Odessa has a Public Institute of the Noosphere (with branches in many cities); and an Orthodox Noosphere University in Moscow has begun to offer courses in "noospheric culturology." Now that the cosmists at the Udmurt State University in Izhevsk have solved—in theory—the problem of human immortality (the practical realization depending, of course, on support from Western sponsors), plans are under way for a World Center of Cosmic Philosophy in the Altai Mountains which will have the task of co-ordinating the worldwide efforts toward the "creation of the noosphere" (*noosferizatsiia*).[41]

And yet one soon discovers that there is something specifically Russian in contemporary cosmism when one considers it as a type of neo-God-building destined to take the place of discredited Western materialistic communism, replacing it with an autochthonous, pseudoscientific religion of the superman. Such an attempt has been made by the "post-industrial patriots," a group of prominent Moscow scientists who propagate a "new humanistic religion" that incorporates allusions to Fedorov, Teilhard de Chardin, and Vernadsky; in their view, this "metaphysics of the common task," a metaphysical doctrine of the "universal cosmic project," is the only ideology capable of conveying to humanity its "historic and cosmic mission," thus overcoming the "cosmic absurdity of human existence."[42] The image of humanity spreading its "noocratic" rule over the universe, whence it can fulfill the "universal cosmic plan" of turning itself into an almighty immortal organism, thus attaining the status of God, is an image that quickly reveals its unmistakably totalitarian character. Even Fedorov's world-delivering common task was totalitarian: no one had

41. Among the founders of the Moscow Tsentr Noosfernoi Zashchity im. Akademika N. D. Zelinskogo and the Pravoslavnyi Noosfernyi Universitet was Iuliia Shishina, a student and former associate of Aleksandr Chizhevsky. On the Obshchestvennyi Institut Noosfery (OIN) in Odessa, see the exhibition catalog *Proekt Zemnogo shara budushchego* (Moscow, 1990) and the volume of essays *Razvitie predstavlenii V. I. Vernadskogo o noosfere* (Moscow, 1991). A Moscow Ob"edinenie Noosfera, which has taken on the task of supplying the atmosphere with ozone, went public in 1989 with the suggestion that the large open-air swimming pool that then occupied the site of the reconstructed cathedral of Christ the Saviour in the center of Moscow should be consecrated and used for mass baptism. Vladimir P. Iaryshkin, chief of the Human Problems Laboratory at Udmurt State University, has communicated to me a number of works on the problem of human immortality and its solution which borrow from Tsiolkovsky. The projected Mirovoi Tsentr Kosmicheskoi Filosofii is a joint effort of the Moscow Cosmic Club, the Rerikh Research Center in Baranaul, and the Institute for Security and Cooperation in Outer Space, Washington.

42. See S. E. Kurginian et al., *Postperestroika: Kontseptual'naia model' razvitiia nashego obshchestva, politicheskikh partii i obshchestvennykh organizatsii* (Moscow, 1990), esp. pp. 58, 71, 82. For a critical view, see Stephen D. Shenfield, "Beware: God-builders at Work!" *Russia and the World* 20 (1991): n.p. The Russian Ministry of Defense has founded an Institute of Noocosmology, and a high-ranking member of the Security Council has suggested that the "national identity of Russia" should be realized through the "ideas of Russian cosmism." See Diakon Andrei Kuraev, "Gosudarstvennyi okkul'tizm?" *Ogonek*, 1995, no. 21, p. 49.

the right to be excluded or forgotten, no one could withdraw from the magnificent project. Tsiolkovsky, too, while scheming to eradicate all evil and suffering and to make every last atom happy, outlined in gloating pedantry the complete extermination of all deleterious and useless forms of plant and animal life, declaring a "battle against the procreation of defective people and animals."[43]

Whereas its conservative critics reject Russian cosmism as the "shadow ideology" of Russian communism, or discredit it by pointing to its Western origins and occult leanings, devotees refer to it as one of the greatest revelations of human culture.[44] This Russian "active-evolutionary, noospheric, cosmic thinking" is, in the words of the philosopher Arseny Gulyga, not only "the last word in philosophy" and the "pride of our national science," but also, by dint of its "general human significance," the "philosophy of the future," capable of solving the urgent problems of humanity by paving the path toward the "divine stage of human development."[45] Cosmism has thus become the catchword for yet another Russian doctrine threatening to save the world.

43. See K. E. Tsiolkovskii, *Budushchee Zemli i chelovechestva* (Kaluga, 1928), pp. 6–8, 16, and *Liubov' k samomu sebe, ili istinnoe sebialiubie* (Kaluga, 1928), p. 37. One is tempted to interpret such formulations as expressions of the totalitarianism of the dawning Stalin era, but the same tone can be found in Tsiolkovsky's earlier works. In an unpublished article of 1917/18 he declares that "the foundation of [our] laws must be . . . the perfection of man and the liquidation of all imperfect forms of life"; "Obshchestvennyi stroi," Arkhiv Rossiiskoi Akademii Nauk, f. 555, op. 1, d. 387, l. 122, quoted in A. V. Khorunzhii, *Problemy organizatsii obshchestva v tvorchestve K. E. Tsiolkovskogo: Avtoreferat dissertatsii* (Moscow, 1992), p. 15.

44. See A. G. Dugin, "Konets proletarskoi ery," *Sovetskaia literatura*, 1991, no. 1, p. 167, and "Le Complot idéologique du cosmisme russe," *Politica hermetica*, vol. 6 (Paris, 1992), pp. 80–89. Dugin, a leading ideologist of the Russian extreme right who calls himself a "metaphysician" and "conspiracy theorist" (*konspirolog*), shows strong mystical and occult inclinations in the tradition of Gustav Meyrink, René Guénon, and Julius Evola; he is the editor of and main contributor to the fascist Eurasian journal *Elementy* and the "esoteric review" *Milyi angel*. A. M. [N. K. Gavriushin], "Voskreshenie chaemoe ili voskhishchaemoe? (O religioznykh vozzreniiakh N. F. Fedorova)," *Bogoslovskie trudy*, 1983, no. 24, pp. 242–59, attempts to connect Fedorov's philosophy and cosmism in general with Western philosophical and occult traditions such as the "religion of Humanity," Masonic gnosticism, and occult-theosophic speculations, to show that they are not only incompatible with Orthodoxy but not even of Russian origin. In "A byl li 'russkii kosmizm'?" *Voprosy istorii estestvoznaniia i tekhniki*, 1993, no. 3, pp. 104–5, this Orthodox philosopher calls "Russian cosmism" a "Trojan horse" that served to hide "Theosophers, occultists, Christian heretics, as well as mystic and positivistic natural philosophers." E. S. Troitskii, *Vozrozhdenie Russkoi idei* (Moscow, 1991), p. 156, rises to its defense.

45. S. G. Semenova, "Aktivno-evoliutsionnaia mysl' Vernadskogo," *Prometei*, 1988, no. 15, p. 221; A. V. Gulyga, "Kosmicheskaia otvetstvennost' dukha," *Nauka i religiia*, 1989, no. 8, p. 34; idem, "Priblizit' filosofiiu k zhizni," *Voprosy filosofii*, 1987, no. 8, p. 60; idem, "Stat' zerkalom dushi naroda," *Voprosy filosofii*, 1988, no. 9, p. 113; idem, "Wir leben im Zeitalter des Kosmismus," *Deutsche Zeitschrift für Philosophie* 40, no. 8 (1992): 874.

CHAPTER NINE

TECHNOLOGY AS ESOTERIC COSMOLOGY IN EARLY SOVIET LITERATURE

Anthony J. Vanchu

The Marxist-Leninist ideology underlying the new culture that the Bolshevik leaders sought to develop was, at least in theory, primarily materialist and rational. The occult and esoteric would seem to have little or no place there. Yet the transition from old to new belief systems in Russia, regardless of how abrupt and totalizing the revolutionary forces at work may have seemed, was a slower and more complex process than the rhetoric of cultural and political ideologues suggests. In fact, the occult proved a curiously palpable presence in early Soviet culture. It manifested itself, however, not in a distinct set of esoteric beliefs per se but rather as a *belief system;* that is, a way of relating to science and technology, two fields of knowledge that the Communist leadership considered essential components of their proposed transformation of life. Yet science did not simply merge with the occult or esoteric and supplant those belief systems; on the contrary, esoteric belief systems were transferred to ways of relating to the actual or promised science and its by-product, technology. Occult beliefs and scientific thought are, in fact, generically related: both function as cosmologies, systems of knowledge and belief through which humans seek to understand the material world and, in some cases, to comprehend or gain access to what lies hidden from everyday perception.

Several chapters of this book attest to the popularity of the occult in both high and low culture in the early twentieth century. A cultural phenomenon of this magnitude could not simply disappear with the declaration of a new cultural program from above. Many people interested in or connected with occult thought or practices were persecuted, forced underground, silenced, or, at worst, "liquidated." As esoteric impulse is palpable in literary works that at the time were generally accepted as ideologically sound and in which representations of science, technology, and engineering play significant roles. In these writings, the aura of mystery and the potential for magical transformation previously associated with the occult was shifted onto science and technology, their practitioners acquiring the status of prophets and magi.

This transfer involved two contradictory processes that could occur simultaneously: demystification and remystification. The "magic" of scientific discovery or technological innovation was demystified, revealed as a phenomenon that could be rendered comprehensible to those willing to acquire the requisite education and abandon nonscientific belief systems (or at the very least, not let those belief systems interfere with the practice of science). The process of remystification takes place during the individual's initiation into this new belief system (a scientific or technological education, followed by apprenticeship), a process roughly parallel to initiation into an esoteric group or occult practices. Such remystification entailed both the learning of science as a replacement for earlier worldviews (including belief in magic) and the acceptance of science as a force akin to magic, two processes that need not necessarily have been mutually exclusive. The similarities between occult and scientific thought are found not in the actual content of their ideas but rather in the mode of their appropriation and apprehension in the cultural sphere. Followers of Nikolai Fedorov, Aleksandr Bogdanov (the head of Proletkult and a leading figure in the early phases of cultural development), and the biocosmists, among others, contributed a great deal to the realization of both these processes in Soviet culture. [1]

Critical accounts of early Soviet literature tend to discuss the occult as a secondary element of little importance, when they mention it at all. Yet the relation of the cultural sphere to science and technology, along with the processes of demystification and remystification, figured prominently in the works of distinctly Soviet prose writers such as Andrei Platonov (1899–1951) and Marietta Shaginian (1888–1982). Their writings establish a relationship with science and technology that is informed by occult cosmological belief systems. For the *prostoi narod* (simple people), science and technology became a magical means not just to realize distant hopes and dreams but also to meet

---

1. See Chapters 7 and 8 in this volume. On the Russian Biocosmists, see Michael Hagemeister, "Die 'Biokosmisten'—Anarchismus und Maximalismus in der frühen Sowjetzeit," in *Studia Slavica in Honorem Viri Doctissimi Olexa Horbatsch*, ed. G. Friedhof et al. (Munich, 1983), pp. 61–76, and "Valerian Nikolaevich Murav'ev (1885–1931) und das 'prometeische Denken' der frühen Sowjetzeit," in V. N. Murav'ev, *Ovladenie vremenem, Moskva 1024: Nachruck nebst einer einführenden Studie von Michael Hagemeister* (Munich, 1983), pp. 1–27. The intermingling of science and ideology in the early Soviet state was an often muddled patchwork of scientific, philosophical, and political theories. For a helpful discussion of the interaction between these spheres of thought, see David Jovarsky, *Soviet Science and Natural Science: 1917–1932* (New York, 1961). Loren Graham's more recent *Science in Russia and the Soviet Union: A Short History* (New York, 1993), provides a concise overview of scientific trends and their relation to culture and society in Russia.

the most basic human needs.[2] Platonov's early short story "Rodina elek-trichestva" (Electricity's homeland, 1926) features the imaginative and resourceful technology of a lone engineer who uses his skills to alleviate a crippling drought in a rural backwater. His activities mark him as both prophet and magus. He is the prophet who introduces a new way of perceiving the universe that is based on scientific knowledge and people's consequent ability to shape their environment, proving that they are no longer dependent on the intervention of supernatural forces to evoke change. He is the type of practicing technological magus who exemplifies the demystification of science and technology through the openness with which he works with materials to implement his plans. The process of remystification later manifests itself in the peasants' inability or unwillingness to be won over to his cause. Because they are still uninitiated, they regard his acts only as invocations of powers beyond the human.

Shaginian's detective-adventure novel *Mess-Mend* (1924) presents the clash of diametrically opposed ideological belief systems—communism and capitalism. As the plot of the American industrialist Jack Kressling to gain power and bring down the Soviet state from within unfolds, technology proves itself a most powerful and coveted force. While Kressling and his henchmen seek technology to gain control over natural resources and workers, the Soviets and the American members of Mess-Mend, a secret workers' guild, use it for other ends. For the Soviets, it is a means to build up their country and improve people's lives. For the American workers, technology is primarily a means to thwart Kressling's designs and to sow the seeds of a system more like that of the Soviets. This novel also presents one of the most enticing fictionalized portrayals of the technology of this period, a cross between homespun craftsmanship and white magic. In *Mess-Mend*, then, technology is demystified both as a way of knowing the world available to the common worker (the Americans) and as an entity that is already a part of everyday life in the Soviet Union. It is remystified by the Mess-Mend members, whose handicraft results in all sorts of "magical" happenings. This group also bears striking outward similarities to an occult order, with set rituals, codes of behavior, secret identities, and so on. Yet another type of remystification is seen in the role of these craftsmen as guardians of esoteric knowledge. In this case, their lack of openness is attributable to the hostile, exploitive capitalist environment in which they struggle to survive.

The parallels between the writings of two authors as diverse as Platonov and Shaginian serve as a clear indication of the occult's lingering significance in the cultural mythologies of the early Soviet era. While science and technol-

2. Here and in the following section on Platonov I do not separate religion from particular occult practices since this distinction was moot in Soviet ideology. Any cosmology or belief system not based on Marxist-Leninist materialism was, by its very nature, occult.

ogy had the power to demystify religion and magic, they themselves came to be perceived as the locus of magical or occult powers that could transform the material world. "Rodina elektrichestva" and *Mess-Mend* both display clearly discernible typological links to the contradictory processes of demystification and remystification.[3]

THE ENGINEER AS PROPHET AND MAGUS: "RODINA ELEKTRICHESTVA"

Several of Platonov's early works depict the engineer as a socially engaged technocrat cum prophet and magus who promulgates and attempts to realize the gospel of a new science.[4] "Rodina elektrichestva" portrays a young engineer who helps a village overcome a chronic and devastating water shortage. Here Platonov presents a much more positive image of engineering and human technological undertakings than in such later works as the short story "Epifanskie shliuzy" (The epiphanic locks, 1927) or his major novels, *Chevengur* (1927–28) and *Kotlovan* (The foundation pit, 1930). All three pieces exhibit a considerably darker, more pessimistic view of the human ability to control nature without destroying the very people such projects are designed to help.[5] The protagonist of "Rodina elektrichestva" is a nameless roving engineer who assembles the materials to construct an electric pump and irrigate the parched fields of the backwater village of Verchovka.[6] Besides the tangible,

3. Other works that are fruitful material for further research include the Platonov works named in n. 4 and his novels *Kotlovan* and *Chevengur;* Yurii Olesha's novel *Zavist'* (Envy) and some of his short stories; Boris Pilniak's novels *Golyi god* (The naked year) and *Mashiny i volky* (Machines and wolves).

4. Here I have in mind the stories "Potomki solntsa" (Heirs to the sun, 1922), "Lunnaia bomba" (The lunar bomb, 1926), "Efirnyi trakt" (The ethereal trail, 1927), and "Epifanskie shliuzy" (The epiphanic locks, 1927). See Andrei Platonov, *Izbrannye proizvedeniia v dvukh tomakh* (Moscow, 1976). These works do not, however, present a uniformly positive and conflict-free picture of the engineer as transformer of nature. See the discussion in Thomas Seifrid, *Andrei Platonov: Uncertainties of Spirit* (Cambridge, 1992), pp. 32–98.

5. Platonov wrote "Rodina elektrichestva" in 1926, but it was published in the journal *Promyshlennyi sotsializm* only in 1939. The cause of the delay is not explained in the sources currently available. Seifrid, for instance, notes only that "in 1926 . . . [Platonov] wrote but was unable to publish 'Rodina elektrichestva' and 'Antiseksus'": *Andrei Platonov*, p. 10. He suggests that perhaps the censors considered this treatment of the ideologically significant topic of electrification insufficiently optimistic at that time (personal communication). He offers detailed discussions of *Chevengur* and *Kotlovan* ibid., pp. 99–131 and 132–75.

6. By leaving the engineer nameless Platonov universalizes him, implying that virtually anyone with the proper education and motivation could do the same. The hero's namelessness also fits well with Fedorov's dictum that the good of all is achieved only when everyone works for the welfare of everyone else—such feats must be performed in a way that is neither selfish nor selfless. This nameless yet assertive, confident, and skilled engineer would be the ideal Fedorovian hero—if only he were Christian.

practical results of his efforts, he introduces a new cosmological system based on scientific knowledge and technological innovation that both allows for and encourages self-sufficiency. This first-person narrative juxtaposes this system with the miracle-seeking religious cosmology to which the villagers have resorted, demonstrating that their withered crops will be revived not by the intercession of outside, nonhuman forces but through the "miracles" wrought by human science and technology.[7]

The literary projection of the engineer as purveyor of a demystified technology has biographical immediacy in Platonov's case—he received a degree in electrical engineering in 1922 and worked as an engineer before turning to writing full-time in 1927. The hero of "Rodina elektrichestva" also bears a striking resemblance to a real-life engineer of this era, Petr Palchinsky (1875–1929). Palchinsky could hardly be considered an ardent supporter of the Bolsheviks, but he had the skills they desperately needed to rebuild and modernize Russia. At the core of his program for industrial planning was rationality, a quality that in principle the Bolshevik government should have received well. Palchinsky, a historian of sciences has observed, "emphasized a rational approach to modernization, never promising more than what could be achieved, and stressed the necessity for fulfilling workers' full social, economic, and educational needs."[8] This realistic, no-nonsense approach to practical problems bears numerous similarities to that of the engineer in "Rodina elektrichestva." The crucial difference lies in the thorough ideological engagement of Platonov's hero, who is committed (albeit not rabidly so) to building a new socialist order.[9]

The first-person narrator of "Rodina elektrichestva" does not describe his work as engineer in rhapsodic patches of purple prose. Indeed, this story reads much like the memoir of a faithful servant who dutifully goes to the provinces simply to solve a public works problem. His narrative does, however, hint at a mystification of technology, for the villagers relate to it as to religion, another outside force that can counteract the forces of nature and have a profound effect on their welfare. In each case they must rely on an intermediary or initiate, either a priest or an engineer.

"Rodina elektrichestva" presents an image of the New Soviet Man that is

7. Other characters who attempt to bring learning and its fruits to the masses can be found in such stories as "Kak zazhglas' lampa Il'icha" (How Il'ich's lamp went out, 1926), "Peschanaia uchitel'nitsa" (The sand teacher, 1927), and "Lugovye mastera" (The masters of the meadows, 1927). The outcome of their respective efforts varies greatly.

8. Graham, *Science in Russia*, p. 163.

9. Palchinsky eventually ran afoul of the Bolshevik authorities, primarily by asserting such unpalatable notions as the need for the engineer to serve as "an 'active' economic and industrial planner, suggesting where economic development should occur and what form it should take": ibid., p. 162. The Soviet political elite clearly was unwilling to allow such autonomy to a politically and ideologically suspect group.

both realistic and idealized. This young electrical engineer, in attempting to alleviate a chronic water shortage, must overcome several hardships—his technology is decidedly of the rough-and-ready variety. He lacks not only the proper materials and tools but also a source of electricity to operate his technology. In the 1920s, the electrification of the country became a top priority, as evidenced by Lenin's famous dictum "Communism equals Soviet power plus the electrification of the entire country." By facilitating industrial development and improving living conditions, electricity would bring Russia into the modern age. It would also aid in the literacy campaign. By providing lighting for workers' libraries and study rooms in the evenings (an important consideration in a country where winter days are long and dark), electrification would speed the masses toward the goal of education, both practical and political.[10] The short supply of electricity was painfully evident even at the inauguration of GOSELRO (State Commission for the Electrification of Russia) in 1920: in order to display the project's model of the Soviet Union, with lights indicating the sites of proposed generating stations, the authorities had to curtail the use of electricity elsewhere in Moscow.

The engineer in "Rodina elektrichestva" manages to construct a source of electricity to power a water pump by putting together an old motorcycle engine and miscellaneous articles found in the village. The pump will divert water from a nearby river. This feat, however, is more an act of bricolage (improvisation with materials at hand) than engineering proper.[11] Whereas an engineer conceptualizes what he will build and assumes the ready availability of raw materials, a *bricoleur* works only with those substances available at the moment, using objects created for other purposes altogether. Platonov's engineer is just such a *bricoleur*, his inventiveness tested by the lack of materials with which to construct his generator. By forcing his engineer to work in this way, Platonov provides a clear picture of the technological backwardness of rural Russia at this time, when other writers were celebrating advances in aviation.

The lack of dramatic allure in these endeavors stands in stark contrast to the high drama, hyperbolized conflicts, and cartoon-like characters of later literary genres, such as the reconstruction and Socialist Realism. Platonov's story portrays the obstacles that a real-life engineer would encounter in his service to the Soviet state. In this story he makes a contribution to socialist literature while retaining some of the spirit of Fedorov's "common task." Indeed,

10. For more on the cultural significance of these electrification efforts, see Richard Stites, *Revolutionary Dreams: Utopian Vision and Experimental Life in the Russian Revolution* (New York, 1989), pp. 48–50.

11. Claude Lévi-Strauss uses "bricolage" to describe the human capacity to create myth from a heterogeneous repertoire of objects, ideas, or symbols. Since the bounds of the repertoire are limited, the *bricoleur* must always "make do with 'whatever is at hand.'" See Claude Lévi-Strauss, *The Savage Mind* (Chicago, 1966), pp. 16–36.

"Rodina elektrichestva" appears to have drawn inspiration from the opening section of Fedorov's *Filosofiia obshchego dela*, which emphasizes the need to use human knowledge *collectively* to overcome natural catastrophes such as drought and famine.[12] Like Fedorov, Platonov's hero seeks mastery of the material world to subdue the blind force (*slepaia sila*) of nature. The sharing and application of knowledge and technology, which constitutes Fedorov's common task (*obshchee delo*), would then benefit all and serve as the basis for building a new society.

The common people in "Rodina elektrichestva" end up perceiving the science and technology that the engineer brings to them as a means of channeling supernatural forces to work on their behalf, something they have attempted before. They turn first to the village priest, who leads a procession behind an icon of the Virgin Mary in an attempt to induce rain. Though these efforts have been to no avail, the narrator reports, the villagers continue to pursue them, perhaps because no other options occur to them.

Since one of the promises of communism is a better life, however, the village leaders eventually petition the government for help. The appeal, penned by Zharenov, the chief clerk, reveals the central role of religion in their worldview. Just as Russians had blended pagan and Orthodox elements in *dvoeverie*, Zharenov mixes Communist rhetoric with religious imagery: "Comrades and citizens, don't waste your breath in the midst of such impoverished world-wide boredom. The power of science stands like a tower, and the Babylon of old with its lizards and droughts will be destroyed by man's knowing hand. It is not we who created God's unfortunate world, but we will finish building it. . . . The Communist's reason sleeps not and no one will deflect his hand. On the contrary, he will subject the whole earth entirely to scientific influence."[13]

The letter mixes official rhetoric, biblical imagery, and folksy informalities in an attempt to reconcile the biblical creation myth with the Communists' promise that they will master the physical world and build a new order (in short, the promise of Fedorov's philosophy). The power of science standing like a tower, for example, clearly alludes to the Tower of Babel (Gen. 11:1–9), and the "lizards and droughts" recall the "fiery serpents, and scorpions, and drought" from which the Lord delivered his people (Deut. 8:15). The Communist's sleepless reason evokes Psalms 121:4: "Behold, he that keepeth Israel shall

12. N. F. Fedorov, *Filosofiia obshchego dela: Stat'i, mysli i pis'ma Nikolaia Fedorovicha Fedorova*, ed. V. A. Kozhevnikov and N. P. Peterson, 2 vols. (1906, 1913; Farnborough, Hants., 1970), 1:1–41. For critical studies that deal explicitly with Platonov's admiration of Fedorov, see Michael Hagemeister, *Nikolaj Fedorov: Studien zu Leben, Werk und Wirkung* (Munich, 1989); Svetlana Semenova, *Nikolai Fedorov: Tvorchestvo zhizni* (Moscow, 1990), esp. pp. 363–72; Ayleen Teskey, *Platonov and Fedorov: The Influence of Christian Philosophy on a Soviet Writer* (n.p., 1982); Seifrid, *Andrei Platonov*, pp. 20–24 and passim.

13. Andrei Platonov, *Izbrannye proizvedeniia v dvukh tomakh* (Moscow, 1976), p. 67; hereafter cited parenthetically in the text by page number. Translations are mine.

neither slumber nor sleep." The Communist, like the keeper of Israel, pursues the just cause, using "scientific influence" rather than divine blessings. Though Zharenov never challenges the idea of divine creation outright, he emphasizes that the Communists' mission is the perfection and completion of "God's unfortunate world," not by the intercession of metaphysical forces but by their own intelligence and labor.

To Zharenov (and, by extension, the other inhabitants of Verchovka), science and religion are similar belief systems; he describes science in precisely the same monumental terms once reserved for religion. Yet the villagers understand science as another outside force that requires an intermediary, though they hope it will yield better results. Their willingness to give science a try appears to have no foundation in a shift in philosophical or moral beliefs, a factor that distinguishes them from the engineer. Since religious cosmology is such a fundamental mode of perception for them, it stands to reason that they would comprehend any system that might provide relief in similar terms.

One consequence is that the engineer, who understands the workings of these forces, becomes a sort of prophet or high priest of this body of knowledge. In the eyes of the people, he is a magus or wizard who marshals the forces of technology and electricity to do his (and ultimately their) bidding. His role as prophet becomes more readily apparent in his initial description of Verchovka as a "naked grave for the people" (p. 66) that is more than parched earth with virtually no sign of growth, its inhabitants locked in—and losing—a life-and-death struggle with nature. In the eyes of the engineer, the religious procession he later observes is an ineffective remnant of a superstitious cosmology that misplaces human energies in fruitless professions of faith in nonhuman forces. His disdain for religion is underscored by his description of the image of the Virgin the villagers carry—this "lonely young woman without God in her hands" (p. 69) emphasizes both the barrenness of the land in Verchovka and the uselessness of the procession. As these people pass, he finally fulfills his role as prophet, telling an elderly bystander that only science and human labor, not the magic of otherworldly forces, can bring the necessary relief from the ravages of natural forces. His words read like a fragment from a Sovietized gospel à la Fedorov: "Better not to pray to anyone, granny. Nature hears neither words nor prayers; it fears only reason and work" (p. 70). The rhetoric of Platonov's engineer is by no means purely materialist, however; when he pictures nature as a hostile force (Fedorov's "blind force"), he makes it clear that nature is to be subdued.

"Reason and work" form the cornerstone of this new cosmology, based in a materialist view of science and technology, which the new Communist state appropriated in its efforts to transform life. But peasants who will still believe that a religious procession can bring rain can see the science of Platonov's engineer only as another body of esoteric knowledge. They seek a miracle to change the natural world, either through the priest, or through the engineer. A crucial difference between the two is that the engineer can actually pass on the knowledge of how to work his "magic," potentially making the villagers self-reliant. Whether or not he will eventually do so is unclear; Platonov does suggest, however, that the engineer's efforts have not been totally in vain, for he leaves instructions for the care of the generator and pump with a local mechanic (p. 89). Perhaps one day, with the proper education, the mechanic will be able to perform similar feats of bricolage.

The question remains as to why Platonov portrays the majority of the villagers as either unable or unwilling to cooperate and learn from the engineer. They make no attempt to find out what he is doing or how his equipment works; they seem to want only to be the passive recipients of its benefits. Yet it is hard to believe that Platonov intended to show the *narod* as primitive and uneducable. It seems most likely that he wished here to dramatize the backwardness of the countryside and the gap between the educated and uneducated. This interpretation fits well with the notion of Platonov as a writer influenced by Fedorovian thinking, for one of Fedorov's main themes was that this gap needed to be closed as quickly as possible. His portrayal of the Verchovka peasantry is then perhaps best understood as evidence that universal education must be established if the nation is ever to develop.

The engineer-hero of "Rodina elektrichestva" is more than a magus who works a miracle that saves a village from likely starvation. He is a prophet bearing the fruits of contemporary scientific and technological knowledge to the far reaches of Russia, ready to help it out of technological darkness. The magic through which he generates electricity to power the pump serves as the first evidence to the *prostoi narod* that education can lead them to self-reliance and away from superstition. He demonstrates that inventiveness and hard work can be used to manipulate the material world and overcome hardships. Platonov's engineer, as exemplar of a demystified approach to the natural world, promotes individual initiative (*samodeiatel'nost'*)—individual, not merely collective efforts to solve problems.

The hero of "Rodina elektrichestva" is a technology-endowed visionary who combines science with social vision. This story may be read as Platonov's idealized conception of a course of action for Soviet Russia involving the demystification of science, the unmasking of religion, with its bogus cosmology and promise of false miracles, and finally, the unleashing of human creative forces against the blind forces of nature. A prophet who spreads the word that human survival need not involve a confrontation with nature as a mystical force, Platonov's engineer seeks solutions by understanding the world of things on its own terms, using knowledge gained from this process to perform the necessary tasks. He is both exemplar and avatar of self-reliance, initiative, ingenuity, and cooperation, qualities that enable problems to be explored and solved. By offering an alternative to religion, he leaves Verchovka with at least a temporary solution to its water problem. He leaves with the knowledge that in completing his mission, he has converted at least a few people to his way of thinking. Now it is time for him to move on and continue his work of spreading the word: "I walked alone in the dark field, young, poor and at peace. One of my life's tasks had been accomplished" (p. 80).

OCCULT FORCES, GOOD AND EVIL: MARIETTA SHAGINIAN

Marietta Shaginian's novel *Mess-Mend, ili ianki v Petrograde: Roman-skazka*, which has been published in English as *Mess-Mend, or Yankees in Petrograd*, first appeared in serial form in 1924.[14] This work was read widely in the Soviet Union until the first five-year plan (1928–33) produced significant changes in the literary climate and lowered the threshold of official tolerance for nonedifying genres such as the detective novel. By 1934, the literary establishment called the detective novel "a weapon for bourgeois ascendancy over the remainder of the petty bourgeois masses and aimed at their demoralization."[15] "Pinkertonism" (*pinkertonovshchina*), fascination with detective novels, was not to be tolerated. In reaction to this change, Shaginian countered that *Mess-Mend* was more than simply an adventure or detective novel; it was "red adventure literature for our reader, for our youth," "an agitational work for the international proletariat." The trilogy of which it was the first part contained "a clearly expressed antimilitarist tendency; they [the three novels of the trilogy] were written by me as agitational adventure novels, directed at the uncovering of fascist aggression."[16]

Shaginian's statement, suggesting that her novel anticipated the rise of Nazism, is symptomatic of a cultural climate in which such claims could obtain official credence. The year Trotsky was expelled from the Party, 1927, is generally considered to mark the beginning of Stalin's reign, but the fear of "capitalist encirclement" already ran deep well before then. Anxiety was amplified as an atmosphere of paranoia seeped out of Stalin's Kremlin, and many of the behaviors it induced in virtually all spheres of life could be said to constitute a sui generis occult belief system. Hidden forces—counterrevolutionaries, fascists, wreckers, capitalist interventionists—lay in wait behind an ostensibly benign exterior, poised to strike at an opportune moment. Only exceptional individ-

---

14. The novel appeared in ten parts, issued weekly. See L. Skorino, "Komentarii," in Marietta Shaginian, *Sobranie sochinenii*, vol. 3 (Moscow, 1987), p. 799.

15. Quoted in Samuel Cioran, Introduction to Marietta Shaginian, *Mess-Mend: Yankees in Petrograd* (Ann Arbor, 1991), p. 20. Skorino remarks that the proletarian writers' group RAPP referred to *Mess-Mend* as a "pseudorevolutionary romance" ("Komentarii," p. 800).

16. Marietta Shaginian, *Sovetskie pisateli: Avtobiografii* (Moscow, 1959), p. 653. The other novels in the trilogy are *Mezhdunarodnyi vagon* (The international railroad car), published in 1925 and later renamed *Doroga v Bagdad* (The road to Baghdad), and *Lorri Len, mettalist* (Laurie Lane, metal worker).

uals could expose this unrevealed enemy (*nerazoblachennyi vrag*) through their special powers (attained usually by their adherence to the proper ideology) and undying vigilance (*bditel'nost'*). Evidence of the prevalence of this rhetoric is seen in Shaginian's phrase "uncovering [*razoblachenie*] of fascist aggression": *razoblachenie* is closely related to *nerazoblachennyi vrag*. The unrevealed enemies in *Mess-Mend* are many, as are the exceptional individuals who combat them. These individuals possess not merely the correct ideology but a variety of unconventional and even fantastic or magical powers. What is unique about these miraculous powers is their origin in and connection to twentieth-century technological advances.

Mess-Mend is set in both the United States and the Soviet Union, sometime between 1918 and 1924. Shaginian's novel is as intricate as it is improbable and fantastic—but then, plausibility is hardly a distinguishing feature of the adventure novel. Its plot centers on the attempt of the American industrialist Jack Kressling to gain control of the world's resources, in order to prevent workers from taking the means of production into their own hands and sharing the fruits of their labor equally. He wants it all for himself. Kressling sends Jeremy Morelander, his right-hand man and most trusted engineer, to the Soviet Union to find a way to bring down the Bolshevik state and take over a secret mine. This mine contains an ore that, when used with an invention developed at his "Secret Works," will allow Kressling mastery over the world.[17] But Morelander, who once shared his employer's strident anticommunism, returns from his trip a convert to the Soviet system, and with the fervor of the newly converted, explains that capitalism and the act of accumulating capital actually limit the possibilities for invention:

> "Their [the Soviets'] creative possibilities are far beyond ours! So what if over there money doesn't grow from dead money—yet all the same, factories are springing up, bridges, machines, roads, canals, stations! So what if they don't have any capital, or as you call it, the 'substratum of psychic energy.' All the same, they have this very energy in an unlimited quantity! And in that energy of theirs remains the same growth factor 'x,' that germinating fungus which is activated in our country by money, forcing the growth of capital. Do you know this can grow and mushroom, Jack?" (pp. 21–22)

His reference to capital as the "substratum of psychic energy" suggests an occult basis to capitalism, since a secondary meaning of "psychic" is "beyond natural or known physical processes; apparently sensitive to forces beyond the physical world." Communist Russia, as Morelander describes it, has demystified this force. Russia no longer relies on the occult potentiating agent of

17. Marietta Shaginian, *Mess-Mend, ili ianki v Petrograde (roman-skazka)*, in her *Sobranie sochinenii*, 3:19; hereafter cited parenthetically in the text by page number. All translations are my own.

accumulated capital; the Soviet system has restored energy and power to its rightful owners, the people who produce and use the creations that power makes possible—the workers.

Kressling greets Morelander's ideas with stony silence, and the engineer is soon eliminated, reportedly killed by the Communists in Russia, although he is in fact murdered by Kressling's agents. Here Shaginian presents us with an unwitting yet eerie foretelling of the liquidation of scientists and engineers who were considered ideologically out of step during the Stalin era. Kressling, in league with a ragtag group of capitalists, fascists, and displaced royalty, sets out to overthrow communism and reestablish autocratic rule not only in Russia but throughout the world. The real power, however, will lie with Kressling, who will finance and retain ultimate control over this undertaking. Central to Kressling's plot is the overthrow of the Soviet state through a series of assassinations of the Soviet hierarchy. One other important player on Kressling's side is the chameleon-like Gregorio Chiche, an elusive and sinister figure with a constantly changing identity.[18] These are the forces of evil in *Mess-Mend*.

The forces of good are led by Michael Thingsmaster, who has been described as a "tall, fair-haired master craftsman . . ., who combines the qualities of Sherlock Holmes, Robin Hood, and Edison."[19] He is the de facto leader of Mess-Mend, a secret workers' organization that engages in a variety of counterespionage activities designed to uncover and subvert Kressling's plot. These workers are craftsmen, however, members of the urban proletariat, not scientists or engineers. They are the ones who make real the ideas and fantasies of the professionals. The counterspies of Mess-Mend gather information about Kressling's plot and take appropriate steps to foil it and bring the transgressors to justice. The novel ends with the collapse of the capitalist's designs and the unmasking of the nefarious forces responsible for this attempt to destroy the Soviet state and deny the will and rights of workers throughout the world.

The occult in *Mess-Mend* is manifested in two ways: in the craftsman Mick Thingsmaster and in the curious amalgam of the occult and materialism with which the workers' organization Mess-Mend does battle with the regressive forces of capitalism.

---

18. The significance of the name is unclear. Its origin could be Italian or Spanish, but neither language yields a likely cognate. The Russian possibilities are slightly more promising. The closest word is *chichiga*, from which comes the adjective *chichigovatyi*, "insolent, troubling, freakish, harmful" (Vladimir Dal', *Tolkovyi slovar' zhivago velikorusskago iazyka*, vol. 4 [Moscow, 1980], p. 609). *Chichigovatyi* describes Chiche precisely, and is also the kind of recherché wordplay Shaginian enjoys. Another possible connection is Chichikov, in Gogol''s novel *Dead Souls*. Chiche's identity, like Chichikov's, constantly changes, depending on who he is with at the moment.

19. Carol Avins, *Border Crossings: The West and Russian Identity in Soviet Literature, 1917–1934* (Berkeley, 1983), p. 58.

Mick Thingsmaster is a colorful figure who, as his name suggests, is a master at manipulating material objects, a technological wizard. But unlike Platonov's hero, Thingsmaster has no training as an engineer and is not concerned with the discovery and development of new technology per se. That is the domain of the likes of Jeremy Morelander. Thingsmaster uses his skills and energies to ensure that the workers, not the industrialists, will reap the benefits of the magic their technology releases.

Shaginian's narrative focuses not on the actual development or implementation of Mess-Mend's technology but rather on the ease with which Thingsmaster and his fellow craftsmen move within the magical world this miraculous technology creates. Feats of technological wonder—the ability to appear out of thin air; to travel great distances along electrical power lines with dizzying speed; to eavesdrop unseen on one's enemies, even to film their meetings—are simply givens. This technology, fantastic and magical at the time, is primarily a means to develop the novel's winding plot. The fascination with the actual workings of technology so prominent in other writers is noticeably absent from *Mess-Mend*.

Thingsmaster, in seeking to democratize the benefits of technology, personifies the idea that the means of production and the distribution of its fruits should be controlled by the workers themselves. Thingsmaster's relationship with material objects is markedly more mysterious and magical than that of Platonov's engineer. The wizardry the Mess-Mend artisans create is revealed at a workers' meeting. When Thingsmaster is reproached for telling "tall tales" (*skazki* or fairy tales), he replies that the workers themselves have the ability to imbue their creations with magical powers:

> "Tall tales? Come on over to our factory, take a look with your own eyes. I say to myself: Mick Thingsmaster, are you not the father of these beautiful little things? Aren't you the one who makes wood into decorative patterns like paper tissue? Don't your wooden panels twitter more tenderly than little birdies as you lay bare the language of wood and the kind of tracings whose existence no teachers of drawing ever suspected? Mirrored cabinets for grand ladies, the cunning surfaces of doors that are always facing in your direction, decorative cases, writing desks, solid beds, secret boxes—are these really not all my own children? I make them with my own hands, I know them, I love them and say to them: Aha, my children, you're going forth into alien quarters to do your service; you, my wardrobe, will stand in some bloodsucker's nook; you, bed, will creak beneath the libertine; you, my fancy little case, will guard some she-spider's diamonds—so take care, my little ones, don't forget your father! Go there with caution, as my faithful helpers." (p. 17)

The craftsmanship of Mess-Mend involves more than the assembly of inert elements into utilitarian material objects; these articles serve the ideological and political agendas of their creators. They perform these functions through a sort of mystical act in which the object is brought to life and imbued with the spirit of its creator. Thus the creative powers of the Mess-Mend artisans are godlike in that they breathe life into inert material:

> Fall in love with your craft . . ., these strips of metal . . . breathe, work, move . . . they radiate for man, yet they are invisible to doctors. You must know how they work. . . . Study every metal, immerse yourself in it, use it and let it flow into the world with your secret instructions and let it do your bidding, do your bidding, do your bidding. . . . The strongest locks, our cunning creations, will unlock themselves merely at our touch. Doors will listen and then tell us what has been said, the mirrors remember, the walls will hide our secret moves, floors will open up, ceilings will fall in, roofs will rise up like lids. (p. 17)

Thingsmaster's creative process thus adds an unseen element to his products, something spiritual. This process seems to have a shamanistic basis, resembling a ritual whereby inert material is re-formed and infused with magical powers. In the case of Mess-Mend, the ritual is the construction of the object by a craftsman who has both its explicit and its hidden goals in mind. This hidden essence is then transferred psychically from creator to final product, at which point it comes to life and is able to do its creator's bidding. The objects produced by Mess-Mend craftsmen are thus inscribed internally and mystically with the bidding of their builders, and externally and concretely with the organization's minuscule double-M insignia.

These creations serve as secret weapons to unmask and eliminate the anticommunist, antiworker conspiracy of Kressling and his ilk. They differ from those of Platonov's engineer in that though they perform everyday functions, their true power lies in their secret function. The craftsmen of Mess-Mend do not make flying machines—and why should they, when they can travel on power lines faster than any airplane? Instead of water pumps for irrigation, they make home furnishings in a traditional style that have a distinctively middle-class character. But these artifacts of bourgeois consumption have been subverted by the magic of their creators—they are tools to infiltrate the world of the ideological Other, the enemy. These spies, inculcated with "the magic of resistance" (p. 17), lie in wait for their master's call to action, which will come at the crucial moment. The magical powers of the craftsman's creation were clearly part of Shaginian's romanticization of the worker. In an essay about the novel, she ascribes magical powers to the worker's hands: "The worker can conquer capital through his *secret power over the creations of his hands, over things.*"[20]

Thingsmaster and his Mess-Mend associates share the open, democratic view of technology of Platonov's engineer. According to Thingsmaster, such knowledge and skills can be learned by anyone, and enable the individual to

---

20. Shaginian, *Sovetskie pisateli,* p. 655.

assert control over his destiny: "Is it difficult? Not in the least! . . . The master of things is the one who makes them, and the slave of things is the one who uses them" (p. 17). But "democracy" in technology also seems to exclude a major portion of the population: women. In *Mess-Mend,* although all workers may contribute to the workings of the organization, Shaginian shows only working-class *men* directly involved in planning and in manipulating the material, creating these products inoculated with the "magic of resistance." Women play solely ancillary roles. A woman who is on the side of Mess-Mend is loving and supportive, but she never takes action or creates objects on her own. Shaginian portrays women as weak and unable to fend for themselves in the hostile world. When the music teacher Miss Orton tries to help the Mess-Mend cause by obtaining vital information, she is knifed by an agent of Kressling. The men of Mess-Mend rescue and help revive her (pp. 52–65). The women in the American capitalist's camp, on the other hand, are cunning and shrewish, using feminine wiles to distract their opponents. Yet even they are supporting players in a drama contrived by men. Kressling's secretary, for example, plays an important part in one of his schemes by pretending to be the widow of the recently deceased Jeremy Morelander. Although she assumes this role willingly, she does so only on her employer's orders. Shaginian certainly makes it clear that she expects men to take charge in all critical situations.

Several of her male characters clearly need to control women or keep them at a distance: Thingsmaster prefers the company of his dog to female companionship, Arthur Morelander is stridently misogynist, and a minor character keeps a "concubine" (one chapter is called "The Bizarre Habits of Banker Westinghouse's Concubine"). Such misogyny in a novel by a woman reflects the extent of sexism in Russian and Soviet culture—a sexism that is still pervasive, despite much rhetoric to the contrary. Men are thought to think more rationally, sharply, and critically, whether for good or for evil. Women's function is to support their men and their respective causes.[21]

As an organization whose identity and mission are known only to initiates and whose membership is based on the possession of special powers over the material world, Mess-Mend qualifies as occult. Shaginian herself referred to it as a "fairy-tale labor union" (*skazochnyi rabochii soiuz*).[22] It is unique, however, in its convergence of political activism with a secret, mystical technology that will allow the creators of its products to call upon them to rebel. The way members identify one another also has esoteric resonance: the password is

---

21. Overwhelming evidence of this tendency is supplied in a variety of critical works on women in Russian culture. See Barbara Clements, ed., *Russia's Women: Accommodation, Resistance, Transformation* (Berkeley, 1991), and Lynne Attwood, *The New Soviet Man and Woman: Sex-Role Socialization in the USSR* (Bloomington, 1990), esp. pp. 33–40.

22. Marietta Shaginian, Author's Introduction to *Mess-Mend,* in her *Sobranie sochinenii,* 3:7. Shaginian wrote this introduction in 1956.

"Mend-mess" and the response is "Mess-mend." Allegedly Shaginian picked the words out of the dictionary at random,[23] but they suggest that this organization's task is to mend the mess capitalism has made of the world.

The Mess-Mend guild is first introduced in the chapter headed "The Hotel Patrician," the name of a hostelry that houses deposed aristocrats and despots. The locksmith Willings, while making adjustments to the hotel locks, meets a fellow Mess-Mend initiate, and their encounter resembles a secret ritual dance:

> . . . instead of beginning the repairs, . . . he made a little jump. He then stopped and listened—not a sound. Then Willings made still another pirouette, pressing with his heels upon some invisible spot, and immediately the square piece of parquet began to move, rose up, and stood on its edge across the room, revealing a dark hole leading downward.
>
> "Mend-mess!" the locksmith said in a whisper, leaning toward the hole.
>
> "Mess-mend!" was immediately heard from inside, and in the opening appeared the head of the plumber, Van Hope. (p. 38)

They discuss whether everything in the hotel interior has the Mess-Mend imprint on it yet (it does not—apparently a wallpaper factory has not yet joined their union, thus hampering their efforts). Van Hope then magically disappears, vanishing into the pipe from which he emerged.

Willings sets to work on the lock in a most unconventional manner: using a magnifying glass, he peers into the tumblers of the door's lock, into its keyholes, and then into the hinges on the doors, dressers, and wardrobes in the room he has entered. He nods approvingly, determining that the Mess-Mend insignia appears on every item. Having reassured himself that these objects are endowed with the "magic of resistance," he then demonstrates how this magic works:

> Willings firmly locked one of the doors, went up to it, and without removing the key ran his nail along some kind of invisible strip. The door immediately opened quietly, although the key was sticking out of the lock as before.
>
> "Mend-mess!" someone called loudly from inside the wall.
>
> "Mess-mend!" Willings replied hurriedly. The wall began to move, opened up, and with a piece of fabric in his hands, the wallpaper hanger entered the room. (p. 39)

Thus, with the help of their creations, the Mess-Mend craftsmen secretly enter and exit the hostile capitalist world, calling upon the magical powers of the objects they have made.

The magic of Mess-Mend is at work primarily in the capitalist United States. When the action shifts eastward, Shaginian portrays her country as a society that has reached and sustains a high level of technological sophistication with-

23. Avins, *Border Crossings*, p. 58.

out magic. As the author later explained, it is "naive and utopian"—"as seen through the eyes of an American."[24] In Chapter 34, "Mr. Vasilov in the Land of Miracles" (the land of miracles is, of course, the Soviet Union),[25] Comrade Rebrov, a laborer at the Putilov works, shows "Mr. Vasilov," who is actually Jeremy Morelander's son Arthur in disguise, an array of Soviet industrial miracles (pp. 155–56). Morelander is duly impressed. The American observes a highly developed technology operated by engaged, knowledgeable, and seemingly happy workers. They understand every aspect of production, thanks to the process of "unified management." An engineer explains to Morelander that this method ensures that "not a single one of our workers from this day forth will approach his work without a complete understanding of all the links of production" (p. 159). Morelander begins a transformation similar to the one his father underwent. He abandons his former hostility to the Soviet system, exclaiming, "This is utopia" (p. 158). The engineer shares his enthusiasm, but also reminds Morelander that what he calls utopia is in fact real, not a figment of the imagination; the technological sophistication before them may seem part of a fantasy world, but it is very much part of this world:

> "You needn't be amazed at all this, there's no sorcery involved. . . . You see the tower in each of the fields. This is the famous Davali regulator that has been adapted to our own invention of an electro-climate. We can determine the moisture and temperature with complete uniformity for a predetermined area, preventing its escape into the atmosphere by means of the fact that we create transmissive magnetic currents of great force all around it just as though we were sealing it in from above." (p. 158)

Such a device never existed in the Soviet Union (or anywhere else, for that matter), but this concept echoes the idealistic optimism over the possibilities of technology that swept the Soviet Union during the first two decades of the twentieth century.[26] In this respect, *Mess-Mend* figures also as a precursor to the Soviet production novel, as Carol Avins has pointed out: "Russia's transition from revolution to utopia is not wholly a matter of magic in *Mess-Mend*. In its attention to Russia's technological progress, it resembles the later production novels that measure national growth in terms of industrial output."[27] Shagi-

24. Shaginian, Author's Introduction, p. 9.

25. The Russian title, "Mister Vasilov v strane chudes," can also be translated as "Mr. Vasilov in Wonderland" (Avins, *Border Crossings*, p. 57). The title invokes, perhaps not inappropriately, the magic and fantasy of Lewis Carroll's *Alice in Wonderland*, which is translated as *Alisa v strane chudes* (Alice in the land of wonders).

26. Fedorov shared in this optimism. The opening chapter of *Filosofiia obshchego dela* mentions the use of electricity to regulate climate: "The regulation of the meteorological process is . . . necessary for the protection of the harvest, . . . for agriculture." Such regulation would also benefit industry, allowing energy to be extracted "from atmospheric currents, from solar power" (1:5).

27. Avins, *Border Crossings*, p. 60.

nian herself later abandoned magical hyperbole in a production novel called *Gidro-tsentral'* (Hydro-central, 1931).

Perhaps the most strikingly occult element in *Mess-Mend* appears with the discovery of the disease *vertebra media sive bestialia*—central or bestial vertebra. The name itself does little more than indicate the location of the disease in the human body, and only implies that it results in the transformation of a human being into a beast. Dr. Lepsius, a character who appears intermittently throughout the novel, presents his findings on this disease at an international psychiatric symposium in Petrograd. He recalls that his first encounters with this degenerative disease were only among

> "so-called claimants: people who had found support with the capitalists of America and who sought through their aid to regain their lost positions in their homelands. All these people sought power against the will of the majority of their own people. And strange as it may have been, among them I discovered several further cases of the aforementioned swelling and protuberance. Their symptoms were all identical. The patients complained about one and the same thing. Treatment wasn't helping. Almost always I observed almost indiscernible changes in the structure of the spinal column." (p. 251)

At first Lepsius suspects that the condition results from an unfamiliar diet and a lack of contact with one's people. But he discovers that it is not confined to exiles when one of his patients, an American capitalist and prominent supporter of exiled rulers, contracts the disease. Lepsius places him under his immediate care so that he can study the symptoms and progression of this affliction in detail. He concludes that this spinal degeneration, which eventually leaves the infected person unable to stand erect, is brought on by an "unbearably powerful feeling of terror . . . in the face of the inevitability of communism" (p. 252).

At the Petrograd symposium, Lepsius prepares to present an individual afflicted with *vertebra media sive bestialia*—and that person happens to be none other than Dr. Hiserton, the previous speaker, who fainted at the podium just moments ago. In an attempt to help his stricken colleague, Lepsius begins to remove Hiserton's clothing. He discovers layer after layer of disguises, until at last he uncovers what appears to be the real person—who is none other than Jack Kressling's henchman Gregorio Chiche. Yet it turns out that this is not the afflicted man's ultimate identity. When Lepsius discovers that Chiche's back is encased in steel, he removes it. "A beast with a spine, rounded in a hump like a cat's, leaped onto the table. On all fours, he leaped off the table into the hall and, barely touching the floor, flew toward the exit" (p. 254).[28]

28. The beast into which human beings degenerate as a result of *vertebra media sive bestialia* is strikingly similar to that of the alien in the contemporary American film trilogy *Alien, Aliens,* and *Alien³*. Both need a human host in which to come into being, and both remain hidden throughout most of their respective narratives, lurking ominously.

The regression of Chiche from human being to hideous monster, he concludes, is clearly "correlated with [the] social devolution from civilization to bestiality."[29] Here again Fedorov's ideas prove helpful, though Shaginian is not known to have been an adherent of his thought. Fedorov viewed civilization as the overcoming of nature, the most elemental expression of which is man's assumption of the vertical position. In an essay titled "Gorizontal'noe polozhenie i vertikal'noe—smert' i zhizn'" (The horizontal position and the vertical—death and life) he wrote: "For what is the vertical position? Is it not the uprising of man against nature, the turning of his gaze from the earth to the sky? In this uprising is expressed . . . the insufficiency of the natural senses for the fruition of life, the consciousness of the necessity for self-initiative for the sustenance of existence, for the use of the most simple tool forces man to raise himself, to stand."[30] Capitalism, then, is nothing more than regression to a most primitive state, in which man has lost the ability to assume the upright position, quite literally to stand on his own two feet.

No one in the hall is quick enough to stop this rushing beast. Even Thingsmaster's faithful and courageous dog, Beauty, fails; when she turns toward the creature to block its exit, her coat bristles and she backs off with a shudder. Apparently it is too horrible even for the bravest animal to face. The hellishly grotesque being is stopped only by the bullet of a Red Army soldier, who shoots it in the head with predictable calm bravery amid the chaos.

The evil supernatural forces of capitalism have been destroyed. The calm, rational, and humane forces of Soviet communism vanquish the freak of nature the opposition has produced. The Red Army soldier who kills this beast is the New Man that the Soviets hoped to produce. He demonstrates a readiness to defend his society against all who would threaten its well-being and is a practical warrior who willingly does battle with occult powers, which have no place in the Soviet Union. Negative occult energies, the result of capitalism, meet their downfall here. The possible fate of the positive occult entity in the novel, the Mess-Mend group, is never addressed directly. This organization, with its magical technology, originates in the world where capitalism reigns. Perhaps, at least for the time being, it is the only means available to the workers there to do battle with the evil forces of Kressling and his kind. Mess-Mend, it seems, is unnecessary in this workers' utopia, where technology is no longer produced by the magic of selected initiates but is a part of everyday life, itself producing "magic" for all to see and use.

The occult was expressed in early Soviet literature in an attitude toward the cosmologies of modern science and technology. Like esoteric practices, these cosmologies were predicated on the possibility of altering the material world.

---

29. Avins, *Border Crossings*, p. 59.
30. Fedorov, *Filosofiia*, 2:264.

Science and technology in a sense became a new type of wizardry, with the engineer and craftsman its new prophets and priests. The traces of the occult stem from the fact that science and technology are attempts to understand the often hidden workings of the world of matter and to exert influence over it, goals that can prove elusive to the uninitiated. While retaining a sense that there are distinct rules to the workings of the universe, Platonov's engineer and the Mess-Mend workers use their technology as a new means to perceive and explain the universe. Not bound by positivistic, mechanistic, or narrowly materialist models of the natural world and its workings, this new science merges the spiritual and the material.

For Platonov and Shaginian, occult knowledge plays a key role in this new science, although the nature and scope of that part vary according to individual aesthetic and ideological goals. In "Rodina elektrichestva" the magic of the new science supplants the clearly ineffective magic of an old cosmology that the Communists tried hard to suppress—religion. Here the ideological lines are clearly drawn, with the story's engineer putting into practice Platonov's plan for the technological development of the Russian countryside and the subsequent transformation of its people. He comes to the village of Verchovka as the bearer of an alternative belief system, one that emphasizes people's ability to take charge of their material surroundings. He uses the magic of his technological knowledge (which, properly speaking, is not magic at all) to overcome the blind forces of nature.

Shaginian's novel abounds in the occult and the fantastic. Here the occult is used by forces positive (quasi-communist workers) and negative (capitalists) alike. The positive forces win out for two reasons: they are guided by the correct ideology and they rely on a magic technology to do battle with the evil occult forces that seek to destroy them. The battle is won only when the action shifts to the Soviet Union. Here the white magic of Mess-Mend becomes unnecessary, for the Soviet state has already created the "miracle" of a workers' utopia. Those involved in capitalism's nefarious black magic come from the outside, and are shown as hideous monsters who meet their end at the hands of the Red Army. Shaginian uses the occult, then, as the ground on which (ideological) good and evil meet and do battle, although the outcome, given the novel's cultural context, can never seriously be in doubt.

Platonov and Shaginian show versions of belief systems connected with the occult as a way of bridging the gap between the old and the new. By the 1930s, interest in the occult was manifested neither in playful contact with other-worldly forces, as in pre-Soviet times, nor in childlike wonder at the magic of technology, as in the 1920s. Shaginian continued to trumpet the triumphs of the Soviet regime for the rest of her career, but Platonov's early enthusiasm faded in the harsh realities of life in the Soviet Union in the 1930s.

PART FOUR

TRANSFORMATIONS OF THE OCCULT IN STALIN'S TIME

CHAPTER TEN
THE MAGIC OF WORDS
Symbolism, Futurism, Socialist Realism

Irina Gutkin

However diverse Russian modernists' language theories and related visions of the future may have been, generally speaking, they were guided by a common historical perspective—namely, a belief in the impending end of the old world and the advent of the new ideal world of the future. In their cosmogonic mythologies the genesis of a new world was conceived principally as a glottogenetic process:[1] the creation of new language obtained the paramount role in the realization of a new ideal world of the future. They shared a utopian dream of a new perfectly "transparent" language, in that their theories implied restoration of the world's original Edenic state, which they conceptualized as the time when human beings spoke a language in which the signifier and the signified existed in complete organic unity. Sacerdotal or magical language provided a model for the new language each of these movements was striving to create, a synthetic magical language of unprecedented epistemological power whose ultimate function was to serve as a means of conjuring new life in the future world. In the course of the revolutionary period (1905–35) the vestiges of these modernist concepts of poetic language found their way, mutatis mutandis, into Socialist Realist aesthetic ideology, both in its manifestation in the official dogma and in popular Soviet beliefs and customs.

The Symbolists were the first among Russian modernists to sense the impending end of the old world and to turn, under the influence of Vladimir Soloviev's philosophy, to diverse occult systems in search of alternative epistemological models that would unite nonrational intuitive ways of cognition

I acknowledge with gratitude an Academic Senate Grant from the University of California at Los Angeles which supported in part my research for this chapter.

1. V. Gofman, "Iazyk simvolistov," *Literaturnoe nasledstvo*, 1937, nos. 27–28, p. 61.

with rational, logical ones. Soloviev's theurgic aesthetics assigned the arts the task of totally transfiguring the world in the light of the future: "Artists and poets once again must become priests and prophets, but in a new, still more important and lofty sense: not only will they be possessed by the religious idea, but they themselves will take possession of it and will consciously control its earthly incarnations."[2] Hence the Symbolist poets modeled the language of their art on that of magicians and hierophants, believing their souls to be better attuned than those of common people to receive the secret knowledge of symbols, which they saw as the ultimate communicative units of a new language. In Aleksandr Blok's words, "The Symbolist from the very beginning is already a *theurgist*, that is to say the possessor of a secret knowledge behind which stands a secret act; but he looks at this secret, which only later turns out to be universal, as his own."[3] The Symbolists conceived of the poet's role in terms of the Gnostic tradition and saw themselves as mystagogues whose exclusive mission was to penetrate the ontological mysteries and to reveal the path to salvation. Like alchemists who believed that the discovery of the elixir of life was a matter of achieving unsurpassed mastery of magic, the Symbolists sought to master the magic of words by means of symbolic correspondences as well as through sound, rhythm, and rhyme.

In magic and the occult, Symbolist poets were looking for ways to overcome space and time, ultimately to attain immortality. They believed that placing the word outside its conventional semantic space allowed the poet-magician to transcend the limits of profane, ordinary time. Andrei Bely wrote that sound frees one from the fetters of space, as well as those of time. Earlier, Valery Briusov in the essay titled, somewhat ambiguously, "Kliuchi tain" (The springs of [or the keys to?] the mysteries, 1904), postulated that "art is a cognition of the world by other, nonrational means. . . . Art is what in other spheres we call revelation. Creations of art are doors open to Eternity."[4] The idea that art defies time and that artists are magicians who can by the power of creative imagination transform sordid reality was explored by Fedor Sologub in a collection of short stories, *Kniga ocharovanii* (A book of charms, 1909) and especially in his novel *Tvorimaia legenda* (A legend in the making, 1908–12). The novel's protagonist personifies the artist-sorcerer: a chemist, or rather an alchemist, a poet, and a magician par excellence, Dr. Trirodov marshals his powers for a Fedorovian task of resurrection.

Generally, the Symbolists' approach to the occult was eclectic; they borrowed extensively from straightforward folk sources and complex esoteric

2. Vladimir Soloviev, "Tri rechi v pamiat' Dostoevskogo" (1881–83) in his *Sobranie sochinenii v dvukh tomakh* (Moscow, 1988), 2:293. See also his "Obschii smysl iskusstva" (1890) and "Krasota v prirode" (1889).

3. A. Blok, "O sovremennom sostoianii russkogo simvolizma" (1910), in his *Sobranie sochinenii v dvukh tomakh* (Moscow, 1988), 2:293. See also his "Obshchii smysl iskusstva" (1890)

4. Valerii Briusov, "Kliuchi tain," *Vesy*, 1904, no. 1, p. 4.

doctrines. When Viacheslav Ivanov spoke of sacerdotal magic, he apparently had in mind chiefly the Eleusinian mysteries of ancient Greece with their cult of Dionysus, which became central to Ivanov's own aesthetic thought and which he reinterpreted in Nietzschean terms. Blok valorized primordial language; he was fascinated by incantational folklore, as were other Symbolist poets, notably Konstantin Bal'mont. While they privileged different sources, all theorists of Russian Symbolist poetics developed analogies between Symbolist language and magical language.

In his "Poeziia zagovorov i zaklinanii" (Poetry of spells and incantations, 1906–08), Blok nostalgically lamented the loss of the primordial wholeness of man and universe, human knowledge and language: "What for primordial man was a living necessity, the contemporary man must reconstruct in a roundabout way of images. . . . Modern consciousness differentiates among concepts: life, knowledge, religion, mystery, poetry. For our ancestors it was all one, they did not have strict concepts." Essentially, he was appealing for an epistemological synthesis that he understood in terms of Vladimir Soloviev's philosophy and in which poetry was tantamount to "life, knowledge, religion, mystery." Blok's desire to fuse scientific logical thought with intuitive irrational cognition was also evident when he emphasized the "practical applicability" of folk incantations and claimed that with the discovery of hypnosis the medicinal powers of incantations were recognized "even by exact sciences."[5]

It is no surprise that critics from the academic establishment, dominated by positivists, found Blok's treatment of incantational folklore unbefitting the scholarly character of *Istoriia russkoi literatury* (The history of Russian literature), for which his essay was commissioned.[6] Propagating the Symbolist perspective and writing in the affected Symbolist idiom, Blok praised the nonrational use of "the word," whose magical powers could tame the chaos of elemental forces. In Blok's characterization, sorcerers are close kin to the Symbolist poets in the way they use language: they "know the word, the essence of things, and know how to turn these things to harm or to good; therefore an inaccessible line separates them from the ordinary people." They create their own world and set laws for it ("koldun—samodavleiushchii zakonodatel' svoego mira").[7] The poet-magician became one of the central images of Symbolist mythologized self-perception.

Like Symbolist poetic language, Blok wrote, the language of folk magic serves "to destroy that old self-satisfied, reasonable mode of daily life [razrushit' tot—staryi, blagopoluchnyi, umnyi byt]," to demolish the petrified "old world." Blok asserted that the magic word can carry those who believe in it

5. A. Blok, "Poeziia zagovorov i zaklinanii," in *Sobranie sochinenii*, 5:36, 37.
6. The essay appeared in vol. 1 of *Istoriia russkoi literatury*, ed. E. V. Anichkov and D. N. Ovsianiko-Kulikovskii, which was devoted to folk literature. For critics' reaction see Blok, *Sobranie sochinenii*, 5:715.
7. Blok, "Poeziia zagovorov," pp. 40, 44.

beyond the limits of ordinary reality, to other unknown realities. Further, when he listed among the most appealing features of folk magic the unity of utility and beauty (*pol'za i krasota*), he evidently followed Soloviev's aesthetic ideas on the future fusion of art and life.[8]

The connections between the occult and symbolic uses of language were explored rigorously and extensively in the theoretical writings of Andrei Bely. An indefatigable erudite, Bely drew on a broad range of occult systems and mystical teachings. The detailed commentaries he appended to his essays "Magiia slov" (The magic of words, 1909) and "Emblematika smysla" (The emblematics of meaning, 1909) bring us into an intellectual kitchen that resembles the laboratory of an alchemist in search of the philosopher's stone: any sort of material that comes into his hands finds its way into the brew. The array of references to occult and mystical sources is indeed dazzling, including various kabbalistic traditions, the arcane hieroglyphic system of ancient Egypt, Pythagorean numerology, and the astrological magic of Marsilio Ficino, along with references to the doctrine of Hermes Trismegistus and to Agrippa's compendium of occult knowledge. There are also brief and baffling excursions into the Vedas, the Vedantas, and the Upanishads, the esoteric teachings of Buddhism recorded in Sanskrit in *The Book of Dzyan*, along with references to traditional Hindu systems of mystical philosophy. Bely's list indicates, however, that much of his knowledge of occult or mystical doctrines came from secondary sources, such as Antoine Fabre d'Olivet's *Langue hébraïque restituée*, Eliphas Lévi's *Dogmes et rites de la haute magie* and *Histoire de la magie*, and Karl Kiesewetter's studies on the occult. Principal among these works were the Theosophical treatises of Elena Blavatsky, whose work Bely characterized as "a motley jumble of marvelous generalizations wherein confusion, fantasy, and sometimes careless use of quotations compete with talent and sharp penetrating [insight]."[9]

The derivative nature of Bely's knowledge of the occult suggests that he was not interested in esoteric doctrines per se, but studied them as part of his search for a comprehensive theory of Symbolism, which he in fact set out to create between 1908 and 1910. This was arguably the most fecund period for Bely the theorist; the programmatic essays he wrote then were collected in *Simvolizm* (1910). At this time Bely was preoccupied with Theosophy; he perused Blavatsky's *Secret Doctrine* and frequented a Theosophical circle in Moscow. Occult doctrines are typically founded on the belief that all phenomena of the universe are connected in a great design or pattern. The highest goal of an occult system has always been to reveal that divine design; to explain relationships between phenomena such as the cycles of human life and the move-

---

8. Ibid., pp. 44, 51.

9. Andrei Belyi, *Simvolism* (Moscow, 1910), p. 624. Commentaries on *Magiia slov* contain frequent references to Blavatsky's *Secret Doctrine* and, to a lesser extent, to *Isis Unveiled*, plus an exhaustive list of major Theosophical journals (pp. 618–26).

ments of the planets, between the proportions of the human body and the structure of the cosmos—ultimately, to construe an overall relationship between spirit and matter. Blavatsky's doctrine was an attempt to bring into one system the mystical notions underlying world religions. Bely, guided by Soloviev's ideas of synthesis, apparently took on an analogous task—to solve the problem of synthetic knowledge.

In Bely's essays devoted to the "theory of the symbol" one discerns a resolve to create a "synthetic epistemology" that would bring together the humanities, the sciences, and the occult doctrines into what may be called an all-encompassing axiology of epistemology.[10] This effort is particularly evident in "The Emblematics of Meaning," the most elaborate if also most arcane of Bely's theoretical works, which, according to an informed contemporary, *"no one understood"* when it appeared.[11] The unintelligible treatise may make more sense, however, if it is read as an occult discourse of sorts, as appears to have been its author's intention. Such a reading is suggested particularly by the visual explications or ideograms Bely supplied in the essay's text. He represented every field of knowledge by a series of paired equilateral triangles, each pair symbolizing the "cognition and creation" of a given field. The triangles were organized into a pyramid symbolizing the ascent from the "technical sciences," placed at the bottom of this pyramid of knowledge, to "value" and on to "symbol embodied" at the apex. This diagram, which to Bely's mind constituted a "synthetic judgment . . . transcending the limits of any monadology," brings to mind illustrations in occult tracts such as Robert Fludd's charts in *De supernaturali, naturali et contranaturali microcosmi historia* (1619), which depicted the relationship between "numerology and the heavens" and between "elemental and celestial harmonies." Bely evidently delighted in his own laborious design, to which he clearly attributed some esoteric significance: he emphasized the fact that within his pyramid the pairs of triangles can be shifted to form a six-pointed star. This hexagram, which "occupies such an important place among the mystical emblems," in his own scheme designated "the appearance of symbolic unity in the symbolization"—that is, the perfect equivalence between the symbol and the symbolized.[12]

10. For instance, the catalog of occult literature that Bely provided in the commentaries on his essays on the "theory of symbol" is matched by a no less impressive list of references to contemporary scholarship in such diverse fields as philosophy (especially epistemology), psychology, musicology, sociology, and philology—an indication that he saw occult teachings as compatible with and complimentary to other scholarly disciplines, including the "technical sciences."

11. Nikolai Valentinov, *Dva goda s simvolistami* (Stanford, 1969), p. 132; Valentinov's emphasis.

12. Andrey Bely, "The Emblematics of Meaning," in *Selected Essays of Andrey Bely*, trans. Stephen Cassedy (Berkeley, 1985), pp. 111–19, 161, and notes pp. 281–95. Unless indicated otherwise, all quotations from Bely's essays are from this translation. In other places Bely alludes to other occultist emblems, such as a cross with a dot at the center of concentric

Bely may be said to have followed in the footsteps of occultist philosophers in yet another sense: they too, while relying on the knowledge and methodology that had been amassed before them, kept the faith in the cognitive superiority of their own systems. Within Bely's theory, the ultimate cognitive power was invested in language used for magic purposes. As Bely confided to Nikolai Valentinov (with whom he was close at the time), "the theory of knowledge, ethics, theology, metaphysics, theosophy, and theurgy constitute intermediate links which bring us to the theory of the symbol," which leads to the ultimate goal of Symbolist art: "the *transformation of the whole of life [v preobrazovanii vsei zhizni].*"[13] Inspired by the theurgic aesthetics of Soloviev (and possibly Nikolai Fedorov), Bely identified control and transformation of nature, together with the prophetic function, as the principal properties of the magic word:

> It is no coincidence that so many ancient traditions refer to the existence of a magic language whose words were able to subjugate and subdue nature . . . [and] that one hears the myths of a certain sacred dialect called *Senzar,* in which all the highest revelations were given to mankind. The natural deductions as well as the myths of a language express, independently of the degree of their objectivity, an involuntary tendency to symbolize the magic power of the word.[14]

In the notes to the essay, Bely added that the "great significance of words is especially promoted in so-called magic literature," and in a five-page endnote he reviewed, with a posture of unbiased detachment, the history of occult traditions that served to preserve and to pass on vestiges of the magical language from the ancient times to modernity. After a swift survey of the Hermetic tradition from its ancient origins through the Renaissance, Bely focused his discussion on "the strivings of present-day occultists to link Hermeticism with the most ancient theosophy of magicians," an aspiration that clearly had a strong appeal for him.[15] Here Bely meant primarily Blavatsky, leaning heavily on suppositions drawn from *The Secret Doctrine,* from which he apparently also culled the information about the legendary magic protolanguage, "Senzar."

If Blavatsky speculated about a historical link through which all sacred languages could be traced to a common source, Bely attempted in "The Magic of Words" to explain the universal magic power of language from a psycholinguistic perspective; that is, to show how an individual relates to the world through language. With the characteristic demiurgist egocentrism of Russian

circles, which, it has been suggested, he derived from the Rosicrucian cross to represent the emanation of the artist's consciousness. See Amy Mandelker, "Synaesthesia and Semiotics: Icon and Logos in Andrej Belyj's *Glossalolija* and *Kotik Letaev,*" *Slavic and East European Journal* 34 (Summer 1990): 165.

13. Valentinov, *Dva goda s simvolistami*, p. 124.

14. Bely, "The Magic of Words," in *Selected Essays*, p. 96.

15. Belyi, "Kommentarii" on "Magiia slov," in *Simvolism*, pp. 619, 621.

modernist artists, he asserted that "creation comes before cognition [*tvor-chestvo prezhde poznaniia*]" and stipulated that "cognition is impossible without words" because for us objects come into existence through "the naming of an object with a word." According to Bely, the process of cognitions the "establishing of relations between words which only subsequently are related to objects corresponding to them."[16] But since "the word is a symbol," naming then is a "creation of symbols" which "unites in one word knowledge, cognition, and magic incantation [*znanie, poznanie, zaklinanie*]."[17]

Evoking the triple meaning of sacred hieroglyphs in ancient Egypt, whereby each sign concurrently expresses a sound representing time, the icon-image denoting space, and the sacred number "symbolizing the word," Bely interpreted symbol as a "conductor" that "connects two unintelligible essences: space which is accessible to my vision, and that inner sense vibrating mutely inside me that I provisionally call . . . time." Moreover, he continued, the word exists in both time and space—in time as a sound, in space as a graphic sign. In Bely's definition, the poetic word serves as the connecting agent between the poet's inner "speechless, invisible world swarming in the subconscious depth" and "the speechless, senseless world" of extrapersonal realities. Just as in magic rites, sounding the words out incantationally is assumed to have the power to conjure up a "third world" in which the master of sounds, the magician and poet, becomes the "creator of reality."[18]

For Bely, symbolic naming is the act of casting a magic spell in order to control the unknown. He contended that invocation enables the artist to defend himself "against the hostile, unintelligible world that presses on me from all sides" and "to subdue the elements," concluding that "connections between words, grammatical forms, and figures of speech are in essence charms."[19] Bely's logic here is analogous to that fundamental notion underlying all magic, the notion that the sign (name or image) is the microcosmic essence of an underlying but hidden reality, and that one who has the knowledge of the sign can, by manipulating it, command that reality. The idea that through the word a poet-magician can act upon the unknown constituted a leitmotif of Bely's essays of the period. In "Symbolism as a World Understanding" he termed this use of the word "theurgy," after Soloviev.

The "magic of words," by means of which the artist obtains the power to conjure up realities inaccessible through common everyday language, was a concept shared by other Symbolist poets; it came to signify the "theurgic" or

16. Bely, "Magic of Words," p. 93.
17. Belyi, "Kommentarii" on "Magiia slov," p. 619.
18. Ibid., p. 432; Bely, "Magic of Words," p. 94. Later, when he became infatuated with Rudolf Steiner's Anthroposophical teaching, Bely attempted to expand on these ideas in *Glossaloliia*, "creating a synesthetic cosmology based on alchemical associations and the form and shape of letters and phones": Mandelker, "Synaesthesia and Semiotics," p. 160.
19. Bely, "Magic of Words," p. 95.

futurological function of art—the creation of a "new" or "future" reality, albeit a reality specific to each theorist. Konstantin Bal'mont, a poet of the older Symbolist generation and a follower of Blavatsky's Theosophy, in his lyric treatise *Poeziia kak volshebstvo* (Poetry as magic, 1915), reiterated many of the ideas expressed by Bely but with a somewhat different emphasis. Bal'mont wrote with nostalgia about the virgin days of the harmonious universe, when there existed "one Sex which knew limit neither in space nor in time." Like Bely, Bal'mont emphasized that invocational verse was always directed "toward the distant goal of changing nature." He discerned magic properties in rhythm and rhyme, in consonants and vowels, and contended that "the sound mystery [*zvukovaia taina*] of Poetry as Magic" consisted in the restoration, through poetry, of the synthesis between the elemental and the human. In support he cited what he alleged to be incantational verses and legends of the peoples from all "corners of the Earth."[20]

Analogies with the views on language characteristic of magic rites and occult philosophies were shaping central tenets of the Symbolist theoretical discourse on poetics in general—such as the concepts of the poetic word, the function of language, and the role of the poet—which in turn informed the Symbolists' poetic praxis. For example, the Symbolists' juxtaposition of *realia*, the "external reality" of the phenomenal world, with *realiora*, the "internal and highest reality" of the noumenal world, as two distinct but related orders of reality has counterparts in the occult notions of *inferiora* and *superiora*, which were current in Renaissance occultist discourse.[21] The paired notion of *realia* and *realiora*, formulated by Viacheslav Ivanov, in Symbolist discourse obtained multiple meanings.[22] Generally, the division explains, if only in part, the principal distinction of Symbolist poetics (which was characteristic of both French and Russian Symbolism), between ordinary and poetic language as expressing "correspondences" in two different orders of reality. Common words were seen as referring to the things and phenomena of mundane reality known to all, while the metaphorical or symbolic words of poetic language were believed to signify the phenomena and experience of other worlds—secret, ultimately higher realms that were open to mediation by those who possessed the knowledge of symbolic language. Through the use of symbols, the Symbolist poet then becomes essentially a mediator linking these two orders of reality. For Russian Symbolists, however, ordinary language signified ordinary reality of the existing everyday world, accessible logically and empirically, while po-

20. Konstantin Bal'mont, *Poeziia kak volshebstvo* (Moscow, 1915), pp. 8, 82, 51.

21. In the writings of Luca Bellanti and Cornelius Agrippa, among others. For a discussion of these ideas in the Renaissance occult intellectual tradition see Wayne Shumaker, *The Occult Sciences in the Renaissance: A Study in Intellectual Patterns* (Berkeley, 1972), pp. 28, 135, and passim.

22. Viacheslav Ivanov, "Zavety simvolizma," in his *Borozdy i mezhi* (Moscow, 1916), p. 134.

etic language denoted the ultimate reality of the future, prefigured through the word-symbol endowed with mythopoetic powers.

Although in Russian Symbolism the distinction between two kinds of languages stemmed in part from Aleksandr Potebnia's linguistic theory concerning the relationship between the "inner" and the "outer" forms of the word, it also has obvious parallels in the esoteric use of the word in magic, in a nonconventional referential setting or function. In "Zavety simvolizma" (The testaments of Symbolism, 1910) Viacheslav Ivanov praised the aesthetic achievements of the Symbolist movement on the grounds that Symbolist poetry resembled the prototypical sacerdotal speech of ancient priests: "In the new poetry Symbolism appears to be the first and vague remembrance of the sacred language of pagan priests and sorcerers who once gave the words of popular speech a special mysterious meaning, open to them alone, due to correspondences, known only to them, between the secret world and the world of common experience." Projecting this model into the future, Ivanov raised to archetypal significance the language created by the Symbolists: he envisioned Symbolism as the historical period in the evolution of poetic language preceding "that hypothetical epoch which will be the religious epoch proper."[23]

Ivanov's visionary and recondite style of writing notwithstanding, by this epoch he meant the ideal future based on apocalyptic doctrines that informed Symbolist mentality, particularly Soloviev's Neo-Gnostic mysticism, which predicated the advent of millenarian utopia. In that hypothetical future, Ivanov contended, language would embrace two different types of speech: "speech expressing empirical things and relationships and speech about things of a different order, available in the inner experience—the hieratic speech of prophecy [*ieraticheskuiu rech' prorochestvovaniia*]." The synthesis of these two types of language would obliterate the division between the logical and intuitive ways of cognition. The logical analytical language, which according to Ivanov was predominant in the present, would give way to "mythological speech [whose] main form will be 'myth' understood as synthetic reasoning." In such new language the word would serve as "symbol-concept" or "myth." More important, such a word-symbol-myth would constitute "the action and the acting power [*deistvie i deistvennaia sila*]"; that is, would be able to affect existing reality directly.[24] Thus Symbolist language was seen as a precursor of the language of the ideal future, which would combine cognitive and aesthetic-mythological functions and therefore would serve as the means of transforming existing reality.

In practice, the poetics of magic embraced by Russian Symbolists evolved

23. Ibid., pp. 127, 129.
24. Ibid., pp. 129–30.

into a predictable pursuit of "magic moments" or breakthroughs to the hidden orders of reality, mediated through symbolic words. In their quest for symbols, they assigned esoteric meaning to the words that in everyday language designated material things or phenomena of the physical world. They believed that this practice could reveal the divine plan of the universe, but in fact it expressed their own mythologies. For example, in the Symbolist lexicon a "red dawn" signified not a spectacle of atmospheric nature, and not even a "sailor's warning," but the imminent apocalypse, the bloodstained beginning of a looming new era. Eventually the arcana of the Symbolist poetic lexicon grew conventional enough to become easy prey to a host of epigones.

Around 1913, the Futurists were rowdily claiming their primacy on the cultural scene and declaring a savage war on the Symbolists, whom they sought to topple from the strategically dominant position as the avant-garde of culture. Despite their bawdy attacks on Symbolist mysticism, the Futurists shared a number of affinities with their modernist predecessors: the Futurists, too, anticipated the advent of the ideal future and set out to create a "new language." The correlation between the guiding millenarian historical perspective, theories of poetic language as the epistemic agent, and interest in occult beliefs was characteristic of the Futurist worldview as well.

The Futurists' background in occult philosophies appears to be by far less illustrious than that of the Symbolists. Unlike the erudite Symbolists, the Futurists did not bother to delve into the arcana of ancient occult and mystical doctrines for appealing models. They deliberately shunned theoretical lucubrations and rarely discussed the sources that contributed to the creation of their poetics. The ideas of Petr Uspensky (1878–1947) may be named as one general source for this generation of the Russian artistic avant-garde. His *Tertium organum* (1911) was read by both Ego- and Cubo-Futurists; the artist Mikhail Matiushin interpreted Uspensky's ideas as compatible with Cubism; his influence is apparent in Kazimir Malevich's treatises; the poet and theorist Aleksei Kruchenykh endorsed Uspensky's tract in "Novye puti slova" (New ways of the word, 1913), an important declaration of the Futurist linguistic program which directly connects it with the first experiments in the "language of the future."[25] Uspensky, a one-time member of the Theosophical Society, took inspiration from the mystical tradition, especially Hindu philosophy, as well as from what may be called futuristic mathematics. He was familiar with the ideas of Claude Bragdon and translated Charles H. Hinton's book *The Fourth Dimension*. Uspensky often expressed his ideas in terms of basic geometrical shapes (which have always had occult significance), of projected

25. See Vladimir Markov, ed., *Manifesty i programmy russkikh futuristov* (Munich, 1967), pp. 66, 72; idem, *Russian Futurism* (Berkeley, 1968), p. 57.

planes and other such graphic images that were dear to technologically and visually oriented Futurists; moreover, his ideas answered their futurological expectations. Following the visionary theory of a Canadian psychiatrist and mystic, Richard M. Bucke, Uspensky heralded a triadic "psychic revolution" in socioeconomic, technological, and ultimately "psychic" realms, which would "literally create a new heaven and a new earth" to be inhabited by a new kind of humanity endowed with superior intuitive cognitive powers ("vysshaia intuitsiia")—a "new category of man for whom there exist different values than for other people," and who therefore promised to transcend the limits of space and time into the "fourth dimension," beyond the boundaries of death.[26] This vision of a future humanity meshed well with the Futurists' cosmogonic mythologies and predilections and validated their search for the language of the future.

The Futurists professed kinship with primitive cultures, especially with the free-spirited Asian nomads, those impulsive destroyers of rational European civilization, and preferred to mythologize themselves as shamans rather than as high priests.[27] The incantational language of folklore and the chants of the mystical sectarians served as their models for a new poetic language that the two leading Futurist theorists, Aleksei Kruchenykh and Vladimir (Velimir) Khlebnikov, conceived principally as transrational or transsense language (*zaum'* or *zaumnyi iazyk*). In "Novye puti slova" and "Vzorval'" (Explodivity, 1913) Kruchenykh valorized the speaking in tongues of some Russian religious sects as the "true" language because it presented a "revelation of things invisible"; in other words, he considered it prophetic speech.[28] Khlebnikov characterized folk magic incantations as the manifestations of "transrational language in folklore [*zaumnym iazykom v narodnom slove*]."[29]

In their search for a "new language" the Futurists maintained the distinction between poetic language and everyday speech. In their desire to strip the word of its rationally perceivable semantics, they were willing to go further than the Symbolists. Not only did they readily discard punctuation, capital letters, and other orthographical and grammatical conventions, but they aimed to change the very act of reading by casting text into cryptogrammatic forms such as palindromes.[30] One of the Burliuk brothers, Nikolai, an "impressionist" poet

---

26. Quoted in Robert C. Williams, *Artists in Revolution: Portraits of the Russian Avant-garde, 1905–1925* (Bloomington, 1977), pp. 118, 119.

27. See Benedikt Livshits, *Polutoroglazyi strelets* (New York, 1978), p. 55 and passim.

28. Markov, *Manifesty i programmy,* pp. 61, 67.

29. Velimir Khlebnikov, *Tvoreniia* (Moscow, 1986), comment 72, p. 665.

30. The Futurists' well-known predilection for cryptogrammatic texts raises the question whether they intended such verbal games as occult. Jerzy Faryno addresses the problem in ahistorical structuralist terms as a travesty of "normative" "sacral" acts. Igor' Smirnov contends in turn that if the employment of cryptic figures provides no substantially new

and a member of the Hylaean Futurist group, argued in favor of intuitively readable poetry whose proper function was to become a "creator of myths [*mifotvortsem*]." Citing the example of ancient hieroglyphs, he proposed that the suprarational communicative properties of the word can be enhanced through the synesthetic use of color and graphic sign; hence, he exhorted verbal artists to experiment with the "graphic life of writings [*graficheskuiu zhizn' pis'men*]," crediting the philosopher Nikolai Fedorov with having understood its importance.[31]

Khlebnikov maintained that the "utmost power over man, the magic spell of sorcery, the direct influence on the fates of man" had always belonged to "incomprehensible words."[32] The concepts of transrational language developed by both Kruchenykh and Khlebnikov presupposed that a cluster of sounds deliberately devoid of any apparent meaning was endowed with great evocative power, since it appealed directly to a person's subconscious. They posited transsense language as the basis for the universal language necessary for future humanity—"a new magic discourse which would reunite all speakers beyond the bounds of ordinary 'rational' language."[33] In 1913 Khlebnikov wrote about Aleksei Kruchenykh's pioneering experiments in transrational poetry: "I agree that the series [of evocative sounds] *aio, eee* has a certain meaning and in clever hands can become the basis for a universal language."[34]

That Khlebnikov took this ambitious task upon himself can be seen in his nexus of essays sketched in 1919, especially in "Khudozhniki mira" (The world artists), "Nasha osnova" (Our foundation), and "O stikhakh" (On verses). Khlebnikov proposed to create a universal "alphabet of truths [*azbuka istin*]." The "letters" of this Cyrillic-based alphabet were to be expressions of concepts, or "units of reason [*edinitsy razuma*]"; the sounds, then, would represent "terms for various kinds of space," and the letters would be corresponding graphic signs of that type of space. This idea was apparently based on "hiero-

---

meaning to the text, they should be recognized as cryptic in form only. See Jerzy Faryno, "Paronimiia-anagramma-palindrom v poetike avangarda," and Igor' Smirnov, "Literaturnyi tekst i taina: K probleme kognitivnoi poetiki," in *Kryptogramm: Zur Ästhetik des Verborgenen*, ed. R. Lachmann and I. Smirnov, Wiener Slawistischer Almanach no. 21 (Vienna, 1988), pp. 48, 289.

31. Nikolai Burliuk, "Poeticheskie nachala" (1914), in Markov, *Manifesty i programmy*, pp. 78–79.

32. Khlebnikov, "O stikhakh," in *Tvoreniia*, p. 633.

33. Boris Groys, *The Total Art of Stalinism: Avant-garde, Aesthetic Dictatorship, and Beyond*, trans. Charles Rougle (Princeton, 1992), p. 45.

34. Quoted in Markov, *Russian Futurism*, p. 131. For the differences in approach to transrational language by Khlebnikov and Kruchenykh see W. Weststeijn, "Bal'mont and Chlebnikov: A Study of Euphonic Devices," *Russian Literature* 8 (1980): 225–96. See also a Weststeijn's *Velimir Khlebnikov and the Development of Poetical Language in Russian Symbolism and Futurism* (Atlantic Highlands, N.J., 1985).

glyphs," by which Khlebnikov evidently meant the pictographs used to write Chinese and Japanese.[35]

Unlike Ludwig Zamenhoff, the inventor of Esperanto, or other visionary creators of artificial international languages, who sought to devise a uniform system of roots, affixes, and a simplified grammar, Khlebnikov attempted to distill pure meaning from every sound by way of paleolinguistic excursions that went far back in time and ranged widely in space. In support of his theory he collected words with the same initial consonant that denoted like concepts. To cite his favorite examples, the sound *ch* was deemed to express the idea of "container"; that is, words denoting vessel-like things were supposed to begin with the *ch* sound (e.g., *chashka*, cup; *cheboty*, boots). Likewise, he contended that words beginning with *kh*, such as *khizhina* and *khata* (hut), indicate that the *kh* sound, denoted by the Cyrillic letter *x*, signifies "the barrier between one point and another, moving toward the first one." This phonetic theory is analogous to Plato's notion of onomatopoeia expressed in the *Cratylus*, where the philosopher observes that in Greek the sound *r* often appears in words denoting motion, and *l* in those referring to smoothness.

In fact, Khlebnikov's search for a universal language was part of a still larger endeavor that may be compared in its intended historical significance to Bely's schema of an integrated theory of knowledge. This larger objective is manifest in the very composition of Khlebnikov's programmatic essay "Nasha osnova," published in 1920. Part 1, headed "Slovotvorchestvo" (Creation of words), contains a general exposition of his theory of a new poetic language. Not unlike the Renaissance occultists, Khlebnikov believed that human activity evolved through time in harmony with the celestial bodies; he aspired to establish the correspondences that would link the laws of physics with putative linguistic ones. Harnessing a motley mixture of notions borrowed from recent scientific discoveries, he worked to establish a "science of language" with laws "similar to Mendeleev's [periodic table of the elements] or Moseley's law."[36] In addition to the English physicist Henry G. Moseley, Khlebnikov referred to the discoveries of the Dutch physicist Hendrik A. Lorentz, which helped Albert Einstein launch his theory of relativity.[37] Khlebnikov's examples indicate his

35. Klebnikov, "Khudozhniki mira," in *Tvoreniia*, pp. 621–22. In Russian the characters used in the Chinese, Japanese, and Korean languages as well as in ancient Egyptian are commonly called "hieroglyphs."

36. Ibid., pp. 624–25. According to Moseley's law, the atomic number is equal to the charge on the nucleus and the frequency of X rays emitted by each element corresponds to its atomic number.

37. Around 1901, Lorentz established (independently of his Irish colleague George Fitzgerald) that the body length contracts as its speed increases, and formulated the law of transformation by which the spatial and time coordinates of one moving system can be correlated with the known space-time coordinates of any other system.

fascination with nuclear physics, then a young but booming field, and also with the theory of relativity (this interest was shared by some other prominent Russian modernist poets and language theorists, such as Andrei Bely, Roman Jakobson, and Vladimir Mayakovsky, who found nourishment for their futuristic aspirations in the newest advancements of science, expecting that they would show how to conquer time and space and to achieve immortality).[38]

Notwithstanding his interest in modern science, Khlebnikov contended that historically "the science of language ran ahead of the natural sciences." Characteristically, his arcane linguistic theories, most of which were based on pseudoscientific analogies and proved to be quite impressionistic, were meant for such visionary tasks as "measuring the wavelength of good and evil" or "establishing an equation of abstract moral laws."[39] The latter idea Khlebnikov illustrated with a rather occult two-column chart that purported to represent the "light nature of morals [*svetovaia priroda nravov*]." Listed in the left column were words designating things and phenomena of "the nether world [*tot svet*]," while on the right side were cataloged the corresponding ones signifying the "relativity principle [*nachalo otnositel'nosti*]."

In Part 2 of "Nasha osnova," headed "Zaumnyi iazyk" (Transrational language), Khlebnikov justified the Futurists' explorations in transsense language, arguing that since transrational poetry was based on intuitive perceptions, it reflected the laws of universal language better than poetry based on the logic of grammar. Finally, Part 3, "Matematicheskoe ponimanie istorii: Gamma Budetlianina" (Mathematical understanding of history: The gamma of the Futurist), was devoted to a comprehensive predictive theory of history which Khlebnikov attempted to explain by analogy with scientific laws, his favorite method of explication. In his calculations, which establish a pattern connecting the births of Jesus Christ, Walt Whitman, Karl Marx, and Buddha, he relied on, among other things, R. M. Bucke's *Cosmic Consciousness: A Study in the Evolution of the Human Mind* (1901), whose mystical scientism he found congenial.[40]

Khlebnikov was also evidently inspired by Plato, perhaps because he saw in Plato a fellow numerological mystic. His innovative emulation of Platonic dialogue in the essay "Uchitel' i uchenik" (The teacher and the disciple, 1913) and in the poem "Zangezi" (1922) suggests the influence of Plato's Pythagorean discourses, such as "Timaeus," and possibly of the recondite passages in Book VIII of *The Republic* concerning the correlation between the divine and human cycles, and the law of the origin and decline of the state (i.e., essentially

38. See Krystyna Pomorska, "Majakovskij's Cosmic Myth," in *Myth in Literature*, ed. A. Kodjak, K. Pomorska, and S. Rudy (Columbus, Ohio, 1985).

39. Khlebnikov, "Khudozhniki mira," p. 625.

40. See Khlebnikov, "Koleso rozhdenii," in *Velimir Khlebnikov: Myth and Reality*, Amsterdam Symposium on the Centenary of Velimir Khlebnikov, ed. Willem G. Weststeijn (Amsterdam, 1986), pp. 286–87.

the law of history, which Plato apparently meant to demonstrate on the basis of Pythagorean numerology).[41] Khlebnikov employed the form of heuristic discourse as a vehicle for exegesis of his own "law governing the fates of the nations [*pravila, kotoromu podchiniaiutsia narodnye sud'by*]," and the pupil surpassed the teacher by connecting a dizzying array of most diverse and distant events in world history, such as "the foundation of China in the year 2852," the fall of Israel "in 723," and the battle of Kulikovo; he predicted the destruction of "a great state" in 1917. After the Russian revolutions of 1917, this prophecy considerably enhanced Khlebnikov's reputation as a diviner in the eyes of his friends, and Khlebnikov himself took great pride in it, though later, when his other predictions failed to come true, he dismissed this law. Besides the apparent shared belief in the divine synthesizing function of contemplative mathematics, a salient affinity between Plato's and Khlebnikov's course of argument lies in the linking of a mathematical event with sensory perception—that is, of the intuitional response with measured definition—which is evident in their respective explorations of the relationship between number ratios and sound frequencies. In Plato's search for the numerical expression of the divine mysteries, for example, the Pythagorean numbers 3, 4, and 5 are related to the harmony of the whole-tone scale as well as to the mysterious number expressing the generational cycles. Likewise, Khlebnikov connected his idea of "the wheel of births [*koleso rozhdenii*]" to the frequencies of tones.

In summary, in the ideas of Velimir Khlebnikov, the fountainhead of Futurist poetic theory, we discern once again a correlation between the theory of poetics, epistemology, and the teleology of history: all are informed with a utopian futurological intent. In general, the Russian modernists' theories of poetics were an integral part of what may be considered pseudo-occult systems guided by the search for a great, all-embracing epistemological scheme that would afford the poets control over the unknown Ideal Future.

The Bolshevik coup put an end to the search for such a design by installing Marxism as the comprehensive doctrine that connected all the phenomena of the universe, thus fulfilling in a way the aspirations of occult philosophers. Most important, Marxism claimed to be the ultimate expression of the "objective laws of history." All that was left for scientists and philosophers was to supplement "the only true scientific teaching [*edinstvenno vernoe nauchnoe uchenie*]"—as Marxism cum Leninism cum Stalinism and beyond came to be officially called—by extending its reach to all spheres of knowledge about life and the universe. Stalin's well-known "great contribution to linguistic science"

41. These analogies suggest that Plato's numerical manipulations, their Hermetic nature notwithstanding, may hold a key to Khlebnikov's visionary computations, which seem to have modified the Platonic system with the figures and formulas borrowed from modern science, as well as perhaps from Buddhism.

may be viewed, historically, as the pinnacle of this epistemological pyramid.[42] Needless to say, the official formula underscores the all-pervading hegemony of Marxism, under which there could be no place for any rival system, particularly a religious or occult one. The mysticism of predictive magic was supplanted by the mystique of science. In the rhetorical climate where any notion deemed politically incorrect was derisively condemned as "pseudo-scientific," all manner of occult beliefs and magic practices were severely ostracized as "unscientific" and therefore harmful.

Nikolai Bukharin's speech at the First Congress of Soviet Writers (1934) is indicative in this respect. This most learned attempt at theorizing Marxist premises for understanding the nature of verbal art at this influential forum opened with a review of the theories of poetic language as magical: citing strictly scholarly papers as his sources, Bukharin mentioned examples from ancient India and China, and the demiurgic "logology," but dwelled on Russian Symbolism, quoting from treatises of Bal'mont and Bely. Although he summarily debunked all theories of the magic properties of language as "pure mysticism" and "fetishism of the word," he credited their adherents with calling attention to the "specificity of poetic thought and speech" at a time when "scientific understanding" of these phenomena was not yet available.[43] His own effort to articulate objective laws of poetics bespeaks a familiar desire to overcome the separation between rational thinking and "thinking in images," albeit from the point of view of materialist "reflection theory," according to which being determines consciousness, and thus phenomena of the empirical world are translated into images representing "condensed emotions." The juggling of such loaded notions as "image," "concept," "symbol," and "type" causes him to revert to Aleksandr Potebnia's authority at a particularly difficult point, when he attempts to explain the relationship between logical thought and emotions. Despite the prominence of scientific determinism (he asserts that the works of the physiologist I. P. Pavlov can explain why some gifted persons become poets and others philosophers), ultimately Bukharin's delineation of Socialist Realist poetics, for all its didactic pragmatism, retains vestiges of the modernist concept of the futurological magic of words: he urges poets to shun mere "realism" in order to "dare to dream"—to make poetic language an active force in shaping new human beings free from the

42. Stalin's essay "Marxism and Problems of Linguistics" (1950) instantly reversed the official course of Soviet linguistic thought (and the good fortunes of Academician Nikolai Marr and his numerous followers).

43. Bukharin's logic brings to mind Fredric Jameson's defense that a comparison of Marxism with religion "may also function to rewrite certain religious concepts—most notably Christian historicism and the 'concept' of providence, but also the pretheological systems of primitive magic—as anticipatory foreshadowing of historical materialism within precapitalist social formations in which scientific thinking was unavailable as such": Fredric Jameson, *The Political Unconscious: Narrative as a Socially Symbolic Act* (Ithaca, 1981), p. 285.

split between will and intellect, and "to pick up the thread of development in the present, to carry it into the future," thus bringing about "victory over the enemy and the conquest of nature."[44]

Likewise, in spite of the professed materialism of the officially dominant ideology, Soviet cultural consciousness was deeply mythic. In the mind of *Homo sovieticus* the world became split into "we" and "they," with "they" representing the forces of the antiworld, the world of the past, and "we" the people of the marvelous wonderland of the ideal future, partially realized in the present. "We" must expose and eliminate every last "enemy of the people," defined broadly in the Soviet Constitution of 1936 as "anyone who seeks to weaken the socialist system." The presence of "wreckers" or saboteurs (*vre-diteli*) was the prerequisite ingredient of the plot in the majority of the Socialist Realist novels of the Stalinist period, especially in the 1930s. In these novels, suspense is typically built on the tension between two plot lines—fulfillment and overfulfillment of production quotas by the good guys on the one hand and resistance orchestrated by an evil wreckers' conspiracy on the other. To be sure, this type of plot provides the detective-story element without which the Soviet novel would be devoid of narrative interest. The struggle with nature that Katerina Clark identifies as "a central image of the Stalinist novel" is usually a struggle against "magicians"; both in literature and in film the ubiquitous "wreckers" are members of secret organizations whose acts of sabotage usually involve water, fire, or other elements (including the chaotic "unconscious masses").[45] Typically the climax occurs when sabotage coincides with a natural calamity of some kind.[46] The invariable connection between the wreckers' plot and tempestuous natural forces suggests that the "enemies of the people" were mythologized as black magicians plotting to unleash the chaos of unorganized elemental forces (*stikhiinye sily*) against the Promethean heroes, who, usually by feats of Soviet "white magic," worked hard to bring communism closer by subduing and transforming those forces.

Evidence of such a perception may be found not only in most Soviet newspapers and novels of the 1930s but also in more unlikely sources. It is curious, for instance, that when Vladimir Propp classified the functions of characters in Russian magic tales in his world-renowned *Morphology of the Folktale* (*Morfologiia skazki*, 1928), he assigned "the antagonist" no other term but "wrecker

44. "Doklad N. I. Bukharina o poezii, poetike i zadachakh poeticheskogo tvorchestva v SSSR," in *Pervyi vsesosiuznyi s''ezd sovetskikh pisatelei: Stenograficheskii otchet* (Moscow, 1934), pp. 481–83, 501.

45. See Katerina Clark, *The Soviet Novel: History as Ritual*, 2d ed. (Chicago, 1985), p. 100.

46. To give but a few examples of novels with this type of plot: Boris Pil'niak's *Volga vpadaet v Kaspiiskoe more* (The Volga falls to the Caspian Sea, 1930); Fedor Gladkov's *Energiia* (Energy, 1932); Leonid Leonov's *Sot'* (The river Sot, 1930) and *Doroga na okean* (The Road to the ocean, 1935); Bruno Iasenskii's *Chelovek meniaet kozhu* (Man sloughs off his skin, 1932); and Il'ia Erenburg's *Den' vtoroi* (Out of chaos, 1933).

[*vreditel'*]," especially since this character's function was defined as presenting obstacles to hamper the protagonist's progress in his or her quest.[47] Propp's book was published in the year of the notorious mining engineers' trial known as the "Shakhty affair," which inaugurated a nexus of infamous "show trials" of "enemies of the people." As mysticism became unfashionable and even dangerous, Andrei Bely reassessed his views on occult practices and associations in the last volume of his memoirs, published in 1934. Attempting to explain away the mystical terror that had seized him in 1908, the hyper-imaginative Bely now attributed his mysticism to his prophetic sense of encroaching capitalism, whose "demonic visage," he confessed, kept arising in his mind as a recurring nightmare. Behind this horrible image Bely professed to have discerned lurking "secret . . . organizations of some capitalists . . . armed with an exceptional power unknown to others." Upon closer inspection, these shadowy figures turned out to be Freemasons, whom Bely claims always to have hated, but "now, in 1933, everybody knows [the names of these persons] . . . , it is now revealed by documents that world war and secret plans were cooking in the Masonic kitchen. I smelled the odors of that kitchen, experiencing them as an 'occult' phenomenon. This is what my mysticism of that time was rooted in."[48]

The vestiges of the fundamental assumption underlying most magic practices, that the identity of the signifier and the signified allows a knowing magician to act upon an object, phenomenon, or person through its image or name, may be found in the uncanny reverence for the images of Soviet leaders. Since any newspaper was likely to contain a speech or a picture of the "Great Leader of All Times and Peoples," an innocuous act such as using a piece of newsprint for some practical everyday purposes could be seen as disrespectful at best and fraught with grave consequences at worst, and was superstitiously avoided by pious Soviet citizens. It would be difficult, of course, to find acknowledgment of this belief or of the punitive practices associated with it either in official directives or in Socialist Realist fiction. From the point of view

47. On the other hand, the epigraphs to the introductory chapters imply Propp's underlying sympathy for Goethe's mystical organicism. See Vladimir Propp, *Morphology of the Folktale*, ed. Louis A. Wagner, trans. Laurence Scott, 2d ed. (Austin, 1968).

48. Andrei Belyi, *Mezhdu dvukh revoliutsii* (Moscow, 1934), pp. 316–17. Among the putative capitalist-Masonic conspirators Bely lists several political figures prominent in the Provisional Government established after the February 1917 Revolution, among them P. N. Miliukov, M. I. Tereschenko, and A. F. Kerensky. Bely's finger-pointing suggests that he took stock in the myth that the February Revolution was a coup d'état orchestrated by a Masonic conspiracy (or that he wanted to give that impression). Hence his attempts to dissociate himself from Decadent, occult, or Masonic trends of prerevolutionary culture and to assert instead his kinship with Marxist revolutionaries by claiming to have always harbored anti-capitalist sentiments, or, in other words, the correct historical intuition. On the myth of a Masonic conspiracy, which eventually descended to the popular imagination and was extended to the Bolshevik Revolution, see A. Ia. Avrekh, *Masony i revoliutsiia* (Moscow, 1990).

of institutional history, the thorough control over the representation of the Soviet leaders was similar to a religious institution's restrictions on the interpretation of icons or saints' lives. "The key," Rolf Hellebust points out, "is the ability of the cultural establishment to limit the interpretive freedom of the consumers of artworks."[49] The fearful awe of the Leader's name, words, and image is still vividly remembered by people who lived in Stalin's times.[50]

The standard practice of relentlessly chanting the Supreme Leader's name or such slogans as "Lenin lived, Lenin lives, Lenin will live!" at Party congresses and public forums suggests invocation of deities or the casting of a magic spell. Even if the initiators and enthusiastic mass perpetrators of this custom had no such conscious intent, these rituals worked to hypnotize participating audiences into a state of ecstatic frenzy. The stenographic reports of the grandiose state and Party congresses of the Stalin era record in formulaic phrases how the "storms of applause" that punctuated the speeches of the Supreme Ideologue escalated into protracted "standing ovations" (a practice that, together with other such ritualistic pomp, persisted into the post-Stalin era, if on a reduced scale).

Letters and numbers in Socialist Realist culture were surrounded by a particular mystical aura; ordinary statistical figures were carefully guarded as "state secrets." The conventional rationale given for this well-known obsession with secrecy was that if the ubiquitous "enemies of the people" obtained this knowledge, they might use it to stall the "march of progress." However, the practice of shrouding statistics on birth and death with a dark veil of secrecy or of inflating productivity rates cannot be explained merely as a tactic to deceive the enemy; evidently it issued from an unacknowledgeable belief that the manipulation of numbers can have an impact on reality. By the same token, a typographical error could be adjudged a crime against the state, especially if it crept into a printed text by or about the Leader.

The rhetoric of miracle permeated all spheres of Soviet discourse of the Stalinist era. Popular songs, those mass-culture repositories of guiding myths, asserted that "we are born to make fairy tale into reality, / to conquer time and space [my rozhdeny chtob skazku sdelat' byl'iu, / preodolet' prostranstvo i prostor]," and that "simple Soviet people create miracles everywhere [prostye sovetskie liudi povsiudu tvoriat chudesa]."[51] The mass media informed Soviet citizens daily about the "miracles of heroism [*chudesa geroizma*]" being per-

49. Rolf Hellebust, "Reflections on an Absence: Novelistic Portraits of Stalin before 1953," in *Socialist Realism Revisited: Selected Papers from McMaster Conference,* ed. Nina Kolesnikov and Walter Smyrniw (Hamilton, Ont., 1994), p. 117.

50. The fear of accidentally inflicting harm on the images of Soviet leaders is satirized in Vladimir Voinovich's *Life and Extraordinary Adventures of Private Ivan Chonkin,* trans. Richard Lourie (New York, 1982), an astute travesty of the Soviet universe of that era (pt. 1, chap. 9).

51. The lyrics to "Marsh aviatorov" (The aviators' march, 1922) and "Sovetskii prostoi chelovek" (Soviet ordinary person, 1936), respectively.

formed by Stakhanovites and other shock workers at factories and collective farms, and about model soldiers guarding "the sacred Soviet borders [*sviash-chennye sovetskie rubezhi*]." In the opening speech at the First Congress of Soviet Writers, Maxim Gorky urged fellow writers to depict the miracles taking place "in the land illuminated by Lenin's genius, in the land where Joseph Stalin's iron will works tirelessly and miraculously [*neutomimo i chudodeistvenno*]."[52]

The reason for the prevalence of these mystical features of Soviet culture in conjunction with vehement denials of the very existence of miraculous phenomena other than those accountable within the framework of the dominant ideology remains debatable. Vladimir Papernyi proposed that these features are the best proof that Soviet culture was "not an invention of a bloodthirsty dictator, nor did it arise as a result of a Zionist, Masonic or any other conspiracy, but took its shape as a result of more *archaic* and *stable* cultural forms subsuming newer and less stable ones."[53] Which archaic forms, though? In sociological terms, such an interpretation implies that Soviet cultural values were a manifestation of triumphant peasant beliefs and tastes, since the "new class" of the Soviet elite (which some scholars consider to have been the power base of Stalinism) were of peasant stock and supposedly brought with them the deep-seated values of their origins. This view is contested by Boris Groys, who faults both Papernyi and (less justly) Katerina Clark for treating Stalinist aesthetics "as a 'lapse' of Russian culture into a 'primitive state' or 'pure folklore.'" He contends that however valuable analogies between Stalinist culture and "the sacred archetypes familiar from the art of other religiously oriented periods" may be, they "neglect to inquire why this quasi-sacred art arose where and when it did."[54] Groys sees the Russian modernist avant-garde as the immediate cultural precursor of Stalinist aesthetics.

It may seem paradoxical, but despite the Stalinists' vehement denunciation of the "formalism" and "idealism" of the modernist avant-garde, in the Socialist Realist notion of artistic language as a powerful tool to conjure up the bright future they in effect institutionalized avant-garde ideas, if in grotesquely mutant forms. The Symbolist theorists thought, of course, in Platonic terms, and their conceptions were rooted in mysticism. Present in both Symbolist and Socialist Realist views, however, is an underlying utopian desire to attain, through symbolic expression, the absolute—to discover and express the ultimate scheme of history. What for the Symbolists meant revealing "the World Soul" or for Khlebnikov "the astral language" was replaced in Soviet aesthetics by Marxist teleology. Nikolai Valentinov, a one-time Marxist revolutionary who came to find a great deal of similarity between the views on art of

52. *Pervyi vsesoiuznyi s"ezd*, p. 1. The pronouncement was met by a "storm of continuous applause [*burnye, prodolzhitel'nye aplodismenty*]."

53. V. Papernyi, *Kul'tura "Dva"* (Ann Arbor, 1985), pp. 156–57; Papernyi's emphasis.

54. Groys, *Total Art of Stalinism*, p. 64.

the Symbolists and the Soviet leaders, wrote that for the latter "art is only a means of 'transformation of life' in accordance with that absolutely true philosophy—or, if you will, materialistic religion—which they, the Kremlin theurgists, claim to possess." [55]

Bely defined Symbolism as "a kind of token or precursor" of the new truly democratic art based on "the method of representing ideas in images." In that synthetic art of the future, he wrote, "the images become the method of cognition rather than something self-sufficient [a]nd their purpose is no longer to arouse a feeling of beauty, but rather to develop the observer's capacity to see for himself the prototypical meaning of these images in the phenomena of life."[56] Bely's prophecy, along with Viacheslav Ivanov's idea of the future language as a "mythological speech" suitable for the "religious epoch proper," were fulfilled by Socialist Realism: the principal tenet of the Socialist Realist doctrine, which demands that writers "show reality in its revolutionary development," put the languages of all the arts precisely to the utilitarian purpose of expressing "the prototypical meaning of images"—only it was the guiding Soviet myths that became the prototypes.[57]

Under Socialist Realism all the words of the language were bonded into a rigid system of politically correct correspondences, so that each signifier was keyed to officially sanctioned mythologemas. This explains the ban on free experimentation with the language of the arts and the striking homogeneity, to the Western ear, of clichéd language on all levels of Soviet discourse, from poetry and fiction to newspapers and Party documents. Every noun had to have a predictable attribute chosen from a limited menu of positive and negative epithets, depending on whether it signified something belonging to the Soviet or the anti-Soviet world. The same rule governed the use of verbs: capitalist politicians, for example, could at best "opine," but usually they "maliciously slandered" whatever it was they were talking about; naturally, Soviet leaders "gave wise directives" even in their casual pronouncements. Such a system of linguistic bondage not only ensured unambiguous legibility of political messages but also fostered automatization of the decoding process by their mass consumers, so that communication took place on the level of the subconscious, thus approximating the effect of transrational speech.

The fact that the Socialist Realist doctrine was introduced at the First Congress of Soviet Writers indicates that verbal art was given principal significance in the new aesthetic ideology. In the Soviet social and cultural hierarchy, artists, and especially writers, were accorded a highly privileged status, comparable only to that of the Bolshevik elite—since together with the Bolsheviks they were regarded as the seers into the future. Aleksandr Blok once described

55. Valentinov, *Dva goda s simvolistami*, p. 127.
56. Bely, "Symbolism as a World Understanding" (1903), in *Selected Essays*, p. 79.
57. *Pervyi vsesosiuznyi s"ezd*, p. 4.

the end product of the Symbolist poet's creative act thus: "Life became art, I performed the magic acts of incantation and at last there appeared before me . . . a terrestrial wonder."[58] Likewise, Soviet artists were expected to conjure up extraordinary artistic images of ordinary life "as it ought to be"—that is, to glorify the "blooming country of socialism" and "the construction of Communist society" by realizing in appropriate symbolic imagery "the sacerdotal speech of prophecies" by Marx, Lenin, Stalin, or the current Party leader. Stalin became "the hierophant over the theurgists," commanding "daring creative endeavors of Soviet art"; his every word had to be incarnated in works of art and in life.[59] In the Soviet political climate writers had indeed to possess exceptional intuitive powers in their alliance, or cooperation, with the Party "theurgists." Since the constantly shifting Party line was accepted as the principal expression of the "only true scientific teaching," the equation of word and deed put artists in a precarious position, making prescience essential for writers' artistic and physical survival.

58. Blok, "O sovremennom sostoianii russkogo simvolizma," p. 430.
59. Valentinov, *Dva goda s simvolistami*, p. 127.

CHAPTER ELEVEN
AN OCCULT SOURCE
OF SOCIALIST REALISM

Gorky and Theories of Thought Transference

Mikhail Agursky

I n fin-de-siècle Europe psychoanalysis, psychic research, and the occult were entangled in the new discipline of psychology. The term "psychic" or "psychical" was used to refer to mental processes, conscious and unconscious, as well as to clairvoyance, and covered areas formerly relegated to the occult, such as dream interpretation. "Occult" came to describe both experiments in parapsychology and esoteric lore. This atmosphere encouraged widespread speculation about and confusion of the scientific, philosophical, and esoteric implications of mental processes. One result of the intellectual confusion was a widespread attempt to discuss occult ideas in positivistic, scientific terms, even to perform methodologically more or less rigorous research on them. In Russia and the early Soviet Union the most prominent scientist to investigate occult aspects of mental activity was Vladimir Bekhterev (1857–1927). Maxim Gorky, among others, was greatly taken with the possibilities the intellectual climate suggested. As both a literary figure and a political activist, Gorky was particularly interested in the idea of thought transference, which promised great power to influence public opinion. His understanding of the matter was that of a lay reader with no scientific training, but his political and literary importance allowed his interpretations to influence both early Soviet psychological research and the premises of Socialist Realism, which after 1932 was the official art form in the Soviet Union.

Mikhail Agursky died in August 1991. The editor has rewritten this chapter from Professor Agursky's first draft, with the aid of comments and suggestions by Irina Gutkin, David Joravsky, and Nina Melechen. I thank them for their help. Unfortunately, some of the author's footnotes remain incomplete.

Further study is needed to pinpoint the exact channels through which Gorsky's ideas were spread, but the impact of his views is evident.

The potential powers of the mind appealed across disciplines. The London Society for Psychical Research was founded (in 1882) "to investigate that large body of debatable phenomena designated by such terms as mesmeric, psychical, and spiritualistic."[1] *Rebus*, the journal of the Russian Spiritualists, regularly published articles on hypnosis, mental telepathy, and extrasensory perception. Hypnosis, a tool of early psychoanalysis, was also called magneticism or mesmerism, after Franz Anton Mesmer, who based his theories on a presumed substance that permeates all being and can be manipulated by persons with special powers or training. Pamphlets such as *Kak peredat' svoi mysli* (How to transmit your thoughts) were part of the Library of Magnetism, a Kiev-based series.[2] Scientists studied thought transference and hypnotic suggestion as neurological or physiological phenomena. The discovery and measurement of sensations was a topic of mainstream medical research. Vladimir Bekhterev came to the idea of thought transference by way of neurology. Ivan Pavlov considered himself a physiologist.

Neo-Kantians who wished to investigate the structure of the mind scientifically (as distinct from only theorizing about it) and to reconcile the Kantian antinomies of mind-body and spirit-matter were among the pioneers of German and Russian psychology. Wilhelm Wundt maintained that sensations are physiological—that is, material, but of a kind of matter that acts upon the psyche, subliminally if the sensations are weak, consciously if they are strong. Georgy Chelpanov, a follower of Wundt, wrote about "empirical parallelism," a modification of Wundt's term "psychophysical parallelism," in *Mozg i dusha* (Brain and soul, 1900). Aleksandr Vvedensky published *O predelkakh i priznakakh odushevlenii* (The limits and signs of animation, 1892) and *Psikhologiia bez vsiakoi metafiziki* (Psychology without metaphysics, 1914). Though they were Kantian idealists philosophically, their methodology was more or less positivist, emphasizing facts, empirical research, and methodological rigor.

Another side to positivism—a search for a grand scheme of the universe, and in some cases for the ultimate nature of substance—led to extravagant speculation, shading off into mysticism and the occult. Auguste Comte, the founder of philosophical positivism, posited three stages of knowledge: religion, metaphysics, and science. But he also advocated a "Religion of Humanity," which included communion with the spirits of departed loved ones and worship of a purely spiritual "eternal feminine." The scientific positivism of the physicist and philosopher Ernst Mach, Robert Williams points out, "was

---

1. See James Webb, *The Occult Establishment* (La Salle, Ill., 1976), chap. 6, pp. 347–63.

2. Prof. Zh. Fabius de-Shanvill, *Kak peredat' svoi mysli: Zametki i svidetel'stva o telepatii ili peredache myslei*, Biblioteka po magnetizmu (Kiev, 1913). The editor is indebted to Woytiech Zalewski, who purchased a reprint edition (n.d.) in the Moscow Metro in 1990.

tinged with both the relativism of modern science and a strong undercurrent of religious seeking." In the 1860s Mach had accepted Gustav Fechner's idea of a "pantheistic universe of interconnected forms where plants and planets had souls in a common universal consciousness reminiscent of the Swedish engineer-mystic Emanuel Swedenborg."[3] By the 1880s, Mach no longer believed in a pantheistic universe, but he continued to accept Fechner's view that death is only a second birth into a freer existence. Mach maintained that the individual's thoughts and deeds leave permanent traces on the macrocosm, thus achieving a kind of social immortality.

Empiriocriticism, the scientific theory Mach and Richard Avenarius developed independently of each other, reduced the world to our sensations of it. Wilhelm Ostwald held that the world is entirely composed of energy in various states of transformation. Both Ostwald's Energetism and Empiriocriticism could be perceived, regardless of their founders' intentions, as compatible with or confirming occult beliefs, because they emphasized invisible or hidden phenomena ("occult" in the literal meaning of the word), eliminated ontological dualism (a perennial occult theme), and "exposed" apparently solid material entities as illusions or maya. From an occultist point of view, Energetism was merely a new form of the alchemical idea of transmutation. We can speak of a positivist occultism, or quasi occultism, grounded in the workings of ultimately explicable natural forces rather than in a transcendent creator God, which was attractive to some Marxists.

Maxim Gorky, the writer and future architect of Socialist Realism, was deeply impressed by early twentieth-century studies of thought transference and hypnotic suggestion. Not a scientist himself, he perceived these studies in quasi-occult terms, mingling their findings with quasi-occult versions of empiriocriticism and Energetism and with Theosophy, Fedorov, and the Symbolist concept of art as a theurgical activity that would magically transform the world. No more a partisan of science for science's sake than of art for art's sake, Gorky was interested in these theories because they seemed to prove the actual existence of the phenomena of thought transference and hypnotic suggestion, and these phenomena provided revolutionary intellectuals with a potentially powerful means to sway the masses. Thus by way of Gorky, early twentieth-century studies of thought transference were a source of Socialist Realism.

As one of the major formulators of Socialist Realism, Gorky taught that writers and artists must cultivate optimism among the Russian people, who he thought had a natural inclination to passivity.[4] He believed that optimism (and pessimism) can be transmitted not only on the cognitive level but also, and

3. Robert C. Williams, *Artists and Revolution* (Bloomington, 1977), p. 29.

4. See Mikhail Agursky, "Maksim Gorky and the Decline of Bolshevik Theomachy," in *Christianity and Russian Culture in Soviet Society*, ed. Nikolai Petro (Boulder, 1990), pp. 69–101.

more important, unconsciously, through its direct influence on the human mind and with no involvement of will on the part of the recipient. As an engineer of the human soul, the writer or artist had the task of inspiring the people to build socialism by offering them "a glimpse of tomorrow," as well as by conveying to them the idea that the fairy-tale reality depicted in the arts already existed. The theory of Socialist Realism can be viewed as an applied mass psychology based on a positivist interpretation of the occult. In this respect, Socialist Realism was heir to the idea of influencing and directing mass psychology which had preoccupied Russian intellectuals since the turn of the century. Let us look at some of these theories and then at Gorky's enthusiastic response to and subsequent use of them.

Russian publications that attempted to interpret psychic or occult phenomena proliferated in the early 1900s. In 1902, for example, Iakov Zhuk published an important article on invisible communications between physical bodies. Zhuk criticized those who rejected the very existence of such occult phenomena as clairvoyance, ghosts, and fortune-telling with mirrors, attempting to explain them scientifically. He especially acknowledged thought transmission: "The senses of one organism can be perceived by another through some specific ways in a more or less clear form."[5] He was not referring to the intervention of spirits.

In an extremely ambitious positivist approach to the occult, the Moscow psychiatrist Naum Kotik conducted experiments in an effort to demonstrate that psychic phenomena were forms of radiation. His experiments in May 1904 with a girl who allegedly proved that she could read her father's mind led him to the concept of N-rays. Kotik concluded:

> The thoughts of one person can be transferred to another through N-rays, which proceed from the vocal centers of the first. N-rays may excite the vocal centers of the second person and produce there corresponding audio images. . . . In our view all humans are linked by invisible threads of N-rays, which play an insignificant role in daily life but may well acquire enormous importance and influence in all mass movements. I think that mass psychology, the law of imitations, and other mysterious phenomena of mass psychology can be seen correctly only as the influence of N-rays.[6]

Kotik believed in a material basis for parapsychological phenomena and sought to discover it. His theory of N-rays was obviously influenced by recent scientific and nonscientific work on radiation. The Russian word *izluchenie*, usually translated as "radiation," can also mean any other kind of emission or transmission of rays, energy, sound, or electromagnetic waves. Many people

5. Yakov Zhuk, "Vzaimnaia sviaz' mezhdu organizmami," *Mir bozhii*, 1902, no. 6.
6. Naum Kotik, "Chtenie myslei i N-luchi," *Obozrenie psikhiatrii*, 1904, nos. 8–9, p. 665.

took the discovery of X rays in 1895 as scientific confirmation of hidden forces or energies that they had believed existed all along.

In 1904 Kotik also published a book that in 1908 was translated into German as *Die Emanation der psycho-physischen Energie* (The emanations of psychophysical energy). Here he went much further in his hypotheses, which can be summarized in the following theses:

1. Thinking is followed by the emission of a special kind of energy.
2. This energy has both mental and physical aspects.
3. As a mental phenomenon, this energy enters directly into the brain of another person and produces the same images there.
4. As a physical phenomenon, this energy has several features.
   (a) It circulates in the human body from the brain to the extremities, and vice versa.
   (b) It is accumulated on the surface of the body.
   (c) It penetrates the air with difficulty.
   (d) It penetrates obstacles (physical objects) with greater difficulty.
   (e) It flows from a body with a stronger psychic charge to a body with a weaker psychic charge.[7]

Interestingly enough, Theosophists had an ambivalent attitude toward Kotik's experiments, despite their mutual interest in thought transference and suggestion. One Theosophist, Konstantin Kudriavtsev, stressed that Kotik was a positivist and that his approach differed from that of the Theosophists, although he agreed with Kotik's conclusions. Kudriavtsev said that "every moment of our life we introduce into the world's space emanations of thoughts that are harmful for us and for others. It depends on us to fill the world with the harmony of beautiful pure thoughts and to shield ourselves from the harmful influences of dark forces."[8] Petr Uspensky, then a Theosophist, later an associate of Gurdjieff, regarded Kotik's experiments and their interpretation more positively. In particular, he supported the concept of "psychophysical emanation."[9] Nikolai Rerikh, the painter and philosopher who developed his own variant of Theosophy, Agni-yoga, also regarded Kotik's experiments very highly.[10]

Later Kotik's work was used by Charles Richet and Albert Schrenk von Notzing, the pillars of parapsychology. As a result of Kotik's experiments,

7. Naum Kotik, *Die Emanation der psycho-physischen Energie* (Wiesbaden, 1908). This work also appeared in French translation in the same year.

8. Konstantin Kudriavtsev, "Emanatsiia psikhofizicheskoi energii," *Vestnik teosofii*, 1908, no. 1, p. 87.

9. Petr Uspenskii, "Chetvertoe izmerenie," *Vestnik teosofii*, 1909, no. 11.

10. Nikolai Roerich, *Altai-Himalaya* (London, 1929), p. 23.

Richet concluded that "thought is an energy that radiates outward," and Schrenk von Notzing said in 1920: "However daring and unconvincing Kotik's experiments may appear at first sight, they indicate a path of research, and offer us a welcome auxiliary hypothesis."[11] Wilhelm Kohlhammer underscored the fact that Kotik's experiments were the foundation of Schrenk von Notzing's theory of mental telepathy.[12]

The Russian scientist Vladimir Bekhterev, on the other hand, cast doubts on Kotik's experiments because of what he considered their methodological weakness. But the sharpest criticism of Kotik was leveled in 1922 by Albert Moll, whose book *Prophezeien und Hellsehen* (Prophecy and clairvoyance) was translated into Russian in 1925. He called Kotik's experiments amateurish, probably on the same basis as Bekhterev did: shoddy hypothesizing and lack of proper control groups.[13] Bekhterev, a rigorous experimenter, criticized even Pavlov for fudging the difference between speculation and proof.

Bekhterev, a student of Jean Charcot and familiar with the ideas of the German scientists Wilhelm Wundt and Emil Du Bois–Reymond, was named professor of psychiatry at Kazan University, where he implemented the use of hypnosis and suggestion in medicine for the first time in Russia. In 1893, after nine years at Kazan, he left for St. Petersburg, where he was appointed professor of mental and nervous diseases at the Military Medical Academy. The major themes of his research were the localization of functions in the cortex, mass psychology and "psychological contagion," and hysteria, hypnotism, and psychoneurosis. He personally had marked hypnotic abilities; hypnotherapy was one of his favorite clinical techniques. He cured hundreds, possibly thousands of psychoneurotics and left interesting records depicting human behavior in the state of somnambulism.[14]

In 1897 Bekhterev delivered a lecture, "Vnushenie i ego rol' v obshchestvennoi zhizni" (Suggestion and its role in social life), which he expanded into a book of the same title, published in 1903. There he asserted that an entire realm of human conduct cannot be explained in terms of rationality or consciousness. Authoritative views, beliefs, and ideologies—all highly influential factors in social life—penetrate the mind beyond conscious control. "Psychological contagion," a wave of excitement that spreads from person to person, creates an endless chain of emotional reactions in the manner of an epidemic. Traditional psychology was helpless in cases of religious hysteria, for example, since

11. Charles Richet, *Traité de métapsychique* (Paris, 1923); Albert Schrenk von Notzing, *Phenomenon of Materialization* (London, 1920), p. 33.

12. Wilhelm Kohlhammer, introduction to Albert Schrenk von Notzing, *Grundfragen der Parapsychologie* (Stuttgart, 1926), p. 79.

13. Albert Moll, *Prophezeien und Hellsehen* (Stuttgart, 1922); in the Russian translation, *Proritsanie i iasnovidenie* (Leningrad, 1925).

14. Vladimir Bekhterev, *Avtobiografiia* (Moscow, 1928); Alex Kozulin, *Psychology in Utopia* (Cambridge, Mass., 1984), p. 50.

it had artificially secluded itself in a world of rational conscious processes and lacked any objective methods for studying complex and extrarational phenomena.

At this time other outstanding Russian scientists, such as Ivan Sikorsky of Kiev, were also working on thought transference, and from the same premise. Sikorsky, however, believed that it was affected by visual contact rather than by emissions: the recipient read the involuntary, subtle muscle movements—what today would be called the "body language"—of the transmitter.[15]

Bekhterev disagreed with Sikorsky. In 1892–93, during his lectures in Kazan, he discussed the case of a certain Malevanny, the founder of a religious sect, who had been forcibly hospitalized in Kiev as a result of Sikorsky's diagnosis that he suffered from hallucinations. While praying, Malevanny experienced extraordinary joy and a feeling of weightlessness. His mood influenced his followers and attracted others, and the sect grew large. Malevanny claimed that he communicated with the Heavenly Father, and proclaimed himself to be Jesus, reincarnated for the second coming. Malevanny taught his followers a prayer that stated that Doomsday was approaching and that Malevanny would then judge humanity. His followers staunchly adhered to him. In 1902, members of his sect desecrated a church in the Ukrainian village of Pavlovka and killed some villagers, for, according to Malevanny, the Orthodox Church was the seed of evil.[16]

Relying on his own clinical experience, Bekhterev explained Malevanny's case by his concept of psychic infection, which he borrowed from the French concept of mass psychology developed by Gustave Le Bon, Gabriel Tarde, and Augustin Cabanès.[17] *Vnushenie*, Bekhterev's term for this concept, can be translated as "suggestion," "hypnosis," or "hypnotic suggestion," depending on the context. "Hypnotic suggestion," he wrote, "can be understood as a direct transmission of a psychic state from one individual to another—a transmission that occurs unknowingly, with no involvement of will (i.e., attention) on the part of the recipient, and often without his clear consciousness." Hypnotic suggestion "influences not only those possessed of normal logical capacity but to an even greater extent those who do not possess sufficient logical capacity"—by implication, the masses.[18]

Bekhterev made a sharp distinction between hypnotic suggestion and tele-

15. Ivan Sikorskii, "O chtenii myslei," *Vrach*, 1884, nos. 51–52.

16. Vladimir Bekhterev, *Vnushenie i ego rol' v obshchestvennoi zhizni* (St. Petersburg, 1903), pp. 78–100; *Delo pavlovskikh krestian* (St. Petersburg, 1902). See also Mikhail Agursky, "L'Aspect millénariste de la révolution bolchévique," *Cahiers du monde russe et soviétique* 29 (1988): 494–95.

17. Bekhterev, *Vnushenie*, p. 5. See Gustave Le Bon, *Psychologie des foules* (Paris, 1895); Gabriel Tarde, *L'Opinion et la foule* (Paris, 1900) and *Les Lois de l'imitation* (Paris, 1890); Augustin Cabanès and Lucien Nass, *La Névrose révolutionnaire* (Paris, 1906).

18. Bekhterev, *Vnushenie*, pp. 5, 19, 23.

communication. The former is only the transfer of a psychic mood; the latter has a specific content. Throughout his life Bekhterev became more and more convinced that telecommunication of thought is an empirically verifiable fact, even though he regarded it as scientifically unproved and perhaps even as unprovable.

The role of faith in the impact of hypnotic suggestion, according to Bekhterev, was very great. In his early experiments he investigated such occult phenomena as collective hallucinations, witch crazes, demonic possession, a type of female hysteria (*klikushestvo*), and the evil eye. The very spread of sects, he held, was a sort of psychic epidemic: consider Malevanny's sect, the orgiastic Khlysty, and the seventeenth-century Jewish followers of the false messiah Shabbetai Tsevi.[19]

Though Bekhterev amended his interpretation of hypnosis many times during his life, he never questioned that it was an empirical, verifiable phenomenon. By the turn of the century, he thought he had found a method to study artificial associative reflexes. In 1907 he founded the Psychoneurological Institute in St. Petersburg. He and Ivan Pavlov, the foremost student of the conditioned reflex, became rivals. Nonscientists who did not perceive the difference between associative and conditioned reflexes lumped their work together as "reflexology."[20]

Bekhterev dismissed the explanation of the occult that was based on the concept of psychic energy as a form of universal energy. In this respect he agreed with Wundt that it was impossible to ignore the radical difference between physical and psychic phenomena. For the same reason, Bekhterev rejected Ostwald's Energetism in its pure form. In his early period, he followed the Wundtian concept of "psychophysiological parallelism." He believed at that time that the psychic and the physical are totally incompatible phenomena, and that no direct transformation of one into the other was possible. If they are always and everywhere parallel, however, this can by no means be explained by the identity of the physical and the psychic, "since both phenomena have one common *hidden* origin, which we can provisionally call *hidden* energy."[21] It is clear that Bekhterev did not identify this hidden energy with Ostwald's universal energy.

Bekhterev categorically rejected the materialist explanation of energy:

Consciousness is the result of an enormous tension of energy that is accumulated by the brain's biomolecules during some specific transformations. Therefore psyche and consciousness are a manifestation of a specific energy stress. Therefore all materialist-mechanist views should be totally excluded from the explana-

19. Ibid., pp. 39, 66.
20. Kozulin, *Psychology in Utopia*, pp. 51–52.
21. Vladimir Bekhterev, *Psikhika i zhizn'* (St. Petersburg, 1904), pp. 38, 39.

tion of the origin of the psyche. The same can be said of the origin of energy and the conditions that bring it to its specific stress.[22]

By "materialist-mechanist" Bekhterev meant the entire worldview associated with Newton, Jacques Loeb, and Pavlov. He said explicitly that energy can by no means be regarded only as a physical or material substance.

Later, perhaps as a result of his objections to Kotik's work and because of the Bolsheviks' insistence on materialist explanations of all phenomena, Bekhterev tried to prevent any suspicion that he himself was gradually moving toward an idealistic interpretation of the occult. He therefore called the occult a superstition, although it is clear that for him superstition was only faith in the supranatural origin of psychic phenomena. Hence he abandoned Wundt and identified himself with Ostwald's Energetism, although without explicitly referring to Ostwald.

Interestingly enough, the Wundtian concept of psychophysiological parallelism was absorbed by a theologian and philosopher, Viktor Nesmelov, who was a professor at the Kazan theological academy when Bekhterev worked at the university there. This does not, of course, mean that they agreed with each other, but they may well have discussed psychophysiological issues. In his treatise *Nauka o cheloveke* (The science of man), Nesmelov examined the relation in which consciousness and thought stand to the physical body.[23] Following Wundt's theory of psychophysiological parallelism, Nesmelov rejected the physical origin of psychic activity and claimed that every activity of a physical body can be only physical.

Nesmelov referred to Wundt's theory but, unlike Bekhterev, he held that the world is dual: body and spirit are born in every organism and develop according to a blueprint in which the inception of the spirit takes precedence over the forms of the physical body. It is not that the human spirit appears in the world before material nature prepares a fleshly container for itself through physical-chemical means; on the contrary, it is the spirit that prepares a body for itself. Yet spirit cannot exist without flesh. It appears with the body of a material seed and all its life it actively correlates with the material world. However, the spirit is not a free agent. It acts within the general constraints of a certain organic type. Note the similarity of Nesmelov's position to that of the Neoplatonist Plotinus, who viewed the soul as a monad that creates a body for itself.

Bekhterev and Nesmelov worked from the latest tenets of Western philosophy and psychology, but Bekhterev tried to remain within the framework of science. Not wishing to rely on theological concepts, as Nesmelov did, he tried to reformulate them in the language of science. Hence his reliance on such obscure concepts as "hidden energy."

22. Ibid, p. 203.
23. Viktor Nesmelov, *Nauka o cheloveke* (Kazan, 1906).

Bekhterev's views were well known to Russian radicals in a general way, for he openly criticized the tsarist government, appointed progressive faculty to the Psychoneurological Institute, and refused to limit the number of Jewish or female faculty and students there. In 1911 he testified for the defense in the trial of Mendel Beilis, a Jew falsely accused of the ritual murder of a Christian boy. Realizing that anti-Semitic hysteria (psychological contagion) had distorted the testimony and the analysis of the evidence, he insisted on an examination of the body, which revealed that the number of stab wounds was fourteen, not thirteen, as alleged by persons who claimed that the murder was a kabbalistic ritual.[24] Bekhterev hailed the February Revolution and remained in Russia after October. By the spring of 1918, he had gained government funding for the Psychoneurological Institute and a pledge of future expansion into an Institute of Brain Research. His *Obshchie osnovy refleksologii cheloveka* (General principles of human reflexology) went through four ever-larger editions during the Soviet period.

Bekhterev deliberately stretched the concept of reflex to include all kinds of animal energy and made speculative leaps from neural facts to psychic and social hypotheses. Reflexology came to encompass the entire universe, nothing less. His ultimate goal was to establish a science that would embrace all the phenomena of human behavior. He was interested in the human being as a body structure, as a network of neural and behavioral processes, and as a healthy or troubled personality. He merged physiology and physiological psychology with biology, physics, and astronomy by interpreting their laws as special cases in a universal pattern grounded in a quasi-mystical "all in all" or "all in one." According to Bekhterev, matter had been shown to be a fiction; energy was the universal substance, whether expressed in solar fire, animal metabolism, or human thought.[25]

During the Civil War, Bekhterev interpreted the Bolshevik Revolution in terms of the French mass psychology of Le Bon, Tarde, and Cabanès, to whom he often referred. He attributed the Bolshevik Revolution to the absence of self-governing habits in the masses, the lapse of their patriotism during World War I, and their susceptibility to "demagogic internationalism."[26] To Bekhterev, the phenomenon of a large group of people becoming possessed by a common impulse and merging into a mob, often observed during the Revolution, was empirical evidence of hypnotic influence on a mass scale. His book *Kollektivnaia refleksologiia* (Collective reflexology) contained a chapter on mutual suggestion and mutual induction. He asked, "Is it possible to transmit energy from nervous centers directly from one person to another?"[27]

24. Kozulin, *Psychology in Utopia*, pp. 55–56.
25. David Joravsky, *Russian Psychology: A Critical History* (Oxford, 1989), p. 273.
26. Ibid., pp. 272, 510.
27. Vladimir Bekhterev, *Kollektivnaia refleksologiia* (Petrograd, 1921), p. 122.

In attempting to answer this question, Bekhterev went much further than he had done earlier. An instance of thought transmission that deserved serious attention, he believed, was described in Mikhail Lermontov's poem "Son" (The dream), which Lermontov wrote shortly before his death in a duel. In this poem, Lermontov dreams that as he lies fatally wounded in a valley in the Caucasus, he sees a woman at an evening feast in St. Petersburg or Moscow, who in turn dreams of his death. He dies in the course of the dream.[28] Although Bekhterev treats the poem as a description of thought transference, the phenomenon it describes could also easily be understood as precognition.

On this question, Bekhterev referred to Richet, Zhuk, and Kotik (while still regarding Kotik's experiments as the "result of a certain carelessness"), and also to his own experiments on the dogs belonging to a famous Russian circus performer, Vladimir Durov, which are mentioned in many books on parapsychology. Bekhterev now acknowledged not only suggestion but also hypnotic influence or thought telecommunication between "nervous" individuals and between animals, although he was aware that it was impossible to prove. "Nervous" individuals can manifest such thought telecommunications even in a nonhypnotic state.[29]

Bekhterev saw the crowd as an ideal medium for the transmission of hypnotic suggestion, and tried to discover its mechanism: "In a crowd, along with mutual cognitive persuasion and so-called infection, which produces direct imitation, another factor should operate in the form of a direct impact through a direct transfer of the stimulus from the centers of one individual to the relevant centers of another." Bekhterev believed in the existence of mediators who can perpetuate collective unity beyond space and time, so that a society whose members are dispersed throughout the world, for example, can retain its unity. "Spiritual unity can exist in a collective of individuals who live in different times, such as in religious communities, states, and other entities, by means of tradition and other mediators, such as oral and written communications." In other words, mediators do not have to be living people: "All subjects that can interest many individuals, whether historical monuments or literary or scientific works, can be such mediums."[30] Though Bekhterev criticized mysticism and the occult, his very use of the word "medium" indicates a certain congruence of thought, or could be interpreted that way, and made his ideas, or simplified and perhaps distorted versions of them, accessible to nonscientists.

Bekhterev continued to study psychic phenomena even after the Bolshevik Revolution, and organized the Committee for the Study of Mental Suggestion. In his own scientific journal, Bekhterev and his school published papers on

28. For an English translation, see the translator's introduction to Mihail Lermontov, *A Hero of Our Time*, trans. Vladimir and Dmitri Nabokov (Garden City, N.Y., 1958), pp. vi–vii.

29. Bekhterev, *Kollektivnaia refleksologiia*, p. 122.

30. Ibid., pp. 126, 127.

hypnosis, telepathy, suggestion, and "miracle healings." One of Bekhterev's articles of the Soviet period deals with mutual suggestion in a community and with collective hallucinations. "Unwittingly," Bekhterev wrote, "we not only change our mood, but acquire to some extent the superstitions, prejudices, inclinations, thoughts, and even some character traits of the people who surround us."[31] It is clear that Bekhterev acknowledged thought telecommunication, and that he also, like Soviet biologists of this period, believed in the inheritance of acquired social characteristics.[32]

Bekhterev was a principal speaker at the first All-Russia Psychoneurological Congress in 1923. The Bolshevik press paid close attention to the congress and reprinted his speech in its entirety. In the 1920s he shifted his emphasis and tried to reduce all behavioral phenomena to one fundamental process, the associative reflex, which at first glance (though only at first glance) seemed scarcely distinguishable from Pavlov's conditioned reflex.

One should also mention in this connection Bekhterev's disciples, such as Iakov Alchevsky and Leonid Vasiliev. Vasiliev (1891–1966), head of the Physiology Department of Leningrad University and a closet parapsychologist in the Stalin years, provided the ideological groundwork for psychic studies in the Soviet Union in the late 1950s and early 1960s. Telephathy was called "biocommunication" and dowsing was labeled "the biopsychical effect." Vasiliev and Alchevsky fully accepted Kotik's concept of psychophysical emanation, though they never mentioned Kotik by name. Petr Lazarev, a prominent Russian physicist who claimed that every thought and every sense emits some sort of energy, was very close to them.[33] The sociologist Pitirim Sorokin was also strongly influenced by Bekhterev. Like Bekhterev, Sorokin relied on Le Bon's, Tarde's, and Cabanès's studies in mass psychology. Sorokin shared Bekhterev's view that the Bolshevik Revolution had given rise to a state of mass hypnotic influence, or "revolutionary illusionism."

> People are bewitched by . . . great illusions. They are hypnotized and do not see what actually takes place around them. All around, ferocity and slaughter reign supreme, but they do not desist repeating that the brotherhood of man is being realized. They don't perceive it and believe that on the morrow the revolution will bring not only plenty, but the beatitude of paradise to all. . . . All

31. Vladimir Bekhterev, "Vzaimovnushenie v soobshchestve liudei i kollektivnye galliutsinatsii," *Vestnik znaniia*, 1926, no. 6, p. 362.

32. Vladimir Bekhterev, "Rol' sotsial'nogo povedeniia v evoliutsii," *Vestnik znania*, 1926, no. 13.

33. See Yakov Alchevskii, "V chem sekret peredachi mysli na rasstoianii," *Ogonek* 50 (1925); Leonid Vasiliev, "O peredache mysli na rasstoianii," *Vestnik znaniia*, 1926, no. 7; Martin Ebon, *Psychic Discoveries by the Russians* (New York, 1971), pp. 10–13, and idem, "The Soviet Dilemma," in *Skeptical Inquirer* 10 (Winter 1985–86): 146.

around, morality crumbles away, license, sadism, and cruelty are everywhere—the masses call it a moral regeneration.[34]

In the 1920s, Bekhterev abandoned his idea that psychic energy is not a modus of energy as a whole and treated immortality in the spirit of pure Ostwald Energetism. "The transformation of matter into energy, though slow and gradual, now turns out to be an obvious fact," Bekhterev wrote. "In the physical world we can speak only of energy, which as a substance includes both physical energy and visible and tangible matter."[35] Like Le Bon, Bekhterev regarded radioactivity as dematerialization. He agreed that the psychic in nature is a special kind of universal energy. Not a materialist in the Marxist sense, Bekhterev held views that were closer to those of Mach or Ostwald, and hence suspect to some Bolsheviks as idealism or mysticism; but this very feature endeared him to some Christians.

"All world phenomena," according to Bekhterev, "including the internal processes of life and the manifestations of 'spirit,' can and should be regarded as 'derivatives of the same world energy.' " He now extended the law of preservation of energy to the concept of a universal field where "no move, no thought that was verbalized or expressed by a simple look, jest, or imitation, disappears without a trace."[36] Therefore each of us becomes a theurgist who can deliberately change the world by merely concentrating our thoughts. A variant of this view was the Symbolist concept of life creation (*zhiznetvorchestvo*), the transformation of the world and of the self through art.[37]

"Throughout his life," Bekhterev wrote, "man diffuses his energy among people who are close or distant. They in turn transmit what they acquire to others, who transmit it to new people. . . . Personality is not destroyed after death but, after manifesting its different sides in life, lives on eternally as a particle of universal human creativity." And through evolution, a new human being of a higher social type will eventually appear.[38] This development is also a quest of Theosophy, Anthroposophy, and mystical Freemasonry, all of which envision a spiritually pure and nonegoistic "new man." It is not surprising, then, that Bekhterev was personally close to the painter and philosopher

34. Pitirim Sorokin, *The Sociology of Revolution* (New York, 1967), pp. 185–86. Sorokin is undoubtedly recalling his own observations at the time of the Bolshevik Revolution, when he was still in Russia.

35. Vladimir Bekhterev, "Sotsial'noe bessmertie chelovecheskoi lichnosti," *Vestnik znaniia*, 1928, no. 1, p. 5.

36. Ibid., pp. 6, 7.

37. See, for example, Andrei Belyi, "O teurgii," *Novyi put'*, 1903, no. 9, pp. 100–112. See also Irina Paperno and Joan Grossman, eds., *Creating Life* (Stanford, 1994); and John E. Malmstad, ed., *Andrey Bely: Spirit of Symbolism* (Ithaca, 1987).

38. Bekhterev, "Sotsial'noe bessmertie," pp. 9, 11.

Nikolai Rerikh.[39] He was also close, however, to people whose ideas he did not necessarily share, such as the religious philosopher N. O. Lossky.

Bekhterev's ideas were taken up by some Russian Orthodox clergymen. The Orthodox priest and Duma member Fedor Vladimirsky (father of Mikhail Vladimirsky, the future chairman of the Central Auditing Committee of the Soviet Communist Party under Stalin) published "Vnushenie, ego sotsial'noe i pedagogicheskoe znachenie" (Suggestion, its social and pedagogical significance) in 1914.[40] He was not the only clergyman who found support for his antimaterialist worldview in Bekhterev's works.

For this very reason, as well as because his ideas were associated with Aleksandr Bogdanov's "Machism," Bekhterev's views were attacked by some party ideologists concerned with eliminating "superstition" and encouraging a rational, scientific worldview. Indeed, in 1924 Petr Ionov called Bekhterev's theories deeply reactionary, and claimed that Bekhterev had overstepped the limits of acceptable research.[41]

At the same time, Bekhterev was attacked by émigrés of the Russian right. In *Bratstvo Viia* (The brotherhood of Viy), a novel of the occult published in Berlin in 1925, Pavel Perov presents Bekhterev as a collaborator of the Jewish conspirators who have brought about the Bolshevik Revolution. It seems that the Jews, with the help of "Professor Bakterev," have invented a method of injecting human energy into robots. Bakterev has discovered the energy of the human soul, which he calls "mortium." By joining mortium (spiritual energy) with "ectoplasm," or matter, Bakterev has invented a "mortomat," a robot that looks like a normal human being. Jews use these robots in an attempt to create an ideal society ruled by one idea. One of the main conspirators says: "We are creating our own paradise. . . . Hasn't the time come for pure intellect to leave its cocoon, this heavy, ignorant human mass that stops it from realizing its ideal being?" Interestingly enough, Perov refers to Schrenk von Notzing, who owed his theory of mental telepathy, as we noted earlier, to Kotik, not to Bekhterev. In the end Bakterev rebels and shouts at the Jewish conspirators: "What I had to do in the name of science, you do in the name of power." His laboratory explodes and humanity is saved.[42]

The idea of an occult mass psychology was also elaborated by the Marxist critic Lev Voitolovsky. For him, social and political psychology existed before economics, when "history descended into the secret hiding places of volcanic passions." He said that "titanic explosions of human will and human passion are the greatest and richest creative element." The mass collective turns out to

39. Petr Belikov, *Rerikh* (Moscow, 1973), p. 108.

40. Fedor Vladimirskii, "Vnushenie, ego sotsial'noe i pedagogicheskoe znachenie," *Vera i razum*, 1914, no. 15, p. 360.

41. Petr Ionov, "Molodaia gvardiia," *Pravda*, October 5, 1924.

42. Pavel Perov, *Bratstvo Viia* (Berlin, 1925), pp. 150, 180, 213.

be a special psychophysical milieu in which "our body seems to become the area of amplification of energy currents."[43]

According to Voitolovsky,

> in the vast majority of cases, the crowd does not limit the personalities of its participants, but it erases hostility and lack of confidence among people, it destroys this cursed conspiracy of aristocrats who set all against all, and by the very fact of melting with others, fills the personality with an enormous, courageous joy and a victorious faith in itself. . . . There is a special power—the power of the masses—which is created by the crowd. The manifestation of the power of the masses is followed by a wave of animal energy and therefore also by an increase of alimentary processes in the body of each participant. As a result, there is a transformation of temperament and all the crowd becomes a prey to emotional infection.[44]

As an example of such a mass effect, Voitolovsky mentions the healing of a paralyzed woman by the psychic energies of a crowd in Gorky's novel *Ispoved'* (Confession, 1908). "The crowd in this case," Voitolovsky wrote, "played the role of an electric battery in the direct sense of the word. The paralyzed body, which was linked to the concentrating activity of the masses by the general elevation of faith, entered into the circuit of this giant will."[45] Incidentally, Lenin detested this work as an example of the Machism he hated.

In the 1920s, Soviet luminaries such as Nikolai Bukharin, Anatoly Lunacharsky, and Nadezhda Krupskaia (Lenin's widow) became interested in psychology in general and in developing a Marxist psychology in particular. Although numerous psychological schools freely contended, the Party tended to favor theories that were, or claimed to be, objective, materialist, determinist, and, like physics and mechanics, quantitative rather than qualitative. Bukharin, the Party's chief ideologue in the 1920s, touched on psychology and neuropsychology repeatedly, but always vaguely. He criticized reflexology (by which he meant both Bekhterev and Pavlov) in a speech to the Comintern in 1924, but on other occasions he praised it as the beginning of a distinctive Soviet psychology, grounded in tangible physiological phenomena, as distinct from introspective, "subjective" bourgeois psychology.[46]

Bekhterev's work in basic neurophysiology, medical neurology, and psychology, as well as in criminology, pedagogy, and the psychophysiology of labor, was funded by the government. In 1924 a long article on psychology in the quasi-official Soviet "thick journal" *Krasnaia nov'* (Red virgin soil) praised Bekhterev as a venerable scientist who was sincerely trying to accommodate

43. Lev Voitolovskii, *Ocherki kollektivnoi psikhologii* (Moscow, 1925), pp. 15, 18, 44.

44. Ibid., pp. 62—63.

45. Ibid., p. 79.

46. Joravsky, *Russian Psychology*, pp. 224, 274.

his theories to Marxism. Pavlov was then openly and vehemently critical of the Bolshevik government. Bekhterev argued that reflexology must not be confused with (Pavlov's) physiology, which is "the science of the function and regulation of the organs of the body, including the brain." "Reflexology is a scientific discipline which sets for itself the problem of studying the responsive reactions to external and internal stimuli."[47] At the Wittenburg Symposium, an international psychology conference held at Springfield, Ohio, on October 19–23, 1927, Bekhterev represented the Soviet Union.[48] He died suddenly on December 27, 1927. The next day *Izvestiia* published a eulogy by Mikhail Kalinin, Politburo member and titular head of the Soviet state, which stressed Bekhterev's genius and his solidarity with the Soviet cause.

Bekhterev's (and Pavlov's) mechanistic theories of personality involved automatic responses to external stimuli. Some Marxist psychologists held that the unconscious "supplied the final link in the chain of determination of human behavior, destroying the illusion of consciously directed behavior." Bekhterev himself called the unconscious "the ideal psychic."[49] Several Soviet psychologists worked diligently to adapt Freud to Marxism.

During the Cultural Revolution, mechanistic and deterministic theories of personality were replaced by dialectical theories that emphasized consciousness and denigrated empirical fact-finding. Attacks on Bekhterev's work intensified, and by 1930 he had been discredited as a Menshevizing idealist. As the Cultural Revolution waned, it was the dialectical psychologists' turn to be attacked and discredited. Between 1932 and 1934, the major psychological journals ceased publication. By 1935, the mechanistic psychology of Pavlov, who had ceased his attacks on the Soviet government after Hitler came to power in Germany, had achieved quasi-official status. Bekhterev's works were not reprinted, but his ideas of mass energy, mass contagion, and mood and thought transmission within the human collective did not disappear without a trace. Research continued in top-secret laboratories, and, unnoticed, Bekhterev's thought came to play an integral role in the creation of the theory of Socialist Realism, mainly by way of Maxim Gorky, its principal formulator.

Any direct connection between Gorky and Bekhterev remains to be researched, but we have written evidence of Gorky's enthusiastic response to Kotik, and we know that he carried love letters to students at Kazan University and listened to Bekhterev's lectures through the half-open doors of the auditorium.[50] We also know of Gorky's long-standing interest in thought transference, hypnotic suggestion, and occult philosophies. In the 1890s Gorky sep-

---

47. Quoted in Raymond Bauer, *The New Man in Soviet Psychology* (Cambridge, Mass., 1952), p. 55.

48. Henri Ellenberger, *The Discovery of the Unconscious* (New York, 1970), p. 850.

49. Bauer, *New Man*, p. 72.

50. Bekhterev, *Avtobiografiia*, p. 19. See also Ivan Galant, "Psikhozy v tvorchestve Gor'kogo," *Klinicheskii arkhiv genial'nosti i odarennosti* 4, no. 2 (1928): 34.

arated ancient magic from religion and claimed that magic preceded religion.[51] Gorky may have been involved in the decision to fund Bekhterev's institute in 1918, for he was close to Lenin at the time. A co-founder, with Bukharin, Lenin, and Krupskaia, of *Krasnaia nov'*, Gorky kept up with the Soviet press after he left the Soviet Union; surely he read the article that praised Bekhterev, and Kalinin's obituary. In May 1927 Gorky was elected an honorary member of the State Psychoneurological Academy, and it was Bekhterev who informed him of this honor.[52]

Upon his final return to Russia in 1932, Gorky was particularly interested in Pavlov's Institute of Experimental Medicine. A week after Gorky met with a group of scientists from the institute, though not with Pavlov himself, the press announced that Pavlov's institute had been raised to All-Union status. In 1935, Pavlov was hailed as a truly Soviet scientists.[53] Bekhterev's ideas were still not forgotten, though, for his views on mass contagion could be applied to political propaganda by persons intent on making sure that the external stimuli came only "from above," and were consciously applied and directed. Gorky frequently referred to Kotik in letters and notebooks written in 1926, but made no mention of him in his public writings.[54] He may have been equally discreet with regard to Bekhterev. Gorky may have appropriated Bekhterev's ideas selectively and without acknowledgment, as he did the views of Bogdanov, Nietzsche, and Fedorov, in his (and Lunacharsky's) own doctrine of God-building. In fact, during the Revolution of 1905, in an article published in a popular science magazine that Gorky may well have read, for he was very interested in science, Bekhterev expressed ideas that were similar to God-building. He argued for a religion of social heroism in the sense of social self-sacrifice; "with this doctrine, he claimed to have provided a scientific basis for the ancient belief in immortality."[55] Gorky's theory of Socialist Realism can be considered a quasi-occult and politicized application of ideas of thought trans-ference and hypnotic suggestion pioneered by Bekhterev and other early twentieth-century Russian scientists.

Gorky expressed deep interest in occult phenomena very early on. It must be stressed, however, that Gorky accepted the occult as an aspect of natural phenomena that needed to be unriddled and explained—a premise he shared with the Theosophists. Having read Schopenhauer in the 1880s, Gorky was aware of the German philosopher's belief in the supernatural and of his state-ment that since time, space, and causality are only categories of the mind, every physical activity of the brain that removes these limitations can mix

51. Agurskii, "Velikii eretik (Gor'kii kak religioznyi myslitel')" *Voprosy filosofii* 1991, no. 8, pp. 62–63, 65.

52. Irwin Weil kindly provided the editor with a copy of Bekhterev's letter to Gorky.

53. Joravsky, *Russian Psychology*, p. 328.

54. Agurskii, "Velikii eretik," p. 64.

55. Joravsky, *Russian Psychology*, p. 84.

events that normally are separated in space and time and that are not causally connected. In dreams, for example, all these categories are removed, since no external signal enters the brain during sleep. In some cases when the brain is isolated from any external excitation, as in total darkness and silence, the same mental activity that produces dreams can produce daydreams.[56] In 1898 Gorky asked a correspondent to send him a book by the well-known German Spiritualist Karl Du Prel, noting that he had already read another of Du Prel's books. Gorky commented that what can be found in Du Prel can also be found in Schopenhauer, but in a deeper and more concise form, and that Du Prel had only developed Schopenhauer's theory of occult phenomena.[57]

Later, according to Rerikh, Gorky met an Indian fakir during his journey through Russia. Gorky told Rerikh that "he himself saw vivid images of Indian cities upon the blank metallic leaves of an album, which was shown to him once in the Caucasus by a Hindu. With all his realism, Gorky absolutely affirms that he saw in vivid colors that which the Hindu pointed out to him."[58] This astonishing event probably occurred in 1892.

Gorky's interest in experiments in thought transference was thus part of a complex weave. The ideas of influencing mass perception and transforming consciousness were part of the ideology for God-building, which was in turn based on Bogdanov's Machism (though Bogdanov himself was not a God-builder): the idea that people can know only their experiences or sensations, and not objective reality. Through Bogdanov, Gorky was also influenced by Ostwald's Energetism, the idea that mental processes are pure energy and hence are transferable. In addition, Gorky was aware of the Symbolist poets' and playwrights' attempts to bypass the intellect and appeal directly to the unconscious. During the Revolution of 1905, in fact, the God-builders and God-seekers exchanged views on using the theater to influence the masses. It is understandable, therefore, that Gorky's belief in occult phenomena was expressed publicly for the first time in his play *Deti solntsa* (The Children of the Sun), written in 1905. A character in the play suffers a premonition of disaster at the moment her absent fiancé commits suicide.[59]

In 1908, when Theosophy and other occult doctrines were reaching large audiences, Gorky's interest in occult phenomena increased and he began to use Kotik's term "psychophysical processes." From that time on, Gorky believed that human relations were determined not only by social factors but

56. See, for example, Arthur Schopenhauer, *Parerga and Paralipomena* (Oxford, 1974), 1:229–68.

57. Gorky to Pavel Batiushkov, in Maksim Gor'kii, *Sobranie sochinenii*, 30 vols. (Moscow, 1949–56), 28:39; henceforth *SS*. Gorky mentions two books by Karl Du Prel: *The Philosophy of Mysticism* (London, 1899) and *Der Rätsel des Mensches* (Wiesbaden, 1950).

58. Roerich, *Altai-Himalaya*, p. 24.

59. Maxim Gorky, *The Children of the Sun* (London, 1973), pp. 98–99.

much more by invisible and unconscious psychophysical processes, which were actually the direct interpersonal flow of mental energy over distances.

Gorky came to the conclusion that the activity of the human mind, especially when concentrated and purposeful, is an extremely important energy process that also has a physical expression, since it results in the transformation of matter into energy and vice versa. Indeed, one can see that, for Gorky, Kotik offered the possibility of accelerating the release of captive energy by concentrated occult activity. There is another possibility: the direct transference of thought through space and the direct psychic influence of one human being on others. A charismatic person who has a strong psychic charge can transfer that power to weaker persons and make them more active.

Gorky first mentioned Kotik in 1908, in a letter to K. P. Piatnitsky: "There is a little book by Dr. Kotik, 'The Emanation of Psychophysical Energy.' If you have time to look it over, you would find surprising experiments of thought transference. These experiments are something marvelous. They prove that thought and will are the same thing! It would be interesting if controlled experiments were made—what would be their result?"[60] Another letter, addressed to Lev Voitolovsky, evidently belongs to the same period:

> May I call your attention to Dr. Kotik's book *Neposredstvennaia peredacha mysli* [The direct transference of thought], published by Sovremennye Problemy? The author is our man—a social democrat. The principal idea of his book: thought is a kind of matter. The conclusion of his work is interesting and I quote it directly: "Taking into consideration the rapid enslavement of human masses by different emotions and their enormous power over the crowd, we should conclude that crowd psychology, the laws of imitation, and actually all the mysterious phenomena of mass psychology would find their correct explanation only from the viewpoint of the direct influence of psychophysical energy."[61]

In still another letter, to one Fedor Erisman, Gorky credited Kotik with having made one of the greatest discoveries in the history of thought.[62]

The most important artistic statement of Gorky's belief in the occult is found in his novel *Confession,* in which he describes the miraculous healing of a paralyzed woman through the concentrated psychic energy (and will) of a praying crowd:

> There was great excitement. They pushed the wagon, and the head of the young girl rocked to and fro, helpless and without strength. Her large eyes gazed out with fear. Tens of eyes poured their rays out upon her; hundreds of force streams

60. Gor'kii to K. P. Piatnitskii, in Arkhiv Gor'kogo, Moscow, vol. 4, 1954, p. 239; henceforth AG.

61. Gor'kii to Lev Voitolovskii, *Literaturnyi sovremennik*, 1937, no. 6, p. 30.

62. Gor'kii to Fedor Erisman, AG.

crossed themselves over her weak body, calling her to life with an imperious desire to see her rise from her bed. . . .

As rain saturates the earth with its live moisture, so the people filled the dry body of the girl with their strength.[63]

Soon after *Confession* was published, Kotik wrote to Gorky: "Recently I happened to read your *Confession* . . . and was stunned by the coincidence of the ideas (especially in the description of the 'miracle') with the results of my work. I am very interested in knowing whether it is only a coincidence or whether you had heard of my book while you were writing it." Gorky replied that he had written *Confession* before having seen Kotik's book.[64]

Shortly thereafter, Kotik was invited to Paris to work in the laboratory of Marie and Pierre Curie, and he appealed to Gorky for money to fund his new experiments. In July 1909 Gorky asked Kotik to clarify the notion of psychophysical energy. Kotik recommended that he read Le Bon's book *L'Evolution de la matière*. Kotik's last letter to Gorky, dated 1913, accompanied a gift of Karl Kroll's book *Thinking Animals*.[65] Kotik contracted tuberculosis and returned to Russia, where he died in 1920.

Frequent references to Kotik can be found in Gorky's notes and letters, but none in his publications. In his notes of 1924 he put Kotik's experiments into the context of Balzac's "Peau de chagrin" and Bernard Shaw's *Back to Methuselah;* the latter is explicitly about immortality. In May 1924, in a letter to N. Orlov, he classed Kotik's experiments with those of Pavlov. Gorky's last known reference to Kotik is dated 1927.[66] It is probable that Gorky was chilled by Albert Moll's book *Prophezeien und Hellschen* (Prophecy and clairvoyance), with its devastating criticism of Kotik, which was translated into Russian in 1925.

But Kotik was not Gorky's only mediator of occult phenomena. In 1910 Gorky read Aleksandr Amfiteatrov's 1895 novel of the occult, *Zhar-tsvet* (Fiery flower). The fiery flower is a power that can resurrect the dead. The novel treats the occult as a reality that the noninitiated regard as mental illness. The action centers on the mysterious Ob' cult. "The North," wrote Amfiteatrov, "is the motherland of mental illness. . . . Our air is live and adhesive, inhabited by spleen, by neurasthenia, by a depressive and jittery mood." He articulated an idea of Gorky's, that "the permanent ecstasy of a group that is tuned to one mood should from time to time produce an outstanding personality who is

---

63. Maxim Gorky, *Confession* (New York, 1916), p. 289. The novel also has Fedorovian and Nietzschean undertones that cannot be examined here.

64. Kotik is quoted in Minna Yunovich, *M. Gor'kii—propagandist nauki* (Moscow, 1961), pp. 61–62; Gorky's response of January 10, 1909, is in *Letopis' zhizni i tvorchestva Gor'kogo* (Moscow, 1958), 2:64.

65. Kotik to Gor'kii, June 20 and 28, 1909; July 27, 1909; July 2, 1913; all in AG.

66. Maksim Gor'kii, "Zametki," in AG, vol. 12, 1970, p. 239; Gor'kii to N. Orlov, May, 1924, in *Literaturnoe nasledie Sibiri* (Novosibirsk, 1969), 1:32; Gor'kii to Gustav Khan Pira, in AG.

extremely strong and also sensitive in its ecstatic manifestations."[67] After read-ing the novel Gorky wrote to Amfiteatrov: "I have read *Zhar-tsvet*—it is inter-esting, it is good. I would wish this book a wide readership. It could cure so many and make so many others more clever."[68]

In 1923 Gorky published *Rasskaz o bezotvetnoi liubvi* (A tale of unrequited love), in which the hero of an unfinished novel comes to life. The fictional author, however, is such a bad writer and has so little psychic energy that the hero's materialization is not complete—he has no shadow (a possible allusion to the devil). This half-incarnated, unhappy creature says:

> They think that a creation of theirs, once set on paper, is the end of the matter. They forget that only the outline remains on the page, while the image itself is thrust into the world to exist there as you and I exist, a psycho-physical emana-tion, the result of the association of the atoms of the brain and of nerve force, something more real than ether. . . .
>
> Fomine [the hero's author] filled me with certain psychological material, and I sprang into existence, but the moment after I realized this, I felt that there were other superfluous thoughts and characteristics penetrating me from the outside, in contradiction to what was already within me. Though I realized that this was disfiguring me, I could do nothing to eliminate it, for at that time I had no genu-ine instinct for life, and Fomine was clouded by a thick emanation of psycho-physical matter. This, as you know, is something so solid and at the same time so elastic that it would have destroyed me had I attempted to reach Fomine's consciousness.[69]

The passage indicates Gorky's knowledge of Theosophy. Fomine represents a kind of astral body, and ether (according to Blavatsky) is the source from which all things came and to which they will return. Gorky was introduced to Theosophy quite early; his interest in occult phenomena and in theurgy was only a part of his Theosophical views. Obviously he had read Blavatsky at least before 1899, because he criticized her then.[70] But later his critical attitude changed, and in 1912 he requested all her writings published in Russian.[71] When one considers that Theosophy never claimed to be a religion, only a system of knowledge, one can understand how Gorky could reconcile his ideas with it.

Actually, Theosophy categorically denies the existence of a personal, tran-scendental, anthropomorphic God, whom it regards only as a giant shadow of man.[72] This was a constant theme of Gorky's. Theosophy denies the physical

67. Aleksander Amfiteatrov, *Zhar-tsvet* (Berlin, 1922); pp. 61, 19.

68. Gor'kii to Amfiteatrov, January 14, 1911 (?), in *Literaturnoe nasledstvo* (Moscow) 95 (1988): 260.

69. Maxim Gorky, *Unrequited Love* (London, 1945), pp. 68, 69.

70. Maksim Gor'kii, "Van'kina literatura," in *SS*, 23: 292.

71. Gor'kii to N. A. Rumiantsev, in *SS*, 29:259.

72. Helene Blavatsky, *Isis Unveiled* (Los Angeles, 1931).

resurrection of the dead, and—even more important for our purposes—it identifies matter with energy.

Blavatsky set three main objectives for Theosophy: the creation of a universal human community with no racial or religious discrimination, the study of
esoteric traditions, and the study of nature's secrets (a code term for occult
phenomena).[73] Moreover, like most occult doctrines, Theosophy opposed acquisitiveness. Gorky shared all these goals.

Gorky was interested in other occult doctrines as well, and in medieval
theosophy (not to be confused with Blavatsky's doctrine) and alchemy. His
favorites were Paracelsus and Emanuel Swedenborg, from whom he may have
taken his view of the human being as a microcosm of the macrocosm—a typical
occult doctrine, reformulated in the God-builders' concept of collective immortality.[74] Paracelsus, a Renaissance physician, introduced the idea of secular
progress into the occult; Gorky liked his thought so much that he managed to
include Paracelsus's biography in the prestigious Soviet biography series, and
it was published in the USSR in 1935.[75] He also liked the works of the French
occultists Fabre d'Olivet and Eduard Schure, which had been translated into
Russian, and he subscribed to Fabre d'Olivet's harsh criticism of the idea that
there had ever been a golden age in human history.[76]

A look at Schure will help us understand why Gorky tried so hard to conceal
his real views on the occult, which we are now trying to reconstruct. It is a
matter of principle in Hermeticism that profound truths may not be disclosed
to those who are unprepared for them. In Schure's view, the revelation of
Truth is a process that starts from Rama and ends in Schure's book on Christ.
"Philosopher-initiates," Schure claimed, "never wished to reveal these profound ideas to the people, for the latter would have understood them only
imperfectly and would abuse them."[77] Apparently Gorky subscribed to this
notion.

For Gorky, God-building was first of all a theurgical action, the creation of
the new Nature and the annihilation of the old, and therefore it coincided fully
with the Kingdom of the Spirit. He considered God to be a theurgical outcome
of a collective work, the outcome of human unity and of the negation of the
human ego. God could become a reality as a result of mass psychic concentration. Consider now Amfiteatrov's ideas about the results of such mass concentration. Gorky first expressed the idea of the creation of God in 1901, in a

73. Helene Blavatsky, *The Key to Theosophy* (Los Angeles, 1930), p. 39.

74. See Paracelsus, *Selected Writings* (New York, 1951), and Jolande Jacobi's Introduction to
George Trobridge, *Swedenborg* (New York, 1938).

75. See Gor'kii to Wolfson, 1926, in AG, vol. 10/1, 1965, p. 28. See also Petr Proskuriakov,
Parasels (Moscow, 1935).

76. Fabre d'Olivet, *Hermeneutic Interpretation of the Origin of the Social State of Man* (New
York, 1915), pp. 31–32.

77. Eduard Schure, *The Great Initiates* (West Nyack, N.Y., 1961), p. 349.

letter to the writer Leonid Andreev: "Now, God is slipping away from the shopkeepers, and the sons of bitches are left without a shelter. That's how it must be! Let them jump about in life naked with their empty little souls and moan like cracked bells. And when they die from cold and spiritual salvation we'll create a God for ourselves who will be great, splendid, joyous, the protector of life who loves everyone and everything. So be it!"[78] Certainly Gorky was also influenced here by the idea of the religion of humanity he had picked up from his friend Vasily Bervi-Flerovsky, who in turn took it from Auguste Comte and from Ludwig Feuerbach's idea that it is the people who create God.[79]

The main artistic exposition of Gorky's God-building, like the main presentation of his acceptance of the occult in general, is to be found in *Confession*. In the novel, the real theurgists are the people, and the most important manifestation of popular theurgy was early Christianity, before it was distorted by the church: "Christ was the first true people's God, born from the soul of the people like the phoenix from the flames." When popular occult energy weakened, however, Christ died; but the people-theurgists can resurrect him: "The time will come when the will of the people will again converge to one point, and then, again, the unconquerable and miraculous power will arise and the resurrection of God will take place."[80]

The Theosophists apparently recognized their common ground with God-building in the idea of the victory of spirit over matter.[81] The occultist Eduard Schure had a similar view. In his interpretation, the Last Judgment "means the end of the cosmic evolution of humanity or its entry into a definitive spiritual condition. This is what Persian esoterism called the victory of Ormuzd over Ahriman, or Spirit over matter. Hindu esoterism called it the complete reabsorption of matter by the Spirit, or the end of a Day of Brahma."[82]

To transform matter into energy and to annihilate the world are not the same thing. In his reformulation of his earlier views, Gorky had introduced a new element, apocalypticism: catastrophe as the release of energy of such magnitude as to create a new world or a new God, thereby replacing the present world, created by an evil demiurge. The latter idea, a Gnostic concept, was widely expressed in early twentieth-century Russian literature, in particular in Fedor Sologub's poetry and prose, which Gorky knew.

This quest for the annihilation of matter directly contradicts the Orthodox

78. Gorky to Leonid Andreev [Crimea, early 1902], in *Letters of Gorky and Andreev*, ed. Peter Yershov (New York, 1958), pp. 39–40.

79. Raimond Sesterhehn, *Das Bogostroitelstvo bei Gorky un Lunacarskij bis 1909* (Munich, 1982), p. 307.

80. Gorky, *Confession*, pp. 219, 245.

81. On November 24, 1909, Anna Kamenskaia delivered a lecture called "Theosophy and God-building." See *Kolokol*, November 28, 1909.

82. Schure, *Great Initiates*, p. 482.

tenet that the body will be resurrected along with the soul. Bekhterev's belief in a kind of social immortality was shared by Gorky, who even interpreted Kotik in that light. Gorky believed that the central place in the historical process belonged to the transformation of matter into energy through the release of nuclear energy. He considered that this energy was released as a result both of matter's natural disintegration and of the conscious and purposeful release of energy by human activity, which is essentially occult. Mass hypnosis, which facilitates the release of such energy, is therefore part of this process.

In the end, all matter must be obliterated. Gorky was certainly aware of Le Bon's theory of the inevitable annihilation of matter, which Le Bon claimed had emerged as the result of some cosmic disaster and was doomed to return to its original state—energy.[83] This view also coincides with Eduard von Hartmann's idea that eventually human beings should somehow coordinate their efforts and annihilate this world, which brings only suffering and is too fundamentally flawed to be improved.[84]

Gorky first hinted at his project of annihilating matter in a public lecture in 1920, when he spoke of his dream: " . . . if man, the human mind, will discover how to transform every single piece of matter into energy . . .";[85] but his most comprehensive statement on the subject was made in his *Fragments from My Diary,* in which he described his project in a conversation with Aleksandr Blok:

> "Personally, I prefer to imagine man as a machine, which transmutes in itself the so-called 'dead matter' into a psychical energy, and will, in some far-away future, transform the whole world into a purely psychical one." . . .
>
> " . . . For at that time [the future], nothing will exist except thought. Everything will disappear, being transmuted into pure thought, which alone will exist, incarnating the entire mind of humanity from the first flashes of it until the moment of its last explosion." . . .
>
> I proposed that he [Blok] should picture in his mind the world in an uninterrupted process of dissociation of matter. Matter, dissolving, continually gives off such species of energy as light, electricity, electro-magnetic waves, Hertzian waves, etc. To these are added, of course, all signs of radio-activity. Thought is the result of the dissociation of the atoms of the brain; the brain is composed of the elements of 'dead' unorganic matter. In the brain-substance of man this matter is uninterruptedly transformed into psychical matter. I myself believe that at some future time all matter absorbed by man shall be transmuted by him and by his brain into a sole energy—a psychical one. This energy shall discover harmony in itself and shall sink into self-contemplation—in a meditation over all the infinitely varied creative possibilities concealed in it. . . .
>
> . . . I am convinced that if we could weigh our planet from time to time, we should see that its weight was gradually diminishing.[86]

83. Gustave Le Bon, *L'Evolution de la matière* (Paris, 1914).
84. Eduard von Hartmann, *Philosophy of the Unconscious* (London, 1890), 3:135.
85. Maksim Gor'kii, "O znanii," in AG, vol. 12, 1970.
86. Maxim Gorky, *Fragments from My Diary* (London, 1972), pp. 145–48.

It is clear that Gorky regarded the creation of such an immortal energetic brain as also the eventual achievement of human collective immortality. In fact, Gorky frequently referred to this issue. In 1912 he claimed that "we shall all rise from the dead, invoking death upon death."[87] In March 1920, he approached the subject once again: "The human mind declares war on death as a natural phenomenon. On death itself. My personal belief is that sooner or later, probably in two hundred years or possibly one hundred years, man will indeed achieve immortality."[88] In 1933 Gorky suggested a specific project to overcome the elemental forces of nature, the last part of which set the objective of "victory over the elements, sickness and death."[89] Here we see Gorky's debt to Fedorov, but without the physical resurrection that is central to Fedorov's vision.[90]

In fact, the annihilation of matter and the achievement of collective immortality is a full-scale occult theurgical project that does not need the intervention of God. In this respect Gorky's project differed from the theurgical projects suggested by Andrei Bely, Pavel Florensky, and Nikolai Fedorov. For Fedorov the conquest of nature was not antimaterial, since he held that nature was a temporary enemy, as in times of flood or drought, but an eternal friend. Humanity would learn to regulate nature, not destroy it. Moreover, Christian theurgy was regarded by its protagonists as a duty to be performed only in cooperation with God; it was also personal, anticipating the resurrection of the dead, whereas Gorky's project was totally impersonal.

Gorky was well acquainted with such writings. But he could not sympathize with Christian theurgy because it looked for the enlightenment of matter by spirit, while he dreamed of the total annihilation of matter. Still, he was very fond of the Christian theurgists because of their active attitude toward life. In 1928 he remarked in *Pravda*: "We had a very fine thinker—not very famous because he was original—N. F. Fedorov. Among his many original theories and aphorisms there is the following: 'Freedom without the conquest of nature is just like the liberation of the peasants without giving them land.' "[91]

Gorky regarded writing as theurgy par excellence: it could be good or bad, and it could influence people not only on the cognitive level but, more important, unconsciously. The exhortation of the Theosophist Konstantin Kudriavtsev is worth repeating: "It depends on us to fill the world with the harmony of beautiful pure thoughts and shield ourselves from the harmful influences of dark forces." Simply substituting socialist ideas for "beautiful pure thoughts"

87. Maxim Gorky, *Tales of Italy* (Moscow, n.d.), p. 294.

88. Gor'kii, "O znanii," p. 107.

89. Maxim Gorky, *On Literature* (Moscow, n.d.), p. 22.

90. For Gorky's debt to Fedorov, see Irene Masing-Delic, *Overcoming Death* (Stanford, 1992), pp. 123–54; Michael Hagemeister, *Nikolaj Fedorov* (Munich, 1989), pp. 368–402; and George M. Young Jr., *Nikolai Fedorov* (Belmont, Mass., 1979), pp. 185, 203, 219, 223, 237.

91. Maxim Gorky, *On Guard* (London, 1933), p. 76.

was not enough. To elicit the desired response, "external stimuli" would have to be applied to the masses "from above," and if they were to prevail over other stimuli, it was necessary to create a political system that would permit the circulation in the "field" of only "pure thoughts" and defend its members from "dark forces," identified to Soviet readers as capitalism, kulaks, fascism, and other perceived enemies. Although there is no explicit mention of Bekhterev or Kotik in Gorky's published writings on Socialist Realism, their ideas, or his quasi-occult, politicized adaptation of them, helped shape the theory and practice of Socialist Realism. Under Socialist Realism the arts, especially literature, were assigned the function of regulating the psychological processes of the masses and organizing them for the epic struggle necessary to construct socialism. Hence the idea of transmitting psychic energy translated into the notion that art was supposed to uplift, inspire, and educate. Gorky, of course, did not intend his theory to be used as ammunition for Stalin's personal tyranny, as ultimately it was. But we are more aware that such theories are always liable to be abused by despots.

CHAPTER TWELVE
SERGEI EISENSTEIN'S GNOSTIC CIRCLE

Håkan Lövgren

S urprisingly, religion and the occult were subjects of great interest to the revolutionary artist and Soviet filmmaker Sergei Eisenstein. His preoccupation with these matters ostensibly emanated from attempts to solve "methodological problems" in art and cinematography, but Eisenstein's personal background and development also shaped his interest in what he called the "imprecise sciences."

Mircea Eliade speaks about the contrast or conflict between archaic or archetypal man, to whom time was cyclical and ahistorical, and modern man, who perceives time as linear and historical.[1] Somewhere between these two extremes, both Christianity, with its eschatological conception of the Fall and redemption, and Marxism, with its revolution and ensuing workers' paradise, maintain the existence of a historical destiny, a destiny that is located in different but equally utopian spheres, so to speak.

Sergei Eisenstein belonged to both of these spheres, and the dualism that marked his perception of artistic creativity and form (his fixation on unity and on symbols of division and wholeness, for example) can be viewed against the background of Eliade's concepts of archetypal and modern man. Eisenstein's focus on pre-Christian, Gnostic, and Christian forms and symbolism also had a dual nature.[2] In his films of the 1920s, he used religious and cultic objects negatively in order to generate signs and images of the old and obsolete world,

---

1. Mircea Eliade, *The Myth of the Eternal Return* (Princeton, 1971).

2. Gnosticism was a profoundly dualist religious system intent on healing the cosmic rift between God and the world, spirit and soul, light and darkness, life and death, through the liberation that comes from gnosis, certain knowledge. Ernst Topitsch has used "gnosticism" as a term for any worldview (fascism and Marxism, for instance) that claims to know salvation and maintains that suffering is only a transitional stage on the path to redemption.

which he set in opposition to the new symbols and forms of Bolshevik political and social organization. As the nominally linear and secular society to which he belonged closed in on itself and grew more interested in its own historical past than in the present or the distant future, Eisenstein ventured to apply his insights into religious forms and symbols differently in his works of the late 1930s and 1940s.

Eliade's polarity of cyclical and linear time, of archaic and modern, has a particular affinity to Russian cultural history, as Jury Lotman and Boris Uspensky have outlined it. Their categories of opposition, such as "Russia versus the West," "true faith versus false faith," and "knowledge versus ignorance," are all subsumed under the historically pervasive dichotomy of "the old and the new." Bolshevism, with its historical "progressiveness," was certainly a "Western false faith," identified with "the new" by Russian Orthodoxy and tsarism. When Christianity was introduced in Russia in the tenth century, however, the dichotomy was reversed, the new ideology challenged the old: "The way in which 'the old' is replaced by 'the new' has deep significance. . . . It may be that for the creation of a new 'Christian' Russia a consolidated and largely artificial image of 'the old' was a psychological necessity."[3]

This psychological necessity—a mythical or "myth-creating" attitude toward both the past (the old) and the future (the new)—may have something to do with the particular maximalist or utopian mode of thinking in Russian cultural and historical development, which was in no sense abandoned by the 1917 revolutionaries. The Bolsheviks and their radical collaborators naturally tried to boost the contradiction between the old and the new by emphasizing "foreign" concepts of secularization and the class struggle in order to keep up the revolutionary steam. In the task of conveying their ideology, they were assisted not only by ardent young revolutionary artists but also by older "fellow travelers," as Trotsky called them, a significant number of whom had been active in or associated with the prerevolutionary Symbolist movement. The Symbolists had originally had an exclusively mystical and religious orientation, which included esoteric and occult traditions that had reached Russia largely through French Symbolist/occultist channels.[4] The particular interaction of these political and intellectual bedfellows makes it difficult to draw a clear line between religion and the occult as well as between religion and politics.

One aspect of the Symbolist-Bolshevik tendency, if I may call it that, was a shared interest in Richard Wagner's musical theater and its theoretical under-

---

3. Jurii M. Lotman and Boris A. Uspenskii, "Binary Models in the Dynamics of Russian Culture," in *The Semiotics of Russian Cultural History*, ed. Alexander D. Nakhimovsky and Alice Stone Nakhimovsky (Ithaca, 1985), p. 34. *Staroe i novoe* (The old and the new) was the revised title Eisenstein gave (or was forced to give) his film *General'naia liniia* (The general line).

4. Cf. James Webb, *The Occult Establishment* (La Salle, Ill., 1976), pp. 145–213.

pinnings. During the early revolutionary years, Wagner's *Die Walküre* was performed more than once, although these productions may have been prerevolutionary in concept and origin. One performance at the Bolshoi Theater in May 1919, for example, was positively reviewed by the Symbolist Viacheslav Ivanov. Symbolists and radicals were, however, separated by the different facets of the Wagnerian legacy they originally emphasized. As Bernice Glatzer Rosenthal has pointed out:

> Mystics of the Russian religious renaissance interpreted Wagner's theater as religious theater, the focal point of a new cult or culture, and viewed Wagner as a religious thinker whose progression from Feuerbach to Schopenhauer to Christ paralleled their own search for faith. Radicals emphasized the revolutionary Wagner of 1848–1849 and developed a political theater designed to create a new revolutionary consciousness.
>
> Wagner's appeal was greatest to Russians who sought synthesis, a "new organic society."[5]

EISENSTEIN'S CONVERSION

The Soviet pioneer film director Sergei Eisenstein was one such "synthesizing" Russian. In some sense, he belonged to both the religious/archetypal and radical/modern categories of Russian artists. A personal and professional "psychological necessity" to challenge the old—his despotic father in particular and "eternal" tsarist society in general—had brought him to join the Bolshevik Revolution. From his Marxist perspective, the old and the new were unambiguous political categories, but from the perspective of his bourgeois family background and his early religious experiences, these categories also represented other, perhaps more ambivalent values and dimensions. Deeply affected by religious emotion during childhood and by mystical experiences in his youth, Eisenstein recognized the power of religion and the irrational to influence human behavior. Eisenstein was born in 1898 into a complicated family situation. His father was an Orthodox Jew who had converted to Russian Orthodoxy, and seemed anxious to deny his Jewishness.[6] His mother had a Russian Orthodox background, and Eisenstein grew up an only child under the eyes of Christian governesses and the pervasive religious influence of his Christian maternal grandmother. This devout and dominating woman introduced young Eisenstein to popular mystical and superstitious notions, ideas that never quite lost their hold on him. In spite of his professed rationalism, Eisenstein remained a very superstitious man all his life.

5. Bernice Glatzer Rosenthal, "Wagner and Wagnerian Ideas in Russia," in *Wagnerism in European Culture and Politics*, ed. David C. Large and William Weber (Ithaca, 1984), p. 245.

6. Because of his Orthodox zeal, his civil servant friends used to jokingly call him *"pravoslavnyi* [Orthodox] Eisenstein."

Two autobiographical texts from the 1940s present partly ambiguous re-nunciations of his childhood religious experiences in the Russian Orthodox Church as well as a half-mocking, half-serious account of his 1920 confronta-tion with the esoteric Rosicrucian order.[7] From an ideological point of view, Eisenstein's negativism in these texts is quite consistent with his revolutionary conversion around 1917, the year he abandoned his civil engineering career and, inspired by Vsevolod Meyerhold's Petrograd production of Lermontov's *Maskarad* (Masquerade), pledged to devote his life to art.[8] Similarly, a desire for initiation, the idea of acquiring exclusive and perhaps secret knowledge from an individual or a group of people, may have developed in Eisenstein's mind from the complex of his religious experiences and his isolated and bookish childhood.

Eisenstein clearly longed for an environment in which he could cultivate his artistic dreams. In a letter to Meyerhold in 1921, probably written to introduce a prospective student, Eisenstein wrote: "The most lamentable, perhaps tragic side of my life is the terrible loneliness, e.g., the total absence up until recently of an artistic 'environment' and links to people who are artistically engaged."[9] The assumption here is that Eisenstein may have been somewhat predisposed to seek initiatory circumstances that would satisfy his quest for what he called the mysteries of art, the secrets of creativity. Such a predisposition could ex-plain his attraction to and initiation into the Rosicrucian order in 1920, an experience that he had both to have and then to reject.

ROSICRUCIAN INITIATION

During the Civil War period Eisenstein traveled about Russia as a volunteer with a Red Army engineering unit, building pontoon bridges and preparing set designs for an impressive number of theatrical plays at an equally impres-sive number of locations. In early August 1920, his unit arrived in Minsk, where a poster announced a lecture on Henri Bergson's theory of laughter by a certain Professor Zubakin. Eisenstein was not impressed by the talk but was intrigued by the man himself, especially during the following day's lecture. Zubakin appeared dressed in a long black cloak, black hat, and black cotton gloves. This is the outfit of Bogori II, a bishop of the Rosicrucian order and "a

7. Sergei Eisenstein's most complete memoirs to date, *YO: Ich selbst Memoiren* (Berlin, 1984) and *Beyond the Stars: The Memoirs of Sergei Eisenstein*, trans. William Powell, vol. 4 of his *Selected Works*, ed. Richard Taylor (London and Calcutta, 1995), are based in part on Sergei M. Eizenshtein, *Izbrannye proizvedeniia v shesti tomakh*, 6 vols. (Moscow, 1964–71), and in part on unpublished Russian manuscripts. They consist of reminiscences, portraits of colleagues, and more strictly creative autobiographical fragments and texts.

8. Cf. Werner Sudendorf, *Sergej M. Eisenstein: Materialen zu Leben und Werk* (Munich, 1975), p. 20.

9. "S. M. Eizenshtein: Here I Am at Last," *Iskusstvo kino*, 1988, no. 1, p. 68.

professor of literature and philosophy," Eisenstein added. Together with a few other people, Eisenstein was taken to a small room in a building inhabited mainly by rowdy Red Army soldiers. An imposing assistant announced that the bishop was ready to receive them. Bogori II entered and washed the feet of the prospective proselytes. "Some words. And we, linking hands, walked past a mirror. The mirror sent our union into the . . . astral."[10] Soon afterward the adepts became Rosicrucian knights.

During the following days the bishop expounded on such subjects as the Kabbala, arcanum, and the tarot. Eisenstein claimed to have slept through the discourse, with the exception of some passages toward the end dealing with the nature of divinity, God, and the manifestations of the divine. Eisenstein wrote: "At the very end it became clear that the initiate was being told that 'there is no God for God is He.' Now that was something I liked."[11]

Another item that attracted his attention is a systematic textbook on the occult, the title of which he did not disclose. A few years later he acquired the book from a used-book dealer in Moscow. It ended up next to Eliphas Lévi's *History of Magic* on a shelf in his library reserved for the "imprecise sciences"—magic, chiromancy, graphology, and the like. After trips to Europe and to the United States in 1929, and a year and a half of filming in Mexico, Eisenstein's library was considerably expanded by books he bought abroad. Many of them were on religious and occult subjects, which he saw as relevant to his search for a creative method as well as to an understanding of "national" or "ethnic" psychology that was partly to supersede the earlier class psychology as a basis for his work.[12] His interest in religion and the occult (James Webb's term "rejected knowledge" is one that Eisenstein might have agreed with),[13] in various forms of religious education and spiritual quests, is reflected in many volumes on the Jesuits—Ignatius Loyola and his method in particular—and on mysticism, the Kabbala, alchemy, and astrology. Eisenstein also shared an interest in "myth creation," "ecstasy," and "unity of the senses" with the Russian Symbolists and early Wagnerians, whose books he had begun to acquire in the 1930s. He owned works by Viacheslav Ivanov, Andrei Bely, Valery Briusov, and Sergei Durylin, who played a part in the dissemination of spiritual and occult ideas in Russia around the turn of the century.

Initiated into the Rosicrucian order along with Eisenstein were Valentin

---

10. Eisenstein, *Beyond the Stars*, p. 82. Boris Mikhailovich Zubakin (1894–1938) belonged to the Mikhail Bakhtin circle. Cf. Katerina Clark and Michael Holquist, *Mikhail Bakhtin* (Cambridge, Mass., 1984), p. 39.

11. Eisenstein, *Beyond the Stars*, p. 122.

12. This notion reflects the revised Marxism of "socialism in one country," which Stalin and the Soviet leadership adopted in the 1930s. The aesthetic tenets of Socialist Realism implied a thematic shift from the "international working class" to the "Soviet working class," "national heritage," and "folk," which Eisenstein continually had to take into consideration.

13. Webb, *Occult Establishment*, p. 10.

Smyshliaev, with whom Eisenstein later collaborated on the Proletkult stage production of *Meksikanets* (The Mexican, 1921), and the actor, teacher, and Anthroposophist Mikhail Chekhov. Their evening discussions centered on Theosophy, Rudolf Steiner, hypnosis, and yoga. Chekhov was both a fanatical proselyte and a heretic, according to Eisenstein:

> I remember conversations about the 'invisible lotus', which flowered, unseen, in the devotee's breast. I remember the reverential silence and the glassy eyes of the believers fixed on the teacher.
> Chekhov and I went out into the street.
> A thin covering of snow. Silence.
> Dogs frisked playfully around the street lamps.
> 'I have to believe there is something to the invisible lotus,' said Chekhov. 'Take these dogs. We cannot see anything and yet they can scent something under each other's little tails . . . '
> Cynicism of this order often goes hand in hand with belief. Such was Chekhov.[14]

Of all the converts in this motley collection of individuals, Eisenstein was the only one to keep a clear head. He was now a man experienced in strong religious sentiments and versed in the traditions of mysticism, but enlightened and "liberated" enough to be able to apply these experiences and this knowledge toward nonreligious and nonmystical goals. After these few days in August 1920, his Rosicrucian education came to an end: "I was finally declared a 'knight errant' and released. I tried, on my errands, to put as much ground as possible between myself and the Rosicrucians, Steiner, and Madame Blavatskaya. Another page of impressions in the past . . . "[15] Like any other declaration of past experiences transcended, this one warrants a certain doubt. As I have already pointed out, Eisenstein definitely returned to the occult sphere and Gnostic traditions in the 1930s, when he acquired a substantial part of his library of "imprecise sciences."

The utopian elation in the arts inspired by the October Revolution prompted the newly converted Eisenstein to try to extract the form and method from religion and the occult as well as from the manifestations of prerevolutionary art. The idea was to discard obsolescent ideologies in all manifestations of culture and reapply the formal distillations to the realization of new social and political ideals.

Eisenstein's rejection of his religious past was essentially focused on the institutional church as bearer and representative of dogma, and not on religious experience as such. The ritual and drama of the liturgy, the dynamic

14. Eisenstein, *Beyond the Stars*, p. 83.
15. Ibid.

form that was capable of generating a sense of mysticism and ecstasy, still seemed relevant and valid to him.[16] Eisenstein's later fascination with dynamic and "ecstatic" form was thus very likely grounded in his own religious experience, in a mysticism that had become ineffaceably imprinted in his mind during the Orthodox services he had attended as a child and young man, so deeply etched that he later felt obliged to describe his infatuation as an affliction.[17]

"When I was not too young I fell prey to the Voltairean germ of disrespect for the Supreme Being," Eisenstein wrote. "This occurred before the Revolution and took a rather aggressive form, since it came after almost hysterical religiosity in my childhood and the cult of mystical feats in my youth." Eisenstein was not ready to charge Voltaire with causing this disrespect, however; he put the blame "on the very ministers of the mystic cults themselves. Or perhaps it is the very balefulness of dogmatism and casuistry that inevitably undermines the essence of emotional passion; that undermines all that in its most mysterious secrecy determines one's adherence to a specific religion."[18]

The fundamental irreconcilability between the cultic function of the priest and his role as a religious instructor with a catechism, "calculated not to educate and deepen the foundations of religious passion, but to educate the experienced casuist," was the dilemma Eisenstein could not resolve.[19] Instead he became a Voltairean atheist, but with one foot still lodged in the aesthetics of Orthodox liturgy with its opposing concepts of Fall and redemption. He became, to paraphrase Anatole France, whom he quotes, an Orthodox who has ceased to be a Christian.

Eisenstein's almost lyrical description of Father Nicholas, his spiritual mentor and guide, reveals the profound impression his visits to the church had made on him:

When at Mass, Father Nicholas, dressed in a silvery chasuble and his arms raised heavenward, stood in a cloud of incense pierced by the slanting rays of the sun. As he performed the sacrament of the Eucharist, the bells, certainly prompted by a mysterious force, pealed from the lofty belfry, and it actually seemed that the heavens had opened and grace was pouring out upon the sinful world.

From such moments springs my lifelong weakness for the ornate in religious services.[20]

16. In this respect he may remind one of Pavel Florensky, whose work Eisenstein does not appear to have known.

17. Cf. Eisenstein, *Beyond the Stars*, p. 73.

18. Sergei M. Eisenstein, *Immoral Memories*, trans. Herbert Marshall (Boston, 1983), p. 201.

19. Ibid. Eisenstein's fascination with the Jesuits and Ignatius Loyola's methods in particular is perhaps a point of reference here.

20. Ibid., pp. 201–2.

An autobiographical essay, "Le bon Dieu," written after his heart attack in 1946, continues the case history approach to his religious past. Eisenstein regarded his religious (and Rosicrucian) education as useful experience, but only because it was confined in time and place, well absorbed, and overcome as a determining factor in his life: " 'You have to have this experience,' or, to avoid generalisations, I shall say of myself that 'I had to have!' Holy Week in the Suvarov Church, my last confession in (?) 1916." Thus, about a year before the political events in 1917, Eisenstein was apparently still a man with a deep religious involvement, with emotions that now suddenly had to be projected onto new "objects" as the social and political reality changed. "It is worth taking the 'fanaticism' out of religion: it can later be separated from the original object of worship, and be 'displaced' to other passions . . . ," he wrote.[21] Although presented in general terms, this was obviously Eisenstein's understanding of how to deal with his own religious emotions: they had to be endured and then relegated to a storehouse of useful experiences, so that later they could be applied to Bolshevik subject matter.

This technique of projecting old passions onto new subjects resembles the psychoanalyst's sublimation and projection. But the fundamental problem of Eisenstein's operative aesthetics—how to redirect conditioned emotional responses, such as religious fanaticism, through the formal and structural adaptation of religious and artistic form—is perhaps better regarded as a resublimation, a rediversion of "energy of primitive impulse into culturally higher activity."[22] That the "fanaticism" in these experiences, and later the new passions, can never be successfully dominated by dogma and ritual seemed to be the implicit assumption in Eisenstein's subsequent thoughts. When he describes the conflict between the church as an official institution and the church as the bosom of persons with a deep individual religious commitment and ecstatic passion, one can sense in which direction his sympathies are leaning: "Every church acknowledges a pope as law-giver and primate in the affairs of the world. And every church has the opposite extreme: a St. Francis, who goes barefoot and embraces lepers and wretched holy curs (domini canes)."[23]

The context of these reflections is the search for a model for Pimen, the Russian Orthodox priest in the film *Ivan Groznyi*, Parts I (1945) and II (1946); that is, for a historical counterpart to this conflict within the Orthodox Church, a Russian Saint Francis. But the climactic confession scene with Ivan in front of the grand mural of the Last Judgment in the third, mostly destroyed part of the film also figures here. In his search Eisenstein settled for one Nil Sorsky, alias

---

21. Eisenstein, *Beyond the Stars*, p. 73. "You have to have this experience" and "I had to have!" are in English.

22. *The Concise Oxford Dictionary* (London, 1982), p. 1062.

23. Eisenstein, *Beyond the Stars*, p. 75. The expression "wretched holy curs (domini canes)" is obviously a play on words, something that Eisenstein loved to indulge in. The Dominicans (domini canes = the Lord's dogs) are a mendicant order.

Nikolai Maikov, a fifteenth-century monk whose radicalism and asceticism met with his approval. "I think that the tendency of this second sort—the ecstasists, dreamers, 'meditators'—can be harmful, in a certain dosage, to one's creative life. If it does not suck away at religion permanently!"[24]

The tradition of *startsy*, Russian monks and spiritual advisers, to which Eisenstein is referring in "Le bon Dieu,"[25] is interesting in relation to *Ivan Groznyi*. Among the Symbolist-affiliated Russian intelligentsia after the turn of the century, one could note an emerging perception of the *startsy* as counterparts to the "initiates" of Western occultism. There was even a belief in "hidden *startsy*," and the veneration of these holy men was seen as a sign of an esoteric tradition within the Orthodox Church.[26] Eisenstein's portrayal of Ivan and his *oprichnina* in black monks' robes, during and after the color sequence of the feebleminded Vladimir Staritsky's mock crowning, gives the impression of an esoteric and demonic sect, whose machinations are justified by the clergy and boyar conspiracy against the tsar. In the mock crowning of Vladimir— perhaps the strongest scene in the film, since we know that Vladimir's delight at dressing up in regal apparel will be the cause of his mistaken murder—Ivan takes on the role of initiator and humble servant. Ivan soon realizes the plot against himself and forces the crowned Vladimir to lead the black monks into the church, where the false tsar is murdered. This "initiation" gone awry could be viewed as a metaphor for Eisenstein's unhappy relation to Meyerhold, who saw his student as a threat, or on a more abstract and unconscious level for Eisenstein's unsuccessful assimilation into the Stalinist Soviet Union, which doubtless contributed to the film director's untimely death at the age of fifty.

MASTERING ART

In the mid-1920s, when Eisenstein left the theater for the relatively unexplored cinematic medium, he set himself the task of putting artistic work in general and filmmaking in particular on a rational footing, attempting to develop scientific theories for the dynamics of artistic form and psychology. Eisenstein wanted to find and explore the principles behind artistic creation through his own practice and rational analysis:

> First master art.
> Then destroy it.
> Penetrate into the mysteries of art.
> Unveil them.

24. Ibid.
25. Eisenstein mentions Father Zosima in Dostoevsky's *Brothers Karamazov* as an example of a Russian Saint Francis.
26. Cf. Webb, *Occult Establishment*, p. 164.

Master art.
Become a master.
And then snatch off its mask, expose it, destroy it![27]

Unfortunately, the analytical tools of the young independent adept were not sharp enough to penetrate the many layers of the phenomenon of art: "Every other line of the theoretical analysis of his new and enchanting acquaintance—the theory of art—was enshrouded with seven veils of mystery."[28]

Eisenstein's favored metaphor of the "seven veils" for the mystery of creation is interesting because of the occult symbolism of its components, especially against the background of his sarcastic reference to Meyerhold's inability to explain his creative work (Eisenstein refers to Meyerhold's "method" as "strip-tease *à l'envers*").[29] Meyerhold's muteness in theoretical matters gave Eisenstein the impetus to develop what he called his own "second tendency":

To rummage, rummage, rummage.
To work my way into the every fissure of a problem; to break inside and dig, trying always to penetrate it more deeply, to get ever closer to its core.
I do not look for any help.
But what I find I do not hide; I bring it out into the open—in lectures, books, magazines, newspapers.[30]

"I've had rotten luck with fathers," Eisenstein noted earlier. His father had failed to initiate him in matters of sexuality, and his mentor (or "second father," as he called Meyerhold) had only allowed him to catch a glimpse of the artistic secrets through a crack in the door he so fervently guarded. But perhaps these matters of artistic creativity were more ambiguous and less susceptible to being explained and revealed in rational terms than Eisenstein imagined. At the time this essay was written, after his massive heart attack in 1946—when, according to all clinical laws, he should have been dead—he concluded with what seems to be a blatant contradiction of his earlier vow of clarity and analytical thoroughness with the mysterious words: "And . . . did you know the most effective way of hiding something is to put it on display?!" That is, trying to reveal everything down to the last detail may have the reverse effect: the deceptive appearances will only consolidate in the clearest of explanations.[31] Such an attitude seems akin to the Renaissance conception of Orphic theology, discussed by Pico della Mirandola and others.[32] Perhaps Meyer-

27. S. M. Eisenstein, *Notes of a Film Director*, trans. X. Danko (New York, 1970), p. 14.
28. Ibid., pp. 15–16.
29. Eisenstein, *Beyond the Stars*, p. 451; English and French in the Russian original.
30. Ibid., p. 453.
31. Ibid., pp. 447, 453.
32. Cf. Edgar Wind, *Pagan Mysteries in the Renaissance* (New York, 1958), p. 9.

hold's theoretical mystifications were fully deliberate and his intention was occult and Hermetic, steeped in Symbolist aesthetics as he was.

As I suggested earlier, Eisenstein's dualism was dependent on conflicting notions of the archetypal and modern mind. Eisenstein had advanced the notion of prelogical/sensuous and logical thought (or nondifferentiated and differentiated thinking) as elements of the fundamental dichotomy in art, which he thought reflected the traumatic mental development of humankind as a whole. This conflict was the driving force behind artistic creativity, the whole complex of which he presented in Greek mythological terms:

> . . . Dionysus and Apollo. Dionysus: prelogic. Apollo: logic. The diffuse and the distinct. The dim and the clear. The animal-elemental and the sunny-wise, etc., etc. (one may add as many as one desires). Out of this arises the question: Is there then somewhere in Greek philosophy a synthesis of the Dionysian and the Apollonian elements? And if there is, where is it? It appears there is. And in the most appropriate place: in Orpheus (the artist!) . . . It is quite right that this synthesis should take place in Orpheus—the singer and father of art.[33]

Orpheus thus symbolized a synthesis of the polar elements in art and artistic creativity, a principle of integration and unification realized by the artist in his work. Symbols and symbolic constellations of unity and unification became a major theoretical and practical concern for Eisenstein in his efforts to reconcile the dualism inherent in art.

THE ALCHEMICAL CONTEXT AND THE OCCULT

There is an alchemical sense to Eisenstein's project of distilling or purifying emotional form in an effort to transform and redirect its energies; and some of his colleagues saw him as akin to an alchemist. Sergei Iutkevich, a film director who worked with Eisenstein on several theatrical productions in the early 1920s, describes in slightly patronizing terms the busy intellectual work to create *the* theory of film in early Soviet cinema, the notion of a political character gallery, *typage*, and a structural principle, *montage*:

> Nowhere is there such a search for a philosopher's stone, so much quasi-medieval Scholasticism, as in the problem of cinema theory. Working as they were in a new art, the artists and innovators really needed to recognize and establish its specific quality. In its time it was montage which was named the philosopher's stone of the cinema, and it was furiously defended, as much in theory as in practice, as the major element in the specificity of the new art.[34]

33. Quoted in V. V. Ivanov, *Ocherki po istorii semiotiki v SSSR* (Moscow, 1976), p. 70.
34. Quoted in Luda and Jean Schnitzer, "Teenage Artists of the Revolution," in *Cinema in Revolution*, ed. Marcel Martin (New York, 1973), p. 39.

The idea of montage in theater and film was, of course, very much associated with Sergei Eisenstein's films and film theories in the 1920s, and Iutkevich's ironic analogy between film theoreticians and medieval Scholastics and alchemists, for whom the philosopher's stone was both the goal and the means of reaching it, seems aimed mostly at his one-time collaborator Eisenstein.

Iutkevich's characterization of the theoretical exertions around montage hints at a specific historical period—the transition between the Middle Ages and the Renaissance, when Neoplatonic philosophy and Gnostic conceptions were widespread in Italy, Central Europe, and England. The cultural and philosophical developments of this period—the resurrection and retransformation of ancient and classical mythology, of the grotesque and ornamental tendencies in religious and occult art and imagery—represent an ideational field of great significance in the development of Eisenstein's creative imagery and conceptual concerns.

Eisenstein was a synthesizer, an artist preoccupied, even obsessed by the idea of division and unity, dismemberment and reconstitution, the relationship between the parts and the whole. In that sense he was not entirely different from great artists and thinkers of the past. What made Eisenstein unique was the fact that he found his artistic career in a new medium, film, which seemed to promise an ultimate realization of the *Gesamtkunstwerk*, a synthesis of the arts, a Symbolist notion derived from Richard Wagner and others.[35] "Film is the most contemporary form of the organic synthesis of the arts," Eisenstein wrote in "Psikhologiia iskusstva" (The psychology of art), a draft not accidentally conceived during the final preparations for his production of Wagner's *Walküre* in 1940[36] (Figure 12.1).

Herbert Silberer maintained that "rosicrucianism is identical with higher alchemy or the hermetic or the royal art."[37] It is conceivable that Eisenstein was introduced to imagery and symbols associated with alchemy during the lectures of Bogori II. Whether they were mentioned there or not, there is one ancient and prominent alchemical symbol of unity that frequently crops up in Eisenstein's sketches and program for *Die Walküre*. Uroboros, the snake that bites its own tail to form a circle, is one of the oldest symbols of the alchemical opus; as a being that in Carl Jung's words, "proceeds from the one and leads back to the one," it is a symbol of return[38] (Figures 12.2, 12.3, 12.4).

35. See Rudolf M. Bisanz, "The Romantic Synthesis of the Arts," *Konsthistorisk tidskrift* 44, nos. 1–2 (1975): 38–47.

36. S. M. Eizenshtein, "Psikhologiia iskusstva," in *Psikhologiia protsessov khudozhestvennogo tvorchestva* (Leningrad, 1980), p. 177.

37. Herbert Silberer, *Hidden Symbolism of Alchemy and the Occult Arts* (New York, 1971), p. 207; first published as *Problems of Mysticism and Its Symbolism* (New York, 1917). Silberer, a psychoanalyst, was a colleague of Hans Sachs and Otto Rank. Rank was the author of *The Trauma of Birth* (1924), which had a great impact on Eisenstein's thinking.

38. C. G. Jung, *Psychology and Alchemy* (Princeton, 1968), p. 293.

Figure 12.1. The cover of Jay Leyda's copy of the program for Sergei Eisenstein's production of Richard Wagner's *Die Walküre* at the Bolshoi Theater, Moscow. The Eisenstein Archive, Special Collections, The Museum of Modern Art, New York.

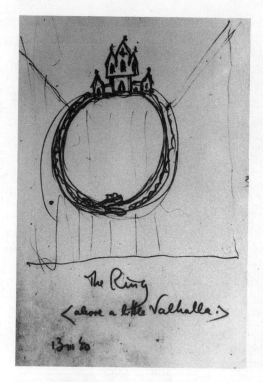

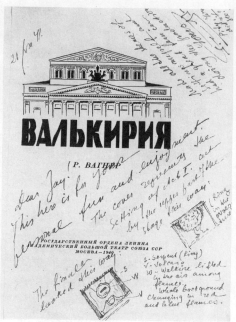

Figure 12.2. (left) The proscenium ring "with a little Valhalla": sketch for Eisenstein's production of Wagner's *Die Walküre*. Russian State Archive of Literature and Art, Moscow.

Figure 12.3. Jay Leyda's dedicated copy of the program for Eisenstein's production of *Die Walküre*. The Eisenstein Archive, Special Collections, The Museum of Modern Art, New York.

Uroboros, the alchemical symbol of the unity of opposites, the synthesis of male and female, conscious and unconscious, apparently attracted Eisenstein in his efforts to resolve the dualism inherent in the development of the human mind—the split into prelogical and logical spheres—which was a real obstacle in his own conception of art. Eisenstein might have reasoned that, if the delicate balance between the Dionysian and Apollonian principles was not maintained in art, then irrational archaic man" would threaten to return and take over at the expense of rational "historical man," an intolerable prospect from the point of view of a socially responsible Soviet film director.

Eisenstein's dilemma was a Faustian one, according to Viacheslav V. Ivanov, in which art became associated with atavistic and profoundly regressive forces:

Figure 12.4. The self-devouring dragon Uroboros in a Greek alchemical manuscript.

Figure 12.5. (left) Siegmund and Sieglinde embrace (are "united in the *coniunctio*") in the world tree in this sketch for Eisenstein's production of *Die Walküre*, February 16, 1940. Mythological figures fill the branches. Russian State Archive of Literature and Art, Moscow.

Figure 12.6. The tree of philosophy, with symbols of the alchemical opus.

The moral crisis Eisenstein experienced in relation to art was essentially tied to the fact that, by accepting the proposition of art's genetic connection with the most regressive parts of the psyche, Eisenstein gave these parts the kind of negative evaluation that was not associated with, for example, Jung's archetypes (which were neutral and capable of being used in any fashion). Following the early Freud in this respect, Eisenstein actually combined two things—research into the genetic roots of art and an evaluation of these sources that went back (with some modification) to dualistic studies in their Christianized form. Art seemed tied to dark, "diabolical" forces.[39]

To Eisenstein, Wagner's opera was a drama about the destruction of the "nondifferentiated" state of early humanity, symbolized by the primordial

39. Ivanov, *Ocherki po istorii semiotiki*, p. 72.

unity of the sexes, the hermaphrodite or androgyne, at a time when the incestuous relationship between the twins Sigmund and Sieglinde in *Die Walküre* was "already banned, but when the new morals had not yet reached into the 'flesh and blood' of the social members." Eisenstein saw this relationship as a symbol of a presocial stage in human development, when "marriage between brother and sister was one of its most natural forms."[40] This self-enclosed and self-sufficient unity, which in a sense represents the self-fecundation of cyclical Nature, was very fittingly embodied in the Uroboros snake.[41] In staging Sigmund and Sieglinde's copulation under the world tree, Yggdrasil (Figures 12.5 and 12.6), Eisenstein intended to hang a gigantic "wheel" over the proscenium in the shape of the tail-biting Uroboros.

Jung has pointed out that Uroboros is generally considered to be a variant of Mercury, "the hermaphrodite that was in the beginning, that splits into the classical brother-sister duality and is united in the *coniunctio,* to appear once again at the end in the radiant form of *lumen novum,* the stone. He is metallic yet liquid, matter yet spirit, cold yet fiery, poison yet healing draught—a symbol uniting all opposites. . . . "[42] The *lumen novum* and the circular Uroboros are thus symbols of polar qualities in harmonic synthesis and the happy return to unity. From a more modern perspective—from a psychoanalytic point of view, for instance—the tail-biting Uroboros would probably seem to be a rather ambiguous symbol. The act of devouring one's own tail has various psychosexual overtones, of which I am sure Eisenstein was not oblivious. For example, the Uroboros could be perceived as a symbol of the ambivalent return to the womb, *Mutterleibsversenkung,* in Otto Rank's terminology—a subject to which Eisenstein devoted a long autobiographical essay[43]—and of castration anxiety during coitus. The notion of coitus as a mildly disguised and ambivalent return to the womb was advanced by the Hungarian psychoanalyst Sandor Ferenczi, whose *Thalassa* (1924) made a deep impression on Eisenstein.

A drawing in Eisenstein's hand is interesting in the context of the *Walküre* production (Figure 12.7). To my knowledge, this is the only Eisenstein illustration that appears to combine Christian, alchemical-occult, and Mexican elements to express the theme of *coniunctio,* the brother-sister pair, the unification of the solar/male and the lunar/female principles (Figure 12.8, 12.9, and 12.10). Eisenstein's eclectic combination of the inverted triangle with God's all-

---

40. Eizenshtein, *Izbrannye proizvedeniia,* 5:337, 336.

41. "This is the ancient Egyptian symbol of which it is said: 'Draco interfecit se ipsum, maritat se ipsum, impraegnat se ipsum.' It slays, weds, and impregnates itself. It is man and woman, begetting and conceiving, devouring and giving birth, active and passive, above and below, at once": Erich Neumann, *The Origins and History of Consciousness* (Princeton, 1970), p. 10.

42. Jung, *Psychology and Alchemy,* pp. 293–95.

43. See Eisenstein, "Monsieur, madame et bébé," in *Beyond the Stars,* pp. 487–507.

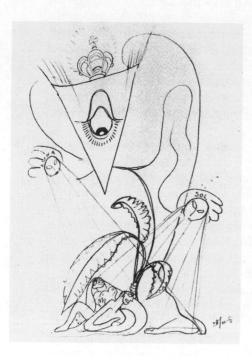

Figure 12.7. (left) A drawing by Eisenstein combining Christian, occult, and Mexican elements. Reproduced by permission of Herbert Marshall.

Figure 12.8. The philosopher's stone and the resurrection of the seven "dead" metals. From Johannes de Monte Snyders, *Metamorphosis planetarum* (1663).

perceiving eye gives the impression of a falling wedge ready to split the paradisal couple under the influence of Sol and Luna. The presocial, innocent unity between brother and sister can be seen as threatened by the snakelike figure behind and above the couple. Is this a variant of the one-eyed Wotan (Odin), who in *Die Walküre* represented the new social morality that sought to destroy this unity and condemn the pair in the drawing—and the world—to eternal division and duality?

Eisenstein's drawing presents an archaic couple, seemingly under the spell and threat of some supernatural being. This Arcadian, presocial world is threatened by a caricatured symbol of the Supreme Being, the inverted triangle (sometimes a sign of the demonic) with the all-seeing eye, a frequent symbol in occult and Masonic contexts (Figures 12.11, 12.12, 12.13, and 12.14). If we see

Figure 12.9. (above) Alexandre Toussaint de Limojon de Saint Didier, *Le Triomphe hermétique* (1689).

Figure 12.10. Hermaphroditisches Sonn- und Mondskind (1752). From C. G. Jung, *Psychology and Alchemy.* Copyright © 1968 by Princeton University Press. Reproduced by permission of Princeton University Press.

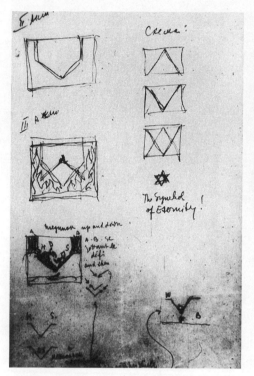

Figure 12.11. (left) Eisenstein's sketch for *Die Walküre,* acts II and III. Russian State Archive of Literature and Art, Moscow.

Figure 12.12. The Great Symbol of Solomon, representing the god of light and the god of reflections.

this image as an anticipation of the conflict between Wotan, who represents the law, and the twins Siegmund and Sieglinde, who together represent passion and innocence, one could also perceive it as a reflection of Eisenstein's contempt for the casuist who kills all genuine (religious) passion with dogma. The implication might also be that only by transcending Christian culture and religion, by simultaneously moving backward and forward in time, would the two cultures, the ancient and the new, close the circle like Uroboros and create a new synthesis. Such a process would guarantee the efficacy of the work of art, according to Eisenstein:

> The influence of an artwork is based on the fact that in it you have two processes going on simultaneously: a swift progressive ascent along the line of the most developed ideological level of consciousness and at the same time a descent

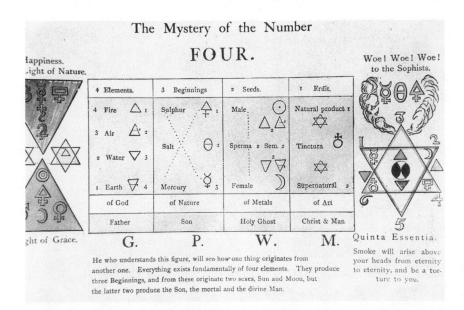

The Mystery of the Number

FOUR.

Happiness. Light of Nature.

Woe! Woe! Woe! to the Sophists.

4 Elements.	3 Beginnings	2 Seeds.	1 Fruit.
4 Fire △ 1	Sulphur 🜍 1	Male ☉	Natural product 1 △△ 2
3 Air △ 2			
2 Water ▽ 3	Salt ⊖ 2	Sperma 2 Sem. 2 ▽▽ 2	Tinctura ♂
1 Earth ▽ 4	Mercury ☿ 3	Female ☽	Supernatural 2
of God	of Nature	of Metals	of Art
Father	Son	Holy Ghost	Christ & Man

Light of Grace.

G.   P.   W.   M.

Quinta Essentia.

He who understands this figure, will see how one thing originates from another one. Everything exists fundamentally of four elements. They produce three Beginnings, and from these originate two sexes, Sun and Moon, but the latter two produce the Son, the mortal and the divine Man.

Smoke will arise above your heads from eternity to eternity, and be a torture to you.

Figure 12.13. Geheime Figuren der Rosencreuzer (1785).

through the structure of form down to the deepest layer of emotional thinking. The polar cultivation of these two lines of aspiration creates the remarkable tension in the unity of form and content, which characterizes the true work of art.[44]

This "descent through the structure of form" is also the *regressum ad uterus*, the return to the womb and point zero, the moment of conception and creation. In the mythology of alchemical creation, work with baser substances and metals in an effort to create gold or the philosopher's stone (symbols of immortality) "should not be understood merely as a primordial condition of the substance but also as an inner experience of the alchemist," according to Eliade.[45] This work represents a return to the womb, embryonic respiration (imitation of the fetus's breathing in the womb), a return to the beginning, preconditions for success in the alchemist's recreation of cosmogony. The alchemical operation represented a fantastic allegorical project of correspondences, of creating resonant structures that would move the forces of macrocosm into a gigantic choral manifestation, into a microcosmic synthesis of all the base metals to yield tangible and symbolic gold, matter and spirit.

44. Eizenshtein, *Izbrannye proizvedeniia*, 2:120–21.
45. Mircea Eliade, *The Forge and the Crucible: The Origins and Structure of Alchemy* (Chicago and London, 1978), p. 119.

Figure 12.14. Illustration from William Law's edition of Jakob Boehme's mystical writings, *The Works of J. Behmen the Teutonic Theosopher* (1764–81). Eisenstein owned a copy of this remarkably illustrated volume.

Eliade's description of the Western alchemist is strikingly similar to Eisenstein's discussion of ecstatic structures and states in artistic creation,[46] and of the artist "killing" (*mortificatio*) the components of the old theatrical art as well as himself through his work, his opus, in an act of redemption:[47]

> The Western alchemist by endeavoring to 'kill' the ingredients, to reduce them to the *prima materia*, provokes a *sympatheia* between the 'pathetic situations' of the substance and his innermost being. In other words, he realizes, as it were, some initiatory experiences which, as the course of the *opus* proceeds, forge for him a new personality, comparable to the one which is achieved after successfully undergoing the ordeals of initiation. His participation in the phases of the *opus* is such that the *nigredo*, for example, procure for him experiences analogous to those of the neophyte in the initiation ceremonies when he feels 'swallowed up' in the belly of the monster, or 'buried,' or symbolically 'slain by the masks and masters of initiation'.
>
> . . . it is interesting to note that the *coniunctio* and the ensuing death is sometimes expressed in terms of *hieros gamos:* the two principles—the Sun and the Moon, King and Queen, unite in the mercury bath and die (this is the *nigredo*): their 'soul' abandons them to return later and give birth to the *filius philosophorum*, the androgynous being (Rebis) which promises the immediate attainment of the Philosopher's Stone.[48]

As Eliade explains, the alchemists adopted and changed the significance of the ancient notions surrounding the processing of ore and metals. Metals were looked upon as organic matter that entered new combinations and "married"; Mother Earth was the womb in which they gestated and out of which they were finally born. The alchemical "marriage" between sulfur and mercury was thus a spiritualization of matter, the expression of

> a mystical union between two cosmological principles. Herein lies the novelty of the alchemical perspective: the life of Matter is no longer designated in terms of 'vital' hierophanies as it was in the outlook of primitive man; it has acquired a spiritual dimension; in other words, by taking on the initiatory significance of drama and suffering, matter also takes on the destiny of the spirit. . . .
>
> . . . The alchemical symbolism of torture and death is sometimes equivocal; the operation can be taken to refer either to man or to a mineral substance. . . . This ambivalent symbolism permeates the whole *opus alchymicum*.[49]

The alchemical *Gesamtkunstwerk* was no mean metaphor for an artist interested in an analogy to his own quest for unity. When Eisenstein explored the

---

46. *Vykhod iz sebia*, the expression Eisenstein used for ecstasy, literally means "coming out of oneself."

47. Cf. Eizenshtein, "Montazh attraktsionov," in *Izbrannye proizvedeniia*, 2:269–74.

48. Eliade, *Forge and Crucible*, pp. 160–61.

49. Ibid., pp. 151–52.

Uroboros snake in the sketches for *Die Walküre,* he was thus employing a very appropriate symbol with the power to express and unify a number of themes in Wagner's opera and the entire cycle—the accursed ring, the unity of sexual opposites, the wholeness of the universe, the synthesis-of-the-arts idea—as well as his own idée fixe, unity in artistic creation, in his own effort as an artist.

Eisenstein's focus on symbols of unity and encirclement became more and more entrenched or obsessive toward the end of his life. One of his last theoretical texts, an eighty-page draft headed "Krug" (Circle), includes discussions of the circular and mandala shapes in Christian art and architecture, especially in Hildegard von Bingen's art, and various forms of womb symbolism. Another text of the same period, "Degas," deals with the circle in Degas's painterly compositions, the significance of the yin/yang symbol, and the like. Similarly, in one of his last autobiographical pieces, "Pro domo sua," written and drawn about a month before his death in February 1948, Eisenstein experimented with his signature in a way that turned it into an embryo-like circular shape containing the actual name. The name is not quite enclosed, however, the circle not completely formed; the small opening, according to Eisenstein, signified an openness to share his insights and knowledge.[50]

Eisenstein's minutely planned Wagner production, the awkward celebration of the Soviet-Nazi nonaggression pact, is fraught with personal and historical irony.[51] The pact that gave him the assignment also resulted in the complete removal of his "antifascist" film *Aleksandr Nevsky* from the Soviet repertoire. His production of *Die Walküre* met with little success and much disapproval, especially from the Germans. Technical factors and a somewhat heavy-handed approach to the Bolshoi ensemble prevented the realization of many of his ideas. Anti-Semitic comments by attending members of the German embassy in Moscow seem to indicate that Eisenstein's handling of the opera's theme was far too "anti-authoritarian" or "Bolshevik" for their taste. "Deliberate Jewish tricks" was the verdict of two German officers as they left the performance.[52] A mythological and esoteric sensibility such as Eisenstein's was apparently not sufficient to satisfy members of a political movement with firm roots in the less appealing traditions and tendencies of occultism and with its own version of Socialist Realism.[53]

Eisenstein's path from Rosicrucian initiation to the production of *Die Walküre* covers some twenty years (1920–40) of intense and often very frustrating

50. RGALI, f. 1923, op. 2, dd. 268, 270.

51. For an account of this production, see Rosamund Bartlett, "The Embodiment of Myth: Eizenshtein's Production of *Die Walküre*," *Slavonic and East European Review* 70, no. 1 (1992): 53–77.

52. Alexander Werth, quoted in Jay Leyda and Zina Voynow, *Eisenstein at Work* (New York, 1982), p. 114.

53. On the occult roots of German Nazism, see Webb, *Occult Establishment*, pp. 275–345.

artistic labor. During that period, Soviet society and its political and aesthetic doctrines fell under the spell of rampant Stalinism. There is no doubt that Eisenstein felt a general allegiance to Soviet policies, even as they played havoc with his own projects. Most of his colleagues of the avant-garde years were dead or in labor camps by the end of the 1930s, but Eisenstein somehow survived, perhaps by luck or because of his international standing, perhaps because the film buff Stalin actually liked his films; no one knows why, when Meyerhold and his earlier close collaborators Sergei Tretiakov and Isak Babel were arrested, Eisenstein was not.[54]

The progression from *Stachka* (The strike, 1925), Eisenstein's first film about the budding political consciousness of the proletariat, to his last uncompleted work, *Ivan Groznyi* (Ivan the Terrible, parts I and II, 1945), about one of Russia's most despotic tsars, reflected the supersession of "the new" by "the old," the return of the ruthless oppressor in the Soviet Union. Stalin's totalitarianism was in a sense an expression of the ultimate occult elitism, Marxism in theory and practice; a small group of people controlling and manipulating far-reaching semiotic systems, including film, in the name of a higher social truth. In the mandatory process of ideological self-control, Eisenstein seemed prone to "dysfunction" because of his artistic involvement, his interests in ancient forms of cultural and artistic expression, in myth and esoteric symbols, in creative psychology, in an artist oppressed by autocratic rule (Pushkin); in short, because of his concern with genuinely artistic issues and problems. As the Soviet Union closed in on itself, began to devour itself, Eisenstein could not stay within the bounds of dogma, but remained open to share and absorb new (artistic) ideas, which the last version of his signature—the open circle—sought to reveal in a somewhat self-conscious yet explicitly occult manner.

54. Eisenstein rescued Meyerhold's papers after the theater director's arrest in 1939, obviously jeopardizing his own life in the process.

CHAPTER THIRTEEN
THE OCCULT IN THE PROSE OF VSEVOLOD IVANOV
Valentina Brougher

I
t has become commonplace to associate the name of Vsevolod V. Ivanov (1895–1963) with a cycle of short stories and novellas about the Red partisan movement in Siberia during the Civil War years. Ivanov's *Partizanskie povesti* (Partisan tales, 1921–23) were republished regularly in the former USSR as testimony of the kind of talent the revolution fostered and nourished. The most famous of these tales or novellas, *Bronepoezd 14–69 (Armored Train 14–69, 1922),* which Ivanov also dramatized for the stage in 1927, became a Soviet classic.[1]

Armored Train 14–69 focuses on the heroic actions of a band of peasants-turned-partisans with the seemingly impossible task of capturing a well-armed train under White control. As Soviet critics who hailed its publication noted, the novella offered "a slice of the Civil War in Siberia" as witnessed by the author himself.[2] Ivanov's descriptions of the partisans brought to the reader's imagination strong healthy men who talked little and analyzed their situation even less. They fought and killed for the land to which they were bound—the land they believed the Whites and various "interventionists" to be taking way from them—with a mystical elemental need. Ivanov's depiction of this band of determined men, joined in their struggle by the whole countryside,

I thank the participants in the Fordham conference on the occult for sharing their knowledge with me; my colleague Valery Petrochenkov, for providing helpful information; and the staff at the Summer Language Lab at the University of Illinois at Champaign-Urbana for their professional assistance and good humor.

1. The Russian *povest'* is a genre that lies somewhere between a short story and a novel. It can be called a tale, a long short story, or a novella. I will adhere to "novella."

2. Valentina G. Brougher, "Vsevolod V. Ivanov," in *Encyclopedia of Russian and Soviet History,* ed. Joseph L. Wieczynski (Gulf Breeze, Fla., 1980), 15:80.

reflected the "mass" character of peasant support for the Reds and was colored with the right degree of optimism. This work is often cited in the West as an early exemplar of what would become known as Socialist Realism.

It is therefore intriguing to discover that Ivanov himself took more literary pride in what he described as "a little volume of short stories," *Tainoe tainykh* (Mystery of mysteries, 1927), and "a colorful novel about Siberia" titled *Pokhozhdeniia fakira*, published in English as *The Adventures of a Fakir.*[3] It is these works that he felt would endure the judgment of time and bear testimony to his "long and fascinating life" (*Perepiska*, p. 367).

If we take Ivanov's self-evaluation seriously and consider what these volumes have to offer, a strikingly different image of the author and his work emerges. The writer whose name evoked immediate association with *Armored Train 14–69*, both in his own country and in the West, was strongly attracted to phenomena that belong to the realm of the fantastic, the magical, the supernatural, the mysterious, the mystical—the world of the occult. Ivanov's three-part semi-autobiographical *Adventures of a Fakir* indicates that as a young boy growing up in prerevolutionary Siberia, he became interested in magic, hypnosis, spiritualism, esoteric systems of thought, and Eastern mysticism. In fact, the attraction of the novel's young narrator to all things occult mirrors the interest in occult phenomena and spiritualism that swept through Europe in the second half of the nineteenth century and seized the imagination of Russians with particular force at the beginning of the twentieth century.[4] His *Tainoe tainykh* evidences that even after Ivanov moved to St. Petersburg in 1921 and settled in Moscow in 1924, his interest in the power of suggestion, word magic, and hypnosis continued to shape his perception and artistic imagination.

Tainoe tainykh played an especially significant role in Ivanov's development as a writer. Its publication in 1927 and the critical attacks that immediately showered on Ivanov's head drew attention to him as a writer whose work ten years after the Revolution was out of step ideologically and artistically with his society. Finding his work under close scrutiny, Ivanov began to make a con-

---

3. E. Krasnoschekova, "Kommentarii," in Vsevolod Ivanov, *Sobranie sochinenii v vos'mi tomakh,* 8 vols. (Moscow, 1973–77), 4:708–12. Ivanov's descriptive phrases are from his *Perepiska s A. M. Gor'kim: Iz dnevnikov i zapisnykh knizhek,* T. V. Ivanova and K. G. Paustovskii (Moscow, 1969), p. 367; henceforth cited parenthetically in the text as *Perepiska. Pokhozhdeniia fakira* first appeared in *Novyi mir,* 1934, nos. 4–10, and 1935, nos. 1–6. Pts. 1 and 2 were published separately in 1934, pt. 3 in 1935. Krasnoschekova brings some evidence that Ivanov planned a fourth part. Pts. 1 and 2, in a somewhat edited form, appeared in 1935 in English (translator unnamed) as *The Adventures of a Fakir,* and this volume was reprinted in 1975. *Pokhozhdeniia fakira* was not republished until its inclusion in the eight-volume collected works, cited above.

4. Maria Carlson, "A Historical Survey of Russian Occult Interests," in her *"No Religion Higher than Truth": A History of the Theosophical Movement in Russia, 1875–1922* (Princeton, 1993), pp. 115–37.

scious effort to depict "the new Soviet reality" that had been found missing in this writing.

In the early 1930s, Ivanov was among the writers who traveled to the construction site of the infamous White Sea Canal and produced a collective volume of ideologically proper observations. His participation appears to be an example of the "moral ambiguity" that would mark his relations with the Soviet regime the rest of his life.[5] Several years later, with the publication of *The Adventures of a Fakir* and accusations of giving in to "formalist tendencies"— that is to say, depicting a life without following the Socialist Realist method of the day—Ivanov was put on notice that he needed to become a more responsible and responsive Soviet writer. In 1938 he published *Parkhomenko*, a biographical novel about a famous Civil War leader, in which the history of the Civil War was distorted on behalf of the Stalin cult. In the 1940s and 1950s he was able to produce short stories, novels, and plays that met the ideological and artistic demands of the day, and his *Partizanskie povesti*, particularly *Armored Train 14–69*, continued to be reissued in new editions.[6]

Yet Ivanov never really abandoned his interest in the mysteries of life or the irrational modes of thinking that people can bring to bear in efforts to order their existence. Sadly, most of this writing languished in "the drawer" and among family and government papers, and appeared only after his death, as the political climate changed. Two satirical novels, *Y* and *Kreml'* (The Kremlin), both written in the late 1920s and early 1930s but published in the 1980s, provide strong testimony that he was, as Konstantin Fedin called him, a *"fantast"*— a writer with a powerful imagination, given to treating the fantastic.[7] The rich philosophical texture of *Y* includes a prophetic dream in the tradition of the Bible, suggesting that intuition and feeling, rather than logic and reason, may be the path to truth (*istina*). The dialogical thrust of *Kreml'* centers on life as a continuous struggle between people's physical (often sexual) and spiritual needs, and includes the appearance of a giant dragon as the "voice *outside time*" who passes judgment on the Soviet era.[8] The "fantastic stories" that he

5. Viacheslav Vs. Ivanov, "Pochemu Stalin ubil Gor'kogo?" *Voprosy literatury*, 1993, no. 1, p. 112.

6. This novella was "edited" a number of times to accord with the Socialist Realist requirements of the day. Conforming to them was not an easy task for Ivanov, as is evident in the number of his manuscripts that were published only after his death, in a more liberal political climate.

7. Konstantin Fedin, "Vsevolod," in *Vsevolod Ivanov—Pisatel' i chelovek: Vospominaniia sovremennikov*, comp. T. V. Ivanova, 2d ed., enl. (Moscow, 1975), p. 6; hereafter cited parenthetically in the text as *Pisatel' i chelovek*. See Vsevolod V. Ivanov, *Y* (Lausanne, 1982) and *Y. Roman. Dikie Liudi. Rasskazy* (Moscow, 1988). *Kreml'* was published in 1990 (Moscow); in 1981 a censored version had appeared under the title *Uzhginskii Kreml'*. Ivanov kept returning to *Kreml'* until his death in 1963.

8. David Bethea, *The Shape of the Apocalypse in Modern Russian Fiction* (Princeton, 1989), p. 42. For an analysis of the two novels, see V. G. Brougher, "Vsevolod Ivanov's Satiri-

worked on during World War II but that, with one exception, appeared only posthumously yield additional evidence of his continued interest in various forms and levels of the occult, particularly in world mythology.

The work that is clearly pivotal to an appreciation of Ivanov's broad knowledge of the occult is *The Adventures of a Fakir*, which was published when Ivanov was already both a celebrated and a much-criticized author. The young first-person narrator of the novel, called Vsevolod or Sivolot, is attracted to all things occult and shares many biographical details with Ivanov.

Prerevolutionary Siberia, where the narrator's spiritual development takes place and where Ivanov spent his formative years, is a land where people point with pride and fear at one of their own, the monk Grigory Rasputin, whose spiritual powers have brought him into a special relationship with the tsar's family; and this is the land where people attribute Maxim Gorky's success to his talent for producing "black books"—books on black magic—which always sell well. In fact, acceptance of the occult underlies both the folk and the religious beliefs that figure in the fabric of daily Siberian life. The shaman and magic healing, talismans, clairvoyance, bewitchments, spells, gods, and spirits (*leshie* [wood spirits], *rusalki* [water nymphs]) are as much a part of Siberian life as the angels and saints depicted in the icons that adorn the village church and the izbas of the people. People in Siberia do not question the Devil's existence; they only wonder about the exact shape and nature of his tail. It is this special dual quality of Siberian spiritual life that shapes the hero's earliest memories of family life in *The Adventures of a Fakir*.

Vsevolod's experiences in a village school and in a variety of jobs he finds as errand boy and apprentice to a tradesman are presented as initial but vital steps in his spiritual evolution: they heighten his awareness that life abounds in mysteries, in phenomena that lie outside the realm of common, observable experience. The unusual, almost symbiotic bond that he senses between his aunt Elizaveta and the wild, vicious wolf she keeps is just one of the moments that suggest a level of reality that is not immediately accessible to human reason.

The narrator's need to escape his harsh life, the almost constant hunger, and the boring grayness that in his perception envelops the Siberian landscape also plays an important role in his spiritual evolution. While his father finds solace in contemplating the wisdom of philosophers through the ages and in direct-

---

cal Novel *Y* and the Rooster Metaphor," *Slavic Review* 53 (Spring 1994); and "Myth in Vs. Ivanov's *The Kremlin*," *Canadian Slavonic Papers* 35, nos. 3–4 (1993). Although insightful references to the spiritual world of Ivanov's heroes can be found in E. A. Krasnoschekova, *Khudozhestvennyi mir Vsevoloda Ivanova* (Moscow, 1980), and to some extent in L. Gladkovskaia, *Zhizneliubivyi talant* (Leningrad, 1988), the role of the occult as such is relatively unexplored. Henceforth Krasnoschekova's work is cited parenthetically in the text as *Khudozhestvennyi mir*.

ing his thoughts to a higher, spiritual plane, Vsevolod retreats into the worlds of Miguel de Cervantes, Jules Verne, and Edgar Allan Poe, which stimulate his imagination and help to develop his attraction to the exotic and fantastic, to magic and the occult.

His fondness for picaresque adventure novels and his search for escape are the genesis of Vsevolod's dream of visiting India, which, in the course of the novel, he attempts twice to reach with several like-minded friends. India, in fact, serves as a kind of leitmotif throughout the novel. As Krasnoschekova (*Khudozhestvennyi mir*, pp. 195–234) rightly points out, India is the distant exotic land to which the adventures of Sivolot's book heroes take them; and India is for him the land steeped in mystery and the source of mysteries, famous for its fakirs and yogis.

It is also clear that Vsevolod's Romantic reading helps to fill the void left by his rejection of organized religion as a source of spiritual nourishment. He mocks its claims of serving as the intermediary between man and God, describing the rituals of the Orthodox Church as reliance on an "external eye" (*vneshnii glaz*) when an "inner eye" (*vnutrennii glaz*) is needed for communion with the divine.[9] His work as an errand boy for some priests makes him passionately anticlerical. Vsevolod's disenchantment with formal religion and his rejection of its role in his spiritual life parallel the negative attitude toward institutional Christianity that fostered spiritism and occultism in Europe less than a century earlier and cannot be attributed solely to Soviet antireligious policy.[10]

Vsevolod's interest in the occult and magic also reflects a vital aspect of Siberian society. Displays of seemingly superhuman physical or psychic powers abound at the outdoor markets, fairs, and circuses that form the center of Siberian town life. The average Siberian does not seem to be able to pass up this form of entertainment, whether out of a need to escape the grayness of Siberian life or to satisfy some deep-seated interest in the mysterious and otherworldly. For a Siberian boy to dream of becoming a world-famous fakir, then, the focus of public attention, is psychologically understandable and, in a sense, in the natural order of things. Moreover, a profusion of books and journals are available at outdoor markets and fairs, dealing with a whole variety of subjects from the world of the occult—black and white magic, psychic phenomena, chiromancy, mental telepathy, tarot cards, graphology and astrology, and various "systems of thought." Vsevolod reports purchasing such books as "Papus's *Practical Magic* (black and white) in three volumes; Paul Sedir's *Magic Plants* including occult botany, hermetic medicine . . . *The Psy-*

---

9. Vsevolod Ivanov, *Pokhozhdeniia fakira*, in *Sobranie sochinenii*, 4:347. Translations of quotations from pt. 3 are my own.

10. Janet Oppenheim, *The Other World: Spiritualism and Psychical Research in England, 1850–1914* (Cambridge, 1985).

chology of Suggestion published by B. Sidiss . . . *Phrenology, Astrology, Chiromancy and Spiritism* by . . . [Synge]; [and] *Magnetism and Hypnotism* by Dr. Okhorovich."[11]

It does not escape the reader's notice that Vsevolod's dream of becoming a famous fakir becomes bound up with his "vanity" (*tshcheslavie*). For a boy who early in life derived immense satisfaction from exploiting his relatives' belief in ghosts and apparitions, standing before people as a fakir is an empowering thought. Fakirism will allow him to become "master of his own fate," to exercise control over others while elevating himself above the crowd (*Khudozhestvennyi mir*, pp. 206–10). His motivation suggests the emphasis Theosophists and followers of Eastern mysticism placed on the role of the will in the individual's path to self-perfection. That Vsevolod does in fact study the occult art of the yogis and is drawn to Buddhist teachings is evident from the titles of some of the books he acquires in Russian translation at outdoor markets: *The Indian Yogis and the Science of Breathing* and *Religion and the Secret Teachings of the Orient*, both by Yogi Ramacharaka, and *How to Become a Yogi*, by Soumi Abendananda. "The advertisements that filled the magazines and papers of our youth and reminded us that there was a 'hidden force within us' and that the best thing to do was to 'train your will-power!' " also lead him to purchase such books as the *Complete Guide to the Training of Will Power* (*Adventures*, p. 125). One bit of advice he follows, to stare at a single point intently, mirrors the advice given in a volume found in Ivanov's personal library.[12] This is not to say that Vsevolod's emphasis on will power and self-perfection owes nothing to Nietzsche. As Bernice Rosenthal has pointed out, even after 1912, when "Nietzsche's influence becomes more difficult to trace . . . his ideas were in the air and continued to influence Russian and even Soviet culture." The extraordinary Napoleonic rooster in *Y*, Ivanov's metaphor for Stalin, who has usurped Lenin's persona for his cult of personality and who wills his own transformation before the masses, hypnotizing them into reverential awe, is fundamentally Nietzschean. Maxim Gorky, Ivanov's early supporter and friend, "privately . . . read, discussed, and praised Nietzsche."[13]

It is noteworthy that descriptions of Vsevolod's first attempts to earn his living by offering the public the kind of entertainment it has come to expect—

11. Vsevolod Ivanov, *The Adventures of a Fakir* (Westport, Conn., 1975), p. 242; henceforth cited as *Adventures*.

12. Viktor Turnbull, *Lektsii o lichnom magnetizme: Somoobladanie i razvitie kharaktera* (St. Petersburg, 1906), pp. 29–30. Krasnoschekova (*Khudozhestvennyi mir*, p. 207) states in a footnote that such books as Papus's *Prakticheskaia magiia: Chernaia i belaia*, trans. A. V. Troianovskii (St. Petersburg, 1912), (Practical magic: Black and white), as well as books on psychology, Indian philosophy, and the teachings of the yoga masters, were to be found in Ivanov's personal library.

13. Bernice Glatzer Rosenthal, Introduction to *Nietzsche in Russia*, ed. Rosenthal (Princeton, 1986), pp. 3, 25. For Gorky's debt to Nietzsche, see Mary Louise Loe, "Gorky and Nietzsche: The Quest for a Russian Superman," ibid.

"swallowing" a sword and piercing his flesh with hatpins—call into question the belief in people's ability to overcome their physical limitations. The "mystery" of sword swallowing quickly becomes one mystery less, for it is a matter of specially designed receding blades, sleight-of-hand, and psychological manipulation of the audience through the power of suggestion. However, his two attempts to perform one of the classic feats of a fakir, to pierce his flesh with pins, do not lead to such quick debunking. Although his flesh bleeds and he feels great pain, he is able, by redirecting his thoughts elsewhere, to pierce his flesh several times through sheer force of will. The question of a practiced fakir's ability to transcend more fully his physical senses and use his spiritual resources is left ambiguous and unresolved.

Vsevolod's conviction that he can become a fakir by training his will leads him to the watershed experience of his life, his "Silvery Enchantment" period ("silvery" [*serebrianyi*] as a reference to the silvery-leaved trees that surround the clearing he uses for his exercises, as well as to the ever-mysterious silvery moon), which serves as the climax of Part II.[14]

Taking to heart the advice found in so many books of the day, that the path to control of one's life is through meditation and sheer concentration of will, Vsevolod decides to turn to Indian mysticism and lead the ascetic life of a yoga. The months he spends sitting in the lotus position, from dusk to dawn, contemplating nature (through a series of breathing as well as mental exercises), convinces him that he has achieved new heights of perception and wisdom. He now can penetrate the secrets of animals and plants; he can "actually hear the grass growing" and sense "the individual soundless voices" of both plants and animals.[15] His new perceptions reflect the Buddhist belief that the acquisition of wisdom or intuitive insight includes the attainment of supranormal faculties, such as "divine ears."[16] Since he sits "by the mysterious light of the moon," there is also the suggestion that the moon—credited since antiquity with influencing human lives, especially emotions[17]—may be responsible in part for his special state of consciousness. But the result of this "Silvery Enchantment" phase of his life is that several old beggar women fall at his feet, calling him a saint. He realizes that his attempt at total denial of his physical body has only brought him full circle to the world he had been so

14. The reader who relies on the English translation may not realize that it represents only two-thirds of Ivanov's novel and may come away with the false impression that the "Silvery Enchantment" phase of Vsevolod's life has largely "cured" the young narrator of his interest in the occult.

15. Krasnoschekova writes only that "the animate nature [*odushevlennost'*] of nature is achieved by the author-narrator's penetration into its 'secret life'": *Khudozhestvennyi mir*, p. 265.

16. Kenneth K. S. Ch'en, *Buddhism: The Light of Asia* (New York, 1968), p. 52.

17. Leonard Zusne and Warren H. Jones, *Anomalistic Psychology: A Study of Magical Thinking* (Hillsdale, N.J., 1989), p. 205.

quick to scoff at: the world of beggars, saintly old women, ascetics, and hermits, the world of his grandmother Fekla.

Vsevolod's experience, however, does not lead him to dismiss entirely the possibility of the existence of the occult—of magical, invisible forces operating in our lives. After plunging with wild abandon into satisfying his craving for meat (he had lived as a vegetarian) and for a bath, he also sates his elemental need for sex with his attractive landlady. It is when he is with her that he notices a special "bright light" (*iarkii svet*) in the room, which "for the life of . . . [him he] can't understand" (*Adventures*, p. 294) as he looks back on the experience.

The "bright light" could be attributed to the subconscious influence of Vsevolod's early religious experience in the Russian Orthodox faith (associating the positive and the spiritual with the halos and brightness of saints in icons) or to his readings in the occult. But the image more likely reflects the claim of Theosophists and other occultists that every human being is surrounded by an aura;[18] the union of two bodies at night in a small dark room would project the light of two auras, resulting in special brightness. Or the "bright light" might have its subconscious source in various theories of animal magnetism, in the belief that all animate and inanimate objects radiate a magnetic fluid that appears luminous to persons of special sensitivity.[19] Whatever explanations readers may be tempted to offer, it is significant that the narrator assigns no explanation to the "special brightness" and leaves it in the realm of mysterious phenomena.

An examination of the key moments and elements in Vsevolod's evolution would be incomplete without attention to the "scientific" dimension of his study of the occult, which, not unexpectedly, mirrors the scientific inquiry that interest in things occult generated in Europe.[20] This aspect of his investigations manifests itself almost as soon as he starts buying books and such journals as *Rebus,* dealing with spiritualist phenomena, and it plays an increasingly important role as the novel progresses. At first he becomes absorbed in finding the *Vol'shebnaia biblioteka* (The magic library), which he had heard contained all the secrets known to magicians, fakirs, and conjurers through the centuries. This is probably a reference to the earliest extant Russian magic books (*vol'-shebnye knigi*), dating from the sixteenth century. These books, Maria Carlson tells us, tapped older texts "translated from European, Byzantine, Arab and Persian sources," and "were copied and recopied by generations of Russian readers over the centuries, with new texts added from time to time."[21] When Vsevolod is not able to find this "library," he begins to compile his own, writ-

18. Ibid., p. 81.

19. Doris V. Falk, "Poe and the Power of Animal Magnetism," *PMLA* 84 (May 1969): 541.

20. See Oppenheim's *Other world.*

21. Carlson, *"No Religion Higher than Truth,"* pp. 15–16.

ing down detailed explanations of feats of magic practiced by mediums at séances, professional conjurers, and fakirs, and including drawings for staging various illusions of his own invention. His notes reveal that what people accept as occult forces at work are often nothing more than cleverly devised tricks relying on mirrors, hidden strings, cooperative cohorts, illusion, collective hypnotism, and the like. Moreover, his descriptions in Part III of the novel are often cynical and ironic in tone. He mocks the mediums and graphologists who work in the restaurants that function also as houses of prostitution; and his comments on his own experiments in mental telepathy are sarcastic. However, as he looks for the descendants of the Decembrists, who he feels possess special "secrets" (a veiled reference to Freemasonry), the door is never entirely shut on the desire to penetrate the worlds he suspects lie hidden from him.

As Part III comes to a close, Vsevolod has not abandoned his dream of reaching India, his "native land" (*rodnaia zemlia*). Neither has he discarded his Romantic imagination,[22] or his attraction to the world of the fantastic and the unknown. He still seeks escape from his daily life, working as an entertainer and writer of comic verses in one of the many houses of prostitution; his escape takes the form of writing outlines for science fiction novels. No stranger to the works of H. G. Wells, Vsevolod looks to fantastic scientific advances to change human life radically, and the unhappy endings to his works echo the negative dimension of Wells's scientific romances.[23] The thematics of these proposed novels—for example, a professor discovering the food secret (left unspecified) behind an ant's strength—suggest not only Wells as an inspiration but also Nikolai Fedorov, whose philosophy of "the common task" envisioned human beings as "regulating" nature.[24] There is a strong possibility that it is in reaction to Fedorov's philosophy, with its emphasis on the Pamir mountain range, that Vsevolod records that it is in Siberia, "at the edge of the world, in the freezing and glistening snows, that the dream of struggling with nature or with people who hinder man from conquering nature is preserved intact."[25] Ivanov's close acquaintance with Fedorov's ideas is borne out by his son, Viacheslav (*Pisatel' i chelovek*, p. 349).

It may strike the reader as curious that *The Adventures of a Fakir* was published in 1934–35, when Socialist Realism was the official artistic method and when literature was expected to model human behavior on utilitarian rationalism. What may have made it acceptable is its setting in prerevolutionary Siberia, at a time before "enlightened" thinking began to "reshape and transform" society. The protagonist's rejection of organized religion and his growing attraction to scientific inquiry as well as to utopian thinking may have given the

---

22. Gladkovskaia (*Zhizneliubivyi talant*, p. 189) apparently concludes otherwise.
23. I am grateful to Christine Rydel for sharing her research on Wells with me.
24. See George M. Young Jr., *Nikolai F. Fedorov: An Introduction* (Belmont, Mass., 1979).
25. Ivanov, *Pokhozhdeniia fakira*, pp. 659–60.

novel further legitimacy. Moreover, Gorky's enthusiastic reaction to the colorful cast of characters in Part I placed the work, at least initially, in a positive light. But Part II and especially Part III were severely criticized for their style, their length, their anecdotal character, and their reliance on "fantasy" as opposed to "real" life. Discouraged by the critical reaction, Ivanov abandoned his plans to continue *The Adventures of a Fakir.*

The thematics and psychological dynamics in *Vozvrashchenie Buddy* (The return of the Buddha, 1923) and *Tainoe tainykh* (Mystery of mysteries) reveal a preoccupation with many facets of the occult that fascinate the young narrator of *The Adventures of a Fakir:* hypnotic suggestion, mysticism, magic, and invisible forces operating in human life.

In *Vozvrashchenie Buddy* the interest in Buddhism that Ivanov's hero exhibits in *The Adventures of a Fakir* is explored through the experiences of one Professor Safonov, a scholar of world literature, who travels through Siberia during the Civil War and the ensuing famine. He is assigned to accompany a gold statue of the Buddha to Mongolia, to make sure it arrives safely. For this well-established scholar, cooking and eating his daily ration of potatoes has taken on the form of a carefully executed religious ritual. His preoccupation with food and his burning (for warmth) books that represent his cultural heritage mark a regressive shift of his life: transcendence not of the spiritual over the physical but of the physical over the spiritual.[26] At the same time, it is Professor Safonov's physical journey through Siberia that leads him to reclaim the spiritual dimension. That reclamation involves the mystical and the fantastic as well as the power of suggestion and the role of coincidence, although the order and force of each is ambiguous.

The mystical element is present in the history of the gold statue of the Buddha. It is also present in the claims of Dava-Dorchzhi, in charge of both the statue and the professor, that he is a *gygen,* "the head of a lamaistic monastic order, the incarnation of the Buddha or one of the Buddhist saints," as Ivanov's note explains.[27] "The incomprehensible call" (*neponiatnyi zov'*) Dava-Dorchzhi heeds in taking upon himself the mission of returning the statue reinforces the mystical dimension, at least in the professor's eyes. But the suggestion that Dava-Dorchzhi hopes to reclaim cattle taken away from him undercuts this dimension, and leaves unclear the extent to which "steppe truths" guide his actions.

In addition, an element of mysticism (or is it coincidence?) is woven into the condition of the statue and the man entrusted with it. Dava-Dorchzhi is seized

26. Ivanov's work brings to mind Evgenii Zamiatin's short story "Peshchera" (The cave, 1922) and Viktor Shklovsky's evocation of the Civil War famine in his "Peterburg v blokade." For the latter, see *Khod konia: Kniga statei* (Moscow and Berlin, 1923), pp. 18–35.

27. Vsevolod Ivanov, *Vozvrashchenie Buddy* (Berlin, 1923), p. 33. Translations are my own.

with typhus after the statue has been taken out of its protective packing and after some gold has been scraped off its body. His physical deterioration seems to parallel the statue's, perhaps suggesting their interconnection, although the possibility of mere coincidence is also left open.

The mystical (or perhaps the power of suggestion) also plays a role in what Dava-Dorchzhi tells the professor as he entrusts him with the mission: " . . . the spirit of the Buddha is passing to you alone . . . you alone are now the embodiment of the *gygen*."[28] From this point on, the professor finds himself growing indifferent to his physical needs, and ensuring the return of the Buddha becomes the pivotal goal in his life. His concern about feeding himself becomes redirected at feeding the sick Dava Dorchzhi, who now is totally preoccupied by his own physical needs.

The architectonics of the work reveal Ivanov to be a masterful craftsman of equivocation. The professor's spiritual transformation can be read as the Buddhist law of moral causality in operation; by denying his "physical cravings and desires," destroying his "false views" and his "ignorance" (he now appreciates the spiritual significance of the statue), the professor achieves a special state of enlightenment.[29] His deeds of compassion, evident in the care he gives to Dava-Dorchzhi and in the total commitment he feels to the Buddha mission, have allowed him to accumulate merit, one of the universal precepts of Buddhism.[30] At the same time, Professor Safonov's spiritual transformation could be attributed to the power of suggestion ("You are now the *gygen*") or as a matter of something more "rational" as well—his interest in "a civilized European gesture"; that is, delivering the statue to its rightful place, and even reaping some recognition and reward.

Professor Safonov's physical life comes to an end in the desert sands at the hands of a Tatar who wrongly suspects that the statue contains jewels. The spiritual dynamics in the work can be interpreted to suggest that it is not important that the professor fails to complete his mission. His very intention and desire to return the statue reclaim for him the "spiritual ecstasy" that the "revolutionary ecstasy" had blotted out, revealing, according to Buddhist teaching, his true being, which "is deep and enduring, and beyond the world of space and time."[31]

Given the emphasis the work places on the role of the supernatural and the mystical in human life, as well as the ironic, satirical light that illuminates the Civil War reality, *Vozvrashchenie Buddy* stands apart from his *Armored Train 14–*

---

28. Ibid., pp. 64–65.

29. Che'n, *Buddhism*, p. 54.

30. "Merit: Buddhist Concepts," in *Encyclopedia of Religion*, ed. Mircea Eliade (New York, 1987), 9:383–85.

31. Che'n, *Buddhism*, p. 58.

69 and from proto–Socialist Realism novels such as Aleksandr Serafimovich's *Zheleznyi potok* (The iron stream, 1924). It raises questions about hypnosis and different levels of reality or "truth," as Iury Olesha's novel *Zavist'* (*Envy*, 1927) does. But unlike Olesha's work, Ivanov's *Vozvrashchenie Buddy* did not arouse controversy at either its appearance in 1923 or even its reissue in 1927 and 1928.[32] It may be that Ivanov's interpretation of reality, shaped in great part by Buddhist philosophy, served to support Soviet efforts to court non-Orthodox nationalities in Mongolia, Tibet, and Central Asia.[33] As John Snelling points out, in the years 1920–24 some intellectuals attempted "to engineer a reconciliation between Buddhism and Bolshevism," and Agvan Dorzhiev, who had served as the Dalai Lama's emissary to the tsar and continued his work after the Bolshevik Revolution, "argued that the 'Buddhist doctrine [was] largely compatible with current communist tradition.'" Snelling also points out that in "the years up to 1929 . . . Buddhism . . . enjoyed a special status among the religions of the Soviet Union." The First All-Russian Buddhist Congress was held in Moscow in January 1927, and the Buddhist temple in Leningrad remained "relatively active during the late 1920s."[34]

Ivanov was a great collector of Buddha statues all his life, and in his study "the air was saturated with the smell of grasses and secrets of the East" (Khodasevich, *Pisatel' i chelovek*, p. 218). He enjoyed visiting Buddhist temples, and his wife, Tamara Ivanova, reports (*Moi sovremenniki*, p. 210) that he even observed the proper etiquette when handed a statue of the Buddha. His son, Viacheslav Ivanov, has written that his "father read and thought especially much about the East. Eastern things, piled up in an unusual fashion all over his study, were not just decoration but the continuation of his thoughts and images. . . . His library contained everything on Buddhism that had been printed in Russian" (*Pisatel' i chelovek*, pp. 347–48).

Ivanov viewed *Vozvrashchenie Buddy* as marking a turning point in his writing (*Perepiska*, p. 411), leading to *Tainoe tainykh*. Certainly the authorial consciousness exploring and questioning the power of invisible forces operating in human life in the former work is also present in "the slim volume" of stories.[35] It is not a mere coincidence that Ivanov's title echoes the title of one of the Old Russian magic books, *Tainaia tainykh*, reissued in St. Petersburg in 1908, to which the narrator of *The Adventures of a Fakir* may have been referring as he searched for the "magic library." Thus *Tainoe tainykh* represents Ivanov's own alchemical manuscript. Instead of "the magical and medical properties of pre-

---

32. First published in 1923 in Berlin, it was reissued in 1927 and 1928 in Moscow. It was not reprinted until the *Sobranie sochinenii* in the 1970s, in a censored version shorn of some of the mystical language. The restored version became available in 1991.

33. Ivanov took Vladimir Soloviev to task for ignoring Buddhism in his views on goodness. See Tamara Ivanova, *Moi sovremenniki, kakimi ia ikh znala* (Moscow, 1984), p. 156.

34. John Snelling, *Buddhism in Russia* (Rockport, Mass., 1993), pp. 205, 234, 225.

35. The volume includes two legends, seven short stories, and one novella.

cious stones" or the "divinatory practices of physiognomy,"[36] however, these short stories provide a creative writer's description of the "alchemical" composition of the peasant soul and of the secrets hidden within. Since the power of suggestion and somnambulistic behavior play important roles in most of them, it is likely that Ivanov's exploration of the relationship between folk beliefs and somnambulistic behavior was partly inspired by the mesmeric themes in Edgar Allan Poe's short stories, for Ivanov read Poe voraciously in his youth. There is no question that to some extent Ivanov found in Poe a kindred spirit.[37]

The influence of Freud, Darwin, and particularly Henri Bergson, whose works Ivanov kept rereading (*Pisatel' i chelovek*, p. 343), can be felt in the questions about reflex, instinct, intuition, knowledge, and consciousness that the stories in *Tainoe tainykh* raise. Critics have pointed out that these stories represent a "delicate weaving together of closely associated experiences," at the basis of which lie peasants' bond with the land and their biological needs as sexual beings—the "dark forces" that hold them in their grip.[38] But critics have not explored the folk beliefs and superstitions that form a vital part of the texture of some of these stories, and that for Ivanov constitute essential properties of the peasant consciousness. These stories are relatively unknown even to Russians and are not available in English translation.

"Plodorodie" (Fertility) is a psychological portrait of a peasant whose life ends violently. Martyn's image among his fellow villagers is drawn with traditional folk references to the occult. Because he spends his days roaming through the woods and hills, the villagers, as well as his wife, call him a wood goblin (*leshii*); after he claims to know the source of the mountain stream that is flooding the village, they label him a sorcerer (*koldun*) as well. They fear that his talk of diverting the floodwaters is a veiled attempt to turn the forces of nature against them by using sorcery. The reader, however, who has been allowed to share Martyn's inner world, understands that no sorcery is involved, only Martyn's desire for the respect and power he has never enjoyed in his village.

Ivanov's portrayal of the villagers' belief in the magical properties of grasses and in the existence of invisible forces in nature, benevolent as well as malevolent, not only gives the story a folkloric coloring but conveys fundamental

36. W. F. Ryan, "Alchemy, Magic, Poisons, and the Virtues of Stones in the Old Russian *Secretum Secretorum*," *Ambix* 37, pt. 1 (March 1990): 46–47.

37. See Falk, "Poe and the Power of Animal Magnetism," and Sidney E. Lind, "Poe and Mesmerism," *PMLA* 62 (December 1947): 1077–94.

38. Zh. El'sberg, "Tvorchestvo Vsevoloda Ivanova," *Krizis poputchikov i nastroenie intelligentsii* (Moscow, 1930), p. 160. For interpretations of *Tainoe tainykh*, see Krasnoschekova, *Khudozhestvennyi mir*, pp. 133–48; Gladkovskaia, *Zhizneliubivyi talant*, pp. 95–103; and the short bibliography found in V. G. Brougher, "The Question of Motivation in Vs. Ivanov's *Tainoe tainykh*," *Canadian Slavonic Papers* 19, no. 3 (September 1977): 352–53.

village psychology. Martyn's friend Turukai encourages him to look for *razryv-trava*, a grass that will magically bring him "treasure, any woman he wants, and [the capacity to inflict] illnesses."[39] What Turukai does not say very clearly is that in village lore this grass was considered so rare that "only people initiated into the mysteries of black magic could find it." It had the power "to cut and render into tiny pieces iron, steel, gold, silver, and copper," and according to folk legend was an effective weapon even against the "unclean spirit" or devil that protected treasures left by robbers.[40] Although Martyn dismisses Turukai's story, he wishes there were such a grass: the reader suspects he would use it to seduce Elena, whose body has him already bewitched.

While Martyn seems to have several motives for his rape of Elena, the magical nature of St. John's (Ivan Kupala) Eve may also play a role in it. On this June night young girls "gather twelve different grasses and put them under their pillows, telling their fortunes by them" (*Tainoe tainykh*, p. 58). They go out carrying handfuls of "magic" grasses, which the informed reader knows serve to enchant the other sex as well as to protect against witches on "the most dangerous night of the year" (*Russkii narod*, p. 240). Martyn himself does not follow any rituals to protect himself from the invisible forces present everywhere. But it is on this night that he spies Elena lying on the bed in her hut and admires her full body. Elena's sexuality, the rituals people observe on St. John's Eve, and the state of nature at harvesttime combine to make him acutely aware of the sense of fertility that envelops the world on this night, underlining for the reader the pagan origin of this holiday as a time to honor "Kupalo . . . the god of earthly fruits" (*Russkii narod*, 67). Martyn's intense sexual frustration and need never leave him, and combined with other factors of a social and personal nature, they impel him weeks later to rape Elena.

Folk beliefs, hypnosis, and the power of suggestion also play key roles in "Noch'" (Night), a story about a village fellow who, under various conscious and subconscious pressures, kills an old woman. The story is initially structured on Ivanov's interpretation of the common folk belief that eyes serve as the medium for the supernatural forces that lie hidden within certain individuals, to be released at will. Glafira's father boasts that his daughter's eyes are like a well, and that they remind him of his own eyes, which have "enchanted many a woman" (*Tainoe tainykh*, p. 26). The omniscient narrator confirms that Glafira's eyes are truly like "the deadly barrel of a gun" and that she does not dare raise them at the groom before and during the wedding ceremony. The bride's father brings the pair to their wedding bed, "tirelessly winking with his

---

39. Vsevolod Ivanov, "Plodorodie," in his *Tainoe tainykh* (Moscow and Leningrad, 1927), p. 64. All translations from this volume are my own. Henceforth stories from this volume are cited parenthetically in the text by page number in *Tainoe tainykh*.

40. M. Zabylin, *Russkii narod: Ego obychai, obriady, predaniia, sueveriia i poeziia* (1880; Moscow, 1990), p. 432; henceforth cited parenthetically in the text as *Russkii narod*.

large and close-set eyes" (p. 26). When Filipp dies that same night, the suggestion that the father and daughter have used their eyes to bewitch and destroy him is very strong. His death may be a case of the "spoiling" (*porcha*) to which, according to peasant beliefs, weddings were highly susceptible.[41]

The rest of "Noch'" focuses on the overwhelming power—and here Ivanov may be drawing on Theosophy—that a thought or suggestion, once released, can have on the course of a village fellow's life. Afonka is being forced to enter into a quick marriage with his brother's widow for the sake of the dowry, a heavy blow to his already low self-esteem. As one of Ivanov's somnambulistic characters, however, Afonka cannot verbalize his feelings; they remain locked deep within him. Instead, his perception of a particular moment in life serves as a moment of personal "truth," and that "truth" gives birth to a self-suggestion that then directs the rest of his life.

As his brother's coffin is being brought into the hut, Afonka notices Glafira standing in the entranceway, "passing her hand over her eyes and mouth as if she were locking within her for the rest of her life the joy she had experienced that one night" (*Tainoe tainykh*, p. 28). This gesture, perhaps not unintentionally, mimics the kind of sweeping hand motion that might be expected of a nineteenth-century mesmerist or a twentieth-century hypnotist. Glafira's hand motion and Afonka's immediate perception that there is nothing left for him, that he would be "better off dead," become inextricably bound. From that moment on, he moves through life as if hypnotized, lacking any will of his own. His life becomes a series of actions and reactions that become increasingly more dark and self-destructive, culminating in his killing of an old beggar woman.

The power of spells and word magic as key ingredients in a peasant's perception of the world receives a sustained artistic treatment in "Zhizn' Smokotinina" (The life of Smokotinin). Shy, awkward Timofei, who is clearly "bedazzled" by a young widow, Katerina, one day forces her to drop a piece of kindling that she has picked up at his work site. He never consciously realizes it, but his life become bound with that piece of kindling, and is ultimately destroyed by it.

When Timofei's feelings of shame and guilt before Katerina settle at some lower level of consciousness and reveal themselves in his "melancholy" (*toska*), and in his inability to enjoy food or sleep, he follows village tradition and turns to "a woman practicing sorcery," a magic healer. She sprinkles water on him and gives him some water to drink as well. Her actions suggest the ritualistic treatment of someone thought to suffer from "the evil eye" (*durnoi glaz*), which in Russian tradition was thought to be at the root of all illnesses.[42]

41. Linda J. Ivanits, *Russian Folk Belief* (New York, 1989), pp. 103–6.

42. I. P. Sakharov, *Skazaniia russkogo naroda* (1885; Moscow, 1989), p. 104. See also Zabylin, *Russkii narod*, pp. 260–61.

That Timofei, too, believes he is under a spell is initially suggested by his reference to his illness as one that he "has been given."

One day, when he finds himself sitting in a tavern, listening to the drunken boasting of a fellow villager, Timofei offers the following "confession": "And I was the ruin . . . of one widow. Just didn't want to get married, and she says to me, 'May he after whom I sigh, into a piece of kindling wood dry'" (*na kom etot vzdokh, tot by v shchepku izsokh* [sic]) (*Tainoe tainykh*, p. 8). That Timofei has cast the words he attributes to Katerina in the form of a spell, thereby confirming his belief that he is bewitched, is clear from the rhythmic nature of the lines, the use of rhyme, and particularly the "drying" imagery he employs, common to Russian love spells. Such spells included the wish that the object of the spell find her- or himself "unable to live, or be, or drink, or eat, or even a word speak," that both dryness (*sukhota*) and melancholy (*toska*) envelop the object's whole being. Some spells also included the formulaic sentence "There's a hut in an open field, boards lie from corner to corner in the hut, and melancholy lies on the boards" (Zabylin, *Russkii narod*, pp. 308, 315). Ivanov has taken the basic ingredients of a love spell—melancholy, drying imagery, and wood—and worked them into the aesthetic and psychological dimensions of his story.

The spell that Timofei attributes to Katerina, but that is in fact shaped and vitalized in his subconscious, brings out his destructive impulses and ultimately leads to his death for attempted horse theft. When Katerina comes to pay her last respects, she kisses Timofei's forehead and utters "*Polno*" (enough), the same word she had uttered when she dropped the kindling. "And now no one would have prevented her from taking any kindling," reads the concluding sentence. The ending leaves open the question whether a spell had been cast against Timofei or whether his own guilt and weakness generated and empowered it. *Polno* can be read as the magic word that removes the spell or as Katerina's comment on his whole misguided life.

After the publication of *Tainoe tainykh*, Ivanov, celebrated as the author of *Armored Train 14–69* just five years earlier, became a center of controversy and polemical attacks. Although the more liberal critics found the psychological dimension to his stories praiseworthy, the critics of the Russian Association of Proletarian Writers (RAPP) and the journal *Na literaturnom postu* (On literary guard) charged that Ivanov was so taken with the theories of Bergson and Freud and so lost in the "dark" Russian village of the past that he was blind to the new society emerging under Soviet rule. Ivanov was genuinely surprised at the negative labels being applied to his writing. Perhaps out of naiveté or misplaced confidence, he had not heeded Viktor Shklovsky's warning about the outcry his *Tainoe tainykh* would produce.[43] When some of the same stories had first appeared, scattered through various journals, his artistic and philo-

43. Vsevolod Ivanov, *Sovetskie pisateli: Avtobiografii v dvukh tomakh*, ed. B. Ia. Brainina and E. F. Nikitina (Moscow, 1959), 1:443.

sophical inclinations were less manifest. But Ivanov may have lost sight of the obvious: concentrated together in one volume, whose very title seemed to challenge the emphasis on the practical and rational in Soviet society, they drew attention to his preoccupation with the irrational, the intuitive, and the elemental at the very time when writers were being enjoined to depict the emergence of the New Soviet Man. It is not surprising, therefore, that after the publication of *Tainoe tainykh* as well as such stories as "Osobniak" (The mansion, 1928), Ivanov's name began to appear alongside that of Boris Pilnyak in the campaign mounted in 1929 against "anti-Soviet" writers. Ironically, Ivanov viewed himself as a Soviet writer, although there was real tension between his desire to be "responsive to the times" (*sozvuchnyi epokhe*) and yet remain true to his beliefs.[44]

That Ivanov continued to be intrigued by the possibility of other worlds, of the fantastic and the supernatural is evident in the philosophical underpinnings of his two novels *Y* and *Kreml'*. Further testimony can be gleaned from his personal life as well as the themes and images he chose for the "fantastic" cycle of short stories he drafted in the 1940s and 1950s.

Anton Ivanov, Ivanov's grandson, speaks of his grandfather as a man "drawn to converting the familiar, devoid of mystery, into the incomprehensible and the mysterious." Even when Anton was old enough to "recognize clearly the unreality of the existence of witches and wizards," his grandfather was still able to make him see "mystically monstrous things." Once he accepted his grandfather's challenge to visit a cemetery at night and look for ghosts. When he reported noticing "a green flickering" above a grave, his grandfather was delighted, for he had read in a book about "the possibility of a person's silhouette appearing in phosphoric outline above a grave" (*Pisatel' i chelovek*, pp. 234, 235, 229).

Y and *Kreml'* can be read as reflections of Ivanov's private rather than public persona and provide vital clues to his perception of the world. Both novels help to explain why Ivanov's depiction of peasant mentality gravitated toward a superstitious cast of mind, with none of the "enlightenment" and rationalism popularized by contemporary rhetoric. In neither novel does Ivanov reject the idea of communism; but he does mock and polemicize with those who envision the future as populated by people almost instantly cleansed of all irrational beliefs and impulses and leading lives structured on logic and reason. For Ivanov, such thinking not only contradicts basic human nature but also leads to an impoverished, hollow "happiness."

Set against the backdrop of the first five-year plan and the destruction of the huge Cathedral of Christ the Saviour, *Y* depicts people's practical concerns about daily life as well as addresses the broader, more philosophical implica-

44. Ivanova, *Moi sovremenniki*, p. 77.

tions of life in a time of fantastically rapid change on all fronts. In counterpoint
to the "Ooh" of delight and wonder on the part of the rationalists and the
utilitarians of his age who tout various strategies for quickly reshaping the
individual and the society, there resounds Ivanov's "Ooh" of fear and despair
at the simplifications and naiveté that underlie those strategies. Irony and
satire illuminate the enormous gulf between reality and utopian objectives in
the areas of communal living, human psychology and the work ethic, and the
spiritual and the practical. In *Y,* the behavior of one of the three main characters, Egor Egorych, at times mimics Dostoevsky's "underground man" as ca-
price and the desire to do something clearly not in his self-interest rule his
actions. Dr. Andreshein, a man of vast learning who enjoys using his mind and
reason, often derives great joy from behaving irrationally, whether engaging in
bloody fistfights or following his animal instincts (as when he is irresistibly
drawn to the smell of Suzanna's sweaty underarms).

Kreml', structured on a struggle between the values of a sect of Old Believers
and of workers at a textile mill, satirizes the simplifications and paradoxes that
abound in an age that emphasizes human reason and touts only the rational.
Vavilov, the Communist worker whose ambition to convert an empty church
into a worker's club is a matter of practicality and logic, is nevertheless unable
to control his irrational fear of machines and blood. And the giant dragon,
Magnat-Khai, with whom Izmail, an old revolutionary, engages in dialogue,
can be understood as Ivanov's insistence that life is a synthesis of the logical
and the illogical, the conscious and the subconscious, the rational and the
irrational. As Magnat-Khai's contemporary tastes illustrate (he likes beer, *vobla*
[dried roach fish], frankfurters, the circus, and musical reviews), life cleansed
of complexity and mystery is life reduced to the banal and the mundane and
ultimately is not worth living.

In one of Ivanov's introductions to his "fantastic stories" (*Perepiska,* 288–94)
he argued the reality of the world described in his tales. He presented as
evidence the details of his own extraordinary experience one day in the Cri-
mea, in Koktebel, when he was observing dolphins. A rock caught his attention, and when it started to move, he assumed it was a mass of seaweed. With
the dolphins still in full sight, he watched with incredulity the round mass
changing to an elongated form some 25 to 30 meters long, the body as "thick as
the top of a writing desk." The "monster" (*chudovishche*) gave chase to the
dolphins, reverted back into a ball, uncoiled again, stuck out its large snakelike
head, and disappeared among the cliffs. Ivanov adds that a local woman who
knew all the local legends told him that in 1921 the newspaper reported sightings of a "huge snake," and that in fact the poet M. Voloshin sent a clipping
about the "snake" to Mikhail Bulgakov, who used it in his novella *Rokovye iaitsa*
(The fatal eggs, 1925). Ivanov concludes with the following question for the
reader: "If I could see a monster in our time at the foot of the Kara-Dag cliffs,
can the fantastic stories that I want to tell you be so surprising?" (*Perepiska,*

p. 294). His argument could be reduced, of course, to a rather standard device on the part of an author trying to give his work a certain legitimacy. In the case of Ivanov, however, there is reason to suspect that a part of him sincerely believed that legends and myths were not simply the stuff of fantasy.

With the exception of "Sokol" (The falcon), the stories in the "fantastic cycle"—which include "Mednaia lampa" (The copper lamp), "Opalovaia lenta" (The opaline ribbon), "Sizif, syn Eola" (Sisyphys, son of Aeolus), and "Agasfer"—first appeared separately in the 1960s, after Ivanov's death.[45] All were included in the fifth volume of the second edition (1973–77) of his collected works. An artistic fusion of everyday reality with elements of the fantastic, these stories follow in the tradition of such writers as V. F. Odoevsky and Nikolai Gogol in the nineteenth century and Bulgakov in the twentieth.[46] They may have grown out of Ivanov's reaction to life during World War II, and his turning to the fantastic stories of E. T. A. Hoffmann for his reading in 1942–43.[47] It is also possible that the more liberal atmosphere of the early war years encouraged him to harbor the hope that he would be able to write more according to the dictates of his artistic conscience. In his "fantastic stories" Ivanov draws on a broad knowledge of world mythology and world literature to explore death, love, happiness, and creativity in the metaphorical language of a very imaginative writer.

In "Mednaia lampa" and "Sokol" Ivanov takes well-known stories from world literature for his "fantastic essence" (Krasnoschekova, *Khudozhestvennyi mir*, p. 285), which he then skillfully sets in the everyday life of another epoch. The first-person narrator of "Mednaia lampa" (who resembles the narrator of *The Adventures of a Fakir*) looks back on his youth, when he rented "Aladdin's lamp" for three hours from a young tramp at an outdoor bazaar. Although he spent his time reviewing his choices and never did manage to rub its "dull bronze luster" to evoke the spirit of the lamp, he did learn that "joy and creativity do not perish even in the hands of drunkards," of men like the young tramp, who demonstrated creative talents that made the narrator want to believe in the lamp's magic.[48] It is vital to note that Ivanov's treatment leaves the magic premise of the *Arabian Nights* story intact. In "Sokol" Ivanov taps a love story, optimistic and naive in its simplicity, from Giovanni Boccaccio's *Decameron*. Ivanov's narrative is structured on a comparison between the "sub-

---

45. For publication history, see Gladkovskaia, "Kommentarii," in Ivanov, *Sobranie sochinenii*, 5:677–87.

46. For a basic introduction to eighteenth- and nineteenth-century writers who incorporated elements of the fantastic and the esoteric in their prose, see Thomas E. Berry, *Spiritualism in Tsarist Society and Literature* (Baltimore, 1985).

47. Gladkovskaia, *Zhizneliubivyi talant*, p. 243.

48. Vsevolod Ivanov, "Mednaia lampa," in his *Sobranie sochinenii*, 5:417. Translations from this volume are my own. Henceforth page references to this volume are cited parenthetically in the text.

lime example of love" in fourteenth-century Italian literature—a man finally wins a woman's love by serving for dinner the last vestige of his vast fortune, his prized falcon—and the "real-life" version, reflected in the life of a seventeenth-century Russian prince. A certain degree of the fantastic is present in the very existence of the love story's living version centuries and thousands of miles removed from the time and space of the literary version. Furthermore, the visit to Prince Podzoliev's estate by Italian craftsmen, including one from Florence, the city where Boccaccio wrote his tale, is built not only on a whole series of coincidences but on an almost mystical relationship between the two versions of the story. The particular coloration in the Russian version, however, introduces the possibility of a hostile supernatural force that influences human life. The object of Prince Podzoliev's love turns out to be a widow, and he continues to pursue her, although Russians believed that passion for a widow was "disgraceful." His "disgraceful passion" leads him to obey her command that he "kill, roast, and eat" a rare white gerfalcon sent to him by the tsar.

The Italian master craftsman's reaction to the Russian version of the tale, that it is all the work of the devil, places further emphasis on the occult. His comment reflects the readiness with which people in medieval times ascribed negative features of life to the devil's influence. More important, it encourages the reader to examine the course of Prince Podzoliev's life for evidence of interference from "the other world." It turns out that the prince is a bitter, gloomy old man who takes no joy in the wealth that surrounds him; and the woman for whom he had burned with such passion now has neither the physical nor the spiritual beauty that merited such sacrifice on his part. It would seem as if an evil force had kindled unbridled passion in the prince, blinding him to the consequences of behaving in ways unacceptable to church and society.

"Opalovaia lenta" and "Agasfer" testify to Ivanov's interest in myths and legends that speak of efforts to understand the greatest mystery of all, death. The former story explores a theme found in *Y*, the genesis of new myths about death and of the various responses people can bring to bear in their efforts to deal with death. The latter story not only focuses on the regenerative power of one of the most famous myths connected with mortality but also, paradoxically, offers its final regeneration.

Ivanov's very title, "Opalovaia lenta," is intended to signal the mysterious quality of the story's "truth." For Ivanov, opaline was "the most elusive, indefinite, and at the same time somatic color" (*Khudozhestvennyi mir*, p. 290). The "somatic" quality of opaline has its parallel in the story's brown-gray clouds, streaked with orange, which are visible to all who look up. The color's "elusive" quality has its parallel in the variety of interpretations that these clouds evoke.

The local townspeople and workers refer to the orange-streaked gray clouds in imagery that comes from the well of their common daily experience: they see "a cart shaft, a cup, or a shuttle [for weaving] . . . in a word, something round" (p. 290). For them this shuttle has the power to cause death. Local legend has it that people who walk in the lake area in the evening and see the shuttle become enchanted. Pulled by some incomprehensible force, they fall powerless to the ground, and after looking into the water in the lake, they die with a smile on their faces.

Against the general response of the town workers stand the responses of five individuals, who bring varying degrees of the practical and the scientific, the imaginative and the fantastic, to their understanding of the unusual clouds above the town. For the student Valerianov, weighed down by the grimness of life around him, the clouds are nothing more than "smoke and dust." For the practical engineer Rumiantsev, they represent harmful factory pollution to be controlled by the huge cauldrons and filters he has designed; and for his rival, the more visionary engineer and dreamer Khorev, the clouds are harmful *aerosoli* (gas particles), to be eliminated with his ultrasound device. The responses of a doctor and a professor, in contrast, include elements of the invisible, the scientifically unproved, and the fantastic. Dr. Afanasiev thinks there could be thousand-year-old organisms, perhaps viruses, in the "orange ribbon," released from the frozen soil by the heat of the burning coal fields. His interpretation speaks of both his scientific orientation and his belief that myths, such as the Greek myth about sirens luring men to a watery grave, are not simply the products of fantasy and invention but reality filtered through human understanding of the observable world at the time. Professor Zavulin, who is steeped in the works of Dante, Shakespeare, and other writers, and decries the contemporary fear of thinking in metaphors in search of higher truth, believes that the "orange ribbon" contains "unprecedented and heretofore nonexistent/fantastic [*svoeobraznye i nebyvalye*) living organisms" (p. 278). His meaning is elucidated by Olga Osipovna: the professor "tried, we could say, to give concrete form to the mystery of life and death. . . . This is an angel or the devil. . . . But in contemporary form" (p. 295).

The ending of the story contains one key paragraph that challenges the reader to share Ivanov's basic philosophical position: in our efforts to understand the world, we use our creative powers to think in images taken from our daily experience. The more freedom we give to our poetic imagination, the better able we are to rise above daily reality and look to the fantastic and the mystical to explain the world. The omniscient narrator tells us that "Khorev, Olga Osipovna, Rumiantsev, and several men in civilian and military clothes, members of a commission, apparently," were walking along the shore of the lake. One member of the commission was "short [*nizen'kii*], round [*kruglen'kii*], completely covered with moisture from emotion, like an object that had broken out in perspiration after being brought into the warmth from the cold. He was shouting and jumping from time to time and, it seemed, beginning to rise from the ground with his short little wings" (p. 330). This image represents a poetic synthesis of the images Dr. Afanasiev, Professor Zavulin, and Olga Petrovna brought to their explanation of the orange-ribbon phenomenon. And it is this collective image that the omniscient narrator is now able to employ for the reader as a metaphor for the immediate presence of death in the lives of the story's characters.

For "Agasfer" Ivanov draws on world mythology and structures his story on a series of visits that "Ahasuerus, the unwilling immortal"[49]—Agasfer in Russian—pays to the first-person narrator. On the realistic level Agasfer's "materialization" is attributed to a series of coincidences: war and the death all around, the narrator's reading of the legend of Agasfer before receiving a serious head wound, bouts of delirium and thoughts of his own mortality, and research on a film scenario about the mortal granted immortality. On a more philosophical level there is a suggestion that anti-Semitism arising out of the Nazi occupation during World War II combined with Russian nationalism and chauvinism is giving new life to Agasfer. Agasfer's description of himself as a cosmopolitan with no registered residence anywhere evokes no particular reaction from the narrator, although the latter's allusion to the "anticosmopolitan campaign" serves to remind the reader of the anti-Semitic campaign against "rootless cosmopolitans" in the late 1940s.

The artistic strength of this story rests on the skill with which Ivanov manages to interweave the fantastic element—the various sightings and recorded accounts of Agasfer's appearance from 1602 on, under various names and in various countries—with both the physical and inner worlds of the narrator. Through what Agasfer reveals about himself and about his creator, Paulus von Eizen, and through what the narrator fills in as he reports on his research, a complex picture emerges for the motivation behind the "continued life" of such a figure: the wish for immortality and yet fear of its implications; desire for fame and money, the motivation attributed to von Eizen; anti-Semitic feelings, suggested in von Eizen's portrait of Agasfer as a man who, "like all Jews," considers Christ "a false prophet"; and attempts to prove Christ's existence through the existence of eyewitnesses to his crucifixion.[50]

The implied author's decision not to continue the film reflects the narrator's moral conclusion that to feature such a figure on film, even with Russian "compassion," is to give new life and energy to a figure whose existence has served to perpetuate anti-Semitism. This suggestion is offered concretely, although with elements drawn from the realm of the fantastic, in Agasfer's taking on features of the narrator and draining his strength each time the

49. *Man, Myth, and Magic: The Illustrated Encyclopedia of Mythology, Religion, and the Unknown,* ed. Richard Cavendish (New York, 1983), 11:2990.

50. To see the skill with which Ivanov incorporated the various myths about the "unwilling mortal" into his portrait of Agasfer, compare the information given in "Wandering Jew," ibid., pp. 2290–91.

narrator becomes more involved with Agasfer. As in von Eizen's case, the created and the creator begin to merge, to become one, and Ivanov's narrator can only reject the implications of such identity on moral grounds.

It is not surprising, given Ivanov's breadth of knowledge and interest in myth and symbols, that Agasfer's death—captured in the image of his disappearance into the ground—is bound to imagery taken from Scythian lore (*Khudozhestvennyi mir*, p. 298). As the narrator finally holds in the palm of his hand "the golden egg," part of the Scythian "treasure" he finds in the roots of an oak tree, he feels new life surging through his body. Immortality embodied in Agasfer is rejected and a thousand-year-old symbol of life, the golden egg, is brought into the twentieth century.

Ivanov's interest in the occult was engendered by his formative years in prerevolutionary Siberia and became a lifelong fascination. More important, it continued to feed his imagination and, in no small measure, to shape the aesthetic, philosophical, and ethical dimensions of his art. It was also Ivanov's interest in the occult—in the mysteries that lay hidden within and beyond human consciousness—that made his life as a Soviet writer difficult and eventually led to a schizophrenic artistic life, a public and a private Ivanov. The challenge and dilemma Ivanov faced as a Soviet author can be appreciated in a comment he made in the 1940s as he reflected on his artistic life:

> Idols of India, with their many hands and many faces . . . to the average cultured person [*intelligent*] can seem ridiculous and unfinished. Without compunction—and he's right in his way—he will cut off their hands and feet and leave them one pair each, according to the laws of logic and reason. Incidentally, I myself often cut off these hands and feet for myself, finding that it was easier to walk on two feet.[51]

Ivanov's indirect admission that he tailored his vision of the world to the rationally ordered world of the day, as the price to be paid for the right to publish, is clear. What is less clear is where the line can be drawn between the occult as material for artistic and intellectual exploration and the occult as a matter of personal belief and conviction. Ivanov's writing, placed in the context of observations by friends and family, certainly suggests that he was *inclined* to view the world through an occultist prism. In that respect even the metaphor he chose is telling. It is also true that Ivanov studied Nikolai Gogol closely and thought highly of Mikhail Bulgakov and Velimir Khlebnikov, all of whom wrote about levels of reality that are not immediately accessible to human reason. A reexamination of the Ivanov archives may yield more direct evidence. Perhaps when the full Gorky archives become available and the real man emerges from the layers of myth in which he has been wrapped, we will

51. Ivanova, *Moi sovremmeniki*, p. 219.

learn more not only about the early mentor and friend who was drawn to the study of esoteric traditions and nature's secrets but about Ivanov as well.[52] By not limiting ourselves to the image of Ivanov that was molded in the early 1920s largely by the ideological interests of the former Soviet Union, and by developing a sensitivity to the occult in his vision of the world, we can come to a new, enriched appreciation of Ivanov's contribution to Russian literature and thought. There is no question that he merits a prominent place in any study of the role of the occult in Russian and Soviet life.

52. See Viacheslav Ivanov, "Pochemu Stalin ubil Gor'kogo," and Mikhail Agursky, "Maksim Gorky and the Decline of Bolshevik Theomacy," in *Christianity and Russian Culture in Soviet Society,* ed. Nicolai N. Petro (Boulder, 1990). Both articles suggest that a great deal remains to be discovered about Gorky.

PART FIVE
THE OCCULT SINCE STALIN

CHAPTER FOURTEEN
DANIIL ANDREEV
AND THE MYSTICISM
OF FEMININITY

Mikhail Epstein

Though Daniil Andreev's works began to be published only in 1989, thirty years after his death, his legacy is already a major factor in Russian intellectual life. His many admirers regard his treatise *Roza mira* (The rose of the world, 1950–58) as one of the highest peaks of twentieth-century Russian spirituality. A mystic and a poet with strong historical, utopian, and philosophical dimensions in his universalist vision, Andreev is often interpreted as the embodiment of the synthetic aspirations of Russian culture. An article about him in the influential newspaper *Nezavisimaia gazeta* stated: "In his study *Lev Tolstoy and Dostoevsky* (1901–1902), Merezhkovsky grasped the imminent emergence in Russia of a poet who will synthesize in his creativity the carnal, paganist, and highly spiritual elements, i.e., the artistic discoveries of Lev Tolstoy and Dostoevsky, respectively. The epic scope of Homer, the visionary gift of Dante, the religious heroism of Milton, the universality of Goethe indissolubly merged in the creativity of D. Andreev."[1] However exaggerated this opinion may be, it conveys accurately the rising influence of Andreev. His legacy belongs to those historiosophical and cosmosophical movements of Russian thought which attempt to synthesize natural sciences, social utopias, and religious inspirations in a kind of occult superknowledge that claims the power to transform the world.

It is difficult to establish strict boundaries between the occult, mystical, and eschatological components of Andreev's teachings. Andreev's cosmology, his vision of the Rose of the World as a hierarchical system of worlds, both visible and invisible, is the most evident occult dimension of his work (a brief syn-

---

1. Boris Chukov, "Most iz mira real'nogo v mir transtsendental'nyi: Daniil Andreev—poet, vizioner, filosof," *Nezavisimaia gazeta* (Moscow), no. 166 (842), September 1, 1994, p. 7.

opsis of this system is provided in the Appendix to this chapter). Andreev's interpretation of the Rose of the World as the "interreligion of the future," uniting all existing churches as "petals," has both mystical and eschatological dimensions. On the one hand, the Rose of the World is based on long-standing traditions of European and Russian mysticism, especially "sophiology," which treats the Eternal Feminine as the Wisdom of God and the soul of the universe. On the other hand, in Andreev's description, the rule of the Rose of the World, as the state of universal theocracy, ends with the accession of the Antichrist, who makes use of the "interreligious" doctrines, including the worship of the Eternal Feminine, to perpetuate his own power and to eliminate the Rose of the World.

Russian-Soviet mysticism has several distinctive features. First of all, it usually represents a mixture of Christian and pagan mythological beliefs (the so-called *dvoeverie*, dual faith). Russian pre-Christian mythology, as is well known, survived only in scattered fragments after Russia became Christian in A.D. 988, thus leaving open a large field for mystical conjectures concerning the qualities of Russian deities and their continued impact on the fate of Russia. Very few of these mystical restorations of Russian paganism are openly anti-Christian, but they attempt to combine Orthodox tradition with archaic beliefs or, more precisely, with the restorers' notions of what these beliefs must have been.

Another important feature of Russian-Soviet mysticism is its combination of national distinctiveness with universalist claims. Russia's location spanning Europe and Asia has fueled speculation about the global destiny of the Russian nation, which was to become a keeper of universal wisdom, blending the best spiritual illuminations of both the West and the East.

Russian-Soviet mysticism has a strong social orientation. Rarely does it lapse into the realm of highly subjective individual contemplation. Usually it is offered as a new social teaching intended to inspire the whole nation and to give a just resolution to the most agonizing problems of contemporary society. Thus the messianic style of Russian mysticism as it tries to appeal to the masses and organize them into an ideal society.

At the same time, Russian-Soviet mysticism has a cosmic dimension. Not only the individual but even society and the earth itself are considered too small to realize the great visions of national prophets. Space must be explored and colonized, and the multiplicity of invisible spiritual worlds must be penetrated.

Russian mysticism has always been closely connected with specifically Russian history, yet it also has striven to overcome history and thus has followed apocalyptic patterns. Russia can fulfill its historical destiny only by being the first *posthistorical* nation, which is fated to experience all the suffering and illuminations imposed on the world by the struggle of Christ and the Antichrist on the Last Day.

Finally, Russian mysticism has included worship of the feminine spiritual essence of the universe and even the feminine hypostasis of the Divine Wholeness, Sophia, in such terms as "the Eternal Feminine" (*Vechnaia Zhenstvennost'*), "the Soul of the World" (*Dusha Mira*), and "the Companion of the Lord" (*Podruga Boga*).

All of these features, which can be traced separately through such prominent mystical and occult thinkers as Vladimir Soloviev, Nikolai Fedorov, Dmitry Merezhkovsky, Nikolai Berdiaev, Pavel Florensky, Andrei Bely, Velimir Khlebnikov, Konstantin Tsiolkovsky, the cosmists, and the Eurasians, are combined in Daniil Andreev's thought. Undoubtedly he is the most important Russian mystic of the Soviet epoch and perhaps gives the most explicit and integrated expression of the ideas of his predecessors.

Since Daniil Andreev is completely unknown in the West, let me provide some biographical background, based on the recollections of Andreev's widow, Alla Andreeva;[2] though the deepest insights into his spiritual life can be gained from his mystical treatise, *Roza mira*.

Daniil Andreev, born in 1906, was the son of Leonid Andreev (1871–1919), an eminent prose writer and dramatist, who fearlessly investigated the darkest depths of the human soul. Daniil confessed that his father's writings remained alien to him: Leonid was a neorealist and a skeptic, partly inclined to a decadent version of Satanism and Nietzscheanism, whereas Daniil received a Christian upbringing and searched for religious revelations throughout his intellectual development. Daniil Andreev did not know his father well. His mother, Aleksandra Mikhailovna Veligorskaia, died three weeks after his birth, and he was brought up by his grandmother Efrosinia Varfolomeevna Shevchenko; his aunt Elizaveta Mikhailovna; and an uncle, a Moscow doctor named Filipp Aleksandrovich Dobrov. It was a very intelligent, tender, and caring family. Visitors to their hospitable home included the novelist Ivan Bunin, the poet Marina Tsvetaeva, the singer Fedor Chaliapin, the composer Alexander Scriabin (who played his "mysteries" for them), and other members of the artistic elite of that time.

Little Daniil inadvertently caused the death of his grandmother, who con-

---

2. The life of Daniil Andreev, rich with spiritual insights and shaped by sudden twists of fate and daily adversity, remains unwritten. One of the most reliable biographical sources is the recollections of Andreev's widow, Alla Aleksandrovna Andreeva, taped in an interview with her on April 28, 1988 (the typescript is 58 pages). A short biographical essay written by Alla Andreeva appears as the introduction to Daniil Andreev's collected works: "Zhizn' Daniila Andreeva, rasskazannaia ego zhenoi," in Daniil Andreev, *Sobranie sochinenii*, 3 vols. (Moscow, 1993), 1:5–26.

tracted diphtheria from him when he was six. Shortly thereafter Daniil tried to commit suicide. It was explained to him that his grandmother had gone "far away" to see his mother, and only at the last moment was he prevented from drowning himself in a pond—he was going to see his mother too. From these episodes one gets a premonition of Daniil's future spiritual wanderings into other worlds. At the tender age of six or seven he was writing a huge cosmic epic, depicting travel between other planets and other universes. During the Bolshevik Revolution, Daniil liked to sit on the roof of his house and observe the stars. Although he may well have been acquainted with Theosophical and Anthroposophical literature, one can infer from his mystical predilections in childhood that most of his subsequent ideas were not borrowed from books.

In the 1920s Daniil Andreev studied at Vysshie Literaturnye Kursy (Highest Literary Courses) in Moscow. He married a journalist, Aleksandra Gorobova, but they soon divorced. Andreev spent a great deal of time reading about history and became so immersed in its details that he devised a game: a friend would pick an arbitrary year (for example, 1246 or 1683) and Daniil would describe all important events that took place around the world during that year. Though he had a natural religious inclination, he was formally reintroduced to the Orthodox Church (*votserkovlen*) only in 1921 by a friend, the actress Nadezhda Butova.

After finishing his literary studies, Daniil spent some time working as an editor for a factory newspaper in Moscow. He published a variety of political materials, but surreptitiously laid aside numerous antireligious articles and finally decided to look for another job. Andreev turned to graphic art, designing maps, fonts, and calligraphy styles, to earn a living at a job that also gave him time to pursue his writing, mostly at night. He wrote many poems and his first, unfinished novel, *Greshniki* (Sinners), during this period. In March 1937 he met his future second wife, Alla Aleksandrovna, an artist, twenty-two years old at the time, and the wife of a close friend, the artist Sergei Ivashov-Musatov.

In the late 1930s, as Andreev wrote his new novel, *Stranniki nochi* (Night wanderers), he read it to a small group of Moscow intellectuals. The book's heroes aspire to transform Russia spiritually: one of them designs the temple of the Sun of the World at the site where, by a strange coincidence, Moscow State University was built ten years later.

During World War II, Andreev worked as a medical orderly; he was with the first Soviet troops to reach besieged Leningrad by the ice road across Lake Ladoga, an experience he describes in his epic poem "Leningradskii apokalipsis." He also worked as a member of a funeral detachment; while burying the dead in communal graves, he prayed for the repose of their souls. In 1945 he returned to Moscow, deeply depressed by everything he had seen. At this point, both Daniil and Alla had divorced their former spouses and married each other. By the beginning of 1947, he had almost completed *Stranniki nochi*.

On April 21 he was arrested by the MVD; the arrest of his wife came two days later. On the basis of his novel, they were accused of a terrorist plot against Stalin and spent thirteen months in Lubyanka Prison and then six months in Lefortovo Prison. Each of them was sentenced to twenty-five years' imprisonment; under Khrushchev's rule, this term was reduced to ten years.

Andreev's last decade (1948–58) proved to be the most creative period of his life. It was in Vladimirskaia prison that Daniil began to hear the voices that dictated his masterpiece, *Roza mira*. Andreev spent these years "communicating" with the highest spirits in Russian and other national "metacultures" (his term); Lermontov, Dostoevsky, and Blok "guided" him in his wanderings through other worlds. During this time, he wrote on tiny scraps of paper, which were invariably confiscated, but he restored his prose and verses from memory and continued to write. It was only after Stalin's death in 1953, when a new warden arrived at the prison, that Daniil was given paper and ink and allowed to write on a regular basis. With his prison roommates, the biologist Vasily Parin and the historian Lev Rakov, Daniil wrote a fictional, very inventive and humorous encyclopedia about outstanding figures of the past who in reality never existed.[3]

Throughout these ten years, Alla was serving her sentence in a concentration camp in Mordovia, and she and Daniil heard almost no news of each other. On April 21, 1957, he was freed and they were reunited in Moscow. At first they were not permitted to live in the city itself, so they settled in an outlying area. Their life was dominated by poverty and they were forced to move frequently. During one of their short residences on the Oka River, Daniil had a chance to see his brother, the gifted writer Vadim Andreev, who had left Russia after the October Revolution and had lived in Paris for forty years.

In spite of chronic diseases and other hardships, within twenty-three months after his release from prison Andreev had completed *Roza mira* and his dramatic poem *Zheleznaia misteriia* (Iron mystery). His book of verses, *Russkie bogi* (Russian deities), which included such long poems as "Navna" and "Smert' Ivana Groznogo," remained unfinished.

His health deteriorated seriously and he died on March 30, 1959, the victim of a heart attack (he had suffered a heart attack as early as 1954, while still in prison). He was buried at the Novodevichie Cemetery in Moscow, near his mother's grave. As Alla Andreeva remarked, his angel kept him alive as long as he needed to finish most of his work. Shortly before his death, as he reread *Roza mira*, he suddenly declared to his wife, "No, it was not a madman who wrote it."

He was a quiet, meek, rather silent man who was not capable of practical leadership, although he certainly exhibited enormous moral courage during the years of persecution. Strong religious faith, although not constrained by

3. D. L. Andreev, V. V. Parin, and L. L. Rakov, *Noveishii Plutarkh* (Moscow, 1991).

church dogmas, enabled him to resist the social pressures exerted on him and to develop his "metahistorical" vision. For Andreev, however, it was a tremendous tragedy that an Orthodox priest refused to grant him Holy Communion before his death because he had confessed to believing in reincarnation. In Alla Andreeva's opinion, Daniil was an inherently faithful Orthodox Christian who never fell into heresy in his writing; he only availed himself of the freedom that is inherent in the creative imagination.

It is impossible to judge the evolution of Andreev's views, since nothing that he had written before his arrest in 1947 was preserved (save for several poems that he managed to restore from memory): the MVD destroyed all his works and even letters from his father after he was sentenced. Nevertheless, one can hypothesize that Andreev's metaphysical views were formed in his youth and gradually increased in clarity and intensity but did not undergo any radical changes.

In the 1930s he was already writing poetry that provided a hint of his mystical vision and a characteristic set of imaginary mythological names and terms. By the time he wrote *Stranniki nochi*, he was committed to the metahistorical and transphysical vision that he later would elaborate in *Roza mira*. One of the novel's heroes, Adrian Gordov, believes that one can rise from the dead and change the world. Another character, Leonid Glinsky, delivers a lecture on the alternation of red and blue epochs in Russian history. In each blue epoch, a red underground movement develops, and vice versa. For example, the beginning of the twentieth century was a blue epoch with a red (politically left) underground, while the period after the October Revolution was a red political epoch with a blue mystical undercurrent. Andreev brought such lifelong visions together in *Roza mira*.

Andreev began *Roza mira* on December 24, 1950, and completed it on October 12, 1958. For a long time his widow was the sole custodian of the only copy, and no one else even suspected its existence. Later Alla Andreeva decided that the time for readers had come; by the late 1970s, the book was circulating in samizdat, and many readers considered it the greatest mystical revelation since the Gospels. During glasnost in the late 1980s, some stories about Daniil Andreev appeared in *Moskovskii Komsomolets* and other Moscow papers. In April 1988 the first official Andreev commemorative meeting was held at the Experimental Creative Center in Moscow. In 1989 and 1990, Andreev's poetry collection *Russkie bogi* and his long dramatic poem *Zheleznaia misteriia* were released by the Sovremennik and Molodaia Gvardiia publishing houses, respectively. The first complete edition of *Roza mira* was released by the Moscow publishing house Prometei in 1991. In 1993, Moskovskii Rabochii and Alesia began to publish Andreev's collected works in three volumes.

The most diverse and incompatible intellectual movements find support in *Roza mira*. Liberal Westernizers, who defend religious pluralism and Christian ecumenism, revere Andreev's legacy as much as neopaganists who draw on the "Aryan" roots of the Russian national spirit and declare Andreev to be the messenger of mythic "proto-Russianism." *Roza mira's* scope of influence stretches from elitist esotericism to stands on topical issues, and from the occult journal *Urania,* which offers an astrological interpretation of Andreev's ideas,[4] to the journalistic articles in *Ploshchad' Svobody* (Freedom Square), where his thought is used to explain the "metahistorical" meaning of the August 1991 Communist putsch.[5]

It is clear that the Soviet system was not merely a political and legislative entity; the ideology on which it was based was informed not only by the theories of Marx as interpreted by Lenin and his successors but by the metaphysical and even eschatological visions of Russian religious philosophers of the Silver Age. The collapse of the Soviet regime left more than a need for governmental reform: it left a metaphysical vacuum. Into that vacuum rushed spiritual and occult teachings that found a ready audience, Andreev's prominent among them.

Roza mira is a multifaceted book that explores the structure of all existing worlds, both visible and invisible, from Paradise to Hell. Many of its terms and expressions cannot be found in any dictionary; they are defined in a glossary at the end of the book. These words, says Andreev, were introduced by supernatural voices into his consciousness, and he rationalized them as signifying the principal elements of the transphysical universe. Andreev defined *Bramfatura,* for example, as the system of various material levels that constitute celestial bodies; *Shadanakar* is the name of our planet's bramfatura, which consists of a great number of planes (more than 240) of different kinds of matter, with various dimensions of time and space. Though the majority of these terms cannot be identified in any language, one sometimes discerns Russian and especially Sanskrit roots. To Andreev's admirers the very fact that these neologisms are from no real language indicates the genuine source of

4. *Urania,* founded in 1991 and edited in Moscow by Tatiana Antonian, is published bimonthly in Russian and three times a year in English. Daniil Andreev's legacy is important for the journal and strongly influences its contributors. It specializes in astrology and, to a lesser degree, extrasensory perception; for this reason, Andreev's teaching is interpreted primarily in occult terms. Several fragments of Andreev's magnum opus appeared in an English translation by Irina Antonian in no. 1, 1992, pp. 28–42.

5. Iuri Arabov, "Perevorot glazami metaistorika," in *Ploshchad' Svobody,* comp. Vladimir Druk (Moscow, 1992), pp. 23–47. Arabov, a poet and screenwriter, has assimilated the metahistorical method and terminology of Daniil Andreev and applies it to the interpretation of the turbulent events at the Moscow White House in August 1991. Arabov presents Daniil as a supernatural figure, in accordance with his contemporary perception as the Teacher with a capital T. "In the midst of the passing twentieth century swirls a gigantic figure of a human being (so may we for the time being refer to him) who succeeded in exposing intelligently on paper the picture of the world as transmitted to him from above. The name of this man is Daniil Andreev" (pp. 27–28).

this mystical inspiration, comprehensible only through spontaneous contact with the highest spirits. Daniil Andreev's entire mythological system is an elaboration of the hidden meanings of these primordial words.

Among the wide range of social, moral, environmental, historical, and theological questions that Andreev addressed, one of the most prominent is the feminine element in the universe. Many Russian visionaries and intellectuals have emphasized the feminine element in Russian popular culture. The philosopher Georgy Fedotov argued that "at every step in studying Russian popular religion one meets the constant longing for a great divine female power."[6] According to Nikolai Berdiaev, "The religion of soil is very strong in the Russian people; it lies deep down in the very foundation of the Russian soul. The land is the final intercessor. The fundamental category is motherhood. The Mother of God takes precedence of the Trinity and is almost identified with the Trinity."[7]

This preoccupation with the feminine is conventionally explained partly by geographical and historical conditions: Russia's vast open plains are often compared metaphorically to a womb that must be safeguarded from foreign invasion; for centuries Russia sustained itself as an agricultural society, which supported a corresponding mythological vision of the earth as a divine mother. Rural rituals of fertilizing the earth survived in Russia into the twentieth century. The very names Rus' and Rossiia are of feminine gender and lead quite naturally to such folkloric and poetic expressions as *matushka Rossiia* (Mother Russia) and *Rus'-zhena* (Rus' wife).

Not all of the consequences of this gender mysticism have been investigated, especially with respect to its contemporary implications. Mythological relics of femininity and maternity are still relevant to twentieth-century Russia, despite its obsession with the tasks of political and social innovation. It is characteristic, however, that even in the most comprehensive and informative Western investigation of feminine themes in Russian culture, Joanna Hubbs's *Mother Russia*, the ideology and practice of Russian communism are not considered at all. Hubbs does not even mention the Russian concept of *materiia* (matter), though materialism, as a tenet of official Soviet ideology, is probably the most important outcome of this traditional worship of Russia as mother.[8]

One often encounters the opinion that materialism was alien to the Russian mentality and was mechanically adapted from the Western European "scientific spirit" of the nineteenth century. According to this stereotype, Russians

6. G. P. Fedotov, *The Russian Religious Mind* (Cambridge, Mass., 1946), p. 362. On the connection between Russia, Mother Earth, and the Virgin see also Andrei Sinyavsky, "Mat'-syra Zemlia i Bogomater'," in his *Ivan-durak: Ocherk russkoi narodnoi very* (Paris, 1991), pp. 181–92. "As the expression of universal Motherhood, the image of the Mother of God sometimes merges with or stands close by the moist Mother earth" (p. 189).

7. Nikolai Berdyaev, *The Russian Idea*, trans. R. M. French (Hudson, N.Y., 1992), p. 24.

8. Joanna Hubbs, *Mother Russia: The Feminine Myth in Russian Culture* (Bloomington, 1988).

are a mystical people, so resistant to rational knowledge of the world that they refuse to rely on objective laws. Despite the kernel of truth in such character-izations, materialism should not be confused with rationalism or empiricism. Indeed, the "average," archetypal Russian is neither a rationalist nor an em-piricist, but nevertheless can be regarded as a materialist; and the most un-yielding materialism does not preclude a proclamation of the mystic qualities of matter.

The Russian word *materiia* is broader and more philosophically loaded than the English "matter." The Academy of Sciences' dictionary of the Russian language defines *materiia* first as "the objective reality that exists beyond and independently of human consciousness," and second as "the substance of which the physical bodies of nature are composed."[9] Only the second meaning is equivalent to the English "matter." The Russian concept of *materiia*, there-fore, has not only physical but metaphysical implications, presupposing the objective nature of matter and even its priority over consciousness, a tenet that is the foundation of Soviet materialism (which in its turn certainly influenced the definitions of ideologically charged terms).

The Russian philosopher Aleksei Losev (1893–1988) argued that the entirety of Russian thought, even its religious components, has a deeply material-istic bias:

> Russian philosophy is, first of all, sharply and unconditionally ontological. . . . This ontology, however, as opposed to the Western strain, is sharpened in *mate-riia*, which has characterized it since the time of archaic mysticism. The very idea of divinity, as it was developed in the Russian Church, puts in the foreground elements of corporeality (such as the teaching about Sophia, "divine wisdom"), in which Pavel Florensky identified the originality of Russian, as distinct from Byzantine, Orthodoxy.[10]

One can suggest that philosophical materialism proceeds from this "archaic mysticism," which claims nature's maternal rights over her creatures and the reciprocal duty of the offspring to Mother Nature. Besides, the words "mother" and "matter" share a Latin origin, as Lucretius noticed in *De rerum natura*. This primordial unity, which explains the mythological origin of philo-sophical materialism, may even be traced back to Plato, as Vladimir Toporov has explained:

> The link between matter and mother, which was outlined by Plato, corresponds to the deep reality of mythopoetic consciousness. . . . To some degree the rela-tionship of the moist Mother Earth and Father Heaven, in Slavonic and in many

9. *Slovar' russkogo iazyka*, 4 vols., vol. 2 (Moscow, 1982), p. 236.
10. A. F. Losev, "Osnovnye osobennosti russkoi filosofii," in his *Filosofiia, Mifologiia, Kul'tura* (Moscow, 1991), p. 509.

other traditions, may be regarded as a distant source of the Platonic relationship between matter ("mother") and idea-model ("father").[11]

If we accept this etymological and mythological explanation, then the entire opposition between materialism and idealism, which for Marxists constitutes the quintessential philosophical issue, can be derived from the ancient cult of the earth mother and sun father. Solar rays carry the energy that fertilizes the earth's womb, giving birth to the vegetable kingdom and to all living creatures. One could even argue that the essence of materialism may be traced to the worship of maternity in the form of Mother Nature.[12]

Before materialism became an official doctrine, another female-oriented philosophy had been developing in Russia, the so-called sophiology. At the end of the nineteenth century and in the first half of the twentieth, this concept was elaborated by Vladimir Soloviev, Pavel Florensky, Sergei Bulgakov, and other thinkers who considered the Russian soul to be especially attuned to Sophia, Divine Wisdom.[13] Both *materiia* and Sophia, they argued, characterized the feminine element in the universe, but there is a major difference between them: *materiia* is nature, which gives birth to living beings; Sophia is Divine Wisdom, which generates nature. Sophia (Hokhma in Hebrew) speaks thus in Proverbs: "The Lord possessed me in the beginning of his way, before his works of old. I was set up from everlasting, from the beginning, or ever the earth was. . . . Then I was by him, as one brought up with him: and I was daily his delight, rejoicing always before him" (8:22–23, 30–31).

Solomon says: "Wisdom I loved; I sought her out when I was young and longed to win her for my bride, and I fell in love with her beauty. She adds lustre to her noble birth, because it is given her to live with God, and the Lord of all things has accepted her" (Wisd. of Sol. 8:2–3).

11. V. N. Toporov. "Prostranstvo i tekst," in *Tekst: Semantika i struktura* (Moscow, 1983), pp. 236–37.

12. According to Engels's foundational definition, materialism is connected with the ancient worship of Nature: "Those who assumed that a spirit existed before nature constituted the idealistic camp. But those who considered nature the primary element formed various schools of materialism. At first, the expressions 'idealism' and 'materialism' implied nothing else": K. Marx and F. Engels, *Sochineniia*, 2d ed., vol. 21 (Moscow, 1961), p. 283. One can suggest that it was Russia's long tradition of dual faith, Christian and pagan, that accounts for the triumph of materialism after Christianity was undermined by the Bolshevik Revolution. With the expulsion of the patriarchal religion of the Heavenly Father, archaic matriarchal elements regenerated in the social unconscious and acquired the form of materialist ideology. Indeed, Paul Federn, a disciple of Freud, argued that Bolshevism is nothing but the replacement of the father's power by the principles of matriarchy. See P. Federn, *Zur Psychologie der Revolution* (Vienna, 1919).

13. Vladimir Soloviev, *La Sophia et les autres écrits français*, ed. Fr. François Rouleau (Lausanne, 1978); Pavel Florenskii, *Stolp i utverzhdenie istiny*, in his *Sobranie sochinenii*, vol. 4 (Paris, 1989), pp. 319–92; Sergei Bulgakov, *The Wisdom of God: A Brief Summary of Sophiology* (New York and London, 1937).

Sophia, or Divine Wisdom, is a mysterious entity that, under various names, is worshiped in several religious traditions: pagan, Judaic, Gnostic, and Christian. In Greek polytheism, Sophia is represented by the chaste goddess of wisdom, Athena, born directly from the head of Zeus. In Christianity, Sophia converges with the image of the Virgin Mary. The essential quality of Sophia-wisdom is her chastity. In Russian, as in Greek, the term "chastity" includes the root "wisdom": *tselomudrie* literally means "whole wisdom." The connection between wisdom and chastity is found in many spiritual traditions. A contemporary Russian scholar, Sergei Averintsev, emphasizes that "according to the stable mythological pattern, widespread in various Eurasian cultures, wisdom belongs to a virgin or, in fact, wisdom *is* a virgin."[14]

Materialism and sophiology in Russian thought have the same mythological origin: both glorify the primary feminine elements, nature and wisdom. Sophia represents the virginal and *materiia* the maternal aspects of femininity. Both are rooted in the deepest mythological archetypes of Russian thought as the two pillars of feminine mysticism. The Soviet intensification of materialism deepened the traditional symbolic rift between the two conceptions of femininity. Materialism, as propagated by Marxism-Leninism, is not merely the glorification of the forces of *materiia;* in alliance with atheism, it strives to tear *materiia* away from its divine origins, from Sophia, and to submit it to human mastery.[15]

Originally the image of Sophia was ambiguous. Thunder, "Whole Mind," one of the Gnostic works found at Nag Hammadi in Upper Egypt in 1945 and probably written during the first century B.C., depicts Sophia as both saint and whore. Gradually, however, these aspects of the feminine divinity became increasingly distinct. As I have indicated, Sophia was identified with the Holy Wisdom of God and the immaculate Mother of God, the Eternal Virgin (*Prisnodeva*). Thus the sophiological preference for chastity begins to betray an ascetic bias, a one-sidedness for which materialism strives to compensate. Virginity is in conflict with the fertile, prolific forces of nature. Thus the other aspect of primordial female divinity—fertility and sensuality (called the fallen Sophia by the Gnostics)—is developed in materialist teachings, where it acts as a counterbalance to virginity, eventually beginning to overcompensate, moving into the excesses of dissipation.

14. Sergei Averintsev, "K uiasneniiu smysla nadpisi nad konkhoi tsentral'noi apsidy Sofii Kievskoi," in *Drevnerusskoe iskusstvo* (Moscow, 1972), p. 28.

15. According to the mythic logic of this materialist conception, the conjugal bond of nature and God must be severed to facilitate her incestuous marriage with her human son. Sophiology is predominantly a cult of chastity, whereas materialism, in mythological terms, is the cult of degraded maternity, since Mother Nature is raped by her own son. For this interpretation see Mikhail Epstein, "Labor of Lust: Erotic Metaphors of Soviet Civilization," in his *After the Future: The Paradoxes of Postmodernism and Contemporary Russian Culture,* trans. Anesa Miller-Pogacar (Amherst, 1995), pp. 177–87.

Many Russian thinkers have lamented the internal division of the Russian national character, which strains in opposite directions, ascetic/angelic and sensual/animalistic, and seldom succeeds in integrating spiritual and material impulses in a human middle ground. The same tragic split occurs within the feminine elements of Russian culture; hence an important task of contemporary Russian thought is to resolve the historical antagonism between the two philosophical tendencies of sophiology and materialism.

Throughout his creative years, Daniil Andreev suffered under the pressure of official Soviet ideology's "stubborn iron materialism," but his inner resistance to this mysticism of *materiia* did not push him to the other extreme of bodiless spiritualism. Nature was the center of his whole system, and he singled out a special category of "elementals" (*stikhiali*), spiritual entities that have an elevating effect on the human soul and are embodied in such natural elements (*stikhii*) as rivers, trees, wind, and snow. Daniil Andreev enjoyed traveling through the wildest and most remote Russian forests, because for him, nature suggested the most genuine way of knowing God and partaking in supreme wisdom. Like Rozanov and Merezhkovsky, he sought the "sanctification of the flesh," and vehemently opposed the ascetic contempt for sensuality. For him, the entire substance of nature was a manifestation of the feminine soul of the universe.

The double materialistic and sophiological context of Andreev's view of femininity becomes clear from his short remark indicating the whole spectrum of traditional Russian worship of the earth as mother and as lover. "Earth is not only our mother; in some deeper sense that still cannot be explicated, she is our lover. One should remember the precept of Dostoevsky, who urged us to kiss the earth constantly at every step" (*Roza mira*, bk. 12, chap. 3, p. 259).[16]

Andreev attempts to elevate this "pagan" worship of the earth to the highest level of Christian theology. Chapter 3, "Femininity," treats this question in terms of the Holy Trinity. Andreev considered himself Christian, but he dared to dispute the doctrine of the Trinity: "I am approaching the decisive thesis. . . . The canonical gospels of Matthew and Luke distinctly and clearly assume the conception of the infant Jesus by the Virgin Mary from the Holy Spirit. Thus one can conclude that it was the Holy Spirit and not God the Father who was the father of the human Christ" (6.3.119). Andreev suggests that God the Father and the Holy Spirit are essentially the same hypostasis of the Trinity. "God the Father is God the Holy Spirit—these are two names for

16. The question of femininity which Daniil Andreev thought to be "the decisive thesis" of the entire *Roza mira* is most extensively treated in bk. 6, chap. 3; bk. 7, chap. 1; bk. 10, chaps. 2–5; bk. 12, chap. 3. There are twelve books altogether. Daniil Andreev's work is quoted from its first edition, *Roza mira: Metafilosofiia istorii* (Moscow, 1991); henceforth cited parenthetically in text. The first figure in parentheses refers to the number of the book, the second to the chapter, the third to the page.

the same first face of the Trinity" (6.3.120). The third hypostasis thus remains vacant. Andreev wants to fill it with the "world's feminine essence." The Trinity, in Andreev's interpretation, is nothing but Father, Mother, and Son. The second, feminine hypostasis simultaneously represents eternal virginity, maternity, spirit, and wisdom.

It is difficult to say whether Andreev was familiar with the ideas of Anna Shmidt, Dmitry Merezhkovsky, or Sergei Bulgakov. Anna Shmidt (1851–1905) postulated that the third hypostasis of God is "God's Daughter, the Eternal Virgin."[17] Merezhkovsky did not deny that the Holy Spirit is God's third hypostasis, but he claimed it to be feminine and identical to the Holy Mother, the symbolic union of divine spirit and earthly flesh.[18] Bulgakov developed sophiology as a specific division within Eastern theology but his deliberately vague doctrine of Sophia as a separate hypostasis outside the Trinity was condemned by the Orthodox hierarchy (1935), even though Bulgakov did not assert directly that Sophia was the fourth hypostasis of divinity.[19] It is likely that church authorities censured sophiology as heresy because it seemed to pattern the Trinity after a trivial family union and it introduced seductive sexual elements into the dogmatic core of Christianity.

Indeed, the mysterious essence of the Trinity is undermined when the Mother of God is substituted for the Holy Spirit. The concept of the Holy Spirit may have derived from the concept of *Hokhma*, or Divine Wisdom, in the Old Testament. But when the "second" hypostasis of the Son was incorporated into the concept of God in the New Testament, the "third" hypostasis had to be revised and purified of any feminine elements in order to avoid any associations with an earthly family structure. Thus the divine wisdom of the Old Testament became the Holy Spirit of the New Testament.

Unlike the Reverend Sergei Bulgakov, the convict Daniil Andreev was not constrained in his theological imagination by church canons. For Andreev, the incorporation of feminine elements into the Trinity had far-reaching implications for Russia: the whole material aspect of life might be spiritualized and sanctified, since maternity, which gives life to all creatures, would be a hypostasis of divinity itself.

Daniil Andreev identified this feminine essence as Zventa-Sventana, whose approximate meaning he conveys as "the lightest of the light, the holiest of the holy" (6.3.124). *Svet* means light, and *zventa* sounds similar to *zvezda*, star. Generally, Andreev preferred to substitute the neologisms he claimed to have received directly from higher spirits for traditional names and terms; in this

17. A. N. Shmidt, *Tretii zavet* (St. Petersburg, 1993), p. 24.

18. For a detailed account of Merezhkovsky's "new religious consciousness" and dogmatic innovations, some of which strikingly anticipated Andreev's conceptions, see Bernice Glatzer Rosenthal, *Dmitri Sergeevich Merezhkovsky and the Silver Age: The Development of a Revolutionary Mentality* (The Hague, 1975), chap. 4, esp. pp. 94–96.

19. Bulgakov, *Wisdom of God*, pp. 43–62.

case, as in many others, he did not care to explicate the semantic difference between Sophia and Zventa-Sventana. There are other modifications of this "Universal Femininity" (*Mirovaia Zhenstvennost'*) in Andreev's vision, such as Navna, or the Communal Soul (*Sobornaia Dusha*). The relation of these names and personifications to one another is sometimes obscure. Zventa-Sventana is defined as the great monad born from God, the expression of eternal femininity, and the bride of a planetary Logos. Navna also is a monad born from God and one of the great sisters, a communal soul of Russian metaculture. When considering the cosmic, global dimensions of femininity, Andreev preferred the name Zventa-Sventana. He reserved the name Navna for the feminine soul of Russia: "The Eternally Feminine principle whose embodiment in Russia, Navna . . . " (10.2.180).

. . . Navna, the ideal communal [*sobornaia*] soul of Russia. . . . Who is she, who is Navna? She is the one who unites Russians into one nation, who calls and directs individual Russian souls higher and higher, who surrounds Russian art with a unique fragrance, who stands above the purest and highest female images of Russian legends, literature, and music, who emits into Russians' hearts a longing for a high, special, purely Russian destination. All this is Navna. Her communal nature [*sobornost'*] consists in the fact that some part of every Russian soul ascends to Navna, preserves itself in her and merges with her inner self. . . . Navna is the bride of the Demiurge of Russia and is the prisoner of the Zhrugrs [the demons of Great Russian statehood]. (4.3.89)

In his long poem "Navna" (1955) Andreev traced the sublime manifestation of this feminine spirit throughout Russian history:

> In each inspiration, in each art
> Of this nocturnal and snowy country
> Only the dawn of Thy distant presentiments
> Slightly gilds our mournful dreams.[20]

According to Andreev's mytho-historiosophy, the Russian demiurge Iarosvet was destined to marry the Communal Soul of the Russian nation and give birth to Zventa-Sventana. But this process was delayed by the interference of Velga, the great demon of a feminine nature, who removes the taboos against blasphemy and destruction. Each people has its own Velga—the goddess Kali of the Hindus, the Hebrews' Lilith, or the Gnostics' fallen Sophia—who represents another pole of the communal soul and attempts to bring society into the fold of demonic materialism. In these terms, Soviet materialistic civilization can be interpreted as an involution of Velga.

According to Andreev, Iarosvet first appeared in heavenly Russia and en-

20. Daniil Andreev, *Russkie bogi: Stikhotvoreniia i poemy* (Moscow, 1989), p. 198.

countered Navna in the tenth century. Andreev described this event as a "happy tempest": "Navna accepted him as a long-awaited groom in the blissful forest expanses of Holy Russia" (7.1.128). Yet until the nineteenth century the feminine element was suppressed in Russian culture; images of women were few and pale in comparison with the powerful male imagery. The reason was that Navna was a prisoner of the Zhrugrs, who personify the demonic aspect of the state, the will to power as the dominant aspiration of patriarchal society.

Daniil Andreev singled out several steps in Russian literature and philosophy which mark the gradual manifestation of Zventa-Sventana. The emanation of this feminine monad into the spiritual world of our planet, Shadanakar, occurred only in the late eighteenth century. This metahistorical event was dimly reflected in the works of Goethe, Novalis, and Zhukovsky.

In Russia the first embodiment of this ideal femininity was Tatiana Larina in Pushkin's *Eugene Onegin*. Then came Turgenev's women, especially Elena in the novel *On the Eve* and Lukeria from the short story "Living Mummy." The highest manifestations of the Eternal Feminine are found in the works of Vladimir Soloviev (1853–1900), though he failed to find a more compelling concept for this mysterious entity than the ancient Gnostic notion of Sophia. In Andreev's view, Soloviev was the first to understand that the religious revelation of the Eternal Feminine is not compatible with the Trinitarian dogma of Orthodox Christianity. This is why he expressed his vision of Sophia in a long poem, "Tri vstrechi" (Three encounters), whose mystical illuminations are deliberately limited by the framework of a slightly humorous autobiographical sketch, in order to conceal their potential heretical implications. In addition, Soloviev was afraid to introduce the feminine principle into the religious sphere, where it might be mixed with sexual elements, thus leading to the blasphemous equation of spiritual marriage with ritualistic depravity, seen in the practice of some Russian orgiastic sects, such as the Khlysty.

These fears, Andreev continued, made Soloviev especially laconic and cautious about revealing his sophiological insights, but they became reality in the works and fate of Aleksandr Blok (1880–1921), who considered himself a spiritual disciple of Soloviev. Blok addressed his first book of poems to the Beautiful Lady, a personification of the feminine soul of the world, but in his subsequent creative work, he fell into the abyss of the demonic feminine, following the steps of the fallen Sophia, who appeared to him as an "unknown woman" (*neznakomka*), a seductive combination of virgin and whore. "Now [Blok] sings about Velga, mistaking her for Navna in his increasing blindness" (10.5.198). This error was not his alone but the entire country's, reflecting the tragic fall of her feminine soul. From the heights of Sophia, to whom many Russian churches were dedicated, the people were slipping into the chasm of revolutionary materialism—the mystical temptation engendered by the great fornicatress, Velga.

Daniil Andreev was one of the first Russian thinkers to proclaim the primary creative role of the feminine in the spiritual growth of humankind, even though he believed that in some fields a woman is less gifted than a man. Though for two hundred years the doors to the arts and sciences had been open wide to women, at least to those of the privileged classes, he pointed out, there were fewer female than male geniuses in music, painting, literature, and science (6.3.123). Nevertheless, Andreev argued,

> it is indisputable that in other respects she possesses gifts that a man lacks and will never have. . . . Motherhood, upbringing of children, the creation of a home, care for the ill, ethical rehabilitation [*vrachevanie*] of criminals, transformation of nature, breeding of animals, some channels [*rusla*] of religious life, creation of love, and finally creative fertilization of the soul of the man she loves—this is where a woman is indispensable and infinitely gifted. . . .
>
> In the spheres of the highest creativity, something opposite to what we see in the physical world occurs. Here the woman is the fertilizing principle while man is the principle of shaping and incarnation. *The Divine Comedy* is the product of two authors and it could not appear without both Beatrice and Dante. If we could penetrate the depths of the creative process of the majority of great artists, we would become certain that it was through a woman that the spiritual seed of the immortal creations was thrown into the depth of their [artists'] unconscious, into the hiding place of their creativity. (6.3.123)

One can see how Andreev combines very conventional views on the predominantly familial or domestic vocation of women with a rather original theory that women impregnate men in the spiritual sphere. According to this hypothesis, there are so few female geniuses precisely because women do not give birth to creative works but fertilize their creators just as men do not give birth to children but impregnate women. This invisible participation of women in the *history* of civilization must be acknowledged; but even more important is to reorient the *future* of civilization according to the increasing role of femininity:

> For thousands of years, the male, masculine element was dominant in humanity—force, audacity, pride, courage, striving afar, cruelty, militarism. . . . Millennium after millennium, waves of wars, rebellions, revolutions, terror, and furiously merciless massacres have been rolling and rolling across the face on the earth. The innumerable drops in these waves are male wills and male hearts. . . . Meek femininity, driven into the depth of family cells, escaped destruction only because without it man himself was as sterile as a piece of lead and because the physical continuation of humankind is impossible without a woman. . . .
>
> Until now it was proclaimed that not only a man but a woman is obliged to be manly. . . . But . . . not only a woman, but a man too, must be feminine. (6.3.123–24)

Thus for Daniil Andreev, the feminine principle will increasingly determine the supreme goals of historical development. Nevertheless, his view does not presume a one-sided dominance of females in the coming epochs. Femininity is asymmetrical in relation to masculinity, in the sense that it is more "capacious" and brings the spirit of reconciliation to both sexes. The male and the female can be reunited on the basis of femininity:

> The growth of feminine forces and their meaning for modernity are seen everywhere. This can primarily account for the general striving for peace, reluctance to bloodshed, disappointment in violent methods of social transformations, the growth of women's social significance, the increasing gentleness and care for children, and a burning passion for beauty and love. We are entering the cycle of epochs when the feminine soul will become increasingly pure and broad, when more and more women will become deep inspirers, sensible mothers, and wise and visionary leaders. This will be the cycle of epochs when the feminine component of humanity will manifest itself with unprecedented strength, balancing the previous dominance of masculine forces in perfect harmony. (6.3.124–25)

Andreev does not imagine a future triumph of femininity as a mere reversal of the present patriarchal establishment; rather, he forecasts a perfect conjugal harmony of feminine and masculine elements that can be seen as an innate quality of femininity.

This synthesis is symbolized by Andreev's central idea—the Rose of the World, which he defines in the glossary as "the coming all-Christian church of the last centuries that will integrate in itself the churches of the past and will connect in a free union all religions of Light. In this sense, the Rose of the World is interreligious or pan-religious. Its main goal is to save as many human souls as possible and to deliver them from the danger of spiritual enslavement by the coming anti-God [*protivobog*]" (274). As Andreev conceived it, the Rose of the World will become the highest manifestation of the feminine soul of the universe. This global religious and social organization is destined to overcome

> the contradiction between two primary tendencies—ascetic spirituality, which rejects the world, and the so-called pagan tendency, which extols the carnal world. . . . Finally, the triumph of the Rose of the World is not possible until the striving of religious humanity toward the Eternal Feminine [*Vechno Zhenstvennoe*] reveals a new, deeper meaning; until the breathing of Zventa-Sventana has softened and lightened the extremely gloomy severity of masculinity, which up to now has completely dominated ethics, religion, and social life. (10.2.180)

A synthesis of two Russian philosophical attitudes, materialism and sophiology, which I would call, for lack of a better term, "materiosophy," is one of the main purposes of Andreev's work. "Materiosophy" can be defined as the "removal of the antagonism between spiritual-ascetic and pagan tendencies and the development of a synthetic attitude toward nature in the consciousness of multitudes of people" (10.2.180). When reunited, these two aspects of femininity, ascetic and pagan, spiritual and sexual, would strengthen the influence of femininity in the future. Certainly the feminine will not remain unchanged; it must embrace not only the purity of a virgin and the fertility of motherhood but the sexuality of a mature woman. The integration of *materiia* and Sophia will imply "the activization of the Eternal Feminine principle, whose embodiment in Russia, Navna, had been weakened, tortured, and taken captive for many centuries" (10.2.180).

The feminine mysticism of Daniil Andreev, as of Russian philosophy, is clearly distinct from those varieties of contemporary Western feminism that postulate separate, self-contained spheres of female culture. Andreev stresses not so much the equality of women in historically male-dominated fields as the superiority of women in those fields that traditionally have been underestimated and underdeveloped by patriarchal civilization. Whereas some Western feminists emphasize female perspectives in writing, reading, and criticism, Andreev emphasizes the privileged position of women in domains of intuitive or integral knowledge which cannot be reduced to scientific disciplines or critical discourse.

Russian feminine mysticism proceeds from the idea of an integral human being in whom heart and mind, body and soul are one. In men, these capacities are usually split and highly specialized because of the division of labor. Women, however, have retained their wholeness because it is necessary for the act of giving birth. Whereas some Western feminists defend gender differences against the power of one male canon, Russian thinkers such as Soloviev and Andreev are inclined to defend androgyny as part of a general desire for "total unity" (*vseedinstvo*) as opposed to gendered specialization. Some Western feminists maintain that women must affirm their social and cultural independence of male-dominated civilization. Daniil Andreev, however, believed that "not only a woman, but a man too, must be feminine."

Despite Andreev's extremely positive and optimistic view of femininity, the underlying ambiguous image of Sophia as virgin and whore unconsciously penetrates his thinking. Andreev's pan-religious system contains an inner drama and inherent paradox: what he glorifies as the Rose of the World is strikingly similar to what he vilifies as the kingdom of the Antichrist. The Rose of the World is the ideal state-church of the future, embracing all existing religions, including Christianity, Islam, and Buddhism, under the rule of one world government and one spiritual leader. (This idea is reminiscent of Soloviev's utopia of global Christian theocracy led by tsar and pope, but in Andreev's vision the future "supreme instructor" (*verkhovnyi nastavnik*) integrates the two roles.) According to Andreev's prophecy, however, after several generations of peaceful rule, the Rose of the World will inevitably fall into the hands of the Antichrist, whose kingdom will finally be crushed by the second coming of Christ, thus ending the current eon of world history. Andreev characterizes the kingdom of the Antichrist, with its horrors and blasphemies, as completely antithetical to his theocratic utopia, the Rose of the World. Nevertheless, the conceptual system underlying his description leads one to conclude that the Rose of the World, the kingdom of God on earth, is implicitly the kingdom of the Antichrist, or at least its antecedent.

Andreev emphasizes, for example, that the "supreme instructor" will combine artistic genius, moral righteousness, and the inspiration of a religious prophet (1.1.15). The same combination of gifts is characteristic of the Antichrist conceived by Soloviev in his "Kratkaia povest' ob antikhriste" (Tale of Antichrist, 1899–1900), a work that Andreev knew well and that he repeatedly cited as a valid prophecy. Moreover, Andreev's Antichrist is endowed with a similar "unprecedented versatility of gifts," and he gains power through his ascension to the leadership of the Rose of the World (12.4.264–65).[21]

Among the features of the Rose of the World that are ironically mirrored in the kingdom of the Antichrist, the cult of femininity is of central importance. As soon as the Antichrist ascends to the throne and is crowned, he "announce[s] himself to be the messenger of World Femininity" (12.4.265). Vladimir Soloviev never reinterpreted Eternal Femininity ironically as a demonic cult: in his "Kratkaia povest' ob antikhriste" he abandons and condemns the ideas of total unity and universal theocracy that he advocated earlier but leaves sophiology intact, as well as the Christian justification of Platonic eroticism attempted in his article "Smysl liubvi" (The meaning of love). According to Soloviev, it is through sexual love that human beings ascend to God and unite with the "Eternal Femininity of God." Characteristically, Andreev considers this erotic moment in Soloviev's theology to be his greatest achievement: "it is precisely the prophecy about Zventa-Sventana and the creation of historical and religious premises for the Rose of the World that constituted his [Soloviev's] mission" (10.4.194).

In Andreev's eschatological vision, the kingdom of the Antichrist releases the sexual drives and raises them to the status of a religious cult. Andreev uses the name of Lilith, an apocryphal female demon and Adam's rebellious first wife, to designate the feminine counterpart of the Antichrist: "The incarnate Lilith, who pretended to be Femininity, will alternately engage in shameless actions with Antilogos and in orgy-mysteries, opened first to hundreds of people, and later, in principle, to everybody. . . . Everything will be directed toward the unbridling of the sexual element" (12.4.266–67).

21. A more detailed analysis of the internal ironies and paradoxes of Andreev's *Roza mira* can be found in my article "Roza Mira i Tsarstvo Antikhrista: O paradoksakh russkoi eskhatologii," *Kontinent* (Moscow and Paris), no. 79, 1994 (1), pp. 283–332; rpt. in Mikhail Epstein, *Vera i obraz: Religioznoe bessoznatel'noe v russkoi kul'ture 20-go veka* (Tenafly, N.J., 1994), pp. 205–50.

Andreev seems to forget that, according to his previous arguments concerning the bisexual nature of God, the intercourse and marriage of the two divine hypostases constitutes the main mystery of the religion of the Rose of the World. This idea was in Andreev's proposal for a future eighth ecumenical council to revise the dogma of the Holy Trinity and to substitute Femininity for the Holy Spirit as one of the three hypostases: "the eternal union between Father and Mother . . . and in this love, the Third is born: the Foundation of the Universe. Father—Eternal Virgin–Mother—Son" (6.3.121). This dogmatic innovation is reminiscent of an atheistic postulate of Feuerbach, who argued that the Christian Trinity is only a reflection of sexual relationships within the earthly family. Andreev humanizes and trivializes the mystery of the Trinity, introducing a male-female polarity that reduces it to the level of the pagan myth of the marriage of heaven and earth.

For Andreev, the replacement of the Holy Spirit by the female aspect of divinity is the "decisive thesis" of his book, though he acknowledges that he dares to break with the "foundation of foundations," the Holy Trinity preached by the Christian churches: "The idea of World Femininity can but grow into the idea of the Female aspect of Divinity, and this naturally threatens to destroy the dogmatic ideas about the hypostases of the Holy Trinity" (6.3.120–21).

The introduction of a female principle into the Trinity is not purely a theoretical proposal. Femininity, as a new dogma crucial for the religion of the Rose of the World, is also realized in the specific hierarchy of the female priesthood, which reflects the second hypostasis of the Trinity. There will be specific temples and rituals designed exclusively for priestesses, the blue hierarchy, functioning along with the golden hierarchy of God-Father and the white hierarchy of God-Son (12.3.258). Moreover, Andreev also anticipates certain cult practices, such as the blessing of young couples seeking marriage not by Christian priests but by the fertile forces of nature, more precisely, by the special order of "nature-priests" under the auspices of the Rose of the World. "[O]ne should not impose wedding vows for more than several years, and it is more appropriate to ask for help not from the hierarchy of Christian transmyth but from Mother Earth and even from the popular Aphrodite of humankind" (12.3.255).[22]

Unconsciously Andreev reveals the demonic side of his utopia: his reverence for a sexually bipolar divinity lays the foundation for the sacrilegious practices of the Antichrist and the eventual doom of the Rose of the World. The Antichrist's main project, and the source of his power over humanity, is sexual permissiveness, for which he will offer religious justification: "Antilogos will announce himself to be the incarnation of God-Father, and the woman whose appearance Lilith has taken by means of a demonic miracle to be the incarnation of Eternal Femininity. . . . Around himself and the incarnate Lilith, the

---

22. In Ancient Greece, the popular Aphrodite, Pandemos, was the goddess of crude, sensual love, as opposed to Aphrodite Urania, who was the goddess of ideal, heavenly love.

Antichrist will create a blasphemous cult of world fornication, and vile actions between the two of them, surrounded by fantastic effects and stupefying splendor, will be performed before the eyes of the everyone, allegedly reflecting, in our world, the cosmic marriage of two hypostases of the Trinity" (12.4.265).

It is clear that if not for the transformation of the Trinity into the cosmic marriage of two hypostases, sanctified and dogmatized by the Rose of the World, there would be nothing for the Antichrist to reflect or imitate. It is impossible to create the cult of world fornication from the relationship of the two traditional hypostases—God-Father and the Holy Spirit—as Christians understand it. The original Trinity simply lacks any premise for such blasphemy, precludes any consideration of it, whereas Andreev's Trinity, presenting "the mystery of the union of Father and Mother" (6.3.121), clears the path for the cult of fornication. How can the sexually bipolar Trinity be reflected in ritual except through an infinite succession of sexual unions, which is precisely what constitutes the seductive appeal of the Antichrist and his female hypostasis?

One wonders why Andreev, who was so sensitive to the spiritual dangers of feminine mysticism—those, in his view, that Soloviev avoided and that proved fatal for Blok—proved to be so susceptible to them himself. Perhaps *Roza mira*, though formally finished, should not be viewed as fully completed, since there is a certain discordance between Andreev's social prophecies and his eschatological visions. (In the end, the author, mortally ill, had less than two years after his release from prison to organize and elaborate on his inspirational fragments.) Andreev understood perfectly that "the intrusion of ideas about the difference of divinely male and divinely female principles into religious organizations and cults is fraught with exceptional dangers. Understood with insufficient spirituality, separated with insufficient strictness from the sexual sphere of humanity, these intrusions lead to the darkening of spirituality with [the loosening of] the sexual element, to the blasphemous identification of cosmic spiritual marriage with sensual love and, in the final analysis, with ritual debauchery" (10.4.194). This was precisely the temptation that haunted Andreev and unconsciously transformed his utopia into the apocalypse.

What Andreev proclaimed as his "decisive thesis" he also condemned as a "blasphemous cult," for it was the selfsame feminine principle polarized as virgin and whore. Andreev's attempt to reconcile these two aspects of the eternal mother, who is both Sophia and *materiia*, proved to be a spiritually dangerous enterprise, since the opposition should not be completely erased. As soon as the desired synthesis of all-comprehensive femininity is achieved in the project of the Rose of the World, it becomes subject to a new doubling, to the materialization of a demonic and purely sensual femininity in the kingdom of the Antichrist, and it is this theoretical irony that ultimately undermines Andreev's theocratic utopia.

Thus the mystical element of Andreev's doctrine, his veneration of the feminine aspect of divinity, comes into a very complicated and controversial relationship with the eschatological element of his doctrine, an apprehension of the "ritual debauchery" at the very essence of the demonic Antitrinity. Andreev never managed to overcome this contradiction, but of all Russian mystics, he most expressively testified to its hidden ironies.

APPENDIX: SYNOPSIS OF *ROZA MIRA*

Roza mira consists of twelve books, each of which is divided into several chapters.

BOOK 1

"The Rose of the World and Its Place in History." In Chapter 1, "The Rose of the World and Its Most Immediate Tasks," Andreev briefly refers to the history of his manuscript, which he had to hide as he was writing it and after its completion in 1958. "I belong to those who have been fatally wounded by two great misfortunes: world wars and one person's [*edinolichnoi*] tyranny" (p. 7). Andreev explains the task of his book as promoting the rapprochement of religions and ideologies that aspire to the spiritual unity of the world. The Rose of the World is the universal teaching of pan-religion, destined to fulfill the integration of humanity, a process begun by the formation of institutions such as world religions and the League of Nations. "If old religions are petals, then the Rose of the World is the flower" (p. 13). "Interreligiousness, the universality of social aspirations and their concrete character, the dynamism of worldview and consistency of historical goals: these are the traits that set the Rose of the World apart from all past religions and churches" (p. 14). "It is a universal, supernational structure [*vsemirnoe narodoustroistvo*] that aspires to the sanctification and enlightenment of the entire life of the world" (p. 16).

In Chapter 2, "The Attitude toward Culture," Andreev looks at the specific scientific, economic, technological, aesthetic, and ethical problems that the Rose of the World is called upon to solve. In particular, he prophesies that visual art in the future will follow the patterns of metarealism, showing many material and spiritual layers of reality through one image.

In Chapter 3, "The Attitude toward Religions," Andreev seeks a way to reconcile the contradictory aspects of the world religions, such as the monotheism of Islam and the Trinity of Christianity.

BOOK 2

"On the Metahistorical and Transphysical Methods of Knowledge." Chapter 1, "Some Peculiarities of Metahistorical Method," lays down the methodological foundation of the book. Metahistory is the unified history of this world and of all others. It is the totality of processes that are implemented in all dimensions of space-time and sometimes shine through the social history of humankind, which is only a tiny part of this metahistory. Andreev categorizes three stages of metahistorical knowledge: illumination, contemplation, and interpretation. He recounts the most important metahistorical illuminations of his own life, which occurred in 1921, 1928, 1932, 1933, and 1943, and then regularly from 1950 to 1953, while he was in prison. In his mystical travels through multiple worlds he was led by the greatest spirits that ever existed in Russia. He did not see them, but was able to talk to them, and he heard their words coming from the bottom of his own heart.

Chapter 2, "Some Thoughts on Transphysical Method," focuses on the perception of nature as a transparent physical reality that reveals its transphysical spiritual essence. Andreev describes his travels across Russia and Ukraine, during which he communicated with the spiritual entities of nature, which he calls *stikhiali*, or elementals.

Chapter 3, "The Initial Conception," describes the most important concepts of the new metahistorical and transphysical vision.

1. Multiple layers. Every layer differs from every other in the number of its spatial or temporal dimensions. Several terms are introduced: *Bramfatura* (a system of layers surrounding each celestial body), *Enrof* (our physical layer, which consists of three spatial and one temporal dimension), *Shadanakar* (our planet's *Bramfatura*, which consists of 242 layers of differing spaces and times), and *Sakuala* (a system of layers, each of which can be entered from another). Andreev writes that elementary particles are living entities that have free will, but it is still impossible at present to communicate with them.

2. The origin of evil. The world's laws. Karma. The root of evil is egoism—the intention to include all other monads, or spiritual entities, in oneself. Only God is capable of creating monads; Lucifer can only try to capture them. Evil is embodied in Gartungr, a planetary demon who has three separate and interrelated identities (antihypostases): the great tormentor, the great whore, and the principle of form (possibly as a demonic counterpart to the third hypostasis of the Holy Spirit). The struggle between Gartungr and the Planetary Logos, who was embodied in Christ, is the force that propels earth's history.

3. The question of free will. History is the progressive development of the freedom of human will, which allows an individual monad to liberate itself from evil and its consequences.

4. Being and consciousness.

5. The various material components of a human being. "A monad is an indivisible and spiritual unit, the highest 'self' of people" (p. 117). Monads materialize in *shelt*, a five-dimensional body, as well as in astral and ethereal bodies. Thus monads can survive physical death and travel into other layers.

6. Metacultures. Andreev introduces the concepts of the supernation (*sverkhnarod*) and its metaculture, which exist simultaneously in many material

layers. Supernations include the Southwestern Roman Catholic Supernation, the Northwestern German Protestant Supernation, the Russian Supernation, and so on. Each supernation creates its own transmyth as a specific vision of multiple realities—a unifying myth, defining the collective identity of interconnected nations. These transmyths include those artistic creations that most deeply express the soul of the given supernation, such as Goethe's Faust and Margarete, or Shakespeare's Hamlet and King Lear.

A supernation is flanked by two metacultural realms. The upper layer, called a *zatomis*, is the metacultural abode of a supernation's enlightened souls, holy cities, and heavenly spirits. The lower layer, called *shrastr*, is home to the concentrated demonic forces of the supernation. Olympus, Sinai, and Kitezh exemplify the transmythical images of the zatomises in the Greek, Jewish, and Russian metacultures, respectively. Andreev explains that Russia's relative youth is responsible for the lack of Russian terms in his description of transphysical worlds. They had already been named in the languages of older metacultures, primarily the Indian.

BOOK 3

"The Structure of Shadanakar: The Ascending Row of Worlds." In Chapter 1, "*Sakuala* of Enlightenment," Andreev describes his most recent death, which occurred three hundred years ago in a non-Russian metaculture. He recalls the layers through which his soul then ascended. The first layer was Olirna, a world in which Andreev met some of his closest relatives and friends. The environment there is similar to the earth's, but it is without earth's extremes of tropical rains and arctic frost. The sky is a deep green and the sun is multicolored. A lonely island in Olirna happens to be the residence of Judas, who has since repented his betrayal of Christ. The way from Olirna to the next, higher worlds is not through death but through transfiguration. The next layer is Fier (Fair), whose inhabitants exult over the abundant light and the appearance of long-expected wings. Those who reach Fier will never come down to Enrof, the earth, unless they have a spiritual mission. Then the worlds Nartis (the land of great tranquility) and Gotimna (the garden of sublime fates) are described.

Chapter 2, "Zatomises." *Zatomises* are the top layers of metaculture and are inhabited by *sinklits*, assemblies of the greatest souls of the supernations. There are nineteen zatomises, corresponding to the number of metacultures. The first zatomis is Maif, the heavenly synod of the metaculture of Atlantis, the society that existed approximately 10,000 years before the birth of Christ. The culture of Atlantis was similar to that of ancient Egypt, only more repressive and gloomy. Other zatomises include Linat (Gondvana land), Ialu (ancient Egypt), Eanna (Babylon, Assyria, and Canaan), Shan-Ti (China), Sumera (or Meru, India, the most powerful of all zatomises), Zervan (ancient Persia), Olymp (ancient Greece and Rome), Nikhord (Judaism), Rai (Byzantium), Eden (Roman Catholicism), Monsalvat (Northwestern Europe, North America, Australia, and some parts of Africa, the most vast of all zatomises), Zhunfleiia (Ethiopia), Jannet (Islam), Sukkhavati (northern Buddhism), Aireng-Daliang (Indo-Malaysia), Heavenly Russia, the zatomis of African culture, and Arimoiia, the emerging, unfinished zatomis of pan-human interreligious culture that is being created by the Rose of the World.

Each zatomis is briefly described and designated by a specific symbol. The symbol of China's metaculture, for example, is a beautiful woman's face under a lotuslike crown; Greek and Roman metaculture is symbolized by a white temple against a sky-blue background; India's metacultural symbol is three mountain chains crowned with golden cities; the Jewish metaculture is symbolized by tentlike buildings surrounded by trees with large red fruits. Finally, Andreev gives a description of Heavenly Russia, a pinkish-white city with many temples on a high shore above a blue river. The highest place in Heavenly Russia belongs to Pushkin, Lermontov, Gogol, Lev Tolstoy, Aleksei Konstantinovich Tolstoy, Dostoevsky, Vladimir Soloviev, and Mikhail Kutuzov (the general who defeated Napoleon), because national geniuses and messengers continue their spiritual activity in the zatomises. Scores of great spirits ascended from the Russian zatomis into the world's sinklit, among them Saint Vladimir, Iaroslav the Wise, Sergei Radonezhsky, Andrei Rublev, and Mikhail Lomonosov.

In Chapter 3, "The Middle Layers of Shadanakar," Andreev presents the yellowish, smoking spaces where Egregors live. These entities of a nonmaterial nature emerge from the psychic essence of great collectives (tribes, states, parties, communities). Seven subdivisions of these middle worlds of Egregors are described. One such subdivision is Foraun, which consists of the dark, ephemeral radiation that comes from congregations of people gathered in churches. The highest category of humanity, known as daimons (demons), inhabits one of the middle worlds. The daimons are similar to angels, except for the fact that they are male and female. They inspire earthbound artists and poets. In Andreev's mind, fictional characters have prototypes in the world of daimons; after a writer dies, a hero's image, such as that of Ivan Karamazov or Andrei Bolkonsky, ascends to one of the other worlds, elevated by the spiritual force of its creator.

BOOK 4

"The Structure of Shadanakar and Infraphysics." Chapter 1, "The Foundation," describes Gartungr, the demon of Shadanakar, who imitates aspects of God, such as the Trinity. He lies on the waves of a turbulent lilac ocean with his black wings spread from horizon to horizon. Gasharva, one of the lowest worlds, has many temporal but only two spatial dimensions. This situation creates a spiritual stuffiness and an enormous density of matter. This world is home to the model for Vrubel's "Demon," as well as for the Velgas, powerful female demons who resemble enveloping black clothing that constantly opens and closes. On the Bottom of the Galaxy, the lowest of all levels, time does not exist. The demonic creatures that live there are one-dimensional, like a black line, and their suffering is indescribable.

Chapter 2 describes the worlds of retribution, which function as purgatories. The first is Skrivnus, a place without God, colors, or flowers. Millions of people live there in trenches dug among low but unclimbable hills. Their sleep is devoid of dreams and their labor is devoid of creativity: they mend old clothes, wash dirty dishes, and so on. Their condition is further hampered by the enormous, frightful beings who live on the other side of the hills and occasionally throw things at them. The people of Skrivnus look almost human, but their features are smooth, like identical pancakes. The most trying torment for them is boredom and tedious work devoid of any sense of the future. The only means of escape from Skrivnus is a black, boxlike ship that occasionally floats ashore swiftly and silently. Those who are taken into the ship's hold see nothing; they only feel a horizontal movement followed by a spiraling downfall.

The layers after Skrivnus are Ladref, Morod, and Agr. Agr is composed of black smoke in which mirror images of the earth's great cities appear. There is no sun, moon, or stars; instead, each object radiates a dim, dark red color. Andreev describes in detail the sight of infra-Petersburg. The next layer is Bustvich, where residents (prisoners) are disgusted by themselves because their ethereal bodies have been reduced to feces. The next purgatories are Rafag, Shim-Big, Dromn, and Fukabirn. These layers are followed by layers of magma (molten rock): Okrus, Gvegr, Ukarvair, Propulk, and Yrl. The levels after the magma descend to earth's core: Biask (infrared caverns), Amiuts (vertical fissures), Ytrech (planetary night), Zhurshch (where only Judas Iscariot ever had resided), and Sufel (or Sufekh), the world in which stubbornly evil people experience a second death and their monads are expelled from Shadanakar.

Chapter 3, "Shrastrs and Uitsraors." Shrastrs are worlds that mirror zatomises from beneath the earth. These satanocratic worlds are inhabited by antihumans who serve the goals of the planetary demon. Among them are the Igvs, who are highly intellectual but have almost no emotional or sexual feelings. They do not need privacy or spiritual love. Uitsraors, another group of subterranean inhabitants, have the most important role in history. They were supposed to be the defenders of nations from outward enemies, but then proved to be tools of demonic will. They are the offspring of the female demon Lilith and the demiurges of the supernations. Uitsraors are enormous; if one imagines the head of this creature to be in the city of Moscow, his tentacles would reach hundreds of miles to the sea. Uitsraors love the human world with a greedy, predatory passion, but they cannot tangibly exist on the earth.

They radiate an enormous amount of psychic energy, which is manifested in national, patriotic feelings toward one's state. All the forces that infuse a great power—chauvinism, tyranny, xenophobia—are concentrated in these huge creatures. The Uitsraors of some previous societies, such as Babylon, Rome, and Byzantium, have perished. The Uitsraor of Russia is named Zhrugr. In the lower world of the Russian metaculture, Drukkarg, Zhrugr uses his power to stifle Navna, the ideal communal soul of Russia.

BOOK 5

"The Structure of Shadanakar: Stikhials." Stikhials (elementals) are the spirits of nature, monads who manifest themselves in physical worlds. Chapter 1, "Demonic Stikhials," describes such elements of physical nature as volcanos, magma, the sea floor, and the earth's core. The worlds of Shartamakhum, Ganniks, Sviks, Nugurt, and Duggur, home to the great metropolitan cities of the underworld, including infra-Petersburg, are portrayed.

Chapter 2, "The Light Stikhials," describes the worlds of Murokhamma (grasses and bushes), Arashamf (souls of the trees), Vaiita (winds), Faltora (meadows and fields), Liurna (souls of the rivers), Vlanmim (upper layers of the seas), Zunguf (clouds and rains), Irudrana (thunderstorms), Nivenna (snow), and many others.

Chapter 3, "The Attitude toward the Animal Kingdom," discusses the spiritual significance of insects, mammals, fish and other creatures. Andreev establishes our moral duty to animals. Zoogogy, the pedagogy of animals, accelerates animals' development to the mental level of human beings.

BOOK 6

"The Highest Worlds of Shadanakar." Chapter 1, "Toward World Salvaterra," describes Salvaterra as the "land of salvation" or, in poetic terms, "the shining crystal of heaven's strivings" (p. 264). The highest souls of humanity, encompassing both individuals and nations, are located here after they have completed their earthly tasks. Andreev believes that world leadership will pass to the demiurge of the Russian supernation in the near future, which will then be succeeded by the demiurge of India.

Chapter 2, "The Logos of Shadanakar," investigates the fate of Jesus Christ. Andreev suggests that Jesus did not fully carry out his mission. The material element of nature and of humanity has not been enlightened on a worldwide scale, but only in the flesh of Christ himself. During the twenty centuries since his resurrection, Christ's spiritual powers have increased immensely; Andreev foresees a second coming in two or three more centuries.

In Chapter 3, "Femininity," Andreev connects the future of humanity with the growing prevalence of femininity; he also revises the traditional concept of the Holy Trinity to include a female hypostasis or essence.

BOOK 7

"Toward the Metahistory of Ancient Rus'." From this book on, the author presents a kind of cohesive explanation of Russian history, from its inception to the foreseeable future.

Chapter 1, "Kievan Rus' as a Metahistorical Phenomenon." The main heroes of this chapter are the Russian demiurge Iarosvet; Russia's communal soul, Navna; and the demonic forces Velga and Gartungr, who were involved in the very conception of Russia.

Chapter 2, "The Christian Myth and Proto-Russianism [*prarossianstvo*]." The relationship between Orthodox Christianity and Russian paganism is investigated. A duality is found in the contrast between the elegant and cheerful exteriors of Russian cathedrals and their dark and severe interiors.

Chapter 3, "The Epoch of the First Uitsraor," is devoted to the birth of Muscovite Rus' and to the personality of Ivan the Terrible.

BOOK 8

"Toward the Metahistory of the Muscovite Tsardom." In Chapter 1, "The Change of the Uitsraors," the period of Boris Godunov and the Time of Troubles are described in metahistorical terms. The Zhrugr of Moscow's statehood was first weakened, then dismembered, and finally eaten by its offspring. Russia was torn apart and a new Zhrugr had to usurp the throne in order to restore the integrity of the country.

Chapter 2, "The Egregor of Orthodoxy and Infraphysical Fear," treats the relationship between the church and the state in Russia, Nikon's church reforms of the mid–seventeenth century, and the birth of metahistorical self-consciousness in Russia.

In Chapter 3, "The Filling of the Space between Cultures," Andreev interprets Russia's eastward expansion and the assimilation of Siberia and the Far East as a great metahistorical event that filled in the space between Catholic, Muslim, and Indian cultures.

Chapter 4, "Rodomysl Peter the Great and the Demonic Distortion of his Mission." Rodomysls (from *rod*, birth, and *mysl'*, thought) are great historical figures, Peter the Great among them, who play prophetic and crucial roles in the fates of their nations. Andreev analyzes the contradictions of Peter the Great, whose activity was instigated by the second Zhrugr of Russian statehood after the first Zhrugr had perished in the Time of Troubles.

BOOK 9

"Toward the Metahistory of the Petersburg Empire." In Chapter 1, "The Second Uitsraor and Exterior Space," Andreev outlines Russian culture as a component of world culture and an intermediary between Western and Eastern civilizations.

Chapter 2, "The Second Uitsraor and Interior Space," describes the peculiarities of the Russian monarchy and of the Romanov dynasty in terms of the laws of karma.

In Chapter 3, "The Removal of Blessing," the reign of Alexander I, his life in Siberia after his apparent death in 1825, his angelic nature, and his burden of karma are viewed as evidence of Alexander's contradictory relation to Providence.

BOOK 10

"Toward the Metahistory of Russian Culture." In Chapter 1, "The Talent of Messengers," Andreev divides artistic geniuses and talents into categories and singles out a specific rank for messengers—people who are inspired by daimons and reveal the highest realities of other worlds.

In Chapter 2, "Missions and Fates," Andreev traces the role of the Eternal Feminine in Russian culture and the spiritual missions of Pushkin, Lermontov, and Gogol.

Chapter 3, "Missions and Fates (Continued)." The missions of Dostoevsky and Tolstoy are regarded as the reconciliation of the two elements of Russian culture, the ascetic Christian and the pagan.

Chapter 4, "Missions and Fates (Conclusion)." The works and fates of Ivan Turgenev and Vladimir Soloviev are considered to reveal the feminine soul of Russia.

Chapter 5, "The Fall of the Messenger." Aleksandr Blok's descent from the idealism of his early poems to the fascination with Russia as a great whore symbolizes the country's mystical fall into the abyss of revolution.

BOOK 11

"Toward the Metahistory of the Last Century." Chapter 1, "The Third Zhrugr's Ascension to Power." The first Zhrugr inspired the state power of Muscovite Rus' and the second one inspired the Petersburg empire. Here the third Zhrugr, a crimson beast who proved to be much more cruel and predatory than the first two, begins his struggle against his predecessor.

In Chapter 2, "The Struggle against Spirituality," Andreev analyzes the doctrine of Soviet ideology as a quasireligion whose aim was to cut all connections of the "new man" with the spiritual worlds. Andreev doubts the cultural potential of the working class, identifying the "faceless" proletariat not as the crown but as the bottom of humanity and as a tragic diffusion and degradation of humanity's truly creative forces, the peasantry and the intelligentsia.

Chapter 3, "The Dark Shepherd." Returning to deep prophecies of Russian literature about the future Antichrist (poems by Lermontov and Blok and the images of Saltykov-Shchedrin are mentioned), Andreev demonstrates their embodiment in Stalin. Stalin proved to be a much more successful manifestation of the Gartungr's demonic will than Lenin or Hitler. The mystical motives of Stalin's behavior and his life beyond the grave at the very bottom of the world are set forth.

Chapter 4, "Toward the Metahistory of Our Days," describes the post-Stalin period, when the hierarchies of both Light and Darkness tried to prevent a planetary catastrophe. The third Uitsraor began to lose its power in Khrushchev's time, though his struggle with Stebing, the Uitsraor of North America, still gave the former Uitsraor many advantages.

BOOK 12

"Possibilities." In Chapter 1, "The Education of a Man with a Noble Spirit," Andreev maintains that the birth of the Rose of the World is foreordained, but no one can predict exactly when it will appear. While critical of the moral doctrines of communism, Andreev also identifies some of its positive aspects, in particular the harmony of the physical and spiritual components of personality, and the coexistence of civilization and nature. He describes the future educational and judicial systems at length.

Chapter 2, "External Measures." The transformation of the earth, the melting of polar ice and snow, the irrigation of desert land into oases, a unified cosmopolitan state, centers of a new religious culture, cities of faith, triumphal gardens, theaters of mysteries, houses of meditation, philosophical institutions—such are the components of Andreev's design for the Rose of the World.

Chapter 3, "The Cult." The liturgy of the Rose of the World will include not only elements of traditional religious rituals but also the spiritual aspects of the arts and literature and the sanctified elements of nature. The sacraments of birth, friendship, love, creativity, childhood, old age, and, most important, femininity will be united in the temples of the future. Andreev foresees five hierarchies of priests that partly correspond to his new concept of Trinity. The first hierarchy, the Father's, will be golden; the second, the Virgin Mother's, will be blue; and the third hierarchy, the Son's, will be white. The fourth, purple hierarchy's religious service will be addressed to the self-consciousness and historic roots of a given nation and will be devoted to the worship of its greatest rodomysls and messengers (for example, the cult of Pro-Russianism). The fifth, green, priesthood will preach the spirituality of nature (pp. 257–58).

Chapter 4, "The Prince of Darkness." The Rose of the World will not prevent Satan's arrival. Thirst for power and sexual freedom will put an end to the golden age by causing the collapse of social harmony. People will worship Gartungr as a rebellious hero against God's tyranny. Antilogos will become the most general and brilliant genius, quickly rising to the pinnacle of the arts and sciences. He will be the same monad whose imperfect draft was Stalin. He will perform miracles that will make Christ's miracles pale in comparison (many details are reminiscent of Soloviev's "Tale of Antichrist"). He will announce himself to be the embodiment of God the Father, but gradually he will be replaced by the great tormentor, Satan. The great fornicatress will take the place of the Eternal Feminine and will seduce myriads of people. The Rose of the World will be banned and all priests and parishes will be destroyed. Anti-humans will rise from beneath the earth's surface and igvs, demonic beings of higher intellect, the inhabitants of the lower worlds, will rule humanity.

Suddenly a catastrophe will overtake Antilogos, when his monad, which was abducted by Gartungr thousands of years ago, is liberated by the Saviour; the Prince of Darkness will fall through all the layers of Hell into the timeless Bottom of Galaxy.

Chapter 5, "The Change of Eons." Unprecedented terror, confusion, and bloody chaos will follow the fall of Satan. There will be sadism, sexual cannibalism, world war between igvs and people, economic collapse, and power in the hands of local tyrants. Nature will become an arena for horrible catastrophes. A few dozen survivors of the Rose of the World, the brothers of the Light, will gather at a single place on earth, presumably in Siberia.

At this time, Shadanakar will tremble from top to bottom, and Christ will manifest himself to everyone. He will descend to the lowest layers of the world and will resurrect the remainders of all souls. During this second eon the worlds of retribution, including the so-called Hell, will be expiated and will become empty.

Gartungr, the Great Demon, will remain alone in the jubilant, transformed universe. If he will finally accept God, then the third eon, the redemption of Gartungr, will begin. The entire Shadanakar will disappear from the physical dimension. "This is about the coming of the third eon that the great angel of the Apocalypse swears by saying that there will be time nevermore" (p. 272).

CHAPTER FIFTEEN
THE OCCULT
IN RUSSIA TODAY
Holly DeNio Stephens

Many of the occult ideas popular in the Russia of the 1990s are based on the fin-de-siècle grafting of Oriental philosophies onto Western occult thought (Theosophy, Anthroposophy, and their spin-offs). The neo-Buddhist philosophies of today, however, contain fewer fundamentally Christian elements than those of the more traditionally devout fin de siècle. These philosophies are also doctrinally less consistent, a development caused mainly by loss of continuity, the impossibility of contact with Western colleagues, a lack of basic texts, and the prohibition of religious and quasi-religious societies during the Soviet years. New doctrines have developed as mutations of Theosophy and Anthroposophy, and a renascence of turn-of-the-century spiritualism has given birth to extrasensatives and belief in energy vampirism.

It is common to find on the streets of Moscow and St. Petersburg reprints (of varying accuracy) of Madame Blavatsky's Theosophical classic *The Secret Doctrine*, as well as other Theosophical books by Annie Besant and C. W. Leadbetter; tracts by the Anthroposophist Rudolf Steiner; abridged and complete editions of *Agni-yoga* by Nikolai Rerikh (Roerich; 1874–1947) and his wife, Elena Shaposhnikova; and other works by fin-de-siècle admirers of the philosophies of India and Tibet such as George Gurdjieff (born Georgy Ivanovich Gorgiades; 1873–1949) and Petr Demianovich Uspensky (1878–1947). Reprints of canonical turn-of-the-century occult classics by Western authors (Papus [Gérard Encausse], Dion Fortune [Violet Firth]) are also available. Small bookshops that

Special thanks to Maria Carlson of the University of Kansas for her very insightful suggestions and comments on this chapter.

provide a more sophisticated selection of occult works, along with crystals, incense, and Western New Age recordings, have sprung up on side streets.

Many occult texts that focus on the "reclamation of the Russian past" appeared after the political events of 1991 and 1993. Reprints of prerevolutionary works that examine Russian mythology, sorcery, witchcraft, and folk belief, as well as new works examining pan-Slavic mythologies and the role of the shaman in all cultures, may be found in virtually every bookstore. Several editions of Russian gypsy fortune-telling cards (based on editions printed in the late nineteenth century) and Russian versions of tarot decks are also for sale at many locations in the cities, from established department stores to office supply stores.

Reprinted and new works, both substantial and ephemeral, have appeared on alchemy, the beneficial healing qualities of stones and crystals, Druidic astrology, the tarot, the Jewish Kabbala, the writings of Hermes Trismegistus, mystical Freemasonry, medieval alchemy, dream interpretation, and chiromancy, as well as on psychic healing, applied and theoretical magic (black and white), spiritualism, and astrology (traditional, lunar, solar, and Chinese). Interest is high in UFOs, abominable snowmen, poltergeists, and Tibetan herbal medicine, both for healing and for attaining supraconsciousness.

In the pop culture arena, the world of the occult has entered the Russian mainstream. Healers and psychics frequently appear on morning and evening talk shows and recount their visions and paranormal experiences. Psychics analyze guardian angels to determine their names, their number, and their role in a person's life;[1] popular museum exhibits focus on the shaman and his role in society; and huge exhibitions of stones and crystals (including crystal balls and pendulums) promote their inherent healing, protective, and divinitory qualities.

Some communication among various groups involved in the occult exists today, but it is limited. Scholars of the occult may contact one group but miss scores of others, since many groups and trends are transitory and will disappear or be absorbed by other groups before it is possible to document them. In early 1995, for example, a small philosophical/occult-oriented group opened a bookstore in St. Petersburg called Deti Solntsa (Children of the sun). They sold books by Blavatsky, Uspensky, Gurdjieff, and Rerikh, as well as stones, crystals, incense, horoscope charts, and tarot decks. Six weeks later the shop was empty; only a small paper taped to the window remained, listing a phone number one could call to receive information about the group's whereabouts. After several days, the paper with the number had also disappeared.

Many messianic apocalyptic sects are also surfacing in the former Soviet

1. One popular idea is that the number of a person's guardian angels, which can range from as many as fifty (some estimates even go into the hundreds) to zero, can be determined by the date and time of birth. A person with no guardian angel is said to live a hopeless and joyless life, unprotected and unaware of the spiritual reminders of divine love.

Union. One such cult, which has lost much influence since 1994, is Beloe Bratstvo (White brotherhood), founded in Kiev in the late 1980s. Its apocalyptic and messianic message appealed to large numbers of people in Russia and several other former republics. Its leaders staged large evangelical demonstrations and predicted that the apocalypse would occur in 1994. Its teachings were so popular among the disillusioned and disadvantaged and it controlled its members so completely that families were filing charges of kidnapping and brainwashing against the cult, and Orthodox priests often intervened on their behalf. In response to concern about the growing numbers of bizarre sects such as this one, the church has established new educational facilities and has increased the number of Sunday schools to serve the spiritual needs of the people. When 1994 came and went with no apocalypse, the White Brotherhood lost many of its followers.

Men and women across the economic spectrum and of all professions (including those in government positions and scholars in the hard sciences) are active in occult groups and sects, organized and informal; curiosity about the occult pervades all elements of society. A survey conducted in the early 1990s revealed that 20 percent of the respondents believed in Buddhism and the Hari Krishna movement, 40 percent were drawn to East Asian philosophies, 50 percent believed in astrology, 66 percent believed in ESP, and 70 percent believed in UFOs.[2]

THEOSOPHY

Events in the Soviet Union after 1985 revealed that occultism in general and Theosophy (and Anthroposophy) in particular had not disappeared from the Russian consciousness. These movements survived the years of forced repression in Russia's occult underground, in exile, and in emigration. Significant numbers of Russian occultists went to Germany, Switzerland, the Baltic states, South America, and Yugoslavia in 1918; after Hitler invaded Eastern Europe in 1939, many occultists emigrated again. Theosophy resurfaced in Russia the moment the climate became even moderately hospitable, although it has not achieved its prerevolutionary popularity and scope. Now Russian Theosophists are once again holding meetings and giving lectures, and Theosophical societies have officially opened their doors in both Moscow and St. Petersburg. The cooperatively printed works of Blavatsky, Besant, and Steiner are readily available.[3]

---

2. Lecture by Boris Falikov, University of Kansas (Lawrence), February 11, 1993.

3. A casual search in Leningrad in the summer of 1991 produced *Vest' E. P. Blavatskoi* (Leningrad, 1991); E. P. Blavatskaia, *Prakticheskoe sokrovennoe uchenie i drugie trudy* (Riga, 1991); E. P. Blavatskaia, *Zakon prichin i posledstvii, ob"iasniaiushchii chelovecheskuiu sud'bu* (Leningrad, 1991); Rudolf Steiner, *Teosofiia, vvedenie v sverkhchuvstvennoe poznanie mira i naz-*

Russian Theosophists have added their voices to the new dialogue about spiritual values to those of the traditional Orthodox, Pentacostals, Evangelicals, Hari Krishnas, and Gurdjievians, as well as the extrasensitives, healers, hypnotists, and other practitioners of popular forms of mass occultism. Like their prerevolutionary predecessors, Russian Theosophists today come from the intelligentsia, the professions, and the middle bureaucracy. They have joined forces with the growing Rerikh movement in an effort to achieve a larger, popular spiritual renewal of Russia through the combined potency of the two "touchstone" names, Blavatsky and Rerikh. Today the search for spirituality continues, through both theosophy and Theosophy—the search eschews Theosophy's fundamentally cosmopolitan point of view and seeks a profoundly Russian solution in the God-seeking philosophies of Vladimir Soloviev, Nikolai Berdiaev, Pavel Florensky, and Konstantin Tsiolkovsky.[4]

GURDJIEFF AND USPENSKY

Books by George Gurdjieff and his disciple Petr Uspensky are also being reprinted, but in lesser numbers than those of the Theosophists, Anthroposophists, and Rerikh. Gurdjieff's basic philosophy was born when he began to seek answers to inexplicable psychic occurrences, and is also primarily Asian-based. According to Gurdjieff, there are four basic states of consciousness: sleep (the private world), waking consciousness (the world that appears to be shared with others but in reality is not, since perceptions of reality are subjective), "self-remembering" (when a person awakens and becomes aware of the real world), and objective consciousness (when the mind is continually aware of reality—a state seldom achieved). People are basically sleeping, helpless victims of circumstance. There are occasional moments of lucidity, when a

---

nachenicheloveka (Yerevan, 1990); Rudolf Steiner, *Khristianstvo kak misticheskii fact i misterii drevnosti* (Yerevan, 1991); S. Tukholka, *Okkul'tizm i magii* (Rostov, 1991); and a variety of Masonic materials. These texts were published in editions of from 5,000 to 100,000 copies, and ranged in price from 5 to 20 rubles (the price early in 1995 was from 600 to 1,200 rubles, or about 10 to 25 cents). They represent but the tip of the occult publications iceberg, for interested individuals have managed to acquire considerable occult libraries in a very few years. Some of the many occult texts now available in Russia are reissues of prerevolutionary translations, but most are completely new, based on definitive Western editions. Several specialized publishing ventures have emerged, such as the Yerevan-based Noi (Noah) publishing house, which plans to issue Steiner's complete works in their series Biblioteka Dukhovnoi Nauki (Library of spiritual science). Several well-produced volumes have already appeared. The Theosophists held an occult conference, "The Creative Contribution of E. P. Blavatsky to Russian Culture," in Leningrad in 1991, claiming (erroneously) that they were celebrating UNESCO's declaration of 1991 as the Year of Helena Blavatsky.

4. Fedorov overlaps oddly with Steiner, in the sense of transforming the physical self and developing spiritual organs of perception. Both would have recognized an evolutionary imperative to develop consciousness and spirit.

person may perceive momentary flashes of ultimate freedom and Truth, but these are ephemeral. Humans must be taught to see beyond the banality of the world and strive for objective consciousness.[5]

In Gurdjieff's cosmology our nature is tripartite and is composed of the physical (planetary), emotional (astral), and mental (spiritual) bodies; in each person one of these three bodies ultimately achieves dominance. "Persons of the physical body" are represented by the fakir (the way of asceticism); "persons of feeling" are symbolized by the monk (the way of religious feeling); and the yogi (the way of reason) represents "persons of intellect." The way of the divine body, the fourth way (a basic aspect of Gurdjieff's philosophy and the later title of a book by Uspensky), is that of complete understanding and self-perfection. Ultimately, one must synthesize these four ways into one single way. Perhaps the most important property possessed by the fully integrated person is immortality.[6]

As recently as ten years ago, the names of Gurdjieff and Uspensky were not recognized in Russia except by people conversant with the occult or with twentieth-century Russian philosophical systems. Today everyone seems to recognize them. Not only have these men been recognized as contributors to the understanding of the occult in general (as well as originators of their own systems), but their teachings have become a way of life for many people— philosophies to be studied and followed. Russians are actively seeking to learn more about these men, and to understand their ideas.

AGNI-YOGA

During the 1920s and 1930s Nikolai Konstantinovich Rerikh (a Theosophist and a Nobel Prize nominee), together with his wife, Elena Ivanovna Shaposhnikova-Rerikh, wrote *Agni-yoga*, a ten-volume work on yogic philosophy allegedly received psychically from Mahatma Moria (who was, coincidentally, also Madame Blavatsky's personal teacher). *Agni-yoga* reflects many of the neo-Buddhist ideas of earlier Theosophical writings. The authors include ideas found in the traditional subdisciplines of yoga, which they dismiss as inferior systems, since each focuses on attaining the ultimate goal through only one method.[7] These are Radzha-yoga (through exercise), Karma-yoga (through

5. Colin Wilson, *The Occult* (New York, 1971), pp. 384–412.

6. Michel Waldberg, *Gurdjieff: An Approach to His Ideas* (London, 1989), pp. 13–15, 87–88. Waldburg also delves deeply into Gurdjieff's numerological systems and the concept of the enneagram. Both of these ideas are central to the complete understanding of Gurdjieff's cosmology but are so complex that they defy brief explanation.

7. According to the authors, yoga is "opposed to magic, for magic stands on cold words, yoga constantly breathes the breath of the Cosmos": (E. I. Rerikh and N. K. Rerikh, *Agni-yoga* (1929; St. Petersburg, 1992), p. 80.

action), Zhnani-yoga (through knowledge), and Bkhati-yoga (through unification with the Absolute).[8]

The Rerikhs emphasize the ancient Agni, Hindu god of fire, who served as a mediator between mortals and the gods. Philosophers explain him as "the all-embracing beginning who penetrates the universe as a light present among people and in Mankind." The Rig-veda characterizes him as a god that "burns, shines, enlightens, controls all forces, . . . opens the doors of darkness, strengthens heaven and earth, knows all paths, all wisdom, all worlds, all Man's secrets."[9] According to the Rerikhs, "all yoga should be a part of life, but Agni-yoga is more definite. . . . [T]he element of fire gives it its name . . . fire does not lead you away from life, it is a . . . guide to distant worlds. . . . Fire is a life-giving element—a sign of perfection. Only fire yoga leads you to future evolutions," for the "Fiery World is the true symbol of uninterrupted evolution."[10]

Through Agni-yoga the fire centers of understanding are ignited in a process similar to *kundalini* (during which all chakras are activated and opened, allowing energy to traverse the spine and exit the crown chakra during communion with the Absolute).[11] During this communion, the unification of human consciousness with that of the Cosmos permits the fire of Agni-yoga to destroy the chaos of human thought. Ideas on psychic energy have their basis in fire, for "all phenomena are produced by fire . . . [it] composes the essence of the spirit."[12] In order to understand Agni-yoga, one must understand the pulsating rhythms of the elements that the fire unites, the psychic energy of which is determined and regulated by the fire of the Cosmos.[13] Realization and participation in a new era is possible for spiritually enlightened people who recognize the purifying cathartic elements of fire, which consumes the past and lights up the future.

One of the Rerikhs' more provocative ideas is the cyclical nature of human creation and spiritual advancement.[14] The manifestations of the ideas of the

8. According to yoga, the Absolute is "the spirit, the source of the entire universe": Iu. M. Ivanov, *Chelovek i ego dusha* (Moscow, 1991), p. 6.

9. S. A. Tokarev, ed. *Mify narodov mira* (Moscow, 1987), pp. 35–36.

10. Rerikh and Rerikh, *Agni-yoga*, pp. 55–56.

11. Fire centers correspond to the chakras, seven main centers of energy found along the spine, starting at the crown of the head and ending at the sacrum, which control various organs and emit vibrations of different frequencies and colors. This is, of course, a rather simplified explanation of a rather complex process of spiritual awakening. For a more complete discussion of this phenomenon, see Mary Scott, *Kundalini in the Physical World* (London, 1983).

12. Rerikh and Rerikh, *Agni-yoga*, p. 106.

13. According to the Rerikhs, the "music of the spheres is created not from melodies but from rhythms": ibid., p. 143.

14. Ivanov devotes a large part of his discussion of human origins to the fundamental beliefs of Agni-yoga: *Chelovek i ego dusha*, pp. 22–30.

Creative Will are perceived as souls who, having been denied rest in the astral plane and having attained great spiritual development, have accepted responsibility for the earth's evolution.[15] One of them, Mahatma, arrived on the earth at the dawn of civilization (and is reincarnated in souls when necessary for the benefit of humankind); other highly spiritually developed beings became gods endowed with the divine gift of creation. These souls migrated from one planet to another. The earth's moon became the source of human generation and evolution by way of the migration of the monads, the "first indivisible immortal spiritual individuals born of the gods or god-created who passed through the animal level of evolution on the moon, and having finished their cycle, needed to start a new level of life on earth, to begin man's evolution here."[16] This immortal first human race, which merged with the second race, was capable of all forms of movement (including flying), but was bereft of a physical body. Ethereal and sexless beings of pure spirit peopled the third race. In time the human body became more dense, androgynous characteristics disappeared, and the separation of the sexes occurred. Procreation precipitated death as we know it, for by this time humans had acquired physical bodies. The actions of the most spiritually developed beings on Venus (the "Sons of Reason") initiated earth's spiritual evolutionary development when they visited the earth as "Divine Teachers" who awakened dormant human reason. The dawn of human spiritual evolution began 18 million years ago as a result of the intervention of these celestial beings.

The giant continent of Lemuria, located along the equator, occupied much of the space now filled by the Pacific and Indian oceans, including the continent of Australia and nearby islands. The Lemurians, under the tutelage of the Venusian Sons of Reason, were a race of giants (attested to, according to the Rerikhs, by the giant statues on Easter Island) with advanced achievements in architecture, mathematics, and astronomy. With the passage of time, morality and ethics declined, but a small number of highly developed spiritual souls remained uncorrupted and survived to become the teachers of the new races.[17] These spiritual teachers migrated from Lemuria to several islands (which now are part of the territory of India) immediately before Lemuria was destroyed by volcanoes and earthquakes and sank into the ocean. They served as re-

15. The Creative Will is the force that emanates from the reason of the Absolute, which attempts to create, defend, and preserve life: ibid., p. 10.

16. Ibid., p. 22, quoting Daniil Andreev, *Roza mira: Metafilosofiia istorii* (Moscow, 1991).

17. The third race included subraces. The first consisted of dark red-skinned peoples; the second had skin of brownish red; the third subrace was the Toltecs; the fourth was made up of yellow-skinned peoples, who were undisciplined, rude, and cruel; the fifth was the Semites, who were warlike, quick-tempered, and mistrustful; the sixth subrace, the Akkadis, comprised white-skinned traders and navigators, who achieved great success in astronomy and astrology, and whose descendants were the Phoenician traders of the Mediterranean; the seventh was the Mongols of eastern Siberia: ibid., p. 28.

positories of knowledge and research to help the next race, the fourth, which occupied the continent of Atlantis four to five million years ago. This civilization was also quite advanced; the Atlantians had airships and electricity, and they were experts in agriculture. After several thousand years, as the Atlantians came to believe that humans were the apogee of the universe, they began to use black magic for personal gain and pleasure. The most highly spiritual members of their society migrated and settled in South and Central America, where they preserved their knowledge and experience for the benefit of the fifth race of people, the cycle to which we belong.[18] The end of the fifth and the entire sixth and seventh cycles in human evolution still remain to be fulfilled; after the conclusion of the seventh cycle the evolutionary development of our universe will be complete. (In 1934, Rerikh estimated the dawning of the new era [the end of the fifth cycle] to be in his near future, the 1940s; contemporary predictions name no exact date.) The Rerikh Society, which he founded, has many of its bases in the ideas set forth in his "Pact of the Banner of Peace" (1933). His society maintained chapters in many nations and gained international repute for its call for cosmopolitan brotherhood, its denunciation of war and human suffering (both physical and spiritual), and its pronouncements against malevolent actions (which could be eliminated through the healing powers of Agni). Since the flag of the International Red Cross (a red cross on a white background) signifies aid for the wounded and ill, Rerikh chose three red dots within a red circle on a white ground for his society's banner. This "Banner of Peace" symbolizes peaceful achievements and the health of the human spirit; the white circle outlined in red is a symbol of eternity, and the three red dots inside are representative of humanity's past, present, and future.[19]

Since the collapse of the Soviet Union the Rerikh cult has gained immense popularity in Russia; it is now possible to find the Rerikhs' reissued works not only in shops dealing with the occult but in all bookstores. People who have long been aware of their philosophy but were forced to remain silent during the Communist period can now discuss it openly and are spreading the word among people unfamiliar with their work. In 1994 and 1995, series of lectures celebrating the Rerikhs' life and works and explicating their philosophy were quite common in both Moscow and St. Petersburg.

18. The fifth race is also divided into seven subraces: those from Central Asia who moved to India and the Himalayas, including not only the Aryan Hindu people but also one of the tribes of ancient Egypt; Aryan Semites and contemporary Arabs; Persians; Celts (who were related to the ancient Greeks and Romans); Spaniards, French, Irish, and Scots; and the Teutons (the Scandinavians, Slavs, English, Germans, and Flemish): ibid., pp. 28–29.

19. N. K. Rerikh, *Sviashchennyi dozor* (N.p., n.d.), p. 73; P. F. Belikov, "Pakt N. K. Rerikh po okhrane kul'turnykh tsennostei," in *N. K. Rerikh: Zhizn' i tvorchestvo*, ed. M. T. Kuz'mina (Moscow, 1978), p. 187.

Even during the period when the Rerikhs' writings were in official disfavor, Nikolai's paintings guaranteed him continued popularity in his native land. Their bright primary colors, their apocalyptic and religious themes, their exotic subject matter, and their stylized and often primitive manner of execution won him a loyal following that continues today. His art often engenders a desire to read and understand his ideas. Rerikh's spiritual paintings are impossible to ignore and are inextricably interwined with his philosophy.

EXTRASENSITIVES (PSYCHICS)

One of the most popular occult practices in Russia today is the traditional discipline of yoga (including Agni-yoga) in efforts to enhance one's psychic energies and abilities and especially to become an extrasensitive (*ekstrasens*) or healer (*tselitel'*).[20] One of the most well received and prolific authors on this subject is Iury M. Ivanov, an extrasensitive who stresses the importance of the more conventional forms of yoga in efforts to achieve unification with the Absolute (*kundalini*). According to Ivanov, yoga enables a person to focus on others' biofields and to examine and interpret the colors of their auras; in short, to develop the dormant psychic abilities necessary to become a healer. In basic occult belief stemming from Oriental paradigms, surrounding the body of every person or object are four "material" energy bodies manifested in the form of radiation: the physical, the etheric, the astral, and the mental, each with its own energy field. The part of the energy field that appears beyond the outline of the body (the aura) represents the sum total of the auras of all the bodies. The physical and ethereal bodies share one energy field; the astral body (which can be separated from the physical body in a state of hypnotic trance or dream) is an exact copy of the physical, but consists of a finer material. According to Ivanov's aural color theories, the basic color of astral radiation is light blue-gray, which changes tone according to a person's moods and feelings. The mental body consists of an oval form of even finer material than the astral body; its aura seems to emit sparks. The colors of this aura change in accordance with the quality of a person's thoughts, while the colors of the auras in general are dependent on the person's temperament, personality, and spiritual development. Calm, reflective people emit greenish auras; those who are unreserved or nervous radiate an aura permeated by reddish-yellow rays. Nonintellectuals also have auras infused with rays of reddish yellow, while those of a more intellectual bent have greater concentrations of green within their auras. The auras of selfless people and empaths emanate rays of a dark

20. It should be noted that yoga and meditation have enjoyed considerable popularity among the Russian intelligentsia, not only in prerevolutionary society but during the Soviet period as well.

blue shade, which turns to light violet in those of a deeply religious and spiritual nature.[21]

The colors and rays have a definite form. Base animal passions are expressed in the form of irregular spots in the auras; fear is shown as a wavy stripe of dark blue with a reddish cast. People who anticipate an event exhibit reddish dark-blue stripes in the form of radii that flow from the center to the outside. Those experiencing strong anxiety caused by external forces periodically emit small orange-yellow points. The aura of a person who is distracted contains ever-changing dark-blue spots. Extrasensitives perceive the auras of both animate and inanimate objects, and are able to affect both through the transfer of either energy or information.

Ivanov focuses primarily on the development of the powers of the extrasensitive as healer. In diagnosing an illness, the extrasensitive analyzes the person's energy field: that of a healthy person is an even background of a definite color; painful or afflicted areas of the physical body are seen as light silver flashes; in the field of a person suffering from a chronic malady, the healer sees dark washed-away spots. By a laying on of hands the healer transfers to the patient his or her own psychic energy, which is developed and maintained by communion with the Absolute through yoga.

General healing affects the entire biofield of the patient; *pranic* (life-force) healing focuses on isolated problem areas. Healers must be careful not to exhaust their own life force while treating patients; they must constantly be aware that, bereft of the human willfulness and pride that can contaminate the healing, the healer is simply a modest "conductor of cosmic energy," a medium for curative psychic forces. The extrasensitive and the healer have highly developed connections between their astral sense organs and consciousness: as the astral light waves pass through material objects, the extrasensitive (often called a "clairvoyant [*iasnovidets*] of space") is able to see the workings of the internal organs, a person's auras, the quality of a person's thoughts. The "clairvoyant of time" is able to see both past and future.[22]

Two objects that are said to aid the extrasensitive are a pendulum and a sort of miniature divining rod (*ramka* or *ramochka*). A ring or needle suspended from a thread held in the hand of preference can function as a pendulum, although some psychics prefer an amber bead on a thread. When the extrasensitive is asked a question, the pendulum swings in one direction for a negative answer in the opposite direction for an affirmative answer. These questions are necessarily less complex and more direct than those addressed by the *ramochka*.

The divining rod, which can be used to find water and ore, buried treasure, and lost items or missing persons, is a 2-mm wire shaped to form a right angle,

21. Iu. M. Ivanov, *Kak stat'ekstrasensom* (Moscow, 1991), pp. 20–21.
22. Ibid., pp. 94–100.

one arm twice as long as the other. The biophysical fields of objects, animals, and people provide the energy emanations that cause the rod to function. Thus the rod can be used to diagnose a medical problem: as the healer moves backward while holding the short arm of the rod, the long arm sways at the edge of the patient's biofield, indicating the distance between the body and the border of the energy field. A shallow energy field indicates poor health, general malaise, blocked chakras, or psychic attack (the patient may be the victim of an energy vampire). A deep energy field in a benevolent person indicates attunement with the Cosmos, innate extrasensitivity (developed or undeveloped), strong spirituality, general benevolence, and respect for life. In a person of a malevolent nature, the values are reversed. An extrasensitive who realizes that the client has a malevolent spirit stops the diagnosis immediately in order to protect his or her own vital life force from contamination by negative energies.

Natalia Vladimirovna Bakhareva is a typical healer in St. Petersburg. She is a devout Orthodox Christian and a follower of Iury Ivanov's basic teachings. She works with children born with the umbilical cord around the neck or with spinal, skull, or muscle injuries. During a series of interviews she explained and described the psychic healing processes that she and her colleagues use: through physical (*kontaktnyi*) and nonphysical (*bezkontaktnyi*) massage (examination and manipulation of a person's auras) she is able to "heal" and to diagnose past, present, and future illnesses. She sometimes uses her *ramochka*, although she considers this the most elementary form of diagnostic reading: an expert healer, in her opinion, is able to read a person in his or her absence either through objects touched or by analyzing the astral image. To prepare for her work with patients, Natalia prays while standing in front of an open uncurtained window at sunrise (a time most optimal for absorbing the psychic energies from the Cosmos and the life-giving force of the sun). At the same time she imagines a silver column of light and pure energy extending from the sun through the open chakra at the crown of her head.[23] This exercise enables her to amass enough psychic energy so that it will not dissipate during the healing process. In addition to healing on the physical plane, many extrasensitives perform "astral operations." In one such operation, the healer psychically placed elastic bands in the heels of the astral body of a paralyzed child to enable him to walk; another extrasensitive divided the image of a little girl's heart into quadrants on the astral plane in order to find the location of her cardiac disease.

Most sensitives have only one clairvoyant skill, which generally manifests itself in early childhood; from this initial skill, however, others may develop. Many practitioners of the occult believe that psychic abilities are born through

23. The *sakhasrarachakra* chakra (the violet chakra of philosophers), which allows one to enter the state of *samadhi* (to understand the essence of things, to acquire unlimited knowledge through union with the Absolute) during the process of *kundalini*.

the natural achievement of the state of *samadhi* (supraconsciousness) through *kundalini*. According to Eastern adepts, *samadhi* is an extremely dangerous state; without the necessary preparation by a qualified teacher, a person may not escape from it. Among people whom Ivanov considers to have achieved *samadhi* naturally, as a result of their actions in previous incarnations, are the Swedish philosopher Emanuel Swedenborg, the American poet Walt Whitman, the Russian poets Mikhail Lermontov and Aleksandr Blok, and the writer Daniil Andreev.[24]

The well-known psychics, healers, and clairvoyants whom Ivanov cites manifest a variety of skills. Their personal philosophies are generally eclectic, for they frequently borrow from others elements that fit their personal worldview. Each has his or her own following. The psychic Diana, for example, is able to "see" through people, sensing their feelings and thoughts. V. I. Safonov, the author of "Nit' Ariadny" (Ariadne's thread), a work widely circulated in samizdat, locates missing persons psychically by means of their photographs. Porfiry Korneevich Ivanov, one of the best-known extrasensitives, healed a woman who had been paralyzed for years. Sentenced to prison for fifteen years, he was at times forced to sit in an ice hole through the night, yet remained healthy. In cold weather Porfiry Ivanov's many followers (the *Ivanovtsy*) are easily recognizable by their lightweight clothing and sandals. Ivanov is also the author of a system of views regarding humans' relation to nature; he was honored by the state in 1989 for his contribution to the understanding of the paranormal. An area in one pavilion at the Exhibition of Economic Achievement in Moscow was dedicated to his life and work. Aleksei Krivorotov, a healer, became acquainted with Semen and Valentina Kirlian in 1964 in Krasnodar, where he helped them develop the process of Kirlian photography: they photographed his hands, from which rays of light emanated. Ninel' Sergeevna Kulagina, a practitioner of telekinesis, was accused of being a magician and charlatan by the editorial board of *Pravda*, who "exposed" the falsity of her claims in a series of articles. In 1988 she successfully defended herself against these charges in court.

Evgeniia Iurashevna Davitashvili, Brezhnev's personal faith healer, conducted a series of experiments in Tbilisi as proof of her healing abilities in 1979. Later in Moscow she began healing in Polyclinic No. 112, and worked for some time in the T. Nikolaev Central Scientific Research Institute of Trauma and Orthopedics, as well as in other scientific institutes. Anatoly Vasil'evich Martynov, a physicist by profession, is also a healer who works with a divining rod; he writes about extrasensory paranormal experiments and occurrences and gives lectures on parapsychology. Boris Evgen'evich Zolotov is director of a center for the preparation of sensitivities, Del'ta-inform, in Rostov-on-Don, where he conducts seminars on telepathy, clairvoyance, and healing.[25]

24. Ivanov, *Kak stat' ekstrasensom*, pp. 108–15.
25. Ibid., pp. 120–26.

By far the most famous psychic healer in Russia—indeed, his reputation has spread to the West—is Anatoly Kashpirovsky, who conducted mass psychic healings, filled stadiums with his followers, and hypnotized scores of people at a time. Kashpirovsky became a television personality when he "purified" cups of tea and coffee, glasses of water, and bottles of hand lotion on an early-morning show, using mesmeric passes. Viewers who used these "blessed" potions were reported to be promptly relieved of their afflictions. A minor scandal erupted, however, when people who believed themselves free of disease began to suffer symptoms again; now Kashpirovsky was widely denounced as a charlatan. In a 1992 pamphlet, *Kto vy, Doktor Kashpirovskii?* (Who are you, Dr. Kashpirovsky?), his most ardent adherents attempted to refute these accusations by documenting his psychic abilities in long lists of success stories. Kashpirovsky's television show was canceled, and he is steadily losing influence and prominence in the arena of the Russian healing arts. Today most Russians feel that he is indeed a charlatan, though some still claim that he did cure their maladies; at the very least, everyone seems to know at least one person who received beneficial effects from his "healing" activities. He has been displaced in the world of the occult by scores of other healers, some well known, others not, but each with a following of believers.

As a psychic Iury Ivanov displays broad vision and is extremely influential in the occult community in Russia, yet his eclectic interpretations of Eastern (primarily Indian) occult thought are highly subjective and are highly colored by the aberrant interpretations that gained currency in the isolated underground occult community in Russia in the years when occult studies were prohibited. In his focus on astrological forecasts for Russia and its messianic mission he resurrects the centuries-old Eastern Orthodox belief in Russia's "holy mission" and the Slavophile philosophies of the nineteenth century. Daniil Andreev, whose *Roza mira* is a quasi-Gnostic mystical vision, also lends credence to this "messianic mission," for it is out of the Russian "cosmic worlds" that Zventa-Sventana will emerge to unite the peoples of the earth in peaceful cosmopolitan brotherhood.

One of the major areas of concern to all occultists, and to all psychics in particular because it directly affects one of their areas of study (the aura), is that of psychic attack, more commonly known in the world of the occult as energy vampirism.

Energy Vampirism (Psychic Attack)

Belief in energy vampirism (psychic attack or psychic vampirism) has become widespread as a result of the fascination with yoga and the paranormal and the spiritualist studies of the past. In contemporary Russian studies dealing with psychic vampirism one finds much in common with the ideas, occult teachings, and paranormal experiences of Dion Fortune, who documents her own experiences with psychic attack in her book *Psychic Self-Defense* (1930).[26] Discussions about energy vampirism may be heard in Russia on city streets, in cafés, in institutes and universities, and in private residences. "Energy vampire" has become a catchword for people with unappealing or exacting personalities, and is frequently followed by a long discourse concerning the negative aspects of that person's character. Descriptions of this phenomenon vary.

Energy vampirism is most commonly believed to consist of attacks on the four basic auras of a person. Attacks on the energy membranes, which involve the physical and ethereal bodies, result in an unpleasant feeling in the physical body; an attack on the astral membrane, which involves the astral body, affects the emotions and gives rise to evil thoughts; and an attack on the mental membrane, which involves the mental body, takes one away from the "paths of truth." Shafika Karagulla, an extrasensitive, refers to people who precipitate these attacks are *sapery* (sappers): they are egocentric, but frequently portray themselves as altruistic and benevolent; they cannot or will not use cosmic energy; they have a locked energy field (Natalia Bakhareva believes that the chakra at the top of the head, which absorbs cosmic energy, is closed in these individuals); and they steal the life force (*prana*) from the auras of others. Diana, a sensitive who works with Karagulla, "sees" in these people a long patterned ribbon surrounding a hole in the solar plexus with which they absorb other people's energy while looking at their victims calmly and decisively until the victims lose the strength to protect themselves.[27]

Methods of defense against psychic vampirism vary. Before one leaves home, one should imagine one's body surrounded by either a golden egg or a revolving golden cross, or should perform the "*kata* of the iron shirt," one of the defensive movements in karate. Upon returning home, a cold or contrasting shower or a rapid dance will eliminate any remnants of vampiric energy one has encountered. Coffee laced with black pepper will function as defense in either situation.[28]

An extremely popular pamphlet, *Kak izbezhat' energeticheskogo vampirizma i samomu ne stat' vampirom* (How to avoid energy vampirism and how not to become a vampire yourself), published by the St. Petersburg School of Spiritual Development of the Personality (under the direction of A. Z. Gromokovsky) in 1992, offers a detailed explanation from a conservative religious and nationalistic point of view. It is collectively written and published by teachers whose basic goal is to help people understand themselves and the system of the universe on the basis of Christian principles.

According to this school, psychic vampirism exhibits Gnostic/Luciferian

26. For a more complete analysis of Dion Fortune's paranormal experiences and her basic occult beliefs, see Wilson, *The Occult.*

27. Ivanov, *Kak stat' ekstrasensom*, pp. 75–77.

28. Ibid., pp. 85–88.

elements and is a result of Lucifer's fall from heaven: since he refused to cooperate with God, he was denied the life force found in Him. Although Lucifer still maintained a reserve of energy, when he understood that he would be destroyed as a result of the absence of the divine life force, he began to absorb pure streams of energy from those still connected with God. The modern vampire is attracted to eating meat; to pornographic books, posters, and films (especially horror films); to rock music, fashion glitz, and superstars; to science fiction; to popular African and shamanistic masks; and to sculptures and graphic portrayals of evil spirits.

The authors propose that the structure of the earth is one of the highest achievements of Satan's creation. It is a highly organized multileveled net laced with mechanisms of automatic regulators and distributors of the energy it has accumulated. Systems of pipes surround the earth, which collect energy from various sources on the surface. The craters and pits seen from outer space function as the basic "sucking" structures, which cosmic vampires supply with pirated energy. These cavities function as energy transformers and are grouped according to the colors of the seven auras; each cavity in the earth is attached to a principal pit of the same color. The appearance of the master of each hole "is similar to that of King Kong," who reflects the "essence of the satanic vampire system."[29] When someone begins to exhibit demonic characteristics, such as malevolence or irritation, the person's astral image is removed and placed in a particular pit. If the demonic behavior continues, an astral image is created which acts independently; thus legions of astral demons who live by means of other people's energy are created.

In the aura system variant, the human body is developed by seven concentric oval-shaped auras in the colors of the rainbow. Those who are highly developed spiritually have an eighth, white aura, which is transformed into streams of gold and silver during spiritual activities.[30] An energy vampire, as defined by the teachers of this school, is one who steals energy from one or all of the seven energy shells of another person; illnesses and weaknesses appear in those areas of the body corresponding to the color of the shell from which the vampire has "sucked" energy. Loss of the orange and red auras causes gynecological problems in women, prostate and lower intestinal problems in men; the absence of the yellow aura causes problems with the liver, stomach, and bile ducts; loss of the green aura causes basic heart disorders; absorption of the light-blue aura causes problems with the lungs and bronchi (such as chronic bronchitis and pneumonia); loss of the dark-blue and violet auras

---

29. *Kak izbezhat' energeticheskogo vampirizma i samomu ne stat' vampirom* (St. Petersburg, 1992), p. 5.

30. These rainbow-colored auras seem to have the yogic chakras as their bases, since the various chakras located in the body vibrate with the energy of a certain color and correspond to locations for specific illnesses.

causes the victim to experience depression, head pain, and insomnia, which prevent one from realizing one's full creative potential.

In contrast to other psychics and healers, the authors of this pamphlet claim that energy vampires do not drain off their victims' energy for their own use; they are only the means by which the demonic energy of the universe replenishes its supply. A person who falls ill without apparent cause may have fallen victim to an energy vampire: the vampire has taken much of the ill person's astral body and either has "placed two or three sucking tubes along the dark-blue, light-blue, violet, and white streams of energy" or enters into the patient's heart "in the form of a snake," which then sucks the person's life force. After this psychic attack, "part of the patient's astral image falls into a pit, where it is torn apart by cats, dogs, snakes, and crocodiles."[31]

Vampirism is not practiced only by people; the concept of "masked vampirism," the draining of energy by ideas and goods imported from the West, has a clear political subtext. Masked vampirism is associated with computers and video games; war matériel, especially rockets, and even toy guns; the entertainment industry in general; bright clothing and jewelry; and homeless domestic animals (especially cats, since they are traditionally thought to be witches' familiars). Since machines absorb the higher planes of a person's consciousness and memory, people who work with computers often experience headaches, poor memory, and irritation at work.

Vampiric "wheels," such as UFOs, are a part of cosmic vampirism, taking energy from computer systems, military equipment, and television and radio broadcasts. According to the authors, one of the most powerful devices of cosmic vampirism is speculative mysticism, of the kind purveyed in works by Madame Blavatsky and in the Rerikhs' *Agni-yoga*.

They advise the erection of defensive "golden streams" to prevent vampirism (much as Iury Ivanov does), but the best defense is an intimate relationship with nature: "people who are happy, who receive a feeling of beauty and harmony from nature, who are sensitive to the higher arts, have an easier time in resisting a vampire." Music also arouses one's life force and courage, drawing one from the psychic pit and cleansing one's various physical planes.[32]

Despite the fantastic elements in this tract, with its crocodiles, King Kong–like monster masters, and bottomless pits for the storage of evil energy, a large number of Russians find a credible core in it. The average Russian does believe in the existence of auras and energy vampires, and in the havoc such people can wreak on a person's biofield and health. Many extrasensitives are now treating people simply for energy vampirism—vampires as well as victims. In the case of a victim, after diagnosing the affected aura, the healer treats the malady with physical massage or astral healing, diet, or exercise. The vam-

31. *Kak izbezhat' energeticheskogo vampirizma*, p. 2.
32. Ibid., p. 13.

pire's cure takes much longer. The healer must diagnose the biofield to make certain that the person is indeed a vampire before implementing the appropriate remedy; perhaps manipulation of the spine in order to release blocked chakras, or infusion of the biofield with the healer's positive energy forces, which are derived from the Cosmos, a special diet or regimen of exercise. The extrasensitive must be very cautious in the healing process, for vampires often deceptively seek help in order to absorb the more pure and concentrated life force of a healer. It takes at least several healing sessions before any results are seen in either a vampire's behavior or a victim's health or mental state. Some vampires may never be healed, no matter how strongly they may wish to be; for biological, psychological, or spiritual reasons they will never be able to tap into the healing energies of the Cosmos or achieve union with the Absolute.

Sorcery, Black Magic, and Demonology

Sorcery and witchcraft (*koldovstvo*) are practiced in Russia today, although the people who profess to practice them are not the sorcerers and witches of the Western imagination. The Russian practitioners of sorcery take pride in their knowledge and their craft, and people seek their advice on everything from marital troubles to illnesses. Most *kolduny* are descended from long lines of village sorcerers, and are proud of their heritage. Some carve talismans for protection from the evil eye, vampirism, and negative energy forces; some read palms and tea leaves; some drive away malevolent spirits with practices similar to exorcism; others, sometimes for a price, will cast spells of protection (or, more rarely, aggression). Some few operate on the dark side of the occult, extolling the beauty and attraction of demons, but most sorcerers view their craft as a beneficial healing art, and maintain a healthy distance from supernatural beings, especially On (He), Satan.

When journalists and commentators discuss black magic, they emphasize the rise of Satanism and demonology, especially in the cities. Newspaper articles discussing Satanists' practices and beliefs, as well as their crimes, appear with increasing frequency. Most Russians feel that Satanism is becoming more pervasive, and that black masses and animal (and occasionally human) sacrifices occur much more frequently than in the past. Making contact with people involved in Satanism is virtually impossible; as in the West, their societies are tightly closed and members are sworn to secrecy, so little information regarding this darkest side of the occult is available.

The goddess movement and wicca (in the United States associated with witchcraft) have not taken root in Russia for several reasons. These ideas are generally based on the neopaganism of Celtic (and less frequently Norse) systems unfamiliar to the average Russian. Texts dealing with these systems have not yet been translated into Russian; even the more canonical works, such as Robert Graves's *White Goddess* and Marija Gimbutas's *Language of the God-*

dess, are virtually unknown. The deification of the Eternal Feminine or Sophia is certainly an ideological element and viable force in many Russian speculative doctrines past and present, but it has not translated into reverence for women and their purportedly occult powers.

Astrology

Solar astrology is extremely popular in Russia today, as it is in the West. Six-month horoscopes include biorhythm charts and numerological values for the letters of the Cyrillic alphabet. Each planet also has a corresponding Pythagorean numerical value, and it is possible to determine one's personality and one's purpose for existence by the total number of letters in one's first name, patronymic, and last name.[33] Numerological and astrological charts are popular among a broad range of the Russian population, even among people who profess to have no other occult interests.

Lunar astrology is also becoming increasingly fashionable. In this sense "lunar astrology" encompasses not only the moon sign (the zodiacal house occupied by the moon at the time of birth) but also the influence of the phases of the moon on personality, the day of the month a person was born in relation to those phases, and the elemental and mythological signs assigned to each. Whereas the sun represents the more masculine attributes and the qualities associated with the spirit, the moon is connected with the feminine, the qualities of the soul: it is the bearer of mysterious and secret information, it affects the subconscious, the soul, and the intuition. In the past the four phases of the moon were connected with the elements. In India these were four elephants of different colors; in Pythagorean terms they were images of goddesses. The closer a person is born to the new moon, the more feminine the soul; people born during the changing of the lunar phase are most unstable; the life choices of those born during an eclipse are more limited.[34]

Other types of astrology that are gaining in popularity are psychological astrology, which helps in choosing a marriage partner; medicinal astrology, which aids in the prevention of health problems; agrarian astrology, for farming; criminal astrology, for analyses of crime; chronobiological astrology, which is the study and research of biorhythms; and a specific branch of astrology regarding the effect of cosmic influences on events in countries, governments, and regions.[35]

33. The bodies of the solar system have the following numerical values: the sun, 1; earth's moon, 2; Mars, 3; Mercury, 4; Jupiter, 5; Venus, 6; Saturn, 7; Uranus, 8; Neptune, 9; Pluto, 10; and in addition Proserpine, 11; and Vulcan, 22.

34. P. P. Globa and T. M. Globa, *O chem molchit luna* (Leningrad, 1991).

35. Ivanov, *Chelovek i ego dusha*, pp. 119–20.

Anomalies

The widespread fascination with UFOs in Russia is attested by two monthly newspapers, *Stalker-UFO* and *Anomalie*, which regularly report on UFO sightings, publish photographs of UFOs, and conduct interviews with people who claim to have met extraterrestrials. *Stalker-UFO* is concerned almost exclusively with UFOs, although it has also begun to publish the prophecies of Nostradamus; *Anomalie* publishes articles about anomalies in general (visions, ghosts, poltergeists, the Antichrist, life after death, missing persons) and about the psychics who track them.

Iury Ivanov explains anomalies as beings who are able to traverse the boundaries between the physical and the astral worlds by controlling the vibrations of their bodies. They possess the inherent abilities of an extrasensitive and can fly through space, levitate, read another's thoughts, and become invisible. Marina Popovich, then a pilot and colonel in the Soviet Air Force, claims that in 1984 she established telepathic contact with an abominable snowman while on an expedition for Kiev University; immediately after the contact her sleeping daughter floated out of her tent unassisted. Ivanov asserts that as our spirituality and psychic abilities become more acutely developed in the future, we will experience these phenomena more frequently, it is simply our inability to perceive matter beyond the physical boundaries of this reality that prevents us from experiencing such occurrences now.[36]

Most of the philosophies widespread today can be traced to East Asia and are outgrowths of trends that gained currency in the late nineteenth and early twentieth centuries. Yet most of the works reprinted today in Russia are by Russian writers and philosophers: the renascence of occult thought is also serving to reclaim the Russian past and prerevolutionary heritage through the writings of Russia's great philosophers and religious thinkers, works previously banned, and the works of émigré writers, thereby validating Russia's own spiritual heritage.

Reactions to the dehumanizing effects of scientific doctrine, the overabundance of prescribed rational thought, and the proscription of alternative systems during the Soviet period have generated much of the energy directed toward the occult today. Many Russians are attempting to find new values and belief systems to replace those that have been jettisoned. As has frequently been the case throughout history, the occult is seen as an attractive alternative, for its philosophies offer an immutable reality that is more consoling than the harsh reality imposed by the instability and chaos of the physical world. Intrinsically apolitical, occult systems serve as spiritual panaceas for the gravest and most trying conditions.

36. Ivanov, *Kak stat' ekstrasensom*, pp. 141–43.

The occult scene in Russia has been changing rapidly. Nontraditional beliefs that occultists on the fringes of Russian society embraced several years ago have now become more acceptable, mainstream, and less shocking as more bizarre cults and doctrines surface and the darker sides of occultism (such as Satanism and demonology) come to the fore. It is impossible to predict what adaptations and mutations will occur in Russia in the future; we can be sure only that adaptations and mutations are inevitable as Russians add their own voices to the established canon of philosophies and occult belief systems.

INSTEAD OF A CONCLUSION

CHAPTER SIXTEEN
POLITICAL IMPLICATIONS OF THE EARLY TWENTIETH-CENTURY OCCULT REVIVAL

Bernice Glatzer Rosenthal

Although occult doctrines per se are apolitical, aspects of them can be politicized and serve as (or be absorbed into) activist ideologies whose formulators wish to transform humanity and change the world.[1] Typically the occultist's claim to higher knowledge fosters contempt for democratic processes and for ordinary people. When mingled with faith in "transmitters" or "initiators," such as magi or high priests, this spiritual elitism can engender a politics of myth and cult, a desire for and expectation of magic and miracles to be performed by a messiah magus, who can create heaven on earth and rid the world of demons. Such figures propagate what Robert Lifton terms the "psychic fallacy," the illusion that one's inner or psychic state is interchangeable with material actuality, "as if there were no external world, as if the universe were nothing but feeling and will." Realistic planning gives way to "insistence on spiritual perfection, mystical strength, and infallibility."[2] Though the psychic fallacy is not synonymous with the occult, it can emerge from the anti-empiricism inherent in many occult doctrines or from the treatment of political ideologies as "illuminated" knowledge.

The occult ideas that circulated in early twentieth-century Russia contributed massively to the politics of myth and cult that culminated in Stalinism. In the twilight years of the empire, politicized occult doctrines had helped to structure perceptions of and receptions to contemporary events, nourishing

1. Donald C. Hodges, *Intellectual Foundations of the Nicaraguan Revolution* (Austin, 1986), pp. 23–71, 256–91, details the formative influence of Spiritualism, Theosophy, and mystical Freemasonry on Augusto Sandino, inspiration of the Sandinistas.

2. Robert Jay Lifton, *Revolutionary Immortality: Mao Tse-tung and the Chinese Cultural Revolution* (New York, 1968), p. 107.

the maximalism and utopianism of the extreme left and the conspiracy theories and anti-Semitism of the extreme right. The Symbolists developed a reservoir of manipulative techniques from which political agitators and propagandists could draw. During and after the Bolshevik Revolution occult ideas were a major factor in Soviet utopianism. Occult-derived symbols and techniques informed early Soviet mass festivals and political theater, as well as the Lenin cult, the Stalin cult, and Socialist Realism. Subtly and not so subtly, occult symbols and themes helped pattern the worldview and rhetoric of persons who probably had no idea that such influences were working on them. In contemporary Russia, occult versions of "the Russian idea" proliferate. Some of them attribute the Bolshevik Revolution, Stalinism, and current political and economic problems to a Judeo-Masonic conspiracy.[3]

Several factors facilitated the politicization of the occult. Occultism was one way in which people tried to orient themselves in a world turned upside down by modernization, war, and revolution. Another factor was the intelligentsia tradition. The intellectuals' commitment to transforming Russia in accord with an ideal and their politicization of areas of life that outside Russia were not usually considered political, such as literature and the arts, shaped the discourse of educated society and affected believers in the occult. The Symbolists, for example, were militantly apolitical in the 1890s, but they considered themselves the progenitors of a new Russian culture nonetheless, and they devised their own visions of social salvation during the Revolution of 1905, when they perpetuated another aspect of the intelligentsia tradition—the view of compromise as a moral lapse. Moreover, early twentieth-century Russian occultism was part of a religious or spiritual quest that took on a political dimension automatically, because it was conducted outside the state-controlled Orthodox Church and it challenged established Orthodoxy.

Certain features intrinsic to the occult invited its politicization along extremist lines, especially in countries such as Russia and Germany, where the liberal tradition was weak.[4] Occult doctrines are characterized by a distinctive

3. The Masons will not be discussed in this chapter; to disentangle fact from fiction and to distinguish political from mystical Freemasonry would require a book in itself. It is noteworthy, however, that mystical Freemasonry was associated with reform since the time of Catherine the Great; that some of the Decembrists were Freemasons; and that historically Freemasonry has been linked with liberalism as well as with radicalism. Tsuyoshi Hasegawa maintains that the lodges to which Kerensky and other members of the Provisional Government belonged had been shorn of their occult elements: *The February Revolution* (Seattle, 1981), p. 194. According to Max Schachtman, the original Russian text of the 21 conditions for membership in the Communist International (Comintern) had a 22d provision that prohibited Russian Communists from being Freemasons: Foreword to Leon Trotsky, *Terrorism and Communism* (Ann Arbor, 1969), p. ix. Presumably the secrecy of the society was seen as a threat.

4. To generalize about the comparative aspects of the politicization of the occult across Europe would be premature, for more research is needed. It is noteworthy, however, that

mode of thought that dismisses empirical reality. This mode of thought does not distinguish between words and things, or between literal and metaphorical language. Words are treated as if they were equivalent to things and could be substituted for them. To manipulate one is to manipulate the other. Analogies are not explanatory devices subject to argument and proof, nor are they heuristic tools to make models that can be tested, corrected, and abandoned if necessary: they are modes of conceiving cosmic relationships that reify, rigidify, and ultimately come to dominate thought, and through which the occultist thinks or experiences the world. This anti-empirical, antirationalist orientation was reinforced by the philosophies of Nietzsche and Wagner, by the mystic theology of the Orthodox Church, and by expectations of the apocalypse. Russian occultists perceived war and revolution as the workings of hidden forces, divine or diabolic or both. Finally, occult symbols are often invested with religious content or intertwined with folk myth and popular culture. The psychological baggage these symbols carry can be transferred to politics by leaders who wish to "summon the forces of the deep." Belief in the underlying doctrine is not necessary. "Politics is magic," wrote the Austrian Symbolist Hugo von Hoffmannsthal. "He who wants to summon the forces of the deep, him will they follow."[5]

OCCULTISM LEFT AND RIGHT IN LATE IMPERIAL RUSSIA

In Western Europe the trajectory of politicized occultism was from left to right. Many early and mid-nineteenth-century socialists perceived capitalism as an occult force personified by demonic Jewish bankers (the Rothschilds) and by Jews generally. By 1900, however, occultism and open anti-Semitism had disappeared from the rhetoric of the mainstream socialist parties, only to become staples of the radical right.[6] In early twentieth-century Russia, politicized occultism appeared on the left and on the right around the same time.

Annie Besant resigned from the Fabian Society after she converted to Theosophy, in large part because she became skeptical of democracy. For India she championed an idealized version of the caste system in which the Brahmins would serve the people instead of oppressing them. Stressing renunciation as part of spiritual self-perfection, she became less sympathetic to the poverty of the workers. See Anne Taylor, *Annie Besant* (Oxford, 1992), pp. 266–67, 312–14. In Ireland and India, Theosophical propaganda stimulated "racial pride" as a way of subverting British rule.

5. Quoted in Carl Schorske, *Fin-de-Siècle Vienna: Politics and Culture* (New York, 1980), p. 134.

6. Occultism remained a factor in utopian thought. Monte Verita, a utopian colony founded in Ascona, Switzerland, in 1899, was a center of the "progressive underground." Its purpose was to show the world a new way of life, featuring "vegetarian socialism." Among its visitors were Prince Petr Kropotkin, Hermann Hesse, Countess Reventlow, Martin Buber, Hans Arp, Stefan George, Paul Klee, Isadora Duncan, Hugo Ball, and reputedly Lenin and Trotsky. See James Webb, *Occult Establishment* (La Salle, Ill., 1976), pp. 58–59. Webb lists Bakunin as one of

On the left, occult ideas were important elements of the eclectic doctrines of Mystical Anarchism, God-building, and Scythianism. Their other elements— ideas derived from Nietzsche, Wagner, Fedorov, apocalyptic Christianity, anarchism, utopian socialism, syndicalism, and revolutionary Marxism—either incorporated occult ideas or were perceived (rightly or wrongly) as compatible with them. Belief in the second coming of Christ is a tenet of mainstream Christianity, hence not an occult doctrine, but apocalypticism and occultism do have some common ground. Gematria and other occult techniques are used to predict the exact date of the Advent, to divine signs and portents of the End, and to identify the forces of evil. Moreover, occultism, like apocalypticism, comes to the fore in times of trouble, the one reinforcing the other. Some occult doctrines such as Anthroposophy have their own eschatology.

On the right, occult ideas and apocalypticism contributed to the obscurantism of the imperial court and were used to instigate pogroms. Every catastrophe that had befallen Russia, including the Russo-Japanese War and the Revolution of 1905, was blamed on the Satanic or demonic Jews and their henchmen.[7] The preoccupation of the Russian right with Satan and with demons, Walter Laqueur finds, "is part of the occult tradition, for it goes far beyond the teaching of the church."[8]

MYSTICAL ANARCHISM

Mystical Anarchism was the brainchild of Georgy Chulkov (1879–1939), an anarchist and a former editor of Merezhkovsky's *Novyi put'*, and the Symbolist writer Viacheslav Ivanov. Assuming that unseen forces are guiding events here on earth, they believed that political revolution reflected realignments in the cosmic sphere, and that a new world of freedom, beauty, and love was imminent. Advocating the abolition of all external authorities and all constraints on the individual—government, law, morality, social custom—they were indifferent to legal rights as merely "formal freedoms" and opposed constitutions and parliaments in favor of *sobornost'*. By *sobornost'* they meant a free community united by love and faith whose members retain their individuality (as distinct from individualism, self-affirmation apart from or against the community). Originally an ecclesiastical concept that connoted the unity of all be-

---

the visitors, but he was dead by then; perhaps Webb meant "Bakuninist." A visit by Lenin and Trotsky does not necessarily mean they were interested in the occult. Lenin may have hoped to use occult symbols for propaganda or been seeking converts to his brand of socialism. Or he and Trotsky may simply have been taking a vacation among friends in a beautiful alpine setting. The mystical socialism of Gustav Landauer is another example of occultism on the left.

7. Abraham Ascher, *The Revolution of 1905*, vol. 1, *Russia in Disarray* (Stanford, 1988), p. 240.

8. Walter Laqueur, *Black Hundred: The Rise of the Extreme Right in Russia* (New York 1993), p. 150; see also pp. 55–56.

lievers in the mystic body of Jesus Christ, *sobornost'* was first applied to secular matters by the Slavophiles, and is compatible with the occult concepts of microcosm and macrocosm.[9] Ivanov and Chulkov also extolled a "powerless" society in which no person ruled another and dominance and subordination had ceased to exist.

They grounded this ideal in their notion of the "mystical person," the soul or the psyche, which seeks union with others and recognizes itself as a microcosm of the macrocosm, as distinct from the "empirical person," the I or the ego, which asserts itself apart from or against others. Evoking and developing this "mystical person" would make feasible a "new organic society" united by invisible inner ties of love (eros, not agape), "mystical experience," and sacrifice—the very opposite of liberal society, based on the social contract and mutual self-interest and characterized by rational discourse. Who or what would be sacrificed and exactly what "mystical experience" entailed were not specified, but it was clear that "mystical experience" included the occult. Chulkov and Ivanov were interested in Theosophy; Ivanov was also interested in "alchemical mysteries" (transmutation).

Mystical Anarchism was part of a genre of Symbolist responses to the Revolution of 1905 and as such incorporated such key tenets of Symbolism as the "magic of words," emphasis on the "inner man," and art as theurgy. To the Symbolists (except for Briusov, who was not a mystic), theurgy was occult praxis.[10] Having regarded the theater as the link between "the poet and the crowd" for some time, the Symbolists centered their hopes for theurgical transfiguration (or transformation; *preobrazhenie* means both) on a new kind of theater as the site and the agency of the theurgical process. Ivanov and Chulkov advocated a cultic theater devoted to "myth creation" (*mifotvorchestvo*), collective creativity, and psychological transformation. Acting as the high priest of the cult, the Symbolist poet would pronounce the salvific New Word in a theater-temple. Here socially unifying myths would be articulated and the dormant "mystical person" activated. The result would be a new person, a new cult, a new culture, and a new organic society cemented by powerful unconscious ties of passion and myth.[11] Although Chulkov was the major

9. Around 1909, when Ivanov became interested in the nationality issue, he treated nations as an intermediate level in a cosmic *sobornost'*. After the Bolshevik Revolution, his lofty *sobornost'* degenerated into an ultracommunalist vision in which the individual virtually disappeared. See Bernice G. Rosenthal, "Transcending Politics: Vyacheslav Ivanov's Visions of *Sobornost'*," *California Slavic Studies* 14 (1992): 47–70, and "Lofty Ideals and Worldly Consequences: Visions of *Sobornost'* in Early Twentieth-Century Russia," *Russian History* 20, nos. 1–4 (1993): 179–95.

10. Briusov sometimes used hieratic language. See, for example, "Kliuchi tain" (Keys to the mystery), *Vesy*, 1904, no. 1, pp. 78–93; and "Sviashchennaia zhertva" (Holy sacrifice), *Vesy*, 1905, no. 1, pp. 23–29, and no. 6, pp. 94–99.

11. For details on Mystical Anarchism, see Bernice Glatzer Rosenthal, "Mystical Anarchism and the Revolution of 1905: The Transmutation of the Symbolist Ethos," *Slavic Review* 36

formulator of Mystical Anarchism, most of the pronouncements on theater were Ivanov's. The cultic theater was his way of bypassing or transcending conventional politics and the institutional church.

Ivanov regarded the theatrical chorus, not the new duma (parliament), as the authentic voice of the people and as the earthly correspondent of a mystical commune (*obshchina*). Proclaiming his democratic ideal, Ivanov wanted the spectators to become a chorus, to dance and sing and praise the god with words, and he criticized "Wagner-sorcerer" for the passivity he induced in his audiences. Ivanov also wanted to abolish the gap between actors and spectators so that all could participate in the "orgy of action" and the "orgy of purification," shedding their sense of separateness by joining in overwhelming mystical ecstasy. Ivanov's inspiration was the Dionysian dithyrambs that had accompanied the ritual sacrifices of ancient Greece. These rituals were not only erotic but frenzied, bloody, and cruel; the sacrificial object was torn limb from limb and pieces of its body were distributed to the celebrants to be scattered in the fields. Ivanov interpreted this practice as symbolizing the eternal cycle of birth, death, and rebirth. Although he highlighted Eros rather than Thanatos, the idea of ritual sacrifice was embedded in his vision of a cultic theater.

The corollary of myth creation was mood creation, to be achieved by a variety of techniques that were already part of the Symbolist inventory. Maurice Maeterlinck's plays portrayed the power of mysterious occult or supernatural forces over people and the illusoriness or insignificance of the material world. The characters were unindividuated marionettes manipulated by mysterious or magical forces. In Symbolist plays generally, orchestration of light, music, and words subliminally engaged the psyche and stimulated trains of associations in a manner akin to hypnotic suggestion. Gestures, music, color, and even smell enriched nonverbal communication, and synesthesia announced the "manmade correspondences that would replace the marriage between Heaven and earth."[12] Pauses, segments of silence, and repetition of words, phrases, or lines, created an incantional effect and in some cases a mood that was downright spooky. The physical aspects of life were deemphasized and material objects were used sparingly. Western Symbolist plays were spiritual in a vague sort of way, for they treated the soul or the psyche. Most Russian Symbolists, by contrast, believed that theater should serve a religious function. Their dramaturgy included mystery plays that extolled sacrifice and resurrection, ideas that were later politicized.[13] During the Revolu-

---

(December 1977): 608–27, and "Theater as Church: The Vision of the Mystical Anarchists," *Russian History* 4, pt. 2 (1977): 122–41.

12. Anna Balakian, *Symbolist Theater* (New York, 1967), pp. 124–25, 151.

13. Examples are Gippius's *Sviataia krov'* (Sacred blood, 1901) and Belyi's *Prishedshii* (He who has come, 1902) and the uncompleted "Antikhrist'." Gippius's play put forward the idea of the murder (or ritual sacrifice) of a dearly loved and venerated being as a way to

tion of 1905, Ivanov, Chulkov, and others attempted to revive the theater of Dionysus, but they failed to attract popular audiences. Some Symbolists concluded that "eternal myths" would have to be reformulated to address contemporary concerns.

As Russia returned to normal in 1908, the Symbolists further reconsidered their views. Chulkov organized a symposium, "On the New Theater." Ivanov was not a speaker, but the symposium was in many respects a response to his ideas. The main speakers were Chulkov, Sologub, Bely, Briusov, and Lunacharsky—all of whom had written plays—and the director Vsevolod Meyerhold.[14] Chulkov, still committed to a theater of myth creation, held that it could play a prophetic, countercultural role in the struggle against bourgeois individualism.[15] Lunacharsky endorsed the idea of a theater-temple as the center of a "free religious cult" and a locus of collective creativity. He welcomed the revolutionary implications of the Symbolist theater's struggle against *byt* (everyday life) and exalted art as a weapon in the "struggle for the human soul." His description of the soul as both individual and collective was similar to the Mystical Anarchists' conception of the empirical and mystical person.[16] Soon after, however, in an essay published in a Marxist symposium, *Literaturnyi raspad* (Literary decadence, 1908), Lunacharsky retracted his views and attacked Symbolist otherworldliness. But the idea of a theater-temple devoted to myth creation and psychological transformation still appealed to him.

Some of the discussions had political ramifications. Discussions of the roles of the actor, the director, and the playwright were also about autonomy and power. Debates about a conditional theater (*uslovnyi teatr*) versus a realistic theater were also about reality versus illusion; in other words, they were about truth. Indeed, the article in which Briusov had first proposed a conditional theater was titled "Nenuzhnaia pravda" (An unnecessary truth, 1904). Deriding the cluttered stage of Konstantin Stanislavsky's Moscow Art Theater, Briusov advocated a stylized theater that minimized externals (the spectators would have to use their imagination) in order to focus on spiritual or psychological truths.[17] In other articles, he argued that "methods of mediumism"

---

salvation, linking salvation with Dostoevsky's and Nietzsche's ideas of transgression; see Avril Pyman, *The Life of Alexander Blok*, vol. 1 (Oxford, 1979), pp. 94–95.

14. Meyerhold was a member of the Fellowship of the New Drama, organized by Aleksei Remizov. As director of the Theater Studio in Moscow and of the Kommissarzhevskaia Theater in St. Petersburg he staged Symbolist plays.

15. Georgii Chulkov, "Printsipy teatra budushchago," in *Teatr: Kniga o novom teatre* (St. Petersburg, 1908), pp. 199–218. Translations of the articles by Briusov, Bely, and Sologub are in *Russian Dramatic Theory from Pushkin to the Symbolists*, ed. Lawrence Senelick (Austin, 1981).

16. Anatolii Lunacharskii, "Sotsializm i iskusstvo," in *Teatr*, pp. 7–40.

17. Although Briusov directed his attack to the minute details of Stanislavsky's staging of a Chekhov play (live frogs croaking, for example), he may also have been responding to Gorky's play *Na dne* (*The Lower Depths*, 1902), in which two derelicts argue about which serves humanity better, the bitter truth or comforting illusions.

would facilitate cognition and enhance the actor's emotional expressiveness. He regarded the actor as the central figure in the theater.[18]

Yet by 1908, the Symbolists' demand for a unified vision was creating a dictatorship of the director and reducing the actor to a kind of marionette, a development that Briusov and Bely deplored. At the symposium, Briusov castigated actor-marionettes as destructive of the theatrical art and advocated a compromise between realistic and conditional theater.[19] Bely wanted to separate theater from mystery and have the actors step off the stage into real life. The very process of acting, he said, induces inner change (and is therefore theurgical); the actor actually becomes a "new man," self-directed and master of his fate.[20] Applied to politics, Bely's view implies that the "new man" is not an obedient subject, nor does he play out a role that others have written. Bely's views on theater were an aspect of his concept of life creation (*zhiznetvorchestvo*), the transfiguration of the world by means of art, the ultimate union of art and life. Other Symbolists developed their own versions of the concept.

Meyerhold and Sologub, by contrast, advocated theater for theater's sake rather than futile attempts to unite art and life. In their versions of a conditional theater, Symbolist techniques of mood creation and subliminal association were separated from theurgical transfiguration and limited to the theater. Meyerhold specified that both the spectators and the actors must be constantly reminded of the artificiality and illusoriness of the production. He believed that the theater removes the masks of everyday life to reveal the soul of the actor, and that the director was the "medium" (his term) through whom the spectator received the efforts of the playwright and the actor. Therefore the director should control every aspect of the performance.[21]

Sologub invoked sacrifice, mystery, and magic. "Black magic is an effective *modus operandi* in our fallen world as in art. Therefore the theater must become incantatory and thaumaturgic, the drama and spell woven by the poet-warlock. God and life are mutually denying, and our mundane sphere is ruled by the Devil: therefore we must lose ourselves in the hectic rhythms of a dervish dance."[22] The dervish dance was Sologub's counterpart to the Dionysian dithyrambs. He believed that the world was created by an evil demiurge—a Gnostic tenet.

Sologub titled his contribution "Theater of a Single Will," specifying that he meant the will of the playwright/poet, an impassive "man in black" who

18. Valerii Briusov, "Nenuzhnaia pravda," *Mir iskusstva*, 1904, no. 2; "Metod mediumizma," *Rebus*, 1900, no. 30, pp. 257–59; "Eshche o metodakh mediumizma," *Rebus*, 1900, no. 41, pp. 349–51.

19. Valery Briusov, "Realism and Conventionality on the Stage," in Senelick, *Russian Dramatic Theory*, pp. 171–82.

20. Andrei Bely, "Theater and Contemporary Drama," ibid., pp. 149–70, esp. 153, 160, 167.

21. Vsevolod Meierkhol'd, "Teatr (k istorii tekhniki)," in *Teatr*, p. 175.

22. Senelick, *Russian Dramatic Theory*, p. xiviii.

reads the play aloud, including stage directions, while marionette performers go through the action. "Why shouldn't an actor resemble a marionette? It does not humiliate a man. Such is the law of universal play-acting, that man is like a wonderfully constructed marionette." "Just as the unique will of I reigns supreme in the Macrocosm, so in the little circle of the theater, only one unique will should reign supreme—the will of the poet." And there is only one hero, sacrificer and sacrifice, "for the sacrament of self-immolation." Other characters are but steps to the hero's unique Visage. The spectator will become a participant in the mysterium, a liturgical ritual, in which he can "join hands with his brother and his sister and press his lips, eternally parched with thirst, to the mysteriously filled cup where 'I shall mingle blood with water.' To consummate in a bright public temple what can be now consummated only in catacombs."[23]

But Sologub also invited the spectators to join in the spectacle, as they did in their youthful sports and games. Not all was solemn and liturgical; there was an element of playful "let's pretend" in Sologub's theatrical vision, and in Briusov's and Meyerhold's as well. Meyerhold employed techniques derived from the commedia dell' arte, for he disliked the pontificating solemnity of most Symbolist plays. Transferred to the political realm, a theater of marionettes would imply dictatorship, but it is important to bear in mind that neither Sologub nor Meyerhold sought a theater that would unite art and life.[24]

Symbolist visions of a new theater had a great impact on their contemporaries. Pavel Gaideburov, the director of a popular theater, adapted Ivanov's idea of audience participation. The writer Leonid Andreev (1871–1919) envisioned a psychological theater in which the spectators would become as mentally active as the performers, and there would be no pretense.[25] In his own plays he fused Symbolism, naturalism, and political protest. Cabaret theaters experimented with audience participation and explorations of the "inner man." Nikolai Evreinov (1879–1953), Meyerhold's successor at the Kommis-

23. Fedor Sologub, "Theater of a Single Will," ibid., pp. 140, 137, 143, 135.

24. In his trilogy *Tvorimaia legenda* (A created legend, 1907–14), Sologub departed temporarily from his cosmic pessimism and exalted the creative power of human beings. The trilogy is structured "around a mirroring principle of opposites that eventually, through a *coniunctio* of polarities, achieves synthesis . . . bestial men become gods and earthly zoologian gardens are changed into Gardens of Eden": Irene Masing-Delic, *Abolishing Death* (Stanford, 1993), p. 155. The protagonist is an (al)chemist, poet, teacher, politician, and spaceship engineer who eventually becomes king. His name, Trirodov, which means "thrice-born" (as in "thrice-great Hermes"), is indicative of the mystic significance of the number 3 and of the protagonist's ability to combine mind, soul, and spirit. Fedorov once said that when the arts and sciences unite, even earths become heavens. Trirodov realizes this idea; he transforms legend into reality. His theurgical activities are a kind of gnosis. We can also describe them as a version of life creation.

25. Leonid Andreev, "Letters on the Theater" (second letter), in Selenick, *Russian Dramatic Theory*, pp. 260, 266, 272.

sarzhevskaia Theater and the future director of *Vziatie zimnego dvortsa* (The storming of the Winter Palace, 1920), integrated the audience into the performance without sacerdotal trappings and liturgical forms. Between 1910 and 1917 he directed the popular St. Petersburg cabaret theater called Krivoe Zerkalo (Crooked mirror), where his monodrama *V kulisakh dushi* (Theater of the soul) premiered in 1910. Evreinov used Freud's ideas to depict what the Symbolists had called "the inner man," adapting Symbolist techniques of mood creation accordingly.

Marxist critics and playwrights countered Chulkov's symposium with one of their own, "Krizis teatr" (The crisis in the theater, 1908), which produced such articles as "Theater or Puppet Show" and "Real Life or Mystery Play." A second volume of *Literaturnyi raspad* (1911) continued the attack on Symbolism and God-seeking. Nevertheless, secular versions of a theater of myth creation and theurgical transformation became part of Bolshevik political culture.

Also absorbed by political activists were Symbolist ideas on subliminal communication, which the Symbolists arrived at by way of art and occult doctrines rather than psychology.[26] They believed that imagery should be used sequentially, for symbol reinforced symbol as an affective momentum was built up. Moreover, the affective value of symbols in general, and of clustered images in particular, was augmented by the use of rhythm, which had its own compelling power, and by repetition. Repetition was said to increase the formation of symbols, intensify their psychological impact, and hammer sensory impressions deep into the psyche, for there was a link between sound and mind.

The Futurists advocated bringing art out into the streets and rejected Symbolist mystification, but in their own way they perpetuated the Symbolist ideas of an active audience, of art as a transformer of life, and of the linkage of sound and mind. One purpose of *zaum*, the transrational language that some Futurists advocated, was to shake up conventional thought patterns.[27] All the Futurists appreciated the incantational qualities of the spoken word and regarded language as a form of power. Khlebnikov, we recall, maintained that the poet could create a new essence merely by changing one letter of a word. In his play *Zangezi* (1922) he used vibrations to awaken the audience to levels of experience buried deep in the psyche. The protagonist (Zangezi) possesses cosmic wisdom; he understands the language of the birds and the language of the stars. Khlebnikov's ultimate goal was a technological utopia, a cosmoswide realm of peace and love in which people are in harmony with nature. Mayakovsky's first Soviet production *Misteriia buff* (Mystery bouffe, 1918, re-

26. For Kerensky's adaptation of their ideas, see Michael J. Fontenot, "Symbolism in Persuasion: The Influence of the Merezhkovskii Circle on the Rhetoric of Aleksandr Fedorovich Kerenskii," *Russian History* 26, nos. 1–4, pt. 2 (1992): 241–68.

27. For the Nietzschean sources of *zaum*, see Bernice Glatzer Rosenthal, "A New Word for a New Myth: Nietzsche and Russian Futurism," in *The European Foundations of Russian Modernism*, ed. Peter Barta (Lewiston, N.Y., 1991), pp. 219–50.

peated 1921), was a communist mystery play that spoofed Christian notions of heaven and hell; the message was the human beings would create their own paradise on earth by forging a new life and transfiguring the world.

GOD-BUILDING

In the Introduction we noted that Gorky and Lunacharsky were interested in Theosophy, that their Marxist surrogate religion was based in part on a quasi-occult interpretation of empiriocriticism and Energetism, and that it was indebted to Nietzsche's description of the cult of Dionysus. Gorky and Luna-charsky also picked up, consciously or unconsciously, and redeployed the cultic elements of Monism. Ostwald was obsessed by sun worship and the "mystical cleansing of eugenics." The God-builders worshiped collective humanity (Lunacharsky maintained that it would turn into a living god) and they were not racists. Energetism was compatible with an interpretation of Nietz-sche in which the masses provided energy and passion, to be channeled and directed by Apollonian leaders. One of Ostwald's slogans was "Waste no energy: turn it all to account." He was concerned not only with thrift but with a proper use of the holy powers given off by the sun.[28] Gorky and Lunacharsky hoped to galvanize the latent energy of the masses.[29] In Gorky's God-building novel *Ispoved'* (*Confession*, 1908), the collective energy of an assembled crowd uses its collective energy to heal a paralyzed girl.

God-building had much in common with Mystical Anarchism and can be considered a Bolshevik form of myth creation. Anarchosyndicalist rather than authoritarian in spirit (which was one reason for Lenin's opposition), God-building promised collective rather than personal immortality and extolled self-sacrifice for the sake of the Revolution. Lunacharsky's familiarity with a broad spectrum of occult ideas, from the folkloric occult to Anthroposophy, is obvious in his early poetry, his plays, and his two-volume *Religiia i sotsializm* (1908, 1911), which discusses such topics as "the destruction of harmony," Pythagoras, Gnosticism, the Logos, and cults. Pythagoras reputedly learned about mystical or magical numbers in Egypt and introduced these concepts to Greece; through him numerology became part of occult lore.

As a youth, Gorky had imagined himself a sorcerer with the power to

---

28. Daniel Gassman, *The Scientific Origins of National Socialism: Social Darwinism, Ernst Haeckel, and the German Monist League* (London, 1971), pp. 66–69; Richard Noll, *The Jung Cult: Origins of a Charismatic Movement* (Princeton, 1994), pp. 47–54, 91.

29. Galvanism, named for the Italian scientist Luigi Galvani (1737–98), involves the thera-peutic application of energy to the body; the idea was taken up by mesmerists, for it struck occultists as related to vitalistic theories that presented health as a state of harmony between the individual microcosm and the celestial macrocosm, involving fluids, human magnets, and occult attractions and affinities of all sorts. See Robert Darnton, *Mesmerism and the End of the Enlightenment in France* (New York, 1970), p. 14.

change grain into apples. As an adult he transferred his hopes from magic to science. He called science the "area of miracles" and believed that scientists could create "new forms of living nature" and change "so-called dead matter into living energy, subject to human will," thereby forming a "second nature."[30] These views are reminiscent of the animated universe of the occultists and their rejection of ontological dualism.

Gorky seized on early twentieth-century studies of thought transfer because he recognized their political potential. His frequent references to the "miraculous force of thought" are usually taken metaphorically, but Gorky meant them literally. He considered Dostoevsky's works psychologically harmful (*vrednyi*) because of the nihilism, sadism, and masochism of the characters. (*Vrednyi* is etymologically linked to *vreditel'*, the Soviets' word for wrecker; plural *vrediteli*, vermin). In 1913 Gorky tried to dissuade the Moscow Art Theater from staging *The Brothers Karamazov* and *Besy* (Demons, usually translated as *The Possessed*). The stage, Gorky wrote, transfers spectators from the realm of free disputation and rational analysis "to the realm of suggestion [*vnushenie*] and hypnosis, to the dark realm of emotions and feelings," in effect taking possession of them. Rather than wallow in barbarism, savagery, self-contemplation, and social pessimism, the stage should depict cheerfulness, courage, and spiritual health, and return to the "energy sources" that people need, to democracy, social consciousness (*obshchestvennost'*), and science.[31]

During the war, Gorky founded a science journal, *Letopis'*, and invited the biologist K. A. Timiriazev to contribute. His goal, he wrote to Timiriazev (October 16, 1915), was to

introduce into the emotional chaos surrounding us the principle of intellectuality. The bloody events of our day are evoking too many dark feelings, and it seems to me that it's time to introduce into this dark storm the moderating principle of a rational and cultured attitude toward reality. People are living in fear, and from fear comes hatred of one another; wildness is growing, respect for man keeps declining. Attention to the ideas of Western European culture is being overwhelmed by calls that summon people to the East, to Asia—from activity to contemplation, from study to fantasy, from science to religion and metaphysics.[32]

Metaphysics included occult doctrines; occultists themselves sometimes used the term as a code word. Trying to promote positive thinking, Gorky hoped

30. *Gor'kii i nauka: Stat'i, rechi, pis'ma, vospominaniia* (Moscow, 1964), pp. 3, 7, 27.

31. Maksim Gor'kii, "O 'karamazovshchine'" and "Eshche o 'karamazovshchine,'" in his *Sobranie sochinenii v tridtsati tomakh*, vol. 24 (Moscow, 1953), pp. 146–56, esp. 154 and 156.

32. Ibid., p. 163. Ivanov and V. Ern, a Theosophist, regarded the war as the work of cosmic forces and counterposed East and West in an eschatological dualism. See Ivanov, "Vselenskoe delo," and Ern, "Ot Kanta k Kruppu," *Russkaia mysl'*, 1914, no. 12, pt. 2, pp. 97–107 and 116–24, respectively.

that reason and science would cast out fear. "Reason" and "science" became his mantras.

The assumption that magic and miracles would be achieved by science and technology became a major feature of Soviet thought. The Futurists virtually worshiped technology. Fedorovian ideas are obvious in Vladimir Mayakovsky's plays *Klop* (*The Bedbug*, 1928), set in the Institute for Human Resurrection, and *Kupal'nia* (*The Bathhouse*, 1930), which assumes time travel. In these plays he satirized not Fedorov or technology but Soviet reality, because it had failed to meet his expectations. Like many of his contemporaries, Mayakovsky had assumed that a "third revolution," a "revolution of the spirit," would follow and complete the Bolshevik Revolution.[33]

"Revolution of the spirit" and related terms should not be construed in a narrow religious sense, because they conflated spiritual, emotional, psychological, and cultural factors, and mingled Christian concepts of spiritual perfection with Masonic, Theosophical, and Anthroposophical expectations of a new, nonegoistic, nonmaterialistic human being and a postapocalyptic world. Russian Anthroposophists spoke of a "worker-artist." Proletkult activists had similar expectations. Said one of them: "*Proletkult* is a spiritual [*dukhovnaia*] revolution. For the old, dark, capitalist world, it is more terrifying, more dangerous than any bomb. They know very well that a physical revolution is only a quarter of the Bolshevik-Soviet victory. But a spiritual revolution—that is the whole victory."[34] In his influential book *Tvorcheskii teatr* (Creative theater) the Proletkult theorist and Party member Platon Kerzhentsev (1881–1940) translated ideas derived from Nietzsche, Wagner, and Ivanov into a language of proletarian "self-activity" (*samodeiatel'nost'*) and collective creativity. Assuming that acting was a self-transforming and socially transforming (theurgical) activity, he called for plays written and produced by full-time workers.

Scythianism

The Scythians, a group of writers clustered around the literary critic Ivanov-Razumnik (1878–1948), "accepted" the Bolshevik Revolution as the prelude to a far-reaching spiritual revolution. (They took their name from the fierce nomads of the Asian steppes who conquered southern Russia in ancient times.) Scythianism was in many respects a replay of Mystical Anarchism except that the dominant occult doctrine was Anthroposophy. The Scythians disdained Marxism as bourgeois, rejected materialism and rationalism, regarded capitalism as a demonic force, and denounced all constraints external to the individ-

33. On Mayakovsky's conception of a "revolution of the spirit," see Bengt Jangfeldt, *Mayakovsky and Futurism* (Stockholm, 1977), pp. 51–71.

34. Quoted in Lynn Mally, *Culture of the Future* (Berkeley, 1990), p. xxix.

ual. They perceived war and revolution as Russia's Golgotha and expected imminent resurrection. Their political position was closest to that of the anarchist "left SRs," a group that seceded from the Socialist Revolutionary Party in March 1918, but they claimed to be adogmatic. Their primary interests were aesthetic, moral, and metaphysical.[35] Vol'fila was a gathering place for intellectuals interested in philosophy, religion, and metaphysics, including the occult. Marietta Shaginian and Olga Forsh attended its meetings.

Bely, the major contributor to Scythian publications and a prominent figure in Vol'fila, illustrates to an extreme degree the distorting and harmful effects of viewing political events through an occult prism. His understanding of Anthroposophy led Bely to believe that the Bolshevik Revolution was a negative apocalypse and that a positive apocalypse, a "revolution of the spirit," would follow and complete the political and social revolution. In essays written between 1916 and 1918, Bely described Russia as "the messiah of the nations," "the God-carrier," "the woman clothed in the sun," and the "conqueror of the serpent." (To Anthroposophists, the serpent represents the lower forms of knowledge through which humanity must pass.)

Occult beliefs had colored Bely's perceptions of contemporary events even before he became an Anthroposophist. In "Apokalipsis v russkoi poezii" (Apocalypse in Russian poetry), written after Bloody Sunday (January 22, 1905) but before the most turbulent phase of the revolutionary year, Bely predicted that disastrous events were about to occur. He perceived these events to be mere external reflections of a more important process, the universal struggle between cosmos and chaos. Waiting for "external signs, hinting at what was happening internally," Bely asserted that the veiling haze "is not reality." It forms itself into phantoms, illusions that are

> an external symbol in the struggle of the universal soul with the horror of the world, a struggle of our souls with the chimeras and hydras of chaos. The struggle against the horrible hydra is futile: new heads will keep growing back until we realize that the hydra itself is phantasmal; it is a Mask thrown over reality, behind which hides the Unseen One; until we realize that the Mask is phantasmal, it will grow, composing bloody worldwide historical pictures.[36]

Bely wanted the intelligentsia to conquer the "chimeras and hydras of chaos" through religious action, but he was unable to overcome his own fears, and projected them onto suffering Russia.

Some years later he wrote, "I found courage in the fact that my fate, the inhumanly vile years of 1906–1908, was a reflection of the illusions that had

35. Details may be found in Stefani Hoffman, "Scythian Theory and Literature," in *Art, Society, Revolution: Russia, 1917–21,* ed. Nils Nilsson (Stockholm, 1979), pp. 138–64.

36. Andrei Belyi, "Apokalipsis v russkoi poezii," in his *Lug zelenyi* (Moscow, 1910), p. 225.

descended upon all of Russia: *'the evil eye, hating Russia.'* " This "dark neurotic mood" was reinforced by Viacheslav Ivanov and Anna Mintslova, who told Bely that he had unwittingly depicted in his poems "the evil illusions that had been spread in Russia by Russia's enemy," and that *"enemies really do exist who are poisoning Russia with negative emanations; these enemies are East-ern occultists acting on the subconscious of the Russian people, unleashing wild passions beneath the crescent of the waning moon."* They also told him that the cultural forces of Russia (the God-seekers) were being attacked by "occult arrows shot from the world of darkness that was consciously demoralizing Russia."[37]

Bely's novels *Serebrianyi golub'* (*The Silver Dove,* 1909) and *Peterburg* (*Pe-tersburg,* 1911) reflect this occult-induced paranoia. Darialsky, protagonist of *The Silver Dove* and symbol of the Russian intelligentsia, cannot withstand the evil occult powers that threaten and ultimately kill him. A hallucinatory terror colors the occult experiences depicted in *Petersburg.* Birth and death loose their meaning. Neither the world nor thought exists. "Cerebral play is only a mask. Underway beneath the mask is the invasion of the brain by forces unknown to us."[38]

Bely's paranoia was exacerbated by Steiner's concept of objectless thinking, a special kind of imagination and meditation in which symbols represent spir-itual facts and states of being to which the senses have no access. This type of thinking dissolves the boundaries between spirit and matter, fantasy and real-ity, self and the world. In a troubled person, it can produce solipsism, the idea that nothing but the self exists. During World War I, Bely came to believe that the sound of gunfire from the battlefields was the sound of his own thoughts on the destruction of Europe. "The catastrophe of Europe and explosion of my personality are one and the same event. One could say that my 'ego' is the war or conversely that the war gave birth to me." "Man these days is like a gun; he is loaded with a crisis. The theme of crisis is interlaced with renascence. . . . Not accidental, therefore, are the voices that call us to spiritual heights: it is time to be reborn." "Politics will dissolve in spiritual war. . . . I am dynamite. I know my fate."[39] The last statement, which Bely meant literally, echoes Nietz-sche's famous prophesy of "great politics" ("Why I Am a Destiny," *Ecce Homo*). Bely identified with the humiliated and suffering Christ to the point of fan-

37. Andrei Belyi, *Vospominaniia o Bloke* (1922–23; Munich, 1969), pp. 623–24, quoted in Maria Carlson, "*The Silver Dove,*" in *Andrey Bely: Spirit of Symbolism,* ed. John E. Malmstad (Ithaca, 1987), p. 64.

38. Vladimir E. Alexandrov, "*Kotik Letaev, The Baptized Chinaman, and Notes of an Eccentric,*" in Malmstad, *Andrey Bely,* p. 157; Andrey Bely, *Petersburg,* trans. Robert A. Maguire and John E. Malmstad (Bloomington, 1978), p. 35.

39. Andrei Belyi, *Na perevale,* 3 vols. (Petrograd, 1918–20), 3: 15, 11; *Zapiski chudaka,* 2 vols. (Berlin and Moscow, 1922), 1:198.

tasizing about his own crucifixion.[40] In such a fantasy, conventional politics was irrelevant. The image of the suffering Christ appears in the writings of other Scythians, but not in the same pathological form.

THE POLITICAL RIGHT

Occult beliefs and practices played a prominent role at the imperial court as well. The influence of the faith healer Grigory Rasputin on the royal couple is well known. Actually, Rasputin was preceded by a long chain of charlatans and mystics, including a Baron Philippe from France. In 1902, before Rasputin's arrival at court, Baron Rothschild told Sergei Witte, then Russian envoy to France, that "great events, especially of an internal nature, were everywhere preceded by a bizarre mysticism at the court of the ruler."[41] Rothschild may have had in mind the popularity of mesmerism and of charlatans such as Cagliostro in prerevolutionary France. In hindsight, we can regard Rasputin as an unwitting herald of the revolutions of 1917. Mircea Eliade's observation is relevant here: "As in all the great spiritual crises of Europe, once again we meet the degradation of the symbol. When the mind is no longer capable of perceiving the metaphysical significance of the symbol, it is understood at levels which become increasingly coarse."[42] Under house arrest in Ekaterinburg after the Bolshevik Revolution, the former empress Alexandra traced a swastika on the window. An ancient Buddhist sun sign, it suggests her knowledge of Theosophy. A propensity to believe in cosmic determinism, perhaps in astrology and other divinatory practices, may help explain the obscurantism and fatalism of the imperial court, its resistance to reform when reform was still possible.

We recall that Blavatsky propounded a racial theory of history, based on her idea of cosmic evolution. She postulated a series of "root races," each embodying a different spirit and stage of development; nineteenth-century humankind was the fifth root race, the Aryan, and a sixth root race, a spiritualized humanity, was being formed. "Archaic root races," such as Jews and gypsies, would die out naturally. Blavatsky did not advocate their extermination. Although an anti-Semite, she was not obsessed by the "Jewish question"; her major concern was "Jesuit plots." Both she and Steiner believed that each race or nation (they used these words interchangeably) had its own destiny. Divid-

---

40. For a description of the Gnostic and Nietzschean elements in Bely's and Ivanov's visions of the kenotic Christ, see Carlson, "*Silver Dove*," pp. 77, 89, 90, 92. In "O Russkoi idee" (On the Russian idea, 1909) Ivanov invoked the descent of the Gnostic Logos and called upon the intelligentsia to descend humbly to the people in a sacrificial act of self-abnegation and giving of self in imitation of Christ.

41. Robert Warth, "Before Rasputin: Piety and the Occult at the Court of Nicholas II," *Historian* 47, no. 3 (1985): 323–37.

42. Mircea Eliade, *Mephistopheles and the Androgyne* (New York, 1965), p. 100.

ing humankind into races does not necessarily involve xenophobia; it can even signify appreciation of difference. Joseph Saint-Yves d'Olveydre, in *La Mission des Juifs* ("The Mission of the Jews, 1884), called the Jews the "yeast in the Aryan blood," and he meant it as a compliment. Steiner envisioned a great destiny for Russia; the Slavic race would supplant the Aryan, which had long dominated world evolution.

But some anti-Semites took up Blavatsky's racial theory of history and fused it with Nietzsche's idea of the Superman (despite Nietzsche's explicit attack on anti-Semitism) and traditional Christian images of the satanic Jew with magical powers.[43] In Germany, Lanz von Liebenfels (1874–1954, born Adolf Josef Lanz), author of *Theozoologie* (1904), preached Ariosophy, a mixture of racism and Theosophy, which heralded an imminent age of Aquarius, in which Aryan heroes would be purified of the sin of mixing their blood with that of ape-men. Humans did not descend from apes, Liebenfels taught; rather, apes were degenerated humans. He advocated war between blond and dark-haired peoples, and between Aryans and Jews, and described Jews as a subhuman racial element that was secretly tyrannizing the world and preventing "true wisdom" from breaking through.[44] In 1929–30 Liebenfels wrote a history of Ariosophy in which he traced the struggle of two eschatological forces, Aryans and subhumans, from ancient times to the present. The ancestors of the present "ario-historic race" were from Atlantis, which was in the North Atlantic. After catastrophic floods submerged their homeland, the northern Atlanteans migrated to the British Isles, Scandinavia, and Northern Europe. The southern ones migrated by way of North Africa to Egypt and Babylonia, where idolatrous beast-cults of miscegenation flourished. Intermarriage with these people produced racial inferiors who should be exterminated. Guido von List (1848–1918; he added the "von" later), a major influence on Liebenfels, held that Arktogaa (from ancient Greek: *arktos*, north; *gea* or *gaia*, land) was the vanished polar continent and the Aryans' original home, and that the real German religion was Wotanism. Ernst Haeckel (not a Theosophist) maintained that Jesus was an Aryan—that his real father was a Roman soldier who had seduced Mary.[45]

43. This is an old theme. For the medieval and early modern periods, see Joshua Trachtenburg, *The Devil and the Jews* (New York, 1944), and R. Po-chia Hsia, *The Myth of Ritual Murder: Jews and Magic in Reformation Germany* (New Haven, 1988).

44. Liebenfels also published a racist magazine, *Ostara* (named for a pagan Germanic goddess), which was in the library of the Nazi Party and which Hitler very likely read. See Webb, *Occult Establishment*, p. 281; Wilfred Daim, *Der Mann der Hitler die Ideen gab: Die sectiereischen Grundlagen des National Sozialismus* (Vienna, 1985); Nicholas Goodrick-Clarke, *The Occult Roots of Nazism: The Ariosophists of Austria and Germany, 1890–1935* (Wellingborough, 1985), esp. pp. 33–106, 153–63, 209–213.

45. Some early members of the German Communist Party also joined the Monist League because it exalted science over religion and the human over the divine. After World War II, East German scholars focused on the similarities between Haeckel and Marx rather than on

French Theosophists were deeply involved in forging the *Protocols of the Elders of Zion* and transferring them to Russia, where long-standing anti-Jewish myths, including the medieval notion that the Antichrist would be a Jew, fused with occult racial anti-Semitism. Sergei Nilus published the *Protocols* in a pamphlet titled *Velikom v malim* (The great in the small).[46] The pamphlet and another fabricated document, *The Chief Rabbi's Speech*, were among the materials disseminated by a new group formed in 1906, the Union of the Russian People, whose unofficial arm was the pogromist Black Hundreds. The most important feature of the Union's ideology was anti-Semitism. Rabble-rousers such as Iliodor and John of Kronstadt blamed the ills of the era on demons, whom they equated with Jews. Pogromists shouted, "Kill the Jews and save Russia!" Occultism and anti-Semitism came together in the writings of Vladimir Shmakov, son of Aleksandr Shmakov, who served as a volunteer attorney for the prosecution in the Beilis case. Vasily Rozanov misrepresented the Kabbala to "prove" that Judaism mandated ritual murder. Some of his articles were so scurrilous that even the reactionary newspaper *Novoe vremia* refused to print them. Merezhkovsky, however, was one of Beilis's most vociferous defenders; partly through his offices Rozanov was expelled from the Religious-Philosophical Society. During the war, Merezhkovsky and Ivanov contributed to a symposium, "Shchit'" (The shield, 1916), organized by Andreev, Gorky, and Sologub, which condemned anti-Semitism and pogroms. Surprisingly, Rasputin advocated equal rights for Jews.

After 1917, émigré writers such as the Baltic German Alfred Rosenberg perpetuated the idea of the Bolshevik Revolution as a Judeo-Masonic conspiracy and reintroduced the *Protocols* to Germany, where they became part of Nazi ideology. Rosenberg was a believer in the occult, as were other Nazi luminaries, most notably Hitler himself, Ernst Roehm, and Heinrich Himmler, head of the SS and organizer of genocide. The ancient Indian sun symbol of the swastika was popularized by Theosophists and Ariosophists. Rosenberg sometimes claimed that the sun-wheel popular in *volkisch* art stemmed from racial memories of the Arctic sun. Himmler claimed that in previous lives SS men had been heroic warriors in a struggle against the Jews that had been going on since biblical times. That Himmler was in charge of the "final solution" was no coincidence. Under his personal protection, the anti-Semitic Russian émigré and occultist Grigory Shvarts-Bostunich became a high-ranking SS officer and specialist on the "Judeo-Masonic-Bolshevik conspiracy." Himmler also believed, as did Hitler, in Hanns Hoerbiger's cosmic ice theory, formu-

---

their differences, and downplayed or ignored Haeckel's racism. Hitler considered Haeckel a prophet of Nazism but not a major one.

46. Webb, *Occult Establishment*, pp. 213–344; Michael Hagemeister, "Wer war Sergei Nilus?" *Ostkirchliche Studien* 40 (March 1991): 49–63, and "Die Protokolle der Weisen von Zion," *Via Regia* 14 (1994): 80–86; "Qui était Sergei Nilus?" *Politika Hermetika* 6 (1992): 141–58.

lated in 1912, which echoes Blavatsky's theory of successive moons. The Nazis used it to "explain" why Atlantis sank: a moon crashing to earth generated huge floods. The Nazi occult incorporated the myth of a northern Atlantis, Third Reich millennialism, Aryan supermen, and Antoine Fabre d'Olivet's theory, which may have influenced Blavatsky, that the white race had appeared near the North Pole and displaced the ruling black race.[47] These myths, and variants of them, are still circulating in Russia today.

Occult Ideas, Symbols, and Techniques in the Soviet Period

When we discuss the selective adaptation and transformation of occult ideas, symbols, and techniques in the Soviet period, we must distinguish between manipulative use of the occult by the leadership and spontaneous developments. We must also note the phenomenon of autosuggestion. Constant repetition of words and images in a controlled environment helped structure the mind-set of the propagandists themselves. The cumulative effect of the

---

47. Antoine Fabre d'Olivet set forth his theory in *Histoire philosophique du genre humain* [Philosophical history of the human race] (1824; Paris, 1910). For Hitler's occultism, see Webb, *Occult Establishment*, pp. 318–34. Hitler's faith in astrology is well known, but his belief in occult forces went much further. It deepened his view of the world as a battleground in which the "Eternal Jew" was the occult enemy. Hitler read widely in the library of the occultic Thule Society, to which Alfred Rosenberg, Dietrich Eckhardt (publisher of *Auf gut Deutsch*), and Gottfried Feder (the Nazi economist) also belonged. Haeckel joined it shortly before his death. At the time of Hitler's putsch (1923), Himmler was reading Ernst Roehm's *Reichskriegflagge*, a compendium of miracles dealing with astrology, hypnosis, Spiritualism, and telepathy. In 1935 Himmler founded an institute, Deutsches Ahnenerbe (German's Ancient Heritage), to research and publish materials on "Germanic" symbols, runes, and mythological archaeology. Wishing to create a purely Germanic occult, Himmler denigrated Anthroposophy as an Asian doctrine and Steiner as a Galician Jew, though Steiner was neither from Galicia nor of Jewish origin. For Fabre d'Olivet, see James Webb, *The Occult Underground* (La Salle, Ill., 1974), p. 270. For the cosmic ice theory, see Webb, *Occult Establishment*, pp. 326–27; for Hitler's private magus and his Ariosophy, see Goodrick-Clarke, *Occult Roots of Nazism*, pp. 177–91, 192–204. For Grigory Bostunich see Rafail S. Ganelin, "Des Leben des Gregor Schwartz-Bostunitsch," pt. 1, and Michael Hagemeister, "Des Leben des Gregor Schwartz-Bostunitsch," pt. 2, in *Russische Emigration in Deutschland, 1918 bis 1941*, ed. Karl Schloegel (Berlin, 1955), pp. 201–8 and 209–18.

The transformation of occult themes is seen in the rhetoric of contemporary black racists. Professor Leonard Jeffries of the City College of New York and former head of its Black Studies Department has inverted the cosmic ice theory to valorize blacks as "sun people" and denigrate whites as "ice people," but like the Nazis, he hates and demonizes Jews. See Jeffries's speech at the Empire State Black Arts and Cultural Festival, Albany, N.Y., July 20, 1991, in *Newsday*, August 19, 1991, pp. 16–18. Black racists quote the *Protocols of the Elders of Zion* frequently and extensively, and they charge that Jews were responsible for the slave trade—an application of Hitler's technique of the "big lie": the more outrageous the lie, the more likely people are to believe it. Louis Farrakhan, head of the Nation of Islam, uses numerology and Masonic symbols in his speeches. See "Excerpts from Farrakhan Talk," *New York Times*, October 17, 1995, p. A20.

occult symbols used to encapsulate or personify ideas, identify real or imagined enemies, and evoke and channel fears and fantasies induced people, including the propagandists, to think in these terms. People came to distrust their own powers of observation and reason, to await guidance from above, and to believe that conspirators were everywhere. The Nazis' use of the occult had similar effects. Hitler, Himmler, Rosenberg, and other Nazi leaders truly believed in the occult.[48] Once they assumed power, they forced (rival) occult groups to disband, but the occult remained a major element of their private beliefs.

In the Soviet Union the interplay of the occult with other elements in the politics and culture was more complicated. In accord with the "ruling idea" of Marxism-Leninism, Soviet leaders constantly invoked reason and science, and they considered themselves to be scientific and rational. But persons who do not believe in the occult can use symbols, ideas, and techniques derived from it to manipulate persons who do. Soviet propagandists drew on (consciously and unconsciously) occult themes and symbols that were familiar to the masses. Early Soviet political theater, the Lenin cult, the Stalin cult, and Socialist Realism all reveal manipulative uses of the occult. Cosmism was a spontaneous development, the work in large part of technocrats, but some of their activities were funded by the government. The cosmists blurred the line between science and magic and created expectations of manmade miracles. The literature of the 1920s, which was relatively free of Party control, did the same. In the 1920s, Bolshevik leaders derided the occult as superstition, but they incorporated occult and quasi-occult ideas in their civil religion nevertheless (as they also used Orthodoxy). In Stalin's time occult and quasi-occult ideas were used in new ways. Particularly striking are the uncanny correspondences between the show trials and the Symbolist theater, the recycling of the occult conspiracy theories of the extreme right, and the deliberately engineered occult paranoia.

The young Soviet Union was an overwhelmingly peasant society. In the villages, people continued to resort to faith healers, witches, and sorcerers rather than consult physicians.[49] Workers who came from peasant backgrounds re-

48. James Webb asserts that Nazi Germany "presents the unique spectacle of the partial transformation of the Underground of rejected knowledge into an Establishment:" *Occult Establishment,* p. 275. Before Hitler assumed power he said that "only when knowledge assumes once again the character of a secret science, and is not the property of everyone, will it assume once more its usual function, namely as an instrument of domination, of human nature as well as that which stands outside man": quoted in George L. Mosse, *The Nationalization of the Masses* (New York, 1975), p. 199; see also pp. 197–98.

49. Much of our knowledge of these practices stems from Soviet ethnographic expeditions of the 1920s and from reports of political activists who complained about the prevalence of superstition.

tained residues of their parents' and grandparents' beliefs. Even Bolsheviks were not immune. Bukharin and Grigory Sokolnikov (1888–1939) visited a renowned fortune-teller in the summer of 1918, when they were in Germany on a diplomatic mission. She read Bukharin's palm and said: "You will be put to death in your own country." Hoping to get a political prediction as well, says his widow, Bukharin then asked whether she thought that Soviet power would collapse. She replied: "Under which power you will perish, I cannot say, but in Russia for certain. In Russia there will be a wound in the neck and death by hanging!" Anna Larina says that Bukharin and Sokolnikov visited the fortune-teller out of curiosity, but they may have been drawn there by more than curiosity. The Civil War had just begun and the outcome was by no means certain. Bukharin was familiar with the writings of the Symbolists and God-builders; though on a conscious level he rejected their "mysticism," some of it may have rubbed off. "Rattled by her prediction," Larina continued, Bukharin asked, "'How can that be?' A person can die from only one thing." But the fortune-teller insisted that "there will be both the one and the other." Bukharin told Larina about this incident shortly before he was arrested early in 1937. He interpreted the prediction as indicating that "the anticipation of terror on a grand scale is choking me. In the language of the palm-reader, presumably, this is the wound in the neck. Later will come death by hanging; it doesn't matter that it's from a bullet."[50] During the Civil War, a reputed witch cursed a commissar who confiscated grain from her, and although he was a young man, he withered and died within the year![51]

Peasant notions of an "unclean force," "spoiling," and witchcraft, and images of demonic monsters and valiant hero-saints were given specifically Soviet political content. Posters that cried "Purge the Unclean!" were clearly alluding to the peasant belief in an unclean force. The very word "purge" (*chistka*) implies a ritual cleansing. Lenin denounced his enemies as vampires and bloodsuckers. A poster proclaiming "Death to World Imperialism!" (1919) depicts an armed worker stopping an enormous green dragon from crushing a factory building around which it is coiled. Another poster, "To the Deceived Brothers" (1918), shows a worker slaying the "many-headed hydra of reaction."[52] Satan and his minions appeared as opponents of Bolshevism. Trotsky was depicted as St. George slaying the dragon. Such mythic and religious images played into popular belief in the existence of powerful occult forces. Capitalist encirclement was represented as such a force, fixated on destroying the workers' state. In Shaginian's novel *Mess-Mend*, the demonic forces of capitalist imperialism actually use black magic, but are defeated by the white

50. Anna Larina, *This I Cannot Forget: The Memoirs of Nikolai Bakhunin's Widow*, trans. Gary Kern (New York, 1993), p. 308.
51. Linda Ivanits, *Russian Folk Belief* (Armonk, N.Y., 1989).
52. The artists were D. S. Moor and A. Apsit, respectively.

magic of the Communists. Early Socialist Realist novels also revolved around occult conspiracies, but technology replaced magic and the emphasis was on "wreckers" and "saboteurs." The new generation of Bolsheviks that came to dominate the Party, most of them from humble backgrounds, were receptive to new myths and cults presented in appropriate Soviet language.

As head of the Commissariat of Enlightenment (or Education; *prosveshchenie* means both) Lunacharsky invited artists to collaborate with the Soviet government. The Symbolists and the Futurists who responded to his call worked in early Soviet cultural agencies and taught in Proletkult schools and studios, as did many Theosophists and Anthroposophists. Ivanov was employed by TEO, the theatrical section of the commissariat, where his ideas had enormous influence. Demystified and politicized, they were one source of the mass festivals and political theater of the revolutionary period. The size of the chorus expanded markedly and many productions were staged out-of-doors, but the intent was the same—myth creation and psychological transformation.[53] When Evreinov staged the storming of the Winter Palace for the third anniversary of the Bolshevik Revolution in 1920, 8,000 actors and 500 musicians thrilled 150,000 spectators.

Evreinov's play *Samoe glavnoe* (*The main thing*, also 1920) was perhaps more important for the future development of the Soviet theater, because it depicted a new kind of fantasy grounded in earthly reality, which supplied people with the illusions they required to face life optimistically. The protagonist is named Paraclete—"advocate" or "comforter" in Greek, but to Christians the Holy Spirit. Paraclete appears in several incarnations, much like a changeling, an archetype of the folk occult. In one incarnation, Paraclete is a female fortune-teller; in another, as a man, he tells the audience that "along with the official theater, a sort of laboratory of illusion . . . we need an unofficial theater, a sort of marketplace of illusions, a theater in even greater need of reform for it is Life itself! Life, where illusion is no less necessary than on these boards, and where, if we are unable to give the deprived happiness, we must at least give them the illusion of happiness."[54] Paraclete is referring to people who are unloved and lonely, not the poor; this play is apolitical. "It is my sincere belief," he continues, "that the world will be transformed through the actor, through the actor's magic art." Evreinov emigrated in 1925, but his idea of necessary illusion anticipated Socialist Realism (and echoed Nietzsche).

That theater could and would transform life was assumed. A character in Mayakovsky's *Mysteriia buff* says:

> We too will show life that's real
> Very!

53. James von Geldern, *Bolshevik Festivals, 1917–1920* (Berkeley, 1993), pp. 137–74.

54. Nikolai Evreinov, *The Main Thing*, in *Theater as Life: Five Modern Plays*, trans. Christopher Collins (Ann Arbor, 1973), pp. 67–68.

But life transformed by the theater into a spectacle most extraordinary![55]

Introspectiveness was shunned; Communists were not supposed to dwell on their own feelings. To quote Mayakovsky once again:

> Don't befoul
> the theater with slobbering psychologism!
> Theater,
> serve Communist propaganda![56]

Meyerhold proclaimed a "theatrical October," a new kind of theater dedicated to sustaining revolutionary passion. The associative techniques that he used in his Soviet productions were in line with his aggressively pro-Bolshevik stance, and also with the reflexology of Vladimir Bekhterev and Ivan Pavlov. Theurgical transformation would be accomplished by physiological or neurological stimuli, or by charges of (psychic) energy or electricity. A series of shocks jolted the spectators into new states of awareness and forged explicitly political associations. Meyerhold described a theatrical performance as a series of passes, each intended to evoke an association in the spectator, some premeditated, others outside the director's control. "Your imagination is activated, your fantasy stimulated, and a whole chorus of associations is set forth. A multitude of accumulated associations gives birth to a new world."[57]

To create a compelling political vision, Meyerhold used radio bulletins, newspaper clippings, and other factographic items. To appeal to popular audiences, he incorporated slapstick, circus clowns, and vaudeville elements, and to make sure the spectators understood the political message, he demonized the villains by having them wear grotesque masks, and had the actors speak directly to the audience. The latter practice involved the audience in the spectacle and incorporated some of the "let's pretend" aspects of conditional theater, as did the minimalist stage decor (there was no money for elaborate sets); the audience had to use their imagination.

Sergei Eisenstein began his career as Meyerhold's protégé. His films of the 1920s were ventures in myth creation and his theory of montage adapted Symbolist ideas on association to the new art form, alternating shots of Kerensky with shots of a peacock, for example, or shots of capitalists with shots of pigs. Like Meyerhold's productions, Eisenstein's were designed to shock the audience into a new level of consciousness.

To trace the steps by which the theater and mass festivals of the early Soviet period turned into the theater of Stalin's time would require a book in itself.

55. Quoted in Harold B. Segel, *Twentieth-Century Russian Drama* (New York, 1979), p. 138.

56. Quoted by Collins in Evreinov, *Theater as Life*, p. xxviiil; name of poem and date not given.

57. Quoted in Robert Leach, *Vsevolod Meyerhold* (Cambridge, 1989), p. 136.

Briefly, during the course of the 1920s, the degree of spontaneity allowed the actors steadily diminished. Mass festivals became mass rallies in which partici- pants / marionettes shouted on cue their adulation of the new high priests and their hatred of the "enemies of the people." Theater and film exalted a single hero, rather than the collective, as "mediator" or "initiator." If the play was about the Revolution, the hero or heroine was the commissar; if it was about the five-year plan, the Party leader or "red" engineer. During the Cultural Revolution (1928–31) and again during the Great Purges (1936–38) there were heroes or heroines who denounced family members or co-workers.

Most important, the difference between reality and illusion, so central to the conditional theater, steadily disappeared. Nikolai Pogodin's play *Aristokraty* (Aristocrats, 1932) depicted the rehabilitation through labor of political pris- oners working on the White Sea–Baltic Canal. In effect, Pogodin was treating labor not only as a form of gnosis but as resurrection, for the laborers emerge as new men and women. He was also idealizing slave labor. Socialist Realist theater presented the illusion on the stage as a "living truth" (that is, a myth). Stage decor became more elaborate and "realistic." The entire nation was be- coming a theater of marionettes directed by Stalin, as if in fulfillment of Sol- ogub's vision of an "impassive man in black" giving directions aloud, except that Stalin's directives were often given obliquely and behind the scenes, and he favored white or light-colored garments.

The show trials of the Old Bolsheviks, writes Robert Tucker, were "basically one-man shows of which Stalin himself was the organizer, chief producer, and stage manager as well as an appreciative spectator from a darkened room at the rear of the Hall of Columns where the trials were held."[58] The chief pros- ecutor, Andrei Vyshinsky (1883–1955), was himself a marionette, as were the defendants and the witnesses, all of whom recited their lines on cue. Inside the Hall of Mirrors (the theater-temple) the spectators (the chorus) demanded the defendants' death (ritual sacrifice). Much of the action—beatings, torture, execution—occurred offstage (Sologub's catacombs). Radio and newspapers brought the trials to new mass audiences, who also demanded the defendants' death. The mystery turned into the monstrous antisoviet conspiracy. Some of the sacrificers became sacrifices in their turn.[59]

The Soviet idea of "building socialism," a rough counterpart to the Symbol- ist concept of "life creation," emphasized the (theurgical) powers of science and technology. The cosmists attributed a messianic role to scientists and engi-

---

58. Robert C. Tucker, "Stalin, Bukharin, and History as Conspiracy," Introduction to *The Great Purge Trial*, ed. Tucker and Stephen F. Cohen (New York, 1965), pp. xvi–xv.

59. In *Darkness at Noon*, Arthur Koestler's fictionalized account of the show trials, the protagonist is urged to sacrifice himself voluntarily as a "last service" to Bolshevism (New York, 1968), pp. 190, 203, 205.

neers and blurred the boundaries between magic and science. Cosmism can be considered a technological version of ocsoc (occult socialism), so designated by Philippe Muray: a hybrid, often incoherent, yet quite fundamental set of discursive practices based on the dream of a universally regimented human order imbued with the principle of Harmony—either the created harmony of the utopian socialist future or the already given harmony of the cosmos.[60] The cosmists were spiritual descendants of Fedorov, the Futurists, the God-builders, and Bogdanov on the one hand, and of nineteenth-century French utopian socialists on the other. To the cosmists, utopia was technology plus socialism. Unlike traditional occultists, who viewed the cosmos as a given, the cosmists wanted to transform it and to colonize (and humanize) outer space in a promethean drive for world domination. New people would be created according to a plan, and they would be immortal. Presumably the cosmists would make the plan—that is, design the new people and their habitat. We know that Fedorov's ideas appealed to engineers and technicians. Whether these people had any input in the five-year plan, as employees of Gosplan, the Soviet central planning agency, requires research. But we can say that the conquest of nature that was so prominent a feature of the first five-year plan derives, at least in part, from Fedorov's goal—the regulation of nature. Research is also needed on the cosmists' view of women and women's role, if any, in the present and future world. I raise this issue because technocrats tend to be male-oriented and because androgyny had been a salient aspect of the pre-revolutionary occult.

Like Fedorov, the cosmists rejected Western concepts of personal freedom. Fedorov had dreamed of a tsar-autocrat who would supervise the labor armies engaged in the "common task" of regulating nature and resurrecting the dead. Participation in this "common task" would be compulsory. Until it was ful-filled, life in a Fedorovian society would be incessant labor. But the cosmists dropped Fedorov's personalism and his emphasis on love. In Konstantin Tsiolkovsky's millennial technocracy all deleterious and "useless" forms of animal and plant life would be exterminated. As early as 1917/18, he began a campaign to prevent the procreation of defective people and animals, by force if necessary. In the writings of the cosmists and of other authors enthralled by technology we find references to "human material" and descriptions of ma-chines that disregarded the distinction between the human and the mechan-ical; a dynamo, for example, might be said to have a "beating heart." We also find allusions to the transmutation (through technology rather than alchemy) of people and things. Soviet admirers of the American efficiency expert Fred-erick W. Taylor wanted to make people into virtual machines.

The literature of the 1920s fostered expectations of manmade miracles. The antiheroes of Iury Olesha's novels and short stories, writes Elizabeth Beaujour,

60. Philippe Muray, *Le Dix-neuvième Siècle à travers les âges* (Paris, 1984).

"have neither the patience nor the capacity for participating in *perestroika*, reconstruction, which demands a long struggle with material more resistant than language. They are interested only in *prevrashchenie*, immediate effortless transformation." Olesha affected a posture of incomprehension of technology throughout his career. For people like him, technology was indeed beyond rational comprehension. "Other men have conquered nature by a knowledge which remains occult to him. Consequently, he is irresistibly drawn to those who exercise some technical competence. They thereby become 'charming,' almost in the etymological sense of the word: they cast a spell."[61] We saw Platonov's and Shaginian's faith in the power of technology in Chapter 9. They were only two of many.

The meshing of the occult and technology helped create an atmosphere that militated against realistic economic planning. Economists who pointed to flaws in the first five-year plan were accused of "creeping empiricism" and "Menshevizing idealism." Max Weber once described politics as a "strong and slow boring of hard boards. It takes both passion and perspective." Occult-derived ideas can supply the passion but distort the perspective. In the same passage, however, Weber also wrote that "all historical experience confirms the truth—that man would not have attained the possible unless time and again he had reached out for the impossible. But to do that a man must be a leader, and not only a leader but a hero as well in a very sober sense of the word."[62] The success of the five-year plans depended on Soviet leaders' ability to arouse and channel the enthusiasm of the masses.

Engineers became the new culture heroes, performing miracles and marvels by means of science and subjugating nature. In Soviet novels of the 1930s, natural disasters "conspire" with the enemies of the plan, and nature is a chaotic, even demonic force that must be defeated by human reason and will. This hostile nature is the very opposite of the benevolent living nature found in esoteric *Naturphilosophie*.

Among the factors that combined to create the Lenin cult, the Stalin cult, and Socialist Realism were the occult (as well as the cultic) elements in Symbolism and God-building. High priests with political power adapted techniques pioneered in the Symbolist theater to a new kind of mood creation that systematically invoked fear and hatred as well as love, directing the feelings and passions of the masses to visible entities, both divine and demonic.

Nina Tumarkin has argued persuasively that the original purpose of the Lenin cult was mobilization, not state power; it was created to enable Party

61. Elizabeth Beaujour, *The Invisible Land: A Study in the Artistic Imagination of Yuri Olesha* (New York, 1970), pp. 37, 125.

62. Max Weber, "Politics as a Vocation," in *From Max Weber: Essays in Sociology*, ed. H. H. Gerth and C. Wright Mills (New York, 1970), p. 128.

leaders to rally the people around their fallen leader and thereby legitimate themselves as his successors. Only later was it harnessed to the state.[63] That the cult-builders appropriated Orthodox terminology and ritual and played on the popular belief that saints' bodies do not decompose is well known. (I call them cult-builders to underscore their connection to God-building.) Luna-charsky was one of the Lenin cult's chief proselytizers. (Gorky was out of the country, but he propagated the cult from his home in Capri.) Other cult-builders were Leonid Krasin (1870–1926), an open admirer of Fedorov, and V. D. Bonch Bruevich (1873–1955), who had preached Marxism to the sec-tarians and was accustomed to couching political ideas in religious terms. Krasin was trained as an engineer; it was he who proposed refrigerating Lenin until Soviet scientists discovered how to resurrect him (literally). Unlike Fedo-rov, Krasin believed that only great men should be resurrected. When Lenin's body began to decompose, the cult-builders decided to embalm him.

Their decision reflected the coincidental discovery of Tutankhamen's tomb, which aroused great interest all over the world. The records of their discus-sions were never published, but their public statements make it clear that they believed that a successful embalming would demonstrate the superiority of Soviet over "bourgeois" science, of philosophical materialism over philosophi-cal idealism, and of communism over Christianity. Communism would pro-vide by means of science what Christianity could only promise—immortal life—and it would be for everyone, not just for the pharoahs and the nobility (Krasin's elitist views were not publicized).[64] Finally, the embalming was a way of tapping into the mystique of Egypt found in recently banned but still popular occult doctrines. Although Freemasonry traces its origins to the ma-sons who built King Solomon's temple, mystical Freemasons hold the mythical Egyptian Hermes Trismegistus in great esteem. And Masonic iconography features the pyramid and other Egyptian symbols. Blavatsky devoted Chapter 14 of *Isis Unveiled* to "Egyptian wisdom." Isis, of course, is an Egyptian god-dess. Steiner taught that ancient Egypt was the third post-Atlantean culture (after the flood that destroyed Atlantis) and that a mysterious thread con-nected ancient Egypt and the present world. The souls of ancient Egyptians were actually residing in the bodies of contemporary Europeans, he said; through them a reawakening of the Third Period has already begun. Egyptian culture will rise again, this time with a Christian principle.

Lenin's tomb was shaped like a cube rather than a pyramid because the cube signified the fourth dimension of life, which, according to the Theosophists, survived the body's disintegration. Kazimir Malevich, the artist who proposed

---

63. The Lenin cult was born after the attempt to assassinate Lenin on August 30, 1918, and developed far more systematically after his death on January 21, 1924. For details see Nina Tumarkin, *Lenin Lives!* (Cambridge, Mass., 1983).

64. Ibid., pp. 179–92.

the cubic shape, held that the fourth dimension enabled one to escape death. Lenin, he declared, had been resurrected from time-bound matter and was now in the world of true art and religion, the "supra-material kingdom of the ideal spirit."[65] Therefore Lenin should be placed in a cube, the symbol of eternity. To Malevich, the cube, signifying metamorphosis, symbolized not only Lenin's immortality but an entirely new culture. Indeed, the cube would actually create this culture as it moved through space, for it possessed theurgical properties. The cube, we might add, expressed the Bolsheviks' prometheanism and future orientation much better than the pyramid, which harked back to remote antiquity and was built by slave labor.

The architect of the tomb, Arkady Shchusev (1873–1949), designed a structure composed of three cubes in evocation of the Holy Trinity. Before the Revolution he had designed churches and had been associated with the aesthetes of *Mir iskusstva,* some of whom were interested in the occult. He had also traveled in Egypt with N. V. Ignatiev, who designed the tomb's interior. Mayakovsky's triadic formula "Lenin lived! Lenin lives! Lenin will live!" became a mantra of the cult.

The German scholar Klaus Vondung maintains that the purpose of political religions and ideological cults is to create a "second [false] reality" and have it accepted as a "higher truth."[66] The Lenin cult was a first step in that direction, but the Bolsheviks were preoccupied with other issues and did not pursue the matter. Moreover, Krupskaia (Lenin's widow), Trotsky, and some other Bolsheviks opposed the embalming as contradictory to Lenin's ideals and as pandering to the superstitions of the masses. The task of developing a psychologically compelling vision of a "second reality" to be purveyed to the masses as part of a coherent cultural policy was taken up by Stalin. The result was a fully worked-out political religion centered on Stalin and proselytized by a new, compulsory aesthetic—Socialist Realism. Total government control of the media—indeed, of the entire economy—created the environment necessary for effective conditioning.

The Stalin cult was launched on Stalin's fiftieth birthday (December 21, 1929), a few weeks after Stalin proclaimed the "great break." The Soviet Union was then in the midst of the first five-year plan and its flaws were becoming apparent. In the factories and on the new collective farms chaos and confusion prevailed, but it was too late to turn back. To rally the people around the "general line," a coordinated media campaign hailed Stalin's wise and calm leadership (he was then first among equals) and the miracles of socialist construction achieved under his direction. The subliminal message was that some-

---

65. Robert Williams, *Artists in Revolution* (Bloomington, 1977), pp. 124–25.
66. Klaus Vondung, *Magie und Manipulation* (Göttingen, 1971; Munich 1979), shows how the Nazis couched their rhetoric in Christian terms, borrowed Christian (mostly Catholic) ceremonial forms, and transformed Christian apocalypticism and millenarianism.

one was in charge, that the confusion and chaos were only apparent, and temporary at that. The "great break" signaled the long-awaited leap from necessity to freedom in a secularized apocalypticism that was also theurgical activity. And it did transform the world, but not by magic.

Lenin had discouraged cult-building during his lifetime, but Stalin (sometimes personally, sometimes through his aides) instigated and orchestrated his own cult. At first, Stalin was hailed as Lenin's disciple, chosen heir, and sole interpreter (compare occultists' carrying on of The Tradition). The second stage coincided with the promulgation of Socialist Realism (1932–34), and shaded into a third stage around 1935–36. Only in this third stage was Stalin described in divine terms—all-knowing, all-powerful, and beneficent. A corresponding shift in the official rhetoric praised the magic and miracles wrought by the cadres (as distinct from the impersonal magic wrought by science and technology), and made it clear that they owed their effectiveness to Stalin. Other people merely shared in his mana, a supernatural force that is concentrated in particular persons or objects. The term itself was not used, but the concept was known to ethnographers and anthropologists, especially those who studied shamanism. Stalin was the sun and the cadres were the moons. Heroes and heroines of labor (the Stakhanovites) proclaimed that the very thought of Stalin inspired them to work harder. Aviator heroes testified that pronouncing Stalin's name gave them courage and protected them from danger. Though the Theosophists could meet only illegally, a legend circulated among them that "Stalin knew something which no one else could ever discover and that he was an incarnation of Manu, the Great Teacher of India."[67] Specially composed "folklore" explicitly invested Stalin with magical powers. "Stalin waves his right hand—a city grows in a swamp, he waves his left—factories and plants spring up, he waves his red handkerchief—swift rivers start to flow."[68] During World War II, Soviet soldiers charged into battle shouting, "For the Motherland! For Stalin!"

Stalin's calm, monotonous speaking style had an almost hypnotic effect on his audience, while his repetition of key slogans ensured that the desired message would get through. Lev Kopelev alludes to the incantational quality of Stalin's speeches; "and these results [of economic campaigns] he repeated—insistently, laboriously, monotonously, like the mumbo-jumbo of a shaman."[69] The incantational quality may have been deliberate. In 1948, Stalin banned hypnotism, suggesting that he feared its effectiveness. His rare, carefully staged public appearances, his inscrutable and remote manner deepened the aura of power and mystery with which he surrounded himself. In *The Master*

67. Andrei Sinyavsky, "The Literary Process in Russia," in his *Continent* (New York, 1976), p. 92.

68. Frank Miller, *Folklore for Stalin* (Armonk, N.Y., 1990), p. 81.

69. Lev Kopelev, *The Education of a True Believer* (New York, 1980), p. 262.

and Margarita, Woland (Satan) is a "somber, black and yet idealized Stalin" who practices black magic. The novel depicts the "mass psychosis [compare Bekhterev's concept of psychological contagion] that has locked society in a vicious circle of denunciations, where the secret police, prison, and interrogations are presented as a sort of theater in imitation of Stalin's own theater of denunciations and repressions."[70]

The Stalin cult awaits its historian. Its surface manifestations are clear enough, but its inner workings are still in the shadows. I suspect that former God-builders and Proletkultists had a hand in its development and dissemination, as well as members of the Change of Landmarks movement (the *Smenovekhovtsy,* émigrés who returned). The latter were ultranationalists intent on maximizing Soviet power; their writings are replete with allusions to the occult. One of their ideologues, Nikolai Ustrialov (1890–1938), even titled one of his books *Pod znakom revoliutsii* (Under the sign of revolution, 1925), an astrological formulation.

The institution of Socialist Realism as the official aesthetic of the Soviet Union (1932–34) coincided with the end of the first five-year plan. Impressive feats of socialist construction such as the Dnepestroi Dam had been achieved and the infrastructure of an industrial economy had been laid. But the standard of living had plunged below 1928 levels. In the cities, bread was rationed and consumer goods were unavailable to ordinary people; in the countryside, resentment at forced collectivization smoldered.

To tell people who had been led by propagandists to expect an overnight transformation that years of hard work still lay ahead could undermine confidence in the Party and result in a dangerous slackening of effort at the workplace; so people were told that the miraculous transformation had indeed been achieved and that even more miracles were imminent. This is the point at which the second stage of the psychic fallacy came into play. (The psychic fallacy is the illusion that one's inner or psychic state is interchangeable with material actuality, "as if there were no external world, as if the universe were nothing but feeling and will." Realistic planning gives way to "insistence on spiritual perfection, mystical strength, and infallibility"). The emphasis on change was replaced with an *image* of change that had already taken place.[71] Socialist Realism purveyed the illusion of an already created "second reality," an image of prosperity and happiness that would spur people on to even greater efforts and dedication. The theme of the 17th Party Congress (the so-called Congress of Victors) was that socialism had won. A popular song told people that theirs was the generation "born to turn fairy tales into reality, to

70. Andrei Sinyavsky, *Soviet Civilization* (New York, 1988), pp. 105–7.
71. Lifton, *Revolutionary Immortality,* p. 135.

conquer space and time." According to Mikhail Agursky, Socialist Realism was a venture in mass hypnosis.

Reflecting Gorky's desire to make optimism ubiquitous, optimism was compulsory in Socialist Realist literature and art. Gorky disapproved of Aleksandr Afinogenov's play *Lozh'* (The lie, 1933), which depicted Party members who lied and cheated as a matter of policy, because it contained negative thoughts that were too close to the truth. Gorky showed the script to Stalin, who had the play suppressed. Negative thoughts were voiced only by villains, if at all. Self-criticism was allowed, but cautiously, for the distinction between constructive and destructive criticism was not always obvious.

In tacit acknowledgment of the "magic of words" and to ensure that the correct political associations were made, language was tightly controlled. The vocabulary of permitted words was sharply circumscribed. Newspapers went through several proofreadings, not only to appear professional and competent, and to provide a model of correct grammar and spelling for the newly literate masses, but also because changing the letter of a word might really change reality (as occultists had taught without calling for such policies). One misprint could spoil an entire project! Statistics on the progress of the plan were inflated for the same reason, to create a new essence, and not just to give the impression of success.

In science, this atmosphere, plus access to political power, made possible the rise of Trofim Lysenko (1898–1976), who purported to be able to transform (transmute) wheat into rye and pine trees into firs. The cult of Lysenko was preceded by a cult of Ivan Michurin (1855–1935), an autodidact whose success in plant breeding created a "garden of miracles" (*sad chudes*).[72] Lysenko denied the very existence of genes and had scientists who disagreed with him purged. He reached the height of his power after World War II, when he was in charge of the attempt to change the climate of Soviet Asia by reforestation—a project that smacks of Fedorov.

Afinogenov's play *Strakh* (*Fear*, 1932), written before Socialist Realism was instituted, depicted new modes of manipulating people. A partisan of psychological drama, Afinogenov set his play during the Cultural Revolution, when "bourgeois specialists" (professionals trained before the Revolution) were being fired from institutes and replaced by *vydvizhentsy* (persons of proletarian or peasant origin who were promoted to professional and managerial positions) and denunciations were routine. The main character is Ivan Borodin, scientific director of the Institute for Physiological Stimuli. Under his auspices the institute did a study that showed that 80 percent of Soviet citizens were paralyzed by fear. As a result, people became "suspicious—shut in—dishonest—careless—and unprincipled," and the effects on the economy were disastrous.

72. *Tridtsat' dnei*, 1934, no. 10, p. 62.

The rabbit who has seen a boa constrictor is unable to move from the spot. His muscles petrify. He waits, submissively, until the rings of the boa constrictor squeeze him and crush him. All of us are rabbits. . . . In view of this can we work creatively? Of course not! [The other 20 percent, the *vydvizhentsy*] have nothing to fear. They are the masters of the country. . . . But their brain is afraid for them. . . . The brain of people accustomed to physical labor is afraid to carry too great a burden, and there develops a persecution mania. They are always striving to catch up and to outstrip everyone; and, choking in this never-ending race, this brain either goes insane or slowly degenerates. . . . Destroy fear—destroy everything that occasions fear and you will see with what a rich creative life our country will blossom forth![73]

Borodin is a composite of the reflexologists Bekhterev and Pavlov. Bekhterev wrote an article on the stultifying effects of autocracy on human personality during the Revolution of 1905, and opposed the excesses of Soviet efficiency experts in the 1920s. Although he described psychological contagion, he certainly did not advocate it as a policy tool. Pavlov was an open and vehement critic of the Bolsheviks until the Nazis came to power.

Borodin is refuted by Klara, a lifelong Communist and a member of the Party Control Commission.

To frighten, to paralyze the will, to break the opposition of those who are oppressed, to transform people into obedient rabbits—this is what the boa constrictors of all times and all peoples have striven for. But the oppressed are not rabbits. . . . Fear gave birth to fearlessness, the fearlessness of those who had nothing to lose, and who are now merciless in the class struggle. . . . When we break the resistance of the last oppressor on earth, then our children will look for the explanation of the word "fear" in a dictionary. But until then temper yourself in the fearlessness of the class struggle.[74]

Borodin is arrested, but he admits his errors and will be reinstated. Not only was he wrong about fear, he wanted science to replace politics and harbored conspirators in his institute—"rabbits" who were actually "boa constrictors."

One of them is Visarion Zakharovich Zakharov (the Russian word for witch doctor, *znakhar*, minus the *n*), professor of the history of ancient Oriental religions, presumably those of Egypt, Babylon, and India. He has attempted to infect the institute with occultism, but his mystic triangles and numerological calculations and books prove to be impotent against Soviet power. Books specifically mentioned are *Occult Intelligence, The Cross and the Pentogram, A Medium's Handbook,* and *Mysticism as the Basis of the World.* Presumably this is what

73. Aleksandr Afinogenov *Fear,* in *Six Soviet Plays,* ed. Eugene Lyons (New York, 1934), p. 451.

74. Ibid., pp. 452–53.

people were reading. The red star is a pentagram, of course, but a pentagram is also an occult symbol; upside down it signifies the devil.

By the time *Fear* was staged, the Cultural Revolution was ending and many bourgeois specialists had been reinstated. Its production throughout the Soviet Union signaled that the worst was over. But fear returned as an instrument of political policy in December 1934, when the murder of Sergei Kirov, head of the Communist Party of the Leningrad region, served as the pretext for a new round of purges, which escalated into the Great Terror. Confessions of monstrous conspiracies by trusted Old Bolsheviks, mass arrests, disappearances of neighbors, friends, and co-workers, and frequent, abrupt, and drastic shifts in the Party line—all contributed to an atmosphere of uncertainty and fear. There were enemies everywhere. Whom could one trust? How could one protect oneself? The results were exactly as described by Borodin in Afinogenov's *Fear*, and by Gorky in 1915 when he noted that fear makes poeple harken to "calls that summon people to the East," to religion and metaphysics. *Fear* is the subtext of Fazil Iskander's novel *Kroliki i udavy* (Rabbits and boa constrictors, 1988), which shows how the boa constrictors deliberately hypnotize the rabbits by fear.

As Stalin's power increased, so did the part played by slogans in yet another application of "the magic of words." There were slogans for all areas of Soviet life. Formulas reduced the current campaign to easily memorized and constantly repeated slogans; first, "Tempo decides everything!" then "Technology decides everything!" then "Cadres decide everything!" Note the triadic form. Slogans, Mikhail Heller has remarked, "provided solutions for *everything*, determining what is the *most* valuable, the *most* important."[75]

To the populace new Soviet words had magical force. After the Revolution, all sorts of neologisms, acronyms, and contracted compound words were formed, and the meanings of key words changed over time. The political police, first known as the Cheka, was renamed GPU, then NKVD, then MGB, and finally KGB. The name of the ruling party changed from Bolshevik to Communist. According to Andrei Sinyavsky, "To the ordinary Russian, this all sounded originally like nonsense language, devoid of meaning yet portending something mysterious and sinister, since certain letters [Cheka, GPU, NKVD, MGB, KGB] threatened life while others constituted its foundation, like some magic formula for reality."[76]

The failures of the five-year plans were blamed on "wreckers and saboteurs," industrial analogues of the peasants' "spoilers." In later trials, treason was added to the charges. Around 1933 a new expression came into use— "double-dealers [*dvurushniky*] masked as Bolsheviks."[77] The scenarios of the

75. Mikhail Heller, *Cogs in a Wheel* (New York, 1988), p. 237.

76. Sinyavsky, *Soviet Civilization*, p. 193.

77. Robert Tucker, *Stalin in Power* (New York, 1990), pp. 243, 397–98.

show trials grew ever more fantastic, the accused ever more demonic, and their "black magic" ever more vicious. The defendants were accused of plotting to spread anthrax, to create accidents in mines, to deliver the Soviet Union to its enemies. All the conspiring "terrorists" were presumed to be members of a single community under the direction of "Judas Trotsky," who was portrayed as a Hydra-headed beast, in league with purged Bolsheviks, Nazi Germany, Japan, and Wall Street in a Stalinist version of the Zionist conspiracy theories of the radical right. Symbols and techniques are transferable. And many of the defendants were of Jewish origin. (The term "Judas Trotsky" was first used by Lenin.)[78] The assumption that empirical reality could be disregarded meant that the accused could not defend themselves; empirical evidence did not count. Stalin's pronouncement that as socialism comes closer to realization, its enemies become more numerous and more desperate, secularized the Judeo-Christian belief that as the millennium approaches, the forces of evil increase in numbers and power. Stalin's "higher knowledge" and "special powers" supposedly enabled him to see conspirators before anyone else did.

The script of the great anti-Soviet conspiracy bears some resemblance to textbook descriptions of paranoid delusions, but the language and imagery of these particular delusions were drawn from Christian demonology and the folkloric occult—"venomous saliva," "foulest of the foul," "perfidy, sacrilege, cunning," "snakes," "loathsome creatures," "cunning duplicity," "foul-smelling underworld of spies."[79] One can almost smell the sulfurous fumes of Hell.

Stalinist rhetoric was a negative theurgy that turned metaphors into reality and converted such phrases as "lackeys of imperialism" into flesh-and-blood people. In Andrei Sinyavsky's words: "The country was suddenly crawling with all kinds of invisible (and therefor specially dangerous) reptiles, snakes, and scorpions with terrible names such as 'Trotskyite' or 'wrecker.' . . . Russia became filled with 'enemies,' no less literal for being invisible, who acted like devils and blurred the line between reality and fantasy. Stalin had brought into play (possibly without suspecting it) the magic powers contained in the language."[80] Sinyavsky was speaking figuratively. He was unaware of the occult genealogy of the Symbolist concept of the "magic of words," and of its subsequent transformations and politicizations.

The "magic," however, was not in the words themselves but in the created

---

78. V. I. Lenin, "Judas Trotsky's Blush of Shame" (1911), in his *Collected Works*, 45 vols. (Moscow, 1963), 17:45.

79. Tucker, *Stalin in Power*, pp. 371, 403; Tucker and Cohen, *Great Purge Trial*, p. 516. Vyshinsky accused the defendants of being ideologically sterile; in Christian theology evil cannot create, it can only destroy.

80. Sinyavsky, "Literary Process," p. 95.

mystery of the political order. When Party cards were exchanged during the purges of the mid 1930s, it was not uncommon for a member who received a new card to wear it on a chain around the neck as a kind of talisman, as if the power of the rulers extended to the card itself. And so it did. The card marked the bearer as a person of special powers, entitled to special privileges.

Stalin's claim that conspirators were lurking everywhere fomented a climate of fear, an occult paranoia that ultimately affected the dictator himself. He trusted no one except, reputedly, Hitler. He related to the pianist Marina Iudina as if she had occult powers. She had no such pretensions (she was a devout Christian), but Stalin was unaccustomed to people who were not afraid of him, so he assumed she must possess such powers or be protected by a supernatural being or force.[81]

There is no direct evidence that Stalin believed in the occult, but we know that he was superstitious. In a letter to Molotov he referred to a critic (Mikhail Riutin) as a "counterrevolutionary unclean force" (*nechist'*) who should be expelled from Moscow.[82] And there are striking similarities between the occultist mode of thought and Stalin's refusal to recognize empirical obstacles. He viewed Marxism-Leninism as a kind of gnosis to which he alone had the key, shared Hitler's view of the world as a battlefield (though the forces were different), and promoted himself as a messiah/magus tirelessly transforming the world and creating new people, the new Soviet man and woman.

Occult symbols and techniques were not needed to rally the population against a real and truly evil enemy during World War II, but they were resuscitated after the war. The cultural xenophobia of the *Zhdanovshchina*—Andrei Zhdanov's campaign against Western cultural influences, formalism in the arts, and objectivism in the sciences—can be regarded as an attempt to draw a magic circle around the Soviet Union through which no dangerous foreign ideas could pass. Anti-Semitism disguised as anti-Zionism underlay the murder of the Yiddish poets, the exclusion of Jews from politically sensitive positions, and the so-called doctor's plot of 1952, which recycled older occult beliefs that Jews used magical powers to poison their enemies.

When Stalin died on March 9, 1953, he was interred in Lenin's tomb, where he lay until 1961. At the 22d Party Congress, a woman (D. A. Lazurkina) who had been a Party member since 1902 rose to announce that Lenin came to her in a dream and told her that he did not want to lie next to Stalin. No one ridiculed or contradicted her "spiritualist" pronouncement. Stalin was removed from the tomb and buried in a plot near the Kremlin wall.

---

81. I am indebted to Olga Meerson for this information.

82. Joseph Stalin, *Stalin's Letters to Molotov*, ed. Lars Lih (New Haven, 1995), p. 215; the letter is dated September 13, 1930. For Stalin's view of Bukharin as a polluting (= spoiling) force, see p. 54.

Politicized Occultism in Contemporary Russia

A politicized occultism of the radical right is a major feature of the contemporary Russian scene. Whether its proselytizers actually believe in the occult or are cynically using occult symbols to manipulate the people or to get media attention by highlighting ideas and symbols that are bound to infuriate "Westernizers" and Americans, or all of the above, is difficult to tell. But there is no question that some Russians do believe in the occult and that the phenomenon of autosuggestion is operative as well. The radical right includes many former Communist apparatchiks who continue to divide the world into saviors and demons. Grigory Klimov, the author of a pamphlet titled *Krasnaia Kabbala* (Red Kabbala), claims to be a former agent of the KGB and of the CIA.[83] According to Klimov, "Hitler's Politburo" was composed of Zionists, who instigated anti-Semitism to control the world. Hitler had no Politburo; whether Klimov meant all of Hitler's entourage, or just some of them is not clear. Such outlandish accusations are impossible to refute because empirical reality is an illusion. With a few exceptions, ideologues of the radical right tend to reject Swedenborg, Rosicrucianism, and Anthroposophy: Swedenborg because he preached universal brotherhood and the equality of women, Rosicrucianism because it is historically linked with Freemasonry, and Anthroposophy because of Steiner's allegedly Jewish origin. The militant Christian right also rejects Theosophy, because it is an eclectic religion. Occult ideas inform Vladimir Zhirinovsky's diatribes on "Zionist influence" and "Zionist plots." Among the members of the editorial board of Russkaia Starina (Russian antiquity), a series that includes reprints of Russian books on the occult, are extreme nationalists and anti-Semites such as Iury Bondarev, Valentin Pikul, and Vladimir Soloukhin. Many are vehemently anti-Israel. Reprints of the *Protocols* and of émigré literature of the 1920s and 1930s that attribute the Bolshevik Revolution to a "Judeo-Masonic conspiracy" and blame Jews for Russia's current problems have been widely available for the past few years.[84] Many are poorly printed on cheap paper, which can indicate their publishers' lack of funding or their desire to appear "home-grown."

Ariosophy is being recycled by Aleksandr Dugin (b. 1962), who combines it with Eurasianism, "sacral geography," "conspirology" (*konspirologiia*), fascism, and Nazism. His publishing firm, Arktogeia (List's firm was Arktogaa), brings out two illustrated journals: *Elementy: Evraziiskoe obozrenie* (Elements: A Eurasian survey) and *Milyi Angel* (Dear Angel), comprising articles by Dugin

83. Grigorii Klimov, *Krasnaia Kabbala* (n.p. [1992]).

84. Two examples are V. O. Ivanov, *Provoslavnyi mir masonstvo* (1935; Harbin, 1992); Grigorii Bostunich, *Masonstvo i russkaia revoliutsiia* (Novyi Sad, 1922). For the Soviet rediscovery of the *Protocols* as a means of explaining the Arab defeat in 1967, see John Klier, "Pamiat and the Jewish Menace: Remembrance of Things Past," *Nationalities Papers* 19 (Fall 1991), esp. pp. 218–22.

and like-minded Russians and translations of works by Western ultraconservatives and fascists. Almost every issue contains something by Julius Evola (1898–1974), who fused fascism with Western occult doctrines, Hindu cosmic cycles, and tantric yoga. Another favorite is René Guenon (1886–1951), who attempted to infuse the Western occult tradition (esoteric Christianity, Hermeticism, and alchemy) with Hindu, Taoist, and Islamic mysticism, and ultimately converted to Islam.[85] Nietzsche is frequently quoted. The cover illustration of the fourth issue of *Elementy* (1993) features the head of an stern-faced Aryan type, but with slanted eyes and a hint of a Mandarin's mustache. On his helmet is a sun wheel (the *Lebensborn* symbol), and wings come out of his head. Above his head are four hammer-and-sickles arranged to form a swastika.

In a 1995 interview, Dugin described himself as a "conservative revolutionary and a National Bolshevik." He calls Mussolini, Hitler, and Stalin "conservative revolutionaries" and believes that Russia and Germany will be the supreme powers of a united Eurasia that stretches "from Dublin [sic] to Vladivostok." The southern boundary is not clear; it could be the Indian Ocean.[86] Going well beyond the Russo-Mongol symbiosis praised by the original Eurasianists, Dugin envisions a union of Russia, the Islamic world, China, and other Asian nations.

Dugin's "sacral geography" is based on Blavatsky's root races, her version of the Hyperborean legend, Eurasianism, Karl Haushofer's geopolitics, and "conspirology." The ancient Greeks had a legend of Hyperborea, a land of perpetual sun beyond the north wind. Blavatsky said that Hyperborea was the home of the second root race (before the Lemurians and the Atlanteans). Dugin claims that it was the home of the "sun people" and was located in what is now northern Russia. Some Russian fascists maintain that Russians were the first Aryans, but Dugin talks more about "cultural-spiritual types"—"sun peo-

85. For a synopsis of Guenon's life and thought see Jean Borella, "René Guenon and the Traditionalist School," in *Modern Esoteric Spirituality*, ed. Antoine Faivre and Jacob Needleman (New York, 1992), pp. 330–58. Borella finds "symptoms of paranoia" in Guenon's hatred of the modern world and his tendency to see evil and conspiracy everywhere.

86. For the interview, see *Knizhnoe obozrenie*, no. 41, October 10, 1995, pp. 22–23. *Elementy* (after the French "new right" journal) began publication in 1992. Six issues have appeared to date. Each issue is called a "dossier" (*dos'e*) and is devoted to one theme: Conservative Revolution, Serbia and the New World Order, The Elite, The Enigma of Socialism, Democracy, and Eroticism, in that order. The press run began at 50,000 copies and is now 10,000. *Milyi Angel* is devoted to metaphysics, tradition, esotericism, angelology, initiations, symbols, eschatology, "sacral geography," and "traditional science" (alchemy). The first issue appeared in 1991 in a press run of 20,000 copies. A second issue appeared in 1996 in a press run of only 1,000 copies, signifying either lack of interest or lack of funding or both. Artogeia also publishes books on the occult, "conspiratology," and religion. Dugin is in close contact with Western European neofascists and other far-right figures; some of them sit on his editorial boards and may be providing him with funding. Thanks to Michael Hagemeister for the *Knizhnoe obozrenie* interview; for excerpts from his paper "The Revival of Eurasianism," presented to the World Congress of Slavists, Warsaw, August 1995; and for the information on Baphomet.

ple" and "moon people"—than about Aryans per se. Sun people are creative, energetic, and spiritual; moon people are materialistic and deeply conservative. Conservatism is not always a fault (Dugin sometimes refers to "sacral conservatism"), but materialism is. Dugin's spirituality is more pagan than Christian.

Dugin posits an eternal, eschatological struggle between continental and sea powers which takes the form of "geopolitical conspiracies" of "Atlantists" (Judeo-Masonic conspiracy) and "Eurasians." The "archenemy" of present-day Russia is not "the Romano-German world" but America and the New World Order, personified on the cover of *Elementy's* second issue (1992) as a demon (see Figure 16.1). This picture, titled "Baphomet" after the idol supposedly worshiped by the Knights Templar, first appeared in Eliphas Lévi's *Dogmes et rites de la haute magie* (1856) and has been reproduced many times. Sergei Nilus included it in his 1917 edition of the *Protocols of the Elders of Zion*. Instead of "Eliphas Lévi," Dugin put "Novyi mirovoi poriadok" (New world order), and he replaced some Russian letters with Hebrew ones, but subtly, in a kind of subliminal suggestion. Aspects of Eurasianism (and of Gumilev's variant of Biocosmism; see Chapter 8) have been taken up by National Bolshevik politicians such as Gennady Ziuganov and Vladimir Zhirinovsky.

Another phenomenon, by no means confined to the radical right, is an occult version of "the Russian idea," a new form of Russian messianism that extols Russia's spiritual superiority over the "materialistic" West. Rejection of materialism is not necessarily occult, but it is part of the constellation of occult ideas we have been discussing. One reason for Rerikh's popularity is that he wrote that Russian spirituality will benefit the whole world. Contemporary Russian astrologers quote Alice Bailey, an American astrologer, who predicted that "out of Russia will emerge [a] new magical religion."[87] Cosmism is very much in vogue, partly because of its Russian genealogy.[88] Valentin Kuklev maintains that "the roots of the new age movement are undoubtedly in Russia." He predicts a "third culture" that is different from and superior to Marxism and liberalism.[89] Such views recall the Slavophile position that Russia must not merely imitate the West, but find its own path. They are also chillingly reminiscent of the claims of Italian Fascists to have found an alternative to communism and capitalism—claims that Dugin and contemporary neofascists echo.[90]

87. Henry Glade, "The Occult Scene in Moscow," *Planet Earth Magazine* 9, no. 11 (1990): 6–30.

88. This is stressed in *Russkii kosmizm: Filosofiia nadezhdyi spaseniia*, ed. V. N. Dudenkov (St. Petersburg, 1992).

89. Valentin Kuklev, "The Inevitability of the Third Culture," paper presented to the conference "The Occult in Modern Russian and Soviet Culture," Fordham University, June 1991.

90. The eminent physicist Peter Kapitsa decries these tendencies in "Anti-Science Trends in the USSR," *Scientific American* 265 (August 1991): 32–38. I am indebted to Robert Randolph for this reference.

Figure 16.1. Baphomet, the goat god supposedly worshiped by the Knights Templar. This picture, first published in Eliphas Lévi's *Dogmes et rites de la haute magie* (1856), was reproduced on the cover of the second issue of Aleksandr Dugin's journal *Elementy* (1992).

The occultism that has flourished in twentieth-century Russia has been a response to acute societal stress, a symptom, like pain or fever. But some symptoms can have permanent effects. Stress can lead to heart attacks, paralytic strokes, and cancer. High fever can damage the brain. Fever-induced delirium or extreme pain can impel actions that cannot be undone. Politicized occultism was that kind of symptom. In prerevolutionary Russia, it fostered escapism, extremism, and demonization, thereby helping to ensure that the political, social, economic, and cultural problems to which it was a response remained unsolved. The belief that All are One had a chilling effect on the fragile idea of the rights of the individual vis-à-vis society and the state. Attempts to destroy or transcend existing political and social hierarchies and structures cleared the ground for even more oppressive ones. In the Soviet period, occultism nourished utopian expectations that no ordinary government could realize, inadvertently making people receptive to the extraordinary measures of Stalin's time. The meshing of technology and the occult facilitated the ultimately dehumanizing view of people as machines. Occultism provided grist for concocted fantasies that attributed shortages and mishaps to a network of conspirators intent on "spoiling" the plan, "harming" the toiling masses, and (later on) destroying the Soviet Union. The occult paranoia that Stalinist conspiracy theory generated took on a life of its own. In present-day Russia, the anti-empirical, antirational mentality that occultism encourages can once again help ensure that political and economic problems remain unsolved. Indeed, as the year 2000 looms ever closer, the occult threatens to fuse with apocalyptic fears in extremist political ideologies. Politically, the occult is dangerous.

APPENDIX

Source Materials

RUSSIAN OCCULT JOURNALISM
OF THE EARLY TWENTIETH CENTURY AND EMIGRATION
Edward Kasinec and Robert H. Davis Jr.

It is unlikely that any survey of the journalistic endeavors of the modern Russian occultists has been published.[1] This lapse is especially poignant because the journalism of the Russian occult is at once rich and a necessary complement to monographs produced by the Russian occultists of the Silver Age. To our knowledge, only one bibliography of Russian occult literature exists, compiled by Ivan Kazimirovich Antoshevsky and published in 1910.[2] Antoshevsky was himself a con-

---

1. For example, neither Thomas C. Claire's *Occult/Paranormal Bibliography: An Annotated List of Books Published in English, 1976 through 1981* (Metuchen, N.J., 1984) nor Cosette N. Kies's *Occult in the Western World: An Annotated Bibliography* (Hamden, Conn., 1986) lists any works immediately pertaining to the Russian occult movement. Nina Vasil'evna Nikitina's *Guide to Bibliographies of Russian Periodicals and Serial Publications, 1728–1985* (Commack, N.Y., 1993) lists only the indexes to *Priroda i liudi* (her entry no. 1020), *Voprosy filosofii i psikhologii* (entry nos. 465–69), and the "indexes in publication" to *Vestnik teosofii* (entry 423) and *Rebus* (entry no. 1051).

2. I. K. Antoshevskii, *Bibliografiia okkul'tizma: Ukazatel' sochinenii po alkhimii, astrologii, germeticheskoi meditsine, gipnotizmu, Kabbale, magii, magnetizmu, spiritizmu, telepatii, teosofii, filosofii okkul'tizma, fakirizmu, khiromantii i pr., 1783–1909* (St. Petersburg, 1910). The first printing sold out so quickly that the book was reprinted the next year. Of the compiler himself we know little. He was born in 1873, and was a graduate of the St. Petersburg Archaeological Institute. From some of the other publications held in Western collections, we know that aside from the occult, two themes occupied his interest: the auxiliary historical disciplines, especially the study of silliography; and the religious question, especially Judeo-Christian relations. In view of Antoshevsky's preoccupations and interests, he was a likely candidate for emigration after 1917, although we have no evidence that he did emigrate.

tributor to and sometime editor of one of the best-known Russian occult journals of the twentieth century, *Izida* (no. 12 below). Interestingly enough, however, though Antoshevsky's bibliography lists several dozen titles in a rather informal and hap-hazard way, it lists no occult periodicals. A 1985 essay on Russian occult literature lost its entire section on occult journalism under the stringent hand of an editor concerned to save space.[3] Other specialized bibliographies—those, for example, by the late Tatiana Ossorguine-Bakounine on Russian Freemasonry; by Nikolai Mik-hailovich Lisovsky (1854–1920) on the Russian periodical press; and by the Soviet bibliographer Liusiia Nikitichna Beliaeva—deal with occult journals only in pass-ing, and in a much broader context; in the case of Ossorguine-Bakounine, the history of Freemasonry; in that of Lisovsky and Beliaeva, the descriptive biblio-graphic history of Russian journalism.[4] The inevitable conclusion is that the listing in this appendix, which includes more than sixty occult titles of the late nineteenth and early twentieth centuries, is the most comprehensive list compiled so far of publications in genre.

The absence of any bibliographical overviews of Russian occult journalism ex-plains in great part the paucity of secondary narrative studies of these journals. The American literary scholar Thomas E. Berry and the Soviet historian Aron Iakovle-vich Avrekh have devoted some attention to individual occult journals such as *Rebus* and to Masonic journals of the early twentieth century,[5] but we looked in vain for any mention of occult journalism in the standard histories of Russian journalism. Much of what we say here, therefore, is based on the empirical evi-dence of the journals themselves.

Three periods in the history of Russian occult journalism may be identified. To the first belongs the period associated with the name of Nikolai Ivanovich Novikov (1744–1818), educator, publisher, editor, scholar, and Masonic activist of the late eighteenth century. Like other major cultural and literary figures of this period, Novikov was very much involved with the religious and philanthropic activities of the Russian Freemasons and Rosicrucians, and published and edited occult jour-nals. By 1789 the government increasingly viewed these activities as politically seditious, and denied his request for renewal of the lease on Moscow University Press. In 1792 Novikov was arrested, his books were confiscated, and his presses were sold. This period of Russian occult journalism has been much studied.[6]

To the second period may be assigned the occult writings and journals of the late

3. Boris Kerdimun and Edward Kasinec, "Russia: Literature of the Occult," in *The Spiritual in Art* (Los Angeles, 1986), pp. 361–65.

4. T. A. Bakunina, *Répertoire bibliographique des Francs-Maçons russes (XVIIIᵉ et XIXᵉ siècles)* (Paris, 1967); N. M. Lisovskii, *Bibliografiia russkoi periodicheskoi pechati, 1703–1900 gg.* (Petro-grad, 1915); L. N. Beliaeva et al., comps., *Bibliografiia periodicheskikh izdanii Rossii, 1901–1916*, 4 vols. (Leningrad, 1958–61); Lauren G. Leighton, *The Esoteric Tradition in Russian Romantic Literature: Decembrism and Freemasonry* (University Park, Pa., 1994).

5. Thomas E. Berry, *Spiritualism in Tsarist Society and Literature* ([Baltimore, 1985]); and A. Ia. Avrekh, *Masony i revoliutsiia* (Moscow, 1990).

6. See the index listings under the heading "Zhurnaly masonskie" in *Istoriia russkoi litera-tury XVIII veka: Bibliograficheskii ukazatel'* (Moscow, 1968), p. 426; and the description of Novi-kov's *Utrennii svet* (1777–80) in *Svodnyi katalog russkoi knigi grazhdanskoi pechati XVIII veka, 1725–1800* (Moscow, 1966), 4:205–8.

Alexandrine period, such as the journal *Sionskii vestnik*, edited by A. F. Labzin (1766–1825) and filled with translations of the mystical, pietist, and occult writings of the late eighteenth and early nineteenth centuries, so popular in France and Germany. This second period, too, has been much studied by eminent specialists of the nineteenth century, such as Aleksandr Nikolaevich Pypin (1833–1904).[7] It is therefore the third period that is the main focus of our remarks.

The earliest modern occult journal began its publication in 1881 under the name *Rebus* (no. 28). Its appearance came at a time of immense growth in the history of the Russian publishing and printing industry. A number of publishing houses, such as that of K. L. Rikker (1833–95), sponsored highly specialized journals dealing with pharmacology, anatomy, and so on. Russian occult journalism, then, appeared at a time when periodicals were becoming increasingly differentiated by subject area.[8] Another development of this period was what might be termed a heterodox Orthodox publishing industry that brought out a wide spectrum of journals and newspapers, ranging from the official bulletins of the dozens of eparchies in the vast empire to academic Orthodox journals sponsored by the theological academies and the edificatory journals issued by the great monasteries of the empire. These are the bibliographical "envelopes" into which occult journalism must be placed. One further point: The late nineteenth and early twentieth centuries saw the establishment of publishing houses that specialized in social, economic, or political works, and some of them were established and controlled by women of the liberal intelligentsia—Mariia Ivanovna Vodovozova (1869–1954), Aleksandra Mikhailovna Kalmykova (1850–1926), and Mariia Aleksandrovna Malykh (1879–1967), among others.[9]

The great flowering of occult journalism came in the early years of the twentieth century, and in some respects coincided with the appearance of a large and significant satirical and humorous press that gained great influence in the wake of the 1905 Revolution. But here the comparison must stop, for the satirical and humorous press has been copiously studied by bibliographers, literary scholars, and art historians, beginning with an early monograph by the Kazan specialist Petr Maksimilianovich Dul'sky (b. 1879) in the early 1920s. If the flowering of Russian occult journalism coincides chronologically with the development of a rich satirical press, the intellectual and spiritual affinities of occult journalism lie with the small private Symbolist publishing houses that flourished after the 1905 Revolution, among them Musaget (fd. 1910), Skorpion (fd. 1900), and Sirin (fd. 1912), to name but a few.

A close reading of Antoshevsky's bibliography reveals that some of the major and most productive occult writers, such as Antoshevsky himself, Viktor Ivanovich Pribytkov (d. 1910), and Anna Alekseevna Kamenskaia (1867–1952), were also either the editors or publishers of occult journals. Among those editors and publishers we see the names of many women and members of the gentry or, in the case of Count Vladimir Petrovich Bykov, the aristocracy. Editors often founded more

---

7. See, for example, A. N. Pypin, *Religioznyia dvizheniia pri Aleksandre I* (Petrograd, 1916).

8. A. I. Akopov, *Otechestvennye spetsial'nye zhurnaly, 1765–1917* (Rostov, 1986).

9. See S. B. Liublinskii, *Podvizhniki knigi: E. N. Vodovozova, L. F. Panteleev, A. M. Kalmykova, O. N. Popova, M. I. Vodovozova* (Moscow, 1988).

than one journal, as is the case with Pavel Aleksandrovich Chistiakov, whose publications included *Russkii Frank-Mason* (no. 29) and *Voprosy psikhizma i spiritualisticheskoi filosofii* (no. 55). Among the contributors to these various journals were members of the Russian Orthodox hierarchy, in a tradition that goes back at least to the late eighteenth century, when some monastics were involved with Masonry.

The cost of these journals varied widely. *Mentalizm* (no. 19), for example, cost a hefty 12 rubles a year, *Russkii Frank-Mason* 10, *Voprosy psikhizma i spiritualisticheskoi filosofii* 4; *Spiritualist* (no. 33) was only 1 ruble. *Voprosy psikhizma i spiritualisticheskoi filosofii* offered a reduction if one also subscribed to *Rebus* (no. 28) and *Russkii Frank-Mason*. By far the largest number of titles—thirty in toto—were published in the capitals of St. Petersburg and Moscow, with two titles appearing in Warsaw and in Smolensk (Belorus'), one in the Ukrainian capital of Kiev, and one each in Kremenets', Volyn, and, surprisingly, Blagoveshchensk, in the Amur region. Until very recently, the titles on this list were available in only some of the great collections in Russia. Now, thanks to the assistance of the U.S. Department of Education's Title II-C program, portions of more than fifteen of the titles on this list are available, albeit the majority on film, at the New York Public Library.[10] Original issues of some of the journals have been available at the distinguished Slavonic Library of the Helsinki University Library, as well as scattered issues at Stanford University, the University of California at Berkeley, Indiana University, the Library of Congress, Columbia University, and even the Carnegie Library in Pittsburgh.[11] None of these titles has yet been made available commercially. According to Iury Masanov, only a handful of occult publications, such as *Vestnik teosofii* and *Rebus,* have cumulative indexes.[12]

Since the Fordham University Conference on the Occult in Modern Russian and Soviet Thought, at which this bibliography was first presented, the wrenching political and social changes sweeping Russia have fostered a surge of popular interest in the occult.[13] This interest is reflected in the supplemented bibliography of serial titles provided below.

10. See Robert H. Davis Jr., "The Imperial Periodicals Project of the New York Public Library's Slavonic Division," *Microform Review* 17 (August 1988): 150–54.

11. In 1987 Stanford University received a major collection of Russian occult literature that is particularly rich in materials from the nineteenth and early twentieth centuries. See Wojciech Zalewski, "Russian Library Goes to Stanford," in *Newsletter* 4 (1988): 30–34 of the Slavic and East European Section of the Association of College and Research Libraries, presented in fine detail at the June 1991 Fordham University Conference on the Occult in Modern Russian and Soviet Thought as "The John M. Constantinoff Collection on the Occult at the Stanford University Libraries." We thank Dr. Zalewski for his assistance in verifying Stanford's holdings.

12. See Iurii Masanov, *Ukazateli soderzhaniia russkikh zhurnalov i prodolzhaiushchikhsia izdanii, 1755–1970 gg.* (Moscow, 1975); and N. F. Andreeva and M. V. Mashkova, *Russkaia periodicheskaia pechat': Obshchie i otraslevye bibliograficheskie ukazateli, 1703–1975* (Moscow, 1977), which complements and supplements Masanov.

13. Many new publications reflect this uncapping in occult studies. See, for example, V. Z. Krivchenok, *Slovar' ezotericheskikh terminov* (St. Petersburg, 1992); *Russkaia Pravoslavnaia zarubezhnaia tserkov' o masonstve, teosofii i okkul'tizme* (Novosibirsk, 1992); *Pravoslavnaia tser-*

The tradition of journalistic endeavors by the Russian occultists has been rich indeed, both in the homeland and in emigration. For the most part, the history of these activities has been little studied; more to the point, these printed sources are widely scattered through collections in North America, Western Europe, and of course the former Soviet Union. If research on the history of the Russian occult is to advance, a concerted effort must be made to collect, concentrate, and preserve the book and periodical literature of the Russian occult movement, past and present. And it is to this challenge that we summon users of the bibliography.

---

kov' ob ekstrasensakh, NLO, teletseliteliakh i okkul'tnykh iavleniiakh (Moscow, 1991); T. F. Antonova, *Okkul'tnye zakony evoliutsii* (Novosibirsk, 1992); and *Put' teosofii* (Petrozavodsk, 1992). The June 1995 *Katalog knig po ezoterizmu-tainovedeneniiu-okkul'tizmu* (New York, 1995) lists some 200 works in these areas.

RUSSIAN OCCULT
JOURNALS AND NEWSPAPERS
Maria Carlson and Robert H. Davis Jr.

The following list is based primarily on occult titles identified and, where possible, personally examined by Maria Carlson.

The amount of information contained in these entries—dates of publication, numeration, editorship, and so on—varies from title to title, dependent on how much data could be gleaned from reference and secondary sources, as well from the journals themselves. Comments, when they appear, are those of Maria Carlson. Holdings information for selected Western institutions and the Russian State Library (formerly the Lenin State Library) is provided. For libraries in the United States, only the Research Libraries Information Network (RLIN) database was used for these searches. Therefore, only Research Library Group institutions, as well as those whose records are crossloaded from the On-line College Library Catalog (OCLC), are represented.

Several bibliographic reference works were consulted in the preparation of this checklist, and are cited in some of the entries below:

Bibliografiia periodicheskikh izdanii Rossii, 1901–1916. Leningrad: Gosudarstvennaia Publichnaia Biblioteka, 1958–61. Hereafter BPIR.

Deimann, Götz. *Die Anthroposophischen Zeitschriften von 1903 bis 1985: Bibliographie und Lebensbilder.* Beiträge und Quellen zur Geschichte der anthroposophischen Bewegung und Gesellschaft. Stuttgart: Freies Geistesleben, 1987. Hereafter Deimann.

Schatoff, Michael. *Half a Century of Russian Serials, 1917–1968: Cumulative Index of Serials Published Outside of the USSR.* New York: Russian Book Chamber Abroad, 1970–72. Hereafter Schatoff.

1. *Alba.* Boston, 195?–?
   Frequency/numeration: No. 1, 195?–?
   Publisher: N. & D. Reincke.

Location: Stanford: 1956, nos. 2, 4, 11.

Comments: The Reinckes had ties to the Theosophical Society, Madras, India. Alba issued an edition of *Teosoficheskii glossarii, sostavlennyi Dzh. R. S. Midom po materialam E. P. Blavatskoi, slovariam i entsiklopediiam kontsa XIX veka* . . . in 1970–73.

2. *Antroposofiia: Voprosy dushevnoi zhizni i dukhovnoi kul'tury.* Paris, 1928–September 1935.

   Frequency/numeration: 1928–29, nos. 1–12; 1930, nos. 1–12; 1931, nos. 1–12; 1932, nos. 1–12; 1933, nos. 1–6; 1934, nos. 1–6; 1935, nos. 1–4, 5/6.

   Editor: G. Kolpaktchy.

   Deimann, pp. 129–31.

   Comments: Assembled by Anthroposophists in Berlin and Chisinau (Kishinev; Bessarabia was then part of Romania, where the Novalis Anthroposophical Lodge had been functioning since about 1924).

   Location: Library of the Goetheanum, Dornach, Switzerland.

3. *Aum: Sintez misticheskikh uchenii Zapada i Vostoka = Esoteric [sic] quarterly of West & East Mistic [sic] Teaching.* Moscow, St. Petersburg, and New York, 1987–93.

   Frequency/numeration: Quarterly. 1987, no. 1–1993, no. 5.

   Publisher: Beginning with 1987, no. 2, issued jointly by Terra (Moscow) and the publishing house of E. P. Blavatsky, Russian Esoteric Society, Inc. [Russkoe esotericheskoe obshchestvo], New York.

   Locations: Library of Congress: 1987, no. 1–1993, no. 5.

   New York Public Library: 1987, no. 1.

   Stanford: 1987, nos. 1–3.

   UCLA: 1987, nos. 1–2.

   Yale: 1987, no. 1; 1993, no. 5.

4. *Azazel'.* Moscow (1992–).

   Frequency/numeration: No. 1–.

   Location: Stanford: 1992, no. 1–.

5. *Belovod'e.* Cheliabinsk, 1991?–.

   Frequency/numeration: 1991?–.

   Publisher: Ural'skii dukhovno-eticheskii tsentr imeni N. K. Rerikha.

   Locations: Berkeley: 1991, ch. 1, no. 5–.

   Stanford: 1991, ch. 1, no. 4–.

6. *Belyi lotos: Teosofiia E. P. Blavatskoi.* Santa Barbara, Calif., etc., 1958–?

   Frequency/numeration: No. 1, 1958 (August)–?

   Editor: Militza Yurieva Cowling.

   Locations: Stanford: 1958–59, nos. 1–2; 1969, no. 14.

   Yale: 1958, no. 1–1965, no. 10.

7. *Dziwy zycia [Chudesa prirody].* Warsaw, 1902–?

   Frequency/numeration: Biweekly.

   Editor: [Vitol'd Khlopitsky] 1902, no. 1 (April)–.

8. *[Fakir].* No information.

   Comments: Journal announced but never published.

9. *Feniks.* Adelaide, Southern Australia, 1983–.

   Frequency/numeration: Annual. No. 1–, 1983.

   Publisher: Russian Phoenix.

Locations: Library of Congress: 1983, no. 1–.

Yale: 1983, no. 1; 1985, no. 3–1986, no. 4.

10. *Golos vseobshchei liubvi.* Subtitle varies: *Spiritualisticheskii zhurnal;* with no. 12, *Sotsial'no-misticheskii zhurnal;* with 1907, *Sotsial'no-misticheskii okkul'tnyi zhurnal;* with 1908, no subtitle, with 1909, *Ezhenedel'nyi spiritual'no-okkul'tnyi illiustrirovannyi vestnik, obsluzhivaiushchii dukhovno-nravstvennuiu storonu chelovecheskoi zhizni i sotsial'no-misticheskoe napravlenie ee.* Moscow, 1906–9.

Frequency/numeration: 1906, nos. 1–36; 1907–8, 52 nos. per year; 1909, nos. 1–27/28.

Editor-publisher: V. P. Bykov i izdatel'skii tovarishchestvo Kardek.

BPIR, no. 1861.

Comments: A subscription cost 2 rubles per year.

Superseded by: *Smelye mysli* (1910–11), weekly; see BPIR, no. 7708.

11. *Idei, fakty i dokumenty = Idées, faits et documents: Sbornik statei po voprosam chelovecheskoi kul'tury.* Brussels, 1939?–?

Frequency/numeration: No. 1 (November 2, 1939)–? Suspended publication 1940–49.

Publisher: C. Platounoff.

Location: Princeton: no. 1 (November 3, 1939)–no. 3 (January 5, 1951).

12. *Izida: Ezhemesiachnyi zhurnal okkul'tnykh nauk.* St. Petersburg, 1909–1916.

Frequency/numeration: 1909/1910–1915/1916, no. 1 (October)–no. 12 (September). 1916, no. 1 (October)–nos. 2/3 (November/December). Indexes for 1910–12 in issue no. 12 of both 1911 and 1912.

Publisher-editor: I. K. Antoshevsky; succeeded by A. V. Troianovsky with no. 11 (August), 1911.

BPIR, no. 3577.

Locations: New York Public Library: god 1, no. 1–g. 7, nos. 11/12 (October 1909–August–September 1916) [FILM *ZAN-*Q1655].

Stanford: 1910, no. 1; 1912, nos. 2, 3; 1913, nos. 4–12.

13. *Iz mraka k svetu: Literaturno-misticheskii i nauchno-filosofskii zhurnal sokrovennykh znanii.* St. Petersburg, 1914.

Frequency/numeration: 1914, nos. 1 (January)–5 (September).

Editor: S. V. Piramidov.

Publisher: L. V. Malai.

BPIR, no. 3251.

Comments: Edited by a woman. The entire corpus of this title amounted to 322 pages.

Location: Helsinki: 1914, nos. 1–5 [Sl.P. 1228].

14. *Izvestiia rossiiskogo Teosoficheskogo obshchestva.* St. Petersburg, 1914–17.

Frequency/numeration: 1914, nos. 1–3; 1915, nos. 1–4; 1916, nos. 1–4; 1917, nos. 1–2. In 1915–16 there were four numbers per year.

Editor-publisher: Ts. L. Gel'mbol'dt.

BPIR, no. 3483.

Comments: This journal, which was edited by a woman, focused on questions and problems of the Theosophical movement. It included articles on religion, philosophy, and science, and chronicled the movement in Russia and abroad. It also published memoirs, historical information on the movement, announce-

ments, a reference section, and letters from the president.
Location: Helsinki: 1914, nos. 1–3; 1915, nos. 2–4; 1916, no. 1 [Sl.P. 1108].

15. *Kinematograf: Ezhenedel'nyi illiustrirovannyi zhurnal tain i uzhasov,* Prilozhenie k zhurnalu *Poprygun'ia-strekoza.* St. Petersburg, 1910.
Frequency/numeration: 1910, no. 1 (n.d.)–no. 12 (May 5).
Editor: V. K. Panchenko.
Publisher: M. A. Lakshin.
BPIR, no. 3928. *Poprygun'ia-strekoza* appears in BPIR as no. 6201.

16. *Kinematograf: Sensatsionnyi ezhenedel'nyi illiustrirovannyi zhurnal. Izdanie sovershenno novogo tipa.* St. Petersburg, 1908.
Frequency/numeration: 1908, nos. 1 (December)–3 (n.d.).
Editor: V. K. Panchenko.
Publisher: M. A. Lakshin.
BPIR, no. 3927.

17. *Lektsii okkul'tnykh znanii: Zhurnal.* St. Petersburg, 1911–12.
Frequency/numeration: 1911, nos. 1 (n.d.)–3; 1912, no. 4.
Editor: S. I. Gal'tsev.
Publisher: Izdatel'stvo Kursov okkul'tnykh znanii [v litse] S. I. Gal'tseva i V. S. Sokolova.
BPIR, no. 4320.
Comments: Issues ranged from 24 to 60 pages.

18. *Mag: Ezhemesiachnyi zhurnal okkul'tizma.* St. Petersburg, 1911.
Frequency/numeration: 1911, nos. 1 (January)–3 (March). Prilozhenie: Knigi po okkul'tizmu.
Editor-publisher: A. Laptev.
BPIR, no. 4547.

19. *Mentalizm: Ezhemesiachnyi illiustrirovannyi okkul'tnyi zhurnal.* Moscow, 1906–8, 1911.
Frequency/numeration: 1906, no. 1 (December 12); 1907, nos. 2 (January)–12 (November); 1908, no. 1 (January)–9 (September); 1909–10, not published; 1911, nos. 1 (January)–7/8 (July/August).
Editor-publisher: N. B. Butovt.
BPIR, no. 4658.
Comments: A subscription cost 12 rubles per year; 15 rubles for foreign subscribers.
In 1910 Butovt published *Sfinks* (no. 31 below; BPIR, no. 8133).
Locations: Helsinki: 1906, no. 1; 1907, nos. 2–5, 7–12; 1908, nos. 1–9; 1911, nos. 1–8.
New York Public Library: nos. 1 (December 12, 1906)–12; 1908, nos. 1–9; 1911, nos. 2–7/8 [FILM *ZAN-*Q1669].
Stanford: 1906–7, nos. 1–12.

20. *Milyi Angel.* Moscow, 1991–.
Frequency/numeration: No. 1–, 1991–.
Publisher: Arktogeia.
Location: Stanford: no. 1–, 1991–.

21. *Ne mozhet byt'.* Moscow, 1990–.
Frequency/numeration: No. 1, 1990–.

Publisher: [Pobratim].

Location: Stanford: no. 1, 1990–.

22. *Novye mysli: Zhurnal, posviashchennyi voprosam probuzhdeniia skrytykh dushevnykh sil dlia dostizheniia zdorov'ia, schast'ia, i bogatstva.* St. Petersburg, 1907–8.

Frequency / numeration: 1907, probnyi no. (n.d.); vol. 1, nos. 1 (n.d.)–6; vol. 2, nos. 7–12; 1908, vol. 3, nos. 13–18.

Editor: L. M. Bliumental'.

Publisher: Psikhologicheskoe izdatel'stvo [v litse] D. Zh. Mak-Donal'da.

BPIR, no. 5522.

23. *Novyia mysli, novye puti.* Vladivostok, 1920–?

Frequency / numeration: No. 1–, 1920–?

Editor-publisher: Izdatel'nitsa, E. Zarina; redaktor, Vladivostokskoe teosoficheskoe obshchestvo.

Locations: Stanford: nos. 1–2, 5–7, 10, 12–13. Some issues lack pages, including initial pages of what is presumed to be no. 7.

University of Washington: no. 2.

24. *Okkul'tizm i ioga.* Belgrade, 1933–36; Sofia, 1937–39; new series: Asunción, Paraguay, 1957–68.

Frequency / numeration: 1933, kn. 1; 1934, kn. 2, 3; 1935, kn. 4, 5; 1936, kn. 6, 7; 1937, kn. 8, 9; 1938, kn. 10. No more published in old series. New series, 1957–68.

Editor: Aleksandr Aseev.

Schatoff, no. 3408 (new series).

Comments: Aseev provided a platform for "proizvedeniia russkikh zarubezhnykh nezavisimykh okkul'tistov."

Locations: Berkeley: new series, kn. 19 (1958)–68 (1982) (lacks 20–21, 30, 62, 65).

Columbia: kn. 25 (1961).

Helsinki: complete run [Sl.P. 3383].

New York Public Library: new series, kn. 18 (1958); 21 (1959); 22–23 (1960); 26 (1962); 30–36 (1964–67); 38 (1968); 42 (1969); 44 (1970); 46–47 (1970–71); 50 (1972); 62–63 (1976); 66 (1977).

Stanford: kn. 20, 27, 44–48, 50–52.

25. *Ottuda: Ezhednevnaia illiustrirovannaia spiritual'no-okkul'tnaia gazeta.* Moscow, 1907–11.

Frequency / numeration: Daily from no. 152 / 155; 1909–, twice weekly. [1907], nos. 1 (December 1)–31 (December 31); [1908], nos. 1 (January 1)–362 (December 31); 1909, nos. 1 (January 1)–362 / 365 (December 31); 1910, nos. 1 (January 3)–104 (December 30); 1911, nos. 1 (January 2)–81 / 82 (December 9). No index for 1910–11.

Editor-publisher: V. P. Bykov, Izdatel'stvo Kardek.

Comments: From 1909 through 1911, this title offered brochures on occultism as an appendix. A subscription cost 3 rubles 60 kopeks per year; 10 rubles for foreign subscribers.

BPIR, no. 5898.

26. *Priroda i liudi.* St. Petersburg, 1889–1917.

Frequency / numeration: Vols. 1–27 (1889–October 1917).

Editors: F. S. Gruzdev; with 1905, no. 1, P. P. Soikin.

Publisher: P. P. Soikin.

BPIR, no. 6416.

Locations: Berkeley: vol. 28, nos. 1–47 (November 3, 1916–September 21, 1917).

Carnegie Library (Pittsburgh): vols. 23–[25].

Indiana: holdings not listed, but obtained on microfilm from Russian National Library, St. Petersburg, and Helsinki.

Library of Congress: vols. 6, 10, 12–13, 27.

New York Public Library: vols. 1, 5, 7, 9–27.

Stanford: 1914, nos. 2, 3, 5, 6, 11, 12; 1916, nos. 7–8, 12.

27. *Rassvet: Ezhemesiachnyi nauchno-okkul'tnyi i khudozhestvenno-literaturnyi zhurnal.* Warsaw, 1914.

Frequency / numeration: 1914, no. 1 (January)–no. 7 (July). Last number unknown.

Editor-publisher: Kh. M. Shkol'nik.

BPIR, no. 6703.

Comments: Edited by a woman.

28. *Rebus: Ezhenedel'nyi zhurnal.* Subtitle varies: to 1905, no. 51, *Nezavisimyi organ russkikh spiritualistov;* from 1905, *Populiarno-nauchnyi zhurnal po voprosam spiritualizma, psikhizma i mediumizma;* from 1909, *Zhurnal psikhizma, mediumizma i spiritualizma.* St. Petersburg, 1881–1903; Moscow, 1904–17.

Frequency / numeration: Vol. 1, no. 1 (October 11, 1881)–vol. 36, nos. 5/6 (May 28, 1917). Weekly until 1903; thereafter 30–52 numbers annually. Jubilee no. 9/1000 (March 4, 1901). [Tsenz. delo: Glavnoe upravlenie po delam pechati, I otd. no. 41 (1881)]. Yearly index, 1901–16. A selective index to articles that had appeared in *Rebus* over the previous twenty years was published in 1901, no. 9, pp. 98–99.

Editors-publishers: V. I. Pribytkov, St. Petersburg, from no. 1 to no. 1125 (December 21, 1903), when he retired because of ill health; P. A. Chistiakov in Moscow from no. 1126.

BPIR, no. 6715.

Comments: The Moscow editorial offices of *Rebus* were on the Arbat, dom Tolstogo. A subscription cost 5 rubles per year; 6 rubles for foreign subscribers. *Rebus* suffered after its change of editors. It came out less frequently and lost dedicated staff members in St. Petersburg. There were conflicts with *Spiritualist,* as well as name-calling and personal animosity between Chistiakov and Bykov. *Spiritualist* labeled *Rebus* a *pseudo-spiritualisticheskii organ,* while *Rebus* accused *Spiritualist's* publisher, A. M. Markov, of murder, among other crimes.

Locations: Berkeley: vols. 5–6.

Library of Congress: vols. [2–10].

New York Public Library: 1881/82–94, 1896–1901, 1903–8, 1910–16 [*QCA + & FILM *ZAN-*Q1815 (1895, 1902, 1907–9)].

Stanford: 1885, 1886, 1891–92, 1904, 1906, 1909, 1910–12: nos. 1523–67; 1914: nos. 1605–37; 1915: nos. 1638–75; 1916: nos. 1676–93; 1917: nos. 1694–99.

29. *Russkii Frank-Mason: Svobodnyi kamenshchik. Populiarno-nauchnyi i literaturnyi zhurnal.* Moscow, 1908.

Frequency / numeration: 1908, nos. 1–2.

Publisher-editor: P. A. Chistiakov.

BPIR, no. 6961.

Comments: A well-produced journal, with a press run limited to 250. A subscription cost 10 rubles per year. The entire run of this journal amounted to only 142 pages.

Locations: Helsinki: 1908, nos. 1–2 [Sl.P. 2156].

New York Public Library: 1908, no. 2 [FILM *ZAN-*Q1894].

Stanford: 1908, nos. 1–2.

30. *Serdtse*. St. Petersburg, 1992–.

Frequency / numeration: No. 1, 1992–.

Publisher: Serdtse.

Organ of Rerikhovskoe teosofskoe obshchestvo "Obshchina materi mira."

Location: Stanford: nos. 1, 2, 1992–.

31. *Sfinks: Illiustrirovannyi okkul'tnyi zhurnal*. Subtitle varies: no. 2 has on cover: *Illiustrirovannyi literaturno-obshchestvennyi, nauchno-okkul'tnyi zhurnal*. Moscow, 1910.

Frequency / numeration: 1910, nos. 1 (January 12)–6 (May).

Editor-publisher: N. B. Butovt.

BPIR, no. 8133.

Comments: The entire corpus of this journal totaled only 168 pages.

Location: Helsinki: 1910, nos. 1–6.

32. *Smelye mysli: Ezhenedel'nyi vestnik prakticheskogo okkul'tizma, obsluzhivaiushchii dukhovno-nravstvennuiu storonu chelovecheskoi zhizni i sotsial'no-misticheskoe napravlenie ee*. Moscow, 1910–11.

Frequency / numeration: 1910, nos. 1–52; 1911, nos. 1–33 / 34.

Editor-publisher: V. P. Bykov.

BPIR, no. 7708.

Comments: A subscription cost 3 rubles 60 kopeks per year.

Supersedes: *Golos vseobshchei liubvi*.

33. *Spiritualist: Vestnik issledovanii v oblasti obshchenii s zagrobnym mirom. Ezhemesiachnyi illiustrirovannyi zhurnal*. Subtitle varies: from 1907, no. 6, *Ezhemesiachnyi illiustrirovannyi semeinyi zhurnal;* 1912, *Vestnik spiritualizma i ego filosofii*. Moscow, 1905–12.

Frequency / numeration: 1905, nos. 1 (October)–3 (December); 1906–11, twelve issues annually; 1912, nos. 1 / 2 (January / February)–5 / 6 (May / June). Appendix, 1911–12; *Al'bom "Spiritualista" 12 l.l. snimkov s tekstom 1912 broshiury po okkul'tizmu*.

Editor: V. P. Bykov.

Publishers: V. P. Bykov, A. M. Markov.

BPIR, no. 7833.

Comments: The editorial offices were located near the Cathedral of Christ the Saviour, Obydenskii pereulok, which was also the location of the offices of *Golos vseobshchei liubvi*. A subscription cost 1 ruble per year (2 rubles if bound in vellum).

Locations: Helsinki: 1907, nos. 3–5, 7–12; 1908, nos. 1–12; 1909, nos. 1–4 [Sl.P. 2396].

New York Public Library: 1906–11, nos. 1–12 for each year; 1912, nos. 1–4 [FILM *ZAN-*Q1773].
Stanford: god 1 (October 1905–December 1906).

34. *Svedeniia o tom, chto proiskhodit v Tsentre antroposofskoi raboty v Dornakhe i na periferii.* Dornach, Switzerland, December 1934–April 1940.
Frequency/numeration: 1934–35, nos. 1–12; 1936, nos. 1–12; 1937, nos. 1–12; 1938, nos. 1–12; 1939, nos. 1–4, 5/6, 7/8, 9–10, 11/12; 1940, nos. 1/4.
Deimann, pp. 143–45.
Location: Library of the Goetheanum, Dornach, Switzerland.

35. *Tainovedenie.* Zikhron Yaakov, Israel, 1982–.
Frequency/numeration: No. 1, 1982–.
Publisher: Tainovedenie.
Locations: Berkeley: 1982, no. 1–1985, no. 12.
Michigan: no. 1, 1982–.

36. *[Tainstvennoe].* St. Petersburg.
Comments: This journal was announced for 1907 but was never published, although there are scattered references to "Izdanie zhurnala *Tainstvennoe.*"

37. *Tainy Zhizni: Nauchno-populiarnyi zhurnal po voprosam khiromantii, gipnotizma, i dr. okkul'tnykh nauk.* Moscow, 1912–13, 1916.
Frequency/numeration: 1912, no. 1 (December); 1913, no. 1 (November 10); 1916, nos. 1–2. Four times per year.
Editor: Ia. G. Stepanov.
Publisher: Tipografiia Reklama; from 1913, Stepanov.
BPIR, no. 8172.

38. *Teosoficheskoe obozrenie: Ezhemesiachnyi zhurnal, posviashchennyi teosofii i teosoficheskomu dvizheniiu v Rossii i za-granitsei.* Subtitle varies: with 1907, no. 3, *Put' k vsemirnomu bratstvu. Zhurnal, posviashchennyi bratstvu chelovechestva, teosofii, i izucheniiu etiki, filosofii, nauk i iskusstv.* St. Petersburg, 1907–8.
Frequency/numeration: 1907, nos. 1 (October)–3 (December); 1908, nos. 4 (January)–12 (September).
Editor-publisher: V. L. Bogushevsky.
BPIR, no. 8315.
Comments: The entire output of this title amounted to 918 pages. A subscription cost 4 rubles per year; 7 rubles for foreign subscriptions.
Superseded by: *Mir* (St. Petersburg, 1908–12), a general journal with no occult content.
BPIR, no. 4729.
Locations: Helsinki: 1907, nos. 1–3; 1908, nos. 4–12 [Sl.P. 2886].
New York Public Library: 1907–8, nos. 1–12 [FILM *ZAN-*Q1874].
Stanford: 1907–8, nos. 1–12.

39. *Teosofskaia zhizn': Posviashcheno teosofskomu dvizheniiu i izucheniiu filosofii, nauk i religii. Organ Smolenskogo Teosofskogo Obshchestva.* Subtitle varies: from 1909, no. 6/7, *Khristianskogo* instead of *Smolenskogo.* Smolensk, 1907–9.
Frequency/numeration: 1907, nos. 1 (September)–4 (December); 1908, nos. 5 (January)–12 (August); no. 1 (September)–2/3 (October/November); 1908–9, nos. 4/5 (December/January); 1909, nos. 6/7 (February/March)–12 (August).
Editor-publisher: V. I. Shtal'berg.

BPIR, no. 8316.

Superseded by: *Zhizn'dukha*; BPIR, no. 2760.

Locations: Helsinki: 1907, nos. 1–4; 1908, nos. 1–2/3, 5–12; 1908–9, nos. 4/5; 1909, nos. 5–12 [Sl.P. 2893].

New York Public Library: 1907, nos. 1–4; 1908, nos. 5–12; 1908–9, nos. 1–12 [FILM *ZAN-*Q1871].

40. *Tropa*. Paris, 1939.

Frequency/numeration: 1939, no. 1.

Comments: An attempt by Natalia and A. Pozzo and Russian émigré Anthroposophists in France to establish a journal of their own.

Deimann, pp. 162–63.

Location: Library of the Goetheanum, Dornach, Switzerland.

41. *Tsyganskaia gazeta [Okkul'tnoe izdanie]*. Moscow, 1908.

Frequency/numeration: Published twice a week. 1908, nos. 1 (May 4)–3 (May 18).

Editor-publisher: S. A. Shimansky.

BPIR, no. 9256.

42. *Uraniia = Urania*. Moscow 1991–.

Frequency/numeration: No. 1, 1992–.

Publisher: Urania Partnership, Ltd.

Comments: Table of contents is in Russian and English.

Location: Stanford: no. 1, 1992–.

43. *Uranus: Zhurnal filosofsko-misticheskoi mysli*. Shanghai, 1939.

Frequency/numeration: Monthly, 1939–?

Publisher: Iupiter. Organ of Sodruzhestvo Uranus.

Location: Stanford: 1939, no. 8–?

44. *Vera i znanie: Ezhemesiachnyi religiozno-filosofskii zhurnal*. Tbilisi, 1914.

Frequency/numeration: 1914, nos. 1/2 (January/February)–12 (December).

Editor: A Bartnovskaia.

Publisher: N. Ivanov; editor and publisher from no. 5 was K. Lomize.

BPIR, no. 721.

Comments: This journal contains a wide range of material, from traditional Christianity to Count Karl Ludwig Du Prel (1839–1899) and magnetism.

45. *Vestnik. Satyan nasti paro Dharma. Net religii vyshe istiny*. Geneva, 1924–40? Now published in Tallinn.

Publisher: Russian Theosophical Society in Exile.

Locations: Berkeley: 1936, nos. 2–3 (September, December); 1937, nos. 5–6 (October, November); 1938, nos. 2–3, 6 (March, May, December), all filmed as part of the Title II-C–funded Russian Émigré Project, based on the holdings of the Museum of Russian Culture, San Francisco [master negative 86–1130].

Bibliothèque Nationale: 1928, nos. 6–12; 1929–30; 1931, nos. 1–3, 6–12; 1932, nos. 1–5, 9–12; 1933–34; 1935, nos. 3, 12; 1936, no. 4.

Columbia: 1939–40.

Geneva: 1924, nos. 1–7 (April–December); 1925, nos. 1–10 (January–December); 1926, nos. 1–11/12 (January–December); 1927, nos. 1–10 (January–December); 1928, nos. 1–12 (January–December); 1929, nos. 1–12 (January–December); 1930, nos. 1–11 (January–November); 1931, nos. 1–12

(January–December); 1932, nos. 1–12 (January–December); 1933, nos. 1–3 (January–September); [4, "Pamiati Anni Bezant"]; 1934, nos. 1–4 (March–December); 1935, nos. 1–3 (March–December); 1936, nos. 1–3 (April–December), of which nos. 2 and 3 were hectographed; 1937, no. 2 (March), 4–6 (July–November), all hectographed; 1938, nos. 1–6 (January–December), all hectographed; 1939, Vesennii vypusk (back to printed format), Letnii vypusk, Osennii vypusk, Zimnii vypusk. Geneva holds all issues except Pervyi and Tretii vypusk 1937, which may not have been published.

Helsinki: 1924, no. 11; 1925, no. 1, 12; 1926, nos. 1–3; 1927, nos. 1–6, 11–12; 1931, nos. 9/10; 1932, nos. 6–12; 1934, nos. [for March], 6, 9, 12; 1935, nos. 3, 12; 1936, no. 4; 1939, Vesennii vypusk, Letnii vypusk, Osennii vypusk, Zimnii vypusk; 1940, Vesennii vypusk, Letnii vypusk, Osennii vypusk, Zimnii vypusk (note this additional year) [Sl.P. 3385].

Stanford: 1928.

46. *Vestnik magnetizma: Ezhemesiachnyi illiustrirovannyi populiarno-nauchnyi zhurnal po voprosam zhivotnogo magnetizma, gipnotizma, vnusheniia, mediumizma, meditsiny i psikhologii.* Kiev, 1914.

Frequency/numeration: 1914, nos. 1 (January 5)–6 (June). Last number unknown.

Editor-publisher: Z. S. Bissky.

BPIR, no. 944.

Comments: A subscription cost 4 rubles per year.

47. *Vestnik Obshchestva druzei Eleny Petrovny Blavatskoi.* Moscow, 1992–.

Frequency/numeration: Irregular. No. 1, 1992–.

Publisher: Mezhdunarodnaia assotsiatsiia Mir cherez kul'turu.

Locations: Berkeley: nos. 1, 1992–6, 1993. Later issues unbound.

Harvard: nos. 3, 1992–5, 1993.

Yale: nos. 1, 1992–6, 1993.

48. *Vestnik Obshchestva spiritualistov goroda Blagoveshchenska: Trekhnedel'nyi zhurnal po issledovaniiu spiritualizma.* Blagoveshchensk (Amur Region), 1910–11.

Frequency/numeration: 1910, nos. 1 (April)–8 (December); 1911, nos. 9 (January)–12 (April); nos. 1 (May)–2 (June). Prilozhenie: 1910, Rech' predsedatelia Lechebno-blagotvoritel'nogo obshchestva—o tseliak obshchestva i o rabote chlenov. Eight pages, in 1910, no. 2.

Editor: G. K. Shneider, from 1911, no. 1, E. G. Konstantinova.

Publisher: R. G. Budzilovich.

BPIR, no. 1000.

Comments: Edited by a woman.

49. *Vestnik okkul'tizma i spiritizma: Nauchno-populiarnaia gazeta.* Moscow, 1914–15.

Frequency/numeration: Published twice a month. 1914, no. 1 (January 10); 1915, no. 1 (March 1).

Editor-publisher: V. D. Filimovich.

BPIR, no. 1012.

Comments: There may be additional issues; these are the only ones held in the Russian State Library, Moscow.

Location: *Russian State Library:* 1914, no. 1; 1915, no. 1.

50. *Vestnik okkul'tnykh nauk: Nauchno-populiarnyi illiustrirovannyi zhurnal, posviash-*

chennyi voprosam khiromantii, khirosofii, khirognomii, psikhografologii, fiziognomii, frenologii, gipnotizma, spiritizma, i iasnovideniia. Moscow, 1906–7.
Frequency / numeration: Published twice a month. 1907, nos. 1 (February 20)–2 (March 12).
Editor-publisher: V. O. Ianchevsky.
BPIR, no. 1013.

51. *Vestnik teosofii: Religiozno-filosofsko-nauchnyi zhurnal.* St. Petersburg, 1908–18.
Frequency / numeration: 1908–16, nos. 1–12; 1917, nos. 1–2, 3 / 5, 6 / 9, 10 / 12; 1918, nos. 1–2. Appendix, 1908–9, 1913: *Knigi po teosofii.* From 1908 to 1915 there was a yearly index.
Editor-publisher: A. A. Kamenskaia; from 1912 published also by Ts. L. Gel'mbol'dt.
BPIR, no. 1154.
Comments: This journal was originally planned for publication on January 7, 1907. In 1911 it had a print run of 700 copies. A subscription cost 4 rubles per year.
Locations: Helsinki: 1910, nos. 1–12; 1912, nos. 1–12; 1913, nos. 1–12; 1914, nos. 1–12; 1915, nos. 1–9, 11–12; 1916, nos. 1–8, 10–12 [Sl.P. 344].
New York Public Library: 1908, no. 1–1915, no. 12 [FILM *ZAN-*Q1654].
Russian State Library: 1908, nos. 1–12; 1909, nos. 1–2, 4, 7–9, 11; 1910–12, nos. 1–12; 1913, nos. 2–6, 11–12; 1914–16, nos. 1–12; 1917, nos. 2–9; 1918, nos. 1–2.
Stanford: 1908, nos. 1–7 / 8; 1909, nos. 1, 5 / 6–10; 1910, nos. 1–12; 1911, nos. 1–12; 1912, nos. 1–12; 1913, nos. 1–12; 1914, nos. 1–12; 1915, nos. 1–12; 1916, nos. 1–12; 1917, nos. 1–12.

52. *Vestnik teosofii.* Moscow, 1992–.
Frequency / numeration: Quarterly. No. 1, 1992–. Continues the journal of the same title, published 1908–18.
Publisher: Izdatel'stvo Sfera, Rossiiskogo teosofskogo obshchestva.
Locations: New York Public Library: no. 1, 1992–.
Stanford: no. 1, 1992–.
Yale: no. 1, 1992.

53. *Voprosy filosofii i psikhologii.* Moscow, 1889–1917.
Frequency / numeration: Vols. 1–28, no. 5 [nos. 1–140], 1889 (November)–1917 (December). Index: 1899–1909 in vol. 20, no. 100.
Editors: S. N. Trubetskoy and L. M. Lopatin; with no. 4, L. M. Lopatin.
Publisher: Moskovskoe psikhologicheskoe obshchestvo pri sodeistvii S.-Peterburgskogo filosofskogo obshchestva.
Comments: A highly respected academic journal that often published materials of interest to the occultists.
BPIR, no. 1560.
Locations: Berkeley: nos. 1 (1889)–3, 5 (1890)–7 (1891); nos. 10, 16–25, 27, 31–34, 39–45, 59, 61, 67–71, 76, 78, 80–82, 94, 96 (1909).
Chicago: vols. 1–[3].
Columbia: nos. 1–105, 107, 109–28, 130, 139–40.
Cornell: nos. [22]–24.
Indiana: nos. 1–140 (microfiche).
Michigan: nos. vols. 1–28 (1889–1917).

National Library of Medicine: vols. 1–13.
New York Public Library: vols. 1–[28].
Northwestern: vols. [3–28].
Ohio State: vols. 19–20, 22.
Stanford: vols. 1–28 (1889–1917) (microfilm).
Yale: vol. 16.

54. *Voprosy khiromantii i gipnotizma: Pervyi v Rossii ezhemesiachnyi illiustrirovannyi zhurnal.* Subtitle varies: from 1914, no. 2: *Ezhemesiachnyi illiustrirovannyi zhurnal.* Moscow, 1912–14.

Frequency/numeration: 1912, nos. 1 (October)–3 (December); 1913, nos. 1 (January)–3 (March); 1914, nos. 1 (January)–2 (n.d.). Last number not known.
Editor-publisher: V. D. Filimovich.
BPIR, no. 1561.
Comments: The print run in 1914 was 20,000 copies. A subscription cost 1 ruble 80 kopeks per year; 1 ruble 20 kopeks outside of Moscow.
Location: New York Public Library: 1912, nos. 1–2 (October, November); 1913, nos. 1–3; 1914, no. 1 [FILM *ZAN-*Q1632].

55. *Voprosy psikhizma i spiritualisticheskoi filosofii: Nauchno-populiarnyi zhurnal.* Moscow, 1908.

Frequency/numeration: 1908, nos. 1–6.
Editor-publisher: P. A. Chistiakov.
BPIR, no. 1557.
Comments: Issues averaged 50 pages. A subscription cost 4 rubles per year; 3 rubles per year for subscribers of *Rebus* and *Russkii Frank-Mason.*
Locations: Helsinki: 1908, nos. 1–5 [Sl.P. 487].
New York Public Library: 1908, nos. 1–6 [FILM *ZAN-*Q1855].
Stanford: 1908, nos. 1–5.

56. *Voprosy teosofii.* St. Petersburg, 1907.

Frequency/numeration: No. 1, 1907–?
Location: Berkeley: 1907, no. 1.
Stanford: 1907, no. 1 [master negative microfilm].

57. *Vozrozhdenie: Ezhemesiachnyi literaturno-nauchnyi zhurnal.* Kremenets' (Volyn Province), 1906–8.

Frequency/numeration: 1906, nos. 1 (March)–7/8 (October/December); 1907, nos. 1 (April)–9 (December); 1908, nos. 1(10) (January)–4 (February).
Editor-publisher: A. I. Kornilovich; ed. N. Ryshkovsky.
BPIR, no. 1425.
Comments: *Vozrozhdenie* printed Russian-language versions of Karl Du Prel's *Die Magie als Naturwissenschaft [Magiia, kak estestvoznani],* translated by K. I. Kniazevicha. Among the unrealized projects of this journal were the publication of Lev Taksil' (1854–1907), *Razoblachenie sovremennogo frank masonstva;* J. Maxwell [physicist James Clerk Maxwell? (1831–79)], *Psikhicheskie iavleniia;* and other occult works.

58. *Vozrozhdenie khiromantii: Nauchno-populiarnyi illiustrirovannyi zhurnal, posviashchennyi voprosam khiromantii.* St. Petersburg, 1906.

Frequency/numeration: Published twice a month. 1906, probnyi no. 1 (October 12).

Editor-publisher: V. D. Filimovich.

BPIR, no. 1431.

59. *Zazerkal'e.* Moscow, 1991–.

Frequency / numeration: Quarterly. No. 1 / 2, 1991–.

Editor-publisher: Eksperimental'nyi nauchno-issledovatel'skii i redaktsionno-izdatel'skii tsentr Zazerkal'e.

Location: Stanford: nos. 1 / 2, 1991–.

60. *Zhizn' dukha: Spiritualisticheskii religiozno-filosofskii zhurnal.* On cover: "Teosofiia. Okkul'tizm. Filosofiia. Religiia. Nauki." Smolensk, 1910.

Frequency / numeration: 1910, nos. 1–11 / 12 (January–November / December).

Editor-publisher: V. I. Shtal'berg.

BPIR, no. 2760.

Comments: Subscriptions cost 2 rubles 50 kopeks; 5 rubles for foreign subscriptions.

61. *Zhurnal psikho-grafologii: Populiarno-nauchnyi illiustrirovannyi zhurnal dlia vsekh.* Subtitle varies: from 1903, no. 12, subtitle reads *Pervyi edinstvennyi v Rossii.* St. Petersburg, 1903–12.

Frequency / numeration: Monthly (quarterly in 1906). 1903, nos. 1 (September 1)–4 (December 1); 1904, nos. 1 (January)–12 (December); 1905, nos. 1 (January)–10 (October); 1906, nos. 1 (January / March)–4 (October / December); 1907–11, 12 nos. annually; 1912, nos. 1 / 4 (January / April).

Editor-publisher: I. F. Morgenshtern.

BPIR, no. 2869.

Comments: A subscription cost 6 rubles per year; 10 rubles for foreign subscriptions.

Locations: Library of Congress: nos. 1, [2–3] [date?].

New York Public Library: 1903, nos. 1–4; 1904, nos. 1–8, 10–12; 1905, nos. 1–10; 1906, nos. 2–4; 1907, nos. 1–12; 1908, nos. 1–12; 1909, nos. 1, 2, 9–12; 1910, nos. 1–12; 1911, nos. 1–12; 1912, nos. 1–4 [FILM *ZAN-*Q1853].

62. *Znamia mira.* Tomsk, 1992–.

Frequency / numeration: Semimonthly. No. 1, 1992–.

Publisher: Alkor Concern.

Location: University of Pittsburgh: 1992, no. 1.

63. *Zvony kitezha.* Minas [Minas Gerais, Brazil], 19?–?.

Frequency / numeration: Irregular. Some issues bear a monthly designation.

Editor: K. Zelentzeff.

Publisher: Gruppa russkikh ezoterikov v Zhuiz-de Fora (Juiz de Fora). "Organ sviazi russkikh zarubezhnykh ezoterikov i okkul'tistov."

Location: Stanford: nos. 2–5, [1960–63].

Topographical Index

St. Petersburg

Izida. 1909–16.

Iz mraka k svetu. 1914.

Izvestiia rossiiskogo teosoficheskogo obshchestva. 1914–17.
Kinematograf. 1908.
Kinematograf. Prilozhenie k zhurnalu *Poprygun'ia-strekoza.* 1910.
Lektsii okkul'tnykh znanii. 1911–12.
Mag. 1911.
Novye mysli. 1907–8.
Priroda i liudi. 1889–1917.
Rebus. 1881–1903; Moscow, 1904–17.
Serdtse. 1992–.
Tainstvennoe. Journal announced for 1907 but never published.
Teosoficheskoe obozrenie. 1907–8.
Vestnik teosofii. 1908–17.
Voprosy teosofii. 1907.
Vozrozhdenie khiromantii. 1906.
Zhurnal psikho-grafologii. 1902–12.

Moscow

Aum. Moscow and New York, 1987–.
Azazel. Dates unknown.
Golos vseobshchei liubvi. 1906–9. Superseded by *Smelye mysli.*
Mentalizm. 1906–8, 1911.
Milyi Angel. 1991–.
Ne mozhet byt'. 1990–.
Ottuda. 1907–11.
Rebus. 1904–17; St. Petersburg, 1881–1903.
Russkii Frank-Mason: Svobodnyi kamenshchik. 1908.
Sfinks. 1910.
Smelye mysli. 1910–11. Supersedes. *Golos vseobshchei liubvi.*
Spiritualist. 1905–12.
Tainy zhizni. 1912–13, 1916.
Tsyganskaia gazeta. 1908.
Uraniia = Urania. 1990–.
Vestnik Obshchestva druzei Eleny Petrovny Blavatskoi. 1922–.
Vestnik okkul'tizma i spiritizma. 1914–15.
Vestnik okkul'tnykh nauk. 1906–7.
Vestnik teosofii. 1992–.
Voprosy filosofii i psikhologii. 1889–1917.
Voprosy khiromantii i gipnotizma. 1912–14.
Voprosy psikhizma i spiritualisticheskoi filosofii. 1908.
Zazerkal'e. 1991–.

Blagoveshchensk (Amur Region)

Vestnik Obshchestva spiritualistov goroda Blagoveshchenska. 1910–11.

Cheliabinsk

Belovod'e. 1991?–.

Kiev

Vestnik magnetizma. 1914.

Kremenets' (Volyn Province)

Vozrozhdenie. 1906–8.

Smolensk

Teosofskaia zhizn'. 1907–9. Superseded by *Zhizn' dukha.*
Zhizn' dukha. On cover: "Teosofiia. Okkul'tizm. Religiia. Nauki." 1910.

Tbilisi

Vera i znanie. 1914.

Tomsk

Znamia mira. 1992–.

Vladivostok

Novyia mysli, novye puti. 1920?–?

Warsaw

Dziwy zycia [Chudesa prirody]. 1902–?
Rassvet. 1914.

Location Unknown

Fakir.

Outside Russia

Alba. Boston, 195?–?
Antroposofiia. Paris, 1928–September 1935.

Aum. Moscow and New York, 1987–.

Belyi lotos. Santa Barbara, Calif., 1958?–?

Feniks. Adelaide, Southern Australia, 1983–.

Idei, fakty i dokumenty. Brussels, 1939?–.

Okkul'tizm i ioga. Belgrade, 1934–36; Sofia, 1937–39; new series, Asunción, Paraguay, 1957–68.

Svedeniia o tom, chto proiskhodit v Tsentre antroposofskoi raboty v Dornakhe i na periferii. Dornach, Switzerland, December 1934–April 1940.

Tainovedenie. Zikhron Yaakov, Israel, 1982–.

Tropa. Paris, 1939.

Uranus. Shanghai, 1939–?

Vestnik. Satyan nasti paro Dharma. Net religii vyshe istiny. Geneva, 1924–40?

Zvony kitezha. Minas Gerais, Brazil 19?–?

PERSONAL AND CORPORATE NAME INDEX

Monographs located in U.S. institutions that participate in the Research Libraries Information Network (RLIN) database, or in the *Dictionary Catalogue of the Slavonic Division of the New York Public Library* are so identified. Some titles listed are not found in any U.S. library or bibliographic database.

The letters "DSD" after some citations refer to the open-shelf Desk–Slavic Division Reference Collection of the Slavic and Baltic Division, kept in the division's reading room at the New York Public Library's Central Research Library. Brackets enclose the RLIN locations of specific works. Numbers in parentheses after the names of individuals and organizations refer to entries in the list above.

Editors

Aseev, Dr. Aleksandr (no. 24). Editor of *Okkul'tizm i ioga* (Belgrade). A medical doctor, he emigrated after the Revolution and lived outside Belgrade. There was a strong Theosophical tendency in his "independent occultism."

Bartnovskaia, A. (no. 44)

Bliumenthal', L. M. (no. 22)

Cowling, Militza Yurieva (no. 6)

Gal'tsev, S. I. (no. 17)

Gruzdev, Favst Sergeevich (1867–1913) (no. 26)

Khlopitsky, Vitol'd (no. 7). Probably Witold Chlopicki, who may be a member of the famous Chlopicki military family, many of whom were intellectuals and interested in occult subjects. See *Polski Słownik Biograficzny,* vol. 3 (Cracow: Nakładem Polskiej Akademii Umiejętności, 1937).

Kolpaktchy, G. (no. 2)

Konstantinova, E. G. (no. 48)

Lopatin, Lev Mikhailovich (1855–1920) (no. 53), *Filosof-spiritualist,* professor at Moscow University, and son of Mikhail Nikolaevich (1823–1900). Their archives are held by GIM, f. 51, 17 ed. khr., 1900-e–1910-e gg. Cf. *Lichnye arkhivnye fondy v gosudarstvennykh khranilishchakh SSSR: Ukazatel'*, vol. 1 (Moscow: Glavnoe Arkhivnoe Upravlenie AN SSSR, 1963), p. 409.

Panchenko, V. K. (nos. 15, 16)

Piramidov, S. V. (no. 13). Occultist and hermeticist.

Pribytkov, Viktor Ivanovich (d. 1910) (no. 28). St. Petersburg Spiritualist and founder of the Anglo-American Spiritualist movement in Russia, Pribytkov became interested in mediumism in 1874 after his wife, Elizaveta Dmitrievna (d. 1896), revealed her mediumistic abilities. An intimate friend of Aleksandr Nikolaevich Aksakov (1832–1903), he edited *Rebus* from October 11, 1881, to December 1903, when illness forced him to give up editorship to P. A. Chistiakov and the Moscow circle. Many major Spiritualist works were published under the aegis of *Rebus*. He was the author of *Vopros o spiritizme v Rossii* (St. Petersburg, 1901) [National Library of Medicine]; *Mediumicheskaia iavleniia pered sudom vrachei* (reprinted from *Rebus*, 1885) [National Library of Medicine]; *Mediumizm Elizavety Dmitrievny Pribytkovoi: Podrobnoe opisanie raznoobraznykh mediumicheskikh seansov* (St. Petersburg, 1897); *Otkrovennye besedy o spiritizme i drugikh iavleniiakh toi zhe oblasti* (St. Petersburg, 1894); *Vopros o spiritizme v Rossii; ot ego voznikovedeniia do nashikh dnei* (St. Petersburg: Izdatel'stvo zhurnala Rebusa, 1901). He died after a long illness.

Ryshkovsky, N. (no. 57)

Shneider, G. K. (no. 48)

Trubetskoy, Prince Sergei Nikolaevich (1862–1905) (no. 53). *Filosof*, professor, and rector of Moscow University. His archives are located in GARF, f. 1093, 162 ed.khr., 1845–1913; RGB, f. 305, 316 ed.khr., 1880-e gg.–1917; GIM, f. 98, 14 ed.khr., 1880–1917. Cf. *Lichnye arkhivnye fondy v gosudarstvennykh khranilishchakh SSSR: Ukazatel'*, vol. 2 (Moscow: Glavnoe Arkhivnoe Upravlenie AN SSSR, 1963), p. 234. DSD; cf. Martha Bohachevsky-Chomiak, *Sergei N. Trubetskoi: An Intellectual among the Intelligentsia in Pre-Revolutionary Russia* (Belmont, Mass.: Nordland, 1976).

Zelentzeff, K. (no. 63)

Publishers

Alkor Concern (no. 62)

Arktogeia (no. 20)

Budzilovich, R. G. (no. 48)

Gruppa russkikh ezoterikov v Zhuiz-de Fora (no. 63)

Iupiter (no. 43)

Ivanov, N. (no. 44)

Izdatel'stvo Kardek. (nos. 10, 25). Allan Kardec (1803–69) was the pseudonym of Hippolyte Léon Denizard Rivail, a prominent French Spiritualist. Author of *Le Livre des esprits* (1856; the revised edition of 1857 became the textbook of Spiritualist philosophy in France); *The Medium's Book* (1861); *The Gospel as Explained by Spirits* (1864); *Heaven and Hell* (1865); and *Genesis* (1867). Kardec founded the Society of Psychologic Studies, and established *La Revue Esprit* (see Arthur Conan Doyle, *History of Spiritualism* [New York: Arno Press, 1975], 2:171ff.). His mystical *Spiritisme* enjoyed considerable popularity in Russia among the French-inclined "Spiritists" (as opposed to the Anglo-American "Spiritualists"), and a publishing house was named in his honor.

His works in Russian include *Evangelie v raz"iasnenii spiritizma,* translated from the 42d French edition (Lublin, 1910; 2d ed. Kiev, 1914); *Kniga mediumov,* translated from the French (St. Petersburg, 1904); *Filosofiia spiritualizma,* 4 vols. (Moscow, 1906–11), all published by the editors of *Spiritualist.* The Russian State Library has a lithographic edition done in Moscow in 1861.

The New York Public Library's general catalog lists 27 works by Kardec, in Spanish, English, French, and Portuguese. His writings have regained popularity in recent years, as reflected by the large number of reprints of his works in many Western European languages.

Kursov okkul'tnykh znanii (no. 17)

Lakshin, M. A. (nos. 15, 16)

Malai, L. V. (no. 13)

Markov, A. M. (no. 33)

Mezhdunarodnaia assotsiatsiia Mir cherez Kul'tura (no. 47)

Moskovskoe psikhologicheskoe obshchestvo pri sodeistvii S.-Peterburgskogo filo-sofskogo obshchestva (no. 53)

Platounoff, C. (no. 11)

Pobratim (no. 21)

Psikhologicheskoe izdatel'stvo (no. 22)

Reincke, N. & D. (no. 1)

Reklama (no. 37)

Russian Esoteric Society, New York. *See* Russkoe esotericheskoe obshchestvo.

Russian Phoenix (no. 9)

Russian Theosophical Society in Exile (Geneva) (no. 45). At the urging of Annie Besant, Anna Kamenskaia, president of the Russian Theosophical Society in St. Petersburg, decided to flee postrevolutionary Russia, and in the summer of 1921 she and her closest friend and Theosophical colleague, Ts. L. Gel'bol'dt (Gel'm-bolt?), made their way illegally to Finland, then to Belgium, and finally were assigned by Mrs. Besant to Geneva, where the Swiss section of the society was in disarray. Anna Kamenskaia not only got the Swiss section into shape; by 1924 she also managed to reorganize the Russian Theosophical Society (Outside Russia). It was rechartered by the Adyar Headquarters on January 1, 1926.

With Gel'mbol'dt's help and support, Kamenskaia ran the worldwide branch until her death in 1952, publishing the Geneva *Vestnik teosofii* to maintain the unity of Russian Theosophists in China, Yugoslavia, North and South America, Europe, and even the East Indies. This indefatigable woman also continued to teach at the university in Geneva and to travel for the Theosophical Society. She and the small Russian Theosophical contingent in Geneva were involved in the League of Nations, as well as various other peace, relief, vegetarian, etc. organizations.

Russkoe esotericheskoe obshchestvo, New York (no. 3)

Serdtse (no. 30)

Sfera Rossiiskogo teosofskogo obshchestva (no. 52)

Sodruzhestvo Uranus (no. 43)
Sokolova, Valentina Stepanova (b. 1916) (no. 17)
Tainovedenie (no. 35)
Ural'skii dukhovno-eticheskii tsentr imeni N. K. Rerikha (no. 5)
Urania Partnership, Ltd. (no. 42)
Vladivostokskoe teosoficheskoe obshchestvo (no. 23)

Editors and Publishers

Antoshevsky, Ivan Kazimirovich (b. 1873) (no. 12). Editor-publisher of *Izida* from October 1909 to September 1911, when he was succeeded by A. V. Troianovsky. On January 15, 1911, he celebrated fifteen years of activity in the esoteric sphere. He received a telegram in honor of the occasion from Papus (pseudonym of Gérard Encausse [1865–1916], one of the most famous turn-of-the-century occultists) and an honorary baccalaureate from Papus's Hermetic School in Paris (the first awarded by that institution to a Russian). He was also treasurer of the Grafologicheskoe Obshchestvo. His most important work was *Bibliografiia okkul'tizma: Ukazatel' sochinenii po alkhimii, astrologii, germeticheskoi meditsine, gipnotizmu, Kabbale, magii, magnetizmu, spiritizmu, telepatii, teosofii, filosofii okkul'tizma, fakirizmu, khiromantii i pr., 1783–1909*, 2d ed., with an introduction by Punar Bhava and a biography of Antoshevsky by E. K. Lossky (St. Petersburg, 1911). His other works include *Evrei Khristiane* (St. Petersburg, 1907) [Stanford] (rpt. Tel Aviv, 1970) [New York Public Library, Florida State, Dartmouth]; *Russkie knizhnye znaki [Ex Libris]* (St. Petersburg, 1913) [Stanford, microform]; *Nadpisi i devizy na russkikh pechatiiakh chastnykh lits* (St. Petersburg, 1903); *Konstantinovskii rubl' 1825 g.* (St. Petersburg, 1904); *Orden Martinistov: Ego proiskhozhdenie, tseli, znachenie i kratkii ocherk ego istorii* (St. Petersburg, 1912); *Drevniaia vysshaia magiia: Teoriia i prakticheskaia formuly*, trans. I. K. Antoshevsky (St. Petersburg, 1907).
Bissky, Z. S. (no. 46)
Bogushevsky, Vasily L'vovich (no. 38). Publisher of *Teosoficheskoe obozrenie* and *Mir*. There is no indication that this publisher of popular reading material was personally involved in any occult movement.
Butovt, Nikolai Borisovich or Boleslavovich (nos. 19, 31). "Potomstvennyi dvorianin." Editor of *Sfinks* and president of the Kruzhok Mentalistov.
Bykov, Count Vladimir Pavlovich (nos. 10, 25, 32, 33, 28 [comments]). Editor of *Spiritualist; Vifezda "teploe slovo bol'nym, bednym, neschastnym (bor'by s otchaianiem"); Smelye mysli; Ottuda;* and *Golos vseobshchei liubvi.* Author of *Spiritizm pered sudom nauki, obshchestva i religii* (Moscow, [1914]) [Berkeley] and president of Moskovskii Kruzhok Spiritualistov-dogmatikov. He also edited publications on self-improvement for railway workers. V. P. Bykov is listed as the publisher of *The Vegetarian Society in Manchester* (in English) (Moscow, 1896), in a press run of 4,000 copies; 2,000 more copies were printed in 1897. Cf. S. A. Vengerov, ed., *Russkiia knigi: S biograficheskimi dannym ob avtrorakh i perevodchikakh (1708–1893)* (St. Petersburg: A. E. Vineke, 1897–99), p. 369, entry 9186.
Chistiakov, Pavel Aleksandrovich (nos. 28, 29, 55). Author of *Bezsmertie* (Moscow,

1908). After Pribytkov's death, Chistiakov replaced him as editor of *Rebus,* where he was noted for a very lively editorial style. Head of Rossiiskoe Spiritualisti-cheskoe Obshchestvo, he was an enemy of Bykov.

Eksperimental'nyi nauchno-issledovatel'skii i redaktsionno-izdatel'skii tsentr Za-zerkal'e (no. 59)

Filimovich, V. D. (nos. 49, 54, 58)

Gel'mbol'dt, Tsetsiliia Liudvigovna (d. Geneva, 1936) (nos. 14, 51). Born into a Russified German family in St. Petersburg, this Theosophist was co-editor of *Vestnik teosofii.* She went abroad with her lifelong best friend, Anna Kamenskaia, in 1921, and headed the Giordano Bruno Russian Theosophical Circle in Geneva and worked on the Geneva *Vestnik.* She was bedridden the last years of her life.

Ianchevsky, V. O. (no. 50)

Kamenskaia, Anna Alekseevna (1867–1952) (no. 51). A major St. Petersburg The-osophist, the first and only president of the Rossiiskoe Teosoficheskoe Obsh-chestvo, and the editor-publisher of *Vestnik teosofii,* Kamenskaia attended nu-merous conferences and read many papers. She was well acquainted with major English and European Theosophists, and was a great admirer and personal friend of Mrs. Besant's. Kamenskaia met Besant for the first time in the summer of 1902, and shortly thereafter she became a member of the English Section of the Theosophical Society. On May 18, 1906, Nina de Gernet and Kamenskaia arrived in Paris for the First International Theosophical Conference (June 3–5). As Kamenskaia was raised in Switzerland, she was very comfortable with French.

Kamenskaia was the translator of *Tupiki tsivilizatsii i kliuchi k nim* (Berlin, 1927), Mrs. Besant's *Civilization's Deadlocks and the Keys* (London, 1924), *In the Outer Court* (3d ed., London, 1903), and *Whatsoever a Man Soweth,* no. 3 of the Three Great Truths Series (1915); *V preddverii khrama* (Tallinn, 1929), originally in *Vestnik teosofii; and Chto chelovek poseet, to i pozhnet* (Geneva and Brussels, 1925).

Listed in St. Petersburg as a *domashniaia uchitel'nitsa* (home teacher), she lived at Ivanovskaia 22 and worked at Stoiunin Gymnasium, from which she retired in 1916 after 25 years of teaching.

The Russian Theosophical Society was closed in December 1919, after mem-bers had been ordered to teach atheism. Kamenskaia refused and left Russia, settling in Geneva. Here, in 1926, she defended a dissertation, "La Bhagavad-Gita, son rôle dans le mouvement religieux de l'Inde et son unité," and was thereafter referred to as Dr. Kamensky. She taught at the University of Geneva, was instrumental in founding the International Theosophical Centre (under the Council of the European Federation in Geneva), lectured all over Europe, and even visited the United States. In 1939 Kamenskaia was still serving as general secretary of the Russian Section Outside Russia when it held its convention in Paris.

In 1943 the members of the Russian Section were spread over the globe, and Kamenskaia was still at the center of the movement. In 1948 she was active on behalf of displaced persons, fielding inquiries about Theosophists from all over the world, and distributing her stockpile of Russian Theosophical texts.

Much information is found in Josephine Ransom, *Short History of the Theosophi-cal Society* (Adyar, Madras, 1938) and *The 75th Anniversary Book of the Theosophical Society: A Short History of the Society's Growth, 1926–1950* (Adyar, 1950).

Kamenskaia died in Geneva on June 24, 1952, aged 84.

Kornilovich, A. I. (no. 57)

Laptev, A. (no. 18)

Lomize (Lomidze), Kaspar Khristoforovich (no. 44). Contributor to *Rebus* and influential in Tbilisi spiritualist and occult circles, as well as the Tbilisi Religious-Philosophical Society.

Mak-Donal'd, D. Zh. [MacDonald, D. J.] (no. 22)

Morgenshtern, I. F. (no. 61)

Pozzo, Natalia and A. (no. 40)

Shimansky, S. A. (no. 41) Author of *Koshmary tsarizma i narodovlastiia*, with an introduction by N. Ia. Abramovich (Moscow: Revoliutsiia kul'tura, 1918), 108 pp. [Hoover].

Shkol'nik [Shiller-Shkol'nik], Kh. M. (no. 27). This psychophrenologist, author, and occultist lived and worked in Warsaw, where she edited and published *Rassvet*, an occult and literary journal, in 1914 (nos. 1–7). She was the author of *Novyi kurs gipnotizma* (1912) [National Library of Medicine].

Shtal'berg, Vladimir Ivanovich (nos. 39, 60). Theosophist, president of the Smolensk Christian Theosophical Society; editor of *Teosofskaia zhizn'*, with strong spiritualist tendencies.

Soikin, Petr Petrovich (1862–1938) (no. 26). Book publisher. His personal archives are located at TRGALI, f. 468, 66 ed.khr., 1894–1929; IRL (Pushkinskii dom), St. Petersburg, A. E. Burtsev collection, op. 2., nos. 449–55, 7 ed.khr., 1896–1915. Cf. *Lichnye arkhivnye fondy v gosudarstvennykh khranilishchakh SSSR: Ukazatel'*, vol. 2 (Moscow: Glavnoe Arkhivnoe Upravlenie AN SSSR, 1963), p. 177.

Stepanov, Ia. G. (no. 37)

Troianovsky, Aleksandr Valerianovich (no. 12). Prolific translator of European mystics and occultists, including Charles Webster Leadbeater (*Astral'nyi plan*) and the French occultists Papus and Paul Desir. He was the compiler of *Slovar' divinatsii i nekotorykh terminov okkul'tizma* (n.d.) and contributed occasional articles to *Teosoficheskoe obozrenie*. In October 1911 he succeeded Antoshevsky as editor of *Izida*. He did not seem to be closely affiliated with any particular occult society or circle, although he was a knowledgeable occultist and respected editor. In St. Petersburg he had his own occult bookshop.

Zarina, E. (no. 23)

LITERATURE ON RUSSIAN OCCULT JOURNALS
Edward Kasinec and Robert H. Davis Jr.

The New York Public Library call Number follows each entry. DSD = Desk–Slavic Division (Room 217, Central Research Library).

JOURNALISM—RUSSIA—HISTORY

Esin, B. I. *Iz istorii russkoi zhurnalistiki kontsa XIX–nachala XX v.* Moscow: Izdatel'stvo Moskovskogo Universiteta, 1973.
*QD 75–2896

—, ed. *Iz istorii russkoi zhurnalistiki nachala XX veka.* Moscow: Izdatel'stvo Moskov-
skogo Universiteta, 1984.
*QD 85–1156
—, ed. *Russkaia zhurnalistika XVIII–XIX vekov.* Moscow: Izdatel'stvo Moskovskogo
Universiteta, 1986.
*QD 87–5555
Lapshina, G. S. *Russkaia poreformennaia pechat' 70–80-kh godov XIX veka.* Moscow:
Izdatel'stvo Moskovskogo Universiteta, 1985.
DSD 86–4836
Literaturnyi protsess i russkaia zhurnalistika kontsa XIX–nachala XX veka. Moscow:
Nauka, 1982.
*QD 88–10851
Zapadov, A. V. *Russkaia zhurnalistika XVIII veka.* Moscow: Nauka, 1964.
*QD

RUSSIAN PERIODICALS—BIBLIOGRAPHY

Andreeva, N. F., and M. V. Mashkova. *Russkaia periodicheskaia pechat' (Obshchie i
otraslevye bibliograficheskie ukazateli, 1703–1975): Annotirovannyi ukazatel'.* Moscow: Kniga, 1977.
DSD 79–51
Davis, Robert H., Jr. "19th-Century Russian Orthodox Church Journals: Structure
and Access." *St. Vladimir's Theological Quarterly* 33, no. 3 (1989): 235–59.
DSD 89–20904
Mashkova, M. V., and M. V. Sokurova. *Obshchie bibliografii russkikh periodicheskikh
izdanii, 1703–1954, i materialy po statistike russkoi periodicheskoi pechati. An-
notirovannyi ukazatel'.* Leningrad, 1956; Nedeln/Liechtenstein: Kraus Reprint,
1977.
DSD 88–4519
Ossorguine-Bakounine, Tatiana. *L'Emigration russe en Europe: Catalogue collectif des
périodiques en langue russe.* 2 vols. Paris: Institut d'Etudes Slaves, 1976–81.
Russkaia satiricheskaia periodika, 1905–1907 gg.: Svodnyi katalog. Moscow: Gosudarst-
vennaia Publichnaia biblioteka imeni V. I. Lenina, 1980.
DSD 84–3091 (Moscow. Publichnaia biblioteka)
Schatoff, Michael. *Half a Century of Russian Serials, 1917–1968: Cumulative Index of
Serials Published Outside the USSR.* New York: Russian Book Chamber Abroad,
1972.
See especially the subject index (pt. 3, S–Z) on p. 529 under "Philosophy and
Religion."
DSD

RUSSIAN PERIODICALS—BIBLIOGRAPHY—CATALOGS

Dindorf, Meinrad, and Edward Kasinec. "Russian Pre-Revolutionary Religious-
Theological Serials in the St. Vladimir's Seminary Library." *St. Vladimir's Theo-*

logical Quarterly 14, nos. 1–2 (1970): 1–8.
DSD

Kuzmin, S. A., et al., comps. *Russkie dorevoliutsionnye gazety v fondakh Biblioteki AN SSSR, 1703–1916: Alfavitnyi katalog.* 2 vols. Leningrad: Akademiia nauk, 1984.

Contains information on two occult newspapers held by the Academy of Sciences Library, p. 49, entry 475: *Vestnik okkul'tizma i spiritizma: Nauchno-populiarnaia gazeta;* and p. 253, entry 2883: *Ottuda: Illiustrirovannaia spiritual'no-okkul'tnaia gazeta.*
DSD 85–1182

——. *Ukazateli soderzhaniia russkikh dorevoliutsionnykh gazet: Bibliograficheskii ukazatel'.* Leningrad: Akademiia nauk, 1986.
DSD 87–3097

Moskovskaia dukhovnaia akademiia Biblioteka. *Ukazatel' periodicheskikh izdanii na russkom iazyke.* [Moscow, 198?].

This rare catalog contains information on occult journals held by the reconstituted Theological Academy Library in Sergiev Posad.
DSD 89–24377 (Moskovskaia)

Russian Serials and Newspapers Held in Helsinki University Library. New York: New York Public Library, 1986.
DSD 86–45 (Helsinki)

RARE BOOKS—RUSSIA

Berezin, N. *Russkiia knizhnyia redkosti.* Moscow, 1902; rpt. Leipzig: Zentralantiquariat der DDR, 1973.
DSD 85–1294

PUBLISHERS AND PUBLISHING—RUSSIA—HISTORY

[Belov, S. V.]. *Kniga v Rossii, 1850–1917: Materialy k ukazateliu Sovetskoi literatury, 1917–1977 gg.* Leningrad: Gosudarstvennaia publichnaia biblioteka imeni M. E. Saltykova-Shchedrina, 1979.

Contains references to the literature of some of the private Symbolist publishing houses of the early twentieth century. See pp. 154–55 (Musaget); 159–60 (Skorpion); 181–82 (Soikin).
DSD 85–93

NEWSPAPERS—INDEXES

Barlmeyer, Werner. *Russkaia mysl', 1905–1918.* Geissen: Wilhelm Schmitz, 1977.

Contains references to occult articles that appeared in this important general Russian periodical. See pp. 222–50.
DSD 84–1774

PERSONAL ARCHIVAL AND MANUSCRIPT SOURCES

Lichnye arkhivnye fondy v gosudarstvennykh khranilishchakh SSSR: Ukazatel'. 2 vols. Moscow: Kniga, 1962–63).

Contains information on the personal papers of individual occult editors and publishers held in archival collections in the former Soviet Union. DSD

Zhitomirskaia, S. V., ed. *Vospominaniia i dnevniki XVIII–XX vv: Ukazatel' rukopisei.* Moscow: Kniga, 1976.

Contains information on Masonic memoirs and diaries held in the rich collections of the Manuscript Division of the Russian State Library. See entries on Masons, p. 616. DSD 88–8165

RUSSIAN LITERATURE—BIBLIOGRAPHY

Kandel', B. L., et al. *Russkaia khudozhestvennaia literatura i literaturovedenie: Ukazatel' spravochno-bibliograficheskikh posobii s kontsa XVIII veka po 1974 god.* Moscow: Kniga, 1976.
DSD 86–5057

Vengerov, S. A., comp. *Istochniki slovaria russkikh pisatelei.* 4 vols. St. Petersburg: Tipografiia Akademii nauk, 1900–1917.

These incomplete bibliographical guides by one of imperial Russia's important literary scholars and bibliographers contain surprisingly rich bibliographical references on some key occult publishers and editors. The card catalog on which these works are based is held in the Manuscript Division of the Institute of Russian Literature (Pushkinskii dom). See vol. 1, pp. 248–49 (Elena Petrovna Blavatskaia) and 412 (V. P. Bykov, "author of a pamphlet on vegetarianism"); vol. 2, p. 147 (Favst Sergeevich Gruzdev); vol. 4, pp. 4–5 (L. M. Lopatin). DSD 84–2508

—, ed. *Russkiia knigi: S biograficheskimi dannym ob avtorakh i perevodchikakh (1708–1893).* St. Petersburg: A. E. Vineke, 1897–99. DSD

Russian Occult Monographs: Titles Listed in Antoshevsky's *Bibliografiia okkul'tizma* Located in the Research Libraries Information Network (RLIN) Database
Edward Kasinec and Robert H. Davis Jr.

Aksakov, Aleksandr Nikolaevich. *Razoblacheniia: Istoriia Mediumicheskoi kommisii [sic] Fizicheskogo obshchestva pri S.-Peterburgskom universitete s prilozheniem vsiekh protokolov i prochikh dokumentov.* St. Petersburg: V. Bezobrazova, 1883. xxxii, 278 pp.
National Library of Medicine

—. *Animizm i spiritizm.* St. Petersburg: Demakova, 1901.
National Library of Medicine

Albertino. *Zerkalo tainykh nauk i otrazhenie sud'by cheloveka*. 7th ed. Moscow: N. N. Bulgakova, 1903.
University of California, Davis
Astrologiia v nashi dni: Otdelenoe izdanie statei pechatavshikhsia v zhurnale "Rebus": *Teoreticheskaia chast'.* Viaz'ma: Rebus, 1908. 465 pp.
Stanford University
Bezant, Anni. *Teosofiia i novaia psikhologiia.* 2d ed. Petrograd: Vestnik teosofii, 1915.
Stanford University
Bitner, Vil'gem Vil'gemovich. *Gipnotizm i rodstvennyia iavleniia v naukie i zhizni.* N.p.: n.p., 1903.
National Library of Medicine
Blavatskii, Elena Petrovna. [*Selections.* Russian. 1928.] *Golos bezmolviia; Dva puti; Sem' vrat': Iz sokrovennykh indusskikh pisanii.* Tallinn: J. & A. Paalmann'i trükk, 1928. 95 pp.
Columbia University
Brodovskii, Boris Maksimovich. *Gipnotizm v prakticheskoi meditsine.* N.p.: n.p., 1888.
National Library of Medicine
Butlerov, Aleksandr Mikhailovich. *Stati' po mediumizmu.* St. Petersburg: A. N. Aksakov, 1889.
Stanford University
Bykov, V. P. *Spiritizm pered sudom nauki, obshchestva i religii.* Moscow: E. I. Bykov, 1914.
Stanford University; University of California, Berkeley
Chatterdzhi, Bramana [Jagadish Chandra Chatterji]. *Sokrovennaia religioznaia filosofiia Indii.* Kaluga: Tipografiia Kaluzhskoi gubernskoi zemskoi upravy, 1914. 4-e ispr. izd.
Stanford University
Chechel, I. *Khiromantiia dlia vsekh.* Jerusalem: Ekspress, 1987.
Stanford University
Chulkov, Mikhail Dmitrievich. *Abevega russkikh sueverii, idolopoklonnicheskikh zhertvoprinoshenii, svadebnykh prostonarodnykh obriadov, koldovstva, shemanstva i proch., sochineniia M. Ch.* Moscow: F. Gippius, 1786. 326 pp.
Yale University / Beineke
Diuprel', Karl. *Zagadochnost' chelovecheskago sushchestva; vvedenie v izuchenie okkul'ticheskikh nauk.* Trans. M. S. Aksenova. (Moscow: I. N. Kushnerev, 1898.
Stanford University
Freimark, Hans. *Okkul'tizm i seksual'nost'.* Moscow: Sfinks, n.d.
Stanford University
Giliarov, A. N. *Gipnotizm.* N.p.: n.p., 1894.
National Library of Medicine
Gartmann, Eduard fon. *Spiritizm.* St. Petersburg: A. N. Aksakov, 1887.
Stanford University
Iasinskii, Ieronim Ieronimovich. *Voskresnuvshie sny.* 2d ed. St. Petersburg: n.p., 1920.
Princeton University; Stanford University
Khalmuratov, A. G. *Khiromantiia (khirologiia).* Moscow: Prometei, 1990.
Stanford University
Kluge, Carl Alexander Ferdinand. *Versuch einer Darstellung des animalishchen Mag-*

netismus, als Heilmittel 3. unveränderte wohlfeilere Aufl. Berlin: Realschul-buchhandlung, 1818. xii, 356 pp.
Library of Congress; National Library of Medicine

Kollinz, M. *Kogda solntse dvizhetsia na sever: Ob"iasnenie shesti Sviashchennykh Miesia-tsev.* Moscow: Dukhovnoe znanie, 1914.
Stanford University

Kotik, Naum Genrikhovich. *Neposredstvennaia peredacha myslei.* 2d ed. Moscow: Sovremennye problemy, 1912. Microform.
University of California, Berkeley; University of Southern California; Stanford University; University of Michigan

Kozlov, Aleksei Aleksandrovich. *Gipnotizm.* Kiev: V Universitetskoi tipografie, 1887.
Stanford University

Lidbiter [C. W. Leadbeater]. *Mental'nyi plan = Le Plan mental.* St. Petersburg: Pechatnyi trud, 1912. 136 pp.
Stanford University

——. *Astral'nyi plan.* Trans. from French by A. V. Troianovskii. St. Petersburg: V. L. Bogushevskii, 1908.
Stanford University

Levinson, Iakov Ivanovich. *Besedy o gipnotizme.* N.p.: n.p., 1890.
National Library of Medicine

Liamin, A. A. *Sny i snovideniia, gipnotizm, spiritizm, telepatiia, iasnovidenie.* Moscow: Russkaia khudozhestvennaia tipografiia, 1904. Microform.
Library of Congress

Mikhailov, Vasilii Iosifovich. *Gipnotizm.* N.p.: n.p., 1886.
National Library of Medicine

Morozov, Nikolai Aleksandrovich. *V poiskakh filosofskogo kamnia.* St. Petersburg: [Obshchestvennaia pol'za], 1909.
Stanford University

Morgenshtern, I. F. *Psikho-grafologiia: Ili nauka ob opredelenii vnutrenniago mira chelo-veka po ego pocherku.* St. Petersburg: A. K. Veierman, 1903.
Stanford University

Osnovy Upanishad (Dukh Upanishad): Sbornik vyderzhek aforizmov, izrechenii, tekstov iz "Upanishad," sviashchennykh indusskikh knig. Trans. and ed. V. Singh. St. Petersburg: I. V. Leont'ev, 1909. 98 pp.
Stanford University

Otkrovennye rasskazy strannika dukhovnomu svoemu ottsu. Paris: YMCA Press, 1973.
University of California, Davis, with its English version, *The Way of a Pilgrim, and The Pilgrim Continues His Way,* 2d ed. (New York: Seabury Press, [1968]; University of Minnesota

Podmore, Frank. *Spiritizm.* St. Petersburg: Slovo, 1904–5.
Stanford University

Pogodin, Mikhail Petrovich. *Prostaia rech o mudrenykh veshchakh.* 3d ed. Moscow: E. A. Vil'de, 1875.
Stanford University

Pribytkov, Viktor. *Mediumicheskiia iavleniia pered sudom vrachei.* Rpt. from *Rebus,* 1885.

National Library of Medicine

Russkii narod: Ego obychai, obriady, predaniia, sueveriia i poeziia. (Moscow: Sovmestnoe sovetsko-kanadskoe predpriiatie Kniga printshop, 1989.
Columbia University

Sedir, Paul *Indiisky fakirizm, ili, prakticheskaia shkola uprazhnenii dlia razvitiia psikhicheskikh sposobnostei. S prilozheniem slovaria terminov indusskogo ezoterizma.* St. Petersburg: I. Lur'e, 1909.
Stanford University

Segno, A. Victor. *Zakon mentalizma: Populiarno-nauchnyi ocherk zakona, upravliaiushchogo vsiakhim myslennym i fizicheskim deistviem, sushchnost' zhizni i smerti.* Translated from English. Moscow: N. B. Butov, 1906.
Stanford University

Tarkhnishvili, Ivan Razmazovich. *Gipnotizm, vnushenie i chtenie myslei.* N.p.: n.p., 1886.
National Library of Medicine

Tukholka, S. *Okkul'tizm i magiia.* St. Petersburg: n.p., 1911.
Stanford University; and, in microform, a later edition (Riga: N. Gudkov, [192?]); University of California, Berkeley

Uspenskii, P. D. [Petr Demianovich]. *Chetvertoe izmerenie: Obzor glavneishikh teorii i popytok issledovaniia oblasti neizmerimago.* 4th ed. Berlin: Parabola, 1931. 116 pp.
Stanford University

Vel'tman, Aleksandr Fomich. *Magii midiiskie kagany XIII stolietiia.* Moscow: V Universitetskoi tipografie, 1860. 72 pp.
Stanford University

Verzhbolovich, M. O. *Spiritizm pred sudom nauki i khristianstva.* Moscow: Universitetskaia tipografiia, 1900.
Stanford University

ABOUT THE CONTRIBUTORS

MIKHAIL AGURSKY is the author of numerous books and articles, including *Ideologiia natsional-bolshevizm* (Ideology of national bolshevism), published in English as *The Third Rome* (Boulder, 1987), and *Maksim Gor'kii: Iz literaturnogo naslediia* (Jerusalem, 1986). Born and educated in the Soviet Union, he emigrated to Israel and was affiliated with the Hebrew University in Jerusalem until his untimely death in 1991.

VALENTINA BROUGHER is Associate Professor of Russian at Georgetown University. She has published several articles on Vsevolod Ivanov and is the editor and co-translator of a forthcoming anthology of Ivanov's prose of the 1920s. Her current research focuses on demonology and folklore in postglasnost literature.

MARIA CARLSON is Associate Professor of Slavic Languages and Literatures at the University of Kansas and director of its Center for Russian and East European Studies. The recipient of numerous fellowships and grants, she has published numerous articles on Russian literature and culture, and is the author of *"No Religion Higher Than Truth": A History of the Theosophical Movement in Russia, 1875–1922* (Princeton, 1993). Her current project is a book tentatively titled "The Novel That Could Never Be Written: Belyi's Unfinished Trilogy, *East or West?"*

ROBERT H. DAVIS is Librarian in the Slavic and Baltic Division of the New York Public Library. He has published numerous articles, reviews, and communications in various North American, Western European, Russian, and Eastern European periodicals, dealing with library history and collections.

MIKHAIL EPSTEIN is Associate Professor of Russian Literature and Culture, Emory University, Atlanta, and a former Fellow of the Woodrow Wilson International Center for Scholars, Washington, D.C. Among his numerous publications on Russian culture are *After the Future: The Paradoxes of Postmodernism and Contemporary Russian Culture* (Amherst, 1995) and *Vera i obraz: Religioznoe bessoznatel'noe v russkoi kul'ture XX veka* (Tenafly, N.J., 1994).

Kristi Groberg is Assistant Professor of History at Moorhead State University, Minnesota. She co-edited, with Avraham Greenbaum, and contributed to *A Missionary for History: Essays in Honor of Simon Dubnov* (Minneapolis, in press) and is the author of "The Feminine Occult Sophia in the Russian Religious Renaissance," *Canadian-American Slavic Studies*, 1992, and of numerous articles on Vladimir Soloviev and on women writers of the Silver Age.

Irina Gutkin is Assistant Professor of Russian Literature, University of California, Los Angeles. She has written articles and conference papers on literature in the context of intellectual history with a focus on modernism and Socialist Realism. Her current project is a book tentatively titled "The Cultural Roots of Socialist Realism as a World View."

Michael Hagemeister is Assistant Lecturer at the Lotman Institute for Russian and Soviet Culture at the University of Bochum, Germany. He is the author of *Nikolaj Fedorov: Studien zu Leben, Werk, und Wirkung* (Munich 1989) and of articles on Pavel Florensky, Aleksei Losev, Eurasianism, utopian thought, and apocalypticism. He is currently working on Sergei Nilus and the *Protocols of the Elders of Zion*.

Linda Ivanits, Associate Professor of Russian and Comparative Literature at Pennsylvania State University, has been the recipient of several fellowships. Her major areas of research are Russian literature and folklore. Her publications include articles on F. M. Dostoevsky and F. K. Sologub and the book *Russian Folk Belief* (Armonk, N.Y., 1989). Her current project is a book on Dostoevsky and Russian folk belief.

Edward Kasinec is Director of the Slavic and Baltic Division of the New York Public Library. His professional career encompasses service as Reference Librarian/Archivist for the Harvard University Library and the Ukrainian Research Institute Library, and Librarian for Slavic Collections, University of California, Berkeley. He is the author of many referred books and articles in the fields of bibliography and librarianship.

Judith Deutsch Kornblatt is Associate Professor of Slavic Languages and Literatures at the University of Wisconsin–Madison. The recipient of several fellowships and grants, she is the author of *The Cossack Hero in Russian Literature* (Madison, 1992) and co-editor, with Richard Gustafson, of *Russian Religious Thought* (Madison, 1996), and has published several articles on Soloviev and Russian religious thought. Her current project is a book to be titled "Meeting of the Chosen Peoples: Judaism and Modern Russian Orthodox Thought."

Håkan Lövgren, an independent scholar, is co-editor, with Lars Kleberg, and a contributor to *Eisenstein Revisited* (Stockholm, 1987); his article "Eisenstein's Pushkin Project," was published in *Eisenstein Rediscovered,* edited by Ian Christie and Richard Taylor (London, 1993). His current project is a book on Eisenstein.

BERNICE GLATZER ROSENTHAL is Professor of Russian and European Intellectual History at Fordham University. The recipient of numerous fellowships and grants, she is the editor of and a contributor to *Nietzsche in Russia* (Princeton, 1986) and *Nietzsche and Soviet Culture: Ally and Adversary* (Cambridge, 1994); co-editor and co-author (with Martha Bohachevsky-Chomiak) of *A Revolution of the Spirit: Crisis of Value in Russia, 1890–1924* (New York, 1990); and author of articles and encyclopedia entries on Russian intellectual and cultural history. Her current project is a book tentatively titled "The Nietzsche Connection in Russia: 1890–1991."

W. F. RYAN, M.A., D. Phil., is Academic Librarian at the Warburg Institute (School of Advanced Study, University of London) and lecturer on Russia at the School of Slavonic and East European Studies, University of London. He is a Fellow of the Society of Antiquaries and of the Akademiia estestvoznaniia Rossiiskoi Federstsii, series editor of the Hakluyt Society publications and two monograph series at the Warburg Institute, and author of many articles in the fields of Russian medieval magic and science.

HOLLY DENIO STEPHENS is a doctoral candidate in Russian literature at the University of Kansas. She has received numerous scholarships for language study.

RENATA VON MAYDELL is Assistant Professor at the Institute for Slavic Philology, Munich University. Her publications include "Dornach als pilgerstaette der russischen Anthroposophen" in *Russische Emigration in Deutschland, 1918 bis 1941,* edited by Karl Schloegel (Berlin, 1995), and "Neue Materialien über Emilij Metner," *Wiener Slawistische Almanach* 36 (1995).

ANTHONY J. VANCHU is Assistant Professor of Russian Language and Literature at Oberlin College. He has published articles on Iury Olesha, Mikhail Kuzmin, and the contemporary authors Liudmila Petrushevskaia, Viktor Erofeev, and Evgeny Popov. His current projects are a book on technology and utopianism in the 1920s tentatively titled "Ambivalent Paradise" and a bilingual edition of early twentieth-century theatrical works.

GEORGE YOUNG JR., an independent scholar, is the author of *Nikolai Fedorov: An Introduction* (Belmont, Mass, 1979); "Toward the New Millennium: Ideas of Resurrection in Fedorov and Solov'ev," in *Russian Thought after Communism: The Recovery of a Philosophical Heritage,* edited by James P. Scanlan (Armonk, N.Y., 1994); and the entry on Fedorov in the multivolume *Encyclopedia of Philosophy,* forthcoming from Routledge.

INDEX